KU-180-227

Cross-cultural psychology is a comprehensive overview of cross-cultural studies in a number of substantive areas – psychological development, social behavior, personality, cognition, and perception – and covers theory and applications to acculturation, ethnic and minority groups, work, communication, health, and national development. Cast within an ecological and cultural framework, it views the development and display of human behavior as the outcome of both ecological and sociopolitical influences, and it adopts a "universalistic" position with respect to the range of similarities and differences in human behavior across cultures: basic psychological processes are assumed to be species-wide, shared human characteristics, but culture plays variations on these underlying similarities.

Cross-cultural psychology

Cross-cultural psychology: Research and applications

JOHN W. BERRY
Queen's University
Kingston, Ontario, Canada

YPE H. POORTINGA
Tilburg University
Tilburg, The Netherlands

MARSHALL H. SEGALL
Syracuse University
Syracuse, New York, U.S.A.

PIERRE R. DASEN
University of Geneva
Geneva, Switzerland

The right of the
University of Cambridge
to print and sell
all manner of books
was granted by
Henry VIII in 1534.
The University has printed
and published continuously
since 1584.

CAMBRIDGE UNIVERSITY PRESS
Cambridge
New York   Port Chester   Melbourne   Sydney

Published by the Press Syndicate of the University of Cambridge
The Pitt Building, Trumpington Street, Cambridge CB2 1RP
40 West 20th Street, New York, NY 10011, USA
10 Stamford Road, Oakleigh, Melbourne 3166, Australia

© Cambridge University Press 1992

First published 1992

Printed in the United States of America

Library of Congress Cataloging-in-Publication Data
Cross-cultural psychology / John W. Berry ... [et al.].
p.   cm.
Includes bibliographical references and index.
ISBN 0–521–37387–5. — ISBN 0–521–37761–7 (pbk.)
    1. Ethnopsychology.   I. Berry, John W.
GN502.C76   1992
    155.8–dc20   91–18275
                                        CIP

A catalog record for this book is available from the British Library

ISBN 0–521–37387–5 hardback
ISBN 0–521–37761–7 paperback

Acknowledgments

We wish to thank the following publishers for permission to use materials that originally
appeared in their publications.
Figure 3-1, from Berkowitz, L. (ed.). (1979). *Advances in Experimental Social Psychology*, vol.
12. "A cultural ecology of social behavior" by J. W. Berry. Reprinted by permission of Academic
Press.
Figure 3-2, from Hofstede, G. (1980). *Culture's Consequences* (Cross-Cultural Research and
Methodology Series, W. Lonner & J. W. Berry, eds.). Reprinted by permission of Sage
Publications, Inc.
Figure 5-1, from Vorster, J., & Schuring, G. (1989). Language and thought: Developmental
perspectives on counterfactual conditionals. *South African Journal of Psychology, 19*, 34–38.
Figures 6-1, 6-2, from Berlin, B., & Kay, P. *Basic Color Terms: Their Universality and Evolution*.
Berkeley: The University of California Press. Permission granted by the Regents of the
University of California and the University of California Press.
Figure 6-4, from Poortinga, Y. H., & Foden, B. I. M. (1975). A comparative study of curiosity in
black and white South African students. *Psychologia Africana*, Monograph, Supplement 8.
Figure 6-5, from Hudson, W. (1960). Pictorial depth perception in sub-cultural groups in Africa.
Journal of Social Psychology, 52, 183–208. Reprinted with permission of the Helen Dwight Reid
Educational Foundation. Published by Heldref Publications, 4000 Albemarle St., N.W.,
Washington, D.C., 20016. Copyright © 1960.

Dedicated to Joan, Heleen, Sally, and Catherine, who
suffered not only our absences, but also our joint presence

Figure 6-6a, from Deregowski, J. B. (1968). Difficulties in pictorial depth perception in Africa. *British Journal of Psychology, 59*, 195–204.
Figure 6-6b, from Dziurawiec, S., & Deregowski, J. B. (1986). Construction errors as a key to perceptual difficulties encountered in reading technical drawings. *Ergonomics, 29*, 1203–1212.
Figure 6-6c,d, from Deregowski, J. B., & Bentley, A. M. (1986). Perception of pictorial space by Bushmen. *International Journal of Psychology, 21*, 743–752.
Figure 6-7, from Deregowski, J. B., & Bentley, A. M. (1987). Seeing the impossible and building the likely. *British Journal of Psychology, 78*, 91–97.
Figures 6-8, 6-9, from Poortinga, Y. H., & Foden, B. I. M. (1975). A comparative study of curiosity in black and white South African students. *Psychologia Africana*, Monograph, Supplement 8.
Figure 7-1, from Whiting, B. B., & Whiting, J. W. M. (1975). *Children of Six Cultures Model of Psychocultural Research*. Cambridge, MA: Harvard University Press, copyright © 1975 by the President and Fellows of Harvard College. Reprinted by permission of the publishers.
Figure 9-1, Table 9-1, from Malpass, R. S., & Poortinga, Y. H. (1986). Strategies for design and analysis, in W. Lonner & J. W. Berry, eds., *Field Methods for Cross-cultural Research*, p. 50. Reprinted by permission of Sage Publications, Inc.
Figure 9-3, from Berry, J. W. (1989). Imposed etics-emics–derived etics. *International Journal of Psychology, 24*, 721–735.
Table 9-3, from Poortinga, Y. H. (1989). Equivalence of cross-cultural data: An overview of basic issues. *International Journal of Psychology, 24*, 737–756.
Figure 14-1, from Gudykunst, W. B., & Hammer, M. R. (1983). Basic training design: Approaches to intercultural training. In D. Landis & R. W. Brislin, eds., *Handbook of Intercultural Training* (vol. 1, pp. 118–154). New York/Oxford: Pergamon Press.
Box 14-1, from Brislin, R. W., Cushner, K., Cherrie, C. & Yong, M. (1986). *Intercultural Interactions* (Cross-Cultural Research and Methodology Series, W. Lonner & J. W. Berry, eds.), pp. 212–213, 223. Reprinted by permission of Sage Publications, Inc.

Contents

Chapter 1	*Introduction to cross-cultural psychology*	1
	What is cross-cultural psychology?	1
	Goals of cross-cultural psychology	2
	Relationships with other disciplines	4
	Ethnocentrism in psychology	8
	A general framework for cross-cultural psychology	10
	Conclusions	14
Part I	*Similarities and differences in behavior across cultures*	
Chapter 2	*Cultural transmission and development*	17
	Enculturation and socialization	17
	Child-rearing practices	20
	The concept of development	30
	Infant development	35
	Conclusions	41
Chapter 3	*Social behavior*	42
	Cultural context	43
	Conformity	46
	Values	50
	Individualism and collectivism	55
	Gender behavior	57
	Conclusions	68
Chapter 4	*Personality*	69
	Traits across cultures	70
	Affective meaning	77
	Expressive behaviors	81
	Indigenous personality	89
	Self and consciousness	93
	Conclusions	98
Chapter 5	*Cognition*	99
	The historical legacy	99
	Language and thought	101

	Contemporary issues	109
	General intelligence	116
	Genetic epistemology	118
	Specific abilities	121
	Cognitive styles	124
	Conclusions	130
Chapter 6	*Perception*	131
	Historical roots	131
	Sensory functions	133
	Color: coding and categorization	137
	Perception of patterns and pictures	145
	Aesthetics	156
	Conclusions	160
Part II	*Pursuing problems across cultures: research strategies*	
Chapter 7	*Cultural approaches*	165
	Conceptions of culture	165
	Ethnography	170
	Culture and personality	179
	Cognitive anthropology	187
	Conclusions	188
Chapter 8	*Biological approaches*	192
	Evolution and adaptation	192
	Behavior genetics	200
	Ethology	205
	Biological models of cultural transmission	214
	Conclusions	218
Chapter 9	*Methodological concerns*	219
	Designing cross-cultural studies	220
	Psychological data in cultural context	228
	Analysis of comparability	236
	Classification of inferences	241
	Conclusions	245
Chapter 10	*Theoretical issues in cross-cultural psychology*	247
	Inferred antecedents of differences in behavior	247
	Relativism, absolutism, and universalism	256
	Culture as a psychological concept	260
	Conclusions	267
Part III	*Applying research findings across cultures*	
Chapter 11	*Acculturation and culture contact*	271
	Acculturation	271

	Contact and participation	275
	Attitudes toward acculturation	276
	Behavior change	280
	Acculturative stress	284
	Conclusions	290
Chapter 12	*Ethnic groups and minorities*	292
	Plural societies	292
	Multiculturalism	296
	Ethnic relations	299
	Ethnic identity	303
	Language issues	305
	Education issues	308
	Conclusions	314
Chapter 13	*Organizations and work*	315
	Organizational structure	315
	Managerial behavior	323
	Work values and motives	331
	Conclusions	337
Chapter 14	*Communication and training*	339
	Intercultural communication	339
	Communication training	344
	International negotiations	347
	Conclusions	355
Chapter 15	*Health behavior*	356
	Psychopathologies across cultures	357
	Cultural factors in psychotherapy	364
	Cultural factors in health behavior	369
	Conclusions	377
Chapter 16	*Psychology and the developing world*	378
	Impact of Western psychology	379
	Indigenous psychologies	380
	Psychology and national development	384
	Conclusions	390
Epilogue		
References		391
Author index		440
Subject index		451

Foreword

The growth of interest in the relationship between psychology and culture began in the main after the Second World War, though some of the fundamental issues have been discussed for well over a century. Until recently mainstream psychology has largely kept aloof from the debate concerning culture and behavior, perhaps because it was felt to be somewhat threatening. For if behavior does vary with cultural setting, this raises the question of the standing of psychological theories elaborated and tested exclusively within a Western cultural setting. Since then the necessity of conducting studies in other parts of the world has come to be more widely recognized, and by 1980 sufficient material had accumulated for a 6-volume *Handbook of Cross-Cultural Psychology*. This remains an indispensable source of reference, but has of course limitations. It was not intended as a textook and does not meet the need for one; moreover, it has inevitably become dated in certain respects and cannot remain the last word in an active field of research whose findings are mostly published in the periodical literature.

It is therefore to be warmly welcomed that a group of some of the most outstanding cross-cultural researchers have come together to produce two volumes, the first intended mainly for undergraduate courses. The present one is at an advanced level, offering a remarkably comprehensive survey of the current state of the art and science of cross-cultural psychology. The coverage is wide-ranging, providing even some sketches of the historical background in such areas as cognition and perception, and encompassing contributions from allied disciplines such as anthropology and biology. Methodological problems are examined in depth, informed by the extensive and varied experience of the four authors. The orientation in this respect tends to be rather tough-minded, favoring rigorous experimental and psychometric approaches, but without neglecting "softer" ones.

Much critical attention is paid to theories, and one encounters some novel ideas and occasional adventurous speculations. Some variations in emphasis and evaluation probably reflect some divergences among the authors' positions, which is hardly surprising in so complex and contentious a sphere. For instance, while all seem to accept in principle "the culture-bound nature of most human behavior," some contributions place the main stress on systematic cross-cultural comparisons, with a view to arriving ultimately at a "universal psychology" that transcends particular cultures. Such an aim is regarded as unrealistic by the adherents of so-called "cultural psychology" who hold that culture and mind are inseparable. Hence not being concerned to establish universal laws, they eschew comparisons and concentrate on intracultural studies. Whether or not one agrees with it, this kind of orientation is sufficiently prominent to have merited more detailed consideration, and it is perhaps worth illustrating its rationale with a brief example.

The authors of the present work cite one of my own studies carried out among Ashanti people in Ghana more than a generation ago. According to traditional Ashanti cosmology the day of the week on which children are born determines the kind of "soul" that enters them, which in turn powerfully influences their character. For instance, the Wednesday boy (*Kwaku*) was believed to be likely to become an aggressive trouble-maker, while for the Monday boy (*Kwadwo*) a quiet and peaceful character was expected. The study of actual behavior significantly confirmed the existence of such differences. While some of my Ashanti friends took this as scientific confirmation of their traditional beliefs, I prefer the alternative interpretation that strong parental expectations led to a self-fulfilling prophecy.

Note that from the standpoint of cross-cultural psychology there are two distinct elements here: a universal one (parental expectations affect children's behavior) and a culture-specific one (the particular operative beliefs). The authors rightly point out that the study has never been replicated. Now let us suppose that someone attempted to replicate at the present time, using an infallible method, and obtained negative results. Such an outcome could mean either that my original work was flawed or that traditional beliefs had ceased to be operative. One might be tempted to regard this as an essentially methodological problem, suggesting for example that appropriate studies of changes in the salience of belief systems would enable us to resolve the question. Unfortunately, there is no such simple answer, since other relevant cultural features might also have changed, so that the precise causal nexus remains obscure. Nontrivial universals in the sense of invariant causal relationships cannot in practice be isolated, because they do not exist apart from a vast variety of changing cultural forms. These forms, moreover, are not just external "variables" influencing behavior, but in the course of development become an integral part of the mental structure.

I have played the devil's — read cultural psychologist's — advocate in order to give some insight into the reasons why they are sceptical about the notion of an abstract "human nature" that could be captured by universal laws. On the other hand they tend to be less united regarding possible constructive alternatives.

In my own view the approaches of cross-cultural psychology and cultural psychology are complementary, since both in their different ways seek to understand human behavior in context. Moreover, there is no sharp boundary between them and some workers occupy a middle ground by using conventional methods for the intensive study of particular cultures, leaving aside any cross-cultural comparisons. Even in the present volume there are accounts of such cases, especially in the applied chapters.

These chapters deal with the actual and potential contributions of cross-cultural psychology to the problems of the third world or ethnic groups and minorities. They are specially valuable, since no such thorough and detailed treatment is available anywhere else. Similarly, far more space than usual has been devoted to the work of non-Western psychologists, whose extensive participation in cross-cultural research is crucial for further advance.

In sum, the dedicated labor of the authors has resulted in a most impressive volume that is stimulating as well as useful, packed with information and ideas. It is likely to remain unrivaled for some time to come, and as such will certainly prove indispensable to all serious students, teachers, and practitioners of cross-cultural psychology.

Gustav Jahoda

Preface

This book provides an examination of the rapidly growing field of cross-cultural psychology for students who have had at least some prior academic training in psychology and related disciplines, and who seek to extend their knowledge of the relationship between culture and behavior. In assuming prior courses in psychology the present book differs from another volume by the same authors (M. H. Segall, P. R. Dasen, J. W. Berry, and Y. H. Poortinga (1990), *Human Behavior in Global Perspective: An Introduction to Cross-cultural Psychology*. New York: Pergamon Press). The two texts were prepared in a way that minimizes overlap in content, which allows for the present volume to follow the earlier one in a student's program.

The book consists of three parts, preceded by an introductory chapter and followed by an epilogue. The introduction orients the reader toward the field by providing a general framework that has guided the organization of the book. Part I critically surveys empirical studies in important areas of human behavior that have long been treated in psychology: these include developmental, social, personality, cognition, and perception. Part II provides essential information from the cognate disciplines of anthropology and biology. It also contains two chapters on the methodological and theoretical foundations of cross-cultural psychology that are needed for a critical appraisal of the literature. Part III builds upon the knowledge and principles established earlier on to consider how cross-cultural psychology can contribute to areas such as acculturation, ethnic and minority groups, organizations and work, communication and training, health behavior, and the role of psychology in the developing world. The brief epilogue makes some concluding observations.

Inevitably, only a portion of the relevant research has been included. The selection of materials was based upon explicit interests of the authors, but also upon some implicit personal and cultural biases. Readers with other cultural concerns are invited to reflect on this book from their own perspectives, informed by knowledge of other traditions.

The chapters are intended to be read in the order in which they appear in the book. However, most chapters can be read on their own by those with specific interests. The Boxes provide background information, extensions of certain arguments, and items of particular interest. They are meant to be read along with the main text, but can be omitted without loss of continuity. For most topics, sufficient references have been provided to enable the reader to pursue them in more detail; such supplementary reading is encouraged. Readers should look, in particular, for supplementary sources rooted in their own culture.

Acknowledgements

We are indebted to many of our colleagues who have contributed in various ways to this volume. We would like to thank in particular: Erik Andriessen, Jan Deregowski, Erwin Hendriks, Rudy Kalin, Roy Malpass, Durganand Sinha, Harry Triandis, and Fons van de Vijver.

Preparation of the manuscript was mainly in the capable hands of Audrey Bailey at Queen's University. We also thank Heather Heintzman, Najum Rashid, Monica Hurt, and Jennifer Sharpe at Queen's; and Xander Jansen, Rianne Smits, Rea Bergmans, and Tinie Aarts at Tilburg University for their contributions.

A fellowship at NIAS (Netherlands Institute for Advanced Study) enabled one of us (Ype Poortinga) to accomplish part of the writing for this book. A year at NIAS also allowed John Berry an early opportunity to reflect on cross-cultural psychology as a general field. Later a year in Geneva, at the Faculté de Psychologie et Sciences de l'Education and the World Health Organization, permitted the writing of other portions of the text. Overall administrative help mainly was provided by the Psychology Department at Queen's University. Syracuse University in many ways supported Marshall Segall's participation in this project. We sincerely thank these institutions for their generosity and support.

John W. Berry
Ype H. Poortinga
Marshall H. Segall
Pierre R. Dasen

1   Introduction to cross-cultural psychology

What is cross-cultural psychology?

According to the definition presented in Segall, Dasen, Berry, and Poortinga (1990), cross-cultural psychology is "the scientific study of human behavior and its transmission, taking into account the ways in which behaviors are shaped and influenced by social and cultural forces." This definition directs our attention to two central features: the diversity of human behavior in the world and the link between individual behavior and the cultural context in which it occurs. This definition is relatively simple and straightforward; a number of other definitions reveal some new facets and point to some complexities:

1. "Cross-cultural research in psychology is the explicit, systematic comparison of psychological variables under different cultural conditions in order to specify the antecedents and processes that mediate the emergence of behaviour differences" (Eckensberger, 1972, p. 100).
2. "Cross-cultural psychology includes studies of subjects from two or more cultures, using equivalent methods of measurement, to determine the limits within which general psychological theories do hold, and the kinds of modifications of these theories that are needed to make them universal" (Triandis, Malpass, & Davidson, 1972, p. 1).
3. "Cross-cultural psychology is the empirical study of members of various culture groups who have had different experiences that lead to predictable and significant differences in behaviour. In the majority of such studies, the groups under study speak different languages and are governed by different political units" (Brislin, Lonner, & Thorndike, 1973, p. 5).
4. "Cross-cultural psychology is concerned with the systematic study of behaviour and experience as it occurs in different cultures, is influenced by culture, or results in changes in existing cultures" (Triandis, 1980, p. 1).

In all these definitions the term *culture* appears. For the time being we can define culture as "the shared way of life of a group of people." Later, in Chapters 7 and 11, we will consider more elaborate meanings of the term. Despite this common focus, each definition attends more specifically to a particular feature, highlighting it for our consideration. In the first the key idea is that of identifying *cause and effect relationships between culture and behavior* ("... specify the antecedents and processes that mediate ..."); the second definition focuses on the *generalizability* of current psychological knowledge ("... determine the limits ..."); the third is more concerned with

1

identifying the kinds of *cultural experiences* ("... speak different languages ...") that may be factors in promoting human behavioral diversity; and the fourth raises the issue of *culture change* and its relation to individual behavior.

Limited attention is given in these definitions to some other interests. For example, cross-cultural psychology is concerned not only with diversity, but also with *uniformity*: what is there that might be psychologically common or *universal* in the human species (Lonner, 1980)? Moreover, there are other kinds of contextual variables (not usually included in the concept of culture) that have been considered to be part of the cross-cultural enterprise. These include: *biological* variables (Dawson, 1971) such as nutrition, genetic inheritance, and hormonal processes that may vary across groups along with their cultures; and *ecological* variables (Berry, 1976a) that view human populations in a process of adaptation to their natural environment, emphasizing factors such as economic activity (hunting, gathering, farming, and so forth) and population density.

Also not included in these definitions is any mention of the term *cross-national*. As pointed out by Frijda and Jahoda (1966), while cross-national methods may be the same as those in cross-cultural psychology, this term seems to refer to studies carried out in two populations that are closely related culturally (for example, Scots-Irish or French-Spanish comparisons), and that usually live in close proximity to each other. While this kind of study is usually excluded from the field of cross-cultural psychology by common consent, another kind of study (while geographically even less far-ranging) is becoming increasingly important: this is the study of various cultural groups *within* a single nation-state. The justification for including such an *ethnic psychology* (Berry, 1985a) in cross-cultural psychology seems to be that some groups represent original cultures that were rather different to begin with (for example, Native Indians, blacks, and Hispanic peoples in the Caribbean region) while others maintain distinctive cultures for generations after migration. This special focus in cross-cultural psychology is reflected in the numerous studies involving changes in behavior that result from contact between cultures; these will be considered in detail in Chapters 11 and 12.

We are now in a position to propose the general definition of cross-cultural psychology that will be used in this book:

Cross-cultural psychology is the study of similarities and differences in individual psychological functioning in various cultural and ethnic groups; of the relationships between psychological variables and sociocultural, ecological, and biological variables; and of current changes in these variables.

Goals of cross-cultural psychology

Implied in the various definitions in the previous section is a set of goals for cross-cultural psychology; these may now be made explicit. Perhaps the first and most obvious goal is the testing of the generality of existing psychological knowledge and theories. This goal has been proposed by J. W. Whiting

(1968), who argued that we do cross-cultural psychology using data from "various peoples throughout the world to test hypotheses concerning human behavior." Dawson (1971) also emphasized this goal when he proposed that cross-cultural psychology is conducted "so that the universal validity of psychological theories can be more effectively examined." This point of view was further reiterated by Segall et al. (1990), who observed that "given the importance of culture as a behavioral determinant, it obviously behooves psychologists to test the cross-cultural generality of their principles before considering them to be established" (p. 37).

This first goal has been called the *transport and test* goal by Berry and Dasen (1974); in essence psychologists seek to transport their present hypotheses and findings to other cultural settings in order to test their applicability in other (and eventually in all) groups of human beings. As examples, we may ask: is it the case that "practice makes perfect" (performance improves over trials in a study of learning) or that items presented early and late in a memory study (primacy and recency effects) are more often remembered by individuals in all cultures? For this first goal, obviously, we start with what we know to be the case in one's own culture and apply the question in another culture; as such, the formulation of the question is not particularly sensitive to discovering psychological phenomena that may be important in the other culture.

A second goal has been proposed by Berry and Dasen (1974) to remedy this problem: to *explore* other cultures in order to *discover* psychological variations that are not present in one's own limited cultural experience. While we may be alerted to the presence of these other psychological phenomena by our failure to find the same results when pursuing the first goal, we could simply come back from our study in the other culture with the conclusion that there are no performance or primacy effects in learning and memory. This second goal makes it clear that we should go beyond such a failure to generalize and seek out the reasons for failure, or find alternative (perhaps culture-specific) ways in which learning progresses, lists are memorized, or cognition is developed. Moreover, this second goal requires us to keep our eyes open for novel aspects of behavior, even when we do find support for the generality of the phenomenon we are studying. For example, individuals may evidence different mnemonic devices during a memory study.

The third goal is to attempt to assemble and *integrate* into a broadly based psychology the results obtained when pursuing the first two goals, and to *generate* a more nearly *universal* psychology (of, for example, learning or memory) that will be valid for a broader range of cultures. This third goal is necessary because of the distinct possibility that in pursuing our first goal we will find limits to the generality of our existing psychological knowledge, and that, in pursuing our second goal we will discover some novel psychological phenomena that need to be taken into account in a more general psychological theory.

It is a working assumption of this textbook that such "universal laws" of human behavior are possible to achieve. That is, we believe that we will eventually discover the underlying psychological processes that are characteristic of our species, *homo sapiens*, as a whole. Our belief is based upon the existence of such universals in related disciplines. For example, in biology there are well-established pan-species primary needs (such as eating, drinking, sleeping) even though their fulfillment is achieved in very different ways in different cultures. In sociology there are universal sets of relationships (such as dominance); in linguistics there are universal features of language (such as grammatical rules); and in anthropology there are universal customs and institutions (such as tool making and the family). In psychology it is therefore plausible to proceed on the assumption that we will also uncover universals of human behavior even though (as in these cognate disciplines) there will likely be wide variation across cultures in the ways in which these universal processes are developed, displayed, and deployed.

Relationships with other disciplines

Clearly cross-cultural psychology has all the hallmarks of an interdisciplinary enterprise (see Box 1-1 for an overview of current activity in cross-cultural

---

Box 1-1   Current activity in cross-cultural psychology

Once a rather exotic subspecialty, cross-cultural psychology became an established, thriving intellectual enterprise peopled by hundreds of scholars from many parts of the world. By 1973, there were 1125 cross-cultural psychologists listed in a published *Directory of Cross-Cultural Research and Researchers* (Berry, Lonner, & Leroux, 1973) and presumably more who were not listed. Although most of them are in departments of psychology in North American and European universities, many are to be found in universities in Africa, Asia, and Latin America. Wherever they may be, they are linked by a variety of institutions. In large numbers they belong to established professional organizations, including the International Association for Cross-Cultural Psychology (founded in 1972), the Society for Cross-Cultural Research (1972), and the French-language *Association pour la Recherche Interculturelle* (1984). The increasing cadres of cross-cultural psychologists now enjoy a diversity of journals in which they publish their research findings. These include the *International Journal of Psychology* (1966), the *Journal of Cross-Cultural Psychology* (1970), *Ethos* (1972), and the *International Journal of Intercultural Relations* (1978). In addition, the older journals in psychology, anthropology, and some related fields are publishing more and more cross-cultural research, with the *Journal of Social Psychology* encouraging such studies by providing priority publication.

The proliferation of reports of cross-cultural research that fill these journals has prompted the publication of numerous reviews and overviews. The most comprehensive are a chapter in the 1972 *Biennial Review of Anthropology* (Triandis, Malpass, & Davidson, 1972), another by the same authors in the 1973 *Annual Review of Psychology*, followed by Brislin (1983), Segall (1986), and Kagitcibasi and Berry (1989).

A brief introduction to cross-cultural psychology for beginning students of psychology was written by Serpell (1976), and a pair of edited volumes dealing with research issues were edited by Warren (1977, 1980a). Both of these served to draw attention to the field among students in Great Britain. In the United States general overviews were edited by Marsella, Tharp, and Ciborowski (1979) and by L. L. Adler (1982), and a textbook by Segall (1979) was widely used during the 1980s. In France a developmental perspective on cross-cultural psychology has been prepared by Bril and Lehalle (1988).

Although primarily concerned with research methodology, a book by Brislin, Lonner, and Thorndike (1973) contains numerous summaries of significant cross-cultural studies, most of them conducted during the 1960s. Lonner and Berry (1986a) have edited a volume concerned with field methods. A series on *Cross-Cultural Research and Methodology* (edited by Lonner and Berry) has been published since 1974. Since then, fourteen volumes have appeared, ranging from research methods to mental health, and from learning to social psychology. The bibliographies in all of these attest to the virtual explosion of interest and activity in cross-cultural psychology.

Conferences devoted largely or even exclusively to cross-cultural psychology are now frequent occurrences. The International Association for Cross-Cultural Psychology has met, starting in 1972, in Hong Kong, Kingston, Canada (1974), and Tilburg, the Netherlands (1976), continuing every two years until the present. Many regional meetings have also taken place, such as the Pan-African Psychology Congress in Nairobi, Kenya, in December 1975. The proceedings of most such conferences are also published, thus adding to the materials available for study by cross-cultural psychologists.

The most comprehensive source of information for the field is the *Handbook of Cross-Cultural Psychology* (1980) under the general editorship of H. C. Triandis. The six volumes were co-edited by specialists in each field: Volume 1, *Perspectives* (W. W. Lambert); Volume 2, *Methodology* (J. W. Berry); Volume 3, *Basic Processes* (W. J. Lonner); Volume 4, *Developmental* (A. Heron); Volume 5, *Social* (R. Brislin); and Volume 6, *Psychopathology* (J. Draguns). Students and other readers who seek a detailed exposition, in forty comprehensive chapters, will be much rewarded by studying this Handbook.

psychology). This is evident from the proposed definition, in which we seek to discover systematic relationships between population-level data (from ecology, biology, and anthropology) and individual psychological data. Wherever scientists approach a topic from an interdisciplinary perspective, it is useful to deal with the issue of *levels of analysis*. This issue is concerned with the legitimacy of studying a phenomenon from various perspectives without the threat of *reductionism*; this latter concept is the tendency, which often appears in interdisciplinary debate, to reduce the phenomena of one discipline to the level of explanation commonly employed in the next "more basic" discipline. Thus, in our frame of reference we need to avoid reducing culture to the level of psychological explanations, of psychological phenomena to biological explanations, biological to chemical, and so on. That is, we must recognize that there are, for example, cultural phenomena that exist and can be studied at their own level. These phenomena canot be rendered in psychological terms; the same is true for all other disciplines with which we are concerned.

To help us see how cross-cultural psychology is related to other disciplines, Figure 1-1 lays out the "geography" of other disciplines with which it is associated. In the portion on the left are population-level disciplines that are largely concerned with describing, analyzing, and understanding features of whole populations, groups, or collectivities; in these disciplines there is rarely a concern with a specific individual. In contrast, the portion on the right of the figure identifies the characteristic domain of psychology as being primarily concerned with individual-level (including inter- and intra-individual) phenomena. From these population-level disciplines cross-cultural psychology can draw a substantial amount of information. This can be employed to establish the general context for the psychological development and functioning of individuals and for understanding variations in individual behavior displayed in different cultural populations. The field of cross-cultural psychology is located at the center of the figure because the field is meant to provide insight into individual behavior as it relates to population-level phenomena. It should be noted that cross-cultural psychology does not "take-over" all of psychology (as may be implied in Figure 1-1), but is simply concerned with many of the same kinds of variables that are included in general psychology. The particular fields indicated in Figure 1-1 are those that we consider in Chapters 2 to 6; other fields of psychology could just as well have been included in the figure.

Another way of thinking about these various levels is to note the arguments, frequently made, that to a large extent anthropology, ecology, and biology are *naturalistic* disciplines, basically concerned with understanding things the way, and where, they are in nature. For example, for anthropology Edgerton (1974) has argued that "at heart, anthropologists are naturalists whose commitment is to the phenomena themselves. Anthropologists have always believed that human phenomena can best be understood by procedures that are primarily sensitive to context, be it situational, social, or

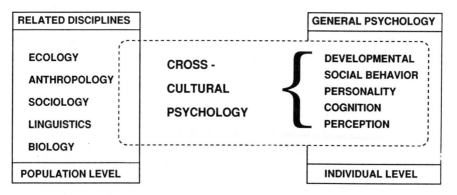

Figure 1-1 Relationships among cross-cultural psychology, general psychology, and population-level disciplines.

cultural" (pp. 63–64). In contrast, psychologists acknowledge experimenta-tion "as their ultimate means of verification" (p. 63). This approach would include not just experiments in the strict sense, but tests, interviews, and other methods in which the researcher constructs an artificial situation within which to control or constrain behavior. Of course, many psychologists have used more naturalistic methods (such as observation) for a long time, but the contrast that Edgerton describes is by and large correct. As he (p. 64) correctly points out, there is no inherent superiority of naturalism over experimentalism; they both are legitimate scientific approaches, at their own levels. He concludes that if there is to be a valid interdisciplinary domain, so that "a convergence between anthropology and psychology can come about, then it must somehow combine naturalism and experimentation" (p. 64). The same argument can be made when we wish to bridge psychology and other population-level disciplines (ecology, biology, population genetics, linguis-tics, and sociology). Without learning how to take both levels of scientific analysis into account in cross-cultural psychology, we may simply be a two-faced Janus, looking longingly at our parent disciplines, but without the means of being a true offspring. An attempt will be made in Part II of this book to show how the problem could be solved, when we consider cultural (including ecological), biological, and psychological approaches in more detail.

In detailed analyses Jahoda (1982, 1990a) has examined the relationship between anthropology and psychology, which is, in many respects, the most substantial of the interdisciplinary relationships identified in Figure 1-1. He has traced the long but sporadic interactions between the two disciplines from the time when they were largely undifferentiated (in the nineteenth century), through a period when many scholars were experts in both fields (around the turn of the twentieth century). Then followed a period of mutual neglect, even hostility, with the exception of the field of "culture and personality" (now known as "psychological anthropology") up to the past few decades, in which there has been a serious meeting of minds between a number of anthropologists and psychologists. Klineberg (1980) has also traced this on again-off again relationship, much of it from the point of view of an active participant.

Ethnocentrism in psychology

The cross-cultural study of *differences* may lead to their being viewed as *deficiencies*; the evaluation of differences between groups (as in "us better — them worse") is known as *ethnocentrism*. The term was coined by Sumner (1906), who noted that there exists a strong tendency to use one's own group's standards as *the* standard when viewing other groups, to place one's group at the top of a hierarchy, and to rank all others as lower. This tendency may even be a universal feature of cultural group relations (LeVine & Campbell, 1972). However, it need not be (and we argue, *should* not be) a feature of cross-cultural psychology. In its stead a value-neutral position has been advocated for anthropology (Herskovits, 1948) and for psychology by many researchers who consider that we too must avoid absolute judgments that are rooted in one's own culture. Essentially, the position is one that assumes no evaluative stance with respect to differences; each varying phenomenon is viewed in its own context and described and interpreted relative to the cultural or ecological situation in which it occurs.[1] An obvious example from the domain of social behavior is that of greeting procedures; in many Western cultures a firm handshake and direct eye contact are considered appropriate, while in other parts of the world a bow, without eye contact, is proper. It is difficult to avoid imposing one's own cultural norms (feeling that looking down is inappropriate) or attributions about the other person (as shy or lacking in manners) even when one has had frequent contact with other cultures. However, it is necessary to avoid these value judgments in cross-cultural psychology.

Apart from leading to incorrect interpretations of observations, the effects of ethnocentrism can enter into cross-cultural research at three more levels. An obvious danger is the introduction of culture-specific meaning with instruments that originally were designed in one particular culture. If there is one message that emerges from knowledge accumulated so far, it is that one should never assume an item or task in a psychological instrument to have the same meaning cross-culturally. A more subtle effect of ethnocentrism lies in the choice of research topics. Psychologists from third world countries have

---

[1] It is useful to note here that Herskovits, who used the concept of *cultural relativism*, limited his concerns to the making of ethnocentric *value judgments*. He did not consider it necessary to prohibit the making of *comparisons*, nor did he argue that no cultural or psychological phenomena are common across cultural groups. In Chapter 10 we will employ the term *relativism* to refer to the general position taken by some researchers that seeks to avoid both value judgments *and* comparisons.

RESEARCHER FROM CULTURE	CULTURES STUDIED A	B
A	STUDY 1	STUDY 2
B	STUDY 4	STUDY 3

Figure 1-2 Multiple studies to distinguish differences across cultures due to the observer and due to the observed.

lamented the lack of societal relevance of cross-cultural research. There is another side to this complaint, namely that a hasty application of presumed scientific knowledge in the past has led to gross and serious errors. A final level at which ethnocentrism is likely to affect cross-cultural research is in the formulation of theories. Our notions and ideas about behavior have cultural antecedents. Consequently, even theory-driven research is likely to be affected by cultural biases.

Cross-cultural psychology attempts to reduce the ethnocentrism of psychology in one important sense: by recognizing the limitations of our current knowledge, and by seeking to extend our data and theory to other (eventually all) cultures, we can reduce the culture-bound nature of the discipline. The pursuit of this goal of reducing ethnocentrism exposes us to the risk of even more ethnocentrism as it involves handling data from other cultures. As a general rule one finds that the greater the cultural or behavioral difference, the greater is the potential for negative evaluations of the difference. Indeed, one critic (Nisbet, 1971) has argued that the comparative (cross-cultural) method is "profoundly ethnocentric" (p. 95), and is just another way (now claiming scientific respectability) of placing other peoples in a hierarchy with European cultures at the top and others ranked below. Similarly, in a thorough analysis of the discipline of history Preiswerk and Perrot (1978) have shown the dangers that social scientists face when looking at our own past in relation to that of others: who can resist the temptation to accept, even in subtle ways, their own superiority? However, resist we must, and an explicit recognition of the potential for ethnocentrism is a first step toward its control.

A second protection lies in a proposal made by D. T. Campbell (1970) to carry out every cross-cultural research project four times, according to the framework in Figure 1-2. The researcher from one Culture (A) studies a phenomenon in one's own Culture (A); no comparisons are made outside the culture and it remains culture-bound. The usual cross-cultural research study is that marked "Study 2"; here a researcher from Culture A does the study in Culture B and compares the results with those obtained in Study 1.

Campbell argues that for both of these studies there is an inherent ambiguity: "for any given feature of the report, it is equivocal whether or not it is a trait of the observer or a trait of the object observed" (p. 70).

To overcome this problem Campbell recommends also carrying out Studies 3 and 4. Here a second researcher, this time from Culture B, studies one's own Culture (B; in Study 3) and then the other Culture (A; in Study 4). In this way comparison across the four studies will enable us to distinguish differences that are due to ethnocentric bias in the researcher from differences that are actually present between the two cultures. The first (bias) would be signaled by a sharp disagreement between the outcome of Studies 1 and 4, and between Studies 2 and 3, usually in reciprocal ways. For example, in the first comparison (1 versus 4) individuals from Culture A are judged to be superior on some trait, while in the second comparison (2 versus 3) the reverse is claimed for the same trait. The second result (valid differences) would be signaled by common findings in the two comparisons. To our knowledge, this type of multiple study has not yet been carried out in cross-cultural psychology. However, the scientific advantages of doing so are clear; so too are the disadvantages, in terms of cost, time, and effort. Still, the very existence of the proposal neatly identifies the nature of the problem and shows us how we can tackle it, if resources are available.

Not meaning to minimize the dangers of ethnocentrism, the working assumption of this book is nevertheless that principles of behavior that have universal validity can be formulated. Psychology as it is known today in all probability contains strong ethnocentric elements reflecting specific manifestations of behavior from the industrial urban societies where psychological science has largely been developed. We acknowledge that until alternative approaches, focusing on other research topics and theories, and rooted in other cultures, have been formulated and extensively tested, psychology will unfortunately remain a Western, ethnocentric, and incomplete science.

The search for non-Western approaches is slowly gaining momentum. Later we shall discuss some attempts to define personality concepts on the basis of non-Western traditions (see Chapter 4). However, such studies are still few in number and so far they have little impact on psychology as a science, even in nonindustrialized countries. In other words the extent of scientific colonialism in psychology is rather great, but difficult to evaluate and even more difficult to remedy (see Chapter 16). We can only hope that we reflect in this book an awareness about the limitations inherent in contemporary psychological knowledge.

A general framework for cross-cultural psychology

It is useful at the outset to have some conceptual framework within which the various bits and pieces the reader comes across can be meaningfully placed. Of course, no single framework can do justice to the variation or complexity of cross-cultural psychology, and as more information and insight are acquired one becomes less comfortable with a simple model. Nevertheless, the advantages probably outweigh the disadvantages, and so we present a general model in Figure 1-3. This framework is a conceptual scheme rather than a theoretical model from which specific testable hypotheses can be derived. It is a general guide to classes of variables and their relevance for the explanation of similarities and differences in human behavior and experience that can be found across cultures.

This framework derives from earlier models proposed by Berry (1971a, 1976a, 1986), where it was called an "ecocultural model." However, as we discuss later (in Chapter 7), the roots of this model go back to the points of view of Kardiner and Linton (1945) and J. W. Whiting (1974), who were working in the field of culture and personality.

Earlier we distinguished between the *population*-level and the *individual*-level of analysis. This distinction is used in Figure 1-3, with the former on the left of the framework and the latter on the right. The *flow* of the figure is from left to right, with population-level variables conceived of as influencing the individual outcomes. This general flow is intended to correspond to the interests of cross-cultural psychology; we wish to account for individual and group differences in psychological characteristics as a function of population-level factors. However, it is obvious that a full model (that is, one that attempts to specify completely relationships in the real world) would have numerous feedback arrows representing influences by individuals on the other variables in the framework.

The notion of feedback is necessary to avoid viewing the developing and behaving individual as a mere *pawn* in such a framework. According to many philosophical and psychological theories, human beings are *active* participants in their relationships with the physical and cultural contexts in which they operate. There is an interactive or dialectical relationship (Boesch, 1980; Eckensberger, 1979; see Chapter 10) that can both filter and alter the very nature of these contexts, so that we must represent this possibility in any overall conception. However, for ease of presenting the framework, only two feedback relationships are illustrated in Figure 1-3 (individuals influencing their ecological and sociopolitical contexts), and this should be taken to signal the presence of feedback in the framework more generally, even though not all relationships are indicated in the figure.

At the extreme left are two major classes of influence (background variables of *ecological* context and *sociopolitical* context), while at the extreme right are the psychological characteristics that are usually the focus of psychological research (including both observable behaviors and inferred characteristics, such as motives, abilities, traits, and attitudes). The two middle sets of variables (process variables) represent the transmission or influence from population variables to individuals. Both biological and cultural factors are included.

In more detail, the ecological context is the setting in which human organisms and the physical environment interact; it is best understood as a set

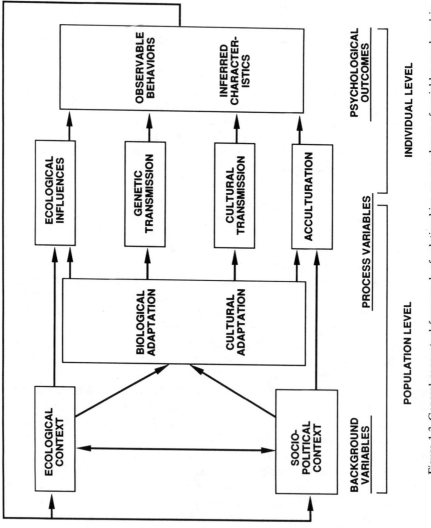

Figure 1-3 General conceptual framework of relationships among classes of variables employed in cross-cultural psychology.

ECOLOGICAL INFLUENCES

GENETIC TRANSMISSION

CULTURAL TRANSMISSION

ACCULTURATION

OBSERVABLE BEHAVIORS

INFERRED CHARACTER-ISTICS

BIOLOGICAL ADAPTATION

CULTURAL ADAPTATION

ECOLOGICAL CONTEXT

SOCIO-POLITICAL CONTEXT

PSYCHOLOGICAL OUTCOMES

INDIVIDUAL LEVEL

PROCESS VARIABLES

POPULATION LEVEL

BACKGROUND VARIABLES

of *relationships* that provide a range of life possibilities for a population. Such an interactive point of view is the essence of an ecological approach (see Chapter 7) and allows us to avoid the pitfalls of earlier approaches, such as that of "environmental determinism" (Feldman, 1975; Berry, 1976a). The central feature of this ecological context is *economic activity*, in which nonindustrial cultural groups are rated with respect to their degree of reliance on five kinds of economic activity: hunting, gathering, fishing, pastoralism, and agriculture. Urban-industrial societies have a way of life in which other dimensions of economic activity have emerged. However, each form of economic activity implies a different kind of relationship between the local human population and the animal and physical resources of their habitat. These relationships in turn imply varying cultural, biological, and psychological outcomes, as we shall see in the chapters to come.

With respect to adaptation at the population level, we take the position that individual behavior can be understood across cultures only when both *cultural* and *biological* features of our species are taken into account. This joint interest in cultural and biological influences on behavior appears to us to be not only balanced, but indeed the only possible point of view to adopt; the exclusion of either culture or biology as factors in the explanation of human variation makes little sense (Freeman, 1983, p. 294; Boyd & Richerson, 1985). We shall later argue (in Chapters 7 and 8) that these two major sources of influence are together adaptive to the contexts in which individuals live. We shall also elaborate the ways in which culture is transmitted, and some important dimensions of this process (in Chapter 2) where *enculturation* and *socialization* are identified as the central concepts used to describe this cultural transmission.

However, not all outcomes can be seen as being the result of ecological relationships. We also take the view that culture and individual behavior are affected by influences stemming from culture contact in the sociopolitical context of one's group. These come about with *acculturation*, because of such historical and contemporary experiences as colonial expansion, international trade, invasion, and migration. This position is elaborated in Part III.

It is important to note that not all relationships between the two major background variables and psychological outcomes are mediated by cultural or biological adaptation. Some influences are *direct* and rather immediate, such as environmental learning in a particular ecology (leading to a new performance), nutritional deficiency during a famine (leading to reduced performance), or a new experience with another culture (leading to new attitudes or values). These direct influences are indicated by the upper and lower arrows that bypass the two forms of population-mediated adaptation. Many of these direct influences have been the focus of the work of Barker (1969) and Brunswik (1957) in the field of ecological psychology. We also accept that individuals can recognize, screen, appraise, and alter all of these influences, (whether direct or mediated) and as a result there are likely to be wide individual differences in the psychological outcomes.

To summarize, we consider that the distribution of psychological character-istics within and across groups can best be understood with the help of a framework such as this one. When ecological, biological, cultural, and acculturational factors are identified and taken into consideration, we should be able to account for how and why people differ from one another, and also why they are the same.

Conclusions

We have argued that cross-cultural psychology draws upon two established scientific traditions: general psychology, which is an individual-level discipline that has gained much of its status from using the experimental method, and a number of cognate disciplines (particularly anthropology) that reside at the population-level and have gained much of their status from using more naturalistic, observational methods. As such, we are an "interdiscipline," operating in a space largely left vacant and unattended by these other disciplines, but one very much in need of attention. This need, to understand population-level influences on individual-level psychological functioning, is best met by attempting to use a nonethnocentric standpoint, while remaining oriented toward the long-term possibility of generating universal psychologi-cal laws.

We believe that two methodological positions will assist us in fulfilling this need. One is that on the continuum from pure phenomenology to unrestricted positivism we occupy a position on the positivistic side, although closer to the middle than most experimental psychologists. We believe that the basis of science is formed by empirical studies, that is, studies that are designed in such a way that the data can show the beliefs and expectations of the researchers to be *incorrect*. In other words, theoretical notions have to be open to empirical scrutiny. This does not mean that all theories mentioned in this book have been sufficiently validated. However, in our choice of ma-terials we introduce a certain bias. For example, historically one of the most important traditions in cross-cultural research, culture and personality, is given little attention. The reason for this is the inaccessibility for critical empirical investigation of the psychodynamic theories that are prominent in the culture-and-personality tradition.

The second methodological theme of this book is the inherent ambiguity that attends the interpretation of any observed behavioral differences be-tween cultural groups: are they a valid indication of differences in psycholo-gical functioning or are they merely an artifact of the methods used? We adopt a critical perspective on the making of intergroup comparisons with psychological data. A cross-cultural psychology that looks critically at the achievements in other areas of the behavioral sciences, but not at its own accomplishments, in our opinion would betray one of its more important functions.

PART I

Similarities and Differences in Behavior Across Cultures

2   Cultural transmission and development

At the end of Chapter 1 we proposed a general framework (Figure 1-3) that related cultural and ecological contexts at the population level to psychological outcomes at the individual level. A key element of the model, one that serves as a way for cultural groups to transmit themselves to their new members (usually children), is *cultural transmission* (including the processes of enculturation and socialization). It is with these issues that we begin this chapter, specifically how a cultural group manages to have its members acquire appropriate behaviors. In a second section the child-rearing practices found across cultures are examined, drawing upon both ethnographic reports and psychological studies. In the last section the focus is on the early stages of development of the child, where biological, anthropological, and psychological evidence is outlined.

Enculturation and socialization

The most general notion to be considered is that of *cultural transmission*. This term was introduced by Cavalli-Sforza and Feldman (1981) to parallel the notion of *biological transmission*, in which, through genetic mechanisms (see Figure 1-3), certain features of a population are perpetuated over time across generations (see Chapter 8, and Thompson, 1980, for a discussion of how these biological factors enter into cross-cultural psychology). By analogy, using cultural transmission a cultural group can perpetuate its behavioral features among subsequent generations through *teaching* and *learning* mechanisms. Such cultural transmission from one generation to a subsequent one is termed *vertical transmission* by Cavalli-Sforza and Feldman (1981), since it involves the *descent* of cultural characteristics from parents to their offspring. However, while vertical descent is the only form of biological transmission, there are two other forms of cultural transmission, *horizontal* and *oblique* (see Figure 2-1).

In vertical transmission parents transmit cultural values, skills, beliefs, motives (and so forth) to their offspring. In this case it is difficult to distinguish between cultural and biological transmission, since one typically learns from the very people who were responsible for one's conception; that is, biological parents and cultural parents are the same. In the case of

17

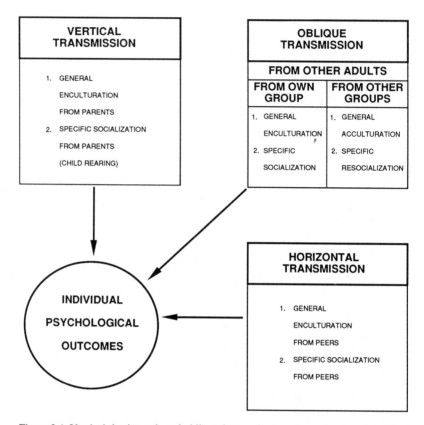

Figure 2-1 Vertical, horizontal, and oblique forms of cultural transmission. (Modified from Berry & Cavalli-Sforza, 1986)

horizontal cultural transmission one learns from one's peers (in primary and secondary groups) during the course of development from birth to adulthood; here there is no confounding between biological and cultural transmission. And in the case of oblique cultural transmission one learns from other adults and institutions (for example in formal schooling), either in one's own culture or from other cultures. If the process takes place entirely within one's own culture, then the terms *enculturation* and *socializaiton* are the appropriate ones (see left side of oblique transmission in Figure 2-1). If the process derives from contact with another culture, the terms *acculturation* and *re-socialization* are employed (see right side of oblique transmission in Figure 2-1). These latter terms refer to the form of cultural transmission experienced by an individual that results from contact with, and influence by, persons and institutions belonging to other cultures than one's own (see Chapter 11).

The concept of *enculturation* has been developed within the discipline of cultural anthropology and was first defined and used by Herskovits (1948). As the term suggests, there is an encompassing or surrounding of the individual by one's culture; the individual acquires, by learning, what the culture deems to be necessary. There is not necessarily anything deliberate or didactic about this process; often there is learning without specific teaching. The process of enculturation involves parents, and other adults and peers, in a network of influences on the individual, all of which can limit, shape, and direct the developing individual. The end result (if enculturation is successful) is a person who is competent in the culture, including its language, rituals, values, and so on.

The concept of *socialization* was developed in the disciplines of sociology and social psychology to refer to the process of deliberate shaping, by way of tutelage, of the individual. It is generally employed in cross-cultural psychology in the same way. When vertical, horizontal, or oblique cultural transmission involve deliberate teaching from within one's group, then we are dealing with the process of socialization; resocialization occurs when the deliberate influences come from outside one's own culture. The net result of both enculturation and socialization is the development of behavioral similarities within cultures and behavioral differences between cultures. They are thus the crucial cultural mechanisms that produce the distribution of similarities and differences in psychological characteristics at the individual level.

The study of both the enculturation and socialization processes tends to focus on two aspects: the cultural *content* or *substance* (for example, items of knowledge, values, skills) that is being transmitted and the *means* or *style* of cultural transmission (child-rearing or child-training practices).

It is useful at this point to clearly distinguish enculturation from another term that is often confused with it – *acculturation*. As we have seen, enculturation is the process by which the group generally incorporates children into the culture and by which the child acquires the appropriate behaviors. In contrast, *acculturation* refers to cultural and psychological change brought about by contact with other peoples belonging to different cultures and exhibiting different behaviors (see lower path in Figure 1-3). For example, many groups in India and Africa became acculturated to aspects of British life-style during the Empire (changing their social structure, economic and other institutions), and many individuals changed their own behaviors (such as their religion, language, and dress). In a sense then acculturation is a second or later form of enculturation, and can take place at any time in one's life, not just during childhood. It involves relearning (including some specific resocialization), and can create both new problems and new opportunities for the individual. The cultural and psychological phenomena of acculturation will be discussed in Chapter 11.

To become a full-fledged member of a culture is a long and difficult process. Our species (*homo sapiens*) is the only one to possess and transmit culture on a significant scale; we also have one of the longest periods of physical dependency of the young on the mature members of the species. Hence the child is attached physically (for nurturance, including food, warmth, and protection) for a period that is sufficiently long to enable the extensive process of cultural transmission to take place.

Physical dependency is not the only factor allowing the transmission of culture. By the time developing children are biologically self-sustaining, they typically continue to live in the family group and continue to acquire important features of their culture. There is a shift from *physical dependence* to *social and psychological dependency*: after puberty, physical needs can be filled by the individual, but the acquired social needs (such as intimacy, love, social interaction, and social support) continue to be met largely by the family group. Thus attachment remains, but its basis gradually shifts from physical to social and psychological dependency, permitting continuing and substantial cultural transmission.

On the other hand, the process of cultural transmission does not lead to replication of successive generations; it falls somewhere between an *exact* transmission (with hardly any differences between parents and offspring) and a complete *failure* of transmission (with offspring who are unlike their parents). Where it falls, of course, is closer to the full transmission end of this spectrum than to the nontransmission end. Functionally, either extreme may be problematic for the society: exact transmission would not allow for novelty and change, and hence the ability to respond to new situations, while failure of transmission would not permit coordinated action between generations (Boyd & Richerson, 1985).

Child-rearing practices

Studies of how a society characteristically raises its children have been reported in the literature for over a century. As we shall see in Chapter 7, many of these reports have been accumulated in an archive mainly composed of ethnographic reports known as the Human Relations Area Files (HRAF). One approach to the study of child-rearing is to employ these files to discover the major dimensions of variation in these practices as they are used around the world; this approach provides us with a broad overview. The archival approach allows us to examine child-rearing practices (the specific socialization of children) in the context of other cultural variables (the more general enculturation) that have also been included in the archives; we are thus able to examine how child-rearing fits into, or is adaptive to (LeVine, 1977), other features of the group's circumstances (the link between socialization and enculturation).

A second approach is to carry out field studies. These can be ethnographic examinations (in a single culture, but sometimes comparatively across cultures) of the child-rearing practices employed by the group. They can also be psychological examinations using standard psychological procedures in selected cultures that differ in some respect. In many psychological theories of child development (e.g., Freud, 1938), the *way* in which children are treated by their parents is judged to be crucial to their psychological growth.

For example, harsh or abrupt weaning (as practiced in some cultures), and the resulting experience of being rejected, is thought to lead to adult personalities that are low in emotional responsiveness, self-evaluation, and generosity (Rohner & Rohner, 1976; Rohner, 1986). Both aspects of child-rearing – substance and method (the *what* and the *how*) – are typically included in cross-cultural studies of child rearing.

Archival studies. Studies of cultural transmission employing ethnographic archives have been carried out over the past thirty years. (These are now termed "holocultural" since they permit the examination of materials from cultures the whole world over.) An early study using HRAF, carried out by J. W. Whiting and Child (1953), attempted to link adult personality to child training by examining the ways in which societies typically explain illness. Ethnographic data from seventy-five societies were employed and five "systems of behavior" (defined as "habits or customs motivated by a common drive and leading to common satisfactions," p. 45) were examined: oral, anal, sexual, dependence, and aggression. The first three of these five behavior systems were derived from Freud's (1938) theory of psychosexual development, in which sexual gratification is thought to be associated over the course of development with different erogenous zones, beginning with the mouth (during the oral stage). Adult personality, in Freudian theory, is described in terms of these developmental stages. J. W. Whiting and Child (1953, p. 45) employed them not only because of their status in psychoanalytic theory, but because of their relationship to three primary needs or drives (hunger, elimination, and sex) that, along with the two other behaviors (dependence and aggression), are likely to be universally subjected to socialization. Judges made ratings of practices in each of these five domains on three dimensions: initial satisfaction or indulgence of the child; the age of socialization; and the severity of socialization.

Two very general conclusions resulted from this study. First, "child training the world over is in certain respects identical ... in that it is found always to be concerned with certain universal problems of behaviour" (p. 63). Second, "child training also differs from one society to another" (p. 64). In this pair of conclusions are the two prototypical and most frequent empirical results found in cross-cultural psychology: first, there are some common dimensions that serve to link humankind together; second, individuals and groups differ in their typical place on these dimensions. We shall see later, in Chapters 9 and 10, that the first conclusion is essential if we are to have some valid basis on which to make cross-cultural comparisons, and that the second is essential if we are to have sufficient variance in our data to discover covariation between cultural and psychological observations.

In two other classical studies Barry and his colleagues (Barry, Bacon, & Child, 1957; Barry, Child, & Bacon, 1959) were able (1) to identify a set of dimensions of child training, (2) to place societies at various positions on these dimensions, (3) to show some characteristic differences between training for boys and girls, and (4) to relate all of these to features of cultural variation such as economy and social structure, thus placing socialization in the broader enculturation context. Let us examine each of these in some detail.

By the mid 1950s, attention had become focused, among users of the HRAF, on six central dimensions of child-rearing thought to be common to all societies. As defined in the work of Barry et al. (1957, 1959) these are:

1. Obedience training: the degree to which children are trained to obey adults.
2. Responsibility training: the degree to which children are trained to take on responsibility for subsistence or household tasks.
3. Nurturance training: the degree to which children are trained to care for and help younger siblings and other dependent people.
4. Achievement training: the degree to which children are trained to strive toward standards of excellence in performance.
5. Self-reliance training: the degree to which children are trained to take care of themselves and to be independent of assistance from others in supplying their needs or wants.
6. General independence training: the degree to which children are trained (beyond self-reliance as defined above) toward freedom from control, domination, and supervision.

Ratings of child-rearing practices used in a particular society were generally made by two or more judges on the basis of the descriptions of societies available in the HRAF. The samples of societies that were drawn from the Files usually represented a wide variety of peoples.

The first issue to consider is whether these six dimensions could provide reasonable definitions of what went on in these societies. In some cases data were absent in the ethnographic description. This could be due to a lack of interest in this particular type of child training on the part of the ethnographer, or it could mean that this dimension is not really relevant; we have no way of knowing which is the case. A second qualification is that ratings varied in the degree of clarity or agreement, and thus ratings may be of differential validity for different societies.

Armed with the ratings, Barry and his colleagues explored the second issue: are these six dimensions independent of each other, or are they related in some systematic way across cultures? Their analyses showed that five of the six dimensions tended to form two clusters. One cluster (termed "pressure toward compliance") combined training for responsibility and obedience; training for nurturance was only marginally part of this cluster. The other cluster (termed "pressure toward assertion") combined training for achievement, self-reliance, and independence. These two clusters were negatively related. Thus, a single dimension was created, along which societies were placed, ranging from compliance training at one end and assertion training at the other end. The six initial dimensions were thus reduced to a single one. The two remaining issues were the presence of sex differences in child training and how a society's place on the dimension might relate to a number of other ecological and cultural variables.

Table 2-1. *Sex differences in child-rearing*

Dimension of Child-rearing	Number of cultures	Percentage of cultures with evidence of sex difference in direction of		
		Girls	Boys	Neither
1. Obedience	69	35%	3%	62%
2. Responsibility	84	61%	11%	28%
3. Nurturance	33	82%	0%	18%
4. Achievement	31	3%	87%	10%
5. Self-reliance	82	0%	85%	15%

Source: Extracted from Table 1, Barry et al. 1957.

To examine the first of these issues Barry et al. (1957) made ratings on five of the six basic dimensions (excluding general independence training) separately for boys and girls. Results showed a fairly clear-cut difference in four of the five dimensions (see Table 2-1). With the exception of the dimension of obedience training, girls were socialized more for "compliance" (evidenced in Table 2-1 by ratings on responsibility and nurturance training); conversely boys were socialized more for "assertion" (evidenced by ratings on achievement and self-reliance). This general pattern was found across the societies in the sample.

In a further analysis Barry and his colleagues (1957) found that the *magnitude* of these sex differences in socialization correlated with other features of culture. First, large sex differences in socialization are associated with "an economy that places a high premium in the superior strength, and superior development of motor skills requiring strength, which characterize the male"; and second, they are "correlated with customs that make for a large family group with high cooperative interaction" (p. 330). To interpret these differences it is useful to turn to their later analysis (Barry et al., 1959) in which the broader cultural context of socialization is explored more fully.

The following questions guided their analysis: "Why does a particular society select child training practices which will tend to produce a particular kind of typical personality? Is it because this kind of typical personality[1] is

---

[1] Barry et al. use the term "typical personality" to refer to basic dispositions in the individual. In Chapter 4 we question the validity of the notion that there are personality types characteristic of a particular society. We accept that there are culture-typical patterns of behavior that have been learned during the process of enculturation. However, we doubt whether this makes it necessary to postulate cross-cultural differences in internal dispositions. The issue is not of great concern here, as the results of Barry et al. appear to be quite meaningful if "typical personality" is read as not more than "typical patterns of adult behavior."

functional for the adult life of the society, and training methods which will produce it are thus also functional?" (Barry et al., 1959, p. 51). They began their search for an answer to these questions by examining one of the most basic functions in a society: the economic mode of subsistence. These were classified as gathering, hunting, fishing, pastoralism, or agriculture. In the view of Barry et al. (1959) with a dependence on pastoralism (raising animals for milk and meat) "future food supply seems to be best assured by faithful adherence to routines designed to maintain the good health of the herd" (p. 52). At the opposite extreme is hunting and gathering. Where "each day's food comes from that day's catch, variations in the energy and skill exerted in food-getting lead to immediate reward or punishment.... If the change is a good one, it may lead to immediate reward" (p. 52). Agricultural- and fishing-based societies are thought to be in between these two extremes.

On the basis of these observations they argued that in pastoral, and to some extent agricultural, societies (which are high in "food accumulation"), people should tend to be relatively "conscientious, compliant and conservative," while in hunting and gathering societies (low in "food accumulation") people should be relatively "individualistic, assertive and venturesome" (p. 53). Assuming that societies will train their children for these appropriate adult behaviors, Barry et al. (1959) predicted a relationship between type of subsistence economy and child-rearing practices.

In order to assess the argument that child-training practices are adaptive to subsistence economy, they were compared in a sample of 104 societies with the degree of food accumulation (defined in terms of exploitive patterns). Before examining these relationships, it is useful to note that other cultural elements (such as social stratification and political integration) and ecological elements in addition to subsistence economic practices (such as population concentration) are strongly related to both the variables of food accumulation and pressure in child training toward compliance. For the societies studied, both the food accumulation and socialization variables are related significantly to other ecological and cultural variables, such as size of settlement and social stratification.

The correlation between food accumulation and socialization is positive for responsibility and obedience training, and negative for achievement, self-reliance, and independence training. When the more global measure of socialization ("pressure toward compliance versus assertion") is employed, these relationships still hold. This global measure combines ratings on "responsibility" and "obedience" on the one hand, and ratings of "achievement" and "self-reliance" on the other. Using this overall compliance-assertion score, Barry et al. (1959) found a correlation of $+.94$ with degree of food accumulation: of the twenty-three societies above the median on the compliance-assertion rating, twenty are high food accumulating, while of the twenty-three societies below the median, nineteen are low food accumulating. There is thus a strong similarity between socialization emphases and the broader enculturation context.

Since these original studies by Barry et al., there have been more extensive codes produced by Barry (e.g., Barry, Josephson, Lauer, & Marshall, 1976; Barry & Paxson, 1971) that both increase the range of societies included and the range of socialization variables covered. There has also been a critical reanalysis of the HRAF data (using newer data analytic techniques now available with computers). Hendrix (1985), using these sophisticated statistical techniques, explored two questions: do the purported dimensions actually inhere in the data, and are the reported variations in child-rearing (and in sex differences in child-rearing) related to subsistence economic activities? The first question was examined by a factor analysis of twenty-four socialization variables in 102 societies. One result was that the "assertion" variables (of self-reliance, achievement, and independence) formed one dimension, and this was independent of the "compliance" dimension (formed by responsibility, obedience, and nurturance). Moreover, sex differences did not appear in either dimension, suggesting that "societies tend to socialize boys and girls somewhat similarly on each substantive emphasis" (p. 252).

The second analysis by Hendrix, relating child-rearing to economic practices, revealed a complex set of results, similar to those reported earlier by Barry et al. In Hendrix's (1985) view, his "re-examination of the links of socialization to the economy shows that the original conclusions were much overly simplified, somewhat misleading, but not completely off the mark" (p. 260).

The issue of sex differences in child-rearing has received rather extensive treatment in the recent cross-cultural literature about sex differences in behavior, leading R. L. Munroe and R. H. Munroe to conclude (1975, p. 116) that (1) there are modal sex differences in behavior in every society and (2) every society has some division of labor by sex. These two phenomena, besides being universal, are also probably interrelated in a functional way.

The correspondence between sex differences in socialization emphases and sex differences in behavior is very strong. That the two sexes behave in ways they are taught to behave is, of course, not surprising, but it still leads to interesting questions. For example, have all these societies observed different inborn behavioral tendencies in males and females and shaped their socialization practices to reinforce such biologically based tendencies? Or are societies' socialization practices merely influenced by certain physical differences between males and females, with those practices responsible for behavioral differences?

Risking oversimplication, we can summarize the picture of sex differences in behavior that is presented by anthropology as showing males to be more self-assertive, achievement-oriented, and dominant, and females to be more socially responsive, passive, and submissive. One key to the explanation is the fact that the behavioral differences just summarized, although nearly universal and almost never reversed, range in magnitude from quite large down to virtually nil. A satisfactory explanation, then, will account both for the universality of direction of difference and the variation in magnitude of the difference. Such an explanation takes into account economic facts, including division of labor by sex, and socialization practices. Key contributors to this explanation have been Barry et al. (1957, 1959, 1976).

The argument begins with an early anthropological finding (Murdock, 1937) that a division of labor by sex is universal (or nearly so) and quite consistent in content. For example, food preparation is done predominantly by females in nearly all societies. Child-rearing is usually the responsibility of females. Sometimes it is shared, but in no society is it the modal practice for males to have the major responsibility. Although there are many cross-cultural variations in the content of sexual division of labor, there are hardly ever significant reversals.

Barry et al. (1957) suggested that this consistent pattern of sex-role differentiation during adulthood represents a set of solutions that societies have invented to deal with what were, for subsistence-level societies, practical problems. These problems are viewed as arising from biologically based physical differences (and not behavioral ones) between the sexes, especially the female's lesser overall physical strength and, most of all, her childbearing and child-rearing functions. Different economic roles for males and females, with the latter consigned mostly to close-to-home activities, would have been a functional response.

The next step in the argument was to suggest that differential socialization of the two sexes evolved as a means for preparing children to assume their sex-linked adult roles. Then the behavioral differences between the sexes could best be viewed as a product of different socialization emphases, with those in turn reflective of and appropriate training for different adult activities (Barry et al., 1959).

Van Leeuwen's (1978) extension of Berry's (1976a) ecological model expands the argument so that it can accommodate other aspects of subsistence mode and variations in degree of sex differences in behavior. Thus, in sedentary, high-food-accumulating societies not only will females be subjected to more training to be nurturant and compliant, but the degree of the difference between the sexes' training will also be high. In low-food-accumulating societies, such as gathering or hunting societies, there will be less division of labor by sex and little need for either sex to be trained to be compliant. Often in such societies (at least in gathering societies, if not hunting ones, as we will see shortly) women's contributions to the basic subsistence activity are integral to it. Hence, women's work is valued by the men, who are then not inclined to denigrate women or to insist on subservience from them.

Some related findings have been reported by Schlegel and Barry (1986) that expand the consequences of the division of labor by sex. One of the ways in which division of labor by sex varies across cultures is in the degree to which women contribute to subsistence. Their participation in such activities may be relatively low or high, depending on the activity. For example, if food is acquired by gathering, women's participation is usually high; in eleven of fourteen (79 percent) gathering societies for which ethnographic reports were coded by Schlegel and Barry (1986) women were high contributors. By contrast, in only two of sixteen (13 percent) hunting societies did women make a high contribution. (Schlegel and Barry defined high contribution as any percentage above the mean contribution, about 33 percent, for their entire sample of 186 nonindustrial societies.) Women are more apt to contribute relatively highly to subsistence where the main activity is either gathering or agriculture (other than intensive agriculture), and less highly where the activity is animal husbandry, intensive agriculture, fishing, or hunting (Schlegel & Barry, 1986, p. 144).

Does the variation in the subsistence role played by women have any consequences? Schlegel and Barry (1986) found that two sets of cultural features, adaptive and attitudinal, are associated with female contribution to subsistence. Where women play a relatively large subsistence role, the features of polygyny, exogamy, brideprice, birth control, and work orientation training for girls prevail. And under these same conditions (high contribution by females to subsistence) men value the contribution of women highly, women have a position of relative independence, and are generally less likely to be perceived as objects for male sexual and reproductive needs.

What we have seen in this discussion is that females do indeed behave differently from males; we will examine these differences more closely in the next chapter. It seems clear that these sex differences are strongly influenced by cultural factors, operating through socialization practices and reflective of ecological factors. Both the consistencies in the cross-cultural data and the variations from society to society help us to understand how cultural values have been defined differently for the two sexes and how individuals come to behave in accord with them.

Field studies. Since studies employing archival data do not reveal underlying psychological processes and mechanisms, a second type of study, employing direct field methods, has been carried out more frequently in recent times. The classic ethnographic study of this type is the "Six Cultures" project in which teams of researchers, armed with a common theoretical approach and with the same methods, carried out ethnographic and psychological work in six cultures in various parts of the world.

The "Six Cutures Study" (Minturn & Lambert, 1964; B. B. Whiting, 1963; Whiting & Whiting, 1975) has been a massive and long-term collaborative project. The volumes produced are well beyond the capacity of this text to review; here we focus on the specific dimensions of child-rearing that were studied and on the similarities and differences found across the six cultural groups: Guisii (from Nyansongo, Kenya); Ilocos (from Tarong, Philippines); Mixtecan (from Juxtlahuaca, Mexico); "Orchard Town" (from New England, U.S.); Rajput (from Khalapur, India); and Taira (from Okinawa).

To understand the findings, consider first the structure of the project. A group of researchers (directed by Irwin Child, William Lambert, and John

Whiting) produced an initial Field Guide for studying socialization (J. W. Whiting, 1966). Pairs of researchers (one male, one female) were trained in its use and worked in one of the six cultures. The plan was to draw a similar sample of children and their mothers in each culture (six boys and six girls in two age groups, 3 to 6 years and 7 to 10 years).

Structured interviews were conducted with the mothers (a total of 133 interviews), from which twenty-eight scales were derived after extensive analysis. There were three types of scales. One type is concerned with the mother's treatment of the child (ranging from physical punishment through to active assistance) in three different situations (child requests help, child is fighting, child is angry). A second type of scale is concerned with other aspects of the mother's behavior on such specific dimensions as mother's caretaking, warmth, hostility, mood variation, rule communication, praise, and physical punishment. The third type is concerned with a variety of specific variables such as age at which child dresses self and plays away from home, and frequency and number of chores.

Data on these twenty eight scales from all mothers in the six cultures were analyzed in a single factor analysis in order to discover patterns in the responses. Ten factors were extracted and rotated (Varimax). Some of the factors, with the scales that define them, are:

1. *Warmth of mother* was assessed by four scales: general warmth, hostility, frequency of praise, and frequency of physical punishment.
2. *Responsibility training* was based on three scales, concerned with general pressures on children for doing things to help the family get its work done: frequency of chores, number of chores, and age of training.
3. *Aggression training (mother directed)*: high punitiveness when child becomes angry in reaction to scolding and when child is angry with mother.
4. *Aggression training (peer directed)*: consistent rules about aggression and reward for retaliation.
5. *Proportion of mother care (past)*: amount of time mother cared for baby and amount of time another adult cared for baby.
6. *Proportion of mother care (present)*: proportion of caretaking by mother at present time and amount of time mother spends now with the child.

Since data from all six cultures were used in this analysis, a case can possibly be made that these factors represent pancultural dimensions on which individuals and societies can vary. If this is so, an important question arises: to what extent does variation in these dimensions reside across societies (*between* cultures) and to what extent does it reside across mothers (*within* cultures)? Given the results obtained from archival studies, one might reasonably expect that there would be important differences between the cultures and that mothers in any one culture might share most child-rearing practices in common. However, Minturn and Lambert (1964) reported that within-culture variance was generally greater than between-culture variance. This was more so for some factors (Responsibility training and Mother care for baby), and less so for others (Aggression toward mother and Aggression toward peers), but overall this is a dramatic finding.

There are three possible reasons for this result. One is that there really is a great deal of similarity across cultures in the way mothers raise their children on average (with individual differences among mothers within cultures). A second reason is that six cultures cannot represent all of cultural variation, since they capture less of the cross-cultural range than archival studies have done. This alternative interpretation means that wide variations in socialization practices may simply have been missed. Such an alternative is a distinct possibility for this study, since five of the six cultures were agricultural in subsistence pattern; hunters, gatherers, and fishers were not included, and as we saw earlier, these societies tend to differ substantially from agricultural societies in their child-rearing practices. The third explanation is methodological. Since all six teams of field researchers were trained to employ common scales, a possible result of this attempt at using standardized procedures is that each team used the full range of ratings for the range of phenomena *within* one culture. Whatever the correct interpretation is of this finding, taken at face value it reminds us that there may be important similarities across cultures in the functional relationship between mothers and their children everywhere.

Another field study, designed to examine more closely the descriptions of Barry et al. (1957, 1959), was carried out by Bolton et al. (1976). It compared pastoral and farming peoples in the Andes of Peru and drew upon a similar comparison made in East Africa earlier by Edgerton (1971). In Peru two communities with a mixed pastoral-agricultural economy were selected, but each had different relative importance of the two economic activities: herding was dominant in one, farming in the other. Eight personality characteristics were examined (among them independence, self-reliance, achievement, responsibility, and obedience) with a sample of eight farming and ten pastoral children (aged 4 to 7 years). Pastoral children were significantly more independent and self-reliant than agricultural children; there were no other significant differences. The authors claim that these findings "support the prevailing stereotype of herders as independent and as given to open and direct expression of emotion ...," and that this finding conflicts with the picture drawn by Barry et al. (1959) of "the pastoral life as requiring responsible, careful tending of the food supply, and an adaptive child-training emphasis designed to build not independence, but an orientation toward conscientiousness, compliance and conservation" (Bolton et al., 1976, p. 464). The critical impact of this work on the Barry et al. (1957, 1959) conclusions has been slight, since Edgerton (1971) and Bolton et al. (1976) contrasted only two types of society (which would be classified as relatively similar to each other by Barry), and they used very small samples. For the time being we are inclined to accept the findings of Barry et al. (1957, 1959) regarding variations in child-rearing across a large range of cultures.

Another type of field study is one that employs a standard psychological procedure comparatively across cultures. For example, Lambert, Hamers, and Frasure-Smith (1979) employed a standardized situation (a tape recording of a child interacting with other children) in eleven national populations (Americans, English-Canadians, French-Canadians, French, English, French-Belgians, Flemish-Belgians, Greeks, Italians, Japanese, and Portuguese), drawing samples of middle- and working-class families (twenty of each). Findings were that responses of parents to these social situations varied more by class than by nation; that is, there were substantial similarities among middle-class parents and among working-class parents, regardless of their nationality, while the major difference was between the two social classes rather than across nations. However, it should be noted that the samples in this study came from a relatively narrow range of cross-cultural variation.

Once again, we have evidence for some transcultural generality in the way parents deal with their children. In this study, as in the Six Cultures Study, while there is obvious variation in child-rearing, this appears to be due to individual and class differences rather than to cultural differences. There is thus a major inconsistency in the literature: the studies employing ratings from archives have revealed a great deal of variation across cultures in child-rearing, while those using direct field observations or standardized instruments tend to find little. Since the archival indices of child-rearing fit into a plausible pattern of relationship with other cultural and ecological variables, it is difficult to dismiss them as invalid. Similarly, the field studies provide compelling evidence that also needs to be taken seriously. This discrepancy clearly sets the stage for future research on these topics.

The concept of development

The notion of development comes into this book at three levels. First, there is phylogenetic development as exemplified in evolution theory. It deals with variation across species and the emergence of new species over long periods of time. This biological form of evolution will be discussed in the next section and in Chapter 8. Second, the term *development* can refer to cultural changes in societies. Development in this sense will be touched upon in Chapter 7 (where the anthropological tradition of cultural evolution will be mentioned). In the present section we are mainly concerned with the course of development of the individual during one's lifetime, which is called *ontogenetic development*.

Differences in behavior as they are found across cultures are not just there at a particular moment in time. They have a history and there is a reason they have come about. For a full interpretation of findings the developmental perspective in cross-cultural psychology is essential (Vygotsky, 1978; Heron & Kroeger, 1981; Munroe, Munroe, & Whiting 1981; Cole & Cole, 1989).

Psychological development will be considered here as the outcome of interactions between a biological organism and environmental influences. This means that we accept the distinction between nature and nurture as a starting point for the discussion. The reason for this position is simple: the relative importance of the biological and environmental-experiential component of behavior has formed the major dimension underlying the differences between the various schools of thinking on individual development in the psychological literature.

There are five such schools that are relevant to cross-cultural research. *Maturation theory* (Gesell, 1940) places great emphasis on biological factors. In his view, development is under the control of genetic factors, continuing well after birth. Gesell's writings influenced early cross-cultural researchers, including Ainsworth (1967) and Geber (1958), who reported evidence of African precocity (to be reported in the next section).

Stage theory (e.g., Piaget, 1970b) proposes that children move through different stages of development and that these stages can be recognized by qualitatively different ways of thinking. Although there are individual and group differences in the *rate* of development, the *sequence* of the various stages is thought to be universally the same. One application of stage theory (to moral development) is examined in Box 2-1.

From the point of view of *differentiation theory* (H. Werner, 1957, p. 126) development implies "increasing differentiation, articulation and hierarchic integration" in the child's psychological life. Greater differentiation implies specialization of psychological functions as well as a more structured organization of these functions. These changes are largely due to environmental experiences.

In the *life span developmental theory* (e.g., Baltes, 1983; R. L. Munroe & R. H. Munroe, 1975) development is considered to be a continuous process of change during the entire course of an individual's life. Emphasis is placed on the context of development and the interaction between the individual and the environment.

In some contrast, *context-specificity theory* (Cole and his colleagues; e.g., Laboratory of Comparative Human Cognition, 1983) emphasizes particular situations (rather than the larger contexts studied by others) and quite specific behaviors that are linked to these situations, but that may not be generalized to other behavior settings. Later, in Chapter 5, most of these theories will be considered in more detail in relation to cognitive development.

An important concept currently used to understand the interaction between environmental and biological factors in development is the notion of the *developmental niche* as described by Super and Harkness (1982, 1986a;

Box 2-1 Moral development

An example of the stage approach to development that has received extensive cross-cultural examination is that of moral development. Kohlberg (1981, 1984) distinguished three major levels of moral reasoning, called the *preconventional*, the *conventional*, and the *postconventional* level. These correspond with three levels of social perspective. In the preconventional stage moral conduct is in the interest of individuals themselves, or in the interest of relatives. Reasons for doing right are the avoidance of punishment and the principle of fairness in an exchange. At the second level concern about loyalty and concern about the welfare of other persons and society at large are given as reasons to justify one's actions. At the postconventional level actions are based on ethical principles to which an individual has committed himself and that serve as absolute standards, even taking priority over laws of society violating these principles.

Kohlberg assumed that the development of moral reasoning would follow the same invariant sequence in all cultures and lead toward the same ultimate level of development, representing universal ethical principles. However, the rate of development and the highest stage reached can show systematic differences. Kohlberg (1981) has proposed a theory of social evolution whereby nonliterate and semiliterate groups living in village communities would lag behind other (more complex) cultures.

Kohlberg's claims have been tested in a fairly large number of cross-cultural studies. In a review article Snarey (1985) included forty five studies from twenty-seven cultural groups. Considerable support has been found for the invariance of the stage sequence postulated by Kohlberg. The first two stages have been identified in a wide range of cultural settings. As far as the highest level of moral reasoning is concerned, no evidence has been found for the presence of postconventional stages in any of the eight "folk tribal or village societies" where data had been collected. Thus, postconventional moral reasoning would seem to be characteristic of complex urban societies (non-Western as well as Western).

For a proper interpretation of these findings one must realize that postconventional reasoning as defined by Kohlberg is derived from the writings of philosophers. It is displayed by a small minority of subjects even in industrial urban societies. The typical level of the responses shows conventional rather than postconventional reasoning, even in the urban societies of North America and Europe. This affects any meaningful empirical test of the universality of Kohlberg's higher stages.

According to C. P. Edwards (1986) cultural groups can be expected to differ in the modal stage or level of moral reasoning, because of differences in values and social organization. Snarey (1985, p. 228) contends that every culture is capable of supporting postconventional reasoning. Other authors have suggested that the higher stages are not separate developmental stages. According to Gibbs (1977), the highest stage represents "second-order" thinking about moral behavior. Eckensberger and Reinshagen (1980) have proposed that the last stage merely represents an extension of earlier stages from individual persons to the social system as a whole. Kohlberg (Kohlberg, Levine, & Hewer, 1983) has accepted many of these criticisms and modified his theory in an attempt to accommodate them.

However, cross-cultural researchers (e.g., Ma, 1988, 1989; J. G. Miller et al., 1990; Shweder, Mahapatra, & Miller, 1990) have raised substantial criticisms, even of this reformulation. For example, Shweder et al., (1990, p. 75) have proposed (on the basis of research in India) the existence of "alternative postconventional moralities" based upon conceptions of natural law and justice, rather than on individualism, secularism, and social contract, and possibly modeled on the family as a moral institution.

The work of J. G. Miller et al. (1990), also in India, has examined the hypothesis of moral behavior as the acceptance of social responsibilities toward persons in need. Earlier studies by Miller and her colleagues suggested that Indians' judgments reflect a moral code that tends to give priority to social duties and Americans' judgments reflect a moral code that tends to give priority to individual rights. In more recent studies Miller et al. found similarities in Indian and American views about social responsibilities when serious (for example, life-threatening) situations were being judged. However, there were substantial cultural differences in the scope of social responsibilities that were considered to be moral in character and in the criteria that were used in judging whether such issues constituted moral obligations: Indians maintained a broad view and emphasized need more than did Americans.

Based on his own work in Hong Kong and on other cross-cultural evidence, Ma (1988) has proposed a revised theory of moral development rooted in Kohlberg's original theory, but extended to include Chinese perspectives, such as the "Golden Mean" (behaving in the way the majority of people in society do) and "Good Will" (the virtue of complying with nature). An empirical examination of some of these ideas with samples from Hong Kong, the People's Republic of China, and England revealed that the two Chinese samples showed a stronger tendency to perform altruistic acts toward others and to abide by the law than did the English sample. "In general, the Chinese emphasize *Ch'ing* (human affection, or sentiment) more than *Li* (reason, rationality), and they value filial piety, group solidarity, collectivism and humanity" (Ma, 1989, p. 172).

It is evident that a more detailed examination of specific cultural features and some variations in findings in these studies in India and China require a reconceptualization of what constitutes moral development, particularly at the highest level of postconventional morality.

cf. Jahoda, 1986a; Segall et al., 1990). The concept is reminiscent of the *ecological niche* in biology (see Chapter 8), that is, the way of life of a species in a certain environment. The developmental niche is described as a system in which the physical environment, sociocultural customs of child-rearing, and psychological conceptions (beliefs and so forth) of caretakers play a role. This view is consistent with the ecocultural perspective adopted in this book.

Super and Harkness (1986a) do not see the child as a passive occupant of a developmental niche. The child not only adapts to a given environment, but also actively influences it, thus contributing to the formation of its own niche. In Figure 2-1 this interaction could be represented by making the arrows show influences in both directions. However, for the sake of clarity, only unidirectional arrows (representing the predominant influence) are shown.

It is important to note that in a growing body of research there is an explicit recognition of the role of biological factors. In one study H. Keller, Schölmerich, and Eibl-Eibesfeldt (1988) analyzed communication patterns between infants (2 to 6 months) and parents in West German, Greek, Trobriand, and Yanomami society. Similar interaction structures were found. For example, infants produce few vocalizations when adults are talking and vice versa; adults respond differently to positive and negative vocalizations. According to the authors the findings are compatible with the notion of intuitive parenting programs that rest on inborn characteristics regulating behavior expression of genetic potential is a function of environmental conditions.[2]

Super and Harkness (1986a) are quite explicit in acknowledging the role of biological factors. These impose constraints on the kind of environment children can effectively cope with and form the basis of universal stages of development. Biological factors are not restricted to the population level. Super and Harkness also noted that individual temperament (which has a genetic basis) can be a determinant of the interaction between the child and its environment. For example, children with irregular sleeping habits (due to their temperament) are seen as "difficult" in the U.S.A, because they interfere with the way of life of their parents, who value their own independence and autonomy. Among the Kipsigis in Kenya, Super and Harkness observed that children sleep with their mothers and are carried around for a large part of the daytime. In this context "sleeping arrangements and the absence of institutionalized work schedules virtually eliminated sleep as a source of difficulty in caring for infants. On the other hand, the Kipsigis niche was not easily able to deal with the baby who did not like being carried around on the back, or who objected to being cared for by someone other than the mother" (Super & Harkness, 1986a, p. 563).

With Super and Harkness's conception of the developmental niche, biological explanations have reentered the cross-cultural developmental literature. The idea that some children genetically are better equipped for (or attuned to) a certain environment points to the possibility of cultural changes in accordance with principles of biological evolution. The relative frequency in a population of an advantageous genetic trait can increase over generations under certain conditions. In other words the door is open for cultural changes stimulated by genetic factors, if different biological traits are advantageous in different cultures. As we shall see in Chapter 8 there is a large distance between the *possibility* and the *plausibility* of genetic causes behind a cultural difference in behavior. In our opinion it is too early to judge whether a new biocultural synthesis will emerge. Nevertheless, suggestions such as those of Super and Harkness differ essentially from earlier biologically oriented approaches in developmental psychology. The relative importance of nature versus nurture is no longer the major point of emphasis, but variation in the expression of genetic potential is a function of environmental conditions.[2]

Infant development

We now turn to an examination of the earliest period of human development, infancy. While it is here that we are likely to be able to observe human activity before cultural factors affect the individual in a substantial way, it is also true that cultural factors (such as prenatal maternal nutrition and activity and postnatal infant stimulation) are known to account for individual and population differences in infant behavior. We begin with a consideration of parallels between infrahuman and human development, and then turn to an examination of some ethnographic and cross-cultural psychological studies.

Phylogenetic approach. This approach (see Konner, 1981) compares human beings with other species on the phylogenetic scale. Particularly in infancy, one can study aspects of psychological development, such as attachment or maternal care, within an evolutionary perspective. Biologists consider human beings to be adapted, anatomically and physiologically, to the hunting and gathering way of life that has been pursued for millions of years. The invention of agriculture that led to sedentarization and the later change to industrialization are only recent events to which mankind has not been able to adapt biologically, only culturally.

More than in any other species human neuromotor development continues after birth; this permits a large environmental influence on development. Although generally the "plasticity" of behavior increases as one goes up the phylogenetic scale, there is nevertheless great variability between closely

---

[2] We would like to comment on the fairly large number of forward references made in this section. In a positive sense this could be taken to signify the central position occupied by the concept of ontogenetic development. However, another explanation seems more correct, namely that in cross-cultural psychology inferences about development often are made on the basis of studies with a nondevelopmental focus. Of the cross-cultural traditions mentioned in this section only that of Piaget is predominantly developmental, also in its cross-cultural applications. Chapters on cognition and perception in books on developmental cross-cultural psychology (e.g., E. E. Werner, 1979; R. H. Munroe, R. L. Munroe, & B. B. Whiting, 1981) tend to contain the same references to empirical cross-cultural studies as those in books without an emphasis on development. Research projects in which developmental changes are studied longitudinally as well as cross-culturally, unfortunately, remain exceptional.

related species. The level of development at birth depends on the specific adaptation to a particular ecological niche (such as the risk of predation). Higher primates and human beings are precocious in their sensory systems, but less developed in their motor systems. Konner (1981) has hypothesized that the relatively slow infant motor development among humans would be a recent adaptation (perhaps a million years ago) caused by the invention of the baby carrier.

The attachment between the baby and its mother, a theme that is important in psychological development (Ainsworth, 1967; Bowlby, 1969; Kermoian & Leiderman, 1986) is seen as an adaptation to the risk of predation. All placental animals have a constant contact between mother and baby from birth, with an important element of tactile stimulation. Almost continuous bodily contact, with the baby held in a vertical position during the day, is characteristic of nomadic hunting societies, but it is also frequent among agriculturalists. The absence of contact and the predominance of a horizontal position are relatively recent developments in human societies.

Weaning takes place among primates at different times (one year for most monkeys, two years for baboons, and four years for chimpanzees) but this nursing period represents a constant proportion (one-quarter to one-third) of the age of female sexual maturity. Among human nomadic hunters, weaning takes place around 3 or 4 years of age (later if there is no new baby), and this corresponds to the same proportion. Most sedentary agricultural societies have a birth spacing (corresponding to the age of weaning) of two to three years. In recent years early weaning and the use of the feeding bottle have spread to much of the world's population, above all to the large cities of the third world, with all the well-known dangers.

Holocultural approach. In the section on archival studies we saw how the holocultural approach can be used to produce evidence for some broad generalizations about relationships between subsistence economic activity and child-rearing practices. A more specific example of the use of this approach is a study by J. W. Whiting (1981) on infant carrying practices in relation to mean annual temperature, which serves as a further example of the ecocultural framework.

Whiting grouped carrying practices into three categories (cradle, arms, and sling). Drawing a 10°C isotherm (coldest month) on a world map and placing the three styles of carrying on the same map revealed a striking correlation with temperature. In a sample of 250 societies cradle carrying was predominant in those whose mean temperatures were lower than 10°C, while arm and sling carrying were predominant in warmer societies. The main exceptions were the Inuit, who carry their babies in the parka hood.

One can speculate on the functional origins of such a relationship between climate and a child-rearing practice. At this level a very basic consideration may be at work: urine on the clothes is disagreeable in cold climates, while it can evaporate quickly in the heat. One can equally speculate on the long-term effects of such practices on young babies. Some of these possibilities will be discussed in Chapter 7 in the section on Culture and Personality.

Psychological approach. The psychological approach to infant development across cultures seeks to observe, describe, and measure individual behavior (particularly in the psychomotor domain) in a variety of field settings. Following the work of the pediatricians Gesell and Amatruda (1947), who first systematized observations in this domain, various psychologists have constructed developmental scales called "baby tests" that allow for quantitative measurement, (e.g., Bayley, 1969; Griffiths, 1970; Brunet & Lézine, 1951). Based on the IQ model, these scales are composed of a number of items (observable behaviors that are characteristic of a given age) that one can use to determine the infant's developmental age. When developmental age is divided by chronological age (and multiplied by 100), one obtains a "developmental quotient" (DQ). These scales, in addition to giving a general DQ, also allow the distinguishing of partial DQ's in particular areas, such as motor, eye-hand coordination, language, and sociability. They can be applied to infants from birth until about 3 years of age.

The state of development at birth is a question that deserves to be considered separately. Just after birth, or at least in the first forty-eight hours, the pediatrician can carry out an examination to establish if the development of the neonate is normal. This examination looks at neuromotor characteristics, particularly at the "archaic" reflexes, which disappear after 6 to 10 weeks in Euroamerican babies. These examinations are not easy to conduct, because of the rapid changes in the infant's state of wakefulness. The first cross-cultural studies were methodologically rather intuitive. More recently, stricter protocols have been established, for example, by Brazelton (1973).

The first cross-cultural study of infant performance, one that has had important repercussions, was carried out by Geber and Dean (1957). They examined full-term neonates who weighed more than 2500 gms in the maternity hospital in Kampala, Uganda. They found a marked precocity in development in relation to Western pediatric norms: an advance of 2 to 6 weeks in holding the head and a nearly complete absence of the archaic reflexes (indicating an advanced state of development). This has come to be known as "African Infant Precocity."[3]

The studies of Geber and Dean (1957) were easy to criticize: the observations and the way in which the results were presented were flawed; the authors did not use statistical tests to establish African differences from the norms; and it would have been better to have both African and American samples tested by the same experimenter. Other, more subtle, factors can also have affected the validity of their results. For example, birthing in Africa (even in a maternity hospital) does not take place under the same conditions

---

[3] The term *African precocity* can be seen as an example of ethnocentrism. The equally appropriate term of Euroamerican *retardation* is used nowhere in the literature.

as in Western hospitals; anesthetics, routinely used in the U.S. and Europe up to the 1970s, are rarely employed in Africa and can have marked effects on the development of neonates. Furthermore, the mean weight at birth of African neonates (as well as Afroamericans) is on average lower than that of white babies, even under optimal nutritional conditions; the limit of 2500 g was not appropriate and led to the elimination of one-third of the potential subjects, who were falsely considered to be premature. Finally, the examination rests in part on the absence of a phenomenon (the archaic reflexes) and should be subject to greater caution than if it had rested on behaviors actually observed.

Differences at birth do not preclude environmental influences (known as intrauterine experiences of the baby). Second, empirical studies generally show smaller differences as measurements are taken earlier in life. An experiment on looking strategies in American and Nigerian children is an instructive example. Bundy and Mundy-Castle (1984; Mundy-Castle, 1983) distinguished three stages in the looking strategies (fixation and fixation duration) of infants aged 5 days to 10 months. The American children tended to reach the third stage at an earlier age, while there was no such difference in the age of transition from the first to the second stage. The study by Bundy and Mundy-Castle suggests that there are effects of environmental conditions even early in life.

Research (e.g., Warren & Parkin, 1974; Keefer, Dixon, Tronik, & Brazelton, 1978) using stricter methods (e.g., the Brazelton exam) has shown that the neonatal precocity found by the first studies was partly exaggerated: there is a certain precocity, but not as general as previously described. Also, cross-cultural differences in the handling of neonates starting almost right after birth points to the possible role of environmental factors (Hopkins, 1977).

Among others Super (1981a & b) observed that this was, in fact, a false debate, based on the fallacious premise that birth is the zero point of development and that it permits the separation of genetic and acquired factors. In fact, the environment influences development already during pregnancy, a period during which the traditional African milieu offers very favorable conditions (such as valuing the woman who is pregnant and her physical activity right up to giving birth). Moreover, there are aspects of development that are genetically determined (such as adolescent hormonal changes) that do not appear at birth. Thus neonatal studies are unlikely to provide us with a method for disentangling genetic and environmental factors in development.

If neonatal precocity has been controversial, psychomotor precocity in the first year of life in different populations (above all in Africa, but elsewhere as well) has been well documented in many studies (e.g., Geber, 1958; Vouilloux, 1959; E. E. Werner, 1972). It is indicated by a general DQ on baby tests between 140 and 180 during the first months of development. It appears certain that this advance is due to particular child rearing practices: bodily and affective contact with the mother, care that promotes motor development (e.g., massage, which exists in one form or another in most of Africa and India), tactile, proprioceptive, visual, and auditory stimulation linked to the baby's participation in daily life, and being in a vertical position (that is, on the back of the mother) compared to Western babies, who spend most of the day lying in a separate quiet place. According to many studies carried out in Africa, the developmental curves (DQ) decline with age, attaining the Western norms (defined as a DQ of 100) during the second year, or even falling below it. For several decades this declining curve has been taken as valid, with explanations given in terms of harsh weaning. In fact, Dasen, Inhelder, Lavallée, & Retschitzki (1978) and others have argued that the ill-effects of weaning have been exaggerated and that the decline in the developmental curves could be explained to a large extent by artifacts.

The use of baby tests has also been criticized because the DQ swamps interesting differences between specific items. Super (1976), by analyzing each item in the Bayley scale separately (for the Kipsigis in Kenya), found that sitting upright unassisted and walking are acquired early (about one month before the Bayley American norms). These are motor developments recognized as important by Kipsigis mothers, that are named, and are specifically trained. In contrast, other motor behaviors, for which infants receive little training, show a delay rather than an advance on the norm (for example crawling).

Super (1976) then studied six ethnic groups in East Africa to find out if crawling was valued and trained or not. The correlation between these data and the mean age of acquisition was 0.77 and reached 0.97 if one took into account the opportunity an infant had to practice this motor skill. Kilbride (1980) has made the same argument concerning sitting and smiling, comparing the Baganda (of Uganda) and the Samia (of Kenya). Thus, informed researchers no longer speak of general precocity, but look for a direct link between "parental ethnotheories" and psychomotor development.

More recently Bril and others (Bril & Sabatier, 1986; Bril & Zack, 1989; Nkounkou-Hombessa, 1988) have made detailed observations on the different postures that accompany child-rearing practices and the care of babies among French infant-mother dyads and among the Bambara (of Mali) and the Kongo-Lari (of the Congo). Rabain (1989), observing African mothers and their babies in Paris, found that migration had little effect on these practices. There is thus evidence of a strong connection between parental ethnotheories and motor development: the Bambara believe that an infant should sit at 3 to 4 months and train them to this end; the Congolese believe that if an infant does not walk by 8 months it is late, and they seek a healer, who practices a therapy that consists of motor manipulation and the application to the joints of a mixture made from the bones of ferocious animals and hot spices (Nkounkou-Hombessa, 1988).

We turn now to a consideration of the development of sensorimotor intelligence. Baby tests (like IQ tests) are empirical constructions: the developmental landmarks that build up the tests are chosen according to statistical criteria, namely a steep slope in the developmental curve, indicating that, in the normative sample, the particular behavior appears at much the same age in all individuals. In contrast to baby tests, the scales of so-called "sensori-motor intelligence" are explicitly based on the theory of Piaget (1936, 1937): items are chosen so as to reflect various stages within the sensorimotor period. During the first two years of life, according to Piaget, the infant constructs his knowledge of the surrounding world; it is knowledge by action rather than representation, hence the term "sensori-motor." This development can be described by a series of hierarchical stages whose order of appearance is constant, and the behaviors of each stage are extensions of those of the preceding stage. Piaget distinguished six such stages, closely matched in the scale developed by Casati and Lézine (1968; translated and adapted in the U.S. by Kopp & Sigman, 1972). Corman and Escalona's (1969) scale deals with the first three stages, and that of Uzgiris and Hunt (1975) differentiates between ten stages. Tests of sensorimotor intelligence typically contain problems to be solved by the infant. Often attractive objects are hidden from sight or are placed outside immediate reach. This can lead to frustration, and much care has to be taken to set up the experimental situation.

There are relatively few cross-cultural studies using scales of sensorimotor intelligence, probably because the examinations are long and difficult to carry out and demand serious theoretical training. The most complete study is a longitudinal one using the Casati-Lézine scale in a rural region of Côte d'Ivoire (Dasen et al., 1978). Goldberg (1972) used a scale developed by Corman and Escalona (1969) in Lusaka (Zambia); Sieye (1975) used the Casati-Lézine scale in Abidjan (Côte d'Ivoire), and Kopp, Khoka, and Sigman (1977) used the American version in India.

The results of these studies demonstrate quite unequivocally the universality of the sequence of the stages of sensorimotor intelligence; at least everywhere the research has been done, the same behaviors have been found in the same order of stages. In contrast, there is a large variation *within* individuals: an infant who is at a certain stage judging by the performance on one task is not necessarily so according to another task. One also finds this lack of homogeneity, not anticipated by the theory, in the following stage (that of concrete operations), but in both cases it is not a phenomenon peculiar to cross-cultural studies.

With respect to the rate of development, the studies have reported various results. For their rural Baoulé subjects, Dasen et al. (1978) found advances over the French norms on certain tasks, but not on all. There was a certain precocity in both motor development and sensorimotor intelligence, but as in the work of Super (1976) it was selective rather than general. Especially advanced over the French norms were the resolution of problems involving the use of instruments to increase the reach of the arm and to combine two objects.

This result is a bit surprising, since the literature leads us to believe that the environment of the African infant is poor in objects. For example, Knapen (1962) suggested that for the Mukongo infant (of Zaire), "The daily environment of the Congolese child is striking in its poverty of intellectual stimulation" (p. 157).

Moreover, African adults seldom use objects as intermediaries in their communication with young children. While a European mother offers a rattle or other toy to calm a crying baby, an African mother intervenes with body contact, especially by offering her breast (Zempléni-Rabain, 1970; Rabain, 1979). Despite the absence of this adult use of objects and the absence of manufactured toys, behavior observations in natural settings show that, in fact, young Africans have available a host of different objects, which they are not prevented from using. Practically nothing is forbidden, not even access to objects considered dangerous by European mothers (Dasen et al., 1978).

These objects, unlike toys, do not have a single function. They are thus particularly relevant to symbolic play, which marks, according to Piaget, the passage from the stage of sensorimotor intelligence to the preoperational stage, which begins by the acquisition of the symbolic function, part of which is language. Behavioral observations made by Dasen et al. (1978) in natural settings, as well as those videotaped under controlled situations, permitted the study of the stages of construction of this symbolic function. Again, there is no reason to doubt that this aspect of psychological development is universal, even if the content of symbolic play is culturally relative. At this stage a Baoulé child pretends to carry a small bowl on its head or a baby on its back, while a French child of the same age pretends to put the doll on the potty or gives it something to eat with a spoon. The structure of these actions, carried out in the absence of the actual model being imitated, and with objects used symbolically, is nevertheless the same.

Conclusions

In this chapter we have sketched the importance of culture-linked antecedent variables in the development of children. Some of the issues raised will appear again in later chapters. We mention two that deserve special attention. One is the initial interpretation at face value of cross-cultural differences in scores on psychological instruments that have been constructed within a particular cultural context. The first studies in an area tend to overestimate cross-cultural differences and to overgeneralize the psychological implications. Such methodological and theoretical problems of interpretation of data are a recurrent theme in this book. A second major theme is the nature of the interactions between genetic predispositions and sociocultural or ecological variables; to a large extent this is unknown territory where it would be premature to make strong statements. One conclusion that is possible is that infants everywhere are set on their life course with much the same apparatus and much the same set of possibilities. Through cultural variations in child-rearing and infant-care practices, some psychological variations begin to appear that can be understood within an ecocultural frame of reference.

3   Social behavior

This chapter considers the domain of social behavior and how it may relate to or be influenced by the general cultural context in which it takes place. We begin with a brief consideration of what social behavior is and some of the issues in cross-cultural psychology that attend its investigation. We then turn to a review of some features of the sociocultural system that have been suggested by sociology and anthropology as being important dimensions of sociocultural variation in human groups. The main part of the chapter is a review of cross-cultural research in a few selected areas of social behavior, including conformity, values, and gender behavior. One other area of social behavior, that of ethnic attitudes and prejudice within plural societies, will be considered in Chapter 12.

A central question addressed in this chapter is the nature of cross-cultural variation in social behavior. On the one hand social behaviors are obviously linked to the particular sociocultural context in which they develop; greeting procedures (for example, bowing, handshaking, or kissing) vary widely from culture to culture, and these are clear-cut examples of the influence of cultural transmission on our social behavior. On the other hand we all do greet, suggesting the presence of some fundamental commonality in the very essence of social behavior. One resolution to these contrasting observations is to make the working assumption that many (perhaps most) kinds of social behaviors get done in all cultures, but that they get done in very different ways, depending on local cultural circumstances.

A typical approach to examining this idea is one that follows closely the three goals of cross-cultural psychology that were outlined in Chapter 1. The starting point is to recognize that the social psychology that is currently available is *culture-bound*; it has developed mostly in one society (the United States), which took "for its themes of research, and for the contents of its theories, the issues of *its own* society" (Moscovici, 1972, p. 19). This culture-bound nature of extant social psychology is now a widely accepted viewpoint (e.g., Berry, 1978; Bond, 1988; Jahoda, 1979, 1986b). An empirical demonstration of the cultural limits of social psychology has been provided by Amir and Sharon (1987), who attempted to replicate (in Israel) some of the more central studies in contemporary American social psychology. Of thirty attempts to replicate, only six were fully successful and four more were only partially replicated; the other twenty studies yielded quite different results. At a theoretical level Berry (1974a) has pointed out the inappropriateness of importing some American social-psychological concepts into Canada (such as studying French-Canadian/English-Canadian relations using an implicit model derived from black-American/white-American research). If there are difficulties in transporting theories, methods, and findings from the United States to Israel and Canada, how much more likely are there to be problems when larger cultural contrasts are involved?

One solution is to create indigenous social psychologies (Berry, 1978) following the proposal of Moscovici (1972): "the social psychology that we ought to create must have an origin in our own reality" (p. 23). This corresponds to the second goal of cross-cultural psychology; as outlined in Chapter 1, the intention is to explore other cultural systems to discover new social behavioral phenomena that correspond to the local sociocultural reality. If we do this, we are likely to end up with a proliferation of "multiple social psychologies" (Doise, 1982; Jahoda, 1986b), each one corresponding to its own sociocultural context.

An obvious advantage of these other social psychologies is that they are likely to match the indigenous realities that nurtured them. However, an equally obvious disadvantage is that such proliferation might hinder the discovery of the possible underlying principles and common dimensions of social behavior; that is, the pursuit of the third goal of cross-cultural psychology (as outlined in Chapter 1) may be impeded. There is little doubt, in the views of many cross-cultural social psychologists (e.g., Faucheux, 1976; Jahoda, 1979; Pepitone, 1976; Triandis, 1978; Pepitone & Triandis, 1987) that these basic universal principles exist in some (if not all) domains of social behavior (see Box 3-1). Put another way, the working assumption with which we started this discussion appears to be widely shared in contemporary cross-cultural psychology. However, *how* to discover these universal principles while wallowing in all the local indigenous social psychologies remains the core problem facing cross-cultural social psychologists. We will return to this issue in Part II of this book, where the topic of universals is examined.

Cultural context

Social behavior takes place in a social and cultural context that varies widely from place to place. In this section we deal with two important dimensions of social and cultural variation found across cultures: role diversity and role obligation.

In every social system individuals occupy *positions* for which certain behaviors are expected; these behaviors are called *roles*. Each role occupant is the object of *sanctions* that exert social influence, even pressure, to behave according to social *norms* or standards. (Readers who are unfamiliar with these terms may wish to consult any introductory sociology text or Chapter 1 of Segall et al., 1990.) The four italicized terms constitute some essential

Box 3-1   Universals in social behavior

Aberle and his colleagues (1950) have proposed a set of *functional prerequisites* or "the things that must get done in any society if it is to continue as a going concern." These are of interest because they probably qualify as *universals*, those activities (in one form or another) that will be found in every culture in which we may work. There are nine of these:

1. *Provision of adequate relationships with the environment* (both physical and social). This is needed to maintain a sufficient population to "carry" the society and culture.
2. *The differentiation and assignment of roles.* In any group different things need to get done, and people have somehow to be assigned to these roles (for example, by heredity or by achievement).
3. *Communication.* All groups need to have a shared, learned, and symbolic mode of communication in order to maintain information flow and coordination within the group.
4. *Shared cognitive orientation.* Beliefs, knowledge, and rules of logical thinking need to be held in common for people in a society to work together in mutual comprehension.
5. *Shared articulated set of goals.* Similarly, the directions for common striving need to be shared, in order to avoid individuals pulling in conflicting directions.
6. *Normative regulation of means to these goals.* Rules governing *how* these goals might be achieved need to be stated and accepted by the population. If material acquisition is a general goal for most people, murder and theft are not likely to be accepted as a means to this goal, whereas production, hard work, and trading may be.
7. *Regulation of affective expression.* Similarly, emotions and feelings need to be brought under normative control. The expression of love and hate, for example, cannot be given free rein without serious disruptive consequences within the group.
8. *Socialization.* All new members must learn about the central and important features of group life. The way of life of the group needs to be communicated, learned, and to some extent accepted by all individuals.
9. *Control of disruptive behavior.* If socialization and normative regulation fail, there needs to be some "backup" so that the group can require appropriate and acceptable behavior of its members. In the end, behavioral correction or even permanent removal (by incarceration or execution) may be required.

More recently a universal model of social relations has been proposed by A. P. Fiske (1991), in which it is claimed that "just four elementary relational structures are sufficient to describe an enormous spectrum of forms of human social relations, as well as social motives and emotions, intuitive social thought and moral judgement." These are:

1. *Communal sharing*: where people are merged, boundaries of individual selves are indistinct, people attend to group membership and have a sense of common identity, solidarity, unity, and belonging; they think of themselves as being all the same in some significant respect, not as individuals, but as "we."
2. *Authority ranking*: where inequality and hierarchy prevail, highly ranked persons control people, things, and resources (including knowledge), frequently take inititative, and have the right to choose and exercise preference.
3. *Equality matching*: where there are egalitarian relations among peers, people are separate but equal, engaging in turn-taking, reciprocity, and balanced relationships.
4. *Market pricing*: where relationships are mediated by values determined by a "market" system. Individuals interact with others just when and as they decide that it is rational to do so in terms of these values, and actions are evaluated according to the rates at which they can be exchanged for other comodities.

In the view of Fiske:

these models are *fundamental*, in the sense that they are the lowest or most basic-level "grammars" for social relations. Further, the models are *general*, giving order to most forms of social interaction, thought, and affect, They are *elementary*, in the sense that they are the basic consitituents for all higher-order social forms. It is also my hypothesis that they are *universal*, being the basis for social relations among all people in all cultures, and the essential foundation for cross-cultural understanding and intercultural engagement. (Fiske, 1991, p. 25)

conceptual building blocks that enable us to understand the flow from background context, to culture, to transmission, and eventually to social behavior as presented in Figure 1-3.

These elements of a social system are not random, but are organized or structured by each cultural group. Such structures are considered in this text to be influenced by the ecological context and are subject to further change stemming from the sociopolitical context (see Chapter 1). Two key features of social structure are that they are *differentiated* and *stratified*. The first term means that societies make distinctions among roles; some societies make few, while others make many. For example, in a relatively undifferentiated social structure positions and roles may be limited to a few basic familial, social, and economic ones (such as parent/child, camp leader/camp member, hunter/food preparer). In contrast, in a relatively more differentiated society there are many more positions and roles to be found in particular domains, such as king/aristocracy/citizen/slave, corporate owner/manager/worker/retiree, or pope/cardinal/bishop/priest/believer. In the former there is minimal *role diversity*, while in the latter there is more.

These differentiated positions and roles may be organized in a hierarchy or not; when they are placed in a vertical *status* structure, the social system is said to be *stratified*. A number of cross-cultural analyses of stratification are available; two of the more straightforward are by Murdock (1967) and Pelto (1968). Murdock is concerned with the presence of class distinctions (for example, hereditary aristocracy, wealth distinctions). At one end (unstratified) there are few such status distinctions, while at the other (stratified), there may be numerous class or status distinctions (for example, royalty, aristocracy, gentry, citizens, slaves). The analysis by Pelto (1968) of these and similar distinctions led him to place societies on a dimension called "tight-loose." In these stratified and tight societies the pressures to carry out one's roles lead to a high level of *role obligation*, while in less tight societies there is much less pressure to oblige.

These two dimensions of cultural variation appear to be related to some basic features of ecological systems. For example, in the work of McNett (1970), nomadic hunting and gathering societies tend to have less role diversity and role obligation while sedentary agricultural societies typically have more diversity and obligation. In urban, industrialized societies many studies have suggested an even higher level of diversity, but lower levels of role obligation (Lomax & Berkowitz, 1972; Boldt, 1978). These two cultural dimensions are thus clearly related to the ecological dimension introduced in Figure 1-3.

With these central dimensions of the social and cultural context displayed, we can now turn to a survey of studies in selected domains of social behavior that have been carried out by cross-cultural psychologists. The general topic is so vast that we will limit our discussion to a small set of specific topics; these have been selected in part to represent a range of typical research in social behavior.

Conformity

The degree to which individuals will characteristically go along with the prevailing group norm has long been a topic of interest in social psychology. As we have seen in the earlier brief discussion of norms there are general expectations in all societies that members will conform to some extent; in their absence it is quite likely that social cohesiveness would be so minimal that the group could not continue to function. However, as we have seen in the discussion of socialization (Chapter 2) there appears to be variation across cultures in the degree to which individuals are raised or trained to be independent and self- (as opposed to group-) reliant. It is thus plausible to expect that there may be a pattern of covariation between where a society is located on the compliance-assertion dimension of socialization and the typical degree of individual conformity to the group's norms.

Moreover, as we have also seen there are some demographic and social variables that tend to go along with compliance-assertion in socialization and that may further encourage conformity; the size of the group and the degree of social stratification may "bear down" on the individual more when one's group is large and highly stratified. We thus can identify a package of influences that suggest that conformity may vary across cultures: there is likely to be relatively more individual conformity in societies that emphasize compliance-training, and are dense and stratified, and relatively less in assertion-training, sparse, and unstratified societies.

Some evidence is available to support this expectation. The tendency of individuals to be influenced by what they believe to be the judgments of a group, even when those judgments conflict with the evidence of the individuals' own perceptions is a phenomenon first demonstrated by Asch (1956). In those studies subjects were presented with a line judgment task in which they had to say which of three lines of differing length were the same length as a standard comparison line. Faced with this task, subjects conformed with the unanimous, but obviously incorrect, judgments (of a group of experimenter's confederates) of line lengths about one-third of the time. Dozens of studies have been done since, mainly with university students in Western countries using Asch's procedures or modifications thereof and have both replicated and extended his findings. A few cross-cultural studies have been conducted with Asch-type materials (e.g., Boldt, 1978; Chandra, 1973; Claeys, 1967; Matsuda, 1985) and with a variety of other estimates of conformity (e.g., Huang & Harris, 1973; Meade & Barnard, 1973; Munroe & Munroe, 1975).

Several of the studies make some assessment of or comment upon the strength of the cultural surround. For example, reference is made to strong traditional group influence (Huang & Harris, 1973; Meade & Barnard, 1973), strong childhood compliance training (Munroe & Munroe, 1975), communal social organization (Boldt, 1978; Matsuda, 1985), or authoritarian social structure (Chandra, 1973). A reasonable interpretation of these various terms (strong, communal, authoritarian, and so on) is that they all point to the influence of a "tight" sociocultural context upon the level of individual conformity exhibited.

A few studies using a modified Asch-type procedure have been done in Japan, a society that is relatively high in role obligation and hence one in which greater conformity might be expected. Frager (1970) obtained findings that he described as contradicting that expectation, including an average number of conformity responses that was less than reported for American respondents and a very minor group prize enhancement effect compared to that reported by Deutsch and Gerard (1955). However, when his data were reexamined by Matsuda (1985), it was noticed that Frager's Japanese subjects in fact did conform on a greater proportion of critical trials than Americans. Moreover, Sako (1975) found no change in conformity by Japanese subjects making their judgments when a group prize was offered.

Matsuda (1985) decided to have a closer look at some details of Japanese notions about proper behavior in a group. In Japanese culture there are, according to Matsuda, distinctions regarding the degree of intimacy involved in collectivities that require different kinds of relations among participants (with these distinctions involving — in Japanese — *uchi*, *seken*, and *soto*.) An analysis of these distinctions and the correlated requirements for behavior led

Matsuda to predict more conformity under *seken* (a moderately cohesive group) followed by *uchi* (groups composed of mutually selected friends) and *soto* (groups composed of persons selected by the experimenter and given no opportunity to develop cohesiveness).

What is very striking about the findings is the very high level of conformity that was displayed by the Japanese women students who were Matsuda's subjects and the partial support obtained for his hypotheses regarding the effects of differing cohesiveness. Overall, these subjects conformed on a very high proportion of critical trials, even though in Matsuda's (1985) procedure their judgments were made privately. And most conformity was displayed under the moderate cohesiveness condition (*seken*), as predicted, but only under certain conditions of information feedback. Matsuda's research demonstrated that behavior in an Asch-type conformity situation is influenced by cultural norms governing relations among members of groups and, in particular, that if a group setting is one in which the role obligation norms of a society are very salient, conformity tendencies are enhanced.

These studies are generally consistent with the view that societies with more role obligation will yield greater conformity among its members. Can we test this general relationship more directly in the context of the ecocultural framework? In a comparative study Berry (1967, 1979a) examined this relationship across seventeen samples from ten different cultures. An Asch-type task of independence versus conformity was developed for cross-cultural use; the study is summarized in Box 3-2.

While the pattern of the sample means found by Berry supports the prediction that conformity in such experimental situations will correspond to the degree of sociocultural tightness in the society, there are some alternative explanations that need to be considered. One is that the researcher (and his assistant) may have been perceived differently by members of the various samples; rather than simply communicating the group norm as intended in the study, they may have served, themselves, as some sort of authority to which participants responded. While this may be a possibility, as an explanation it requires showing some basis for a systematic relationship to the outcome of the study. Why should the researcher and his assistant be more of an authority in Sierra Leone communities and less in the Arctic; and why should this variation in authority status show a systematic decline along the ecocultural dimension?

A second alternative explanation has been advanced by Boldt (1978) and Boldt and Roberts (1979) based upon their work with Mennonite and Hutterite samples in Canada. They argue that the "tight-loose" (cf. role obligation) dimension is confounded in some comparisons with another dimension of cultural variation, that of "simplicity-complexity," which is similar to the role diversity dimension outlined earlier. This second dimension raises a question about the actual cultural variable that best explains the distribution of results on the Asch-type test, and also about *which* "others" the respondent is sensitive to (the respondent's entire cultural group, as

> ## Box 3-2   A cross-cultural study of conformity
>
> In the study by Berry (1979a) the task was to make judgments of the lengths of lines after having been provided with a fictitious group norm. In the Asch prototype the task was to indicate which of three clearly different-length lines was the same as a standard; one of the three was obviously the correct one, while another of the three was unanimously indicated by a group of phony subjects (confederates of the experimenter). For field purposes there are two difficulties with such a test, although its general nature is suitable. The first is that experimental confederates are not possible in settlements or villages; word about the deception would soon spread and the test would be rendered useless. Second, the use of obviously right or wrong lines as alternatives makes plain the deception; the whole research effort would soon be discounted if one element were considered to be a trick.
>
> To remedy these problems, a new task had to be designed that avoided the use of confederates and obvious deception. The second of these can be handled easily by increasing the ambiguity of the stimulus array. However, the first problem was more difficult and its solution had to make use of an early observation by Sherif (1935) that individuals in experimental settings accepted the norms of their group even when members of the group were not present. Thus, it was decided that a group norm could be presented during the administration of the test by one line marked as "the one most . . . people chose." Pilot trials prior to field work indicated the acceptance of this manipulation.
>
> An initial series of items was presented, without any norm being suggested, so that basic ability on this kind of task might be assessed independently of distortions introduced by social influence. The initial series also introduced some element of control over the possible individual and group differences in line discrimination accuracy. Then the actual test items were presented with suggestions of the group norms indicated by an x beside one line. The main results are indicated in Figure 3-1, where the samples are arranged (on the horizontal axis) according to their relative societal emphases on role obligation (high on the left) in tight, stratified agricultural societies and on the vertical axis according to the mean sample score on the independence-conformity task. It is clear that the seventeen subsistence-level samples are distributed widely on the independence task and that their scores are related to their position on the ecocultural dimension. In fact, the Pearson correlation between the sample means on the independence task and their scores on the ecocultural index was $+.70$. When individual scores (rather than samples means) are employed in the correlation, the coefficient across the 780 individuals is $+.51$.

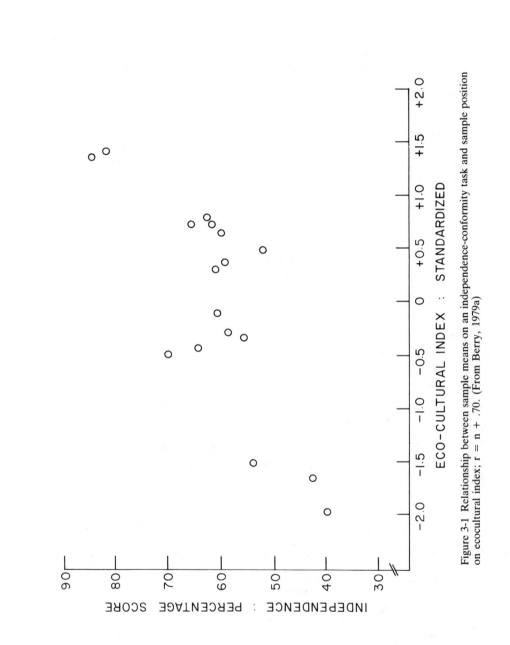

Figure 3-1 Relationship between sample means on an independence-conformity task and sample position on ecocultural index; $r = n + .70$. (From Berry, 1979a)

intended in the Berry study, or those who are present and administering the test).

Nevertheless, this study, taken together with the evidence presented earlier, suggests quite strongly that in loose societies, where there is child training for assertion, there will be relatively independent performance on an Asch-type task, while training for compliance in tight societies is associated with greater conformity. As Barry et al. (1959) predicted, child-rearing practices do apparently relate to adult behavior; in this case there is a clear theoretical and empirical link between how a society characteristically trains its children on compliance-assertion and the typical score obtained by a sample from that society on a conformity-independence task.

Values

The study of societal values has a long history in sociology and anthropology (e.g., F. Kluckhohn & Strodtbeck, 1961), and the study of individual values has a similarly long history in psychology (e.g., Allport, Vernon, & Lindzey, 1960). The cross-cultural study of both societal and individual values, how-ever, is relatively recent (e.g., Feather, 1975; Hofstede, 1980; Zavalloni, 1980).

In both disciplines values are inferred constructs (held collectively by societies and individually by persons). In an early definition the term *values* refers to a conception held by an individual, or collectively by members of a group, of that which is *desirable* and which influences the selection of both means and ends of action from among available alternatives (C. Kluckhohn, 1951, p. 395). This complete but rather complex definition has been simplified by Hofstede (1980) to: "a broad tendency to prefer certain states of affairs over others" (p. 19). Values are usually considered to be more general in character than attitudes, but less general than ideologies (such as political systems). They appear to be relatively stable features of individuals and societies and hence correspond in this regard to personality traits and cultural characteristics.

In anthropology and sociology values became included as one aspect of a culture or society; they appear in definitions of culture and often appear in field-based descriptions of particular societies and cultures. Soon, such single culture studies gave way to comparative survey studies, the most renowned being that of F. Kluckhohn and Strodtbeck (1961) based on a classification of values earlier proposed by C. Kluckhohn (1951); the general scheme is presented in Box 3-3. Drawing samples from five groups, they presented a series of short stories with alternative outcomes to respondents who indicated their own preferred outcome. By aggregating responses to statements embodying these alternatives, F. Kluckhohn and Strodtbeck (1961) were able to present a general statement about preferred value orientations in a particular cultural group; this method contrasts sharply with the earlier anthropological approach of discerning value preferences from natural cultural indicators (such as myths or political institutions).

Box 3-3   Variations in value orientations

The empirical study of values was greatly advanced by the research of Florence Kluckhohn and Fred Strodtbeck (1961) with samples of individuals from rural communities in the southeast U.S., representing five different cultural groups: Texan, Mormon, Hispanic, Zuni, and Navaho. Their classification of value orientations used five dimensions:

1. *Man-nature orientation* concerns man's relation to his natural environment. There are three alternatives: man's mastery over nature, man's subjugation to nature, and man's harmony with nature.
2. *Time orientation* concerns one's orientation to the past, present, or future.
3. *Activity orientation* concerns a preference for being, becoming, or doing; essentially these represent the enjoyment of one's current existence, of changing to a new existence, or of activity without any change.
4. *Relational orientation* concerns man's relation with others and emphasizes individualism, collateral relations (preference for others in extended group), or lineal relations (ordered succession within the group).
5. *Nature of man* is judged to be good, bad, or neither on one dimension, and mutable or immutable on another dimension.

Short stories that pose a problem are presented to respondents, who are asked to indicate which alternate solution to the problem is the best; answers are scored as indicative of one of the values on one of the five dimensions. Results indicated that it was possible to measure *cultural* value orientations through the use of *individual* responses. Moreover, systematic differences appeared across cultures: Mormons and Texans were higher on *doing* than the other groups; Hispanics were *present-* and *being*-oriented and valued man's *subjugation* to nature more than others; the Zuni preferred *doing* and a *mastery* over nature; while the Navaho preferred the *present* in time orientation and the *with* nature relationship rather than mastery. These now-classic findings showed that some general characterizations of cultural groups were possible using standard values measures. However, in some respects these characterizations approach the overgeneralizations that were so problematic for the culture and personality school (as noted in Chapter 1 and to be discussed in more detail in Chapter 7).

Perhaps the best known and most widely used approach to studying values in psychology is that of Rokeach (1973). Drawing upon the distinction by C. Kluckhohn (1951), Rokeach developed two sets of values, namely *terminal* values, which were defined as idealized end-states of existence, and *instrumental* values, which were defined as idealized modes of behavior used to attain the end-states. Rokeach identified eighteen values of each kind, and his instrument (the Rokeach Value Survey) requires that the respondents rank order the values within each set of eighteen. For example, included in the list of terminal values are goals of "equality," "freedom," "happiness," "salvation," and "self-respect"; in the instrumental values are such behaviors as being "courageous" "honest," "polite," and "responsible." The cross-cultural use of the Rokeach Value Survey has been pioneered by Feather (1975), who has drawn samples of students in a number of countries (Australia, Canada, Israel, Papua-Niugini, and the United States).

An extensive survey using a modified Rokeach instrument has been carried out by Ng and his colleagues (1982) in nine East Asian and Pacific countries. The modifications were to add four values (self-determination, social power, social justice, and equity) in order to include some values that are relevant to countries experiencing political and economic changes. Discriminant function analyses revealed two dimensions that maximally discriminated the country samples. The first function "reflects on the negative pole, societal-oriented values that emphasize the submission of self to a hierarchical society (obedient, polite) and the country (national security); and on the positive pole, self-oriented values with a strong Dionysian tendency" (that is, self-indulgence and self-satisfaction). The second function "reflects, on the positive pole, self-oriented values, which (unlike their counterpart of Function 1) emphasize the cultivation of inner strength; and on the negative pole, materialistic-oriented values (Comfortable Life, Equity)" (Ng et al., 1982, p. 200).

More recently, work by Schwartz and Bilsky (1987, 1990) has extended the Rokeach tradition. In a study of the thirty-six values in a number of societies (Australia, Finland, Germany, Hong Kong, Israel, Spain, and the United States) seven distinct *motivational domains* emerged in all societies: achievement, enjoyment, maturity, prosocial, restrictive conformity, security, and self-direction; an eighth (social power) existed only in Hong Kong. Some value *oppositions* were evident in all societies (for example, the opposition between prosocial and achievement values), and some in at least four societies (for example, the opposition between achievement and security values). Some value *compatibilities* were also present in all societies (for example, restrictive conformity, prosocial, and security). These patterns of similarities are taken by the authors to indicate the presence of *universals* in values, although they recognize that other (non-Western, nonindustrial) societies will need to be studied before the claim can be substantiated. Another universal claimed is the distinction between values that are broadly "individualist" and those that are "collectivist"; we will consider this distinction in the following section.

Before doing so, it is important to note that in all of this work the question of cultural relevance arises: to what extent do the Rokeach values match those that are of concern to people in their daily lives in these various cultures? There is also the question of the meaning of these terms (whether translated or not): do individuals from different cultures interpret the value terms in exactly the same way? These methodological issues will be considered in more formal terms later (Chapter 9), but in the meantime they can be considered as impediments both to understanding value preferences in any particular culture and to comparing value preferences across cultures.

The studies of major current interest have been stimulated by the gigantic study of Hofstede (1980, 1983b). For many years Hofstede worked for a major international corporation and was able to administer over 116,000 questionnaires (in 1968 and in 1972) to employees in fifty different countries and of sixty-six different nationalities.

Four main factors were distinguished and four "country scores" were calculated based upon responses to questionnaire items that defined each of the four factors. These four factors are:

1. *Power distance*: the extent to which there is inequality (a pecking order) between supervisors and subordinates in an organization.
2. *Uncertainty avoidance*: the lack of tolerance for ambiguity and the need for formal rules.
3. *Individualism*: a concern for oneself as opposed to concern for the collectivity to which one belongs.
4. *Masculinity*: the extent of emphasis on work goals (earnings, advancement) and assertiveness, as opposed to interpersonal goals (friendly atmosphere, getting along with the boss) and nurturance. The first set of values is thought to be associated with males, while the second more with females.

For each country a score is provided on each of the four value dimensions. In Figure 3-2 a plot of two of these values (power distance and individualism) reveals a number of "country clusters": in the lower right quadrant is the "Latin cluster" (large power distance/high individualism), termed "dependent individualism" by Hofstede (1980, p. 221); the opposite pattern, called "independent collectivism" is exhibited for Israel and Austria, most of the third world countries are located in the upper right quadrant (a kind of "dependent collectivism"); and most Western industrialized nations are in the lower left quadrant ("independent individualism"). The figure also reveals a clear negative correlation between the two value dimensions ($r = -.67$), and both are correlated with economic development indicators, such as gross national product ($r = -.65$ with power distance; $r = +.82$ with individualism). These data are presented here to provide a basic introduction to Hofstede's work on values; their relevance to the cross-cultural study of organizations will be discussed in Chapter 13.

The work by Hofstede has led to a blossoming of research both within and across cultures on these four value dimensions. In particular, work on the individualism dimension has become very active, mainly influenced by

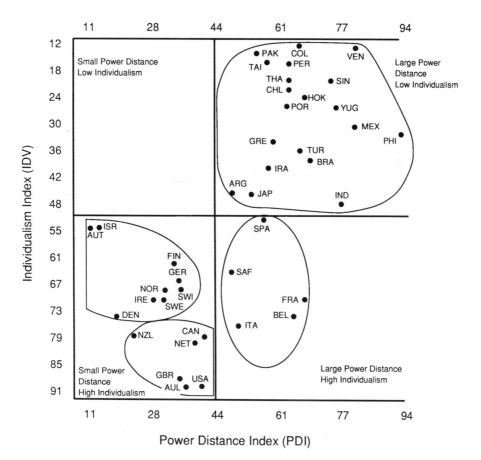

Figure 3-2 Positions of the forty countries on the Power Distance and Individualism scales. (From Hofstede, 1980)

Triandis (1988; Triandis, Leung, Villareal, & Clack, 1985). In this program of research, Triandis distinguishes the group level (which he terms "individualism-collectivism," following Hofstede) from the personal level of the value: this latter he terms "idiocentric" and "allocentric" tendencies. The reasons for making this distinction are that the conceptual status of such values is different for groups and individuals (pertaining to social system and personality, respectively), and that the measurement of individual values necessitates more comprehensive assessment than is possible using the few items per value employed by Hofstede. A number of scales have been developed to measure personal idiocentrism and allocentrism, and it is expected that these scores will vary by culture in a systematic relationship with Hofstede's individualism country scores.

In a follow-up study to the cross-cultural use of the Rokeach Value Survey by Ng et al. (1982) and Hofstede value dimensions, Hofstede and Bond

(1984) attempted to cross-validate the two approaches by employing data from six countries (Australia, Hong Kong, India, Japan, New Zealand, and Taiwan). Across the six countries two of Hofstede's dimensions (power distance and individualism) are significantly related to the two Ng et al. (1982) discriminant functions. The authors argue that this approach is an important step in cross-cultural research, one they call "synergy"; and they propose that more studies seeking such convergence should be carried out in all domains in the future.

However, Ellis (1988) has raised some questions about the reliability of these relationships by pointing out that correlations between the two values measurements *across* cultures do not necessarily hold up *within* cultures. Using samples of German and American university students, she hypothe-sized (on the basis of large intercountry differences on uncertainty avoidance and individualism dimensions) that Germans would rank the Rokeach values of politeness, obedience, and comfort (related to uncertainty avoidance) higher than Americans, while Americans would rank exciting life and beauty (related to individualism) higher than Germans. Neither of these predictions was borne out, providing a useful reminder that we need to be wary of generalizations made on data obtained cross-culturally when similar rela-tionships cannot be replicated within cultures.

Individualism and collectivism

In the last section we saw that Triandis et al. (1985) proposed that individualism-collectivism be retained as the name for the dimension at the national level, but that *idiocentric-allocentric* be employed to refer to the individual value orientations. Others have proposed additional terms (such as indiocentric-sociocentric by Shweder and Bourne (1984) and "culture of separateness" and "culture of relatedness" by Kagitcibasi (1985). Examples of some scale items are provided in Box 3-4 to illustrate this domain.

In what is now a vast and burgeoning research domain it is clear that there are substantial relationships between the two levels: persons living in indi-vidualistic cultures tend to have idiocentric values and behaviors, while those living in collectivistic cultures tend to have allocentric values and behaviors. For example, Forgas and Bond (1985) compared Australian and Chinese subjects' perception of social episodes; Australians emphasized competive-ness, self-confidence, and freedom, while Chinese emphasized communal feelings, social usefulness, and acceptance of authority.

In other Asian studies Hui (1988) found an association between an indi-vidual's collectivism score and sharing responsibility among Chinese subjects (but not among American subjects), and Kashima and Triandis (1986) showed that individual coping mechanisms (such as self-serving attribution) were used more by Americans than by Japanese. In a study of distributive justice Berman, Berman, and Singh (1985) found that Japanese and Indian subjects (but not Australian or American subjects) considered family need

---

Box 3-4 Individualism and collectivism

Hofstede (1980) found his dimension of individualism-collectivism to be defined by a very few items in his country-level factor analyses. These items were later found not to be particularly useful to place either individuals or work organizations on the dimensions (Hofstede & Spangenberg, 1987), and so both Triandis, Bontempo et al. (1986, 1988) and Hui (1988) have developed individual-level scales for use in placing persons on the individualism-collectivism dimension. Some items from each of these scales will serve to illustrate the quality of this domain.

Triandis et al. (1988)

1. If the group is slowing me down, it is better to leave it and work alone (Ind.).
2. To be superior, a man must stand alone (Ind.).
3. If you want something done right, you've go to do it yourself (Ind.).
4. In the long run, the only person you can count on is yourself (Ind.).

Hui (1988)

1. It is reasonable for a son to continue his father's business (Col.).
2. I enjoy meeting and talking to my neighbors every day (Col.).
3. I like to live close to my good friends (Col.).
4. The bigger the family, the more family problems there are (Ind.).
5. I am not interested in knowing what my neighbors are really like (Ind.).
6. I would rather struggle through a personal problem by myself than discuss it with my friends (Ind.).

---

above merit. Other studies with children (L. Mann, 1986) and adults (Kashima, Siegel, Tanaka, & Isaka, 1988; Leung, 1987) showed that subjects from collectivistic Asian cultures used equality more than equity (that is, equal distribution, rather than according to one's contributions), but this was not the case for subjects from more individualistic cultures.

Three important issues have arisen from this expanding literature. First, the question of *who* the others are seems to make a difference. Triandis, Bontempo, Villareal, Asai, & Lucca (1988) found that subjects from more collectivist cultures exhibited these justice behaviors only with members of their in-group; with out-group members, their behavior was similar to subjects from individualistic cultures. Moreover, the definition of who belongs to the in-group changes from culture to culture and has to be understood in indigenous terms. The second issue is the status of the person-level variable: is it traitlike and stable across time and place, or is it situationally variable, as suggested in the above discussion about the person's definition of in-group? A third issue is related: are individualism and collectivism polar opposites on a

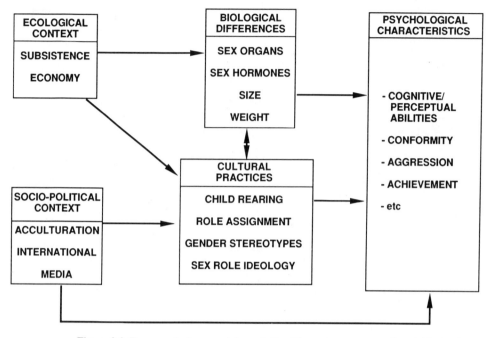

Figure 3-3 Framework for examining relationships among contextual variables and gender differences in behavior.

unidimensional scale and thus mutually exclusive (Schwartz, 1990), or are they independent tendencies? It has been argued that both orientations can be seen in the same person at the same time (Kashima, 1987; Kagitcibasi, 1987), and factor analyses have suggested that individualism and collectivism may best be conceptualized as independent factors (Triandis, Bontempo, Betancourt, Bond, & Leung, 1986). Leung and Bond (1989) have attempted to resolve these issues, but as in the case of all evolving areas of research it is likely to be some time before they are clarified.

Gender behavior

In Chapter 2 we considered the question how boys and girls are socialized differently in various cultures. We noted that girls generally are socialized more toward nurturance, responsibility and obedience, while boys are raised more for independence, self-reliance, and achievement. We also noted that these differential socialization patterns are themselves related to some other cultural factors (such as social stratification) and ecological factors (such as subsistence economy and population density). In this section we raise the question whether there are any social and psychological consequences of this differential treatment and experiences of boys and girls.

A framework is presented in Figure 3-3 (really a subset of Figure 1-3) that draws our attention to how some of these elements may be related. As in the case of the overall framework, this submodel is very much interactive, with all main features potentially influencing all others. Where we start our examination is thus somewhat arbitrary. However, since in psychology we are interested primarily in explaining individual behavior, we will enter the model at the point of an individual's birth.

At birth a neonate has a sex, but no gender. At birth one's biological sex can usually be decided on the basis of physical anatomical evidence; but culturally rooted experiences, feelings, and behaviors that are associated by adults with this biological distinction give individuals their gender. Much of the evidence we will review about how males and females differ, and how they are similar, will be interpreted as a cultural construction on a biological foundation rather than as a biological given. This is not to deny a role for biological differences between males and females, but merely to understand that they are the starting point rather than the whole story.

Biologically males and females have different sex organs and sex hormones; there are also differences in average size and weight. However, on the basis of these, all the extant collective images, including values, cultural beliefs (stereotypes), and expectations (ideology) swing into action, leading to sex differences in child-rearing and role differentiation and assignment, and eventually to sex differences in a number of psychological characteristics (abilities, aggression, and so forth). While all cultures build upon these early and minimal sex differences, the core question to be addressed in this section is whether cultures vary widely or are rather similar in what they do with these initial biological differences. We will also be taking into account the increasing acculturative influences being placed on most cultures (mainly by external telecommunications media) that are likely to be changing stereotypes, ideologies, and practices in other cultures.

Gender stereotypes. Widely shared beliefs within a society about what males and females are generally like have been studied for decades in Western societies. A common finding is that these stereotypes of males and females are very different from one another, with males usually viewed as dominant, independent, and adventurous and females as emotional, submissive, and weak. Only recently have studies examined whether distinctions are made in other cultures between male and female stereotypes and exactly what these beliefs are like.

The central cross-cultural study to be considered is that of J. E. Williams and Best (1982), who posed these questions to samples in thirty countries (three in Africa, ten in Europe, seven in Asia, two in North America, and six in South America). With the help of colleagues in these countries the researchers obtained the views of university students (a total of 2800 persons, ranging between 52 to 120 respondents per country, and usually close to a 50-50 split between males and females) on a 300-item adjective check list

(ACL) describing psychological characteristics of persons. The original ACL is an English-language person rating task developed by Gough and Heilbrun in 1965. For the cross-cultural survey, translations were made where required, usually employing forward and back translation procedures advocated by Brislin (1980).

The task for respondents was to decide for each adjective "whether it is more frequently associated with men rather than women, or more frequently associated with women than men" (J. E. Williams and Best, 1982, p. 51). Participants were reminded that "you are being asked to serve as an observer and reporter of the characteristics generally said to be associated with men and women in our culture. You are not being asked whether you believe that it is true that men and women differ in these ways, and you are not being asked whether you approve of the assignment of different characteristics to men and women" (J. E. Williams & Best, 1982, p. 51). The task was a "forced choice" for respondents; characteristics had to be judged as being associated more with males or females rather than equally associated. While instructions were designed to require such a dichotomous choice and to discourage "equal" answers, in fact when respondents found it impossible to make such a choice, a "cannot say" response was accepted by the researchers.

Results indicated a large-scale differentiation in the views about what males and females are like in all countries, and a broad consensus across countries (see Box 3-5). This degree of consensus is so large that it may be appropriate to suggest that the researchers have found a psychological universal when it comes to gender stereotypes. However, before such a conclusion is accepted, some further dimensions of the study need to be considered.

Beyond this apparently universally shared description of males and females, Williams and Best (1982) carried out a factor analysis of the adjectives assigned to each category. Based on earlier research of Osgood May, and Miron (1975), they sought the underlying meanings of the set of adjectives consensually used to describe men and women in the various countries. In keeping with previous studies of this type Williams and Best (1982) found three factors, which they called favorability, activity, and strength.

The first represents an evaluation of males and females (cf. an *attitude*), and across all countries there was little overall mean difference on this dimension; male favorability was 505 while female favorability was 498, scores that are just slightly above and below the standardized midpoint of 500. However, there were some clear cross-cultural differences on this dimension: the male stereotype was most favorable in Japan, Nigeria, and South Africa; the female stereotype was most favorable in Italy and Peru.

The second dimension represents a judgment about how action-oriented males and females are thought to be. In this case overall mean activity scores varied substantially (males scoring 545 and females 462). This difference is substantial, indicated by the nonoverlapping distribution: the countries in which females were considered most active (Japan and United States) are

---

Box 3-5 Characteristics associated with males and females in twenty-five countries

In the large cross-cultural study by J. E. Williams and Best (1982) forty nine adjectives were consensually assigned to males and twenty five to females. Consensus was defined as having two-thirds of respondents make an assignment within a country sample, and the cross-cultural agreement was defined as having at least nineteen of twenty five countries meet this degree of consensus. The adjectives are:

Male-associated items (N=49)

Active (23)	Energetic (22)	Realistic (20)
Adventurous (25)	Enterprising (24)	Reckless (20)
Aggressive (24)	Forceful (25)	Robust (24)
Ambitious (22)	Hardheaded (21)	Rude (23)
Arrogant (20)	Hardhearted (21)	Self-confident (21)
Assertive (20)	Humorous (19)	Serious (20)
Autocratic (24)	Independent (25)	Severe (23)
Boastful (19)	Ingenious (19)	Stern (24)
Clear-thinking (21)	Initiative (21)	Stolid (20)
Coarse (21)	Inventive (22)	Strong (25)
Confident (19)	Lazy (21)	Unemotional (23)
Courageous (23)	Logical (22)	Unkind (19)
Cruel (21)	Loud (21)	Wise (23)
Daring (24)	Masculine (25)	
Determined (21)	Obnoxious (19)	
Disorderly (21)	Opportunistic (20)	
Dominant (25)	Progressive (23)	
Egotistical (21)	Rational (20)	

Female-associated items (N=25)

Affected (20)	Fearful (23)	Sexy (22)
Affectionate (24)	Feminine (24)	Shy (19)
Anxious (19)	Gentle (21)	Softhearted (23)
Attractive (23)	Kind (19)	Submissive (25)
Charming (20)	Meek (19)	Superstitious (25)
Curious (21)	Mild (21)	Talkative (20)
Dependent (23)	Pleasant (19)	Weak (23)
Dreamy (24)	Sensitive (24)	
Emotional (23)	Sentimental (25)	

---

lower than the two countries in which males were considered most passive (France and India).

Similarly, on the third dimension of strength there was a large overall mean difference (males at 541, females at 459). And once again there was no overlap in the distributions: the two highest ratings of females on strength (in

Italy and U.S.) were lower than the two lowest ratings of males on strength (in Venezuela and U.S.).

In summary, while males and females were described in very different terms within every culture, they were also described in very similar terms across cultures. And while in terms of favorability they were evaluated on average equally, they were judged on average rather differently on the other two dimensions, with males more active and stronger. Some variations between cultures occurred on all three dimensions, but these variations were rather limited when viewed in the context of overall similarity.

How can we account for this pattern of results? One possibility is that all cultures follow the sequence outlined in Figure 3-3: Original biological differences have given rise over time to cultural practices, differential male-female task assignment and child-rearing, that actually make males and females everywhere psychologically different; gender stereotypes are thus merely an accurate perception of these differences. But such a sequence can also be turned around: a sex role ideology (see next section) that specifies how males and females *should* be may lead to differential cultural practices and to distorted perceptions of what males and females are like. Thus, bias in perception may be sufficient to generate the findings obtained and even to enhance any underlying biological differences.

Finally, we need to consider a third alternative: that some combination of acculturation influences and sampling decisions have contributed to the dramatic similarity in gender stereotype descriptions. University students share much in common worldwide: age and generation, high educational attainment, and exposure to international media images of males and females. In other words, university students all over participate to a large extent in an international "youth culture" that may override more traditional, locally rooted cultural phenomena. Only a repeat study, with samples that do not have so much in common, will really help us assess this possible explanation. However, some data from Williams and Best's own study suggest that this third alternative may not be particularly potent. They also examined the gender stereotypes of children in twenty-four countries, in two age categories (5 to 6 and 8 to 9 years). Once again, their evidence indicated substantial cross-cultural similarity in male and female stereotypic descriptions, and these are virtually identical to those obtained in the adult samples. The question obviously arises: is it really possible that children as young as 5 or 6 years have everywhere been exposed to an international "children's culture" that has propagated these gender stereotypes? The likely answer is "no," leaving us with the conclusion that these children have acquired the stereotypes from enculturation and socialization into their own society.

Sex-role ideology. While gender stereotypes are the consensual beliefs that are held about the characteristics of males and females, sex-role ideology is a normative belief about what males and females *should* be like, *should* do, and so on. In a second major cross-cultural study using the ACL

J. E. Williams and Best (1990) examined how individuals believed themselves to be (actual self), how they would like to be (ideal self), and how males and females should be. For this last variable they used a sex role ideology scale (SRI) developed by Kalin and Tilby (1978) with scores ranging between "traditional" and "egalitarian."[1]

As in the previous study university student samples were obtained with the help of colleagues, who administered the ACL and SRI instruments. This time only fourteen countries were included (five from Asia, five from Europe, two from North America, and one each from Africa and South America), and approximately fifty male and fifty female respondents participated in each country (total $N = 1563$). Translations were employed where appropriate, and data were collected and analyzed by Williams and Best (1990).

Results showed little variation across cultures in the ACL ratings by males and females on either actual or ideal self; however, rather large differences appeared on the SRI instrument (see Box 3-6). In general the more egalitarian scores were obtained in countries with relatively high socioeconomic development, a high proportion of Protestant Christians (and a low proportion of Muslims), a high percentage of women employed outside the home and studying at the university level, and a high country score on the Hofstede value dimension of individualism. Unlike the first study, where gender stereotypes were virtually universal, this study has shown rather large variation in sex-role ideology. If we examine the content of the female stereotype presented earlier (Box 3-5) and the content of the traditional SRI items (Box 3-6), it is apparent that they have much in common. Thus it appears that females are viewed in contrasting (perhaps even contradictory) ways in those countries where strong female stereotypes as well as a more egalitarian ideology exists. In the two studies there are thirteen common countries (though, of course, not identical samples). The four countries with the most egalitarian SRI scores (Netherlands, Germany, Finland, England) obtained differential male-female stereotype favorability scores averaging near zero, while the four countries with the most traditional SRI scores (Japan, India, Pakistan, Nigeria) obtained a mean differential stereotype favorability score averaging around +40 (that is, males are more valued on average than females). Thus while gender stereotypes are widely shared across cultures (in *both* traditional and egalitarian countries), there is nevertheless quite a different evaluation of males and females in traditional and egalitarian societies.

Psychological characteristics. In the previous chapter we encountered evidence for differential child-rearing practices and role assignment for boys

---

[1] The term *egalitarian* is employed by us to refer to the pole opposite, *traditional*. Kalin and Tilby (1978) used the term *feminist*, while Williams and Best (1990) used the term *modern* for this pole. We avoid the term *modern* in this text, since it is used elsewhere (Chapter 12) to refer to a broader set of attitudes related to social change.

Box 3-6   Sex role ideology in fourteen countries

In a second cross-cultural study J. E. Williams and Best (1990) examined the views of males and females in fourteen countries about how males and females should be and should act, using the Sex Role Ideology scale of Kalin and Tilby (1978). Sample items representing the traditional ideology are:

- When a man and woman live together, she should do the housework and he should do the heavier chores.
- A woman should be careful how she looks, for it influences what people think of her husband.
- The first duty of a woman with young children is to home and family.

For the "egalitarian" ideology sample items were:

- A woman should have exactly the same freedom of action as a man.
- Marriage should not interfere with a woman's career any more than it does with a man's.
- Women should be allowed the same sexual freedom as men.

The scores obtained by men and women in each country varied rather widely:

Country	Males	Females
1. Netherlands	5.47	5.72 (More
2. Germany	5.35	5.62 "egalitarian")
3. Finland	5.30	5.69
4. England	4.73	5.15
5. Italy	4.54	4.90
6. Venezuela	4.51	4.90
7. United States	4.05	4.66
8. Canada	4.09	4.54
9. Singapore	3.61	4.39
10. Malaysia	4.05	4.01
11. Japan	3.70	4.01
12. India	3.81	3.88
13. Pakistan	3.34	3.30 (More
14. Nigeria	3.11	3.39 "traditional")

In every case (except two, Malaysia and Pakistan) males scored more toward the "traditional" end and females more toward the "egalitarian" end of the scale. However, significant differences in the views of male and female respondents were limited to nine items (three "egalitarian" items on which women agreed more than men, and six "traditional" items on which men agreed more than women).

and girls, and differential role activity for men and women. In this chapter we have discovered variations in gender stereotypes and sex-role ideology. On the bases of these factors (identified in Figure 3-3) can we predict differences in psychological characteristics between men and women; and can we discover how these differences may themselves be differentially related to ecological and cultural factors? We attempt to answer these two questions with respect to three behavioral domains: perceptual-cognitive abilities, conformity, and aggression.

In Chapters 5 and 6 we will examine a variety of perceptual and cognitive ability dimensions in some detail; here we are concerned only with the issues of sex differences and the possibility that the magnitude of any sex differences may be related to ecological and cultural factors. We highlight two studies, one (Berry 1976b) that examines the issues within a single research program, and the other (Born, Bleichrodt, & Van der Flier, 1987) that provides a meta analysis across many research studies.

It has been a common claim that on spatial tasks (and those tasks that have a spatial component) males tend to perform better than females (e.g., Maccoby & Jacklin, 1974). However, it has been reported (Berry, 1966; MacArthur, 1967) that this difference does not appear to be present in Inuit (Eskimo) samples in the Canadian Arctic. The interpretation offered by Berry (1966) was that spatial abilities are highly adaptive for both males and females in Inuit society, and both boys and girls have ample training and experiences that promote the acquisition of spatial ability. (That such experience is related to test performance has been shown in other societies, for example, by R. L. Munroe and R. H. Munroe (1971) in East Africa.) In an analysis of sex differences on Kohs Blocks (a task requiring the visual analysis of a geometric design and the construction of the design by rotating and placing blocks) in a set of seventeen societies correlations between sex and test score varied from +.35 to −.51. (A positive sign, in this analysis, means a superior male score, a negative sign a superior female score.) When these correlation coefficients are ranked from most positive to most negative and then related to an "ecocultural index" (basically a standardized score for a society, derived from the ecocultural model, which takes into account subsistence economy, settlement pattern, population density, social tightness, and socialization practices), a clear pattern emerges: male superiority on this task exists in relatively tight, sedentary, agricultural societies, but is absent or is reversed in relatively loose, nomadic, hunting and gathering societies. Similar analyses with two other spatial perceptual tasks (across only eight samples) showed a similar pattern. We take this to indicate that sex differences on spatial tasks are not universal, nor are they inevitable. Since they are present in relatively tight societies, but not so in looser societies, there is an interaction between sex differences and ecological and cultural factors that, as we have seen in the previous chapter, underlie differential male/female socialization and role assignment.

In a metaanalysis incorporating the results of many research studies Born et al. (1987) noted that typically in the Western literature there are no over-all sex differences in general intelligence, but that differences are present in various subtests: females tend to perform better than males on verbal tasks, including verbal fluency, and on memory and perceptual speed tasks; males tend to obtain higher scores on numerical tasks and a variety of other perceptual tasks, including closure, spatial orientiation, and spatial visualization.

Their cross-cultural analysis drew together a massive literature, but it was really a cross-continent or cross-region analysis, since they used geographical areas as categories in their analysis rather than cultures; they also lumped all "minorities" together, ignoring cultural variation within that category. These problems make it difficult to understand the results obtained: in general, sex differences were smallest in "minorities," greatest in "African" and "Asian" samples. On specific tests sex differences were greatest (males superior to females) on spatial orientation (in "Africa" and "Asia") and on spatial visualization (in Western samples). As we have noted, it is not at all clear how "culture" might be involved to explain these patterns, since no particular cultural variables were identified in the review. Nevertheless, the Born et al. (1987) study confirms that there are differences in cognitive test scores between males and females and that the patterns of difference are variable across cultures.

We earlier noted a variation across cultures in the degree to which individuals vary in their responses on conformity tasks. In the Western literature there is some evidence that females may be more susceptible to conformity pressures than males, but this has been subject to heated con-troversy (e.g., Eagly, 1978). Once again, it is possible that the cross-cultural examination may put the issue in perspective. Using the same samples referred to in the earlier discussion of conformity in this chapter (Berry, 1979a), and employing the same strategy used by Berry (1976b) to examine sex differences in spatial ability, a clear pattern emerged. Across the seven-teen samples greatest sex differences (females more conforming than males) were present in the tighter samples and fewer (sometimes even a reversal) in the looser samples. The overall correlation between magnitude of sex differ-ence and the "ecocultural index" was +.78. Thus, once again we find that the presence and magnitude of a sex difference in a psychological characteristic is variable across cultures and predictable from a knowledge of sex differences in child-rearing, male-female role allocation, and degree of social stratifica-tion (in which women tend to occupy the lower ranks in society).

One of the best-documented sex differences in behavior is that on average males (particularly adolescents) quite consistently commit more aggressive acts than do females. In industrialized nations in Europe, North America, and elsewhere, they account for a disproportionate number of violent crimes (Naroll, 1983, Goldstein, 1983). So, too, do they in nonindust-rial societies (Bacon, Child, & Barry, 1963). A thorough analysis of studies relating to gender, culture, and aggression was provided in Segall et al.

(1990). This analysis considered several alternative explanations for the sex difference in aggression (and, by implication, for aggression itself). Here is a summary of this analysis.

Since it is the behavior of male adolescents that we are trying to explain, need we consider anything other than the high concentration of circulating testosterone that characterizes the physiological status of male adolescents? Evidence that testosterone levels are linked with dominance striving is available (Mazur, 1985), but more for primates like baboons than for humans, who often express dominance striving in ways that do not inflict harm on others, in other words, nonaggressively. There is also evidence that testosterone levels are linked to antisocial behavior in delinquent populations (Dabbs & Morris, 1990). One student of aggression who places considerable weight on the role of sex-linked hormones notes, however, that while the human organism is "already primed for the sex difference, cultures can dampen or exaggerate it" (Konner, 1988, p. 34).

Surely, aggressive behavior is a product of cultural influences acting largely through culturally mediated childhood experiences. If males and females have different experiences that impact on their tendencies to behave aggressively, then knowing what those experiences are is necessary in any attempt to understand aggression. One class of such experiences is the well-known set of differences between the sexes in inculcation of aggression (Barry, Josephson, Lauer, & Marshall, 1976). They found a sex difference in deliberate teaching and encouragement of aggression to children *on the average* over a sample of nearly 150 societies. If it were generally true that in most societies little boys received more inculcation of aggression than little girls, we would have a simple, strictly cultural answer to the question of why there is a sex difference in aggression. But it is not the case. The average difference found by Barry et al. (1976) was produced by relatively few societies in which the sex difference in inculcation was very large. Indeed, in only 20 percent of all cases was there a significant difference. So other factors than inculcation differences or hormonal differences, separately or in combination, must be implicated.

In Segall et al. (1990) an expanded biocultural model of the development of sex differences is presented. It begins with the universally present division of labor by sex and the fact that a very salient feature of it is the nearly universal tendency of child-rearing to be a predominantly if not exclusively female role. From this is derived a mechanism whereby in many societies, especially those with very distinct divisions of labor that result in low male salience during early childhood, young boys develop a cross-sex identity that is later corrected either by severe male initiation ceremonies for adolescent males (J. W. Whiting, Kluckhohn, & Anthony, 1958) or by individual efforts by males to assert their manliness (a phenomenon dubbed "compensatory machoism"). In this model aggression is seen partly as gender-marking behavior.

To appreciate the details of this argument, readers should refer to Chapter 12 in Segall et al. (1990). There one may also find additional examples of cultural factors that currently exist to differentially set the stage for the many different forms of aggressive behavior that continue to plague humankind.

Conclusions

Social behavior is often thought to be the most likely area in which to find substantial influence on human characteristics from cultural factors. However, as this chapter has shown, there is evidence for widespread cross-cultural similarity as well as difference in the social behaviors reviewed. While conformity and sex-role ideology are clearly patterned according to cultural factors, others (such as gender stereotypes and some shared values) are not. Both social and biological factors have panhuman features and can contribute to cross-cultural similarity. These, along with some basic psychological processes (such as the perception and categorization of social stimuli), clearly attenuate the possibility of cultural variation in social behavior. We agree with Aberle et al. (1950) that the cross-cultural coordination of social relationships is possible only when such shared characteristics are present. Nevertheless, cultural factors do play variations on these common underlying processes, producing some support for the assumption of many observers that social behavior is where cultural variation is most widespread.

4   Personality

Personality research is concerned with behavior that is typical of a person and distinguishes that person from others. Personality is the outcome of a lifelong process of interaction between organism and environment. The effects of external factors make it likely that there are systematic differences in the person-typical behavior of people who have been brought up in different cultures. For this reason many traditions in personality research have been extended cross-culturally. There is a wealth of information available of which only a selection can be presented here.

A dominant theme in personality research concerns the question whether observable differences in behavior between various individuals should be understood in terms of more permanent psychological dispositions or whether these differences are restricted to specific situations. A global distinction can be made between psychodynamic theories, trait theories, and (social) learning theories. The psychodynamic tradition that has the oldest roots will be discussed in the chapter on cultural approaches (Chapter 7). Most research in this tradition, which goes by the name of culture and personality, has been carried out by cultural anthropologists.

Research based on trait theories and social learning theories is discussed in the first section. Personality research tends to emphasize differences between individuals, or in the cross-cultural tradition between members of different cultures. The second and third sections point to important similarities in psychological functioning underlying diversity in behavior patterns. The arguments developed in these sections have important implications for the theoretical position of universalism that will be presented in Chapter 10. The second section deals with the subjective culture approach, in which the focus is on how people experience themselves and the sociocultural context in which they are living. The recognition of emotional expressions and gestures is discussed in the third section. The similarity across cultures in these nonverbal expressions provides important insight why we so often can understand the behavior of people in other cultures despite differences in the repertoire of beliefs, opinions, attitudes, and knowledge.

These first three sections mainly reflect research based on dominant theories and notions of personality. In the fourth section, on indigenous

---

Box 4-1   Ashanti names and personality

According to Jahoda (1954) among the Ashanti a child is given the name
of the day on which it was born. The name refers to the "kra," the soul
of the day. Among boys (no such ideas appear to exist about girls) the
kra implies a disposition toward certain behavior. Those born on
Monday are supposed to be quiet and peaceful. Boys called by the name
given to children born on Wednesday are held to be quick-tempered and
aggressive. An analysis by Jahoda of delinquency records in a juvenile
court indicated a significantly lower number than expected of convic-
tions among youngsters called "Monday." There was also some evidence that those called "Wednesday" were more likely to be convicted
of crimes against the person of others (for example, fighting, assault).
Although relationships are weak and, to the best of our knowledge, the
study has not been replicated, Jahoda's conclusion stands that the
"correspondence appears too striking to be easily dismissed."

---

personality, attention will be paid to some conceptions of personality that are
based in other traditions of thinking. In the last section we shall look at two
substantive aspects of personality to which cross-cultural psychology has
contributed: the self and altered states of consciousness.

Before continuing we would like to call attention to Box 4-1, about a
possible relationship among the Ashanti between a man's name and his
tendency toward criminal behavior. It is an example of one of the myriad and
often unexpected interconnections between personality variables and sociocultural environment. Whether or not the results reported in the box will
prove to be valid on replication is difficult to tell. This uncertainty shows
that our understanding of the relationship between the behavior of a person
and the cultural environment remains limited and tentative.

Traits across cultures

In the field of personality research there are various terms, such as *motive*,
trait, and *temperament*, that refer to enduring characteristics of a person.
These concepts imply consistency over time and situations in the behavior
pattern of an individual. The presumed origin of consistency is not always the
same. Temperament, for example, refers more to the biological basis of
behavior, while motive and trait can be associated with influences of the social
environment. Whatever way the alleged consistency has come about, it is
thought to reflect a psychological disposition in the person that is manifest in a
wide range of actions.

Personality traits are usually measured by means of self-report personality questionnaires (for specific traits) or personality inventories (omnibus instruments covering a range of traits). The most important empirical support for the validity of traits in these self-report instruments has been obtained from factor analytic studies. The information contained in the items can be reduced to a limited number of factors without an appreciable loss of information. Each factor is taken to represent an underlying psychological disposition.

When interpreting cross-cultural differences in scores, a researcher has to choose between three possibilities:

1. An observed cross-cultural difference in mean score is an adequate reflection of a difference in the underlying trait that presumably has been measured.
2. The difference is caused by errors in translation, a culture-bound specific meaning of some of the items, and other factors that have little to do with the trait measured by the scale.
3. Behavior cannot be explained in different cultures with the help of the same set of traits. This means that different sets of traits have to be postulated in different cultures.

We shall deal with this interpretation problem more extensively in Chapter 9. Here it has to be mentioned because it plays an essential role in the evaluation of cross-cultural research with data from trait scales.

Locus of control. The concept of locus of control developed by Rotter (1954, 1966) derives from a theory of social learning in which reinforcement occupies a central position. It is believed that an individual's learning history can lead to generalized expectancies about reinforcement. One can see a (positive or negative) reward either as dependent upon one's own behavior or as contingent upon forces beyond one's control. In other words, the locus of control can be perceived as *internal* or *external* to oneself. Success in life can be due to "skill" or to "chance" and so can failure. Many events that happen in persons' lives can be taken by them as their own responsibility or as beyond their control.

The most important instrument is Rotter's I-E Scale (1966). It consists of twenty-three items that offer a choice between an internal and an external option. Rotter concluded on the basis of factor analysis that the scale represents a single dimension. Hence, locus of control can be expressed in a single score that indicates the balance between externality and internality in a person.

There has been much research and theoretical debate on the precise conceptualization and assessment of locus of control (e.g., Lefcourt, 1976, 1981). One concern is whether locus of control can be generalized over various domains of behavior or whether distinctions have to be made between various reinforcement areas. In the case of specificity each domain would need to be assessed separately and a single scale would be inadequate. In a cross-cultural comparison this would imply that a single measurement may result in a rather inadequate representation of the differences between cultural groups.

Another question is whether the external agents can be taken together or whether a distinction is needed between, for example, fate or luck (chance) and other persons who can exert control over an individual (such as powerful others). This problem is of great interest for a precise analysis of cross-cultural differences, since there have been findings pointing to intercultural differences in the factor structure of locus of control measurements (Dyal, 1984). A valid interpretation of quantitative differences in score levels is hardly possible when factor structures are not identical across the cultural groups to be compared (see Chapter 9 for more details). Another finding hampering interpretation is that cross-cultural differences on various items within a scale are not always similar, indicating that there is cultural bias in at least some of the items. In a thorough and detailed review of the cross-cultural literature on locus of control Dyal (1984) describes these methodological problems of comparison in detail.

The locus of control construct has led to a large number of studies. One of the more salient results is that persons in Western countries on average are more internal than those in the Far East. Also, people in developing nations are less internal than those from industrial countries. This has to be considered against the background of findings showing that men tend to be somewhat more internal than women and that internals are more achievement-oriented.

Within the U.S., where by far the largest body of cross-culturally relevant research has been conducted, it has been repeatedly found that blacks are more external than whites (Dyal, 1984). Low socioeconomic status tends to go together with external control, but the black-white difference remains when socioeconomic differences have been controlled for. In the case of other minority groups in the U.S., such as Hispanics, the results vary and depend on the level of education and socioeconomic status of the samples tested. According to Dyal (1984), the results with minorities are generally consistent with the explanation that the locus of control scores correspond with the actual degree of control that people can exert on the course of their own lives in the real world.

Differences between European countries and between Europe and the U.S. tend to be small. In contrast, there are consistent differences between Americans and East Asians; the Japanese in particular score relatively high on externality.

Locus of control has been related to an array of other variables. One of the most consistent findings is a positive correlation between internal control and (academic) achievement. In general the locus of control concept represents a behavior tendency that seems to fit life expectations that are reasonable for individuals belonging to certain groups, given their social conditions. Of particular interest are findings to the effect that relationships between locus of control and other variables are not invariant over cultures. For example, the U.S. literature indicates that externals are more compliant and conforming. In a cross-cultural experiment on source credibility McGinnies and Ward

(1974) replicated this finding, but found an absence of the expected relationship in New Zealand and even a reversed relationship in Australia.

In summary, locus of control appears to be an interesting concept for cross-cultural psychology, not least because scores on locus of control scales are contingent upon specifiable conditions in the environment.

Other trait traditions. Cross-cultural research on traits tends to be centered around certain instruments (Guthrie & Lonner, 1986). Apart from studies with locus of control scales, traditions have developed around the MMPI (Minnesota Multiphasic Personality Inventory; cf. Butcher & Pancheri, 1976), Eysenck's Personality Questionnaire (cf. Box 4-2), Gough's (1969) California Personality Inventory (CPI), and Spielberger's STAI (State-Trait Anxiety Inventory; cf. Spielberger & Diaz-Guerrero, 1983).

A multitude of studies have been carried out with these and other instruments, which far more often than not have resulted in cross-cultural differences in scores. Some of this work has shown awareness of the pitfalls of cross-cultural research. For example, for the CPI it has been claimed on theoretical grounds that the various scales have universal validity. Available evidence from Israel has been interpreted to support this claim (Levin & Karni, 1970). Nevertheless, Gynther (1978) referred to (unpublished) results indicating that differences between black and white Americans may have to be attributed to variables like socioeconomic status and are not a function of the personality traits presumably measured by the CPI scales. The sheer mass of the findings and the lack of coherence between them, which undoubtedly has to do with the methodological difficulties, in our opinion make it difficult to derive from this literature an integrated view about the nature and extent of cross-cultural differences in personality traits.

The research traditions mentioned so far have in common that traits are identified at the level of individuals. One can also imagine sociocultural influences that differ from culture to culture, but show little variation within cultures. This means that there could be personality traits defined at the level of cultural populations.

An example of such a trait approach is the research by Peabody (1967, 1985). He draws a sharp distinction between national stereotypes (considered to be irrational and incorrect) and national character, that is, "modal psychological characteristics of members of a nationality" (Peabody, 1985, p. 8). To identify national characteristics Peabody makes use of ratings of judges (usually students) on trait descriptive adjectives about people in various nations including their own. In order to distinguish between the *evaluative* (stereotypical) and the *descriptive* aspects in the ratings of the judges Peabody uses an elegant method. He works with pairs of adjectives with an opposite meaning, using two pairs for each trait. Of the two adjectives with a factually similar meaning one has a positive and the other a negative connotation. An example is *thrifty* (+) and *stingy* (−) versus *generous* (+) and *extravagant* (−). Combinations of ratings on the four adjectives are used by Peabody to

Box 4-2   Eysenck's personality scales

One of the more frequently used personality scales for cross-cultural comparison studies is the Eysenck Personality Questionnaire (H. J. Eysenck & S. B. G. Eysenck, 1975). The EPQ is developed from earlier scales such as the MPI (Maudsley Personality Inventory) and the EPI (Eysenck Personality Inventory). In a review published in 1981 Lynn referred to data from twenty-four countries collected with these scales. Since then the number has been increased substantially (e.g., Perera & S. B. G. Eysenck, 1984; S. B. G. Eysenck & Opolot, 1983).

In the EPQ four personality factors are distinguished, namely, psychoticism, extroversion, neuroticism, and social desirability. According to Eysenck there is substantial evidence that the first three of these factors have a biological substratum and form temperament dimensions. But, as we shall soon see, this does not imply that cross-cultural differences are necessarily attributed to genetic determinants.

Neuroticism or emotionality represents a dimension ranging from instability, with being moody and touchy as characteristic features, to stability, characterized by an even temper and leadership. Extroversion stands for a dimension from quiet and passive or introverted behavior, to social and outgoing or extroverted behavior. The third dimension, psychoticism, has tough-mindedness and tender-mindedness as its opposite poles. It is a later addition to Eysenck's theory and conceptually somewhat less developed. Social desirability, finally, refers to the tendency to give responses that are socially acceptable and respectable. This tendency has been mentioned as the most important determinant of responses in self-report personality tests (A. L. Edwards, 1970).

The first objective of cross-cultural studies with the translated EPQ is to show whether the same four factors emerge in other cultures that were originally identified in Great Britain. If this is found to be the case, a second and third objective can be pursued, namely the computation of local norms and the interpretation of quantitative cross-cultural differences in the scores on the four personality scales formed by the four factors.

The observed similarities in eighteen studies (in each of which samples from another culture were compared with the results of subjects from Britain) attain such high values that, according to H. J. Eysenck and S. B. G. Eysenck (1983), "essentially the same dimensions of personality emerge from factor analytic studies of identical questionnaires in a large number of different countries" (p. 46). The correspondence of factors is expressed in the form of an index of factor comparison ranging from 0.00 (no similarity) to 1.00 (identity). This index typically shows values in excess of 0.95 and even values higher than 0.990 are not uncommon.

Scores on the four factors have been related to various social and political antecedents and to climatic factors. For example, high stress is thought to lead to high neuroticism. Political and economic instability, war and military occupation, and a hot climate are considered to be stressful. In various samples (of students) in India a rather low level of neuroticism is found, which in view of the political instability was considered surprising. Lynn (1981) has suggested that possibly the rural farmer population of India is "relatively little affected by the political struggles taking place in New Delhi and the stresses experienced by the mass of the population are in fact fairly slight" (p. 277).

If the evidence were as clear as suggested, cross-cultural research would provide rather strong support for the position that identical trait concepts can serve to explain behavior anywhere and, in addition, that the same set of items can be used across a wide range of cultures if not universally. However, the evidence is not so clear-cut.

By the Eysencks' own account, drastic changes in the loadings of items are found occasionally (e.g., H. J. Eysenck & S. B. G. Eysenck, 1983, p. 43). In a study by Perera and Eysenck (1984) in Sri Lanka, nine items in the twenty-five item (British) psychoticism scale had their highest loading on one of the other three factors. For a proper evaluation of the results one has to realize that the technique for intergroup comparison used in the studies mentioned invariably leads to fairly high values for the factor similarity index. Even with random data values in excess of 0.90 are not too unusual (Bijnen, Van der Net, & Poortinga, 1986).

This has implications for the comparison across cultures of score *levels* on the four factor scales. A slight shift in the meaning of an item can lead to major changes in the endorsement rate. Even if this happens for only a few items, a significant cross-cultural difference in scores is a likely outcome. The reported similarities in factors do not preclude this possibility. It follows that interpretations such as that by Lynn of the low neuroticism scores in India are premature. This finding would require further scrutiny in any case, as it ignores the hardships of poverty and the local political strife and violence that more than occasionally disrupt life in an Indian village.

separate the effects of likes and dislikes of the judges from effects due to their factual opinion. Thus, if a rater is of the opinion that the Scots are likeable but not exactly big spenders, he will tend to rate them higher on thrifty than on stingy and higher on generous than on extravagant. In the case of dislike this pattern will be reversed. Peabody has collected data mainly in Western countries. He has identified three descriptive dimensions on which nations differ (namely, tight versus loose control over impulse expression, assertiveness versus unassertiveness, as well as a general evaluative dimension). In his opinion the data provided by the raters fit with descriptions found in other sources, such as the anthropological and historical literature on various nations.

Objections have been raised against the validity of national characteristics and judges' opinions about them. It has been argued that ratings reflect ethnocentric attitudes, that nations change, and that judges rarely have extensive firsthand experience with other countries. Peabody (1985) has discussed these objections and concluded that by and large they have to be rejected for lack of any supporting evidence. However, in our opinion the case for national characteristics has not been clearly established. Particularly, we do not believe that the secondhand knowledge of students about other nations can be a valid basis for scientific knowledge. Peabody argues that virtually everything we know is acquired from others and that we do not even know that the world is round on the basis of our own experience. Of course, there is much substance to this argument, but only if we have no reason to doubt what we are told. It is clear from Peabody's own discussion that the validity of national characteristics has been seriously questioned. Therefore, it seems undesirable to rely on the evaluations of judges who lack extensive firsthand knowledge to decide the issue.

To the criticisms raised about the validity of cross-cultural differences in personality traits more general questions on the theoretical value of the trait concept can be added. If individual behavior can be described as a function of stable traits, future behavior should be predictable on the basis of trait scores. Notably Mischel (1968, 1973) has criticized the trait approach because of the low validity of predictions found in empirical studies. He has argued that to a large extent behavior is determined by the situation in which the person finds himself rather than by internal psychological dispositions that differ from person to person. Between this social learning approach and the trait approach one finds a tradition of interactionism (e.g., Magnusson & Endler, 1977) in which the interaction between person and situation (some persons show behavior consistency in some situations) is emphasized.

The idea that traits do not reflect stable dispositions, but are merely convenient labels to reduce the information about other persons to manageable proportions, finds support in the research indicating that we *attribute* stable traits mainly to other persons. For our own behavior we tend to refer more to situational determinants or to our intentions (Nisbett & Ross, 1980).

Intergroup research within attribution theory has shown that explanations of behavior by observers are dependent on group membership (own or other group) and on the relationship between the groups (for example, in terms of status) (Taylor & Jaggi, 1974; Hewstone & Ward, 1985). To complicate matters further, there is also evidence of cultural differences in the extent to which subjects refer to general personality dispositions as opposed to situational factors (e.g., L'Armand, Pepitone, & Shanmugam, 1981). In Box 4-3 a relevant project is discussed.

In summary, there are various reasons why modal cultural traits may well

---

Box 4-3 Reference to dispositions and to contextual factors

J. G. Miller (1984) asked Hindu subjects in India and subjects in the U.S. to mention two prosocial behaviors (doing something good for someone else) and two deviant behaviors (a wrong thing to have done) of persons they knew rather well. The subjects were also asked to give the reasons for the behaviors. These were coded in a scheme with actor's general disposition (for example, personality, capability, value), situation-specific aspects of the actor's reaction (for example, purpose, physical state), and the context in which the behavior took place included in the scoring categories.

Miller found that adult Americans made more references to general dispositions, particularly personality characteristics, than did adult Hindu subjects. The difference was more marked for deviant than for prosocial behavior. For samples of 8-year-old children she reported little difference between the two countries. With 11- and 15-year-old children in the U.S. an increase in the dispositional answers was found, but not for samples of Indian children in these age groups.

Miller conducted a second study to rule out the possibility that the *behaviors* mentioned in the interviews rather than the *attributions* were culturally different. She asked American subjects to give the reasons for behaviors that had been reported by Indian subjects. The answers more closely resembled the previously found pattern for American adults than the pattern of attribution of Indian subjects.

The research by Miller, of which only a part of the results has been mentioned here, forms an indication that the explanation of individual behavior in terms of inferred characteristics such as traits in itself may be a phenomenon more prevalent in some cultures than in others.

---

reside in the eye of the beholder. Later in this chapter we shall suggest an alternative explanation of cross-cultural personality differences that relies less on trait-like dispositions.

Affective meaning

In this section we consider a research tradition in which the central theme is how members of various cultural groups experience themselves and their social environment. A distinction can be made between objective and subjective aspects of culture (Herskovits, 1948). The objective aspects are reflected in indicators about climatic conditions, number of years of schooling, national product, and so forth. Subjective indices reflect how members of a culture view themselves and how they evaluate their way of life, their "subjective culture."

In the analysis of subjective culture people are asked how they perceive themselves and how they see others. Triandis and Vassiliou (1972) found that Greeks tend to describe themselves as *philotimous*. As much as 74 percent of a sample of subjects used this term in self-description. There is no direct English equivalent of the concept of *philotimo*. Triandis and Vassiliou (1972) write: "A person who has this characteristic is polite, virtuous, reliable, proud, has a 'good soul,' behaves correctly, meets his obligations, does his duty, is truthful, generous, self-sacrificing, tactful, respectful, and grateful" (pp. 308–309). They summarize by stating that a person who is *philotimous* "behaves towards members of his in-group the way they expect him to behave."

Apparently Triandis and Vassiliou were of the opinion that they could communicate the meaning of the Greek concept to their English-language readers. The question can be asked whether this is indeed possible. Does the description capture all essential aspects of *philotimo* as experienced by the Greeks or is there still something missing? In case the former alternative is correct a second question can be asked, namely what are the implications of the emphasis on *philotimo* in Greece?

Words do not only have a *denotative*, but also a *connotative* meaning. A word points to a certain referent; it has a designative or referential meaning, which is called denotative. In addition a word has an emotional and metaphoric tone; this is the connotative meaning. The terms *objective meaning* and *subjective meaning* capture more or less the same contrast. The Semantic Differential Technique (Osgood, Suci, & Tannenbaum, 1957) is a method to describe the connotative meaning of words. A subject is given a word that has to be rated on a number (for example, 20) of 7-point scales. The poles of each scale are marked by a pair of contrasting adjectives, for example good versus bad, light versus dark, or quick versus slow. Factor analyses in the U.S. demonstrated that the ratings on all kinds of words could be represented by three factors that were labeled *evaluation* (good–bad), *potency* (strong–weak), and *activity* (active–passive). These three factors together defined a three dimensional space of affective meaning. The affective meaning of any word can be identified in terms of its position in this three-dimensional space. For example, the word "kind" has a high positive value on the evaluation factor, a low positive value on potency, and a slightly negative value on activity.

In a project that took more than fifteen years data were collected with the Semantic Differential Technique in thirty communities (Osgood, May, & Miron, 1975; Osgood, 1977). In each culture one hundred nouns were used as the concepts to be rated. These included, "house," "fruit," "cloud," "hunger," "freedom," "money," and "policeman." These presumably culture-common notions were first used to elicit in each culture a large number of adjectives associated with these nouns. In a computer analysis fifty bipolar pairs of adjectives were selected from the data set in each culture. It may be noted that these scales were chosen by means of a computational procedure in which the meaning of the adjectives did not play any role; the adjectives were not even translated into English.

The 100 nouns were then rated in each culture by 100 teenage boys on each of the fifty bipolar scales. These results were analyzed for the thirty cultures together in what is called a *pancultural* factor analysis. The three-dimensional structure described earlier emerged very clearly. For each of the three dimensions bipolar pairs of adjectives with a high loading could be found in each of the thirty cultures. On translation of these adjectives into English it was evident that there was a high similarity in meaning. Consequently, it could be concluded that the three dimensions have equivalent meaning in all thirty countries.[1]

For more practical use of the Semantic Differential Technique a short form was developed for each culture consisting of the four local scales with the highest loadings on each of the three factors, evaluation, potency, and activity. This short form with twelve bipolar rating scales was prepared for large-scale application in the thirty cultures.

The short forms were used in each culture to rate 620 concepts. These data form the basis of the famous *Atlas of Affective Meaning* (Osgood, May, & Miron, 1975). Chunks of data from the Atlas have been used to identify *universals* (nonchance trends across all societies), *subuniversals* (clusters of societies sharing certain patterns of deviations), and *uniquenesses* (deviations of individual societies from universal trends). In respect of color words, to which we shall come back in Chapter 6, it was found universally, for example, that "brightness" is more positively evaluated than "darkness," but that "darkness" is higher on potency. "Red" is less positively evaluated than "blue," but it is higher on activity.

Among the culturally unique features are a relatively high positive evaluation of "being aggressive" in the U.S. Osgood gives as a reason that in this country aggression also implies being competitive in sports and at school and that it does not so much imply intentional injury to others, the more common meaning elsewhere. Other examples include a unique meaning of the color black among Indian students in Delhi. Black showed unusually negative potency and positive activity. By local informants the high activity was ascribed to the association of black with the god Krishna and hair and the low potency to the lower status of a dark skin. It is well recognized that uniquenesses may reflect method artifacts and that the interpretations can only be tentative until supported by other evidence. The emphasis in the Atlas is on the universal rather than on the specific.

---

[1] In a later study (Tzeng, Osgood, & May, 1980) a denotative semantic space was also identified. Seven dimensions were found that can be seen to represent the shared "affect-free" semantic character of various objects and entities that are common to societies. It may be noted that these dimensions of objective meaning were far less well defined than the three dimensions defining the subjective meaning space.

The research by Osgood and his colleagues provides some means to answer
the two questions asked earlier in this section. The results in the Atlas are
suggestive of a common structure of affective meaning. This implies that
differences in person-characteristic behavior, such as the emphasis on *philotimo* among the Greeks, should indeed be communicable to members of other
cultures. Of course, we cannot be perfectly sure that Triandis and Vassiliou
have indeed rendered correctly the meaning of *philotimo* for their readers.
However, the research by Osgood and his associates indicates that at least this
should be possible in principle.

Inasmuch as "culture" can be identified with subjective culture the Semantic Differential Technique can be used to assess the distance between populations defined in cultural terms. It seems intuitively likely that a society
culturally is not equally different from all other societies. If differences are
large, ratings on denotatively identical concepts can be expected to show
larger connotative discrepancies than when differences are small.[2]

Still, it is difficult to know what the implications are of the emphasis among
the Greeks on the concept of *philotimo*. As we saw, in the Atlas uniquenesses
have also been identified. Perhaps the concept of *philotimo* can be seen as
representing a location in the affective meaning space for which there is no
specific word in American English.

Triandis and Vassiliou mention that *philotimo* is a rather central concept
for people in Greece. For example, a *philotimous* young man in traditional
Greek society will not marry before he has earned the dowry that is needed
for his sister's marriage. It is likely that Greeks will often refer to *philotimo* as
the reason for an action. In other societies an obligation in respect of the
marriage of one's sister may not exist. However, there will be other obligations or in a more general sense other prescriptive norms for social behavior.
When asked for, the reasons given for such obligatory acts presumably will
include concepts such as doing one's duty, truthfulness, respect, and other
terms from the list that we quoted earlier from Triandis and Vassiliou. Thus,
the area in semantic space covered in the Greek language by *philotimo* is
represented by other terms in other languages.

In other words, whether or not the emphasis of the Greeks on *philotimo*
has behavioral implications in distinction to non-Greeks cannot be established from the analysis of subjective meaning alone. Our second question is
unanswerable without additional information. Examples of studies are available where findings with the Semantic Differential Technique are placed in a
broader context (Triandis, 1972; Osgood, May, & Miron, 1975), but the
additional data do not match the Semantic Differential ratings in extent and
quality.

Considering the evidence, we are inclined to conclude that the study of

[2] There are other methods to assess "psychocultural distance" that are somewhat similar to the
Semantic Differential Technique. For example, Szalay and Deese (1978) have used the method
of *associative group analysis*. With this method subjects of different cultures are asked to write
down associations evoked by a particular word.

subjective culture has pointed to common elements in the subjective experience of humans independent of their cultural background. However, some reservation has to be expressed as Osgood's work was limited to young students in all cultures investigated, thus systematically excluding all illiterate populations.

Expressive behaviors

Recognition of emotional expression. Research on the expression of emotions can be traced to Darwin. He considered the universal occurrence of the same expressions as important evidence that emotions are innate. From a survey among British residents in various countries Darwin acquired information that he took as a validation of his viewpoint. Ekman (e.g., 1973) has pointed out that Darwin's criterion of universality of emotional expression does not provide sufficient proof for the biological inheritance of emotions. Early experiences common to all humans in infancy and childhood form an alternative explanation.

When in the first half of this century the biological basis of behavior was challenged by social scientists, the casual results of Darwin were also questioned and it became popular to argue that there are major cultural differences in emotional expressions. According to authors like Klineberg (1940) and Birdwhistell (1970) these differences mean that human emotional expression is acquired in the process of socialization, at least to a considerable extent. Impressive illustrations have been quoted. Samurai women in Japan, according to one of these examples, will smile when they have lost their husband. Ekman (1973, 1982) has reviewed the evidence favoring culture-specific views. He found that these results rest as much as those of Darwin on casual observations and anecdotal data.

The best-known studies that systematically probe the question of cross-cultural invariance of facial expression are those conducted by Ekman among the Fore in Papua-Niugini. Ekman (1980a) has published a series of photographs that show a similar range of emotional expressions to those found in the industrialized countries. Although subjectively convincing, this does not constitute strong scientific evidence. Ekman and his team also conducted two types of experiments. In one type they presented the subjects with three photographs, each displaying a different emotion, and asked them to indicate the person to whom something had happened (for example, whose child had died). In the other type of experiment subjects were asked to make the face they would show when they were happy to see their friends, angry enough to fight, and so on. These facial expressions were recorded and later analyzed to determine whether the same emotion-specific muscular patterns in the face could be found as previously established for Western subjects.

In contrast to some previous studies the photographs displaying an emotion had been selected on the basis of a theory that suggested links between central nervous system activity and movements of the facial muscles. Ekman and Friesen (1969) suspected that most facial expressions reflected a blending of more than a single emotion. One of their postulates was that there is a characteristic pattern of the facial muscles for each basic emotion. On this basis they selected photographs that showed one of six "unblended" emotions: happiness, sadness, anger, fear, surprise, and disgust. Subjects in five societies (U.S., Brazil, Chile, Argentina, Japan) were shown these photographs. The six emotions just mentioned were given as response alternatives with each stimulus. The overall rate of correct identification was quite high and, most important, no significant difference between cultures was found when the results for the six emotions were combined.

Although this pleaded strongly against culture-specificity, there was still a possibility that the emotional content of photographs from the U.S. could be recognized in other countries because of previous exposure to American movies and other cultural products. To rule out the alternative explanation of acculturation (see Chapter 11), the research was extended to groups isolated from Western visual materials and Western persons. After some initial attempts, the studies among the Fore, already mentioned, were carried out. Apart from a confusion between fear and surprise, the agreement between the Fore and Western subjects on the meaning of (Western) facial expressions for various emotions ranged from substantial to near perfect (Ekman & Friesen, 1971). In the reverse case, where posed emotions of the Fore were shown on videotape to American students, similar results were obtained, again with a confusion between fear and surprise.

The results of Ekman and his associates do not stand alone. Their work was replicated among the Dani, a group living in the mountains of West Irian (Indonesian New Guinea). The results again showed that the basic facial expressions of emotion were interpreted in a similar way as in the industrialized urban world. Independent studies by other researchers, for example, Izard (1971), have also provided results that were compatible with the findings of the Ekman group. Some studies have elaborated on aspects of the research procedure. The main reason is that, despite the overall similarities, the recognition rate of facial stimuli appears to be somewhat lower when subjects have less previous contact with Western culture. Among the Fore the rates of agreement were mostly of the same order of size as in the earlier study by Ekman and Friesen with subjects from six countries, but the task had been simplified from a six-choice to three-choice format.

The obvious question is to what extent the somewhat lower recognition rates reflect artifacts of the test method (for example, cultural ideosyncracies in the stimuli) and to what extent they reflect effects of cultural factors on emotions. Studies designed to probe this problem (e.g., Boucher & Carlson, 1980; Ducci, Arcuri, Georgis, & Sinseshaw, 1982) have yielded ambivalent results. There appears to be *some* cultural variation in the ease of recognition of specific emotions, but more precise evidence is still lacking. In the meantime Ekman and Friesen (Ekman et al., 1987) have demonstrated in a ten-culture study (Estonia, Germany, Greece, Hong Kong, Italy, Japan, Scotland, Sumatra, Turkey, and U.S.) with students as subjects that blended emotional expressions are also recognized very well across cultures. A comparison between the Asian and Western samples of the intensity ratings for the stimulus faces that were all Caucasian showed somewhat lower ratings for the Asian subjects. Therefore, Ekman et al. suggested that possibly less intense emotions are attributed to expressions on foreign faces.

Research on cross-cultural recognition of emotional intonation in the voice has yielded similar results. Albas, McCluskey, and Albas (1976) collected speech samples meant to express happiness, sadness, love, and anger from English- and Cree-speaking Canadian subjects. These expressions were made semantically unintelligible by means of an electronic filtering procedure that leaves the emotional intonation intact. Subjects from both language groups recognized the emotions intended by the speakers far beyond chance level, but the performance was higher in the subjects' own language than in the other language. In another study McCluskey, Albas, Niemi, Cuevas, & Ferrer (1975) made a comparison between Mexican and Canadian children (6 to 11 years of age). With a procedure similar to the one just mentioned they found that the Mexican children scored higher than the Canadian subjects on the identification of Canadian English emotional expressions.

Van Bezooijen, Otto, and Heenan (1983) tried to explain why the vocal expression of certain emotions appears to be recognized more easily than others. They compared Dutch, Taiwanese, and Japanese subjects, using a single brief phrase in Dutch that had been expressed by different speakers in nine different emotional tones (that is, disgust, surprise, shame, interest, joy, fear, contempt, sadness, anger) as well as a neutral tone of voice. With one exception all emotions were recognized at better than chance level by all three groups, but the scores of the Dutch subjects were much higher, suggesting a fair amount of loss of information because of cultural and/or linguistic differences between the three samples. On the basis of an analysis of the rate of confusion between the various emotions Van Bezooijen et al. suggested that emotions are more difficult to distinguish when they reflect a more similar level of activation or arousal. Activation level was found to be more important for recognition than the evaluation component (that is, positive or negative emotions). In a scaling analysis the distance between, for example, the passive emotions of shame and sadness and between the active emotions of joy and anger turned out to be small, while the distance between shame and anger was much larger. This is in line with the general literature on the recognition of vocal expression of emotion (e.g., Scherer, 1981).

Although facial expressions of emotions have been most extensively studied, there are other aspects of personality reflected in the face. In Box 4-4 we discuss a cross-cultural study on dominance versus submissiveness as reflected by the position of the eyebrows. Although among nonhuman primates the meaning of raised and lowered brows appears to be unambivalent, systematic differences were found across human cultures.

Box 4-4   A nonuniversal expression of social dominance

In nonhuman primate species dominant or threatening individuals tend to have their eyebrows lowered. Raised eyebrows are a sign of submissiveness. On the basis of evolutionary continuity in behavior a similar finding in humans would be expected. Observers in the U.S. saw models with lowered brows more often as dominant than models with raised brows. In addition, smiling models were seen less often as dominant than nonsmiling models. Smiling in college girls has been reported as indicative of approval-seeking behavior. In observations of children lowered brows and assertiveness have been found to be related. Against this background Keating et al. (1981) designed a study to test the universality of brow position and smiling as expressions of social dominance and submission.

Two sets of photographs were prepared with reversed poses by the same models; a model with raised brows in one set would appear with lowered brows in the other set. Subjects rated one set of photographs either on dominance or on happiness. There were two scores based on the frequency of selecting a certain eyebrow position (raised versus lowered) and a certain mouth position (smiling versus nonsmiling). By comparing results for the two sets with reversed poses, ideosyncracies of the models and other incidental sources of variance could be eliminated. Results were collected on fairly large samples in nine countries.

In all countries smiling models were chosen more often as happy and nonsmiling models as dominant. Models with lowered brows were judged as dominant more often in Brazil, Canary Islands, China, Germany, and the U.S. However, raised brows were chosen as dominant more often in Thailand, while no significant differences were found in Colombia, Kenya, and Zambia. The Thai were also the only group where lowered brow position was associated more often with happiness than the raised brow position.

The smile had a similar meaning in all the cultures included in the study. This is in agreement with other findings on the expression of emotions. The meaning of the discrepancies with respect to brow position is not clear. Method artifacts, which in this carefully designed study are not very likely, can never be excluded entirely. However, Keating and her coauthors rightly suggest other possibilities. Dominance gestures may be in part a product of socialization. Socialization practices in some cultures may have obscured the hereditary underpinnings of dominance expressions in the face. These interpretations argue against a too-easy acceptance of the general trend of similarity in facial expressions reported in the main text.

Antecedents to emotions. Each emotion is triggered by certain kinds of events. Are there cross-cultural differences in the *appraisal* or *evaluation* of events? Is the same emotion evoked by a given situation or do cultural groups differ in this respect, and to what extent? In the Ekman research among the Fore the aspect of appraisal entered into the experiments when the subjects were asked to select the photograph of the person whose child had died or of the person who was angry and ready to fight.

More systematic studies into the antecedents of emotions have been conducted by Boucher. The largest study (Brandt & Boucher, 1985) is based on samples of subjects from Korea, Samoa, and the U.S. A large pool of narratives was collected by asking informants to write stories about events causing one of six emotions, namely, anger, disgust, fear, happiness, sadness, and surprise. A selection of these stories was translated and stripped of specific cultural referents and of all emotion terms. A set of 144 stories was presented to subjects from the three countries. The subjects indicated in each case which of the six emotions the person in the story had experienced. Substantial overall agreement was found in the assignment of emotions to stories between cultures as well as within cultures. This means that the "right" answers could be identified unambiguously. In an analysis of these responses it was found that, contrary to expectation, subjects did *not* do better overall on stories from their own cultures. This result, which needs further replication in other cultures, suggests that the emotional appraisal of antecedent events is quite similar for people in different cultures.

In another series of studies initiated by Scherer (cf. Scherer, Wallbott, & Summerfield, 1986) an open-ended questionnaire was used to ask for antecedents of four emotions (joy, sadness, anger, fear) and for various aspects of the reactions beyond the emotional feeling per se. Few differences were found between European countries. Between the U.S., Europe, and Japan there were major differences in the relative importance of eliciting situations. It was also found that the American subjects reported higher and the Japanese subjects lower emotional reactivity than the Europeans. So far in this section patterns of similarities in findings rather than differences between cultures have been emphasized. With reliable data similarities are not likely to be due to method artifacts, in contrast to cross-cultural differences for which this often is a very real possibility (e.g., Malpass & Poortinga, 1986). Scherer and his colleagues (Scherer, Matsumoto, Wallbott, & Kudoh, 1988) appear far less reluctant than many other authors to make quantitative comparisons between various cultures. They write for example: "The lower fear intensities in Japan might be due to the fact that the fear of crime, which seems to lead to fairly high fear intensities, is less pronounced there and that there might still be more of a feeling of being safe in a network of social support. It is difficult to see why American subjects report higher intensities throughout, particularly for joy and anger. These findings may be attributable to either a higher emotionality or emotional responsivity on the part of the American subjects" (p. 21). However, to entertain these interpretations seriously, one would first have to make sure that differences in response styles and other method artifacts could be ruled out.

Our criticism seems to find some support in a study by Wallbott and Scherer (1986) with a standardized questionnaire. This instrument was administered to approximately eighty subjects in each of twenty-seven countries. They were asked to recall an everyday occasion in which, respectively, joy, fear, anger, sadness, disgust, shame, and guilt had been experienced. The questionnaire contained items asking for the duration, intensity, physiological concomitants, and effects on feelings about self and on relationships with others. There were two main findings. First, there were differences between the separate emotions for most parameters included in the questionnaire. Second, while there were some significant differences between countries, these tended to be much lower than the differences within countries among the seven emotions.

What has been said so far does not rule out systematic differences between cultural populations in the frequency and intensity with which emotions are expressed. Ekman has introduced the notion of *display rules*, that is, "norms regarding the expected management of facial appearance" (Ekman, 1973, p. 176). Within each culture there are rules about what face to put up on certain occasions and whether one should or should not show certain emotions. It was mentioned earlier that Samurai women will smile while feeling grief about a lost husband. The cultural rules prescribe the emotional expression that should be simulated. There are few controlled experiments in which the suppression or production of expressions in social situations has been demonstrated. An exception is a study by Ekman and Friesen (1971).

Japanese and U.S. students were shown stressful films in isolation and in the presence of an experimenter. Without the subjects' awareness the emotional expressions on the face were recorded in both conditions. For the two samples similar expressions were found in reaction to the same movie episodes when the subjects were alone. However, in the presence of the other person the Japanese subjects showed far fewer negative expressions than the Americans. Needless to say, this result fits the existing notions in the West about the impassive and inscrutable Japanese.

Nonverbal communication. According to Frijda (1986, p. 60), it is a mistake to think that emotional expressions exist for the purpose of communication. Nevertheless, they can often serve communication and sometimes are produced for that purpose. There are other channels of nonverbal communication, some of which will be mentioned here. For a general overview of this literature we refer to Argyle (1988). In our treatment of this topic we are particularly interested in the question to what extent other channels confirm the impression of basic similarities across cultures that have emerged from the study of facial and vocal expressions.

Gestures are a well-studied form of nonverbal communication. Interest in gestures has cross-cultural roots. In earlier times explorers often managed to acquire goods and even engaged in some kind of bargaining with people with whom they did not share a common language. Many modern-day tourists have similar experiences. In the eighteenth and nineteenth centuries the idea of gestures as a universal, albeit rudimentary, form of language gained some popularity (e.g., Kendon, 1984). However, D. Morris, Collett, Marsh, & O'Shaughnessy (1979) found that common, well-defined gestures can have a different meaning in various regions of Europe and even within countries are not always interpreted in the same way.

Most gestures are not made with the intent to communicate a message. Ekman and his coworkers (for example, Ekman & Friesen, 1969; Ekman, 1980b) have distinguished various categories of gestures, such as *adaptors* (or body manipulators), *illustrators*, and *emblems*. Adaptors, such as scratching one's nose, have developed from movements connected with bodily needs or interpersonal contacts. In the course of development they can become fragmented and lose their function. Illustrators are directly tied to the content and flow of speech; they serve to underline or depict what is being said and are related to features of the language. Emblems have a cognitive meaning that is usually familiar to members of a culture. They are meant to communicate this meaning and usually there is a verbal equivalent.

Presumably all these types of gestures are shaped in the process of socialization and enculturation. Child-training includes the modification of adaptors, especially those that are considered improper in the presence of others.

On the other hand, even with respect to emblems there is cross-cultural commonality. Many emblems can be understood even when the receiver has no knowledge of the culture of the sender. Argyle (1988) argues that some of the more common gestures, such as the shrug, may well be innate; others may be common because they follow from the nature of physical space. The arm gesture "come to me" may well be understood everywhere. But a fist with an outstretched finger to indicate a gun presumes knowledge of a cultural product not found everywhere and offers no basis for recognition for someone who has no prior knowledge of guns. Ekman and Friesen (1969) have made a distinction between referential emblems, where the distance between the form of a gesture and the referent (what is being depicted) is small, and conventional emblems, where this difference is large and dependent on prior cultural knowledge. Poortinga, Schoots, and Van de Koppel (1990) found that Dutch students could not only give the meaning of most referential emblems generated by Chinese and Kurdish actors, but also reported that these gestures were present in their own culture. This suggests that there is a repertoire of referential emblems common to a broad range of cultures. The rate of recognition for conventional emblems varied, but some were not interpreted correctly by a single one of the Dutch subjects.

However, the importance of cross-cultural differences may well lie in the frequency of usage of gestures of various types or (analogous with facial expression) in the display rules concerning the use of gestures. Italians tend to make an excited impression to visitors from more Northern countries presumably because of their more lively movement patterns. Efron (1972) compared gestures of Italian and East European Jewish immigrants in New York and found differences in gesturing style. Among other things quite different illustrators were used. A comparative study of Italians and inhabitants of Great Britain showed that the presence of gestures with the verbal description of complex geometrical shapes aided Italian subjects in the accuracy of understanding more than it did British subjects (Graham & Argyle, 1975).

The notion of personal space (see Altman & Chemers, 1980, for a review) is based on the idea that every person is surrounded by a private sphere. When somebody comes and stands too close to us, this is experienced as an intrusion. The anthropologist Hall (1966), who has paid extensive attention to cross-cultural differences in personal space, noted that Arabs, southern Europeans, and Latin Americans stand close together when talking. They tend to touch each other and even breath in each others' faces, while people of northern European descent keep a much larger physical distance. Subsequent research has only led to a very partial corroboration of Hall's dimension of high-contact and low-contact cultures. Intracultural variations due to social class and situational determinants obscure the postulated dimension. For example, Sussman and Rosenfeld (1982) found that Japanese students in the U.S. were seated farther apart than students from Venezuela when talking in their own languages. When speaking English, this difference disappeared and students from both countries sat at a similar distance as observed for students from the U.S.

Display rules for emotions, gestural style, and rules governing interpersonal distance may well be a component of the "personality" of the members of a culture as attributed to them by the visitor from outside. For example, in Peabody's study, mentioned in the second section, German raters described the Italians (with their lively movements) as highly active and agitated (Peabody, 1985, pp. 144–145).

If this suggestion is correct, the evidence presented in this section does not only explain why we can understand much of the behavior of persons from other cultures and why we may assume that this understanding as a rule will be correct. It also points to a basis for the impression of consistent differences around which so much of cross-cultural personality research has been centered.[3]

---

[3] In this context studies with the PONS-test can be mentioned (Rosenthal, Hall, DiMatteo, Rogers, & Archer, 1979). This is a test for assessing the ability to decode nonverbal cues from the face, body gestures, and voice tone. A fairly high correlation was found (in Western countries) between the mean score on the PONS-test and the rated cultural similarity of subject samples with the U.S. sample that served as a reference group (cf. Rosenthal et al., 1979, p. 218).

Indigenous personality

As used here the term *indigenous* refers to phenomena not generally found in Western cultures. As such it is somewhat a misnomer (see Chapter 16). It can be argued that most personality theories are the product of scientific traditions that are *indigenous* to Western industrial-urban cultures. Many studies by non-Western psychologists have built on to these traditions (cf. Blowers & Turtle, 1987). However, there are also personality theories based on non-Western traditions of reflection on human existence. We shall mention some of these, constructed by authors writing on the culture in which they were brought up. There are unmistakably Western influences, but also authentic insights not easily achieved by outsiders.

African personality. During colonial times, the descriptions of African personality made by Western psychiatrists were largely marked by prejudices and stereotypes. An upsurge in the 1960s and 1970s of writings by African authors claiming a separate identity for African people can be seen at least in part as a reaction against the generally negative picture prevalent in colonial times. Many of the writings are politically inspired (e.g., Makinda, 1982) and appear to have little relevance for our purposes.

In contrast, the work of the Senegalese psychiatrist Sow (1977, 1978) provides an extensive theory of the African personality, psychopathology, and therapy based on anthropological and psychological argument.

A schematic representation of the African personality as described by Sow is found in Figure 4-1. The outer layer (1) is the body, the corporeal envelope of the person. Next comes a principle of vitality (2) that is found in human beings and animals. It can be more or less equated with physiological functioning. The third layer represents another principle of vitality, but one found only in humans. It stands for human psychological functioning not shared with other species. The inner layer is the spiritual principle (4), which never perishes; it can leave the body during sleep and during trance states and leaves definitely upon death. This spiritual principle does not give life to the body, but has an existence of its own, belonging to the sphere of the ancestors and representing that sphere in each person.

These concentric layers of the personality are in constant relationship with the person's environment; Sow describes three reference axes that represent the relations of a person with the outside world. The first axis links the world of the ancestors to the spiritual principle (4) passing through the other three layers. The second axis connects the psychological vitality principle (3) to the person's extended family, understood as the lineage to which the person belongs. The third axis connects the wider community to the person, passing through the body envelope to the physiological principle of vitality (2). These axes represent relations that are usually in a state of equilibrium.

According to Sow, the traditional African interpretations of illness and

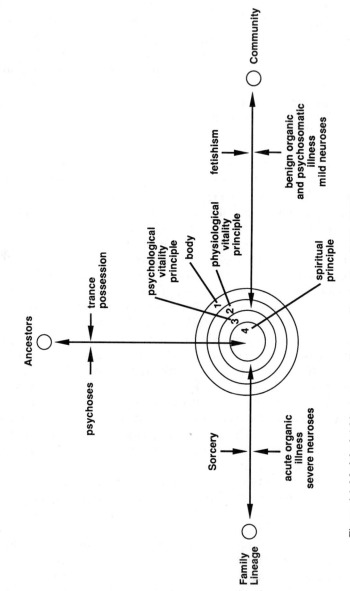

Figure 4-1 Model of African personality according to Sow (1977, 1978).

mental disorders, and their treatments, can be understood in terms of this personality theory. A disorder occurs when the equilibrium is disturbed on one or the other of the axes; diagnosis consists of discovering which axis has been disturbed, and therapy will attempt to reestablish the equilibrium. Note that in African tradition illness always has an external cause; it is not due to intrapsychic phenomena in the person's history, but to aggressive interference from outside.

If there is a rupture of the equilibrium on the first axis (linking the spiritual principle to the ancestral pole), serious chronic psychotic states may occur, but this cannot lead to death since the spiritual principle cannot be destroyed. The disturbance is due to spirits who are transmitting messages from the ancestors. A state of trance as a psychotherapeutic technique, during which the person is possessed by one of these spirits, can serve to reestablish the relations with ancestral tradition. Therefore, possession trance can have important psychotherapeutic effects.

A rupture of the equilibrium on the second axis (linking the psychological vitality principle to the family lineage) leads to organic illness, acute anxiety states, severe neuroses, and wasting away. This is likely to be a very serious illness, which can lead to death through the destruction of the vitality principle. It is due to sorcery and can only be cured through sorcery. A disequilibrium with the third, community, pole leads to more benign organic and psychosomatic illnesses as well as neurotic states. It is due to aggressions from enemies and can be cured through fetishism. As a general rule, healing requires the resolution of conflict (with the community, family, or ancestors) and the consequent restitution of equilibrium.

We have given here only a simplified account of this personality theory; for example, the model takes a slightly different form in matrilineal and patrilineal societies. In Sow's conception the supernatural, for example in sorcery, has to be understood in its cultural meaning replete with symbolic interpretations.

The importance of symbolism is emphasized by Jahoda (1982; cf. Cissé 1973) in his reference to the very complex personality conceptions of the Bambara, who live in Mali. They distinguish sixty elements in the person that form pairs, each with one male and one female element. Examples are thought and reflection, speech and authority, future and destiny, and first name and family name. Jahoda sees some similarities with psychology as it is known in the West, but also important differences. Bambara psychology forms part of a world view in which relationships between various elements are established by symbolism rather than by analytic procedures.

Amae in Japan. Amae (pronounced ah-mah-eh) has gained prominence in the writings of the psychiatrist Doi (1973) as a core concept for understanding the Japanese. Amae is a form of passive love or dependence that finds its origin in the relationship of the infant with its mother. It is the desire for contact with the mother that is universal in young children and that plays a role also in the forming of new relationships among adults. Amae is more prominent with the Japanese than with people in other cultures. Doi finds it significant that the Japanese language has a word for amae and that there are a fair number of terms that are related to amae. In Doi's view culture and language are closely interconnected.

He ascribes to the amae mentality of the Japanese many and far-reaching implications. The seeking of the other person's indulgence that comes together with passive love and dependency leads to a blurring of the sharp distinction found in the West between the person (as expressed in the concept of self) and the social group. As such it bears on the collectivistic attitudes thought to be prevalent in Japanese society. Mental health problems manifest in psychosomatic symptoms and feelings of fear and apprehension can have their origins in concealed amae according to Doi. The patient is in a state of mind where he cannot impose on the indulgence of others. In a person suffering from illusions of persecution and grandeur "*amae* has seldom acted as an intermediary via which he could experience empathy with others. His pursuit of *amae* tends to become self-centered, and he seeks fulfilment by becoming one with some object or other that he has fixed on by himself" (Doi, 1973, p. 132). In an analysis of the social upheavals in Japan, in particular the student unrest during the late 1960s and early 1970s, Doi points out that the present time is permeated with amae and that everyone has become more childish. There has been a loss of boundaries between generations; amae has become a common element of adultlike child and childlike adult behavior.

Although we want to present rather than critically discuss indigenous ideas about personality, it may be noted that Doi's conception has been questioned on important points by others (e.g., Kumagai & Kumagai, 1986).

Indian conceptions. According to Paranjpe (1984, p. 235 ff.) the concept of *jiva* is similar to that of personality. "The *jiva* represents everything concerning an individual, including all his experiences and actions throughout his life cycle." Five concentric layers are distinguished. The outermost is the body. The next is called the "breath of life"; it refers to physiological processes. The third layer involves sensation and the "mind" that coordinates the sensory functions. Here egoistic feelings are placed that have to do with "me" and "mine." The fourth layer represents the intellect and the cognitive aspects of the person, including self-image and self-representation. The fifth and most inner layer of the *jiva* is the seat of experience of bliss.

Paranjpe sees many similarities with Western conceptions such as that of William James, but notes an important difference. In addition to the *jiva* there is a "real self" or *atman*, that is the permanent unchanging basis of life. Paranjpe (1984, p. 268) quotes the ancient Indian philosopher Sankara on this point. "There is something within us which is always the substrate of the conscious feeling of 'I.' ... This something knows every thought that passes through the mind, but is not known by them. This inner Self (*antar-atman*) is an eternal principle, which is always One and involves an integral experience of bliss.... This *atman* can be realized by means of a controlled mind." To achieve the state of bliss one has to acquire a certain state of consciousness.

We have summarized Paranjpe's description of only one school of thinking (Vedanta), but other ancient Indian scholars agree that there are different states of consciousness, including Patanjahli, who described yoga, the system of meditation that nowadays has many adherents outside of India. It is seen as highly desirable to attain the most superior state of consciousness. Restraint and control of the mind to keep it steadily on one object, withdrawing the senses from objects of pleasure, and enduring hardship are means toward this desirable condition.

To reach the ultimate principle of consciousness, the ultimate reality, transcending space and time, is a long and difficult process. Should the complete state of detachment and inner quietness be reached, then one's body becomes merely incidental (like one's shirt) and there is a change to fearlessness, concern for fellow beings, and equanimity. Ordinarily people have a low impulse control, which implies that they cannot detach themselves from the always present stimuli and vicissitudes of life. It will be clear that those trained in detachment are far less subject to the stresses and strains of life.

On the basis of considerations as described here Naidu (1983) has taken detachment as the basis of a research program on stress. Contrary to Western psychology where control over the outcome of one's actions is seen as desirable, the ancient Hindu scriptures value detachment from the possible consequences of one's actions. Western studies are on *in*voluntary loss of control and this can lead to helplessness and depression. Detachment amounts to voluntarily giving up control and is assumed to have a positive effect on mental health. Naidu's approach is one of the few attempts to translate directly a non-Western notion of a philosophical and religious nature into a personality index that can be studied experimentally.

In a review on personality published in the early 1970s Shanmugam (1972) dealt with studies of indigenous personality in India on a single page, complaining that practically no systematic empirical validation of the ancient Hindu concepts of personality had taken place until that time. In a survey published in 1988 this situation had not markedly changed (Asthana, 1988). This complaint is relevant not only to India. The conceptions by Sow and by Doi that we mentioned earlier also remain speculative.

Self and consciousness

Two longstanding issues in personality psychology have been the nature of the self and consciousness. In this section we consider the possibility of cross-cultural variation in the very notion of self and some findings (in a number of cultures) that consciousness can be deliberately altered to achieve various cultural and personal goals.

Conceptions of self. The notion of a person as a bounded individual has been central to the discipline of psychology. Indeed, it is the description and understanding of the unique individual that has been at the core of personality psychology. Despite this established position, the possibility that person and selfhood are cultural constructions, and hence likely to vary cross-culturally, has become an issue in theoretical and empirical research over the past decade. The central question was first posed by Shweder and Bourne (1984): "Does the concept of person vary cross-culturally?" Their answer, based upon research with Indians in the state of Orissa, is that persons are believed to be altered by the social relations into which they enter and are described not so much in terms of enduring traits, but in terms of social relationships. The links between this conception of the person and the dimension of individualism and collectivism (discussed in Chapter 3) are quite apparent.

A wide-ranging examination of this issue has been reported in Marsella, De Vos, and Hsu (1985) for both Western and Asian cultures. Rooted in anthropological explorations of personhood (e.g., Burridge 1979; Carrithers, Collins, & Lukes, 1985) and of interdisciplinary considerations of self (e.g., J. G. Miller, 1988) current cross-cultural research on the self attempts to bridge personality and social psychology (e.g., Yang & Bond, 1990). The claim is made generally that the Western conception of self is of an individual who is separate, autonomous, and atomized (made up of a set of discrete traits, abilities, values, and motives), seeking separateness and independence from others (Markus & Kitayama, 1991). In contrast, in Eastern cultures relatedness, connectedness, and interdependence are sought, rooted in a concept of the self not as a discrete entity, but as inherently linked to others. The person is only made "whole" when situated in one's place in a social unit.

A major theoretical review by Triandis (1989) may serve to illustrate this emerging field. Triandis has examined three aspects of self (private, public, and collective) as they are exhibited over three dimensions of cultural variation (individualism-collectivism, tightness-looseness, and cultural complexity). His review of a wide range of literature led him to conclude that: the more individualistic the culture, the more frequent is the "sampling" of the private self and the less frequent is the sampling of the collective self. (By "sampling" Triandis means attending to self-relevant information.) Societal tightness is also linked to high sampling of the collective self; while the more complex the culture, the more frequent is the sampling of the private and public self. Child-rearing and other ecological and cultural factors are proposed to account for these patterns, but they remain largely unspecified. These generalizations, if borne out by future empirical tests, will go a long way to integrate many of the findings in cross-cultural psychology that have been discussed in this and the two previous chapters. However, at present they are rather grand and require a good deal more precise operationalization (of both the aspects of self and cultural dimensions), as well as a detailed examination of the nature of the links between them.

Altered states of consciousness (ASC). This is the generic name for phenomena that include mystic experiences, meditation, hypnosis, trance, and possession (see Ward, 1989). In the Protestant tradition of the Christian religion and among agnostic scientists ASC had a strong flavor of abnormality. Even today practising of yoga tends to be frowned upon in more traditional groups in Western societies. The use of psychoactive substances such as marihuana remains largely restricted to social deviants in these societies. Still, the use of some of these substances goes back to prehistoric times and excepting instances of misuse apparently has been integrated in the life of the groups who for long periods have been familiar with their effects.

There are four criteria to distinguish ASC from other states of consciousness (that is, sleep, dreaming, and wakefulness). The most important is introspection, i.e., the self-reports of persons who have experienced a temporary state that they see as different from the usual state of consciousness. During ASC sensations, cognitive processes and emotions are reported to be changed.

Observations by outsiders of the behavior persons display during ASC form the second criterion for identification. Unusual patterns of motor behavior often make it immediately obvious to the observer that a person is in an unusual state. Combining these first two criteria, the following are characteristic of ASC in distinction to a "normal" state of consciousness: (1) alteration in thinking, (2) disturbed time sense, (3) loss of control, (4) change in emotional expression, (5) change of body image, (6) perceptual distortions, (7) change in meaning or significance (increased significance of subjective experience), (8) sense of the ineffable, (9) feelings of rejuvenation, (10) hypersuggestibility (Ludwig, 1969).

Induction is the third criterion. Classifications of ASC states tend to be based on the various means of induction (Dittrich, Von Arx, & Staub, 1985; Ludwig, 1969). The three most important techniques are the use of hallucinogens, reduction of environmental stimulation (or its opposite, sensory bombardment), and physical strain. The intake of hallucinogens is nowadays the most widely known method of induction due to the popularization of certain psychoactive drugs. Reduction of environmental stimulation is the basic induction technique for meditation. Stimulus deprivation can be self-imposed by shutting off external events and by inner-directed concentration. In other instances physical isolation and loneliness are important factors in bringing on an altered state of consciousness. Overstimulation also can take different forms. Sometimes light but rhythmic stimulation leads to the desired effect, sometimes a bombardment with varying stimuli (clapping, dancing, singing) is used. Physical exertion leading to exhaustion, hunger, and thirst, and sometimes even self-mutilation are applied to facilitate the onset of ASC.

The fourth criterion for identification are characteristics in psychophysiological measures during an ASC experience. Studies have been conducted with practitioners of yoga and Zen meditation. The abundance of high-amplitude alpha waves in the EEG is a finding reported by several investigators. Other remarkable results have been obtained, but they tend not to be consistent across studies. For example, alpha activity disappears from the EEG record when an intensive external stimulus is presented. Anand, Chhina , and Singh (1961) found with two yogis that their alpha activity was not blocked by external stimulation. They could keep their hands submerged in ice-cold water for three-quarters of an hour and still show persistent alpha activity with high amplitude.

Kasamatsu and Hirai (1966) observed the onset of alpha activity within fifty seconds after the beginning of Zen meditation in their sample of forty-eight Buddhist priests and trainees. This happened despite the fact that the subjects were meditating with their eyes open, while usually abundant alpha waves can be recorded only when subjects have their eyes closed. Another finding was that alpha blocking did occur in response to an outside stimulus (contrary to the findings of Anand et al., 1961), but that there was no habituation with repeated presentation of the same stimulus. Such an habituation effect was to be expected and it was actually observed in a sample of control subjects. More research is needed to decide whether differences such as between the two studies mentioned are a function of differences between the two forms of meditation or whether some artifact of method was involved. (See Box 4-5.)

ASC is a widespread phenomenon. In a survey by Bourguignon and Evascu (1977) some institutionalized form of ASC could be identified in a large majority of all the societies sampled. Institutionalization implies a religious, medical, or other social function and presupposes certain specified conditions and persons (for example, medicine men or shamans).

Much of the research on ASC is focused on the question whether there are differences in the incidence and in the type of ASC found in a society that can be explained in terms of cultural variables. Bourguignon (1976, 1979) attaches importance to a distinction between trance (or visionary trance) and possession trance. A person in trance may be experiencing hallucinations. Quite often these take the form of an interaction with spirits, whereby the spirit or soul of the person in trance may even have left the body and gone somewhere else. The experience must be remembered in order to pass it on to others (for example, clients seeking advice from the spirits) or to use it for curing purposes.

The possessed becomes another being, namely the spirit that has taken over the body. The possessed often will not remember what happened during the episode of possession; others will have to be present to hear what the spirits are communicating. Bourguignon sees trance as an *experience* and possession as a *performance* that requires an audience. Possession is usually brought on by drumming and dancing, trance by fasting, sensory deprivation, and drugs.

Box 4-5 Psychophysiological variables

For the first time in this book reference is made to psychophysiological measurements. This reflects the relatively rare use that is made of these methods in cross-cultural research. There are various reasons for this state of affairs. One has to do with the historical development of cross-cultural psychology; many of the researchers have been trained in the social science approach to psychology, an area in which psychophysiological registration is largely absent. Another reason is that careful recording of most psychophysiological events requires elaborate and sensitive equipment that is difficult to transport and operate under field conditions. The most important reason is probably that psychophysiological events are believed to be pretty much the same across all cultures. They are thought to be not much affected by cultural factors and fall largely outside the sphere of interest of cross-cultural researchers.

Perhaps the relevance of such variables is being underestimated. Not only can they provide measurements of psychophysiological processes in interaction with cultural conditions, they can also serve to control for unwanted effects. An example of the former use is the registration of the EEG record as a measurement of the state of consciousness mentioned in the main text. The control function is illustrated in Chapter 6, where a study by Poortinga and Foden (1975) is discussed. They made psychophysiological measurements to control for possible cross-cultural differences in arousal or activation that might have affected scores on their measures of curiosity.

Bourguignon has found some relationships between the type of ASC (trance or trance possession) and cultural variables. Although there are many exceptions, trance is more typical of men, possession of women. Among hunter-gatherers trance is more common; in more complex societies possession is the more frequently occurring form. There are also differences between major cultural regions. Among the original inhabitants of America the use of psychoactive plants leading to trance was widely practised. In some parts of Africa possession is more frequent. A number of explanations have been suggested for these variations. For example, the inferior position of women among agriculturalists has been mentioned as a possible cause for the higher frequency of possession trance. ASC would then be used for self-serving purposes, making the spirits express the wishes of the possessed. It has also been suggested that the high incidence of trance possession has to do with a poor nutritional state sometimes aggravated by food taboos for women (e.g., Gussler, 1973).

The effect of cultural variables has also been discussed by Wallace (1959). There are quite remarkable differences between North American Indians using peyote for religious rituals and Anglo-Americans. The Indians reported feelings of reverence and relief from physical ailments. In other users the drug had a wide range of effects on mood, from agitated depression to euphoria. They showed a breakdown in social inhibitions, a shift in behavior not observed in the Indians. The changes in perception were threatening to the Anglo-American control subjects, who experienced all kinds of things. The Indians reported visions that were in accordance with their religious beliefs and fitted their expectations about what would happen. Apparently, cultural expectations and knowledge are important determinants of subjective (experiential) and objective (observable) aspects of behavior (cf. also L. G. Peters & Price-Williams, 1983).[4]

In recent years there has been a tendency to argue that the variety of altered states of consciousness described in the literature are expressions of the same underlying process. This point has been made by L. G. Peters and Price-Williams (1983) from a phenomenological perspective. In their opinion a search for meaning and insight is fundamental to all the different cultural manifestations of ASC. Various theories about the neurophysiological mechanisms of ASC have been developed in psychopharmacology, especially in relation to neurotransmitters (e.g., Mandell, 1980). A somatic basis for the unity of altered states exists according to some authors in a common neurophysiological state characterized by parasympathetic dominance in the EEG (e.g., Winkelman, 1986). As long as there is a good deal of uncertainty on the regulation of EEG wave patterns precise psychophysiological theories should be seen as tentative. Nevertheless, research has opened a perspective on a common psychological basis underlying various culturally modulated expressions.

Conclusions

There are many traditions in cross-cultural psychology emphasizing modal personality differences that should be consistent over a wide range of situations. In this chapter we have mainly presented evidence that questions such an orientation. From this point of view cross-cultural differences find their origins in specific beliefs, norms, and conventions. The similarities in affective meaning, emotional expressions, and modes of experiencing provide a common psychological basis that underlies differences in overt culture-characteristic behavior patterns.

---

[4] The findings of Wallace are also in rather close agreement with the well-known experiments by Schachter and Singer (1962) where a divergent range of effects was observed in subjects who had taken unwittingly the arousal heightening drug epinephrine.

5   Cognition

In this chapter we shift our focus from those domains of behavior that are social and affective in character to those that are cognitive. The chapter begins with a consideration of the historical background of contemporary cross-cultural studies of cognition, followed by a review of the historically rooted work on the relationship between language and thinking. We then turn to an examination of some contemporary issues in the study of the role of cultural factors in cognition and to presentations of the four major conceptual orientations in the study of cognitive functioning in cultural context. A more detailed treatment of culture and cognition can be found in Segall et al. (1990), Chapters 5 to 9.

The historical legacy

Observations on the intellectual qualities of the various peoples of the world have been recorded throughout history. Along with the correctness of religious beliefs and manners, and taste in food and clothing, judgments about the intelligence or stupidity of others have been popular topics. We have little concern here with these writings, except to note that they likely reflected the social norms and relationships of the time rather than being valid accounts of intellectual life. However, some trained and astute observers produced detailed and insightful accounts; for example, the *Jesuit Relations* (of the seventeenth century), as interpreted by Hallowell (1946), exhibited a high degree of psychological sophistication. Similarly, work in the philology tradition (essentially the comparative study of languages) in Germany gave rise in 1860 to the first cross-cultural journal, *Zeitschrift für Völkerpsychologie und Sprachwissenschaften* edited by Steinthal and Lazarus, who were both linguists and psychologists. It is within this context that Wundt wrote his ten-volume opus, *Völkerpsychologie*.

Formal cross-cultural studies began only toward the end of the nineteenth century, just as psychology itself was becoming organized as a distinct discipline. Following some early studies on basic sensory and perceptual functioning (to be discussed in Chapter 6), there appeared a series of monographs on higher-level cognitive phenomena that were less experimental. The two classics to appear within a year of each other were

99

Boas's *The Mind of Primitive Man* (1911) and Wundt's *Elements of Folk Psychology* (1912 in German; 1916 in English). Both writers stemmed from a rigorous scientific background (Boas in physics and geography, and Wundt in linguistics, physiology, and experimental psychology) and both brought as much of this rigor as possible to the study of the "native mind." Surprisingly, perhaps, to the psychologist who often considers his experimental approach to be more rigorous than the anthropologist's field observational method, it is Boas's volume that is the clearer and less dated of the two.

Boas asserted that "the possession of language, and the use of tools, and the power of reasoning" (pp. 96–97) distinguish man from other animals. By implication, Boas may be said to consider that human uniqueness lies in their cognitive capacities rather than in their emotional or motivational life.

Within psychology, a major figure was Wundt, who in addition to his great physiological and experimental studies wrote extensively in the field of folk psychology *(Völkerpsychologie*, in ten volumes between 1912 and 1921). His translator ventured the opinion that "One may hazard the prophecy, that the final verdict of history will ascribe to his latest studies, those in folk psychology, a significance not inferior to that which is now generally conceded to the writings of his earlier years" (p. vi). This prophecy turned out to be generally incorrect (Berry, 1983; Danziger, 1983); much of Wundt's writing in this domain is not free of ethnocentrism, especially in his classification of cultures into "ages" of "Primitive Man," "The Totemic Age," "The Age of Heroes and Gods," and finally "The Development to Humanity."

For Wundt the question was not as it was for Boas (what is the cultural content and context of mental development?) but what is the mental basis for cultural development? If we consider the:

general cultural conditions of primitive man, and recall the very meagre character of his external cultural possessions as well as his lack of any impulse to perfect these, we may readily be led to suppose that his intellectual capacities also have remained on a very low place of development. (p. 110)

However Wundt, like Boas, declined to consider these to be intellectual *deficiencies*:

It is characteristic of primitive culture that it has failed to advance since immemorial times, and this accounts for the uniformity prevalent in widely separated regions of the earth. This, however, does not at all imply that within the narrow sphere that constitutes his world, the intelligence of primitive man is inferior to that of cultural man. (p. 112)

He concluded that:

the intellectual endowment of primitive man is in itself approximately equal to that of civilized man. Primitive man merely exercises his ability in a more restricted field; his horizon is essentially narrower because of his contentment under these limitations. (p. 113)

Wundt thus echoed the opinion of Boas that intellectual processes and competence are basically the same in "primitive" and "civilized" man and that the cultural and environmental context and content of the intellect provide sufficient basis for differential individual and group behavior and attainment.

The universality of thought processes soon came under attack from Lucien Lévy-Bruhl, (1910/1928 and 1922/1923; see Segall et al., 1990, Chapter 5, for a review). His basic argument was that "the mental processes of 'primitives' do not coincide with those which we are accustomed to describe in men of our own type ..." (1928, p. 14).

Challenges were soon forthcoming to Lévy-Bruhl's arguments and assertions. As Hallowell (1955a) points out in his review originally entitled "The Child, The Savage and Human Experience," the recapitulation theory of the evolutionists was a compelling model for anthropologists. This theory proposed that individual development from conception onward mimics the evolution of animal species ("ontogeny recapitulates phylogeny"). Consistent with the belief in evolutionary stages in cultural development was the assumption of concomitant stages in mental development through history and the findings of psychologists that there were definite stages in ontogenetic development were taken as support for their assumption. However, in later years Lévy-Bruhl's insistence upon different processes among groups of men was somewhat relaxed and, as psychologists began to explore varieties of intellectual functioning within subgroups of Western man, they discovered reason and logic to be less pervasive than originally thought (Wason & Johnson-Laird, 1972). Thus the clear gulf, which was so strenuously debated for decades, now appears to have been a matter of bias of observation.

In summary, the early workers on the problems of culture and cognition passed from primary concern with basic sensory and perceptual processes to elaborate discussions of "world view" complete with highly ethnocentric assertions regarding animistic, concrete, and prelogical thought. Despite the dated flavor of many of these passages, the major themes of current research are contained in them. First among these are a continuing concern for the relationship between language and cognition.

Language and thought

Thinking and language are intimately connected. It is difficult to imagine how we could think at all if we had no language in which to think. Therefore, it is not surprising that the question has been raised whether people who speak different languages also think in a different way.

Linguistic relativity. The principle of linguistic relativity is based on the notion that there are relationships between characteristics of a language and the thoughts that occur in the culture in which that language is spoken. According to some authors, the influence between language and culture is reciprocal. Others ascribe to language a determining influence on the thought patterns of the members of a culture. The notion of linguistic relativity has a long history, but today it is usually referred to as the "Whorfian hypothesis," after the linguist Benjamin Lee Whorf, or as the "Sapir-Whorf hypothesis," because the anthropologist Edward Sapir, with whom Whorf studied, had already formulated similar ideas.

In Whorf's view (1956) "the background linguistic system (in other words, the grammar) of each language is not merely a reproducing instrument for voicing ideas but rather is itself a shaper of ideas, the program and guide for the individual's mental activity, for his analysis of impressions, for his synthesis of his mental stock-of-trade" (p. 212). From this passage it is quite clear that language is seen not only as a means to communicate ideas and thoughts, but as intrinsic to their formation.

Whorf based his theory of linguistic relativity on a comparison of Standard Average European (SAE) with Native American languages. Between the European languages such as English, French, and Italian, Whorf saw much commonality; hence the term SAE. Major differences occur when one compares Indo-European languages with languages from other familes. An example is the sense of time among the Hopi. Whorf (1956) has argued that a Hopi-speaking person has no general notion of time as "a smooth flowing continuum in which everything in the universe proceeds at an equal rate, out of a future, through a present, into a past" (p. 57). The reason is that the Hopi language contains no words or grammatical constructions to refer to time, either explicitly or implicitly. In Whorf's opinion this shows that just as there can be other geometric systems besides the Euclidean, it is possible to have valid descriptions of the world in which our familiar concepts of space and time do not occur.

The Hopi language and culture have a metaphysics that differs from that of English and only can be described properly in the Hopi language. However, an approximate description in English is possible according to Whorf. The major distinction in Hopi is not between past, present and future, but between the manifest (or the objective) and the unmanifest (or the subjective). The manifest comprises everything that is accessible to the senses, that is, the physical world of the past and the present. The unmanifest includes the future, but also everything that exists in the mind (the Hopi would say the heart) and the realm of religion and magic. To the unmanifest belong desire and purpose. The term also implies that which is in the process of becoming manifest. As such it pertains to part of what in English is the present time. In the Hopi verb there is a form that refers to the emergence of manifestation, like going-to-sleep. However, most of what in English is the present time belongs to the realm of the manifest and is not distinguishable in the Hopi from the past.

The SAE notion of time also emerges in the use of plurality and numbers. In English one can as easily speak about ten days as about ten men. Whorf has pointed out that ten men can be perceived as a group. Ten days cannot be experienced objectively; we can only experience today. A group of days is a mental construction. It is a linguistic usage that is patterned on the outer world. "Concepts of time lose contact with the subjective experience of 'becoming later' and are objectified as counted QUANTITIES, especially as lengths, made up of units as a length can be visibly marked off into inches. A 'length of time' is envisioned as a row of similar units, like a row of bottles" (Whorf, 1956, pp. 139–140). In Hopi there are no imaginary plurals. The expression "ten days" will not be found. Rather reference will be made to the day that is reached after the number of ten days has passed. Staying for ten days will be expressed as staying until the eleventh day. Length of time is regarded by the Hopi as "a relation between two events in lateness. Instead of our linguistically promoted objectification of that datum of consciousness we call 'time,' the Hopi language has not laid down any pattern that would cloak the subjective 'becoming later' that is the essence of time" (p. 140).

This example shows that Whorf extended the principle of linguistic relativity to the level of grammatical characteristics of a language and that he saw these as cultural themes shared by the speakers of the language. The evidence on which these interpretations are based was rather anecdotal. It has certainly not been demonstrated by Whorf that the Hopi cannot discriminate between past, present, and future in much the same way as SAE speakers. Among others, Lenneberg (1953) has criticized Whorf's method of translation that led to such strong inferences about cross-cultural differences in thinking.

Later attempts were made to better specify the nature of linguistic relativity. An important distinction is that between the lexical or semantic level and the level of grammar and syntax (e.g., Fishman, 1960). Another distinction can be made between the influence of language on perception and cognition and the influence on verbal communication.

There are numerous examples that demonstrate noncorrespondence of denotative word meaning across languages. The Inuit have several (approximately twenty) words for the semantic category that in SAE languages is represented by the single word "snow." On the other hand the Aztecs have only one word where SAE languages use cold, snow, and ice. This leads to two expectations. First, the availability of words for certain categories presumably makes it easier to discriminate certain nuances in the outer world. Second, the availability of more words within a certain category should lead to greater ease of communication. If words are taken as codes, a larger number of words for a given range of phenomena implies a more accurate codability of these phenomena. Hence, verbal communication about them should also be more accurate.

The linguistic relativity hypothesis requires an answer to questions such as the following. Do the Inuit *perceive* more varieties of snow than speakers of SAE languages? And do Africans speaking Bantu languages in which there are no words for geometric forms such as triangle and square *experience* special difficulties with mathematics (cf. Du Toit, 1968)?

Whorf's hypothesis has been investigated extensively in one area, namely color perception. This research will be discussed in the next chapter, which deals with differences in perception. Here we merely note that sensory discrimination was found to be quite independent of the availability of semantic categories (basic color words) in a person's language. It was also established that focal colors (the colors that are most typical of color names) are much the same in any language; color perception has a neurophysiological basis that makes it largely invariant over all cultures. As we shall see, cross-cultural research on color perception has led to doubts about the effects of linguistic relativity at the lexical level.

Of course, this does not mean that vocabulary is irrelevant. Language in the form of labeling influences the organization and recall of representations in memory (e.g., Santa & Baker, 1975). However, the effect of the absence of certain words in a language appears to be limited. At most it reflects different interests of people in their interactions with the environment in which they live. Within the realm of shared experience we can communicate a particular state of affairs with a string of words if there is no single label available.

We have seen already from the example on the Hopi that linguistic relativity for Whorf included grammatical aspects of language. There have been a large number of reports, especially in the anthropological literature, in which some difference between two languages has been linked to a difference in other behavior patterns between the speakers of those languages. With few exceptions these links were made *post hoc*. Since any two cultures differ in many respects, nonlinguistic differences may have nothing to do with linguistic factors; they can be due to some other cultural variable.

One of the few experimental studies into linguistic relativity of grammar was carried out by Carroll and Casagrande (1958). They used a feature of the Amerindian Navaho language in which the conjugation of the verb differs according to whether the form or some other feature of an object is referred to. For this reason they hypothesized that the concept of form would develop early among Navaho-speaking children. Carroll and Casagrande found that Navaho-speaking children more than English-speaking children of Navaho origin would use form rather than color as a basis for the classification of objects. However, this support for the Whorfian hypothesis lost much of its significance when a control group of Anglo-American children showed an even stronger tendency to classify objects by form.

Another study (Bloom, 1981) focused on a particular difference between English and Chinese. English has a conditional construction that can indicate that a statement is counterfactual. The sentence "If I knew French, I could read the work of Voltaire" implies that the speaker does *not* know French. The listener deduces that the premise is false and that the meaning of the sentence is counterfactual. Chinese does not have such a conditional mode of expression. If the listener has no advance information, the sentence has to be preceded by an explicit negation. For example, "I do not know French; if I knew French, I could read Voltaire." According to Bloom, the absence of a counterfactual marker negatively affects the ability of speakers of Chinese to think counterfactually.

He presented Chinese- and English-speaking subjects with a story in which counterfactual implications were mentioned following a false premise. The counterfactuals were presented in a conditional form in the English version, but not, of course, in the Chinese version. Bloom found substantial differences when he asked whether the counterfactual events had actually occurred. The percentage of counterfactual responses varied from 6 percent to 63 percent among samples of Chinese students in Taiwan and Hong Kong, depending on the wording of the stories and the level of education of the subjects. For samples from the U.S. the proportion varied from 96 percent to 98 percent. In Bloom's (1981) opinion the differences in linguistic form "may well be highly responsible for important differences in the way English speakers, as opposed to Chinese speakers, categorize and operate cognitively with the world" (p. 29).

Au (1983) conducted similar experiments, but her results contradicted Bloom's. She found hardly any differences in counterfactual responding between speakers of English and Chinese.

New evidence was reported by Liu (1985), working with Chinese speakers who had minimal prior exposure to English. Using subjects in various school grades and various presentations, she concluded that education level and the presentation and content of the story are crucial variables for the level of performance. But she found no cross-cultural effects of linguistic markers of counterfactuality. Another study in which counterfactuality is manipulated within a single language is reported in Box 5-1.

In general, we can conclude that there is at best limited support for the linguistic relativity hypothesis at the lexical level, but the last word has probably not been spoken on this issue. Hunt and Banerjee (1988) have pointed out that contemporary models of memory and thought presume that language provides the concepts used in thinking. At the grammatical level there is only limited evidence, but this has been so negative, at least until now, that the hypothesis that the structure of a language has a broad effect on thinking can be shelved.

Universals in language. The anatomical properties of speech organs and the nervous system are among the universal features of language. However, according to many psychologists, the emergence of language cannot be explained in biological terms; it is not innate. Piaget (1975), for example, sees language development as a concomitant of the cognitive structures of sensorimotor intelligence. In this sense cognitive development is considered to be a necessary condition for language. However, cognitive development can take place, at least to a certain extent, independent of the availability of speech. Research with deaf children has shown this quite clearly, (e.g., Lenneberg, 1967; Eibl-Eibesfeldt, 1979a). Is it, in view of this evidence, not more reasonable to assume a genetic basis for human language? In a classic work on the biological foundations of language Lenneberg (1967) has argued that the processes by which language (including its structural properties) is realized are innate.

Box 5-1   Counterfactuality in northern Sotho

Vorster and Schuring (1989) presented a story with counterfactual statements to South African subjects from three languages, namely English, Afrikaans, and Sepedi, or Northern Sotho. Samples consisted of schoolchildren from grades 3, 5, and 7. The authors do not mention this, but the Sepedi-speaking subjects probably must have had prior exposure to English and/or Afrikaans. Nevertheless, meaningful data could be collected. Vorster and Schuring made use of a feature of the Sepedi language, namely that there are two modes of expressing counterfactuality, one of which is stronger than the other. It is also noteworthy that these authors asked questions about factual as well as counterfactual statements in the stimulus story. They argued that group differences in responses cannot be ascribed to the effects of counterfactuality if it has not been shown that similar differences are absent for factual statements.

The results are summarized in Figure 5-1. They show that the percentage of correct responses to factual items was very high even for the youngest children. Counterfactual statements led to large percentages of wrong answers, especially with younger children. The crucial finding is that with the less strong counterfactual cueing the Sepedi-speaking children show a similar pattern of results as the children from Afrikaans- and English-speaking backgrounds, while with the stronger cues the percentages of correct responses are much higher for the Sepedi. The differences in reactions by these Sotho-speaking subjects to the two versions of the same story indicate that the way in which counterfactuality is formulated in a specific instance should be seen as the determining factor rather than as a general mode of thinking. This is clearly not compatible with the Whorfian hypothesis.

In line with Lenneberg's ideas Chomsky (e.g., 1965, 1980) has suggested that there is a universal grammar to which any human language conforms. This grammar corresponds with the nature and scope of human cognitive functioning. According to Chomsky, there is an innate organization that determines the potential for language in the human being. At birth the mind is equipped with a mental representation of the universal grammar. Essential in Chomsky's writings is the distinction between the surface structures of a sentence and the deep structure. The surface structure (that is, the sentence as it appears) can be changed through a series of transformations to the deep structure (that is, the meaning of the sentence).

In Chomsky's view all languages have a common universal core. The existence of a universal grammar in this sense is difficult to demonstrate. As

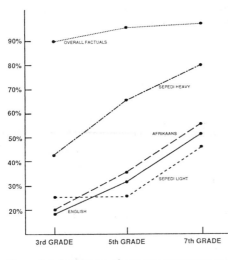

Figure 5-1 Percentage of correct responses to questions on factual statements (over all subjects) and on counterfactual statements (for four samples separately) (from Vorster & Schuring, 1989).

far as we know no studies have emerged in cross-cultural psychology aiming to test this theory. Rather, the available evidence is mostly based on detailed rational analyses of abstract structures (such as the deep syntactic structure) in one language.

There has been a fairly extensive amount of cross-cultural comparative research on other aspects of psycholinguistics, ranging from directly observable phonological variables, via word order in sentences, to semantic meaning. Sometimes data have been collected in a wide range of cultures. Much of this research has been inspired by Greenberg (1963, 1978). As in most other fields it is possible to emphasize cross-cultural similarities as well as variations. For example, all languages have nouns and verbs, but adjectives as they are known in English apparently are not found everywhere (see, for example, Hopper & Thompson, 1984). Intonation is a universal feature of speech, with a high pitch indicating that the speaker is placing emphasis. Also, toward the end of a discourse there tends to be a lowering of pitch (Bolinger, 1978). On the other hand, there are tone languages in which the semantic meaning of words can be dependent on the level of pitch at which phonemes are pronounced. In Papiamento, a language spoken in the Caribbean, pàpá (low-high) means daddy and pápà (high-low) means porridge. Tonality is widely spread; it is found in many African languages as well as in America and in Asia (for example, Chinese languages). Although the number of tone levels usually is two, up to five distinctive levels have been found (Maddieson, 1978).

Far-reaching implications for cognitive functioning have been ascribed to tonality (e.g., Wober, 1975). Even the neurological processing of tonal information in tonal and nontonal language speakers has been investigated. Verbal information tends to be processed more in the left hemisphere; processing of nonverbal information, including emotional aspects of speech, is more located in the right hemisphere (e.g., Bradshaw & Nettleton, 1981). Contrary to some earlier reports, Van Lancker and Fromkin (1973) found among Thai-speaking subjects a left-hemisphere dominance for tone words.[1] This indicates that semantic aspects of tonality are processed as verbal information. A replication showed similar results for English-speaking subjects (Van Lancker & Fromkin, 1978). This points to cross-cultural uniformity rather than differences in the processing of verbal information.

Further negative evidence for the hypothesis that tonality has extensive effects on cognition comes from a study by Joe (1991). With tonal-speaking (Papiamento) and nontonal-speaking (Creole English) children from the Caribbean she found that the Papiamento children could better discriminate between tonal and nontonal words in a foreign language (Mandarin Chinese). In a series of other perceptual and cognitive tasks there was only some indication of a better pitch discrimination with sequences of pure tones. On all the other tasks, including paired associates learning and sensitivity for emotional cues in spoken stories, no effect of tonality was found. Joe also found no differences in hemispheric preference with a series of dichotic listening tests. Except for the understanding of tonal words, there appears to be little connection between tonality and cognitive functioning.

In addition to structural (for example, word order) and prosodic (for example, intonation) aspects of language there is semantic meaning. The most important research tradition is that of Osgood; he has drawn on the work of Greenberg (1963), as well as his research on affective meaning that was discussed in Chapter 4. There we saw that Osgood's data base extended over thirty cultures. Among the features presumably shared by all languages Osgood (1980) postulated the principle of affective polarity. Each of the three factors, evaluation, potency, and activity, has a positive and a negative pole. Affectively negative words will be "marked" more often and positive words will be "unmarked" more often. The marking of a word implies extension with an affix. A clear example in English is the prefix "un" as in *un*happy, or *un*fair. In all the language communities studied by Osgood and his associates adjectives with a positive meaning, particularly on the evaluation dimension, are also used more frequently and over a wider range of situations than adjectives with a negative meaning.

Apparently, positive words are also easier to process cognitively. This was demonstrated for English and Chinese by Osgood and Hoosain (cf. Osgood,

---

[1] Hemispheric dominance or lateralization can be assessed by means of dichotic listening procedures in which separate stimuli are presented simultaneously to the right ear and to the left ear. When subjects reproduce better the stimuli presented at their left ear, this is an indication of right hemisphere dominance; with better reproduction of stimuli to the right ear there is left hemisphere dominance.

1980). When subjects were asked to respond "positive" to positive words and "negative" to words with a negative affective meaning, response times (measured with a voice-key) tended to be longer for negative words.

Another study by Osgood (1979) concerned the use of "and" or "but" in various languages. He argued that the polarity of positive and negative is a basic characteristic of human cognition, already expressed in the ancient Chinese principles of yang and yin. Osgood anticipated that subjects, when asked to connect two adjectives with either "and" or "but," would use "and" for adjectives with an affectively congruent meaning. When the meaning of two adjectives is affectively incongruent, they would use "but." For example, we tend to speak about noble *and* sincere, strong *but* nasty, happy *and* beautiful, and so forth. From his large-scale project on affective meaning discussed in Chapter 4 Osgood calculated a similarity index between pairs of adjectives within the three-dimensional semantic space defined by evaluation, potency, and activity. A positive correlation between proportion of subjects using "and" as a connective for two adjectives and similarity in their con-notative meaning was expected. A positive correlation was indeed found in all twelve languages, including American English, Finnish, Turkish, and Japanese. The average of these correlations was $r = 0.67$, indicating the universality of these basic cognitive structures.

Our understanding of cognitive universals in language is still far from complete; there are language families that were not included in the research mentioned here, and there are many aspects of language that have not been systematically investigated. Nevertheless, the available evidence in experimental psycholinguistics indicates that language as an instrument for thinking has many cross-culturally invariant properties. As humans we may not all be sharing the same thoughts, but our respective languages do not seem to predestine us to different kinds of thinking.

Contemporary issues

From this concern with language and its possible relationships with individual cognition we turn to a consideration of some current issues and then to the four major psychological approaches to cognition that have emerged in the cross-cultural literature. For all four approaches there are clearly articulated theoretical positions and a large set of empirical studies that speak to these positions. However, all four share difficulties in relating the empirical to the theoretical domains: how can valid inferences be made from cognitive be-haviors (the data) to cognitive processes and to cognitive organization; how can these psychological aspects be validly linked to cultural (or other antecedent) variables; and how can generalizations be validly made from cognitive behaviors (usually test scores) to broader domains of cognitive life to be found in daily activities in the culture? These theoretical and methodological problems will be discussed in Chapters 9 and 10. Here we provide part of the substantive information and argument on which these later chapters will be based. Some of these issues relating to the cross-cultural use of cognitive tests are outlined in Box 5-2.

We begin our consideration by asking the question, "What do people do, cognitively, in their daily activities that can tell us about their cognitive life?" This question is the one that is posed frequently in contemporary writing on cognition and is referred to as "practical intelligence" (e.g., Sternberg & Wagner, 1986) or "indigenous cognition" (e.g., Berry, Irvine, & Hunt, 1988). One term that has been employed to refer to these mundane daily cognitive activities is *bricolage* (Berry & Irvine, 1986). The term was originally employed by Lévi-Strausss (1962/1966) to refer to work of an odd-job sort. The term *bricoleur* has no precise equivalent in English. He is a person who undertakes odd jobs and is a jack-of-all-trades, or a kind of professional do-it-yourself man, but he is of a different standing from an "odd job man" or "handyman."

The approach taken in this book is that cognitive processes are very likely to be universal[2] (a view now widely espoused in cross-cultural psychology and one based on a considerable amount of research). Moreover, these day-to-day behaviors are not to be lightly dismissed; rather, they are the very stuff on which we may be able to build a more culturally relevant, more comprehensive, and less ethnocentric conception of human cognitive functioning.

A second question is the local cultural meaning of "cognitive competence" (incorporating the cognitive values toward which cognitive development is likely to take place). It is essential to understand these values and meanings since one cannot assess how far a person has gotten unless one understands where he is going. Studies of the meaning of intelligence in differing cultures (see Berry, 1984b, for a review) and of cognitive socialization more generally constitute an important set of data in our attempt to understand the kinds of cognitive competence children are directed toward. These studies exhibit a wide and diverse set of cognitive goals, often diverging sharply from the Western "quick, analytic, abstract" cluster so much inculcated by the school system and so thoroughly incorporated in psychological assessment devices.

Whether from anthropological or psychological sources, the essence of this approach is that we view cognitive (and other psychological) functioning as situated in an ecological and cultural context; the task is to specify the general life requirements for the group as a whole and then to identify how these are communicated to the developing individual. The ecocultural approach demands that work of this sort be accomplished prior to beginning individual assessment. It is basically making sure that we know the cognitive values or

[2] The theoretical notions of *absolutism*, *universalism*, and *relativism* will be discussed in detail in Chapter 10. However, some orientation to them is needed here. For the time being, absolutism can be understood as positing invariance across cultures with little or no role considered for the influence of cultural factors. Universalism proposes the existence of common psychological processes that are panhuman; cultural factors affect the development and display of behavior rooted in these common underlying processes. Relativisim claims the uniqueness of human behavior in each culture.

Box 5-2 The cross-cultural use of cognitive tests

In no other area of cross-cultural research have tests been used more extensively than in the area of cognition. For a proper understanding of tests and testing one has to be familiar with principles of assessment such as standardization, reliability, validity, and utility. Readers are advised to consult a textbook on the subject (e.g., Anastasi, 1988) if they are not familiar with these principles. Two important books on the cross-cultural use of tests have been edited by Cronbach and Drenth (1972) and Irvine and Berry (1983).

The use of a test in a cultural group other than the one for which it was originally designed has often led to sharp controversies. The central question is whether a given score has the same meaning independent of the cultural background of the test-takers. This issue of psychometric equivalence or comparability (which is not restricted to psychometric tests, but applies to all psychological data) is discussed in Chapter 9.

It is now generally recognized that culture-fair tests of cognitive abilities (that is, tests in which each person independent of cultural background has an equal chance of knowing the correct answers) are a fiction. Some tests more obviously than others require culture-specific knowledge, but the belief in general rules, for example that verbal tests are more unfair than nonverbal tests, has no empirical basis.

Tests are used in a culture other than the one in which they originated mainly for two purposes. The most important is the assessment of individuals for educational or job selection, or for clinical diagnosis. In a culturally homogeneous population (when there is one language, equal exposure to media, equal access to education, one ethnic identity) the question is whether the test reflects the same aspect of behavior as in the original culture; this is the problem of *test transfer* (see below). In culturally heterogeneous societies an additional question has to be asked, namely whether the test leads to a disproportionate number of low scores in ethnic or minority groups. This is the problem of *test fairness*, which has been the subject of extensive research (e.g., Schmitt & Noe, 1986).

The second purpose is the comparison of test scores. Usually one wants to find out whether certain cultural conditions lead to a higher score than other conditions. There are numerous examples of such comparative studies in this book. It may be noted that culture-fairness is not a requirement for comparison. (In fact, if a test were completely culture-fair it could not be used to assess any cultural group differences.)

The administration of tests, especially among subjects to whom such a procedure is utterly strange by an obtrusive foreigner, can lead to all kinds of unintended reactions and misunderstandings. Reuning (Reuning & Wortley, 1973) administered tests to nonliterate Bushmen, making sure that: (1) understanding of the actual task is not dependent on verbal explanation, (2) the task setting invites a response of the kind required, (3) the meaning of the stimuli is unambiguous for the subjects, and (4) the response is given in terms of some action rather than verbally.

A condition for all testing, but especially relevant for groups unfamiliar with the stimulus materials, is that extensive training should be given until all subjects know exactly what kind of problem they have to solve. A minimal requirement is that during the instruction at least one example is given of each type of item (and its solution) that occurs in the test. In this way the range of possible solutions that the subject has to take into consideration is defined beforehand. The importance of prior training can hardly be overestimated. Since an early report by Ombredane, Robaye, and Plumail (1956), there is evidence that with subjects who are unfamiliar with tests scores tend to increase rapidly with repeated administration of a test and that validity coefficients for the second or third score tend to be higher than for the first score.

Among the more frequently used tests in cross-cultural studies up to the 1960s are maze tests (subjects have to find a path to a goal in a maze schematically drawn on paper) and block designs (subjects have to construct a pattern of real blocks from an example on paper). The most widely used test has been and probably still is Raven's Matrices (Raven, Court, & Raven, 1982); it is supposed to provide a measurement of general intelligence. An overview of much of the earlier work on tests used cross-culturally, including many designed for use with nonliterate subjects, can be found in Ord (1972).

The transfer of tests for use in another culture according to Poortinga and Van der Flier (1988) presupposes an answer to three questions. The first is whether the behavior sampled by the items has at least approximately the same meaning; for example, there is no point in administering a mathematics test to unschooled subjects. The second question is whether the ability or trait measured plays approximately the same role in the organization of behavior of members of the new culture as in the original culture. This can be investigated by psychometric analysis. A test measuring a corresponding aspect of behavior should show the same intercorrelations (or factor loadings) in both cultures. Before a test is used, it is necessary to investigate especially the correlations of test performance with measurements of criteria that the test is supposed to predict. The third question is whether a score in a quantitative sense has the same meaning as in the country of origin of the test. Only if this is the case can the original norms be applied. However, unless the repertoire of behavior in the two cultures is very similar, new norms will certainly be needed. In general the use of translated tests with the original norms will lead to serious errors of interpretation and should be strongly discouraged.

Testing programs, notably for educational and personnel selection, have taken two forms: the transfer of existing (Western) tests with minimal adaptation of content and the construction of new tests that are suitable for the new culture. Among the most extensively used tests designed for nonliterate and semiliterate subjects is the General Adaptability Battery (Biesheuvel, 1954) and its revision, the Classification Test Battery (Grant, 1970). The instruction takes place by means of a silent film. For many years these batteries have played an important role in the selection and placement of personnel in Africa.

Examples of tests for educational selection can be found in the work of Drenth and colleagues (e.g., Drenth, 1977). The rationale for such testing is to provide information on a broader range of mental abilities than school achievement data and to compensate for unevenness in school quality. Ability tests that were constructed in the context of this program have been applied in various countries in Africa, Indonesia, and Surinam (e.g., Drenth, Van der Flier, & Omari, 1983; Bali, Drenth, Van der Flier, & Young, 1984). In addition, some of the tests were included (with modifications) in a Dutch battery of intelligence tests to make it more suitable for use with migrant children living in Dutch society (Resing, Bleichrodt, & Drenth, 1986).

goals being pursued by a particluar cultural group and being transmitted to developing members of the group before assessment is begun.

A third question is: once the values and meanings have been identified, is it possible to attempt to discover how far individuals have traveled toward them? Evidence from a review of cultural definitions of intelligence (Berry, 1984b) shows that in some groups holistic rather than analytic problem solving is culturally valued and that deliberation rather than haste is the proper course of action; moreover, collective discussion rather than individual reflection may be the preferred mode. In a society with this cluster of values about cognition an individual confronted with a standardized Western psychological test may exhibit "minimal development" according to the analytic-fast-individualistic criteria, but be maximally developed with respect to the holistic-reflective-collectivistic criteria. The cognitive competence of an individual in a particular culture should thus be conceived of as actual progress toward a number of culturally valued cognitive norms.

To set the stage for a consideration of the four approaches, we present Figure 5-2. Distinctions are made between the approaches of *general intelligence*, *genetic epistemology*, *specific abilities*, and *cognitive styles* on the basis

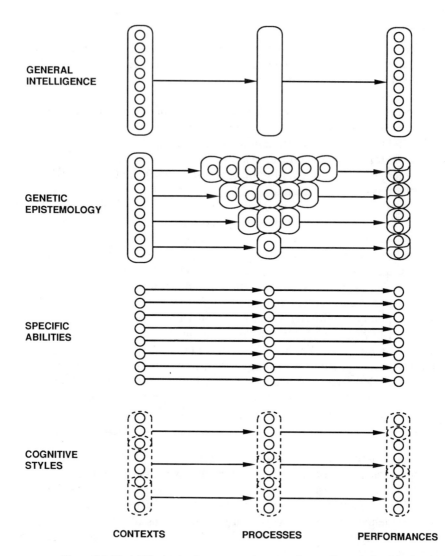

Figure 5-2 Model illustrating four approaches to understanding relationships between culture and cognition.

of three issues: conceptualization of ecological and cultural contexts (including cognitive values and cognitive socialization, on the left), cognitive performances and their organization (on the right), and the link through various cognitive processes between these two (across the center). After a preliminary portrayal and contrast among the four approaches guided by Figure 5-2, we will turn to a more detailed exposition of each. No attempt will be made to achieve comprehensiveness, since the literature is vast and readily available in other volumes (see, e.g., Berry & Dasen, 1974; Cole & Scribner, 1974; Irvine

& Berry, 1988; Segall et al., 1990, Part II). Rather we will limit our discussion to the issues identified above.

In the *general intelligence* approach (e.g., Vernon, 1969) there is claimed to be a unitary cognitive competence (called "general ability") that is evidenced by a set of positive correlations among performances on numerous cognitive tasks. This is illustrated on the right of Figure 5-2 at the top, where there is a single all-encompassing boundary drawn around a number of small circles (representing specific cognitive performances on various tasks such as verbal, spatial, and numerical). This unitary general ability is taken to imply (in the organism) the presence of a central cognitive processor that underlies the varying levels of intelligence found distributed across individuals in a population. Ecological and cultural contexts (comprising biological, social, cultural, educational, and nutritional stimulation) are often observed to come in a cluster (represented by the encompassing boundary, on the left, around these particular experiences); a large cluster represents an "enriched" environment, while a small one represents a "deprived" one. Overall (going across the top of Figure 5-2) an individual who has an enriched context will have greater opportunity to develop the central processor and hence will exhibit a greater general intelligence.

In the approach of *genetic epistemology* (e.g., Piaget, 1966), at least in its initial form, uninformed by the cross-cultural and differential studies of the last two decades, there are assumptions shared with the general intelligence view, but with a greater concern for a sequence over time of qualitatively different forms of cognition: the well-known sensorimotor, preoperational, concrete operational, and formal operational stages (represented by the increasingly complex processes in the middle). Within each stage, the theory postulates a particular logical structure of thought, which corresponds to the assumption (as in the general intelligence approach) that cognitive performances will be intercorrelated. There is also a set of postulated contextual antecedents to cognitive development that can promote or hinder (advance or delay) the appearance of the stages.

In the *specific abilities* approach (e.g., Cole, Gay, Glick, & Sharp, 1971) single abilities (represented on the right by discrete small circles) are studied individually; rarely is there any search for relationships among them. Each ability is considered to have a specific cognitive processor underlying it, and there is a particular experience in one's ecological and cultural context that stimulates the development and use of the processor, which in turn is revealed by the performance of the specific ability.

In the *cognitive styles* approach (e.g., Witkin & Berry, 1975) there are considered to be variable patterns of relationships among cognitive performances (indicated by dotted lines around small circles at the right). They are not assumed to be fixed into a single package (as in general intelligence), nor are they unrelated to each other (as in specific abilities). Underlying these variable clusters are a number of cognitive processors that together define an individual's characteristic way of exhibiting one's cognitive life (hence called an individual's cognitive "style"). These varying cognitive styles are thought to be developed as a result of variable sets of experiences (indicated on the left by dotted lines around particular aspects of one's ecological and cultural context).

With these initial orientations as background, we turn to a fuller description of each approach.

General intelligence

The history of the notion of *general intelligence* is well documented by Fancher (1985) for psychology generally and by Vernon (1969) and Irvine (1983) for cross-cultural psychology specifically. Within the psychometric tradition, Spearman (1927) pursued Galton's idea that there is an orderly mathematical relationship among all cognitive abilities: that is, they are positively intercorrelated. These positive correlations suggested to Spearman that there is a fundamental source of energy at work in all mental test performance, which he called "g" (for general intelligence). Subsequent theories of intelligence (e.g., Thurstone, 1938; Guilford, 1967; Carroll, 1983 ; Sternberg, 1985) have all involved the notion of positive intercorrelation, and so have had to deal to some extent with the concept of "g."

Vernon proposed a hierarchical model that incorporates "g" and other named factors at varying levels of increased specificity. In his empirical examinations of such a model cross-culturally (e.g., Vernon, 1969) he claimed to find support for the existence of "g" and the other levels. In his comprehensive overview of cross-cultural studies, Irvine (1979) also finds evidence for "g" and other more specialized factors, such as reasoning, verbal, figural, mathematical, and conceptual reasoning.

Even while obtaining these other factors, "g"-theorists maintain, like Spearman, that some basic underlying feature of an individual's cognitive life is responsible for the commonality. To identify what this might be Vernon (1969) called upon Hebb's (1949) distinction between "Intelligence A" and "Intelligence B": the former is the genetic equipment and potentiality of the individual, while the latter is the result of its development through interaction with one's cultural environment (compare the *genotype-phenotype* distinction of geneticists; see Box 8-1).

However, Vernon went further, introducing the notion of "Intelligence C" to refer to the performance of an individual on a particular intelligence test. This distinction between intelligence B and C allows another role for culture, since the developed intelligence (B) may or may not be properly sampled or assessed by the test, yielding a performance (C) that does not represent what is actually there. Numerous cultural factors (such as language, item content, motivation, and speed) may contribute to this discrepancy.

It should be clear that testers are able only to obtain data that speak directly to intelligence "C". As we shall see later, tests often are biased against members of other cultures; sometimes observations of people's daily activities (by culturally knowledgeable observers) may lead to a more valid assessment. Only by drawing inferences from data can researchers say something about "Intelligence B"; it should be clear that biased tests and observations will lead to wrong interpretations. This holds even more when inferences are extended to the remote concept of "Intelligence A."

Despite these obvious points, the long sad history of measuring the "intelligence" of peoples of various cultures is full of such biases (the "C-B" discrepancy) and impossible inferences (the "B-A" discrepancy). For a long time (Shuey, 1958; Porteus, 1937; Maistriaux, 1955, 1956; Rushton, 1988) comparisons have been made of "Intelligence C" presuming them to be valid estimates of "Intelligence B," and then claims were made about fundamental differences in "Intelligence A" on this basis. Cross-cultural psychologists generally distance themselves from such faulty use of the scientific and comparative methods. The persistence of such comparisons may be explained only by a combination of ignorance of cross-cultural methods and of ethnocentrism on the part of such researchers.

If test performances are generally related to each other (the basis of the IQ score), and if there is a unitary cognitive operator that is considered to underlie general intelligence, what cultural factors are usually identified by intelligence theorists as being responsible for an individual's general intelligence? For some there is a role claimed for a biological substrate; this position is epitomized by H. J. Eysenck (1988), who attempts to gain direct access to Intelligence A by way of psychophysiological techniques (for example, evoked potential measures of brain activity). Others emphasize a range of cultural experiences, sometimes packaged as the concept of "cultural advantage — disadvantage."

McShane and Berry (1988) have critically examined a number of these *deficit* and *difference* or "D-models" of explanation for cultural differences in cognitive test performance. In addition to the *genetic* and *physiological deficits* proposed in the literature, they identified individual *deprivation* (poverty, poor nutrition, and health), cultural *disorganization* (a group-level version of deprivation in which whole cultural groups experience the deculturation and marginalization that will be discussed in Chapter 11), and *disruption* (or uprooting, leading to maladjustment and loss of coping skills). In contrast to these deficit explanations a number of *difference* models were identified that do not share the negative value-laden character of the deficit models. Instead, it is assumed that processes and levels of competence are widely shared across cultural groups; performance differences arise because of cultural or other differences in the way these underlying qualities are expressed. This *difference* class of explanation is the one proposed earlier in this chapter during the discussion of cultural variation in cognitive norms.

When general models of contexts are employed, the single package of cultural experiences (illustrated on the left of Figure 5-2) is appropriate. However, many cross-cultural psychologists (such as Vernon and Irvine) who espouse the general intelligence notion use a more differentiated set of cultural experiences to account for variations in intelligence test performance. For Vernon (1969, p. 230) these factors include: perceptual and kinesthetic experience; varied stimulation (including play); "demanding" but "democratic" family climate; linguistic and conceptual stimulation (for example, books, travel); absence of magical beliefs; tolerance of nonconformity in the family; regular and prolonged schooling; positive self-concept; and broad cultural and other leisure interests that provide varied experience.

Irvine (1983), in an analysis of the influence of "non-test" variables (those not part of the actual test) on intelligence test performance, divided them into categories: low inference and high inference. Low-inference variables are those for which there is a rather clear and direct relationship between test performance and the proposed explanatory variable (such as practice, coaching, incentives, school streaming, and school quality). High-inference variables are those for which a bigger leap is required to link test performance to the presumed cause (such as ethnicity, socioeconomic status, gender, ecological press). According to Irvine, the evidence indicates that in industrialized countries, low-inference variables have little effect, but high-inference variables have a more pronounced effect on test scores. However, for reasons unknown, in many third world countries (particularly in Africa) this pattern is reversed. Because of this differing pattern, it is necessary to keep hypothesized antecedent variables conceptually and operationally distinct in cross-cultural studies.

Referring to the ecocultural framework (Figure 1-3), one factor has not yet been mentioned: acculturation. One possible reason for test scores to intercorrelate and produce a general factor in the cross-cultural studies is "a" (for common acculturation) rather than the more fundamental "g." Education (a frequent indicator of acculturation because it is usually formal Western-style schooling) has been identified by Vernon and Irvine as having a role in the distribution of intelligence test scores; it is common to find "years of schooling" to be the single best predictor of test scores in many studies. It is thus plausible, in the absence of statistical controls for acculturation experience, to consider that such coherence of test scores may be due not to a uniform "g" across cultures but to a uniform "a." That is, the reason for finding a single factor in the analysis of cognitive test performance may not be within the person's cognitive apparatus, but due to a common experience of formal Western-style schooling.

Genetic epistemology

Like the approach of general intelligence, the theoretical contribution of Jean Piaget posits coherence among cognitive performances when various tasks are presented to an individual. However, in contrast, four sequential stages are proposed (each with its own underlying cognitive structure), appearing one after the other as a child develops (Piaget, 1972). The first of these intelligences (sensorimotor) has already been described in Chapter 2, and the cross-cultural evidence for the theory has been treated extensively by Segall et al. (1990). Hence, in this chapter we present only a brief summary of the basic ideas, followed by a consideration of recent developments in the approach (called "neo-Piagetian").

In the course of development a child is considered to pass through four stages in a fixed sequence: sensorimotor, pre-operational, concrete-operational and formal-operational. At each stage "cognitive structures" (middle of Figure 5-2) appear, incorporating the previous structures. The two processes by which these changes take place are "assimilation" (the integration of new external elements) and "accommodation" (the adaptation of internal structures to external novelty).

As we have seen (Chapter 2), in the sensory-motor stage (up to 2 years of age) the child deals with reality in basic ways through its peripheral sensory and motor activity. At the concrete-operational stage (starting in Western industrialized settings around 6 or 7 years and continuing until around puberty) the child is able to perform the well-known "conservation" tasks, implying the "reversibility" of thought. In between these two stages (2 to 6 years) is the pre-operational stage, during which the child begins to organize its world of ideas. With the formal-operational stage (after puberty) comes the capacity to carry out hypothetico-deductive reasoning and scientific thinking. While the performance of various tasks within a stage is thought to be related to each other (hence the groupings of performances at the right of Figure 5-2) there is, nevertheless, some temporal sequencing (called "horizontal decalages") of performances, for example, with conservation of quantity usually appearing before weight and weight before volume.

With respect to factors that are antecedent to cognitive development, Piaget (1966) proposed four categories. First, *biological* factors lie at the root of the maturation of the nervous system and are unrelated (in Piaget's view) to social or cultural factors. Second are *equilibration* factors, involving the autoregulation that develops as the biological organism interacts with its physical environment; for Piaget, this factor also probably has little to do with one's social environment. Third are *social* factors, ones that are common to all societies (compare Aberle's "functional prerequisites to society" discussed in Chapter 3). While these involve the social environment, for Piaget they are not likely to be cross-culturally variable. Fourth are the *cultural transmission* factors that are highly variable across cultures, including education, customs, and institutions. If Piaget is correct, it is only these latter factors that can be properly included on the left of Figure 5-2, since the hypothesized invariance of the first three kinds of factors could not account for cross-cultural variance in cognitive performances (on the right of the figure).

The cross-cultural enterprise has been rich and controversial; it has also been reviewed frequently (see Dasen, 1972; Dasen & Heron, 1981) and is described in some detail in Segall et al. (1990). Our interest here will be mainly in the epistemological shifts that have occurred in cross-cultural psychology inspired by Piaget's work. We will in particular point out some of the advantages that the so-called "neo-Piagetian" theories have over the more orthodox versions of Piaget's theory when it comes to taking cultural diversity into account.

Despite its reference to a single theory, and most often to a set of more or less standardized tasks, Piagetian psychology is not any longer a homogeneous research venture. The "orthodox" tradition tends to follow an absolutist orientation, taking the sequence of stages and the definition of the end state of development as the same everywhere and paying little attention to the cultural validity of the assessment contexts. Piaget himself posited the invariance of the theory, even though he paid lip service (Piaget, 1966) to the need for empirical, cross-cultural tests. In orthodox Piagetian theory no attempt is usually made to account for cultural differences. The theory deals with an "epistemic" subject that often has no counterpart in a "real" child. The stages are defined by unitary structures that lead to the expectation of overarching "developmental levels," not unlike "general intelligence."

Such an absolutist Piagetian approach has been criticized repeatedly, notably because the interpretation of cultural differences in terms of a standard developmental sequence may easily lead to value judgments in terms of "retardation" or "deficit" against an ethnocentric, middle-class Western norm (Cole & Scribner, 1977). However, Dasen, Berry, and Witkin (1979) have argued that it is not necessary to link developmental sequences to value judgments if an ecocultural framework is used as a guiding paradigm, since each adaptive context sets its own standards for development.

Cross-cultural research using this paradigm has led to the conclusion that ecological and cultural factors do not influence the sequence of stages, but the rate at which they are attained (Dasen, 1972). Cultural differences are expected to occur at the performance (surface) level for concepts that are culturally valued (that is, needed for adaptation in a particular ecocultural setting) and also at the competence (deep) level for concepts that are not valued. Research using training techniques (e.g., Dasen, Ngini, & Lavallée, 1979) has shown that the asymptote in the development curves (the apparent leveling off in the attainment of some concrete operational concepts) is usually a performance phenomenon that disappears in many cases after repeated testing and after a small number of training sessions.

The link between the ecocultural contexts and the developmental (performance) outcomes is established using the concepts of enculturation and socialization practices during infancy and childhood. Dasen (1984) has paid some attention to the developmental niche of concrete operational thought. The relationships between operational development and locally valued aptitudes have been studied among the Baoulé of Côte d'Ivoire in terms of the parental ethnotheory of intelligence (Dasen et al., 1985), and Dasen (1988) has used behavior observations to document the relevant learning contexts. Other work along this paradigm is Saxe's (1981; Saxe & Moylan, 1982) research on the development of number and measurement concepts among the Oksapmin of Papua-Niugini (cf. Box 7-4) that integrates Piagetian theory with a local number system and counting practice that is related to parts of the body.

Occasionally, an extreme culturally relativistic approach is advocated for cross-cultural Piagetian research (e.g., Greenfield, 1976), but no convincing empirical work has been carried out using this approach. Furthermore, while cultural validation is obviously necessary, a totally relativistic strategy precludes the search for commonality through cross-cultural comparisons. Cognitive development, according to the existing cross-cultural data (reviewed by Dasen & Heron, 1981), is neither exactly the same everywhere nor totally culturally specific.

Thus, by the end of the 1970s a revival of structuralist approaches occurred in an attempt to integrate both structural and contextual aspects. The new models look for structural invariants accounting for developmental changes or for commonalities across situations, while insisting on the necessity to take situational variables into account. These so-called neo-Piagetian theories have been developed by a number of authors, notably Pascual-Leone (1970, 1980), Case (1985), and Mounoud (1979). In a special issue of the *International Journal of Psychology* statements by most of these authors have been brought together, and Demetriou and Efklides (1987a; 1987b), who also propose their own model, have attempted to search for an integration.

Neo-Piagetian models combine a Piagetian qualitative-structuralist framework (the existence of qualitatively different stages) with functional approaches; they draw heavily on Piaget's description of development, while refining it (by describing more stages and substages), but most of them reject the use of general logical structures such as those favored by Piaget. Some of the theories import contributions from information-processing approaches, such as the necessity of task analyses and the concept of attentional capacity (or working memory). The latter plays an important role in most neo-Piagetian theories and corresponds to the quantitative aspects of individual development. Attentional capacity refers to the number of units of information that a subject can process simultaneously. For Case (1985) this quantitative mechanism is seen as coexisting with qualitative changes, whereas for Pascual-Leone (1980) "M-power" (the chronological increment in the number of elements that can be integrated) is seen as sufficient to account for the qualitative changes. Dasen and de Ribaupierre (1987) have examined these neo-Piagetian theories in terms of their potential for taking cultural and individual differences into account. In their view cross-cultural psychology has an important theory-testing role. However, this is made difficult by the jargon and the technicalities that abound.

Specific abilities

In sharp contrast to both the general intelligence and genetic epistemology approaches other cross-cultural psychologists (notably Michael Cole and his colleagues) have criticized grand theories that attempt to link all cognitive performances together into a single intelligence (or sequential set of stages), with a presumed underlying general cognitive processor. Instead, in a series of monographs (Cole et al., 1971; Cole, 1975; Laboratory of Comparative Human Cognition, 1982, 1983; Scribner & Cole, 1981) they outline a theory and methodology that attempts to account for specific cognitive performances in terms of particular features of the cultural context and the use of specific cognitive operations.

In their 1971 monograph Cole and his colleagues proposed that "people will be good at doing the things that are important to them, and that they have occasion to do often" (p. xi), and concluded their volume with the proposition that "cultural differences in cognition reside more in the situations to which particular cognitive processes are applied, than in the existence of a process in one cultural group and its absence in another" (p. 233). Their "context specific approach" is characterized as a "formulation that retains the basic eco-cultural framework, but rejects the central processor assumption as the organizing metaphor for culture's effect on cognition" (Laboratory of Comparative Human Cognition, 1982, p. 674). Thus, in terms of Figure 5-2, specific abilities (on the right) are tied back to specific contexts (on the left) through specific (rather than general, central) processors (in the middle):

Instead of the universal laws of mind that control development "from above," the context-specific approach seeks to understand how cognitive achievements, which are initially context-specific, come to exert more general control over people's behavior as they grow older. The context-specific approach to culture and cognitive development takes "development within domains of activity" as its starting point; it looks for processes operating in the interactions between people within a particular setting as the proximal cause of the increasingly general cognitive competence. (Laboratory of Comparative Human Cognition, 1983, p. 299)

To substantiate their approach, Cole and his colleagues have produced a large volume of empirical studies and literature reviews. Their early studies (e.g., Gay and Cole, 1967; Cole et al., 1968, 1971) were carried out among Kpelle schoolchildren and adults in Liberia and American subjects in the U.S. in a set of projects concerned with mathematics learning, quantitative behavior, and some more complex cognitive activities (classification, memory, and logical thinking). For example, with respect to Kpelle precision in measurement (for example, of rice in a market setting), Gay and Cole (1967) concluded:

The most important thing is that measurement is used where it is needed. ... units of measure are, in general, not parts of an interrelated system but are specific to the objects measured. ... measurements are approximate unless there is a real need for exactness [and] ... measures are made quantitative primarily in economic activities. (p. 75)

Their general conclusion from these and many similar studies is that much Kpelle cognitive behavior is "context-bound" and that it is not possible to generalize cognitive performances produced in one context to other contexts. In their more recent writings (Laboratory of Comparative Human Cognition, 1982, 1983) they claim support for their position by critically reviewing the work of other researchers in such areas as infant development, perceptual skills, communication, classification, and memory.

A related line of work has been the examination of the relationship between cognitive performances and one important cultural feature: literacy. In their major report of this work Scribner and Cole (1981) challenge the common view (Goody & Watt, 1968) that literacy has served as a "watershed" in the course of human history, that preliterates cannot, while literates can, do certain abstract cognitive operations. Among the Vai people (also of Liberia) Scribner and Cole were able to find samples of persons who were literate in the Vai script but who had not attended formal schools, thus eliminating the usual confound between schooling and literacy as contributors to cognitive test performance.

Using a battery of tasks covering a wide range of cognitive activity (for example, memory, logical reasoning), Scribner and Cole sought to challenge the idea that literacy transforms the intellect in a general way. They found that there were no general cognitive effects of literacy, but there were some specific test performances that were related to particular features of the Vai script. They concluded that:

Instead of generalized changes in cognitive ability, we found localized changes in cognitive skills manifested in relatively esoteric experimental settings. Instead of qualitative changes in a person's orientation to language, we found differences in selected features of speech and communication . . . , our studies among the Vai provide the first direct evidence that literacy makes some difference to some skills in some contexts. (Scribner & Cole, 1981, p. 234)

In interpreting their results they noted that Vai literacy is a "restricted" one in the sense that not many people know and use it, and those who do use it for only limited purposes: "Vai script literacy is not essential either to maintain or to elaborate customary ways of life. . . . At best, Vai script literacy can be said to engage individuals with familiar topics" (p. 238) rather than opening up new experiences. Further, "Vai script literacy does not fulfill the expectations of those social scientists who consider literacy a prime mover in social change. It has not set off a dramatic modernizing sequence; it has not been accompanied by rapid developments in technology, art and science; it has not led to the growth of new intellectual disciplines" (p. 239). Thus, one possible reason for a lack of a general change in intellectual life is the rather limited role that literacy plays in Vai society.

A partial replication of this study among the Cree of Northern Ontario was carried out by Berry and Bennett (1989). Once again, literacy is present in a form (a syllabic script) that is not associated with formal schooling. The Cree are functionally literate; the script is less restricted than among the Vai since it is very widely used by many people and for many purposes. However, it is restricted in the broader cultural senses noted by Scribner and Cole above. The results of this study also found no evidence for a general cognitive enhancement (assessed by an elaborated version of Raven's Progressive Matrices), but some evidence for abilities that involved the same mental operations (rotation and spatial tasks) that are important in using this particular script. Thus, in two studies on the effects of literacy there is no evidence that a major shift in ways of thinking has taken place. The "watershed" view of the role of literacy in the course of human history thus has to be rejected, at least with respect to its effects on individual thought; however, the social and cultural consequences of literacy are not addressed by these studies.

In the Berry and Bennett (1989) study the interrelationships among test scores were examined, and all cognitive test performances were found to be positively intercorrelated. However, most of all they were found to be positively correlated with years of formal Western-style schooling, once again reminding us of the power of this acculturative influence.

Rooted in the traditions of experimental psychology, Cole and his colleagues have not typically posed the question of intertest relations of their data; this issue has not been of central importance to their research goals.

On the "context" side Cole and his colleagues have typically considered the influence of one single cultural experience on one cognitive performance. The problem with considering culture as a set of discrete situation-linked experiences has been identified by Jahoda (1980) in his perceptive critique of the specific abilities approach. For Jahoda (1980) this approach "appears to require extremely exhaustive and in practice almost endless exploration of quite specific pieces of behavior with no guarantee of a decisive outcome. This might not be necessary, if there were a workable 'theory of situations' at our disposal, but as Cole admits, there is none" (p. 126). However, Cole does appear to subscribe to the view that cultural experiences are intertwined rather than being a discrete set of situations: "the real stuff of culture is believed to reside in the interaction among elements; *the independent variables are not independent*" (Laboratory of Comparative Human Cognition, 1982, p. 645).

In the end, then, there may be an evolving rapprochement between Cole and those who seek some generalization on both the context and performance side. Still Cole appears to be convinced of his early assertion, namely that nonperformance on a particular cognitive task should not be generalized either to an expectation of nonperformance on other tasks or to the absence of the necessary underlying cognitive process or operator.

Cognitive styles

The cognitive style approach begins, as does that of specific abilities, with an attempt to understand how particular cognitive performances might be important in particular ecological and cultural contexts. It also draws upon an early proposal by Ferguson (1956), who asserted that "cultural factors prescribe what shall be learned and at what age; consequently different cultural environments lead to the development of different *patterns* of ability" (p. 121). In the cognitive styles approaches (as was the case for genetic epistemology and specific abilities) there is an interest in an "ecological analysis"

(Berry, 1980b) of the demands of the situation, posing the two questions: "What has to get done around here in order to survive?" and "What are the cultural practices that lead to the development of the required cognitive performances" (Berry, 1966)? The approaches differ in that the cognitive styles approach searches for the *patterns* of cognitive activity identified by Ferguson, while the specific abilities approach is generally unconcerned with relationships among cognitive performances.

The most influential conceptualization of cognitive style has been that of Witkin, Dyk, Paterson, Goodenough, and Karp 1962), who developed the dimension of the Field-Dependent Field-Independent (FDI) cognitive style. Their starting point was a concern with perceptual and orientation abilities in air pilot trainees, but they soon noticed that a number of abilities were related to each other in a way that evidenced a "pattern" (in the Ferguson sense). However, the construct that best explained this pattern was far less comprehensive than that of general intelligence: it was the tendency to rely primarily on internal (as opposed to external) frames of reference when orienting oneself in space. Subsequent studies extended this pattern of covariation to include cognitive and social behaviors. At one end of the FDI dimension are those (the Field-Independent) who rely on bodily cues within themselves and are generally less oriented toward social engagement with others; at the other end are those (the Field-Dependent) who rely more on external visual cues but are more socially oriented and competent. For any psychological dimension few individuals fall at the extreme ends; most fall in the broad middle range of the dimension.

The FDI cognitive style is referred to by Witkin, Goodenough, and Oltman (1979) as "extent of autonomous functioning" (p. 1138). The notion of *cognitive style* itself refers to a self-consistent manner (or "style") of dealing with the environment. In the case of FDI the construct refers to the extent to which an individual typically relies upon or accepts the physical or social environment as given in contrast to working on it, for example by analyzing or restructuring it. As the name suggests, those who tend to accept or rely upon the external environment are relatively more field-dependent, while those who tend to work on it are relatively more field-independent. The construct is a dimension, the poles of which are defined by the two terms; individuals have a characteristic "place" on this dimension, reflecting their usual degree of autonomy. However, individuals are not "fixed" into their usual place. Overall, the FDI cognitive style is a pervasive dimension of individual functioning, showing itself in the perceptual, intellectual, personality, and social domains, and it tends to be stable over time and across situations. It "involves individual differences in process rather than content variables; that is to say, it refers to individual differences in the 'how' rather than the 'what' of behaviour" (Witkin & Goodenough, 1981, p. 57).

Much of the cross-cultural use of the FDI construct has been carried out in relation to the ecocultural framework (Figure 1-3). Early studies (e.g., Berry, 1966; Dawson, 1967) employed a rudimentary version of the emerging

ANTECENDENT VARIABLE	PREDICTION OF COGNITIVE STYLE	
	FIELD INDEPENDENCE	FIELD DEPENDENCE
Subsistence pattern	Hunting, Gathering	Agriculture
Settlement pattern	Nomadic	Sedentary
Population density	Low	High
Family type	Nuclear	Extended
Social/political stratification	Loose	Tight
Socialization	Assertion	Compliance
Western education	High	Low
Wage employment	High	Low

Figure 5-3 Relationships between ecological, cultural, and acculturation variables and cognitive style.

framework (mainly the ecology and socialization components). For example, Berry (1966) was interested in what hunters and gatherers need to know in order to be successful and survive. An "ecological analysis" suggested that visual discrimination, visual disembedding, and spatial orientation would be important abilities for hunter-gatherers to possess; these were called the "ecological demands" placed upon developing individuals in hunting and gathering societies. The next step was to search for some "cultural aids" (for example, socialization practices and linguistic distinctions) that were present in a cultural group and that would promote such development (Berry, 1966, pp. 211–212). Later studies (e.g., Berry, 1976a; Berry et al., 1986b) have used the full ecocultural framework. Work up until the mid-1970s has been reviewed by Witkin and Berry (1975), while more recent work has been reviewed by Berry (1990). Only a summary of the evidence can be provided here.

The ecocultural framework has some obvious relevance for the theory of psychological differentiation. This relationship between the model and the theory is most succinctly presented in Figure 5-3, which illustrates the major ecological, cultural, and acculturational variables along with their expected relationships with the FDI cognitive style.

There is a theoretically important relationship between the FDI cognitive style dimension and the dimensions in the ecocultural framework: nomadic hunters and gatherers, who are relatively loose in social structure and who emphasize assertion in child-rearing, are likely to be relatively field-independent; in contrast, sedentary agriculturalists, who are tight in social structure and who emphasize compliance in child-rearing, are likely to be relatively field-dependent. Furthermore, those undergoing acculturation, particularly those with higher Western schooling, are likely to be more field-independent than those with less such experience.

In the literature reviewed by Witkin and Berry (1975) self-consistency correlations were found to be significant among tests representing the perceptual domain, but this was not always the case, particularly in Africa. Less consistency appeared in the literature between the perceptual and other domains.

With respect to sex differences there was a variable but interpretable pattern. An early "anthropological veto" was provided by Berry (1966) and replicated by MacArthur (1967), demonstrating that the usual sex difference (females more field-dependent than males) did not appear in a variety of Inuit and North American Indian samples. This was interpreted as an outcome of the relatively similar child-rearing and other ecological and cultural experiences of boys and girls in these hunter-gatherer societies. In most such societies a relatively field-independent cognitive style was judged to be highly adaptive for both males and females in individual economic roles, in family life, and in hunting and gathering activity more generally. In tighter and more structured societies (such as agricultural peoples) the usual sex differences were typically in evidence.

One of the clear theoretical points of contact between Witkin's theory and the ecocultural framework is that the description of characteristic family and child-rearing practices (leading to variation in cognitive style development) matches the descriptions of these practices as they vary across cultures from an emphasis on assertion to one on compliance (Barry et al., 1959). The conclusion was drawn from a review of over a dozen studies within and across cultures that the socialization of cognitive style as proposed by the theory was generally supported.

Turning to other cultural factors, within which these family practices are set, the conclusion was drawn that:

The evidence from these studies together suggests that a relatively field-dependent cognitive style ... is likely to be prevalent in social settings characterized by insistence on adherence to authority both in society and in the family, by the use of strict or even harsh socialization practices to enforce this conformance, and by tight social organization. In contrast, a relatively field-independent cognitive style ... is likely to be prevalent in social settings which are more encouraging of autonomous functioning, which are more lenient in their child-rearing practices, and which are loose in their social organization. (Witkin & Berry, 1975, p. 46)

Ecological factors, within which both cultural and family practices are set, focused on variations in cognitive style across groups that engage their environment differentially (for example, the contrast between nomadic hunting and gathering societies and sedentary agricultural ones). This ecological perspective provided the broadest context for examining the origin of differences in cognitive style. The conclusion reached on the basis of almost two dozen studies was that:

Overall, there is an accumulation of evidence which indicates that individuals from hunting-based samples tend to be more field-independent on tasks of perceptual differentiation, while those from agriculture-based samples tend to be relatively field-dependent. There may also be a congruent difference in degree of personal autonomy. Whether this ecocultural patterning of differentiation is due primarily to one factor or another is not easily answered since all work to date has sampled from groups characterized by a coherent cluster of antecedent variables. Since it is virtually impossible to disentangle ecological setting from adaptive cultural patterns, a test of individual variables is very difficult. (Witkin & Berry, 1975, pp. 61–62).

The last major section of the review was concerned with adaptation and change, particularly in relation to acculturation (contact with other societies, primarily through formal schooling and the experience of industrialization). Virtually all of the studies reviewed provided evidence for increased field-independence with acculturation experience. However, it was unclear whether such experiences fundamentally alter the cognitive style of individuals, or whether they alter the approach to the test materials through greater familiarity and practice in acquiring "test-taking tricks." Despite this uncertainty about the mechanism or the "depth" of these changes, the empirical evidence is unequivocal in showing more field-independent performance with greater experience of acculturation.

Since 1975 cross-cultural empirical work has continued on the theory. By far the largest program of cross-cultural research has been conducted by Durganand Sinha and his colleagues in India. Generally, Sinha has adopted the ecocultural framework and sought out populations in India with whom he could test and extend predictions from the model. In a first study, D. Sinha (1979) worked with two subgroups of the Birhor tribal culture, one of which remains nomadic hunter-gatherers, the other of which has made the transition to being sedentary agriculturalists. A third group, of long-standing agriculturalists (the tribal Oraon), was also included. Predictions were that with the expected variations in socialization practices (but no variation in acculturation) mean scores would vary according to ecological engagement. Samples of boys and girls 8 to 10 years of age from each of the three groups were administered the Story-Pictorial Embedded Figures Test (S-P EFT). This is a version of the Embedded Figures Test (EFT) in which a simple figure has to be found in a complex background (that is, by "disembedding"). Such tests are frequently used for the assessment of the FDI cognitive style. In most EFT tests geometric forms are used. However, the S-P EFT designed by D. Sinha employs local, natural small figures (for example, snakes, rodents, butterflies) embedded in larger organized natural scenes (for example, forests, gardens), in order to make it more suitable for children who are generally unfamiliar with geometric shapes. Results showed a significant group effect, and Sinha interpreted this finding as support both for his hypothesis and for the ecocultural framework.

In later studies Sinha looked to northern India for important variations in ecological and cultural arrangements. In one D. Sinha and Bharat (1985) located a group in the Cis-Himalayan region of India where three forms of marriage (and hence family type) were to be found: *monogamous*, in which there is one husband, one wife, and their children; *polyandrous*, in which there is one wife and two or more husbands (usually brothers, with the eldest brother being the head of the family) and their joint children; and *polygynandrous*, in which there are two or more husbands (again, often brothers) sharing two or more wives and their common children. They predicted the highest psychological differentiation in children in the first, intermediate in the second, and lowest in the third, based upon specific practices thought to diffuse parent-child interactions and upon increasing maternal indulgence of the child. The S-P EFT and Block Design were administered to children at two ages (7 to 9 and 13 to 15 years) more or less evenly split across the three family types. Analyses of variance revealed no significant difference for family type on either test but a clear age effect and an age by sex interaction (less sex difference among the younger sample).

Another Sinha (G. Sinha, 1988), in association with the research program just reviewed, studied the roles of three possible acculturative influences on cognitive style. Frequently the experience of formal *schooling, industrialization*, and *urbanization* come as a "package," so that their relative influences on cognitive style cannot be examined. Working with the Santhal tribal peoples, who have begun to experience all three acculturative changes, G. Sinha found (with children aged 7 to 10 years, again employing the S-P EFT) that all three factors were significant, with industrialization showing the strongest effect. There was also an interaction showing that the effect of industrialization was stronger when it was coupled with exposure to urban life and formal schooling. Unlike most previous studies, schooling did not appear to be the most important contributor to cognitive style, perhaps because of some specific qualitative feature of the schools in this area.

A second program of recent reseach (really a single extended study from 1975 to 1986) was initiated by Witkin and carried to completion by an interdisciplinary team, ending in the publication of a research monograph (Berry et al., 1986b). Until the beginning of this project most studies involving ecological contrasts compared the cognitive style of Amerindian hunter-gatherers to that of African agriculturalists. Two replications were needed, one of agricultural North American Indians and one of hunting and gathering Africans. The first study (Lonner & Sharp, 1983) showed that agricultural Amerindians (Yucatecan Maya) tended to be field-dependent relative to the hunting and gathering Amerindians in the literature, thus providing one of the two critical test cases. The second was a study of cognitive style in Africa (Berry et al., 1986b) comparing an African Pygmy (Blaka) hunter-gatherer sample with a sample of agriculturalist villagers living in the same geographical region as the Pygmy. Results showed that there was a difference between the two cultural groups on an African EFT, but only when differences in acculturation were taken into account. This finding was taken as evidence for the joint importance of both variables and was predicted from the ecocultural framework.

Conclusions

It is clear from the material in this chapter that ecological and cultural factors affect human cognition. It is equally clear that such effects cannot be explored in relation to naive questions about which groups are smarter than others. Rather, some important distinctions between cognitive process, competence, and performance reveal the complexity of the relationships. Further, theoretical differences between the four major schools of thought drew attention to the various ways in which these cognitive distinctions can be employed in empirical research. Hence, no simple summary or conclusion is possible in the face of such diversity. However, guided by the ecocultural framework, we can offer our own reading of this varied set of ideas and data: cognitive processes appear to be common to all human beings as universally shared properties of our intellectual life; cognitive competencies are developed according to some common rules, but can result in highly varied performances that are responsive to ecological contexts and to cultural norms and social situations encountered both during socialization and at the time of the performance.

It seems to be part of contemporary wisdom that cross-cultural differences in perception are of minor significance. The universal similarity in the anatomy and physiology of human sensory organs and nervous system seems to make it likely that sensory impressions and their transmission through the perceptual system are invariant across cultures. In the first section of this chapter, in which we trace some historical roots, we shall see that such ideas were not self-evident around 1900 when the first empirical studies in cross-cultural psychology were undertaken.

In the other sections more recent evidence will be reviewed. We begin with studies of sensory functions ranging from sensory acuity to information transmission. Thereafter we shall turn to perception in a more strict sense. When contrasted with sensation, perception implies stimulus selection and other forms of active engagement of the organism. Two topics that are salient in the literature will be given attention, namely the perception of color and the perception of pictorial materials. The chapter concludes with a section on aesthetics with emphasis on perceptual aspects.

The larger part of the discussion is on studies concerning the visual modality. There are some references to auditory perception and an infrequent mention of the other senses. In the available research literature a similar distribution in emphasis is found.

Historical roots

Many psychologists consider W. H. R. Rivers (1864–1922) the founding father of cross-cultural psychology. His main work (Rivers, 1901) was based on data collected with Torres Strait Islanders. The Torres Strait is located between Papua-Niugini and Australia. Rivers took part in the famous Cambridge Anthropological Expedition organized by the anthropologist Alfred Haddon. The main body of data was gathered during a period of four months by Rivers and some students on Murray Island. Measurements were taken on visual acuity, color vision, color blindness, afterimages, contrast, visual illusions, auditory acuity, rhythm, smell and taste, tactile acuity, weight discrimination, reaction times to visual and auditory stimuli, estimates of time intervals, memory, muscular power, motor accuracy, and a number of similar topics. The data were organized around three main subjects; visual acuity, color perception, and visual/spatial perception. Here we shall concern ourselves mainly with the first topic.

In many respects Rivers' study could be called exemplary even today, although the data analysis is not in every respect up to present standards. In his report Rivers shows great concern for issues of method. He worried that a task might not be properly understood and tried out different methods to find out which one worked most satisfactorily. His report is especially readable because the quantitative data are backed up by all kinds of supporting evidence, mainly obtained from observation. For example, in his analysis of color vision Rivers not only studied color naming and the sensitivity for different colors, he also asked for color preferences and even took note of the colors of the scarfs that people would wear on Sundays in church.

Rivers had an eye open for possible alternative explanations. When discussing the then popular notion of extraordinary visual acuity of non-Europeans, he distinguished between the power of resolution of the eye as a physiological instrument, powers of observation, and familiarity with the surroundings. Data on visual acuity were mainly collected with Snellen's E-chart. The E-figure is placed with the opening in one of four different positions; the correct one has to be indicated by the subject. A poster with Snellen figures in decreasing sizes was used by Rivers, who further manipulated the difficulty of the task by varying the distance between the poster and the subject. Rivers examined the eyes of his subjects for defects and diseases. He measured visual acuity with and without correcting lenses for deficient eyesight.

Rivers found the visual acuity of the Torres Strait Islanders not in any way extraordinary. He analyzed the available literature, which was already quite extensive around the turn of the century. However, many of the available studies were lacking in methodological rigor, and observations were often casual rather than systematic. On the basis of his own work and what information he had gained from other sources Rivers (1901) concluded "that the visual acuity of savage and half-civilized people, though superior to that of the normal European, is not so in any marked degree" (p. 42). Rivers discussed at length differences that he attributed to accurate observation of the "savages" and their attention to minute details. He was of the opinion that the predominant attention to objects of sense are a distinct hindrance to higher mental development. "If too much energy is expended on the sensory foundations, it is natural that the intellectual superstructure should suffer" (pp. 44–45). This complementary relationship between the sensory and the intellectual domain is repeatedly mentioned. In our opinion it shows that despite the openness of mind that is so manifest in his writings, even Rivers was deeply influenced by the ideas prevalent in his time.

The work of Rivers did not mark the beginning of a continuous research tradition in cross-cultural psychology. In the miscellaneous studies on perception that were published between 1910 and 1950 race remained the dominant antecedent factor in explanations of differences, but often without gross implications of inferiority. An example is the work of Thouless (1932) and

Beveridge (1935, 1940) on constancies, or phenomenal regression. From most angles of vision the projection of a circular disc on the retina of an observer forms an ellipse. When asked to draw what they see, subjects tend to make an ellipse that is between the form of the actual retinal projection and a full circle (the phenomenon). This regression toward the phenomenon is found not only for form, but also for size, color brightness, and so forth. For example, when a grey paper is illuminated at a higher intensity so that it reflects more light than a white paper, it may not appear lighter to the subject who knows that it is grey.

Thouless found that a small sample of Indian students, compared to Scots, showed a greater tendency to phenomenal regression for two tasks (relative size of two discs and circular versus ellipsoid presentation of a disc). He related this finding to Indian art, where, in the absence of perspective, objects are drawn as they are rather than as they actually present themselves to the observer. In Thouless's opinion the most simple explanation for this finding is that there are differences in how people perceive. These make Indian artists, compared to Europeans, see objects in a manner that is further removed from what can be expected according to the principles of perspective. Beveridge (1935) found a greater tendency to phenomenal regression among African than among British students for shape and size. In a later study (Beveridge, 1940) he extended the range of tasks and concluded that Africans are probably less affected by visual cues than Europeans.

The suspicion that preconceived ideas about the mental status of various races affected the outcome of research is strengthened when the work of Oliver is considered. He took an almost modern position on racial comparisons of intelligence test scores and argued for the incorporation of indigenous elements in test items recognizing the difficulties of language and instruction (Oliver, 1932, 1934). In a study with the Seashore Test for Musical Abilities he found that West African students, when compared with American students of a similar level of schooling, acquired higher scores for loudness discrimination, tone duration discrimination, and identification of rhythm, but lower scores for pitch discrimination, discrimination of timbre, and tonal memory. Oliver noted that the tests for timbre and tonal memory were the only two that correlated with intelligence, presumably because the instructions were difficult to understand.

Recapitulating this section, it can be stated that in the past differences in perceptual and sensory processes were considered important. Depending on the prior beliefs of an author, they were seen either as the outcome of cultural experiences or of racial inheritance. In the following sections we shall explore more contemporary notions.

Sensory functions

There are four classes of explanations of cross-cultural differences in reaction to simple sensory stimuli, namely (1) conditions in the physical environment that affect the sensory apparatus directly, (2) environmental conditions that affect the sensory apparatus indirectly, (3) genetic factors, and (4) cultural differences in the interaction with the environment.

An example of the first kind of explanation can be found in Reuning and Wortley (1973). They reported a better auditory acuity in the higher frequency ranges (up to 8000 Hz) for Kalahari Bushmen than the reference values given for samples in Denmark and the U.S. The differences were more striking for older subjects, suggesting that in the Kalahari desert there is less hearing loss with increasing age. Reuning and Wortley emphasized that other factors, such as diet, can provide alternative explanations. Still, they were inclined to see the low levels of ambient noise in the Kalahari as the critical factor, citing findings by other authors on slow deterioration of hearing in nonindustrial societies. It may be pointed out in passing that Wortley and Humphriss (1971) did not find Bushmen to have a better visual acuity (although they needed correcting lenses less often) than some urbanized groups.

An indirect effect of an environmental factor, namely poor nutrition, was suspected when black recruits to the South African mining industry were found to have a slower dark adaptation than white South Africans (Wyndham, 1975). It was thought that deficiencies in the diet could have led to a low level of vitamin A.[1] When a change in diet did not lead to the expected improvement, it was suggested that many of the mine workers might suffer from subclinical forms of liver ailments (cirrhosis), which in turn were associated with a high incidence of nutritional diseases in early childhood. This example is informative because it mentions both major factors that are nowadays seen as causal to cultural differences in sensation or motor performance, namely nutritional deficiencies and diseases. It is understood that certain diseases can have a debilitating effect on behavior, even if there are no clear signs of clinical symptoms.[2]

It has been established that some genetic traits occur with different frequency in various populations. Most famous is the difference in the incidence of red-green color blindness. It was already known in the time of Rivers (1901) that the frequency of red-green color blindness was much lower in some non-Caucasian groups than among Caucasians. Later on it was found that the mode of economic subsistence is probably an important factor. Hunters and gatherers have a much lower incidence of color blindness than populations that have a long history of agriculture. Within an evolutionary framework this has been attributed to a poorer discrimination that could be

[1] A low level of Vitamin A leads to insufficient functioning of the so-called rods in the retina that are used for (colorless) vision under conditions of low illumination.

[2] This was demonstrated for psychomotor abilities as well as cognitive abilities in research on the effects of endemic goiter by Bleichrodt (1986; Bleichrodt, Drenth, & Querido, 1980). Goiter is an enlargement of the thyroid gland that is caused by iodine deficiency. It is associated with cretinism, a syndrome characterized by mental deficiency and neurological abnormalities. It was found in Indonesia as well as in Spain that not visibly afflicted children in iodine-deficient areas obtained much lower scores on a wide variety of tests than children from neighbouring areas where the water contained sufficient iodine.

disadvantageous to the color blind when hunting and gathering (cf. Post, 1962, 1971). We shall come back to this point in Chapter 8. Another example is the inability to taste substances that contain PTC (phenylthiocarbamide) or another thiocarbamide group. About 30 percent of Caucasians are "taste blind" for these substances that taste bitter to others. Africans and American Indians have only a few percent nontasters (Kalmus, 1969; Doty, 1986). A further illustration of differential sensitivity for the effects of certain chemical compounds is the "alcoholic flush," a reddening of the face that is common among Oriental people after the consumption of only a few alcoholic drinks (Wolff, 1972, 1973), but is rarely found in people of European descent.

Socialization and enculturation practices are generally seen as the main antecedents of differences in sensory sensitivity and discrimination. Of the differences in sensation that have been reported many have to do with a socially conditioned preference or dislike for stimuli. For example, Kuwano, Namba, and Schick (1986) have argued that small differences in the evaluation of loudness of neighborhood noise between Japan, Great Britain, and West Germany should be interpreted with reference to sociocultural factors (how much do you tolerate) rather than in terms of sensory impact or some other perceptual variable. Several differences in preference or hedonistic value of sensory stimuli have also been found in studies on taste. For example, Chinese subjects rated sucrose at low concentrations as more pleasant than white subjects in the U.S. (Bertino, Beauchamp, & Jen, 1983). It seems likely that experience plays a role, since sucrose preference can be manipulated by dietary exposure. Also, it has been demonstrated in conditioning experiments that a more or less neutral taste becomes more appreciated when it is coupled with a well-liked flavor (cf. Doty, 1986, for a review).

An important question is whether observed differences in sensory functions stand by themselves or whether they have wider ramifications. It is an important scientific premise that complex behavior is an assembly of more elementary abilities and skills. Children learn to pay attention to certain stimuli and to acquire certain preferences, and these in turn lead to the development of more complex abilities.

In this context we can refer to the belief that Africans excel in auditory tasks while Europeans are more oriented to visual stimuli. This view, which has been expressed by well-known cross-cultural psychologists like Biesheuvel (1943) and Ombredane (1954), is an example of a "compensation hypothesis." In the previous section we mentioned that even Rivers was of the opinion that paying a great deal of attention to sensory stimuli would be to the detriment of intellectual development. More recent compensation hypotheses were less encompassing; they concerned the balance between various modalities. In the 1960s McLuhan (1971) emphasized the dominance of the visual modality in Western people and Wober (1966) coined the term *sensotypes* to indicate differences between cultural groups in the relative importance of one sensory modality over the others. The popularity of these ideas has extended to the field of art and literature where the concept of

Négritude was used to refer to the philosophy of life of African societies. According to Nursey-Bray (1970), a "study of the writings of Négritude shows that, as a cultural reaction to colonial arrogance, it vaunts a mode of perception that is asserted as specifically African; it is a mode of perception that is in essence audile, tactile, and at variance with the visual culture of the coloniser" (p. 241).

There was never a good theoretical account of cultural antecedents that would have led to a relative predominance of auditory perception in Africans. Nevertheless, there was a variety of observations that authors like Biesheuvel (1943) offered in support of this compensation hypothesis. Reference was made to generally poor scores of Africans on tests of spatial relations, and this was contrasted with a performance level on auditory tasks by and large on par with U.S. norms (compare the study by Oliver mentioned in the previous section). It was also observed that Africans appeared to have difficulty with the study of mathematics, but displayed a high facility for learning languages and a good sense for rhythm and music. Rhythm and dancing also lie behind the emphasis that Wober (1967) placed on the importance for Africans of both proprioceptive and auditory cues.

Direct empirical evidence on the salience of auditory or kinesthetic cues for Africans is very limited. Wober administered field-dependence tests with stimuli for different senses to Nigerian subjects and compared the patterns of scores with those reported in the literature on subjects from the U.S. He found relatively high scores for proprioceptive cues, but the results have been questioned on methodological grounds (cf. Deregowski, 1980b). Poortinga (1971, 1972) conducted a series of experiments on information transmission with corresponding auditory and visual stimuli. Black and white South African students served as subjects. In one of the experiments they were required to make judgments on the brightness of a white spot and on the loudness of a pure tone. With these two scales no evidence was found in support of a relative superiority of the black students in auditory judgments or the whites in visual judgments. In another experiment Choice Reaction Times to visual and auditory stimuli were used to assess the rate of information transmission for both senses. Even after fairly extensive practice the CRTs of the white subjects remained faster. However, the difference was of approximately the same size for the two kinds of stimuli, so that this experiment also failed to support the notion of relative differences between visual and auditory information transmission.

Since the early 1970s notions such as sensotype or relative auditory versus visual predominance have largely disappeared from the cross-cultural literature on perception.[3] Here a similar shift in emphasis has occurred from

---

[3] Biesheuvel (cf. Poortinga, 1971) has raised the possibility that Africans may perceive and communicate more readily through the auditory modality. Such a preference would not necessarily depend on or lead to greater acuity or powers of discrimination. To our knowledge there is no research on preferences that support this version of the compensation hypothesis.

broad domains of behavior to more limited and specific ranges of stimuli, as was noted for cognition in the previous chapter.

Cross-cultural studies with simple sensory stimuli have fallen far behind in the general growth of the field since the 1950s. In a bibliography with 3122 entries on Africa south of the Sahara, covering the period from 1960 to 1975, Andor (1983) listed only nine studies on the sensory bases of perception. This probably more than anything else reflects the contemporary belief that sensory differences are only small. Following the traditions of the field, we have mainly been dealing with *differences* in this section. The overall impression one gains from the accumulated literature is that cross-cultural differences in the sensory impact of stimuli are exceptions rather than the rule and that if they do occur, a variable outside the perceptual system should be sought for an explanation.

In the remainder of this chapter we shall pay attention to perceptual variables. Traditionally sensation implies a more passive role for the organism as a recipient for stimuli, whereas perception presumes an active engagement on the part of the organism in the selection and organization of stimuli.

Color: coding and categorization

For a proper understanding of this section it is important to realize that color is a physical quality of objects as well as an impression or sensation with the human observer. On the one hand each color can be defined unambiguously in terms of physical qualities. On the other hand one can ask subjects to name colors, to remember colors, to categorize them, and so on. The physical measurements can then be related to the psychological reports. In early studies color terms were taken as indices of what people in a particular culture apparently perceived. Later on sets of papers or chips came into use in which the whole range of visible colors is represented. The most well known of these sets is the Munsell system.

The history of cross-cultural research on the perception of color is usually taken to start with the work that the British politician William Gladstone published in the middle of the nineteenth century. He called attention to certain oddities in the poetry of Homer, such as the absence of words for brown and blue, which he attributed to a limited differentiation of color vision among the ancient Greeks. Somewhat later Geiger (1880) extended this idea about the differentiation of sensitivity for color from early history to modern times. Originally only black and red were distinguished; later came yellow and green and finally blue. Geiger obtained the evidence for his thesis from old literary sources, such as Homer and the Germanic epic poems.

Magnus (1880) was the first to report on an empirical investigation with contemporary data. He collected information from colonial foreign residents in a number of countries, using a questionnaire as well as chips of different colors. The objective was to establish the range of color vision of "uncivilized" peoples as well as the verbal expressions for various colors. Thus, a distinction was made between physiological and linguistic issues. So far Magnus had believed that evidence on color vision could be derived from the study of color names. Against his own expectations he found that the range of perceivable colors was invariant across cultures, while in many languages words for certain colors were lacking. This concerned colors with a short wavelength (green, blue, violet), rather than long wavelength colors (red, yellow). In particular a single word only for green and blue was found frequently, while there was always a separate term for red.

Because of this consistency in the pattern of findings, Magnus kept on looking for some physiological explanation. Through the spectrum from violet to red he suggested an increase in vividness of the colors. The less vivid colors would be less salient to non-Europeans and for that reason less likely be identified with a separate word. Rivers (1901) took up the study of color vision and color naming during the Torres Strait expedition. He found a frequent confusion between green and blue and between saturated blue and dark or dull colors. Also, his subjects detected a faint red more readily than a faint blue, taking the thresholds of Europeans as a standard.

Rivers was struck by a parallel between these results and linguistic expressions. Although none of his subjects was found to be color blind, he argued that their color vision is characterized by a certain insensitiveness to blue and (probably) green as compared to Europeans. He wrote (1901):

I have already described how many of the older natives [of the island Mabuig] compared every colour to some natural object, apparently showing, as regards most colours, a high degree of appreciation of differences of hue and shade, and yet these natives would deliberately compare a brilliant and saturated blue to the colour of dirty water or to the darkness of a night in which nothing could be seen. Every detail of the behaviour of the natives in connection with the naming of colour was consistent with the idea that blue to them was a darker or a duller colour than it is to us. (p. 94)

To account for his findings Rivers suggested that racial differences in pigmentation play a role. Short wave length colors are absorbed to a greater extent by pigment in the retina and dark-skinned people have more of this pigmentation. Below we shall see that much later this idea was mentioned again for the explanation of cross-cultural differences in geometric illusion perception.

Interest in the work on color perception of these early cross-culturalists soon dwindled. Only in part this had an empirical reason. Titchener (1916; cf. Lloyd, 1977) replicated some of Rivers' research with students in the U.S. and showed that they also had a relative insensitivity to blue when tested under similar conditions of illumination as used by Rivers. The findings on physiological differences fell into disregard mainly under the influence of cultural and linguistic relativity, culminating in the Sapir-Whorf hypothesis (see Chapter 5).

The domain of color is excellently suited to test Whorf's hypothesis, because any color can be unambiguously defined in terms of objective physical measurements. The mediation of language in color naming was advocated among others by Ray (1952), who concluded from his own studies with Amerindians that each culture has divided the visible spectrum into units on a physically quite arbitrary basis. Even the famous confusion between blue and green was rejected and attributed to a greater rather than a lesser subtlety in classification. Where Western cultures use only blue and green, he found a three-way division. The middle region is then not identified as blue-green but as a separate color. However, there has been no further empirical validation of Ray's observations.

A new line of research was started by Brown and Lenneberg (1954) with the introduction of the term *codability*. This was a composite measure of (1) agreement in the naming of a color chip, (2) the length of the name, and (3) the response latency in naming. It was expected that more codable colors are better remembered and more easily identified in a recognition task. Some positive results were found in the U.S., but the research was not replicated elsewhere. Lantz and Stefflre (1964) suggested another measure, namely *communication accuracy*. They asked listeners to identify a certain chip in an array of colors on the basis of color terms that were presented to them. Some terms were found to lead to more accurate identification than other terms. When used in a recognition experiment, the more accurately communicable terms also were better recognized. Although this work showed the influence of language on communication and memory, it was not very relevant to the basic issue, namely the relationship of color terms with the visible spectrum that they represent.

The linguistic relativity hypothesis was radically challenged in a book by Berlin and Kay (1969) with the title *Basic Color Terms: Their Universality and Evolution*. These authors asked bilingual subjects resident in the area of San Francisco to generate basic color terms in their mother tongue. A basic term had four main characteristics: (1) it is monoleximic, that is, the meaning cannot be derived from the meaning of its parts, as in lemon-colored; (2) the color it signifies is not included in another color term (for example, scarlet is a kind of red); (3) its usage must not be restricted to certain classes of objects; and (4) it must be psychologically salient. This is evaluated with several indices, such as stability of reference across informants and occasions of usage.

After a listing of basic color terms had been obtained, a subject was given a panel with 329 differently colored chips from the Munsell system and asked to indicate for each term (x) that had been previously generated: (1) all those chips that would be called x under any condition; and (2) the best, most typical, example of x in the Munsell display. It is important to note that the subjects worked with terms that they had generated themselves. The experimenter had no idea which color shade was signified by a particular x.

The results of subjects from twenty languages are summarized in Figure 6-1. The map shows that the most typical, or focal, chips for basic colors are neatly clustered. Apart from clusters for black and white with terms in all

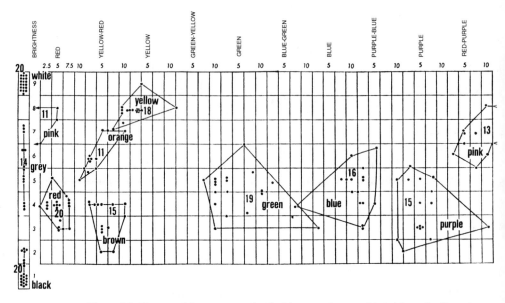

Figure 6-1 Clusters of dots representing foci (averaged over subjects) in each of twenty languages. The number in each cluster indicates the number of languages that had a basic term for the color concerned. (Numbers in the margins refer to parameters of the Munsell color system.) (Berlin & Kay, 1969, p. 9)

twenty languages, there is also a word in all these languages for the area that is called red in English. Then the number decreases to 19 for green, 18 for yellow, 16 for blue, 15 for brown and purple, 14 for grey, and 11 for pink and orange. Large parts of the diagram remain outside the areas covered by the basic color terms. Berlin and Kay (1969, p. 10) concluded that "color categorization is not random and the foci of basic color terms are similar in all languages."

Many cultures do not have names for all the eleven basic colors in English. The second important finding by Berlin and Kay was that there is a strong relationship between the number of basic color terms in a language and the subset of focal colors for which there is a basic term. They claimed that the focal colors become encoded in the history of a language in a (largely) fixed order. The sequence of stages is summarized in Figure 6-2.[4] In the most elementary stage there are two terms, one for white, encoding also for light and warm colors (for example, yellow) and one for black that includes dark and cool colors (for example, blue). In the second stage a separate term for red and warm colors emerges. From the third stage onward the order is not

[4] In more recent work (Berlin & Berlin, 1975) a somewhat more complicated scheme has been proposed. However, the deviations from the original sequence are small and need not concern us here.

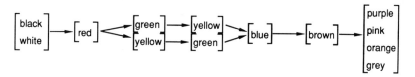

Figure 6-2 The sequence in which terms for focal colors emerge in the history of languages. (Berlin & Kay, 1969)

precisely fixed. It is possible that either green or yellow is the next term, but one also finds the opposite order. Thereafter follow blue and then brown. It can be seen from the figure that pink, orange, grey, and purple are added to a language in the last stage.

For Berlin and Kay the various stages are steps in the evolution of languages. To support their evolutionary scheme they drew on a large number of reports in the (mainly ethnographic) literature. There were a few color vocabularies that did not readily fit, but by and large the available information showed a striking agreement with the proposed order. Later studies in which the fit of the scheme was tested in various cultures also did not show much incompatible data.

Berlin and Kay's research can be criticized on a number of points. Their definition of basic color terms is somewhat fuzzy, although it seemed to work quite well. More serious is the objection that the subjects from San Francisco had all been living for a longer or shorter period in the U.S. Rather fundamental is the objection by McNeill (1972) that Berlin and Kay ignored the functional meaning of colors in a culture.

The subjective meaning of colors has also been emphasized by Sahlins (1976). His reproach to Berlin and Kay is that with their approach they reduce culture to nature. He emphasizes the social meaning that colors carry, in particular when they are used in symbols and rituals. In Sahlins's view this social meaning has a logic of its own that cannot be explained with reference to biological features. Culture makes use of nature rather than that nature should determine culture.

While anthropologists like McNeill and Sahlins defended a relativistic or cultural viewpoint, further experimental evidence was collected mainly by psychologists. Rosch (1972, 1977) established that focal colors had a higher codability in the sense that they were named more rapidly and were given shorter names than nonfocal colors by subjects from twenty-three language areas. She then tested the hypothesis that focal colors would also have a higher codability than nonfocal colors even for those focal colors for which there is no basic term in a subject's language. She studied the Dani, a group in Niugini with only two basic color terms (that is, a language at the first stage in the Berlin and Kay sequence). When the Dani were shown color chips, they did indeed recognize focal colors better than nonfocal colors after a 30-second interval (as did American students).

In a second study with the Dani, eight focal colors and eight nonfocal colors were paired with a separate response word. The number of trials it took a subject to learn the correct response for each stimulus was the dependent variable. It was found that the focal colors required significantly fewer trials than the nonfocal colors. In Rosch's view the results should be explained with reference to physiological factors underlying color vision rather than linguistic factors. She concluded (1972) that "far from being a domain well suited to the study of the effects of language on thought, the color space would seem a prime example of the influence of underlying perceptual-cognitive factors on the formation and reference of linguistic categories" (p. 20).[5]

More direct evidence on the role of possible physiological factors in the linguistic categorization of colors was reported by Bornstein (1973). He related the wavelength of the focal colors found by Berlin and Kay (see Figure 6-1) to the spectral sensitivity of four types of cells found in the brain of Macaque monkeys. These cells were found to be sensitive for wavelengths corresponding to red, yellow, green and blue, respectively.

In fact, Bornstein has reopened the debate on biological differences in color perception. He pursued the suggestion that Negroid and Mongoloid groups have a more dense pigmentation of the retina than white-skinned groups, which acts as a filter for blue light. On the basis of a survey of color names in almost 150 societies he noted a relationship between distance to the equator and color terms. As one comes closer to the equator there is more often only a single term for blue and green. In the same direction there is a deepening of skin color (which is correlated with retinal pigmentation). High pigmentation may form a protection against the ultraviolet component of sunlight. Bornstein suggested further that a certain diet (rich in carotenoids) may lead to more yellow pigments in the eye that have a similar effect.

There is some indirect evidence against Bornstein's ideas. In the next section we shall see that the retinal pigmentation hypothesis failed to account for intercultural differences in illusion susceptibility. In summary, it appears that a physiological basis for cross-cultural differences in color terms has not been firmly established, although this line of research would seem to deserve further attention.

In a further study (Bornstein, Kessen, & Weiskopf, 1976) the technique of

---

[5] Rosch's studies were criticized by Lucy and Shweder (1979). They carried out experiments on recognition memory as a function of both communication accuracy (referred to earlier in this text) and focality of colors. They found that the linguistic factor, that is, communication accuracy, was the best predictor of recognition memory. When the effect of the linguistic factor was partialed out, the correlation between focality and memory came close to zero. The study was carried out with colors of equal discriminability, rather than equal distance on physical parameters (wavelength). In a sense this amounts to making more difficult what subjects can do well and less difficult what they can do less well, so that performance becomes more equal for all stimuli.

stimulus habituation was used with 4-month-old babies, using red, yellow, green, and blue stimuli. When the same stimulus is presented repeatedly, looking time will decrease. At the presentation of a different stimulus there will be a dishabituation effect that is stronger as the new stimulus is more dissimilar. All stimulus changes in this experiment were identical in one respect; the size of the change, measured in wavelength, was always equal. However, with some of the changes the new stimulus remained within the same color category as the original stimulus (for example, both would be designated as red by an adult observer), while with other changes the new stimulus would be classified in another color category (for example, a shift from red to yellow). It was found that the infants showed a stronger reaction to the new stimulus when the latter type of change occurred. This indicated that the categories and boundaries between categories for babies are much the same as those for adults long before the onset of speech. In the debate on the primacy in color identification of either language or perception this quite convincingly suggests the primacy of perception.

Can we conclude that over the last 100 years the pendulum has merely been swinging between biological determinacy and linguistic-cultural relativity? In our opinion this is certainly not the case. In the nineteenth century the observations on differences in color naming were interpreted within an evolutionary framework that allowed for a hierarchical order between human subspecies or races. When Berlin and Kay used the word "evolution," they referred not to the biological but to the linguistic domain. They explicitly stated that differences in color terminology do not reflect differences in the perceptual apparatus of the groups concerned.

The more recent psychological findings point to a universal identity of the physiological system and the programming of color perception. In addition, there seems to be a convergence between anthropological and psychological approaches. For example, Kay (cf. Kay & McDaniel, 1978) has accepted a neurophysiological theory of color categories that presumes the same four focal colors mentioned by Bornstein and that imposes strict limits on the cultural relativity of color perception. Only on the formulation of the linguistic stages or the emergence of a particular color term are debates continuing (e.g., Van Wattenwyl & Zollinger, 1979; Greenfeld, 1986).

At a more pragmatic level we now know that all focal colors are readily perceivable independently of the culture people live in and that verbal labels, if they are not available in the lexicon of a language, can be readily learned should any need for categorization arise.

It has to be noted that the flexibility found for learning new color categories later in life is not necessarily matched by a similar flexibility in other perceptual skills. In Box 6-1 some findings are discussed that seem to point at considerable difficulties in the auditory perception of speech categories not present in one's own language. Cross-cultural differences in visual skills also exist; some will be discussed in the next section.

Box 6-1   Categories in the perception of speech

The smallest identifiable units of speech are called *phonemes*. For example, the words "bad" and "sad" are distinguished by their initial phonemes, indicated as b and s. Many studies have been carried out with phonemes that differ on a single phonetic dimension, such as (in English) b, d, and g (as in good). Speakers of a particular language usually have no difficulty in making the correct identifications of phonemes that occur in their language. We shall not concern ourselves with vowels, but for consonants the boundaries of phoneme categories tend to be very sharp. When pairs of artificially produced sounds belonging to different categories are presented, discrimination is nearly perfect. But when acoustically equally different sounds are presented that fall in the same phonemic category, discrimination is hardly better than chance (Strange & Jenkins, 1978).

There are differences between languages in the set of phonemes that are used. Well-known examples include the l and r, two sounds in English that are not distinguished in Japanese, and an aspirated "b" in many Arab languages that does not occur in English. When artificially produced sounds are presented, subjects will categorize them in accordance with the categories of their own language. Abrahamson and Lisker (1970, mentioned in Strange & Jenkins, 1978) found, for example, that subjects from the U.S. distinguished two categories (d, t) for a series of sounds where Thai subjects used three (d, t, and an aspirated t). Miyawaki et al. (1975) demonstrated that subjects from the U.S. could discriminate well between synthetic stimuli like la and ra, while Japanese hardly did better than chance.

There is some evidence suggesting that infants differentiate between phonemic categories before they produce articulated speech. They even appear to distinguish categories that are not found in the adult language of their environment (e.g., Eimas, 1975). The facility for distinctions that are never used disappears in the course of development. When learning a second language, the discrimination of category boundaries that do not coincide with one's own language can be a difficult process. This is illustrated by Goto (1971), who recorded English words with l and r (for example lead and read) spoken by Japanese with knowledge of English and by subjects from the U.S. Japanese discriminated poorly between l and r also when they heard the words spoken by the Americans. Even when asked to discriminate their own earlier word productions they could not accurately do so.

Research on speech perception suggests that there are natural categories, as in the case of color. However, it also would seem that the ability to discriminate between certain phonemic categories that do not occur in one's own language may decrease in the course of development. The difficulties in acquiring the correct phonemic understanding of a foreign language provides rather convincing anecdotal support.

In summary, it appears that experience has a rather profound effect on the perception of phonemic categories, while an equivalent effect in the domain of color perception has not been established.

Perception of patterns and pictures[6]

In a study of pictorial representations among the Mekan of Ethiopia Deregowski, Muldrow, and Muldrow (1972) used fairly detailed and clear drawings of animals as stimuli. The Mekan are a remote group in Ethiopia with little exposure to pictures. With few exceptions the subjects identified the animals, but only after some time and not without effort. In the process of examination some subjects would go beyond visual inspection; they would touch the cloth on which the pictures were painted and sometimes even smell it. These results are in line with various miscellaneous reports to the effect that the perception of clear representational pictures and even (black and white) photographs is not always immediate in cultures without a pictorial tradition.

Not only lack of recognition, but also the possibility of culturally idiosyncratic depiction can lead to difficulties in understanding. Winter (1963) asked black South African industrial workers what they saw on a series of safety posters. There were many instances where the intention of the artist was not understood, because symbolic meanings (such as a red star to indicate that someone is hit) were misinterpreted. The number of misinterpretations was much lower for urban than for rural subjects and also decreased as a function of the number of years of schooling of the subjects. A striking example of the kind of discrepancy between intended and perceived message occurred in a scene where a person is holding out a hand to receive something. This was often seen as an act of giving. Winter could relate this to the local custom that a person accepting something will hold out two cupped hands.

The two examples bear on an important controversy. Among artists the opinion is not uncommon that all portrayal makes use of cultural codes (cf. Gombrich, 1977). Pictures are perceived in a certain manner mainly because of cultural traditions about how to represent an object or scene. Codes are conventions that members of particular cultures learn and adhere to, even when they are not aware of this. An opposite viewpoint is emphasized by psychologists like Gibson (1966). He argues that a picture can represent an object or scene because it contains information for the perceiver that is similar to information from the real environment.

---

[6] A more extensive coverage of most of the topics discussed in this section can be found in the work of Deregowski (especially 1980a,b).

Simple patterns and figures. Most pictures are fairly complex and obviously subject to artistic style. Therefore, it may be useful to look at more simple figures.

First of all there is a large body of data on the susceptibility of visual illusions. For an overview we refer to Segall et al. (1990). A summary of the findings is presented in Box 6-2. Although the effects of physiological factors on illusions cannot be ruled out, long-term exposure to environmental conditions, summarized in the concept of carperteredness, seems to account for most of the cross-cultural differences. It may be important to note explicitly that all populations are at least to some degree susceptible to all illusions that have been explored in cross-cultural comparisons.

We make this point because a basic identity in processing appears to exist even for perceptual tasks that have clear cognitive-analytical aspects. An interesting example is provided by work on symmetry by means of a symmetry completion test designed by Hector (1958). In the most extensively used version each item of this test consists of a drawing of three narrow rectangles, two grey and one black. The subject is given an oblong of the same size as the rectangles. This has to be placed in such a position on the paper that it forms with the three rectangles already there a pattern that shows bilateral (or mirror) symmetry. Two examples of items are given in Figure 6-4.

Reuning and Wortley (1973) administered this test to various nonliterate groups, including Bushmen in the Kalahari desert. It was found that the idea of bilateral symmetry was easily grasped. The authors noted (1973) "... it was one of our greatest surprises to see how easy the Bushmen found it to deal with these unfamiliar patterns. Even the least intelligent from them could find the solutions to a few items, the majority to about half and some bright ones to nearly all of them" (p. 58).

Analyses of incorrect answers on the symmetry completion items made by the Bushmen and several other groups in southern Africa have shown that most errors can be classified in two categories (cf. Deregowski, 1980a, for a summary). The first is a lack of accuracy in placing the oblong precisely in the right position. The second consists of errors that lead to regular patterns but not in accordance with the required principle of symmetry. Instead of bilateral symmetry often translational symmetry was found. (In this case the two halves of a pattern are identical, but they do not form mirror images.)

Jahoda (1978) found that children in Ghana made much larger errors of orientation than children in Scotland in the reproduction of patterns with Kohs blocks. Part of this could be related to the notion of "sameness." When asked whether two patterns, identical in composition but different in orientation, were the same or different, Ghanaian schoolchildren more often than children in Scotland would respond that they were the "same." Jahoda further observed that Ghanaian subjects who had been instructed to pay attention to orientation and did so during initial trials would lapse into neglecting this aspect of the task during the course of the experiment. He

---

Box 6-2 Susceptibility to visual illusions

An extensive body of cross-cultural research on visual illusions was triggered by the landmark study of Segall, Campbell, and Herskovits (1966). This study had its origin in a difference of opinion between the anthropologist Melville Herskovits and the psychologist Donald Campbell. Herskovits, whose ideas about cultural relativism implied almost unlimited flexibility of the human organism, believed that even such basic experiences as the perception of the length of line segments would be influenced by cultural factors. Campbell was sceptical of this viewpoint. The project they started together with Marshall Segall was rooted in the work of Brunswik (1956). He believed that repeated experience with certain perceptual cues will affect how they are perceived. This is expressed in the notion of *ecological cue validity*. Illusions occur when previously learned interpretations of cues are misapplied because of unusual or misleading characteristics of stimuli.

Three hypotheses were generated:

1. The carpentered world hypothesis. It postulates a learned tendency among those raised in an environment shaped by carpenters (rectangular furniture, houses, and street patterns) to interpret non-rectangular figures as representations of rectangular figures seen in perspective. If the hypothesis is correct, people in industrial urban environments should be more susceptible to illusions such as the Müller-Lyer and the Sander parallelogram (see Figure 6-3).
2. The foreshortening hypothesis. It pertains to lines extending in space away from the viewer. In pictorial representations these appear as vertical lines. People living in environments with wide vistas have learned that vertical lines on the retina can represent long distances. They should be more susceptible to the horizontal-vertical illusion than people living in an enclosed environment, such as a rain forest.
3. The sophistication hypothesis. Learning to interpret patterns and pictures should enhance geometric illusions that are presented two-dimensionally. Exposure to pictorial materials makes people more susceptible to visual illusions.

It may be noted that according to these hypotheses the illusion effect arises because of a three-dimensional perceptual interpretation of two-dimensional figures. This suggests close links between figural depth perception and susceptibility for illusions (cf. Deregowski, 1980a, 1980b).

Fourteen non-Western and three Western samples were tested by Segall et al. (1966) with a series of stimuli for each of the six illusions presented in Figure 6-3. The reasons for selecting the first four illusions have been indicated already. The fifth figure is a modified Ponzo illusion. It was expected that in more carpentered societies the perception of the figure would be toward orthogonal angles and parallel lines. This would lead to a correlation in susceptibility between this illusion and the Müller-Lyer and the Sander. The last figure, the Poggendorff, has been included for the sake of completeness. Segall et al. did not find reliable data for this illusion, partly because of instructional difficulties.

On both the Müller-Lyer and the Sander Parallelogram the Western samples were more illusion prone than any of the non-Western samples. Subjects from regions with open vistas were more susceptible for the two versions of the horizontal-vertical illusion than subjects from regions where such vistas are rare. Also compatible with the second hypothesis was the finding that on the whole non-Western subjects were more prone to the horizontal-vertical illusion than Western subjects. The patterning of the findings with non-Western subjects being more susceptible to some but less to other illusions rules out an explanation in terms of an overall factor, such as test sophistication. All in all, the results were clearly in support of the hypotheses.

The version of the Ponzo illusion used by Segall et al. showed only weak effects. In subsequent cross-cultural studies with the original Ponzo illusion (where the highest of the two horizontal line segments does not intersect one of the two other lines) clearer illusion effects were obtained. Susceptibility for the Ponzo illusion was shown to be influenced by enrichment of the context (cf. Leibowitz, Brislin, Perlmutter, & Hennessey 1969; Brislin, 1974). Brislin and Keating (1976) even worked with a three-dimensional version constructed from wooden planks and placed at a larger distance (approximately 10 meters) from the subject. They found that subjects from the U.S. were more prone to this version of the illusion than subjects from Pacific islands.

Apart from context enrichment, effects of attention (Davis & Carlson, 1970), training in drawing (Jahoda & Stacey, 1970), and race have been investigated. The latter variable provided a challenge to the environmental interpretation of the data given by Segall et al. as well as most other cross-cultural researchers.

The implication of race rested on a series of findings. Pollack (1963) established that at older age the ability for contour detection decreases. Pollack and Silvar (1967) found a (negative) correlation between contour detection and susceptibility for the Müller-Lyer. They also found correlations between skin color and both retinal pigmentation and contour detection (Silvar & Pollack, 1967). Since most non-Western samples in the study of Segall et al. came from Africa, an explanation in physiological and genetic terms could not be ruled out.

Initially some empirical support for the retinal pigmentation hypothesis came from cross-cultural studies by Berry (1971b) and Jahoda (1971). The latter tested subjects' illusion susceptibility for the Müller-

Lyer with blue- and red-colored stimuli. Pigmentation affects the transmission of blue light more than of red light. Jahoda found no difference for Scottish students with presumably low pigmentation under the two conditions, but a sample of Malawian students with high pigmentation was indeed significantly less susceptible to the illusion effect with the blue stimuli.

Soon the tide turned. In an extended replication Jahoda (1975) found no further support for the retinal pigmentation hypothesis. In other studies race (that is, skin color) was varied in a constant environment (Armstrong, Rubin, Stewart, & Kuntner, 1970), or the environmental carpenterdness was varied, keeping race constant (Stewart, 1973). The results were clearly more in line with the environmental than with the physiological explanation.

Not all the data fitted the carpentered world hypothesis or the foreshortening hypothesis. The most important discrepancy was the finding by Segall et al. that the susceptibility for nearly all illusions decreased with age, while the ever increasing exposure to the environment would lead one to expect the opposite, at least for the Müller-Lyer and related illusions. Among others Wagner (1977) and Brislin (1974) found results, mainly with various forms of the Ponzo illusion, that were more ambiguous and sometimes showed an increase of susceptibility with age.

Although the effect of cultural variables in the perception of visual illusions remains a somewhat contentious issue (see especially Deregowski, 1989), we are of the opinion that the hypotheses mentioned at the beginning of this Box are by and large supported by the available evidence.

comments (Jahoda, 1978): "The disposition to respond in this manner appears strongly established in some subjects, but readily susceptible to situational modification in others" (p. 56).

Another experiment in which cross-cultural differences were found in the way information is handled has been reported by Cole, Gay, and Glick (1968). They presented arrays of dots with a brief exposure time (0.25 sec) to Kpelle children in Liberia and to children in the U.S. The subjects had to assess in each stimulus the number of dots. This varied from three to ten. The experimental variable was a distinction between stimuli with a random array of dots and stimuli in which the dots formed a pattern. Cole et al. found that the American children did better on the ordered arrays than on the random patterns. For the Kpelle hardly any difference was observed between the two kinds of stimuli. Apparently the two groups differed in the extent to which

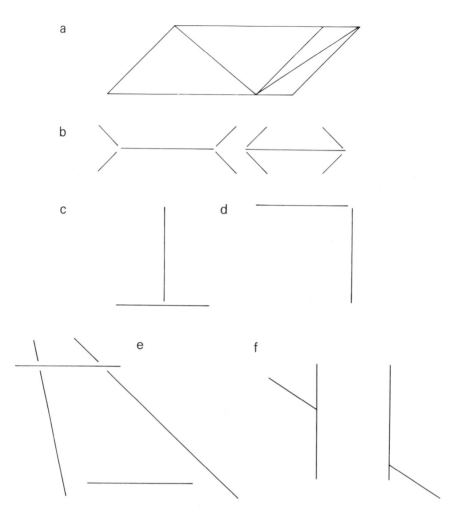

Figure 6-3 Visual illusions used by Segall, Campbell and Herskovits (1966). The respective patterns are (a) Sander parallelogram, (b) Müller-Lyer illusion, (c and d) two versions of the horizontal-vertical illusion, (e) modified form of the Ponzo illusion, and (f) the Poggendorff illusion.

they made use of the structural information that was present in the patterned stimuli.

Only a few of the studies on cross-cultural differences in the perception of simple patterns have been presented. Various antecedent factors, such as the carpenteredness of the environment, have been mentioned in explanation; they all emphasize specific experiences (or a lack of them), but do so retrospectively. This kind of explanation does not allow us to predict with much accuracy whether a certain task will be easy or difficult for a certain

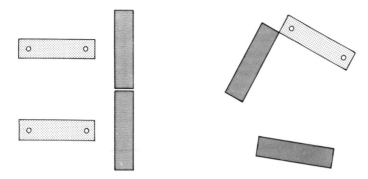

Figure 6-4 Two bilateral symmetry items. The left-hand figure is completed; the right-hand figure shows an item as it is presented to the subject. (The subject indicates an answer by making a mark with a pencil in two small holes in the oblong indicated by the small circles on the oblong-figure and the matched figure.) (After the Symmetry Completion Test, NIPR, Johannesburg.)

group. Reuning and his associates were surprised to find that the Bushmen could deal with symmetry so well, but the finding by Jahoda that Ghanaian children tended to neglect orientation despite elaborate instructions was similarly surprising. Apparently, even the effects of cultural conditions on relatively simple perceptual tasks are far from clear.

Depth in pictures. The systematic study of depth cues in pictures was started by Hudson (1960, 1967). Two stimuli of the set he used are shown in Figure 6-5. Hudson wanted to include the depth cues of object size, object superimposition, and perspective in the pictures. Subjects were asked first to identify the man, the antelope, and so on to make sure that the elements in the picture were recognized. Thereafter they were asked what the man was doing and whether the antelope or the elephant was closer to the man. If there was an answer to the effect that the man was aiming the spear at the antelope or that the antelope was nearer to the man than the elephant, this was classified as a three-dimensional (3D) interpretation. Other answers (that the elephant was being aimed at or was nearer to the man) were taken as evidence of a 2D interpretation.

Hudson's test was administered to various groups in South Africa that differed in education and cultural background. School-going subjects predominantly gave 3D answers, the others responded almost entirely two-dimensionally. Hudson was criticized on a number of points, but in essence his results were confirmed by later research; the ability to interpret Western-style pictorial materials increases as a function of acculturation and school education (cf. Duncan, Gourlay, & Hudson, 1973).

Potentially the most destructive objection is that a 3D answer can be derived analytically by considering that the elephant is much smaller than the

Figure 6-5 Two of Hudson's (1960) pictures.

antelope and thus has to be farther away. Deregowski and Byth (1970) investigated this possibility with Pandora's Box (Gregory, 1966), an apparatus that allows the subject to adjust a light spot according to the distance between himself and an object in any selected part of a figure. Support was found for the hypothesis that 3D responders more than 2D responders saw the man, the antelope, and the elephant in different planes. At the same time, not all 3D responses coincided with differential settings of the spot. This means that verbal responses have to be treated with some suspicion.

There have been other criticisms of Hudson's work (e.g., Hagen & Jones, 1978; Jahoda & McGurk, 1974b). Questions have been raised about his use of verbal procedures: do subjects indeed see what the experimenter concludes from their verbal reports? It has been shown that Hudson's drawings are geometrically inaccurate. The relative position of figures in the drawing does not match their distance to the horizon. In addition, the probability that a correct response is given by chance is rather high. A considerable amount of research has been carried out, mainly in the 1960s and 1970s, to expand on Hudson's work. We shall mention a few of these studies.

The most important development has been the design of alternative methods to measure depth perception in pictorial representations. Deregowski (1980a), who contributed more than any other cross-cultural psychologist to this development, has made extensive use of construction methods in which subjects have to build a 3D construction after a drawing. In one of these tasks subjects were asked to build with sticks and small balls of plasticine models of abstract geometrical drawings. An example of a stimulus is shown in Figure 6-6a. In another task drawings of assemblies of cubes (Figure 6-6b) had to be copied with real blocks. Maybe the most interesting, because of its simplicity, is an experiment with a pair of large wooden calipers. The subject has to set the calipers at the same angle as shown in simple drawings of the kind presented in Figure 6-6 c and d. The right-hand figure can be perceived as a rectangular object photographed at an obtuse angle. If it is seen as such, the perceived angle should not be the same as for the flat figure but more rectangular. If no depth is perceived in the right-hand figure, the subject can be expected to set the calipers at the same angle for both figures.

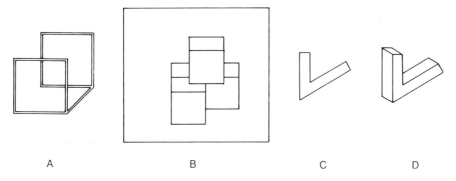

Figure 6-6 Stimuli for two construction tasks (a and b) and the calipers task (c and d). (After Deregowski, 1968; Dziurawiec & Deregowski, 1986; Deregowski & Bentley, 1986.)

A study with both Hudson's tests and items of the kind given in Figure 6-6a showed that Zambian domestic servants and schoolchildren produced more 3D responses on the latter (Deregowski, 1968). Apparently, the responses of subjects vary with the nature of the task. It may seem somewhat counter-intuitive that performance should be better on the abstract figures than on Hudson's pictures, which are closer to the recognizable environment. How-ever, it is in line with theoretical notions mentioned in Box 6-2 that the effect of illusions such as the Müller-Lyer can be explained as a consequence of a 3D interpretation by the perceiver. It is also consistent with findings on the calipers task. A discrepancy was observed between settings for the two kinds of stimuli, which showed that most subjects in a sample of Bushmen settlers in Namibia were influenced by the depth cues. The proportion of 3D responders was higher than anticipated on the basis of previous findings with the Hudson pictures (Deregowski & Bentley, 1986).

Jahoda and McGurk (e.g., 1974a; McGurk & Jahoda, 1975) used a test in which elevation (that is, the position of a figure higher or lower in the picture) formed the most important depth cue. They relied on nonverbal responses, asking their subjects to place models of human figures on a response board in similar positions as these figures occupied in the stimulus pictures. Even young children (4 years old) showed evidence of depth perception. Children in various cultures, including Ghana, Hong Kong, and Zimbabwe, with hardly any exception gave responses that demonstrated the effect of elevation and some other depth cues. Jahoda and McGurk argued that Hudson's test procedure tends to overemphasize the difficulties of perceiving depth in pictures, particularly by African subjects.

There are two depth cues that deserve special attention. The first is the gradient of texture. When one is looking along a brick wall, details of separate bricks can be seen in the foreground. As the distance from the observer increases, less and less detail of texture can be perceived; hence the term *gradient of texture*. It is a powerful depth cue in photographs, but is absent from virtually all stimulus sets used in cross-cultural studies. This is one reason these stimuli are lacking in important information and to the first-time observer may display unusual qualities.

The second cue is linear perspective. In many pictures, including some of Hudson's, a horizon is drawn on which all lines converge that represent parallel lines from real space. It has been a point of considerable debate whether this depth cue, which has an evident impact on the perception of depth for Western subjects, should be seen as a convention. One of the arguments for the conventional character of this cue is the existence of many art traditions in which linear perspective does not occur. In fact, it became commonly used in Europe only during the Renaissance. In addition, linear perspective in drawings does not correspond as closely to reality as often thought. Parallel lines converge at infinity, but the horizon of our visual field is never at infinity. If we stand on a railway, the tracks may be seen to come closer together at a large distance, but they do not visibly converge into a single point. On the other hand, it can be argued that under most circumstances drawings based on the prescriptions of linear perspective better resemble the optic array of real space than drawings constructed following other principles.[7] In other words, linear perspective is not a convention in the sense of an arbitrary agreement. It leads to more realistic representation than other conventions (Hagen & Jones, 1978). The debate cannot be resolved on the basis of extant empirical evidence. Data would be needed on the exposure to Western drawings by individuals brought up exclusively with another art style. There are only some anecdotal reports that Orientals familiar with their traditional art style but not Western art in the first instance perceive pictures of rectangles drawn in perspective as nonrectangular.

In his analyses of pictorial perception Deregowski (1980a, 1989) has made a distinction between epitomic and eidolic perception. Certain pictures can be recognized to represent an object without evoking an illusion of depth. Such pictures, of which silhouettes are the best illustrations, Deregowski calls *epitomic*. There are also pictures that evoke the notion of depth. Deregowski then speaks about *eidolic* pictures. Some pictures have eidolic qualities when they cannot even be associated with a real object. Impossible figures such as the two-pronged trident in Figure 6-7 are the clearest examples. The eidolic character of this picture is so strong that it evokes the impression of an object that cannot exist in most adult Western subjects, though the 3D character is not perceived universally (e.g., Deregowski & Bentley, 1987). We are aware of epitomic cues; clouds are perceived to form epitomic pictures, such as a face or an animal. We are usually not aware of eidolic cues, we accept them as

---

[7] Instances where linear perspective does not lead to a good representation have been discussed by Ten Doesschate (1964).

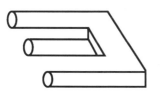

Figure 6-7 The "two-pronged trident" (Deregowski & Bentley, 1987).

they appear. The link between visual illusions and depth perception, mentioned in Box 6-2, is a plausible one if we accept that visual illusion figures have some eidolic quality. Deregowski has suggested that on a dimension from epitomic to eidolic the pictures by Hudson are more to the epitomic side and tasks such as those used by Jahoda and McGurk and the calipers are more to the eidolic side. This would be the reason there are more 3D responders on the latter tasks than found by Hudson.

The epitomic-eidolic distinction is also important insofar as it reminds us that the perception of figures should not be seen as a unitary psychological process.

Together with Serpell (Serpell & Deregowski, 1980) Deregowski has arrived at a conception in which picture perception is considered as a set of skills. A skilled perceiver can deal with a wide variety of cues and use those cues that are appropriate in a given situation. Basic is the recognition by the perceiver that a situation requires the application of certain skills. This means that one has to learn to treat pictures as a representation of real space. As mentioned before, the Mekan had some initial difficulty with this. Another skill is required when interpreting impoverished cues. Apparently Western subjects have learned to interpret linear perspective cues as drawn in some of Hudson's pictures.

The term *skill* is used in different ways. On the one hand it refers to such general phenomena that it almost borders on the term *perceptual mechanism*. On the other hand knowledge of specific symbols (such as multiple depictions in cartoons for representing movements) is also called a skill. This raises the question whether the various skills stand by themselves or whether they are hierarchically organized in some way.

Theorizing about pictorial perception as a set of skills makes clear that cultures can differ in the cues that are used and the relative importance attached to each of them. It is reasonable to assume that culturally specific conditions will determine which skills will develop. In this respect an approach postulating a set of skills does justice to the variations in cross-cultural differences in responses to pictures that from a Western point of view all contain depth cues. However, it fails to go much beyond the observation of a given state of affairs.

One can evaluate this in two ways. It can be emphasized that over the last decades we have gained important insights into difficulties of pictorial communication. It can also be argued that an integrated theoretical approach that specifies how perceptual mechanisms and environmental experience interact is still beyond our reach. In what direction we have to proceed is rather unclear. If conventions are arbitrary, it would be foolish to search for more encompassing explanations. But insofar as certain conventions more than others lead to representations that closely simulate real space there is scope for the scientific exploration of the perceptual principles that govern the relationship.

Aesthetics

A cross-cultural analysis of art leads to two perplexing findings. The first is the tremendous variation in conventions and styles of expression. The second is the flexibility of the human perceptual mechanism in coping with this range in variation. In this section it will be shown how despite the tremendous variation in art styles there are common perceptual mechanisms that lead to similarities across cultures in aesthetic appreciation. For an evaluation of what follows it is necessary to keep in mind how little formal similarity there is between Bushman rock paintings, the stylized drawings of classical Egypt, post-Renaissance landscapes from the Dutch school, and Japanese landscapes painted in the traditional style, just to mention a few major styles in pictorial art.

We have seen that conventions play a certain role in perception, especially of depth cues. They certainly are important in the making of art, witness the large variation in styles. If conventions play a dominant role in appreciation, there is no reason to expect much agreement betweeen subjects from different cultures. A few comparative studies of aesthetic preferences have been reported that support this expectation. For example, Lawlor (1955) showed eight designs from West Africa to subjects from that region and to British subjects, asking them to indicate which two they liked best and which two they liked least. There was considerable agreement among the subjects within each sample, but the preferences of the two groups did not correlate. Lawlor concluded that there was little evidence for a general factor that depended on the designs. Rather the cultural background of the judges was the important determinant of agreement in ratings.

Still, the weight of the evidence is that there is at least a moderate agreement in aesthetic preferences between cultures. For example, C. R. Morris (1956) found positive correlations between rankings of Western paintings by students from China, India, and the U.S. Research along similar lines was carried out by Child and his coworkers (e.g., I. L. Child, 1969). It included evaluations of art objects from the Congo, Japan, Fiji Islands, and the U.S. Positive and sometimes substantial correlations in appreciation were found between local artists and American experts. Child often worked with artists, because he believed that becoming an artist is a matter of certain personality characteristics regardless of culture. Evidence for a transculturally stable relationship between some personality variables and aesthetic interests have been reported for Japan, Pakistan, and Greece (Anwar & Child, 1972; I. L. Child & Iwao, 1968; Haritos-Fatouros & Child, 1977).

Quite another approach was followed by H. J. Eysenck and his associates (H. J. Eysenck & Iwawaki, 1971; Soueif & Eysenck, 1971, 1972). They used polygons that differed in the number of angles or vertices. Pleasantness ratings in Britain correlated positively with complexity. In cross-cultural comparisons with students in Japan and Egypt considerable agreements in ratings with British data were found. In a subsequent analysis on the Egyptian data set, which contained ratings from art students as well as non-art students, twelve identifiable factors were extracted that had some similarity to factors found in Britain.

Psychological aesthetics. Eysenck's results are in line with expectations that follow from the theoretical work of Berlyne (1960, 1971). He postulated psychological determinants of aesthetic appreciation that are independent of the artistic style of a culture. Berlyne related appreciation to certain stimulus characteristics, referred to as *collative variables.* Aesthetic appreciation was seen by him as a special instance of curiosity or stimulus-seeking behavior. There is a close relationship with a complex of psychophysiological events known as the Orientation Reaction (e.g., Kimmel, Van Olst, & Orlebeke, 1979). Stimulus-seeking is intrinsically motivated behavior. Certain stimuli are sought because the activity of dealing with them is satisfying or pleasurable in its own right. From looking at art people can derive satisfaction; it is a behavior that can be rewarding for its own sake and not because it leads to other rewarding consequences. Strictly speaking Berlyne's theory deals with motivation as well as with perception. As we shall see, an analysis of the informational content of stimuli forms the major concern of research in this tradition. As such it can be seen as a natural extension of research in perception.

The stimulus characteristics that evoke curiosity and appreciation include novelty, uncertainty or ambiguity, incongruity, and complexity. These are formal or structural properties that can be defined independently of a particular art style. This does not mean that the reactions of the subjects from different cultures to a given stimulus should be the same. For example, what constitutes a novel stimulus in one setting may be highly familiar somewhere else. The relationship between collative variables and curiosity is often curvilinear. This implies that a moderately complex or incongruous stimulus will evoke the strongest reaction.

Berlyne and his colleagues (1975; Berlyne, Robbins & Thompson, 1974) made use of pairs of patterns that differed in complexity in various ways. The number of elements could differ, the shape of a depicted pattern could be regular or irregular, the patterns could be symmetrical or asymmetrical, and so on. Measurements included the looking time for a stimulus, paired comparisons for pleasingness, and ratings of the separate stimuli on 7-point rating scales for attractiveness and some other dimensions. Data were collected in Uganda among urban, semiurban, and rural subjects, in Canada among students, and in India among students and villagers. Berlyne (1980) emphasized that the results showed more similarities than differences across cultures. Looking times increased with complexity, the numbers of subjects preferring the same stimulus in a pair correlated positively across all six samples, and factor analyses of ratings also showed similarities across cultures. As was to be expected the intercultural differences were larger than the differences between samples within the same country.

Bragg and Crozier (1974) obtained ratings on various scales for a set of sound patterns in which the informational complexity was varied systematically. The tones of which the patterns consisted were sine waves (pure tones) differing in frequency, loudness, and duration. Small samples from Canada, India, Japan, and Ivory Coast were tested. Graphs for ratings such as complexity and pleasingness of the varous stimuli showed a large degree of similarity across cultures.

Poortinga and Foden (1975) used visual stimuli in a compartative analysis of curiosity in black and white South African students. They collected four kinds of data; these included measurements of collative variables (incongruity, ambiguity, complexity, and novelty), self-reports on stimulus-seeking behavior, psychophysiological indices of arousal, and intelligence tests. These measurements were administered twice to control for effects of unfamiliarity with the experimental situation and with the various tasks. As it turned out some of the precautions had been unnecessary. There was hardly any session effect. There were a few differences in the psychophysiological indices, but these were not correlated with the scores on the various collative variables. The correlations of the intelligence tests with the collative variables also were very low. Consequently, it could be ruled out with some confidence that the scores on the collative variables would be determined by unfamiliarity with the situation, arousal, or intelligence.

Two of the tasks of Poortinga and Foden (1975), namely two measurements of complexity, will be discussed in some more detail. In the Non-Representational Complexity Test items consisted of symmetrical patterns of line segments generated by a computer; the location and orientation of the lines in the first segment were selected randomly. There were eight levels of complexity. A stimulus of level 6 (on the right) and one of level 7 (on the left) are given in Figure 6-8. In each trial two patterns differing in complexity were projected for three seconds. Subjects indicated which one of the two they wished to see for a second time. The selected pattern was projected for a further three seconds. The percentage of choices for the stimuli at each level of complexity are presented on the left in Figure 6-9. The graph for the black group has a peak below the highest level of complexity. In the white sample there was no peak, probably because the level of complexity had not been

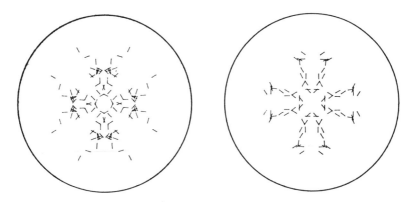

Figure 6-8 Two stimuli from the Non-Representational Complexity task (complexity level of left = 7; of right = 6). (The original stimuli where white on a black background.) (Poortinga & Foden, 1975.)

extended far enough for these subjects. This was confirmed in further analyses in which curves for subsamples from both groups with similar levels of preference for the more complex patterns were found to be almost identical over the whole range of stimulus complexity.

The second measure of complexity, the Representational Complexity Test, was based on existing visual art expressions from six different cultural traditions, varying from Bushman rock paintings to abstract modern art. Negative slides in black and white were prepared so that the complexity of the original was retained, but much of the color, tone and shading was eliminated. To establish the complexity level of the stimuli ratings by black and white judges were obtained for slides from each art tradition separately and in combination. This test was administered in the same way as the Non-Representational Complexity Test. The relative preference of the samples for each level of complexity is presented on the right in Figure 6-9. The similarity of the graphs is striking.

Poortinga and Foden (1975) did not offer any interpretation for the discrepancy between the results of the two tests. They merely noted that such discrepancies show that a quantitative cross-cultural difference in scores on any single variable has to be interpreted very cautiously.

The score distributions of the two groups in Poortinga and Foden's study generally showed a remarkable degree of overlap for the self-report questionnaires as well as the collative variables. The mean of the black sample, averaged over all collative variables, was only 0.30 standard deviation units below that of the white sample. This value dropped to only 0.15 sd when the test with the most atypical results, namely the Non-Representational Complexity Test, was eliminated.

The overally results of this study give considerable support to the general tenet of research in psychological aesthetics. Underneath the different con-

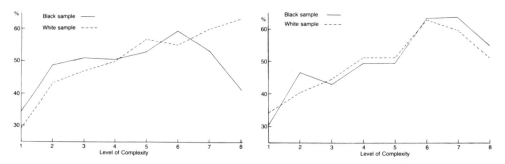

Figure 6-9 Preference for stimuli at different levels of complexity on the Non-Representational (on the left) and the Representational (on the right) Complexity task (Poortinga & Foden, 1975).

ventions about aesthetic expression there appear to be the universal psychological mechanisms in the perception and appreciation of visual stimuli.

Conclusions

It is obvious from this overview that not all perceptual variables are equally likely to show cross-cultural differences. On tasks for basic sensory functions, such as perceptual constancies and stimulus discrimination on psychophysical scales, an approximately equal level of performance is to be expected for all cultural groups.

At a higher level of stimulus complexity the pattern of findings changes. Object recognition in clear representational pictures does not create many problems anywhere in the world, provided there has been some exposure to pictorial materials. Depth cues are readily experienced in certain kinds of pictures and geometric patterns, but contrary to naive expectation, culture-specific conventions can play a dominant role in the perception of depth in simple schematic drawings, such as in Hudson's test.

Perceptual habits that are transferred from real space to pattern perception have been mentioned as antecedents of cross-cultural differences in the susceptibility for certain visual illusions. Some of these illusions are pictorially very simple, consisting only of a few line segments. On the other hand, seemingly difficult perceptual notions such as symmetry appeared to be readily grasped by a population where pictorial art is almost absent.

As the discrepancy between real space and pictorial representation becomes larger cross-cultural differences increase. However, research on aesthetic appreciation has shown that underneath the conventions of various artistic traditions there are universal mechanisms.

As more emphasis is placed on common mechanisms, the explanation of cross-cultural differences in perception is shifting to conventions in the sense of cultural agreements that have a certain arbitrariness. Most conventions are limited to fairly specific classes of stimuli. They are not compatible with broad generalizations as have been made in the past, for example in the formulation of compensation hypotheses. However, it would be a mistake to think that an emphasis on conventions means that cross-cultural differences are trivial. If their number is large enough, together they can have a profound influence on the repertoire of behavior. Maybe this is the most important lesson that cross-cultural psychologists can learn from variations in artistic styles. Such styles appear to be rather arbitrary from the viewpoint of basic perception, but sometimes they have retained distinctive characteristics for centuries.

PART II

Pursuing Problems across Cultures: Research Strategies

In earlier chapters we have frequently used the term *culture* as if it needed no lengthy discussion. In Chapter 1, however, we did indicate that we would use the term to refer to the "shared way of life of a group of people." In this chapter we examine the notion of culture in more detail, drawing mainly upon the anthropological literature, and then consider some anthropological approaches to topics of interest to cross-cultural psychology.

The relationships between anthropology and psychology have been thoroughly examined by Jahoda (1982); his book should be read by those wishing an in-depth treatment of these issues. In the first two sections of this chapter we attend to those specific features of the anthropological tradition that have direct bearing on the development and conduct of cross-cultural psychology, including various conceptions of culture and the practice of ethnography. We then turn to a consideration of two domains of anthropological research that are related to cross-cultural psychology: culture and personality, and cognitive anthropology.

Conceptions of culture

While the term *culture* first appeared in an English dictionary in the 1920s (Kroeber, 1949), the first use in an anthropological work was by Tylor (1871), who defined culture as "that complex whole which includes knowledge, belief, art, morals, laws, customs and any other capabilities and habits acquired by man as a member of society."

Two rather short but now widely used definitions were later proposed: Linton (1936) suggested that *culture* means "the total social heredity of mankind" (p. 78), and Herskovits (1948) said that "Culture is the man-made part of the human environment" (p. 17). In contrast to these concise definitions we also have lengthy listings of what is included in *culture*. One of these is by Wissler (1923), who included: speech, material traits, art, knowledge, religion, society, property, government, and war. This list is similar to the general categories that are used in the Human Relations Area Files that will be presented later in this chapter (see Box 7-2).

In a classic survey of many definitions Kroeber and Kluckhohn (1952) suggested that there are six major classes of definition of culture to be found in the anthropological literature:

1. *Descriptive* definitions are those that attempt to list any and all aspects of human life and activity thought by the writer to be an example of what one means by "culture." Both Tylor's and Wissler's definitions are of this type. To Kroeber and Kluckhohn, descriptive definitions tend to emphasize the view of "culture as a comprehensive totality" (p. 85).
2. *Historical* definitions, such as in Linton's, tend to emphasize the accumulation of tradition over time rather than enumerating the totality or range of cultural phenomena. The term *heritage* is frequently used in these definitions (also the term *heredity*), but the context clearly indicates that no biological factors are thought to be involved in the accumulation.
3. *Normative* definitions emphasize the shared rules that govern the activity of a group of people. Unlike the descriptive and historical definitions, where the cultural life being referred to is clearly observable, normative definitions require us to dig into the overt activity and to try to discover what lies behind it. Later in this chapter we will refer to this distinction using the terms *explicit* and *implicit* culture.
4. *Psychological* definitions emphasize a variety of psychological features, including notions such as adjustment, problem solving, learning, and habits. For example, culture permits a group to adjust to its recurrent problems, culture is learned, and the result of this learning is the establishment of habits in a particular group. This category is rather broad and includes both implied (for example, adjustment) and observable (for example, habits) cultural phenomena.
5. *Structural* definitions emphasize the pattern or organization of culture. This view is related to the first (descriptive) category in that the overall or total picture is emphasized. However, structural definitions require going beyond the overt features in order to discover the arrangements that exist. The central view is that culture is not a mere list or hodgepodge of customs, but forms an integrated pattern of interrelated features.
6. *Genetic* definitions emphasize the origin or *genesis* of culture. Within this category there are three main answers given: culture arises as *adaptive* to the habitat of a group, out of *social* interaction, and out of a *creative* process that is a characteristic of the human species.

Concluding their review with a definition of their own, Kroeber and Kluckhohn (1952) proposed that: "Culture consists of patterns, explicit and implicit, of and for behavior acquired and transmitted by symbols, constituting the distinctive achievements of human groups, including their embodiments in artifacts; the essential core of culture consists of traditional (i.e., historically derived and selected) ideas and especially their attached values; cultural systems may on the one hand be considered as products of action, on the other as conditioning elements of further action" (p. 181).

Since the term *culture* is now part of our daily vocabulary, it is useful to consider briefly how it differs in anthropology and cross-cultural psychology from these colloquial uses. First, it is not restricted to "high culture," referring only to painting, classical music, and so forth, but to *all* products of human life, ranging from comic books and pop music to those products normally preserved in museums and performed in concert halls or opera houses.

Second, culture is not "civilization"; *all* human groups possess culture, including those ethnocentrically referred to as being "civilized" or "primitive." Most anthropologists (as well as cross-cultural psychologists) avoid the terms *civilized* and *primitive* because they are value judgments about the quality of culture (see section below on cultural evolution).

Third, *culture* is not the same as *society*, although they are closely linked. One definition of society refers to "an organized collectivity of interacting people whose activities become centered around a set of common goals, and who tend to share common beliefs, attitudes and modes of action" (Krech, Crutchfield, & Ballachey, 1962, p. 308). From this definition we can see that a *society* is composed of people, while *culture* is the way of life they hold in common. This distinction between culture and society is often blurred; even in the literature of cross-cultural psychology writers occasionally slip and use "culture" when they mean "society."

In Chapter 1 we considered the idea that different disciplines employ different levels of analysis and do so legitimately without having to protect themselves from reductionistic attacks by more basic disciplines. In anthropology the concept of *culture* is clearly a group-level or collective phenomenon. Just as clearly, though, biological and psychological variables may be related to cultural variables, and from time to time there have been attempts to use them to *explain* cultural phenomena.

One protection against this reductionism has been proposed by Kroeber (1917), who argued that culture is *superorganic*, above and beyond its biological and psychological bases. Two arguments were presented by Kroeber for the independent existence of culture at its own level. First, particular individuals come and go, but cultures remain more or less stable. This is a remarkable phenomenon; despite a large turnover in membership with each new generation, cultures and their institutions remain relatively unchanged. Thus, a culture does not depend on particular individuals for its existence, but has a life of its own at the collective level of the group. The second argument is that no single individual "possesses" all of the "culture" of the group to which one belongs; the culture as a whole is carried by the collectivity and indeed is likely to be beyond the biological or psychological capacity (to know or to do) of any single person in the group. For example, no single person knows all the laws, political institutions, and economic structures that constitute even this limited sector of one's culture.

For both these reasons, Kroeber considers that cultural phenomena are collective phenomena, above and beyond the individual person, and hence his term *superorganic*. This position is an important one for cross-cultural psychology since it permits us to employ the group versus individual distinction in attempting to trace the influence of cultural factors on individual psychological phenomena. Whether "culture" can constitute the "independent variable" in such studies is a matter of debate and will be addressed in Chapter 10 in the section on culture as a psychological concept.

In the comprehensive definition of culture offered by Kroeber and Kluckhohn (1952), the terms *explicit* and *implicit* were used to qualify the term *culture*. The distinction between explicit and implicit culture is similar to one that has become well-known to psychologists since the advent of behaviorism. Some cultural phenomena are overt, readily observable, and fairly concrete; these are the day-to-day customs, practices, and usages that can be gauged by virtually any observer, whether an insider (member of the culture) or an outsider. These phenomena correspond, in psychology, to the overt behaviors that are the basic data for all psychologists, but that usually constitute the only acceptable data for behaviorists. *Explicit culture*, then, is the set of observable acts and products regularly found in a group.

In contrast, *implicit culture* refers to the organizing principles that are inferred to lie behind these regularities on the basis of consistent patterns of explicit culture. This corresponds in psychology to the inferred traits or characteristics of individuals that we postulate to account for behavioral consistency. Whether implicit culture and traits actually exist in their own right or only exist in the cognitive life of observers is an epistemological and methodological question of long standing. Inferred characteristics cannot be observed directly by an outsider (anthropologist or psychologist) and often cannot even be articulated by the persons exhibiting these regularities. Grammar that controls speech, rules of address that regulate interaction, and norms that guide proper conduct are all examples of implicit culture; so too are the fundamental features of social structure, myth, and ritual, all of which result from cognitive activity (inference, comparison, generalization) on the part of those seeking to discover the meaning behind cultural regularity.

Cultural evolution. The dimension of cultural variation underlying the "civilized"–"primitive" distinction is essentially one of *cultural evolution*: historically, cultural groups have appeared in an identifiable sequence from small hunting and gathering bands, through societies based on plant and animal domestication (agricultural and pastoral peoples), to industrial and now postindustrial societies (see, e.g., Lomax & Berkowitz, 1972). In the past it has been thought by many and is probably still thought by most people living in Western industrial societies that this historical sequence somehow displays "progress" (see analyses and criticisms by Preiswerk & Perrot, 1978). There is sometimes thought to be a parallel between biological evolution (from amoeba to mankind; see Chapter 8) and cultural evolution (from hunters to industrial societies), a sequence termed *social Darwinism*. Critics (Nisbet, 1971; Poggie & Lynch, 1974) reject the idea that over time there has been "improvement" (in some absolute sense) in the quality of culture. This rejection is based upon the belief that such judgments do not have any scientific basis and must inevitably rest on personal preferences about what is "good" and what is "bad" in human existence. In this book we also reject such absolute notions of progress and improvement in culture over time.

In an attack on this general position Sahlins and Service (1960) have made an important distinction between *specific evolution* and *general evolution*. In the former cultural diversity and change appear, often in adaptation to new ecological (both physical and social) conditions. In the latter general evolution "generates progress; higher forms arise from and surpass lower forms" (1960, pp. 12–13). We accept the first view of evolution (diversity through adaptive modification), while not accepting the second (progress and higher forms resulting from change). The reason for this position is that there is ample objective evidence for ecologically induced change, but there are only subjective value judgments to provide a basis for claiming one adaptation to be better than another. As Sahlins and Service (1960) have phrased it: "adaptive improvement is relative to the adaptive problem; it is so to be judged and explained. In the specific context each adapted population is adequate, indeed superior, in its own incomparable way" (p. 15). Not everyone, however, accepts this judgment. Hallpike (1986), for example, has argued that modification through adaptation is not the whole of the story. There is indeed a "directional process" (p. 375) at work that needs to be taken into account when attempting to understand cross-cultural variations in social systems. Despite this alternative view, we espouse in this book a basically functionalist perspective in which culture and behavior are considered to be an adaptation to ecological and sociopolitical factors.

Cultural relativism. The alternative to a position of social Darwinism is *cultural relativism*, first introduced by Boas (1911) and elaborated by Herskovits (1948). As introduced to cross-cultural psychology by Segall et al. (1966): "... the ethnographer attempts to describe the behavior of the people he studies without the evaluation that his own culture would ethnocentrically dictate. He attempts to see the culture in terms of its own evaluative system. He tries to remain aware of the fact that his judgments are based upon this own experience and reflect his own deep-seated enculturation to a limited and specific culture. He reminds himself that his original culture provides no Olympian vantage from which to view objectively any other culture" (p. 17).

This position of cultural relativism provides a nonethnocentric stance from which to view cultural and psychological diversity. It can range from a general awareness of the problems inherent in ethnocentric thinking about differences, through to a "radical cultural relativism" (Berry, 1972). This more extreme position has been advocated for cross-cultural psychology where the social and political consequences of scientific ethnocentrism can be harmful. Especially in the areas of cognition and psychopathology scientific errors due to ethnocentrism (generalizations such as "they're all dumb!" or "they're all crazy!") can have important consequences for large numbers of people. Here the "radical" position is to avoid comparisons completely (rather than by just tempering them with our awareness of the problems of ethnocentrism) until thorough local analyses have been carried out. In this way scientific caution is maximized and potential error and harm can be minimized. We will return to the issue of relativism in Chapter 10 when we consider the advantages and disadvantages of this stance and of some alternatives to it (the absolutist and universalist positions).

Cultural universals. One of the more subtle features of cross-cultural psychology is the balance sought between seeking to understand the local phenomena, while at the same time attempting to develop panhuman generalizations. The position of cultural relativism assists us in the first endeavor, while the existence of cultural universals provides a basis for the second. Similar to the claim of Aberle et al. (1950) that there are certain functional prerequisites for a society (see Box 3-1) is the position that there are certain common features to all cultures: these are basic qualities of culture and consist of those phenomena that one can expect to find in any and *every* culture (see Wissler's list). Activities that all peoples engage in (even though obviously carried out in very different ways) are the basis for claims about uniformities in psychological functioning. In other words, cultural universals reflect psychological universals.

These cultural universals may be derived theoretically or generated empirically (Lonner, 1980). For example, Malinowski (1944) posited a set of universal aspects of culture based upon a set of (universal) basic biological needs. With the biological need for reproduction there comes the cultural response of kinship systems; with a need for health there comes a system of hygiene, and so on. However, these have been termed "fake universals" by Lonner (1980) and described as "vague tautologies and forceless banalities" by Geertz (1965, p. 103). The claim that families and socialization practices exist in all societies does not take us very far, except to alert us to the fundamental role of such institutions in genetic and cultural transmission.

More concrete and useful for psychological research are listings based on a wide range of work in many cultures. Such elaborated lists do more than provide a "handy checklist"; they provide a comprehensive set of descriptive categories that may form the basis for comparative work. One candidate for use as a comparative tool is the set of categories developed by Murdock (1949) and used in the Human Relations Area Files, which will be discussed later in this chapter (Box 7-2).

Ethnography

Research in anthropology has a long experience of working in virtually all of the world's cultures. The legacy of this tradition resides in thousands of published volumes of "fieldwork" in particular cultures. These ethnographic reports are a rich source of information and serve as an important foundation for cross-cultural psychology. Two other scientific activities are based on this ethnographic foundation: *ethnology* and *archives*.

In the field of ethnology researchers attempt to understand the patterns, institutions, dynamics, and changes of cultures. This search for the larger picture requires the use of ethnographic reports from numerous cultures, comparing them and drawing out similarities and differences. In so doing ethnologists work with original ethnographic materials (sometimes their own, sometimes those of others), seeking what may lie behind or account for the ethnographic variation. In a sense, while ethnography remains descriptive of explicit culture, ethnology becomes interpretive, using scientific inferences to comprehend implicit culture (using the terms introduced earlier). In practice, however, most anthropologists do not maintain such a strict distinction between doing ethnography and ethnology.

In the case of archives research is conducted using a vast array of ethnographic reports, sometimes organized into a systematic framework that is amenable to comparative use.

Ethnographic fieldwork. Cross-cultural psychologists will inevitably need to have a good grasp of how to conduct ethnographic work in the field. Long-standing problems, such as how to enter the field and how to carry out ethnographic research, have been major issues for anthropology, and much has been written to assist the field worker (e.g., Royal Anthropological Institute, 1951; T. R. Williams, 1967; Pelto & Pelto, 1973, 1981). Other problems, such as interviewing and testing, reside in the psychological tradition, while still other, such as sampling and the use of observational techniques, belong to both disciplines. Two recent discussions of these issues, written expressly for cross-cultural psychologists, can be found in Goodenough (1980) and in R. L. Munroe and R. H. Munroe (1986).

The first approach to and contact with a cultural group or community can be the single most important act in a program of research: how can it be done with sensitivity and without major gaffes? In a discussion of the problem (R. Cohen et al., 1970) experienced field workers concluded that there is no single best approach to the field, each situation requiring attention to local standards and some degree of self-knowledge on the part of the researcher. Indeed, the field worker as a sojourner experiences acculturation and may also experience *acculturative stress* (see Chapters 11 and 14) in which self-doubt, loss of motivation, depression, and other problems may become great enough to hinder the work.

Perhaps the most effective and ethical way to enter the field is to establish a collaborative relationship with a colleague in another culture. In this way local knowledge and acceptance may be acquired easily and quickly. With this sort of arrangement it is also probable that research questions that are important to the population are addressed and that results obtained can be made relevant to local problems. We have already noted the methodological advantages of such an arrangement in Figure 1-2, where the elimination of ethnocentrism was established as a goal for cross-cultural psychology. Some practical aspects of carrying out field work are discussed in Box 7-1. (See also Irvine & Carroll, 1980; Pareek & Rao, 1980.)

While a complete ethnographic study is probably not necessary (and likely

Box 7-1 Some practical aspects of fieldwork

Upon entering the field a number of personal, practical, and bureaucratic issues have to be dealt with. With respect to personal issues, the foremost is health. One should prepare well in advance with appropriate inoculations against diseases and take other prophylactic measures. Mental health problems may also be avoided by thinking in advance about how one might respond to isolation, reduced communication, and changes in living conditions (particularly diet and sleeping arrangements). Some of these issues can arise equally in cross-cultural work with Western samples by researchers from developing countries and in work with ethnic groups in plural societies.

Practical arrangements made on arrival can very much affect one's adaptation to field conditions. Appropriate shelter, arrangements for receiving and sending mail, and a reliable source of favored foods all need to be worked out soon after entry; the very success of one's project may well depend on an adequate solution to these problems.

One's social roles and relationships deserve special consideration on entry; should one be friendly to all (and risk both loss of objectivity and perhaps befriending the local outcasts), or be somewhat aloof (and risk being judged as unsympathetic or even undesirable)? No single answer is possible, but the best course, at least in the short run, is to be polite and open and to accept roles assigned by the local community; later, once entry is established, corrections and rearrangements can be made. For example, one of the most frequent role attributions made to the cross-cultural psychologist entering the field is that of the "schoolteacher." Immediate denials ("No, I'm not; I'm a psychologist!") may be true, but of no use, and may even destroy one's acceptance. Responses such as "Not exactly, but ..." followed by explanations are more likely to be useful as well as being honest. Other role attributions frequently made are of "anthropologist" (everybody, it seems, has heard of *them*), "doctor," "missionary," or "government agent" of some sort. Attempts to explain oneself should be gentle and honest and within the hosts' frame of reference; in the end you will be what your hosts believe you are, and strong denials may only reinforce their belief.

Formal presentation of oneself to authorities often begins with an embassy official in one's home country and ends with negotiating for acceptance in a local community. In between, each official (immigration on entry, followed by state, provincial, or county officials) and finally local chiefs or mayors all need to be assured of your good intentions, nonthreatening goals, and general willingness to cooperate. One way to signal these personal qualities is to offer to share research findings with the local community (in a way that will be both comprehensible and useful). Another, more contributory way is to ask if one's research might be extended in some way to include issues or questions of interest to the local community. As a psychologist there are often educational, health, or developmental issues of concern that fall within one's competence, and minor extensions of a research project can be of major assistance in peoples' understanding of local problems.

Beyond the research role there is usually an opportunity to be of practical help to individuals seeking medical assistance and general information. To the extent possible, first aid (and if within one's competence, more extensive medical aid) is often expected and should be provided. Minimal treatments (such as with disinfectants, oral antibiotics, fever reducers) can all be lifesaving in their consequences, and one should be prepared to provide these services in the field. In addition, all of these "contributions to the community" will be of value not only to one's own research in the short run but to those who follow in later years.

to be beyond the capabilities of a psychologist), there is, nevertheless, the need to verify the information contained in a previous ethnography of the people involved in the study. To do this, we need to have some familiarity with ethnographic methods. Full treatments of this topic can be found in Naroll and Cohen (1970) and Lonner and Berry (1986a). We focus here on some broad but central questions that need to be considered when learning to do cross-cultural psychology in the field.

First, some basic features of the culture need to be examined in order to understand the general context in which one's research participants developed and now carry out their lives. The list of features studied by most anthropologists of what constitutes a *culture* has been presented earlier. Foremost on these lists is the language, and this is often the correct place to begin learning about another culture; it not only provides cultural knowledge in its own right, but also provides a vehicle to learn about most other aspects of culture.

While field anthropologists usually acquire a functional fluency in the local language, cross-cultural psychologists rarely do. Herein lies a major difference and a major problem. Anthropologists learn the local language because it is an important part of the culture-to-be-understood; cross-cultural psychologists do not because their research question (unless it is in psycholinguistics) may have little to do with language. However, it can be argued that psychological understanding is so subtle, so dependent on interpersonal communication, that learning the local language should be a primary, preliminary objective for cross-cultural psychologists.

An alternative to this rarely achieved goal is to rely on others as vehicles for understanding; this can be done by way of bilingual assistants or by collaborating with bilingual co-researchers. The use of local research assistants, with whom one shares a common language, is probably the most frequently employed alternative. The researcher can locate, hire, and train members of the community who then serve as linguistic informants, translators of research instruments and instructions, and actual research assistants during the course of data collection (see Brislin 1980; 1986). Care should be taken both in deciding whom to hire (taking local advice into account, in addition to one's own impressions) and in training (not to bias the data collection in favor of one's hypothesis). Indeed it is an interesting question whether to reveal or disguise one's research theory or hypothesis. By disguising them the risk of bias may be reduced, but the assistant (like the curious subject) may spend much of the time attempting to guess the hypothesis. By revealing them the risk of bias may be increased ("giving the researcher what he wants"), but a full sharing of the research hypothesis with one's assistants may very much improve one's understanding of the issue in local terms and the degree of rapport and trust in the working relationship.

Other cultural variables that are implicated in one's research framework need to be examined. For example, economy, material goods, social stratification, political organization, religion, and myth may play a role in one's research. The most commonly used approaches to obtaining such information in field anthropology are by intensive interaction with *key informants* and by the use of *observational techniques*.

Key informants have a central role in anthropological research because of the presumed *normative* nature of most aspects of culture. That is, culture is thought to be a widely shared phenomenon, and hence any (or a few) individuals should be able to give a detailed account of their culture. Extensive, followed by intensive, questioning, checking and rechecking of previously obtained information, and trying out one's formulations for comment from informants all contribute to the growing body of knowledge about the cultural group. Over time, with the help of only a few individuals, a comprehensive picture can be built up.

Observations made of daily life also serve to check on the information gained from key informants (Pelto & Pelto, 1981) and as a way of verifying one's own formulations about the culture (Bochner, 1980, 1986b; Longabaugh, 1980). Discrepancies will be encountered (between formulations and observations), and a return to one's key informants will be required to help sort them out. Hence, there is often an iterative process, moving back and forth between asking informants and direct observations until one is satisfied that the cultural variables of interest are adequately understood.

Ethnographic archives. By far the most frequently used ethnographic archive in cross-cultural psychology is the vast set of materials known as the Human Relations Area Files (HRAF). If one wanted to locate a set of cultures for a comparative project that met certain criteria, it would be a long and difficult task to wade through hundreds of ethnographic reports searching for specific groups that would serve this purpose. Fortunately, a good deal of the ethnographic literature has been organized (assembled, categorized, and coded) into these files.

The HRAF were started in 1936 and are based upon two classification of societies and topics thought to be applicable worldwide (Moore, 1971). One is the *Outline of World Cultures* (Murdock, 1975) and the other is the *Outline of Cultural Materials* (Murdock, Ford, & Hudson, 1971). The first of these (*Outline of World Cultures*) is a comprehensive listing of many of the world's cultural (including ethnic and political) units, and this constitutes the population from which researchers may identify and sample cultures. A related inventory of societies is the *Ethnographic Atlas* (Murdock, 1967), which includes 863 societies, arranged into six "culture areas" (Sub-Saharan Africa, Circum-Mediterranean, East Eurasia, Oceania, North America, and South America). Another listing of societies contains the Standard Probability Sample (Murdock & White, 1969) selected to provide a representative set of sixty independent societies (arranged in eight culture areas) for use in the search for patterns of correlations among characteristics across cultures.

The *Outline of Cultural Materials* contains seventy-nine topics that are considered to be a universal set of concepts or categories to be found in all cultural groups. These have been arranged into eight broad categories by Barry (1980). Box 7-2 provides a complete listing of these topics.

Thus, there are two major dimensions cross-cutting each other: a universe of cultures and a universe of cultural characteristics. With this massive archive virtually any feature of a society can be sought and found by the researcher. For example, one can search for a subset of all cultures in a particular part of the world and count the proportion of cultures in these regions that are hunting, as opposed to agricultural, in their basic economic activity. Given the availability of geographical information (on latitude, altitude, temperature, and rainfall) for these cultures, one could then raise the question: "Is basic economic activity distributed in a way that is predictable from geographical information?" Prior to the availability of the HRAF, researchers interested in these ecological questions (such as Kroeber, 1939) had to go to numerous original sources for their information.

Actual uses of the Files have largely been to discover patterns of regular associations (correlations) between two sets of cultural variables across cultures. This "holocultural" or "hologeistic" approach incorporates the "whole-world" range of data and findings (Naroll, 1970b). We have seen one specific example in the search for a relationship between child-rearing practices and subsistence economy (reported in Chapter 2). For ease of use many numerical codes have been produced so that each researcher does not have to convert verbal descriptions of a custom (such as child-rearing) to a digit each time a category of cultural activity is employed. A massive set of codes is available in both the *Ethnographic Atlas* (Murdock, 1967) and in the survey *A Cross-Cultural Summary* (Textor, 1967). Further, more specialized, codes continue to be produced (Barry & Schlegel, 1980).

A number of problems have attended the use of the Human Relations Area

Box 7-2   Cultural topics contained in "Outline of Cultural Materials"

In Murdock's "Outline of Cultural Materials" variations in cultural practices around the world are placed under seventy-nine topics or categories; these in turn are organized into eight major sections. The first section provides general information about the culture (what, where, how studied, which language spoken, and so forth), while the other sections give specific information about various material (sections II, III, & IV) and social (sections V, VI, VII, & VIII) culture of the group. It is interesting to compare this listing to that contained in Wissler's earlier definition of "culture" by listing its essential attributes.

The seventy-nine cultural categories of Murdock, as arranged by Barry (1980), are:

I   General characteristics
    10 Orientation
    11 Bibliography
    12 Methodology
    13 Geography
    14 Human Biology
    15 Behavior Processes and Personality
    16 Demography
    17 History and Culture Change
    18 Total Culture
    19 Language
    20 Communication
    21 Records

II Food and clothing
    22 Food Quest
    23 Animal Husbandry
    24 Agriculture
    25 Food Processing
    26 Food Consumption
    27 Drink, Drugs, and Indulgence
    28 Leather, Textiles, and Fabrics
    29 Clothing
    30 Adornment

III Housing and technology
    31 Exploitative Activities
    32 Processing of Basic Materials
    33 Building and Construction
    34 Structures
    35 Equipment and Maintenance of Buildings
    36 Settlements
    37 Energy and Power
    38 Chemical Industries
    39 Capital Goods Industries
    40 Machines
    41 Tools and Appliances

IV Economy and transport
    42 Property
    43 Exchange
    44 Marketing
    45 Finance
    46 Labor
    47 Business and Industrial Organization
    48 Travel and Transportation
    49 Land Transport
    50 Water and Air Transport

V   Individual and family activities
    51 Living Standards and Routines
    52 Recreation
    53 Fine Arts
    54 Entertainment
    55 Individuation and Mobility
    56 Social Stratification
    57 Interpersonal Relations
    58 Marriage
    59 Family

```
        60 Kinship                    75 Sickness
        61 Kin Groups                 76 Death
                                      77 Religious Beliefs
   VI Community and government        78 Religious Practices
        62 Community                  79 Ecclesiastical Organization
        63 Territorial Organization   80 Numbers and Measures
        64 State                      81 Exact Knowledge
        65 Government Activities      82 Ideas About Nature and
        66 Political and Sanctions       Man
        67 Law
        68 Offenses and Sanctions  VIII Sex and the life cycle
        69 Justice                    83 Sex
        70 Armed Forces               84 Reproduction
        71 Military Technology        85 Infancy and Childhood
        72 War                        86 Socialization
                                      87 Education
   VII Welfare, religion, and science 88 Adolescence, Adulthood,
        73 Social problems               Old Age
        74 Health and Welfare
```

Files, leading to many criticisms and attempts to deal with them (Naroll, Michik, & Naroll, 1980). We examine briefly here three of these problems and the solutions proposed within anthropology; further consideration, from the point of view of cross-cultural psychology, will be given in Chapter 9. The first problem is to define what is a *cultural group* exactly; what are its limits and boundaries, and who is a member? Naroll (1970a) has proposed the notion of *cultunit* (short for "culture bearing unit"). The key issue in the statistical use of cultunits is the question of their independence. This issue has been termed Galton's Problem (see Naroll, 1970b), and it has been a substantial thorn in the side of those who wish to use correlational analyses in holocultural studies. The essence of the problem is the *diffusion* of cultural traits from one cultunit to another; the presence of a particular practice in many adjacent cultunits may be due to borrowing and not to independent development. Thus, for example, the correlation across twenty cultunits between the emphasis on assertion in child-rearing and reliance on hunting and gathering for subsistence might be due to one society establishing such a link and then sharing it with other societies. Since correlations of this sort require independence of cases, the apparent linking of these two factors in the twenty cultunits may represent only a single case diffused rather than twenty independent cases. The solution that has been proposed by Naroll (1970b) is the "double language boundary"; two cultunits may be considered to be independent of each other for statistical purposes if there are at least two language borders between any two cultunits in the study. The standard cross-cultural sample (mentioned earlier) was chosen in part to meet this independence requirement.

A second problem is that the quality of the data is extremely variable in the HRAF. Some were collected by explorers and merchants, some by military invaders and missionaries, and some by anthropologists. While it would be tempting to claim the greatest data accuracy and quality for those trained to be objective field workers, this may not necessarily by the case. To evaluate this problem and to control for it, Naroll (1962) has introduced a procedure called "data quality control," in which one "assumes that there is variation in the degree of accuracy of holocultural data, and that this variation is related to characteristics of the data generation process" (Naroll et al., 1980, p. 497). For example, whether the report is from a person who knew the language or not may be correlated with variations in reported cognitive ability, or missionary status may be correlated with reported religious beliefs. Five control factors have proven to be valuable in assessing data quality: length of field work, knowledge of language, description of current life as observed versus remembered life as recalled by elders, number of data sources and crosschecks employed, and number of publications cited in the formal written presentation of the ethnographic account.

A third problem to be noted here is that of the categories of culture used in the HRAF. In Box 7-2 there were seventy-nine categories or topics presented into which all cultural data are slotted. The question is whether these categories are a perfect fit, an approximate fit, or a poor fit for the whole range of cultural data being reported from around the world. In other words, are these really *universal* categories of culture or do some cultural data become selected or distorted in order to match such a neat conceptual scheme; are the data within each category truly *comparable* (see Chapter 9)? The solution proposed by Naroll et al. (1980) is to make quite explicit all of the coding rules to be employed when taking material from an ethnographic report and entering them into the HRAF. For example, is cannibalism to be understood as any eating of human flesh or must it also be *known* (not accidental), *customary* (not one time only), and *approved* of (not under duress)? Similar coding rules may be generated and applied to distinguishing between such cultural practices as science, religion, magic, witchcraft, myth, and ritual. With such rules coding errors and forced categorization may be avoided. However, numerous data that cannot be categorized may require an expansion or reorganization of the present system of categories.

While cross-cultural psychologists may wish to use the Files to search for systematic covariation between population-level variables, two other uses are suggested here. One is that an "initial reading" of a psychological theory or hypothesis (prior to the effort and expense of going to the field) may be possible using variables already in the Files; and in this way one may be able to direct one's activity more effectively toward fruitful questions when one eventually goes to the field. The second one (as we noted at the outset) is that with the help of the Files specific cultures can be identified as providing particular cultural contexts and experiences that are required for a particular comparative psychological study. For example, if our interest were in the effects of variations in child-rearing practices, we could select a set of societies varying from the extreme assertion to the extreme compliance ends of the severity dimension and then go to the field and use psychological assessment procedures with a sample of individuals to see if the expected behavioral outcomes are indeed present.

Culture and personality

In Chapter 1 we noted that another subdiscipline shares the interspace between psychology and anthropology: culture and personality (also known as psychological anthropology). There are some features that distinguish culture and personality from cross-cultural psychology: the latter is conceptually and methodologically rooted in academic psychology, while culture and personality is rooted primarily in anthropology and to some extent in psychoanalytic psychiatry. Those wishing to have a more extensive discussion of the field of culture and personality are referred to Bock (1980, 1988), Bourguignon (1979), and Spindler (1978). Earlier expositions include the texts by Barnouw (1973) and Wallace (1970), the two readers of Hsu (1961, 1972) and one by Kaplan (1961). A recent evaluation by Shweder (1979a; 1979b; 1980) is also of value in understanding the current status of the field, and a perusal of the journal *Ethos* will reveal some current topics and issues. The most committed exposition of the field has been by LeVine (1982), whose ideas we will return to at the end of this section.

At the outset the name of the discipline needs to be explained. Originally referred to as the field of "culture and personality," it has now become generally known as "psychological anthropology" following a proposal of Hsu (1961). The two terms will be taken as synonyms in this book.

One definition of the field (Bock, 1980) is that "psychological anthropology comprises all *anthropological investigations* that make systematic use of psychological concepts and methods" (p. 1). Its development "has been influenced by the interplay between *anthropological problems* and the psychological theories that were being formulated" at the time (Bock, 1980, p. xi). In these two assertions the added emphasis draws our attention to the fundamentally *anthropological* nature of the field.[1] What does this mean? First, it signals that most of its practitioners are anthropologists, whose education, theoretical preferences, and methodological practices are firmly rooted in that discipline. In contrast, cross-cultural psychologists are usually rooted in psychology with its own disciplinary biases. Second, the theoretical

---

[1] In his 1988 revised text, however, Bock goes on to make the provocative statement that "all anthropology is psychological." This can be interpreted in at least two ways. One is as a form of scientific reductionism (see Chapter 1) in which cultural phenomena are reducible to psychological ones. The second more likely explanation is that it signals a search for a rapprochement between anthropology and psychology, a goal we heartily endorse.

level of analysis (compare Figures 1-1 and 1-3) remains distinctive: population-level concerns predominate in psychological anthropology (with some inferences occasionally made to individual dispositions), while individual-level issues (individual differences and processes) predominate in cross-cultural psychology. Third, there is, as noted by Edgerton (1974), a long-standing methodological commitment to "naturalism" in anthropology and psychological anthropology and to "experimentalism" in psychology and cross-cultural psychology. Phenomena are typically observed in the field in one case, while they are stimulated in the laboratory or other standard situations in the other. These characterizations are only general modal descriptions; the use of tests and interviews is not uncommon in psychological anthropology, while field observations are also employed by cross-cultural psychologists.

The origin of the field of psychological anthropology is usually traced to the simultaneous interest of anthropologists (mainly from the U.S.) in psychological explanations of cultural phenomena and the availability of the Freudian theory of psychoanalysis. The major period of development was in the 1920s and 1930s, and the central issue was the "relationship between culture in the widest sense (including economic, sociopolitical, and even ecological) and personality characteristics, as mediated by the socialization process" (Jahoda, 1980, p. 76).

While chronological overviews of the development of the field are presented in most of the general works cited earlier, the clearest is that of Bock (1988), who distinguishes four main approaches: *Configurationalist* (1920–1940) with Ruth Benedict and Margaret Mead as the main figures; *Basic and Modal Personality* (1935–1955) with Abram Kardiner, Ralph Linton, and Cora Dubois; *National Character* (from 1940 on) with Clyde Kluckhohn and Alex Inkeles; and *Cross-Cultural* (from 1950 on) with John Whiting and Robert LeVine. The first three are largely concerned with single culture analysis, while the latter approach studies relationships comparatively. For Jahoda (1980) these two trends are easily distinguishable: "one is concerned with the analysis of the role of socialization processes and personality factors *within* a cultural group; the other concentrates on attempts to identify the general processes whereby culture shapes, and is shaped by, personality factors *across* human cultures" (p. 76). We turn now to a portrayal of each of these four approaches, drawing to a large extent on the Bock typology and description.

The *configurationalist* approach derives its name from the writings of Sapir (1949), who proposed that "personality conceived of as a distinctive configuration of experience which tends always to form a psychologically significant unit ... creates finally that cultural microcosm of which 'official' culture is little more than a ... mechanically expanded copy" (pp. 201–203). In this view, and put in its simplest terms, culture is the personality of a society: "cultures ... are individual psychology, thrown large upon the screen, given gigantic proportions and a long time span" (Benedict, 1932, p. 24). Like personalities, cultures are complex, organized and patterned.

In Benedict's main work (*Patterns of Culture*, 1934) the influence of Gestalt psychology is also apparent: patterns or forms are emphasized and give meaning to the details that constitute them; indeed, details are often downplayed, even ignored, in her preference for understanding the overall configuration. Such an orientation led Benedict to describe and label whole cultures with diagnostic terms derived from clinical and psychoanalytic psychology: Pueblo Indians are termed "Apollonian" (avoiding extremes, seeking the middle way); Plains Indians are "Dionysian" (seeking excess in sensory and motor life); Dobuan Islanders are "Paranoid" (with lives full of suspicion, fear, and conflict); and Kwakiutl Indians are "Megalomaniac" (indicated by competitive gift giving and the destruction of one's own property). These brief sketches give the flavor but do not convey the richness of Benedict's description and interpretation.

Margaret Mead is also usually identified with the configurationalist approach. Her views on the nature and origin of sex differences have become very well known and have tended to overshadow her early and important role in configurationalist studies. Even this work on sex differences (*Coming of Age in Samoa*, 1928) has now been severely criticized for its ethnographic inaccuracy (Freeman, 1983).[2]

The *basic and modal personality* approach developed during a seminar at Columbia University in New York; "anthropologists 'presented' the cultures with which they were most familiar, after which psychologists 'interpreted' the data to reveal their dynamic significance" (Bock, 1980, p. 86). Kardiner (a psychiatrist) and Linton (an anthropologist) worked out the concept of *basic personality structure*, which "places the focal point of culture integration in the common denominator of the personalities of the individuals who participate in the culture" (Kardiner & Linton, 1945, pp. viii–ix).

This approach asserts a causal link between personality and culture, not just a similarity or identity between the two concepts (as proposed by the configurationalists). The causal chain begins with *primary institutions* (such as the subsistence activity, family organization, and socialization practices

---

[2] The book by Freeman pointed out numerous discrepancies between Mead's description of Samoan culture generally (and Samoan female adolescents specifically) as lacking in guilt, conflict, and turmoil, and the observations of other ethnographers. Freeman's own view emphasized such Samoan cultural and psychological qualities as violence, jealousy, competitiveness, and stress, as indicated in high rates of rape, assault, and homicide. The publication of Freeman's book unleashed a storm of controversy that soon entered the realms of ideology and politics (including cultural versus biological determinism, the women's movement, sexual liberation, and permissive parenting). The subjective nature of the ensuing debate has revealed to a substantial degree the subjective nature of the anthropological enterprise itself. Most explanations of the discrepancy between the two views are based on their different *a priori* ideologies. Access to different sectors of Samoan culture and their varying command of the Samoan language appear to take second place to the preconceived expectations with which different researchers approached their informants.

present in a culture), leading to the *basic personality* found in the culture and then leading to the *secondary institutions* (such as religion, myth, and folk-lore) of the culture. For Kardiner and Linton secondary institutions are to be understood as the effects of the primary institutions acting on the human mind; put another way, basic personality is an adaptation to the fundamental realities of life in a particular culture.

Following the basic personality approach, DuBois (1944) proposed the notion of *modal personality* in which the more *global* notion of basic personal-ity was replaced by a *statistical* one that expresses greater frequency (mode) rather than a fundamental or basic uniformity in personality. This permitted her to deal with variability in personality and with discrepancy and incongru-ity between personality and culture. For DuBois personality assessment was likely to give "multimodal rather than unimodal results." Moreover, there is a "high probability that only a small percentage of people in a society belong to these modal groups" (p. xx).

In Chapter 1 we briefly mentioned that cross-cultural and cross-national studies have been conventionally distinguished from each other by one focusing on small-scale traditional and usually nonindustrial cultures and the other on contemporary industrialized nation states. So too in the field of psychological anthropology we find studies of *national character* as a distinct approach, one that attends to the psychological qualities of present-day nation states. For example, both Clyde Kluckhohn (1957) and Ruth Benedict (1946) worked on characterizations of the Japanese. Benedict sought to explain the contradiction in Japanese character between restrained aesthetic-ism (seen in art and ceremony) and fanatical militarism (typified by the ideal of the samurai warrior). A similar analysis of German national character (Fromm, 1941) during the Nazi period was rooted in the national characteris-tic of the "authoritarian personality" (see also Adorno et al., 1950), which was thought to be present in German society. Russian national character was also analyzed. Gorer and Rickman (1949) proposed that swaddling (the prac-tice of babies being alternately swaddled and released) could account for the supposed Russian mood swings between "long periods of introspective de-pression and short bursts of frantic social activity" and political swings between "long periods of willing submission to a strong external authority punctuated by brief periods of intense revolutionary activity" (Bock, 1980, p. 115).

It should be noted that other approaches, which do not originate from culture and personality, fit the modal personality or national character orientation. For example, Hofstede (1980), whose four value dimensions we mentioned in Chapter 3, argues that national character traits can be revealed by survey studies of the kind he carried out and that the "mental programs of members of the same nations tend to contain a common component" (p. 38).

Finally, the *cross-cultural* approach to culture and personality emerged when attention switched from *intensive* examinations of single cultures and the collective personality of their members to *extensive* examinations of relationships across cultures between cultural and personality variables. As we saw in Chapter 2, J. W. Whiting and Child (1953) drew on psychoanalytic theory and data in the HRAF to explore the possibility that there might be systematic relationships between the ways in which children are socialized and their adult personalities. Earlier studies in this tradition had been carried out at Yale University, where George Murdock founded the HRAF and Miller and Dollard (1941) explored the relevance of learning theory to the development of complex human behaviors.

In this approach, as we have seen, correlations are sought between cultural characteristics (usually rated as present or absent for a particular culture) and some other characteristic (of the culture or of individuals in the culture). Using these correlations, links are established between child personality and adult personality, antecedents to the former are sought in cultural characteristics (usually child training practices), and consequents of the latter are sought in cultural outcomes (compare the secondary institutions of Kardiner).

An elaborate model has been proposed J. W. Whiting (see Box 7-3) that is similar to the ecocultural framework (Figure 1-3) that is employed in this text. These similarities are in part due to the obvious general influence of the early culture and personality schools on contemporary cross-cultural psychologists, in part to the specific influence that Whiting has had on the field, and in part to the similarities (both metatheoretical and methodological) between the cross-cultural approach in psychological anthropology and cross-cultural psychology.

We end this overview of early work in culture and personality with some evaluative comments and critical observations. From the point of view of cross-cultural psychologists many would agree that the field of culture and personality is "untidy" (Jahoda, 1980) and "fuzzy" (Hsu, 1972). These judgments arise for a number of reasons, some theoretical, some methodological.

On the theoretical side there is the widespread attachment to the psychoanalytic theory of Freud. Given that the theory is often judged by psychologists to be untestable and unprovable, not to say unscientific, this attachment was bound to raise doubts about the scientific status of the field of culture and personality.

More specifically, both Bock (1980, 1988) and Shweder (1979a,b; 1980) have presented similar criticisms, often employing similar terms. First is the issue of characterizing whole societies with a single label ("global traits" for Shweder, 1979a; and the "uniformity assumption" for Bock, 1980). Psychologists usually discover distributions within populations; there are variations within groups and individual differences between persons in virtually every psychological study ever conducted. This common finding is ignored in most research in psychological anthropology, where differences within groups are ignored or minimized and differences between groups are magnified. From current work on social categorization (e.g., Tajfel, 1978) we know this to be a frequent occurrence in intergroup perception by people in their daily lives. However, it is risky when it occurs as a part of a scientific strategy.

Box 7-3   Whiting's model for psychocultural research

The model proposed by John W. Whiting (1974) is the most recent of a series of models guiding research into personality and its relationships to culture. The core, from Freud's writing, was that a child's socialization experiences should be predictive of adult personality. To this core concept Kardiner added antecedent primary institutions and consequent secondary institutions in the culture. Whiting has elaborated all of these components, often renaming them as their nature became more clear or more specific. For example "primary institutions" became differentiated into a set of three interrelated contexts in Whiting's model: physical *environment*, social *history*, and cultural *maintenance systems*. "Child rearing" became elaborated into the child's *learning environment*, now including physical as well as social aspects. "Adult personality" became a set of more specific attributes, with a basic distinction between *innate* and *learned* outcomes, and including cognitive and motivational characteristics, in addition to those conventionally included within the notion of "personality." Finally, "secondary institutions" evolved into a large range of *projective expressive systems*, including subjective aspects such as beliefs and myths, as well as objective social indicators, such as crime and suicide rates.

A comparison of this model, Figure 7-1, with Figure 1-3 in this text reveals many similarities; however, one major difference is that Whiting's model continues the flow of variables until it ends again (at the right) with population-level outcomes. As an anthropologist, psychological outcomes (the end point of the cross-cultural psychologist's main interests, as in Figure 1-3) are placed by Whiting as a variable that leads to and may help to explain a number of important eventual cultural expressions.

Also dubious is the premise rooted in Freudian thought that the "child is father to the man" ("search for childhood origins" for Shweder, 1979a, and the "continuity assumption" of Bock, 1980). Research examining relationships between child training and childhood experiences on one hand and adult personality on the other has not been so clear. As suggested by the review of Orlansky (1949) and by the more recent analysis of Shweder (1979a), individual adult personality is not *determined* solely by individual childhood experiences. This does not rule out the possibility that some aspects of behavior are influenced by characteristic socialization practices used in a particular society; the contentious issue is whether or not such practices are predictive of broad personality traits in adults.

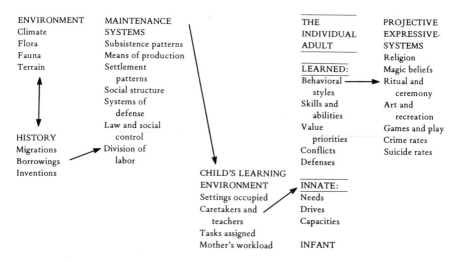

Figure 7-1 Model for psychocultural research (Whiting, 1974).

With respect to method researchers in psychological anthropology have not been able to "make really independent assessments of the two major sets of variables relating to culture and to personality" (Jahoda, 1982, p. 87). This problem has arisen because ethnographic accounts are often the source for evidence regarding *both* cultural and personality variables. Correlational techniques, at the very least, require some independence in measurement. In part, this problem is overcome by the use of personality tests by field workers. However, most tests used by anthropologists have been projective tests and provide scope for substantial subjective involvement of the ethnographer in their interpretation (compare the "projective assumption" of Bock, 1980).[3]

The "objectivity assumption" (Bock, 1980) is related to this issue: can an outsider like an anthropologist ever really take an unbiased or objective view of the personalities of other peoples? Anthropological field methods require personal immersion, whereas psychologists often distance themselves with the use of "objective" tests. There are, of course, advantages and disadvantages to both approaches, but it can be argued that systematic data collection that is repeatable by others, with culturally appropriate and standard tests, protects the researcher (and the participants!) from gross subjective assessments and interpretations.

Future directions have been suggested, for example by Jahoda (1982, p. 96), who has expressed the view that "there are extensive and important areas of behavior about which academic personality theory has little if anything to say." He refers to the study of *envy* as an example; while the psychological

---

[3] See also the discussion in Segall et al. (1990) of Lindzey's (1961) warnings about the use of projective techniques in personality research.

literature is virtually silent on this widely distributed psychological phenomenon, the anthropological literature is rich and is largely based on the
very methods and theories that have been so much criticized by psychologists.

A comprehensive effort to revitalize the field of culture and personality has
been made by LeVine (1982), who considers the field to encompass the three
subfields of psychological anthropology, cross-cultural psychology, and transcultural psychiatry. This master discipline is defined as the "comparative
study of the connections between individuals (their behavior patterns and
mental functioning) and their environments (social, cultural, economic,
political" (p. 3). The scope of this field is virtually identical to the one we
have taken for cross-cultural psychology in Chapter 1. We should therefore
examine LeVine's views in more detail to differentiate his view of "culture
and personality" from our view of "cross-cultural psychology."

In his definitions of the two central terms of *culture* and *personality* we find
no means of distinguishing the fields. LeVine (1982) defines *culture* as "both
the distinctively human forms of adaptation, and the distinctive ways in which
different human populations organize their lives on earth" (p. 3), and
personality as "the organization in the individual of those processes that
intervene between environmental conditions and behavioral response....
These processes include perception, cognition, memory, learning, and the
activation of emotional reactions as they are organized and regulated in the
individual organism" (p. 5). It is clear that the specific definition of culture
used by LeVine is similar to that employed in the present text. Moreover, his
notion of personality incorporates all the domains of psychology (not just
those features emphasized in our more current use of the term) and hence
matches in scope the concerns of cross-cultural psychology as we have
identified them. Similarly, one general theoretical perspective is shared —
that of culture and behavior as adaptive to ecological context. LeVine (1982)
is quite explicit in his acceptance of this fundamental point of view, as we are
in Chapter 1. However, in two other theoretical perspectives we find substantial divergence: one is LeVine's adoption and rather uncritical acceptance of
the psychoanalytic theories of Freud; the other is his central concern (rooted
in anthropology) for how people are *similar* within cultures.

The acceptance of the psychoanalytic tradition has long been a central
feature in the culture and personality field (as we noted earlier). While we
consider this problematic, LeVine considers psychoanalytic theory to be a
sure guide for the future evolution of the field. Further, rejecting the usual
"testing methods" of academic psychology, LeVine argues for the superiority
of the "clinical method." While critical of most previous work and of the view
that "much psychoanalytic anthropology is based on superficial or misguided
field work, or both" (p. 205), LeVine proposes (in a chapter entitled "The
Couch and the Field") to follow closely the methods of psychoanalysis that
have proven useful to clinicians.

The second differentiating feature lies in LeVine's primary concern for the
second level of C. Kluckhohn and Murray's (1948) famous dictum: "Every

man is in certain respects: (a) like all other men, (b) like some other men, (c) like no other man" (p. 35). For LeVine:

Culture and personality studies are primarily concerned with those respects in which a man is like some other men, particularly his fellow group members, in contrast to members of other groups. The respects in which he is like all other men are the biosocial and psychological universals that form the background categories within which significant between-group variations are found. The respects in which he is like no other man are the objects of inquiry in the psychology of individual differences, which are a function of the variability within any population, no matter how clearly defined. Investigators of culture and personality can ill afford to ignore biosocial universals, psychological universals (such as those in semantic structure), and individual differences, but their special attention is reserved for variations between groups." (p. 22)

While cross-cultural psychology is certainly interested in this second level, our roots lie partly in the study of individual differences (the third level), and the field is moving toward the explication of universals (the first level), as we shall see in Chapter 10.

Cognitive anthropology

Another branch of anthropology that has close links with psychology is cognitive anthropology. Its goal is to understand how people in various cultures describe, categorize, and organize their knowledge about their natural (and supernatural) world. It shares with psychological anthropology a concern for normative knowledge, what and how people in general know, rather than for psychological processes or individual differences, and differs from the cross-cultural psychological study of cognition (reported in Chapter 5) on these same dimensions.

Another name for this general area is *ethnoscience* (e.g., Sturtevant, 1964); it is defined as a branch of anthropology that seeks to understand the scientific knowledge of other cultures. In principle there could be any number of branches, such as ethnobotany, ethnogeology, ethnoastronomy, even ethnopsychology. This initial orientation has led, in psychology, to a concern with indigenous knowledge systems, including practical know-how (*bricolage*, Lévi-Strauss, 1962; Berry & Irvine, 1986) and larger-scale cognitive systems ("indigenous cognition," Berry, Irvine, & Hunt, 1988).

In the early studies in cognitive anthropology a key to understanding cognition is to recognize the very great importance given to language as a cultural phenomenon. As we saw earlier in this chapter, language is one constituent element of culture, and along with tool-making may be one of the few really distinctive qualities of human culture (after all, many nonhuman species have social organization, territory, and even games).

Language is also readily identified with the cognitive life of the human species, since it is clearly implicated in learning, remembering, and thinking. Anthropologists interested in human cognition thus sought to gain their particular entry to cognitive phenomena by way of this particular cultural phenomenon, that of language.

Historically, two main influences made this language-cognition link the focus of cognitive anthropology. First, as noted in Chapter 5, Whorf (1956) argued that language categories (both the words and relations among words) serve to codify and organize the world on the one hand and mould the cognitive life of the individual on the other. The empirical evidence for this view is slight (see Chapter 5); nevertheless, the links are intuitively compelling and were sufficient to move anthropologists in this direction. Second, formal linguistic analyses (e.g., Greenberg, 1957) provided a model method for examining categories and the structure of categories that was easily adopted by cognitive anthropologists. Linguistic analyses of the way people *talked about* a domain (for example, kinship, animals, hunting technology) thus formed a basis for an analysis of their cognitive organization of the world that is, how they *thought about* the domain). A well-known early example is the work of D'Andrade, Quinn, Nerlove, and Romney (1972) on the conceptual organization of disease categories in American English and Mexican Spanish. Examples of more recent studies can be found in Holland and Quinn (1987). This approach is concerned with collective cognition (how people in general understand their world), not with individual cognition (how persons are similar or different from each other or the nature of the underlying cognitive processes). Indeed, Jahoda (1982, pp. 214–225) expresses a commonly held view among cross-cultural psychologists that such "collective representations" (cf. Moscovici, 1982) cannot really provide access to any individual psychological processes, be they cognitive, motivational, or attitudinal.

In this conclusion we find a correspondence with that drawn from studies in the culture and personality area (in the previous section); individual differences and individual processes (the core of psychological enquiry) are simply beyond grasp with population-level data. However, this should not be a basis for dismissing the work of cognitive anthropologists; indeed, like those working in culture and personality they have opened up whole new domains for enquiry by cross-cultural psychologists and have provided a language-based method for studying individual behavior.

More recent approaches have shifted away from a focus on language to a concern with actual behavior (Gatewood, 1985). In the terms of Dougherty and Keller (1982) there is less interest in "taxonomy," and more in "taskonomy." That is, individual differences in how people actually use the cultural knowledge have become the object of study (see Box 7-4).

Conclusions

Other than psychology it is clear that the most important parent of cross-cultural psychology is the discipline of cultural anthropology. The central concepts of culture, of relativism, and of universalism have been contributed

Box 7-4 The Yupno number and counting system

During his ethnographic studies of the Yupno (in Papua-Nuigini), the anthropologist Wassmann documented their number system on the basis of information provided by his main informant, one of the most important men of the community. The Yupno start counting on the left hand, folding down each finger in turn from the little finger to the thumb; distinct number words exist for 1, 2, and 3; number 4 is "2 and 2," and 5 is called "the finger with which one peals bamboo shoots," namely the thumb; the sum is indicated by showing the closed fist and saying "one hand." Numbers 6 to 10 are counted in the same way on the left hand and 11 to 20 on the feet. For numbers 21 to 33 symmetrical body parts are designated two by two, intermixed, to mark each group of five (and number 33), with parts on the central body line. Once the last body part (called "the mad thing") is reached, the sum is expressed as "one man dead." The process can be repeated on a second person if there is a need to count beyond 33. This number system is illustrated in Figure 7-2.

The following aspects appeared to be interesting from a psychological perspective:

1. The use of the number system in daily life in various segments of the population (old and young men, women, schooled and unschooled children).
2. The use of the system in unfamiliar situations, such as performing calculations (addition, subtraction, multiplication) and counting to infinity.
3. The development of the understanding of the number system in children and their ability to abstract the system from particular body parts (following Saxe, 1981, 1982, 1983, 1985).

The details of the results of the first two questions are available in Wassman & Dasen (in press). In fact, it proved impossible to study women, because Yupno women are not supposed to know the number system and therefore refuse to answer any questions. Neither was it practicable to study children and younger men, because the former only use the decimal system taught in school and the latter use the traditional system only up to 20, as is done on the coast of Papua-Niugini. Any attempts to replicate, among the Yupno, Saxe's developmental studies was therefore impossible, which shows the limits of psychological research in some field situations.

One most interesting finding, however, emerged from the psychologist's insistence on asking several older men to demonstrate counting with the number system: Although four of them used the system described above, ending with 33, one of them produced a system ending

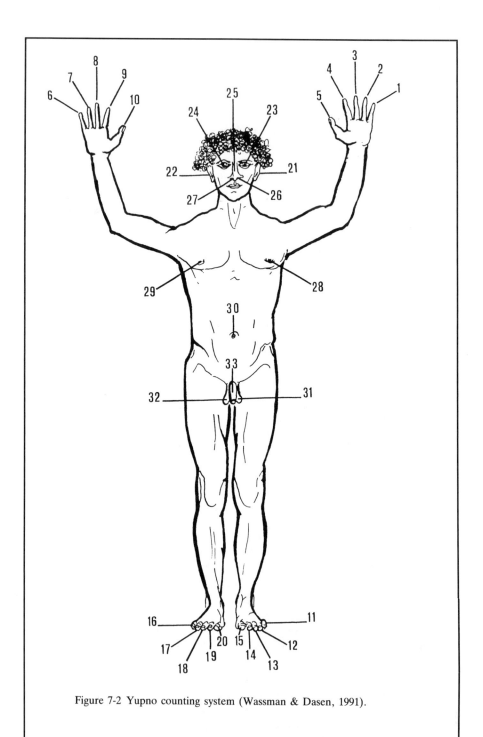

Figure 7-2 Yupno counting system (Wassman & Dasen, 1991).

with 30, two with 32, and one with 37. With one exception (a man starting from bottom up), counting always ended on the penis, but the number of intermediate body parts could vary.

How is it possible to have a functional number system that is not absolutely standardized? Possibly the variations occur because the traditional number system is nowadays used rather infrequently, being replaced with the decimal system and number words in Pidgin. However, it is also possible that idiosyncrasies have always existed. In fact, counting always occurs in public (for example, in the exchange of bride price or even in the recently introduced trade stores), and counting always starts with one, going through the whole system. Thus the partner in a deal can witness how a result is arrived at, and individual variations do not matter, since no one ever speaks in terms of the end result only.

by anthropology; so too have the methods used in field settings. While these notions and practices have had to be translated from the language of the collective to that of the individual, the task for cross-cultural psychology has been informed in many ways by this pioneering work in anthropology. Despite this assistance, occupying the middle ground between the population and the individual has not been all that easy for cross-cultural psychology. The study of the individual in context (particularly the concern with individual differences) has meant some distancing from, even some conflicts with, our anthropological ancestor. Similarly, a concern for the cultural context has distanced us from our more experimentally oriented psychological parents. It should be clear, however, that cross-cultural psychology has been informed in major ways by the anthropological traditions, only a portion of which we have been able to present in this chapter.

8   Biological approaches

Within cross-cultural psychology biological bases of behavior are seldom emphasized. The focus is usually on the sociocultural environment and how it moulds the members of cultural groups. This is an unbalanced view of reality. In the framework presented in Figure 1-3 we have included biological adaptation and genetic transmission among the concepts that have to be taken into consideration in cross-cultural psychology. To understand behavior, its similarities as well as its variations, the study of the biological basis is as essential as the analysis of sociocultural influences. The complex pattern of interactions between the human organism as a biological entity and environmental factors cannot be understood unless the partial knowledge available within the various scientific disciplines is somehow integrated.

In the first section of this chapter we give a brief overview of some core concepts of evolution theory. The subject area of the second section is behavior genetics. In the third section biological approaches to the study of the interaction of the organism with its ecological and social environment are the subject of discussion. In ethology, as the study of animal behavior in natural settings is called, the immediately observable behavior is the starting point. The fourth and last section of this chapter is devoted to models of cultural transmission that have been developed from a biological perspective in analogy with models of genetic transmission.

Evolution and adaptation

The theory of evolution formulated originally by Charles Darwin and further developed in the course of the last 100 years is central to the biological sciences, including their perspective on behavior. Of the core concepts in the theory there are two that are of particular interest in the present context, namely that species can change over time and that natural selection is the key to such change.

Essential to the theory of evolution is the diversity among individual organisms within a single species. In most species parents produce a large number of offspring. Many of these fail to reach maturity and to procreate in turn. If for some reason a certain heritable characteristic enhances the probability of survival and reproduction, the frequency of this characteristic in the population will increase over successive generations. In other words, a differential rate of reproduction leads to systematic changes in a population over time. This is how Darwin explained natural selection as a causal process under the influence of environmental factors. At the time of Darwin the reasons for individual variation were not well understood, although it was known from the breeding of domestic animals and plants that systematic changes in morphological or behavioral traits could be brought about. Through the mating of individual organisms with desired characteristics a breeder could increase the probability that these characteristics would be found in subsequent generations. It was only much later that genetic principles were discovered that could account for these observations.

Artificial selection practised by breeders clearly serves a specific purpose. However, the presence or absence of a purpose or goal in natural evolution has been vigorously debated for many decades. At the present time most biologists share Darwin's opinion that changes in species can be seen as the outcome of random variations in genetic materials and the interaction between organisms and their environments. We shall briefly describe how these mechanisms of change operate. Since an understanding requires some knowledge of genetics, a brief summary of a few basic principles is given in Box 8-1. The reader unfamiliar with this field is advised not only to consult this box, but also the relevant literature (e.g., Cavalli-Sforza & Bodmer, 1971; E. J. Gardner & Snustad, 1984; F. Vogel & Motulsky, 1979).[1]

The Hardy-Weinberg law, mentioned in Box 8-1, states that in an environment that does not change the relative frequencies of alleles in a population remain constant over generations. How then do changes in species come about?

First of all, new alleles emerge from time to time. This can happen under the influence of external factors that affect the genetic material. Nuclear radiation and certain chemicals are known causal agents. New alleles can also be formed without any known external determinant being present. In the complex process of DNA synthesis during sexual reproduction an occasional replication error occurs. Changes in the genetic meterial lead to *mutations*. These are relatively rare and most mutants are not viable. However, the actual occurrence of an event is not only a function of its probability, but also of the number of times it potentially can happen. In rapidly reproducing microorganisms mutations provide a realistic prospect for change within a limited time period (compare the various strains of the influenza virus); in higher organisms with a longer life cycle other factors are likely to have a more appreciable effect on the rate of change.

These factors include natural selection, migration, assortative mating, and chance fluctuations. The Hardy-Weinberg law presupposes an infinite

---

[1] There are also several textbooks written for students of psychology that treat more extensively the topics touched on in this chapter, for example, by Plomin, DeFries, and McClearn (1980), and V. Reynolds (1980), and a chapter by Thompson (1980) in the *Handbook of Cross-Cultural Psychology*.

Box 8-1   Genetics

The account given here is concerned with the human species, but is, with some variations, valid for all species that multiply through sexual reproduction. The genetic material consists of DNA molecules, which form long double strands made up of pairs of nucleotides. Each nucleotide contains a base. This base occurs in only four forms, often indicated with the letters A, C, T, and G. Various sequences in which the ACTG groups occur correspond (in triplets) with the structure of aminoacids. Long strings of aminoacids form polypeptides which, as enzymes, have an effect on specific biochemical reactions. Through a kind of copying process polypeptides originate from the DNA.

A *gene* is a DNA segment that can be recognized by its specific function. The gene is the functional unit of genetic material. Each gene has a certain place (locus) within a *chromosome*. Of a single gene (identified by locus and function) often more than one variation is found. These variations, which are called *alleles*, form the most important basis for individual variation within a species.

The chromosomes, in which the genetic material is contained, form long coiled strings of DNA. In humans there are twenty-three pairs of chromosomes, which by common convention are numbered from 1 to 23. In the process of cell division the chromosomes replicate so that each cell of an organism contains all the genetic materials. There is one important exception, namely in sexual reproduction. In the process by which reproductive cells (*gametes*) are formed, the chromosomes are reduced to half. There is an extra division in which only one of each pair of chromosomes is transmitted to each gamete. With fertilization the chromosomes of two gametes, one from the father and one from the mother, combine to form a new cell with a complete set of chromosomes.

The chromosomes of a pair closely resemble each other, with one exception. Males have an X and a Y chromosome, females two X chromosomes. This determines biological sex differences. The other chromosomes in a pair show, in the normal case, only small differences. They are *homozygous* for a particular gene when the alleles at a certain locus are identical; they are *heterozygous* when unlike alleles of that gene are present in the two chromosomes of a pair. In the case of heterozygosity the one allele can suppress the other; the *dominant*, but not the *recessive*, allele finds its expression in the phenotype of the organism. Alternatively, the two chromosomes can both contribute to the results of the genetic process of protein production. This leads to some combination of the expression that the two alleles have separately.

A distinction is often made between *genotype*, that is the genetic constitution of an organism, and *phenotype*, which refers to the characteristics of the organism as they can be observed and reflects also the influences of the environment.

The chromosomes contain an enormous amount of information. There is no doubt about this, although estimates differ considerably. Dobzhansky, Ayala, Stebbins, and Valentine (1977) put the number of pairs of nucleotides in man at 2,900 million. Assuming 2,000 pairs of nucleotides per gene, there would be enough material for 1.5 million gene pairs. For reasons we shall not go into it is likely that not nearly all DNA codes for specific genes. Still, according to Dobzhansky the number of genes in man can easily be as high as 100,000 or 150,000. For a large proportion (say half) of the genetic loci there will be more than one allele.

These numbers, although far from exact, give an indication of the genetic variability present in the human species. Through sexual reproduction each organism acquires a specific combination of the total pool of the genetic material available in the species. Only monozygotic (identical) twins are genetically identical.

Nevertheless, in an environment that remains constant, existing genetic variation within a species does not lead to systematic change. This follows from the Hardy-Weinberg law, which states that the ratio between different alleles of the same gene remains constant over generations. If at a certain time there are two alleles of a gene with the relative frequencies of p_1 and p_2, then the same values will be found for p_1 and p_2 at any later point in time if other factors remain constant. The conservation of gene frequencies results in a genetically stable population.

---

population with random mating patterns and a constant environment. In reality mating populations can be quite small, for example because they are geographically isolated. Random fluctuations in the distributions of alleles will occur in all breeding populations. This *genetic drift* is negligible in large populations, but not in small groups. A single individual among the founding parents of a group of settlers can sometimes have an appreciable effect on the frequency of a certain characteristic in the descendants many generations later.

Nonrandom or assortative mating patterns are very much in evidence among humans, where the choice of a marriage partner is governed by social rules. In certain societies marriages between blood relatives are encouraged and even customary; this can give rise to inbreeding.[2] In other societies such close-relative marriages are prohibited.

[2] Many deleterious but recessive alleles exist with low frequency in a population. Two relatives have far more genes in common than two randomly selected individuals. Hence, there is a larger probability that a certain deleterious recessive allele will be transmitted by both parents (and thus express itself) when they are relatives than when they are not relatives. The resulting higher probability of a defect is called inbreeding.

Another factor in assortative mating is the selection of partners on the basis of similarity in psychological characteristics. In many contemporary societies level of education, which is associated with intelligence, is important for partner choice. If intelligence has a heritable component, the expected variation on this trait is larger in a population with, than in a population without, partner choice made on the basis of intelligence. In itself this does not lead to any change in the population as a whole. Only when there is a correlation between level of intelligence and number of offspring can assortative mating have a long-term effect on the population. Few if any such effects are known (e.g., Cavalli-Sforza & Bodmer, 1971).

Disturbance of the Hardy-Weinberg equilibrium can also occur when the condition of a constant environment is violated. Certain changes in the environment can lead to differential reproduction of a given genotype. This is the principle of natural selection mentioned previously. Selection effects have actually been demonstrated in experiments. There are also field studies in which it has been shown that in certain species of moth the most frequently found color can change from light to dark under the influence of industrial pollution. One moth in Great Britain, which was almost always light in preindustrial times, is now predominantly dark-colored in smoky and sooty industrial areas. A possible explanation is that moths that blend with their environment are less conspicuous for predators and hence have a higher survival and reproduction rate. This explanation was validated in an experimental study in which both dark and light moths (with markings to distinguish them from nonexperimental animals) were released in light and dark environments. When the surviving moths were trapped again, a differential survival rate in each of the two environments was found in favor of the moths with the matching color (Kettlewell, 1959).

In the human species a selective mechanism is known that has caused a high incidence of sickle-cell anemia in some populations. This is described in Box 8-2.

Adaptation. Population change through natural selection in reaction to demands of the environment is called *adaptation*. The concept of adaptation used to have wide usage in biology, but nowadays can be found more frequently in psychological and anthropological writings, as we have seen in Chapter 7. Broadly speaking, adaptation in the social sciences refers to changes that take place during the lifetime of an organism in response to environmental demands. In evolutionary biology adaptation refers to the adjustment of a population to an environment over many generations. However, when a biologist concludes that a certain change is the result of an adaptive process, this is often merely a *post hoc* inference. Such inferences are risky because there are always alternative explanations that may be overlooked. Similarly risky are *post hoc* inferences about cultural influences on behavior. Therefore, we shall discuss the analysis of adaptation in some detail following Lewontin (1978).

Box 8-2 Sickle-cell anemia

Sickle-cell anemia is a genetically transmitted defect in which the hemoglobin (red blood corpuscles) are easily deformed from round to sickle-shaped. It leads to a severe form of anemia, and patients usually do not live until they have children. The condition is caused by a single nucleotide that occurs in two forms, called *S* and *s*. There are three ways in which these two alleles can be combined in the genetic material of an individual. The two chromosomes of the relevant pair both can be *S*, both can be *s*, and one can be *s* while the other is *S*. The (homozygotic) carriers of *s/s* suffer from sickle-cell anemia. *S/S* homozygotes are normal and the heterozygotic carriers of *S/s* can suffer from a mild form of anemia.

The striking feature about sickle-cell anemia is its very unequal distribution in the world. In equatorial Africa frequencies of up to 35 percent of (mostly heterozygotic) carriers of *s* have been observed in certain populations. The incidence is much lower in northern and southern Africa. The *s* allele is also found around the Mediterranean and in certain aboriginal groups in India. In the North European populations it is practically absent. Given the low rate of reproduction of the *s/s* homozygotes, it is incomprehensible at first sight that the incidence of the *s* allele can be so high.

What is the reason for this unequal distribution? F. Vogel and Motulsky (1979) offer three possible explanations.

1. The mutation rate may be different for some external reason (for example, climate) or due to some other internal genetic factor.
2. Chance fluctuations (genetic drift) have played a role.
3. There is some selective advantage to sickle-cell anemia in areas where it is found frequently.

The size of the populations make it highly unlikely that the differences in incidence can be due to random error, and for this reason the second possibility can be rejected.

The first alternative has been investigated. For example, in theoretical studies the rate of mutation needed to maintain the high frequencies actually found in certain areas was calculated. Also, the rate of inheritance was studied empirically by comparing children with their mother. On both counts it could be ruled out that mutations provide a feasible explanation.

A selective advantage for the *S/s* heterozygote was indeed found after it was noted that there is a coincidence between the presence of malignant forms of malaria and sickle-cell anemia. In a number of studies, which we shall not review here, support for a causal relationship was found. Perhaps the most important evidence is that the incidence of malaria infections is higher in young children who are S/S homozygotes than in heterozygotes. A ratio of 2:17 between these two categories has been reported (Allison, 1964; quoted by F. Vogel & Motulsky, 1979). Given the overall high mortality of children because of malaria, this provides a sufficient selective advantage to maintain a high frequency of the s allele in the population despite the mortality of the s/s homozygotes. Thus, the higher incidence of sickle-cell anemia in equatorial Africa and some other regions in the world very likely reflects a genetic adaptation to long-term conditions in the environment.

First, the environment that imposes the demands leading to adaptation has to be defined. But this can only be done with reference to the way of life of an organism. Each species occupies an *ecological niche* in the environment. This niche defines the way of life of the species in the total environment: how the organisms of a species cope with the prevailing temperature, how they move around in the environment, what food they use, how they collect it, and so on. Since the world can be broken up in many different ways, it is easy to define an ecological niche. If there is an infinite number of alternatives available, it becomes trivially easy for a species to find a niche. Thus the concept of adaptation, which implies adaptation to a particular niche, could lose all explanatory value.

Second, organisms are not passively shaped by their environment, they interact with it. For example, the soil can change because of the excreta that are deposited; and insects contribute to the fertilization of plants from which they draw honey and thus help to ensure a future food supply. It can be said that an organism contributes to establishing its own ecological niche through the way it interacts with the environment. This would mean that all organisms are always already adapted. So there would be no scope for evolutionary change.

To cut through this dilemma it can be suggested that a species as it exists in a particular ecological niche at a particular time has to be taken as a starting point for analysis. On a large time scale the environment is not constant and the ecological niche will change. If the species is not to die out, it must change. From this perspective adaptation is the process of keeping up with the changing environment. This is expressed in the notion of *environmental tracking*. Subpopulations of the same species can come to face different environmental challenges, depending on their geographical location, and can evolve differentially into new species.

This still does not solve the problem of *post hoc* interpretation, unless a precise functional relationship can be specified between a well-defined property of the environment and an equally well-defined property of an organism. Skin color may be seen as an adaptation to the environment; however, we do not know whether an increase in the pigmentation of darker people or a decrease in the pigmentation of the lighter-skinned has been the likely direction of change. Another example is that in humans the chin protrudes much further than in primates. Articulated speech is facilitated by the form of the human chin. Attempts to explain the larger chin as an evolutionary change failed until it was realized that it is not our chin that has grown larger. Taking the primates as a standard, the part of the human jaw where the teeth are set is small in relation to the bony part of the jaw (perhaps due to changes in diet). Compared to other primates we appear to have less-protruding teeth rather than a more-protruding chin.

A functional relationship can only be specified when a functional unit of analysis can be defined in both the organism and in the environment. It has emerged that the protruding chin is not such a functional unit. Presumably it is merely a byproduct of some other evolutionary change.

The difference between two alleles often is not restricted to a single effect on the phenotype. A gene can have various effects on the development of an organism. This is called *pleiotropy*. In a process of natural selection where a directional evolutionary change takes place in a gene all effects of that gene on the phenotype will be affected. This implies, for example, that human speech, a main condition for the development of culture, may have to be explained biologically as coincidental to the functionally unrelated change of recession of the teeth rather than as an adaptation in its own right.

So far a number of traps have been indicated that one can fall into when inferring an adaptive process based on the principle of natural selection. The question how such an inference can be more validly made still remains to be answered. Lewontin (1978) refers to the analysis of the adaptive value of a trait as an *engineering analysis* of organism and environment. This is a procedure in which a particular idea is tested in a number of coherent ways. If none of the expectations has to be rejected, that would constitute confirmatory evidence. This research strategy is like the internal and external validation of theories used by social scientists. The systematic analysis of the various possible explanations for the high incidence of sickle-cell anemia mentioned in Box 8-2 provides an example of this approach.

Human "races." The biological mechanisms of change mentioned earlier in this section and their interactions are responsible for the emergence of "races" in the human species. Social scientists sometimes refuse to recognize "race" as a valid concept. Biologists more often argue that differences in environmental conditions, such as climate and geographical separation with limited possibilities for interbreeding, have led to genetic divergence between groups. Skin color is easily the most distinguishable characteristic in which human groups differ genetically. It is affected by a number of genes. Possibly dark pigmentation has had a selective advantage against sunburn in tropical areas. More likely there have been changes in the direction of a light skin in areas with little sunshine (F. Vogel & Motulsky, 1979). Sunlight is needed for the synthesis of vitamin D, which prevents rickets (a bone disease). Other visible traits on which human populations differ include body height, the shape of the nose, hair color, and the implantation of the hair. There are also noticeable differences in the distributions of various blood groups between races (Cavalli-Sforza & Bodmer, 1971).

However, it should be noted that racial differences are very small compared to the genetic diversity within races. Lewontin (1972) has reported a study in which he surveyed seventeen blood markers in seven races, all represented by a number of populations. In this study "race" accounted for 6.3 percent, population for 8.3 percent, and individual variation for 85 percent of the variance. To our knowledge there have been no such comparative studies on factors other than blood markers. Since the genetic basis of most human characteristics is still unknown, this is hardly surprising. Nevertheless, the limited evidence available points to individuality rather than race or populations within race as by far the most important factor in genetic variation between humans.

Behavior genetics

In genetics a distinction is made between morphological, physiological, and behavioral traits. The search for direct links between phenotype and genotype has been most successful at the morphological level, that is, the level of physical characteristics. The heritable basis of certain morphological traits in the pea plant was clearly established in the famous experiments of Mendel in the middle of the nineteenth century. Genetic mechanisms for behavioral traits have been more resistant to analysis. Most of the evidence derives from laboratory studies with animals and is difficult to transpose to the human species. Because this book is about human behavior we shall deal very little with animal studies, although this decision makes the present section rather unrepresentative of the biological field of behavior genetics.

Environmental variables exert a limited effect on the expression of traits encoded by a single gene, such as eye color. Simply stated, there are no influences in the natural environment that will change the color of someone's eyes from brown to blue or vice versa. Hence, the range of modifiability of this trait is small. With respect to many other traits, the amount of change under the influence of environmental variation is much larger. We shall not attempt to explain the genetic basis for environmentally controlled modifiability (about which knowledge is still very incomplete anyway), but mention just one factor. A distinction can be made between *structural* and *regulatory* mechanisms. Structural genes control the structure of polypeptides (see Box 8-1). The rate of expression of a structural gene (that is, how much of an enzyme is produced) is controlled by regulatory genes. A regulatory gene need not be limited in its effects to one or more structural genes, but can also trigger other regulatory genes. In this way complex sequential biochemical events can come about, such as the hormonal changes in puberty or during a pregnancy. However, the interaction between various processes is not exclusively genetically determined. There is evidence that environmental events can influence regulatory processes in an organism.

This makes the distinction between genetic and environmental influences rather fuzzy. Nevertheless, many social scientists are of the opinion that it does not make sense to assume any direct genetic effects on those aspects of behavior that are typically human. They will accept only that the genetic code imposes certain constraints on the range of behavior of an individual. For example, genetic processes define important stages in individual development, such as the onset of sexual maturity. However, so it is argued, from a psychological perspective the plasticity of behavior under the influence of external factors is so large that for all practical purposes genetic constraints are of little relevance for understanding human behavior and experience. The genes may set the stage, but they have little to do with the play performed on it. We shall try to avoid taking sides in this rather fruitless and ideologically tainted nature-nurture debate and try to give a balanced summary of the evidence.

The impact of gene action on behavior is direct, broad, and unmistakeable in the case of certain malfunctions, such as Down syndrome (or Mongolism) and phenylketonuria (caused by the absence or inactivity of one particular enzyme that is needed for the metabolism of the amino acid phenylanine found in milk). Among the diseases in which some genetic predisposition is strongly suspected but not (yet?) clearly demonstrated at the level of genes or chromosomes are the major mental disorders schizophrenia and depression. Their genetic basis has been mainly inferred from family and twin studies. In the context of this book it is significant that all major mental disorders appear to occur universally, although cross-cultural differences in the rates of incidence cannot be excluded. In Chapter 15 we shall return to this point.

Personality and intelligence. Are findings about genetic abnormalities relevant to variations in typically human behavior, or is "normal" behavior more or less exclusively a function of environmental variables? Behavior genetic research on personality traits and cognitive abilities is relevant to this question.

In the older literature the term *temperament* was associated with the inheritable components of personality. In early conceptions such as that of Heymans (1932; Van der Werff, 1985) temperament referred to a dominant mode of reacting that was characteristic of a person across a large range of situations. In certain traditions of personality research strong associations with a biological basis for individual differences have remained, such as in the work of the neo-Pavlovians (e.g., Nebylitsyn & Gray, 1972) and of H. J. Eysenck (1967). The dimension for which most inheritability estimates have been obtained is that of extroversion-introversion. Fuller and Thompson (1978), who reviewed the evidence, report that the heritability estimates (h^2) in twin studies vary from 0.03 to 0.83, with relatively few results below 0.40.[3] In a summary (p. 359) they point out that the work on the inheritance of human personality traits has led to somewhat ambiguous conclusions. However, they ascribe this mainly to the poor methods of assessment in this area.

Despite these shortcomings, strong genetic effects have been reported also for large samples. In a study with 573 pairs of twins Rushton, Fulker, Neale, Nias, and Eysenck, (1986) derived estimates of approximately 0.60 for the heritability of individual differences in scores on self-report questionnaires for altruism and aggression.

In many studies on the genetic basis of personality dispositions a genetic component is inferred from the difference in correlations between scores obtained by subjects who are genetically related and subjects who only share the same environment. For scales in personality inventories Loehlin, Willerman, and Horn (1985) report an average correlation of approximately 0.05 between adoptive parents and their adopted children, against an average of around 0.15 for the correlation between children and their biological parents. The difference between the two values corresponds to an estimate of genetic heritability (h^2) of about 0.20. From the available evidence it appears that adoption studies generally tend to result in lower heritability estimates than twin studies.

In recent years there has been a revival of the term *temperament*, for example in the notion of *difficult temperament*. Some researchers in this area see it as characteristic of certain children that they are fussy and difficult to handle. The psychometric basis for this difficulty variable rests mainly on reports by parents to questionnaires rather than on observational studies. Although there are some dissenting voices, it is generally agreed among those involved in this research that temperament implies genetic inheritance (e.g., Bates, 1986). A summary of the (few) relevant cross-cultural studies is presented by Super and Harkness (1986b). They specifically refer to the findings of Freedman (1974) that Oriental babies are less excitable and irritable than Caucasian American babies. Super and Harkness warn against overinterpretation, mentioning some contradictory evidence as well as methodological concerns, which we shall discuss in Chapter 9.

There is no personality trait that is controlled by a single gene and for which a pattern of inheritance is found in the same way as for eye color and other physical traits. In fact, there is not a single personality dimension for which a direct link with a certain genetic configuration has been established. This implies that the evidence is circumstantial and that a discrepancy such as that between twin studies and adoption studies is difficult to resolve.

---

[3] The index of heritability, h^2 is an estimate of the ratio between genetic variance and total (phenotypic) variance. It can range in value from 0.00 (all variance is environmental) to 1.00 (all variance is genetic). Estimates of h^2 can be derived from correlations between relatives. For the transformation from correlational statistics to heritability estimates we refer to other sources (e.g., Cavalli-Sforza & Bodmer, 1971; F. Vogel & Motulsky, 1979). It may be noted that computations of heritability and environmental effects require simplifying assumptions that are unlikely to be satisfied by the data.

Another problem is the large variation between studies in the amount of variance attributed to genetic causes even when the same method (for example, twin studies) is used. Even more critical is the finding that approximately the same average emerges for the amount of explained variance when the results of a number of studies are combined, independent of the personality dimension under consideration. This would mean that for all traits the degree of heritability would be about equal. This is an unexpected and consequently worrisome state of affairs.

The most serious criticisms focus on the nonexperimental nature of the research designs in studies on the genetic basis of complex human behavior. As mentioned before, these studies are aimed at estimating the correspondence in trait scores as a function of the genetic relationship between subjects. A person has more genes in common with one's father or mother than with an uncle and still more than with a cousin. Twin studies in which the concordance in scores of monozygotic (identical) twins is compared with that of dizygotic (fraternal) twins are a special category of family studies. A complicating factor is the covariation of genotype and environment because most close relatives live together in a family, at least for part of their lives, and as such share much of their environment as well (see Chapter 2). This is the reason similarities between family members do not provide good heritability estimates. This problem plays a smaller role in adoption studies, where the incidence of a certain trait is compared for nonrelatives (the case of adoption) and for relatives raised in the same (family) environment.

In modern studies different approaches are sometimes combined. However, an unbiased estimate of heritability is impossible even in the most sophisticated nonexperimental study. Certain simplifying assumptions have to be made. In adoption studies a major assumption is that adoption is carried out randomly. In fact, a substantial proportion of adopted children are raised by relatives, thus confounding genetic and environmental influences.[4] When comparing monozygotic and dizygotic twins, it is assumed that variation in the environment is the same for both kinds of twins, despite many indications that the monozygotes are far more often treated as alike.

These methodological criticisms apply as well to research on intelligence, which is by far the most controversial area of human behavior genetics. For summaries of the available empirical information we refer to Vernon (1979) and Plomin, DeFries, and McClearn (1980). We shall restrict ourselves to some general observations.

Studies purporting to estimate the relative contributions of genotype and environment to the performance on intelligence tests invariably show effects that point to a genetic origin of the variance. The heritability estimates usually are higher than those reported for personality variables. For example, Jensen (1969, 1973) claimed an average heritability coefficient (h^2) of 0.80. In

---

[4] A further complication arises in cross-cultural research, since the role of relatives in adoption apparently varies greatly across cultures (Silk, 1980).

a large-scale adoption study Horn, Loehlin, and Willerman (1979) obtained estimates corresponding to an h^2 of approximately 0.50. Although there is variation in outcome, the results of typical studies suggest a stronger influence on measured intelligence by hereditary factors than by the environment.

Nevertheless, the potential importance of the role of genetic factors has been strongly doubted, among others by Lewontin, Rose, and Kamin (1984). They emphasize the shortcomings in studies designed to estimate genetic variance. It would carry us too far to even summarize all the objections (see Segall et al., 1990, p. 101), but we shall mention one. Lewontin and his coauthors argue, in our opinion quite convincingly, that as more factors are controlled the genetically explained variance decreases. As we indicated previously, theoretically unassailable estimates cannot be obtained; critics can point out flaws in all studies. However, it is difficult to see how even the combined effect of all valid objections can reduce the genetic variance component in IQ tests scores to zero.

Culture by gene interactions. If genetic influences on individual human behavior are possible, we have to ask ourselves what the implications are for intergroup differences, especially when the groups have not been in contact for a large number of generations. With respect to personality variables there is little cross-cultural research in which genetic as opposed to sociocultural differences are proposed. The work on the Eysenck Personality Questionnaire, discussed in Box 4-2, is one of the rare examples.

With respect to intelligence the evidence on genetic and environmental causes of cross-cultural differences has been reviewed by Vernon (1979). Most of the research originates from the vigorous debate in the U.S. on the nature of IQ test score differences between groups of black and white Americans. Toward the end of his book Vernon provides a summary of the findings regarding racial-ethnic differences, listing thirty relevant points. The number of these points that are more in line with an environmental explanation is about as large as those more in line with a genetic explanation. However, according to Vernon the points fitting a genetic explanation tend to be more convincing.

We would like to add that there is no logical basis for inferences about *inter*group variation on the basis of *intra*group variation. Even if within all human groups a large proportion of individual differences could be accounted for in genetic terms, this would not imply that an observed difference between groups also has a genetic basis. The underlying argument has been presented by Furby (1973) among others. She gives the imaginary example of a population in which individual genetic differences exist for height. The phenotypical height is affected by the daily consumption of milk. For each glass of milk per day a quantity c is added to a person's stature. Suppose that groups drawn from this population are exposed to environments characterized by different quantities of milk. Between-group differences in height will then be entirely determined by the drinking of more or less milk, while the within-group variations are entirely determined by genetic factors. It is easy to see that in this example the mean height of two groups drinking one and two glasses of milk respectively will differ by a quantity c.

The example of body height is not entirely arbitrary. It is known, mainly from military archives in which the height of all army conscripts has been recorded, that over the last century the average height of young people in West European countries has increased by about 10 centimeters. Improvements in the diet are a major reason, but other environmental factors should not be excluded. On the basis of such archival data on intelligence test scores an increase of 15 to 20 IQ points in a single generation (since 1950) has been computed for Western countries by Flynn (1987). Since such a rapid change cannot possibly be due to evolutionary genetic processes, environmental factors have to explain most if not all of it.

For less controversial evidence of interactions between cultural and genetic variables we have to look at other phenomena than personality traits and cognitive abilities. The clearest example so far of such an interaction is that of cross-cultural differences in lactose tolerance, discussed in Box 8-3. Population differences in the incidence of color blindness (e.g., Post, 1962; 1971) constitute another example. There is evidence that in hunter-gatherer populations the frequency of red-green color blindness is not more than 2 percent compared to about 5 percent in groups that are furthest removed from a hunting existence in mode of subsistence. This form of color blindness is usually linked to the X-chromosome and is far more prevalent in men than in women. The most suggestive explanation is that hunter-gatherers are more dependent for their survival on accurate color vision (spotting of game) than agriculturalists and people living in industrialized societies. The higher survival rate of color blind mutants in agricultural societies would then be the most likely genetic mechanism.

In summary, the literature reviewed in this section leaves open the possibility of genetically based differences in behavior between human races. However, it has also become clear that there is little substantive evidence that such differences exist for such complex aspects of behavior as personality traits and cognitive abilities.

Ethology

Ethology is the study of animal behavior in natural environments, often involving elaborate and detailed field studies. The resulting descriptive accounts form the basis for theoretical explanations that are further developed along three lines of inquiry: through additional observations, through experiments to test specific hypotheses, and through the comparison of findings across species. It is particularly via the third strategy that ethologists are able to cross-validate their conceptualizations in a broader biological framework. In this section we shall briefly examine what the ethological approach can contribute to cross-cultural psychology.

Box 8-3   Differences in tolerance for lactose

Lactose is the most important carbohydrate in milk. It cannot be absorbed in the intestine, but needs to be split in two molecules by the enzyme lactase. In newborns the (very rare) absence of lactase is lethal. In adults lactose intolerance is manifested by diarrhea, abdominal pain, and flatulence after consumption of, let us say, half a liter of cow's milk. Until fairly recently it was considered normal that in older children and adults the activity of lactase was maintained. We now know that persistent tolerance is the norm only among West Europeans and their descendants in other countries. In many other populations the continuation of lactase activity in older children and adults is virtually absent. This holds for many Mongoloid groups, for Melanesians, Amerindians, and for most of Africa. Groups of nomadic pastoralists in Africa, such as the Fulani, form a notable exception, with a high prevalence of lactose tolerance. In southern Europe and in certain regions of India intermediate values (from 30 to 70 percent) are found. (See Dobzhansky et al., 1977, or Vogel & Motulsky, 1979, for further references.)

Although there is no perfect correlation, the relationship between lactose tolerance in adults and animal husbandry is striking. Two explanations have been suggested, one cultural and the other referring to physical qualities of the environment (Flatz & Rotthauwe, 1977). In the cultural explanation it is postulated that the consumption of milk, because of its nutritional value in proteins, should give a selection advantage. There are always some individuals who can tolerate milk and this trait could slowly spread through the population over a large number of generations. The fact that there are cattle-farming populations with a low frequency of tolerance weakens the hypothesis. In addition, when milk has fermented, it is low in lactose content and is digestible even in the absence of lactase in the consumer's intestinal tract.

The second hypothesis postulates an advantage of lactose tolerance in areas with relatively little ultraviolet sunlight, such as northern Europe. Sunlight plays a role in the production of vitamin D, which is needed for calcium metabolism. A too-low level of vitamin D leads to rickets, a bone disease. It has been suggested that lactose is an alternative substance to vitamin D in the metabolism of calcium. Another version of this hypothesis bears on the direct absorption of vitamin D contained in milk and milk products.

Whatever the correct explanation, lactose intolerance explains why milk is considered repulsive by adults in many countries (for example, China). Sometimes it is considered good for children and by extension for other weak and sickly persons, but not for strong and healthy people. Obviously such opinions have a much more valid basis than originally thought by Westerners, laymen as well as scientists.

Of more interest to us are possible wider ramifications. To what extent has the intolerance for fresh milk been a barrier against the development of animal husbandry in various societies? The form of economic subsistence is thought to influence major cultural variables in a number of ways, as we have seen in Chapter 2. Thus, variations in the digestion of milk may well have been a factor in the shaping of cultures, even if it is not clear at this stage how this factor has actually operated.

The work of Lorenz (e.g., 1966) is often seen as the beginning of modern ethology. In the 1930s he reported observational studies on the social behavior of jackdaws, a kind of crow. Probably the most influential ethologist after Lorenz was Tinbergen, who is well-known for his work on the stickleback, a small fish.[5]

The early ethologists were struck by distinct patterning in much of the behavior of animals. Often one can observe behavior sequences consisting of a number of distinguishable acts. Once such a sequence is set in motion, it cannot be interrupted and then continued; after interruption it has to be started again from the beginning. Hence the notion was proposed of *fixed action patterns*. These patterns are triggered by specific stimuli, which act as *releasers* of an available behavior process. Another important notion is that of *imprinting*. It was observed that young birds tend to react to the first moving object they see after hatching as they normally respond to their parents. For example, animal keepers in zoos have found themselves in the position of substitute parents. They are then followed by young birds, just as chickens normally follow the mother hen. As adults such animals have been known to make sexual advances to members of the substitute human parent species rather than to their own species. For this reason Lorenz postulated *critical periods* in the process of development. What an animal acquired during such a period was considered fixed and irreversible.

A sharp distinction was made between instinct and learning. This divide also marked more or less the boundary between ethology and psychology from before World War II until the 1970s. The term *instinct* referred to genetically inherited and thus preprogrammed and rather immutable behavior. At that time psychology was dominated by learning theories. It was believed by many that through classical conditioning in the tradition of Pavlov and operant conditioning as developed by Skinner virtually any reaction an

---

[5] General introductions to ethology can be found in a chapter by Tinbergen (1969) or in book-length treatments by Manning (1979), Hinde (1982), or Alcock (1984).

animal is capable of making can be linked to any stimulus that an animal can perceive.

This conclusion proved to be premature. Rats can be conditioned easily to avoid foods that later make them ill if these foods have a certain taste, but conditioning is difficult if the consumption of these foods is accompanied by electric shock to their feet (Garcia & Koelling, 1966). Conversely, rats have great difficulty in learning to jump for food, but can easily be taught to jump for shock avoidance. Visual cues have also been found to be ineffective in rats for learning food avoidance. For other species, such as monkeys, visual cues are quite effective in avoidance learning of toxic foods. Apparently, cues are most effective when they match the natural life-style of a species (Bolles, 1970; Gould & Marler, 1987). Some ethologists had argued earlier that the learning abilities of animals are greatly dependent on context. There are predispositions for certain stimulus-response associations, and a reward that will reinforce a certain response may not work well for other responses.

The distinction between learning and instinct has also lost some of its importance because ethologists have drawn back somewhat from the earlier position of Lorenz on imprinting as a special kind of learning dependent on "critical" periods. They now tend to speak about "sensitive" periods instead. Genetic factors will facilitate or constrain the learning of certain associations in a relative, rather than in an absolute sense. These factors are not necessarily constant; they can differ in effect during various phases of individual development (Hinde, 1982). The animal is seen as innately equipped to learn what it needs in the particular ecological niche it occupies. On the other hand, it is also recognized that "instinctive" responses cannot develop without environmental influences and that an ecological approach to behavior is needed. It requires only a small step to argue that learning in the human species, with its own evolutionary history and adapted to its own particular niche, is subject to the same considerations.

Human ethology. The extension of ethological methods and theories to the human species is sometimes referred to as human ethology. In their quest for a variety of evidence ethologists more than psychologists are combining results from different disciplines. Almost inherent to this strategy is the danger of overinterpreting the findings from research areas other than those in which one has firsthand experience. An example of a controversial ethological book can be found in Box 8-4.

The scope of human ethology is well illustrated in an eloquent article by Eibl-Eibesfeldt (1979a). Central to this article is the biological heritage of human behavior. For Eibl-Eibesfeldt:

the comparative approach is a basic source of information, but it has been criticized for making too much of "similarities." Yet if we compare the structure or the behavior of animals and man, we do indeed encounter striking similarity. In greeting rituals, for example, weapons are turned away in a conspicuous fashion to indicate peaceful intent. Boobies [a small sea bird] sky point with their beaks, the Masai thrusts his

---

Box 8-4 On aggression

The first book on ethology that created a furor was published (in English) with the same title as this Box in 1966 by Konrad Lorenz. It contained a few chapters extending an instinct theory on aggression to humans. Lorenz adhered to a "hydraulic model" of instinct: if there is no outlet for pressures that build up in the organism, they will eventually explode with force. According to Lorenz, aggression in humans is to be understood as an adaptation developed in the course of phylogenetic evolution. If aggression is part of "human nature," aggressive behavior can be seen as unavoidable and perhaps to some extent excusable. The moral implications of such a viewpoint are a major reason the book triggered many negative reactions.

However, Lorenz did not consider aggressive acts as inevitable or excusable. Investigating the natural causes of aggression would in his opinion lead to a better understanding and indicate how to regulate its expression and to prevent its undesirable manifestations, as for example in warfare. He argued that aggression can be redirected through sublimation (as proposed in psychoanalytic theory) and through forms of ritualization, of which the playing of sports was seen to be the most important. Sports are supposed to have educational value in teaching self-control and respect for rules. It even diverts national militant enthusiasm (in Lorenz's opinion motivated by aggression) into positive expression at international matches.

Most ethologists do not share Lorenz's theory of aggression. For example, Hinde (1982) denied the inevitability of the building up of aggression. He emphasized that environmental conditions (such as exposure to aggressive acts and frustrations) stimulate violence, and that factors in the socialization of the individual play an important role. Similarly, Archer (1988), in a book on aggression from a biological perspective, explicitly considers aggression as a mechanism to react to external threats rather than as an internal drive.

---

spear into the ground, and in our culture we salute state visitors with twenty-one averted guns. Similarities of this kind call for an explanation. They can be accidental, but most of the time they are not, being due to similar selective pressures that have shaped behavior during phylogenetic and cultural evolution alike, or else to a common heritage resulting from a shared ancestor. (1979a, p. 2)

Only in a footnote does Eibl-Eibesfeldt add to these statements a small reservation about cultural traditions that can be passed on through human communication and in different cultures may not have evolved independently. He continues his main text by drawing a distinction between homologies and analogies. Similarities genetically transmitted from common ancestors are called *homologies*. In Eibl-Eibesfeldt's opinion we can confidently infer that most behavior patterns that we share with the great apes are homologies. *Analogies* are similarities between species in morphological or behavioral traits that have arisen in response to similar environmental demands. The eye of an octopus, which is remarkably similar anatomically to the human eye, obviously also has the same function. There are also functional similarities in behavior, the cross-species comparison of which can be helpful for the explanation of human behavior.

After presenting evidence from animal behavior, Eibl-Eibesfeldt discusses evidence from humans to show that phylogenetic adaptation has also prepro-grammed our behavior to a significant extent. One of the sources of evidence is cross-cultural research; we would like to discuss this a little further.

Eibl-Eibesfeldt refers to the extensive recordings on film of unstaged social interactions that he and his collaborators have made in various so-called "primitive" cultures.[6] The films have revealed a large number of universal motor patterns. An example is the kiss, which is universally found as a sign of affection to children. It may well have derived from mouth-to-mouth feeding and is linked to similar behavior in nonhuman primates. Another example is the display of "coyness," which is clearly recognized independent of the culture in which it has been filmed. There are also differences between cultures, for example in the nonverbal communication of expressing "no." In most cultures people shake their head. Other gestures are used; for example, the Greeks throw back their head and turn it sideways and the Ayoreo Indians wrinkle their nose (as if smelling something bad) and pout. According to Eibl-Eibesfeldt all these patterns are found universally and all express some denial or rejection. Apparently, it is possible that one of these patterns becomes the standard convention in a group instead of the more common horizontal head shake that seems emotionally the most neutral way to express a factual "no."

Eibl-Eibesfeldt also finds important basic similarities in the structure of *rituals*, which are complex behavior patterns of a symbolic nature (cf. Eibl-Eibesfeldt, 1979b). He argues that in a friendly encounter there are universally three phases, each with a specific function. The first or opening phase is characterized by a mixture of aggressive displays and appeasement. As an illustration Eibl-Eibesfeldt refers to a Yanomami Indian going to another village, who will perform an aggressive display dance, but will be accompanied by a child waving green leaves. He continues (1979a):

---

[6] When subjects notice that they are being observed, they tend to start acting. In order to obtain unstaged recordings Eibl-Eibesfeldt and his team made use of a lens with a mirror device so that events were filmed to one side at an angle of 90 degrees rather than directly in front. Reuning (personal communication to YHP), who is an expert on the Bushmen, has questioned who is being tricked by this device: persons who are not familiar with movie cameras and have little idea about how these are supposed to function or investigators who underestimate the social skills of nonliterate peoples.

The Yanomami salutation is certainly a culturally specific ritual. We in the West do not perform war dances on such an occasion. But consideration of the more general principles expressed does reveal comparable displays in our way of saluting. A visitor of state, for example, is greeted by a welcoming canonade, and in addition is received by a child with a bouquet of flowers. In the most diverse salutations we discover the same principle. So, too, in our culture the handshake — and squeeze — are partly display and partly challenge, mitigated by smiling, nodding, and embracing (p. 21).

Eibl-Eibesfeldt goes so far as to suggest that bodily characteristics have evolved to serve as releasing signals. It was noted already by Lorenz that babies possess certain qualities that make them look "cute" and that solicit care-taking and affective responses. Among other things are the relatively large head, the rounded body shape, and the round protruding cheeks . The latter are sometimes said to have a function in sucking, but this is not entirely clear. Eibl-Eibesfeldt (1975) argues: "Such an additional function is feasible, of course, but we notice that monkeys and other mammals can get along without this formation. This argues for a specifically human organ that evolved in the service of signaling" (p. 490).

Eibl-Eibesfeldt (1979a) concludes that "there exists a universal 'grammar' of human social behavior" (p. 22). It may be noted that genetic mechanisms are presumed to underlie what many consider to be qualities that are acquired in the process of socialization. Even symbolic behavior can be reduced to inborn behavior patterns in Eibl-Eibesfeldt's opinion. We would argue that the validity of such claims cannot be demonstrated by similarities such as those mentioned in the last few paragraphs. The examples show that Eibl-Eibesfeldt has not heeded the warnings by Lewontin, mentioned earlier in this chapter, that certain changes may not be adaptations, but have come about as a byproduct of other changes (for example, pleiotropy). More important, the interpretations cannot be accepted at the present time because plausible alternatives in many instances are not considered, let alone ruled out.

If the range of modifiability of human behavior is so large that a short handshake or even a verbal greeting can have the same meaning as an elaborate dance display, there is a dramatic and essential difference between human behavior and the fixed action patterns that ethologists have observed in animal behavior. The essential similarity between such different forms of greeting can only be derived from their common meaning. However, meaning is a psychological attribute that is not identical across cultures. Examples of cultural differences are abundant, even in behaviors in which a strong genetic component at some time appeared to be present. Perhaps most telling is the study by Keating et al. (1981; see Box 4-4) in which it was shown that lowered brows, identified in nonhuman primates as a signal of dominance, had that meaning in most human populations *but not universally*.[7]

However, the basic question is not whether a few specific interpretations are valid or have to be replaced by more appropriate explanations. The real

---

[7] For more extensive comments we refer to the discussion following Eibl-Eibesfeldt's (1979a) review article in *The Behavioral and Brain Sciences*.

concern is to what extent human behavior can be reduced to genetic mechanisms and to what extent it reflects experiences that are transmitted from one generation to the next in a process of cultural learning or socialization. For the human ethologists the genetic basis of much uniquely human behavior is axiomatic; it is only a matter of finding the correct genetic pathways along which it developed. To us the more fundamental questions relate to the validity of the axiom.

Sociobiology. Human ethology as presented here can be seen as the European counterpart of the American school of sociobiology. Although the adherents of both traditions will point out certain differences, these are only small from the perspective of the present book. The foundation of sociobiology is the book *Sociobiology, the New Synthesis* by E. O. Wilson, published in 1975. It contains a powerful attempt to explain social behavior, including that of the human species, within the evolutionary framework. Central to the sociobiological doctrine is the axiom that the behavior of an individual organism is geared toward maximizing its *inclusive fitness*. The concept of fitness refers to the reproductive success of an organism; simply stated, high fitness implies a large number of offspring. Inclusive fitness is not limited to an organism's own offspring, but is extended to encompass also the organism's biological relationship to other relatives than direct descendants. An organism without its own children can be biologically successful when it has many procreating sisters, nephews, and other relatives with whom it shares many of its own genes. To promote the interests of its kin is in the evolutionary interest of the organism.

Classical evolution theory had been unable to account for altruistic behavior, except when it promotes the interests of direct descendants. Not only among humans, but also in other species one can frequently observe behaviors that seem incompatible with self-interest. Clear examples are found among insects such as bees and ants, where workers that do not produce their own offspring devote their entire life to the care of other members of the society. W. D. Hamilton (1964) demonstrated that the behavior of worker bees can be understood as self-serving given the principle of inclusive fitness. In the insect societies in which the kind of altruism mentioned is found among workers the genotype of males and females tends to be quite different. Females (including workers and queens) are *diploid*; they receive a double set of genes, just like, for example, human beings. One set comes from the father and one from the mother. Males are *haploid*; they only get one set of genes, namely from the mother. A queen bee can lay both unfertilized and fertilized eggs. The unfertilized eggs develop into males and the fertilized eggs into females. This implies that "sisters" have 3/4 of their genes in common; they share the entire genotype of their (homozygous) father and they share, on average, 1/2 of the genes they receive from their mother. Under these conditions "sisters" share even more genes than mothers and daughters, namely 3/4 as against 1/2.

Hamilton argued that worker bees may increase their own inclusive fitness more by looking after their "sisters" than by caring for their own offspring. This argument is strengthened by the role of male bees, who do not take part in the caretaking activities of the workers, do nothing to gather their own food, and live almost as parasites in the community. In evolution theory the key to the differences between workers and males is the genetic relationship, which between "brothers" and "sisters" is only 1/4 and thus much lower than that between "sisters."

Wilson had no hesitation in extending sociobiological arguments to human behavior. In the last chapter of his book, dealing with the human species, he argues that from an outsider's perspective "the humanities and social sciences shrink to specialized branches of biology; history, biography, and fiction are the research protocols of human ethology; and anthropology and sociology together constitute the sociobiology of a single primate species" (Wilson, 1975, p. 547).

Wilson's book has triggered a large amount of discussion about whether human cultural patterns can be reduced to evolutionary principles. The criterion for a biological origin is that a phenomenon occurs in a preponderance of human societies. Examples are male dominance, sexual taboos, and extended socialization of children. An area of particularly intensive study and speculation is that of human sexuality (e.g., Alcock, 1984, Chapter 15; Daly & Wilson, 1983; Symons, 1979). Men and women tend to differ systematically in their expressed desire for variety in sexual partners, with men being clearly more adulterous. Men are also more jealous about the promiscuity of their partner than women. These patterns fit different strategies for reproductive success, characteristic for the male and female sex not only among humans, but in most species (at least of mammals).

A woman can have only a limited number of offspring, given the energy, resources, and time she has to invest in each child during pregnancy and lactation. Pair bonding is in her interest so that her partner can help provide for her and her offspring. One mate should be enough to provide her with the maximal number of children she can have. The human male, like the male sex in most species, has a large capacity for reproduction. To achieve a large number of biological descendants the man's best strategy is to inseminate as many females as possible and to fight for this opportunity. However, there are factors that redress the success of this strategy. For example, the period of receptivity in the female menstrual cycle is not noticeable among humans, as it is among most other species; this is considered to be an adaptation with an advantage for the female. Presumably, her escort has to stay with her for a longer period if he wants to make sure that she will bear his child (Alcock, 1984). An alternative hypothesis is that females among our hominid ancestors who made themselves sexually available were more successful in obtaining meat from the hunters when hunting became a predominantly male activity (Symons, 1979).

A major dimension of reproductive strategy is represented by the notion of the r/K continuum. A high r-value refers to a large number of offspring with a low investment in parental care per individual offspring. Oysters producing enormous numbers of eggs left to develop on their own are an example. A K-oriented reproduction strategy implies a small number of offspring, but high parental investment in the survival of each of them. Most species of birds and larger mammals follow this strategy, but there are significant differences even between evolutionary closely related species. The r/K dimension is correlated with a variety of variables, ranging from the rate of maturation and the number of years in the life span to social organization and display of altruism.

Rushton (e.g., 1988), in a sweeping interpretation of various sources of data, has inferred that slight but consistent differences in reproductive strategy exist between the major human "races." In his opinion "Negroids" are more sexually active than "Mongoloids," with "Caucasoids" occupying a medium position. According to Rushton, these differences coincide with differences in maturation rate, personality variables, intelligence, and social organization. Obviously, Rushton's extraordinary claims have not gone un-challenged (e.g., Zuckerman & Brody, 1988). Such generalized claims draw-ing together highly divergent and impressionistic information are far too speculative to be scientifically acceptable and have a distinct flavor of racism.

Sociobiologists have no argument with the major findings of psychology and cultural anthropology. Learning mechanisms, for example, whether they are based on conditioning or imitation, can easily be incorporated in a genetic framework. Principles of learning can be seen as adaptations to certain ecological demands that have developed in the process of evolu-tion. For the sociobiologists, differences between cultural groups are merely variations on a common theme. As they see it, genetic constraints on human behavior allow only a small margin for cultural differences. Most social scientists disagree. What to sociobiologists like Wilson is merely a small margin is to many social scientists something much more. As Sahlins (1977) has stated: "Within the void left by biology lies the whole of anthropology."

Biological models of cultural transmission

In the first section of this chapter we described how genetic information is transmitted from generation to generation. The cultural transmission of information between members of a cultural group during the process of socialization, which does not necessarily require a biological relationship, was discussed in Chapter 2. Biologists have developed formal models in which the transmission of both genetic and cultural information is dealt with. Some of these models may be useful in cross-cultural psychology. The distinction between vertical, oblique, and horizontal transmission (cf. Cavalli-Sforza & Feldman, 1981) outlined in Chapter 2, is an example. Cavalli-Sforza and Feldman have developed a mathematical theory of the nongenetic transmis-sion of aspects of culture. One of the areas they discuss is the diffusion of innovations, for which mathematical descriptions can be made similar to those used to describe the spread through a population of an advantageous biological mutation.

The scope of most models goes beyond mere description. They are intended to put biological and cultural phenomena within a single explanatory framework. The sociobiological orientation of a unified evolutionary framework in which cultural phenomena are incorporated requires that the same mechanisms hold for both genetic and cultural transmission.

A sophisticated attempt to construct models of cultural transmission meeting this requirement is contained in a book by Lumsden and Wilson (1981). They postulate the notion of *culturegen*, which forms the basic unit of culture. A culturegen is a more or less homogeneous set of artifacts, behaviors, or mentifacts (Lumsden and Wilson's term). Transmission takes place via *epigenetic rules*. Epigenesis is the process of interaction between genes and the environment, but it is essentially a process controlled by genes. Any regularity in development that gives direction to behavior forms an epigenetic rule. Examples in Lumsden and Wilson's book include principles of perceptual information transmission and incest taboos. However, they go beyond these principles:

Human beings are thought [by cultural anthropologists] to pursue their own interest and that of their society on the basis of a very few simple structural biological needs by means of numerous, arbitrary, and often elaborate culturally acquired behaviors. In contrast to this conventional view, our interpretation of the evidence from cognitive and developmental psychology indicates the presence of epigenetic rules that have sufficiently great specificity to channel the acquisition of rules of inference and decision to a substantial degree. The process of mental canalization in turn shapes the trajectories of cultural evolution. (Lumsden & Wilson, 1981 p. 56)

These few sentences do not do justice to the sophisticated arguments presented by Lumsden and Wilson; however, they suffice to indicate the kind of concepts, essentially those found in genetics, that the authors use to describe cultural transmission.

Besides sociobiologists, who try to deal with cultural and biological transmission within a single framework, there are those who more clearly distinguish between biological and cultural transmission. They do not question the evolutionary basis of cultural variation and cultural change, but accept, contrary to orthodox sociobiologists like Lumsden and Wilson, that other mechanisms have to be postulated in addition to the natural selection of alternative alleles in the genetic constitution.[8]

---

[8] Among the authors who have constructed formal models we can also mention Cavalli-Sforza and Feldman (1981) and Durham (1982). Plotkin and Odling-Smee (1981) present a rather differentiated framework distinguishing three additional levels of evolution beyond genetic selection, namely development, individual learning, and socioculture. Of special importance is D. T. Campbell's evolutionary epistemology. Campbell (1960, 1975) has argued that natural selection provides an explanation of phenomena at a range of levels. He has postulated a hierarchy of knowledge processes, ranging from genetic adaptation via habit and instinct and via observational learning to science.

We shall pay somewhat more attention to the Dual Inheritance Model of Boyd and Richerson (1985). In addition to the genetic inheritance system that has been described in the first section of this chapter they postulate a cultural inheritance system that is based on learning. What an individual has learned during one's lifetime is not transmitted genetically; only the capacity for learning that is part of one's genotype is passed on to one's offspring and remains in the population. However, during a person's lifetime one can pass on cultural information to other members of one's group. This information can stay in the possession of the group from generation to generation. The transmission of cultural information has "population-level consequences" according to Boyd and Richerson (1985, p. 4).

The cultural and genetic inheritance systems differ, among other things, in the nature of parenthood. Cultural traits can be transmitted by cultural parents who may well be different from the biological parents. It is likely that an individual has a fairly large number of cultural parents, including teachers, sibling, and peers, from whom one acquires information. As we have seen in Chapter 2, Cavalli-Sforza and Feldman (1981) speak in this context about oblique and horizontal transmission. Also, in the cultural inheritance system specific experiences gained during an individual's lifetime can be transmitted to one's cultural offspring and become part of the inheritance of the group. This is in contrast to genetic transmission, which can only have an effect through a differential rate of reproduction.

The close analogy between biological and cultural transmission in the theorizing of Boyd and Richerson is especially evident in the mechanisms that they postulate for explaining cultural change. Apart from "mutations" (that is error rates due to imperfect memory) and chance variations due to selective retention of information in certain groups, an important place in the transmission of information is attributed to social learning and systematic biases.

Social learning is distinguished from individual learning. The latter is based on trial and error or conditioning principles. Boyd and Richerson believe that a large cultural repertoire cannot be acquired by socially controlled conditioning of youngsters. This process would be too uneconomical. They attach great importance to Bandura's (1977) social learning theory, in which imitation of behaviors that have only been observed, is seen as a sufficient condition for learning. Social learning by observation and imitation leads to cultural stability of behavior patterns. Individual learning shaped by specific environmental conditions leads to change. However, behavior patterns acquired in an individual learning process can be dependent on contingencies of a specific situation that do not apply in other situations to which the pattern is generalized. Hence, individual learning has a higher rate of error than social learning. Considerations such as these are reflected in formal models of transmission that Boyd and Richerson have constructed in analogy with models of genetic transmission. The relative incidence of individual and social learning is one of the parameters in these models. The consequences of a change in this parameter, for example on the rate of responsiveness to changes in the environment, can be calculated.

The models are further elaborated through the inclusion of the concept of *transmission bias*. An individual within a culture is exposed to different variants of the available cultural repertoire. In a static culture the relative frequency of the variants presumably would remain constant (in accordance with the Hardy-Weinberg law). But Boyd and Richerson assume that the available options can be evaluated and the most adaptive variant selected. This is illustrated with the example of a child learning to play table tennis and observing that there are two ways to hold the bat, the "racquet" grip and the "pencil" grip. No bias occurs when the child chooses randomly one player as a role model, but there are other possibilities. After some practice, the child can choose the grip with which one obtains the best results. If it takes too much practice to find this out, another option is to use the most successful player as a model. Still another option is to simply follow the majority in one's choice.

This strategy, a *conformist* one, is linked by Boyd and Richerson to altruism, or cooperation, and to ethnocentrism. The conformist strategy, which makes people follow the most popular variant in a group, leads to a decrease in cultural variation within groups relative to the between-group variation. Even though cooperation with group members rather than the pursuit of self-interest can be disadvantageous to the individual (and thus should have disappeared in the process of evolution according to traditional evolution theory), the lower fitness of cooperators within groups can have been offset by a higher survival rate of groups with a high frequency of cooperators. If this is the case, a high frequency of cooperators is maintained more or less indefinitely. At the same time the conformist bias can only have this effect if the cooperative behavior is restricted to a limited group. One kind of group that seems to meet the requirement of the models is the cultural group with the associated characteristics of ethnocentrism, including cooperative behavior toward members of the in-group and uncooperative behavior toward the out-group. It may be noted that in this paragraph the fitness of groups is defined in terms of the biological mechanism of natural selection. Boyd and Richerson explicitly assume that natural selection can operate on the cultural inheritance system as well as on the genetic inheritance system. However, the Boyd and Richerson theory is not the same as sociobiology. It leads to predictions that deviate from an exclusively genetic theory.

The precise relationship between biological and cultural transmission remains largely unclear, but models such as those of Boyd and Richerson may make possible the quantification of transmission effects, including those that are cultural rather than biological. Behavioral and social sciences have long treated both constancy and change in cultural behavior patterns as a given, without paying much attention to how they evolve. Cross-cultural psychology should attend to this issue, and approaches like that of Boyd and Richerson can help us to do so.

Conclusions

Evolutionism in ethological and sociobiological writings does not meet the requirements of a testable scientific theory (compare Popper, 1979, p. 267). Even if the genetic basis of behavior in a general sense is accepted (and we have no intention to question this principle), one still can ask to what extent the genetic predisposition determines behavior. Biologically speaking we cannot really go against our genes, but behavior implies a range of responses and the question is what is the space in which we can operate.

The human species, although morphologically and physiologically quite similar to other species, occupies a unique position psychologically. The facilities for conscious reflection and the formulation of long-term goals and plans that can be reached by a variety of routes add a dimension to human behavior not found in other species. To the extent that behavior patterns are not genetically fixed, it is a dimension of possibilities (see Chapter 10). To define its parameters, much more insight into cross-cultural variations and invariances of behavior is needed than is presently available.

In the meantime we have to be careful not to fall into the dogmatic and ideological traps either of those ethologists and sociobiologists who are so convinced about gene-culture interrelations that they are inclined to see any coincidence as a causal relationship or of those environmentalistically minded social scientists who cling to the view that the biological basis is largely irrelevant to the study of human behavior.

Inasmuch as it makes sense to accept sociocultural evolution as a relevant determinant of cultures as we find them today, there is an important warning issued by D. T. Campbell (1975), who argued that in an evolutionary framework, cultural inheritance has to be regarded as adaptive. He pleads that when we come across puzzling and incomprehensible features of a culture, including our own, we should search diligently for ways in which it might make adaptive sense.

This chapter will capture methodological aspects of the cross-cultural re-search process, emphasizing concerns that are prominent in this enterprise. As already noted in Chapter 1 there is much more to a cross-cultural study than collecting data in two countries and comparing the results. In Chapters 4 and 5 we have seen that differences in test scores may not reflect differences in the traits supposedly measured by the tests. Here the interpretation of cross-cultural data will be explored more systematically. We shall see that interpretations have to be guarded carefully against *alternative explanations* and against the effects of *cultural bias* in measurement procedures.

In a sense this chapter provides the skeleton of cross-cultural research, showing little of the flesh and the skin. Methodological principles are pre-sented as rather rigid standards, but we realize that these standards rarely can be met in practice and that cross-cultural research would come to a grinding halt if they were rigorously applied. Still, research has to be guided by these standards, even though they usually cannot be met completely but only approximately. Students of cross-cultural psychology have to know them in order to be able to critically evaluate the extant literature and to pinpoint weak spots in design and analysis. In laying out these standards we provide criteria in terms of which empirical studies can be evaluated. This determines how much confidence one can have in findings that have been reported.

The two major methodological issues in an empirical research project, the design of a study and the analysis of the results, constitute the two themes of this chapter. The first section discusses the design of cross-cultural studies and the controls that are available to researchers to protect their results against alternative explanations. In addition problems of sampling at the level of cultures, groups within cultures, and individual subjects are dealt with.

The second section presents a classification of psychological variables. Few data in cross-cultural studies are responses to specific stimuli manipulated under laboratory conditions. The study of behavior in more naturalistic contexts knows a range of approaches from experimental to holistic. One of the major questions in cross-cultural psychology is whether behavior has to be understood in the context of the culture in which it occurs or whether cultural differences can be conceived of as variations on a common theme. Two contrasts, between the *emic* as opposed to the *etic*, and between the *cultural* as opposed to the *cross-cultural* approach, are discussed.

In the third section, dealing with analysis of data, the central question is how one can decide whether or not psychological data are "equivalent" or "unbiased," that is, whether equal scores obtained by subjects from a different cultural background do or do not have the same meaning. Judgmental methods employing expert ratings on the culture appropriateness of stimuli as well as psychometric analyses of bias are reviewed.

In the last section, on the interpretation of data, a distinction is made between levels of inference made from results of cross-cultural studies. With some inferences researchers stay close to the data; the validity of comparisons is then open to statistical analysis. Other inferences move much further away from the data; these amount to sweeping claims, which, as we shall see, escape all empirical examination.

Designing cross-cultural studies

A cross-cultural study usually starts with a psychologically interesting difference in behavior between two or more cultural groups. A tentative explanation of the difference is then formulated on the basis of some theory. To test this explanation, a study is designed for which data have to be collected in various cultures. As discussed in Chapter 10, in such studies "culture" entails some sort of "treatment" or "condition," in the sense of an experiment (Strodtbeck, 1964).

The leading research paradigm in academic psychology was for a long time that of the controlled experiment; however, it is seldom available to cross-cultural researchers. This is somewhat unfortunate, because the results of a well-designed experiment are less open to alternative interpretations than those obtained with other forms of scientific inquiry. In the experimental paradigm a distinction is made between the independent variable (denoting a set of stimulus conditions or treatments) and the dependent variable (describing a set of behaviors or responses). An experiment is meant to investigate the antecedent-consequent relationship between these two variables.

In a well-designed experiment the researcher has control over the treatments administered to the subjects in the various experimental conditions as well as over ambient variables. In addition, the researcher can assign subjects at random to the various conditions so that any prior differences between them that may affect their responses are randomly distributed across conditions. However, for many studies in real-life situations, intact groups are used that differ from each other in many ways. Each variable that potentially has an effect on the dependent variable has to be taken into account in the explanation of the observed differences; otherwise it leaves room for an alternative explanation of the differences (D. T. Campbell, 1969; Cook & Campbell, 1979).

In cross-cultural research it is difficult to rule out all plausible alternative explanations. This will be explained with reference to two points: the allocation of subjects and the lack of "experimental control" over cultural condi-

Table 9-1. *Control over treatment conditions and the assignment of subjects* (after Malpass & Poortinga, 1986)

	Control over treatment			
Control over subject allocation	Control over treatment and *most* ambient events	Control over treatment and *few* ambient events	No control of treatment or ambient events	
			selection of populations	ad hoc choice of populations
Random assignment of subjects to treatments	True experiment			
Group membership, *weak* effects on exchangeability		Quasi-experiment		
group membership, *strong* effects on exchangeability			Cross-cultural comparative study	Cross-cultural studies with post-test only

tions that are taken as independent variables. Much of our argument is summarized in Table 9-1. Down the vertical axis three categories of subject allocation are indicated. On the horizontal axis there are four categories that differ in the degree of control by the researcher over the actual treatment and over confounding variables.

In a laboratory experiment subjects are allocated at random to experimental conditions. It is a plausible assumption that there would be no essential change in results if the outcome of the allocation procedure had led to a different distribution of subjects over conditions. There are no apparent factors on which the subgroups assigned to the various conditions will differ systematically.

In studies with already existing groups of subjects the allocation of subjects is not strictly random. Such studies of nonequivalent groups are referred to as *quasi-experiments.* Consider an educational research project where different teaching methods are administered to school classes with a view to comparing the effectiveness of these methods. On some variables there will be systematic differences between schools, for example in the competence of the teaching staff and the average socioeconomic status of pupils. However, the set of variables on which differences will occur is limited and will generally be small. A researcher would not be concerned if children moved from one school to another prior to the start of the study.

In the case of cultural populations the set of variables on which subjects differ is immense and the differences tend to be much larger than within a single society. Socialization practices, availability of words for certain concepts, education, religious beliefs, and access to mass communication media are only some of the many variables that can differ between groups. The impact becomes evident when one tries to imagine subject exchange between cultures; this is impossible, since any one subject is inherently linked to one culture.

Another feature that distinguishes an experiment from a nonexperimental study is the control over the treatment administered to a subject. In the laboratory the researcher defines the treatment, although even there control over the motivation of the subject and other ambient variables is imperfect. In field testing, for example of educational programs, the lack of precision in control tends to be far greater, especially when the treatment extends over weeks or even months. In addition to the treatment, pupils undergo many other experiences that can affect their performance. However, within the limitations of administration accuracy the researcher still has control over the treatment as such.

Direct control over treatment is usually not available in cross-cultural research. Cultural factors extend their influence over a long period of time. The effect of a postulated cultural factor is typically inferred *post hoc* from differences between groups on a measurement. Cross-cultural researchers have to be aware of this when interpreting their findings.

In the cross-cultural literature some powerful psychological influences have been identified, each of which has an effect on a broad range of measurements. The most important is school education, Western style. It forms part of a complex of which literacy in a foreign language, test taking experience, urbanization, economic wealth, and acculturation all can form part. It is hard even to imagine a psychological measurement unaffected by such variables.

Controls available in cross-cultural research. The absence of direct control through manipulation of treatment and through subject allocation does not mean that valid explanation is out of reach; it is only more difficult to achieve than in other areas of psychology. We shall briefly mention four kinds of measures for reducing plausible alternative explanations of differences between cultural groups (cf. also Malpass & Poortinga, 1986).

The *a priori* selection of cultural populations is the form of control that distinguishes cross-cultural studies from the type of study in which measurements are taken only *post hoc* (the post-test-only design) and where the vulnerability to incorrect interpretation is so high. It is only within the context of a theory that differences between cultural groups on some dependent variable can be predicted from their position on an independent variable (Malpass, 1977). If the actual results fit the predictions, the plausibility of the theory from which the predictions were derived increases.

When groups are included for reasons other than their position on the independent variable, the most important form of experimental control in a comparative study is lost. Many studies of ethnic or minority groups are a case in point. In this kind of research the selection of a minority and the majority within a society is confounded. Differences between these groups can be ascribed to factors in the minority, the majority, or the interaction between the two. Prevailing notions of social scientists are often an important determinant in the choice of a particular interpretation (Howard & Scott, 1981; Pettigrew, 1983). Preference should be given to minority research projects that are comparative, extending across societies (cf. Berry, Kim, Minde, & Mok, 1987).

A second strategy for eliminating competing alternatives is available if the dependent variable can be expressed as a function of two or more separate scores. An example is the score that can be obtained by taking the difference between scores on two measurements. The approach can be illustrated with the study on visual information processing among Kpelle and North American subjects (Cole, Gay, & Glick, 1968) mentioned in Chapter 6. It was found that the Kpelle did less well in estimating the number of dots in a tachistoscopically presented display than subjects from the U.S. This finding is of little interest, since many explanations can be thought of that have nothing to do with the processing of visual information. Of interest is that Cole and his associates found the intercultural difference to be larger when the dots formed regular patterns than when they were randomly scattered. Of many uncontrolled variables (such as motivation of the subjects, comprehension of the task), it can be reasonably assumed that they had an equal effect in the experimental conditions. Therefore, it is a plausible conclusion that the American subjects made more use of the organization of dots in the stimulus display.

A third form of control open to the cross-cultural researcher is the elimination of effects of irrelevant variables through statistical analysis (e.g., by means of analysis of covariance or regression techniques). Although some alternative explanations can be ruled out, statistical control remains a poor alternative to experimental control (e.g., D. T. Campbell, 1969; Holland & Rubin, 1983). Of course, the elimination of a particular explanation through statistical analysis requires that relevant information is available. This means that the variables that can provide this information have to be included in the design of a study.

The fourth type of control involves the extension of the data base from which an interpretation is derived. An important strategy is to use more than one method of measurement. One can have more confidence in a finding (such as black-white differences in the U.S. on external versus internal locus of control as described in Chapter 4) if this is established not only by means of self-report scales, but also with interviews, analyses of life histories, and so forth.

The distinction between convergent and discriminant validity (D. T. Campbell & Fiske, 1959) is relevant here. Evidence about validity can be obtained from relationships between variables that are expected on theoretical and/or empirical grounds; this is *convergent validation*. Evidence can also be derived from the absence of relationships between variables for which no relationship should theoretically be found. This is *discriminant validation*. For example, if in none of the cultures investigated there is a correlation between the scores on a test and the level of education of subjects, it becomes less likely that an intercultural difference in education is the reason for cross-cultural differences that have been found for the test scores.

Before concluding this subsection we want to emphasize that extension of the data base is certainly not a panacea for better cross-cultural research. In Box 9-1 it is illustrated how with more data the probability of finding an *in*valid difference can sometimes also increase.

Sampling. Three levels of sampling will be distinguished. First a choice has to be made regarding which cultural groups are to be included in a study. Then the question arises whether or not the selection can be restricted to certain groups within each culture. Finally, it has to be decided how individuals are to be selected within each culture or group (cf. Lonner & Berry, 1986b).

There are two acceptable strategies for the *selection of cultures* in comparative studies. Most common is the choice of only a few cultures clearly differing on some variable that is of interest to the cross-cultural psychologist. The second and less common strategy is to draw a sample of cultures that can be considered representative of all the cultures in the world.

Often a particular culture is included in a study as the result of a chance meeting at a conference with a colleague who is willing to collect data in another culture or the opportunity to visit a particular country. As we have seen, however, the research topic should be dictated by a theoretically interesting contrast between the cultures concerned rather than by mere opportunity.

This means that cultures should be selected that differ on the postulated independent variable that is the focus of research. The initial selection has to be made on the basis of available information, for example from the ethnographic literature (see Chapter 7). It is recommended that a check be carried out whether the presumed differences on the independent variable indeed are present. This was done by Segall, Campbell, and Herskovits (1966), who in their study on visual illusions (see Chapter 6) included a questionnaire with items on environmental features. It was to be completed by local researchers for the group in which they collected the data.

What is being described here as the ideal resembles theory-driven research in the tradition of experimental research. In actual practice much of the ongoing cross-cultural research is concerned with dependent variables, that is, the identification of phenomena that can be considered important and worthy of explanation (LeVine, 1970).

Sometimes a culture is included in a study to serve as a reference standard. If researchers take their own culture as a reference, they can check whether the results (levels and patterns of scores) conform to prior expectations. This

---

Box 9-1   The questionable null-hypothesis

In an experimental study the research hypothesis is accepted when the null-hypothesis can be rejected with a certain level of confidence. When testing the null-hypothesis, two errors can be made. A Type I error occurs when the null-hypothesis is wrongly rejected. There is no difference between conditions, but the outcome of the test leads the researcher to believe there is. A Type II error is made when the null-hypothesis is actually false but not rejected (e.g., Hays, 1988). For the ideal experiment the probability of both types of errors can be estimated. The accuracy of a statistical test of the null-hypothesis can be improved by increasing the number of subjects or by replication studies. In other words, the margin of error can be reduced by investing more effort. However, if a difference between groups is due to some other factor than the one intended to be measured, extension of the data base does not lead to a more accurate assessment of the probability of a valid intergroup difference, but to an increased confidence in the *erroneous* rejection of the null-hypothesis.

This is illustrated in Figure 9-1. The vertical axis gives the probability that a significant difference is found (alpha < .05). On the horizontal axis the sample size is given. The broken line gives the probability of a Type I error in unbiased data; it is independent of the sample size. The solid lines show that the probability of a significant difference is higher when a "bias" is added to the scores of one of two groups with an otherwise equal score distribution. As we shall see later in this chapter the term *bias* refers to all unwanted factors that unequally affect scores in different cultural groups. The size of the bias is expressed in standard deviation units (i.e., 1/16 sd, 1/8 sd, and 1/4 sd). The solid lines also indicate that the probability of a significant difference between the means of the two groups increases with the sample size.

The thrust of this argument is that the null-hypothesis is a fairly meaningless proposition unless the presence of even a small amount of bias can be ruled out with confidence. The implications have been formulated by Malpass and Poortinga (1986) as follows: "In view of the high *a priori* probability of ambient factors contributing to the observed differences, the likelihood of erroneous inference is so high that in general the results of cross-cultural comparative studies cannot be taken seriously if alternative explanations are not explicitly considered and, preferably, excluded on the basis of empirical evidence. We feel strongly about this point since it can be argued that the high probability of finding differences in the long run will tend to have cumulative effects on our insights about the impact of cultural variation on behavior" (pp. 51–52).

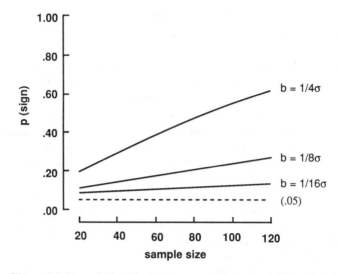

Figure 9-1 The relationship between sample size and the probability (p) that a significant difference (alpha <.05) will be found resulting from a bias effect (b). (After Malpass & Poortinga, 1986.)

is particularly useful when newly constructed methods are used. If the findings in a familiar culture do not fit expectations, the validity of the results in other cultures is highly questionable.

Additional cultures can be included in a study to obtain a better distribution over the range of an independent variable; this is the technique of stratified sampling (e.g., Kish, 1965.) With an extension of the number of cultures, sooner or later the strategy of drawing a sample at random from all the cultures in the world has to be considered. The size of such a sample depends on the degree of accuracy required, but for most variables it should certainly not contain less than twenty or twenty-five cases.[1] For Osgood's *Atlas of Affective Meaning* (Osgood, Suci, & Tannenbaum, 1957) data were collected in thirty countries, but the populations concerned cannot be considered a random sample of all cultures. For one thing, the subjects all had to be literate. This is also true for the sampling in other large-scale psychological studies that have been reported, for example, by Hofstede (1980) on work-related values and by J. E. Williams and Best (1982) on gender stereotypes, mentioned in Chapter 3.

There is a fairly large number of hologeistic studies (that is, studies that employ a sample of cultures from all over the world) in cultural anthropology that include nonliterate societies. They are based on available descriptions,

---

[1] A general rule cannot be given. The accuracy of results is dependent on how reliably societies can be distinguished from each other on the variable concerned. (See J. Cohen, 1988, for further information.)

mainly from the Human Relations Area Files (HRAF) that were mentioned in Chapters 2 and 7.

There are two aspects of sampling that have received far more attention in anthropology than in cross-cultural psychology. The first is known as Galton's problem (Naroll, 1970b; Naroll, Michik, & Naroll, 1980). It has to do with the spreading of cultural characteristics through contacts between groups. If two cultures have a similar score on a variable, this may be due to the exchange of knowledge and artifacts through contact and communication. As we have seen in Chapter 7, Naroll (1970b) has suggested ways to avoid this problem, which are based on the assumption that similarities between neighboring groups are more likely to reflect diffusion than are similarities between groups living at a large geographical distance from each other. After all, probability of diffusion over great distances is less than between neighbors.

The second problem is at what level cultures should be defined. At the most general level there are the six cultural areas distinguished by Murdock (1967), namely Sub-Saharan Africa, Asia, Australasia, Circum-Mediterranean, North America, and South America. On many dimensions of interest to psychologists (for example, literacy, socialization practices, collectivism) the range of variation *within* certain cultural areas is about as large as the variation *between* these areas. Therefore, selection of a sample stratified according to areas (for example, picking an equal number of cultures from each) serves a useful purpose in only a limited number of instances.

At a somewhat less general level societies are confounded with nation-states. In articles published in the *Journal of Cross-Cultural Psychology* and the *International Journal of Psychology* "culture" quite typically coincides with "country." In cultural anthropology this is considered an unacceptable practice. The definition of a culture, more properly named a "culture bearing unit" (or "cultunit"), has to coincide with the level at which a variable is operating. If political organization is of interest, the nation-state is the appropriate unit of selection. But in a study of the psychological effects of tonality in language the unit of selection should be the language group. Child-rearing practices usually will have to be defined on smaller culture-bearing units, as there can be large differences within a country, for example between urban and rural groups.

The underlying principles can be summarized in two points. First, the definition of a culture-bearing unit depends on the nature of the independent variable studied. Second, culture-bearing units have to be selected to cover adequately the range of variation on this variable.

The relative lack of concern among cross-cultural psychologists for a precise definition of culture-bearing units can also have implications for the *selection of subgroups* within these units. It is usually a fallacy to assume homogeneity of cultures with respect to the factor studied. Most, if not all, psychological variables show systematic variation between the members of a culture-bearing unit. This implies that there are virtually always groups that are distinguishable in terms of high and low scores. Therefore, the size of a cross-cultural difference will depend directly on the selection of particular groups.

It is almost impossible to select a group in one culture that will precisely match a group in another culture. Strong warnings have been issued against the use of matched samples in comparative culture studies (Draguns, 1982; Lonner & Berry, 1986b). The crux of the objections is that matching on one variable almost without exception leads to mismatching on other variables. Suppose a researcher would like samples of Americans and Africans matched on education. Educated Africans are more likely than the average citizen of their country to have a high income and a high social status, while they are less likely to value traditional norms and customs.

In a representative sample each member of the population of interest has an equal probability of selection. This requires random *selection of individuals*. The samples used in cross-cultural research seldom if ever even get close to meeting this requirement. It depends on the distributions of relevant variables in the populations to be investigated whether deviations from a random selection procedure have serious effects on the outcome of a study. Again, the sampling procedure is rather immaterial when individual differences (within-group variance) are small compared to the differences between cultures (between-group variance). But for many psychological variables the former clearly exceed the latter.

The following conclusions emerge from this discussion. First, cross-cultural researchers should be careful not to generalize their results to large cultural populations of which the subjects tested are not selected by some random procedure. As far as we can see this does not lead to serious methodological or theoretical problems. The contrast between Southeast Asia and North America is rarely of more psychological interest than between the people of two small groups within the two areas. A consequence of this recommendation is the need for a fairly detailed description of the populations in a comparative study. Second, the requirement for random selection of individuals within the population of interest applies in cross-cultural psychology just as much as in other areas of psychology.

Psychological data in cultural context

Apart from the experimental approach that was discussed in the previous section there are other approaches in cross-cultural psychology to which we shall now turn.

Classification of contexts. In earlier chapters we have come across methodological approaches at the individual level (using psychological tests and behavioral observations) as well as population-level research (with data from the HRAF and field ethnography as methods). To bring these two levels as well as related notions together we propose the scheme presented in Figure 9-2.

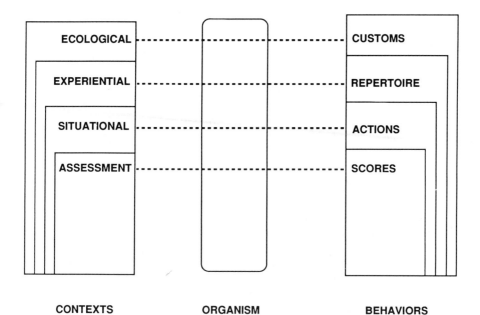

Figure 9-2 Scheme for integrating contexts and outcomes at four levels. (After Berry, 1980a.)

The goals of the scheme are to link psychological effects or outcomes (on the right) to their contexts (on the left) across the scheme; to do so at four distinct levels (down the scheme) ranging from naturalistic (at the top) to controlled (at the bottom) forms of research; and to link the four levels of contexts by "nesting" each one in the level above it.

Traditionally, much of the discipline of psychology has attempted to comprehend behavior as a function of stimuli impinging upon an individual. The approach of ecological psychology (e.g., Brunswik, 1957; Barker, 1969, 1978) has noted that the stimuli usually employed in psychology represent only a very narrow range of all possible stimuli and that they are excessively artificial in character. As a result, ecological psychology has emphasized the need to study behavior in more naturalistic contexts. Similarly, as we have mentioned frequently, cross-cultural psychology proposes that we should be attending to broad ranges of situations drawn from a cross-section of cultures. Sampling from new cultures also means sampling from the new physical environmental contexts in which the cultures are situated. Thus, it is essential that the extension of research cross-culturally be accompanied by increased attention to the natural environmental settings of the cultures studied, a position similar to that espoused by ecological psychology and presented in our general framework (Figure 1-3). Figure 9-2 represents four relationships (perhaps sometimes causal linkages) between environmental contexts and behavioral outcomes. Toward the top of the model are natural and holistic contexts and outcomes, while at the bottom they are more experimental (controlled and reductionistic).

Looking in more detail at the environmental contexts, the *ecological context* is the "natural-cultural habitat" of Brunswik (1957) or the "preperceptual world" of Barker (1969). It consists of all the relatively stable and permanent characteristics of the habitat that provide the context for human action and includes the population-level variables identified in Figure 1-3: the ecological context, the sociopolitical context, and the general cultural and biological adaptations made by the group.

Nested in this ecological context are two levels of the "life space" or "psychological world" of Lewin (1936). The first, the *experiential context*, is that pattern of recurrent experiences that provides a basis for individual learning and development; it is essentially the set of independent variables that cross-cultural psychology tries to spot as being operative for individuals in a particular habitat during the development of behavioral characteristics. These variables include such day-to-day experiences as child-rearing practices, occupational training, and education. The other, the *situational context*, is the limited set of environmental circumstances (the "setting" of Barker, 1969), which may be observed to account for particular behaviors at a given time and place. They include features such as specific roles or social interactions that can influence how a person will respond to that setting.

The fourth context, the *assessment context*, represents those environmental characteristics, such as test items or stimulus conditions, that are designed by the psychologist to elicit a particular response or test score. The assessment context may or may not be nested in the first three contexts; the degree to which it is nested represents the ecological validity of the task.

Paralleling these four contexts are four behavioral outcomes. The first, *customs*, refers to the complex, long-standing, and developed behavior patterns in the population or culture that are in place as a traditional response to the ecological context. Customs include established, collective, and shared patterns of behavior exhibited by a cultural group.

The second, *repertoire*, is the relatively stable complex of behaviors that have been learned over time in the recurrent experiential or learning context. Included are the skills, traits, and attitudes that have been nurtured in particular roles or acquired by specific training or education whether formal or informal. The third effect, *actions*, connotes those behaviors that appear in response to immediate stimulation or experience. In contrast to repertoire they are not so much a function of role experience or long-term training, but appear in reply to immediate situational experiences.

The fourth effect, *scores*, is comprised of those behaviors that are observed, measured, and recorded during psychological assessment (experiments, interviews, or testing). If the assessment context is nested in the other contexts, the scores will be representative of the repertoire of the organism and the customs of the population.

Relationships can be traced between the environmental contexts and the behavioral outcomes across the scheme (dotted lines in Figure 9-2). The first level is concerned with the life situation (in physical, environmental, and cultural terms) and its relationship to daily customs and practices of the population. It is here that other disciplines (such as anthropology and ecology) can supply valuable information to cross-cultural psychology. The second level is concerned with tying together recurrent experiences of individuals with their characteristic repertoire of behaviors. The third level is interested in more specific acts as a function of immediate and current experience. And the fourth level is devoted to the systematic study of relationships between stimuli and the scores obtained by individuals.

A recurrent problem for general experimental psychology, in terms of this scheme, has been the difficulty of contributing to an understanding of relationships at the three higher levels while collecting data almost exclusively at the lowest level. The problem facing cross-cultural psychology is more complex. Rather than ascend the reductionistic-holistic dimension to achieve ecological validity, cross-cultural psychology has typically failed to work systematically at all levels to achieve a specification of context variables that are responsible for task performance and behavioral variation across natural habitats. In our view only when tests and experimental tasks and outcomes (scores) are understood in terms of their relationships with variables in the upper levels of the scheme will cross-cultural psychologists be able to grasp the meaning of their data.

Statistical techniques for analyzing data from more than one culture and more than one level are available. An approach for analyzing the effects of context variables (those variables on the left side of Figure 9-2) on outcome variables has been described by Poortinga and Van de Vijver (1987). They see a cross-cultural study as successful when all differences between cultures on an outcome variable have been explained in terms of context variables. Their analysis includes a dependent variable, samples of subjects from two or more cultures, and one or more context variables (measured at the individual or the population level).

The analysis starts with determining whether there is a significant differ-ence between cultures on the outcome (dependent) variable. If this is the case, the next step of the analysis establishes how much of this between-culture variance can be explained by each of the available context variables. More and more of the variance is "peeled off," until ideally no difference between the cultures is left to be explained. The goal of the analysis is to split the total "culture" effect on the dependent variable into components that can be accounted for by various context variables.[2]

---

[2] Statistically the analysis takes the form of a stepwise multiple regression analysis or an analysis of covariance (e.g., Pedhazur, 1982; J. Cohen & P. Cohen, 1983). Poortinga and Van de Vijver (1987) point out that context variables have to be carefully chosen; they should not be in any way confounded with the outcome variable and they should be measured at least at an ordinal and preferably at an interval scale level.

Table 9-2. *The emic approach versus the etic approach (Berry, 1969)*

Emic approach	Etic approach
studies behavior from within the system.	studies behaviour from a position outside the system.
examines only one culture.	examines many cultures, comparing them.
structure discovered by the analyst.	structure created by the analyst.
criteria are relative to internal characteristics.	criteria are considered absolute or universal.

The need to distinguish in the analysis of data between population and individual differences has been advocated by Bond and Leung (Chinese Culture Connection, 1987; Leung and Bond, 1989; Leung, 1989). They follow up on a concern expressed by Hofstede (1980). However, little has been done to develop appropriate analytical techniques in cross-cultural psychology. For this reason we refer to the education literature where the problem of multiple levels (for example, pupil, class, school, district) has not only been recognized, but statistical techniques for separating their effects in a single analysis have been developed (Burstein, 1980; Aitkin & Longford, 1986).

In summary, researchers should employ methods that will give them access to both population- and individual-level information that is sufficiently rich to provide a full interpretation of their results. All too often in cross-cultural psychology we find studies that leap from a very limited knowledge of the *ecological context* (for example "they are herders," or "they are immigrants") to an explanation of the *scores* obtained from an experiment or test. The argument being made here is that such interpretations are only valid when both contexts and outcomes at all four levels are included in the research.

Emic and etic orientations. Many cross-culturalists make a distinction between culture-specific and culture-general (or universal) aspects of behavior. The former are referred to as *emic*, the latter as *etic* aspects. As explained in Segall et al. (1990) the terms *emic* and *etic* were originally coined by Pike (1967) in analogy with phonetics and phonemics. In the field of linguistics phonemics is the study of the sounds used in a particular language; phonetics refers to the study of general aspects of vocal sounds and sound production. Berry (1969) has summarized Pike's comments on the emic-etic distinction as it applies in psychology. This summary is presented in Table 9-2.

Many researchers argue that behavior in its full complexity can only be understood within the context of the culture in which it occurs. In the emic approach an attempt is made to look at phenomena and their interrelationships (structure) through the eyes of the people native to a particular culture. One tries to avoid the imposition of *a priori* notions and ideas from one's own culture on the people studied. This point of view finds its origin in cultural anthropology, where, via the method of participant observation, the researcher tries to look at norms, values, motives, and customs through the eyes of the members of a particular community.

In personality research a distinction is often made between idiographic and nomothetic research (e.g., Pervin, 1975). The emic approach is reminiscent of the descriptive idiographic orientation with emphasis on the uniqueness of each individual, although a culture rather than an individual is the unit of analysis. In this analogy there is also a parallel between the nomothetic and the etic orientations. In both, the identification of lawful relationships and causal explanation are the primary goals.

The danger of an etic approach is that the concepts and notions of researchers are rooted in and influenced by their cultural background. They are working with "imposed" etics (Berry, 1969, p. 124) or "pseudo" etics (Triandis, Malpass, & Davidson, 1972, p. 6). The goal of empirical analysis is to change progressively the "imposed" etics to match the emic viewpoint of the culture studied. This should lead eventually to the formulation of "derived" etics that are valid cross-culturally.

More extensive listings of distinctive features between emic and etic than the one given by Berry have appeared in the literature (Pelto & Pelto, 1981; Ekstrand & Ekstrand, 1986). These tend to further subdivide the contrasts listed in Table 9-2. On the other hand the emic-etic distinction has also been criticized, notably by Jahoda (1977, 1983). Jahoda notes that in cultural anthropology, where they originated, the terms emic and etic are used at the level of cultural *systems*; they are research orientations. In cross-cultural psychology interest is primarily focused on the measurement of *variables* and the analysis of relationships between variables. To label research orientations with the same term that one uses for types of variables may be confusing. Jahoda thus recommends that the emic-etic distinction be abandoned. He suggests that at the empirical level the contrast between universal and culture-specific is entirely adequate and that this pair of terms does not have any undesirable surplus meaning.

The literature is not very informative when one is looking for empirical procedures to separate the emic from the etic. Berry (1969, 1989) has suggested an iterative approach, which is outlined in Figure 9-3. Researchers will typically start with an imposed etic. They will scrutinize their conceptions and methods for culture appropriateness and modify them in an emic phase. When the investigation is successful, they will end up with a modified or derived etic in terms of which valid comparisons can be made, at least across the cultures concerned. Extension of the research will ultimately lead to so

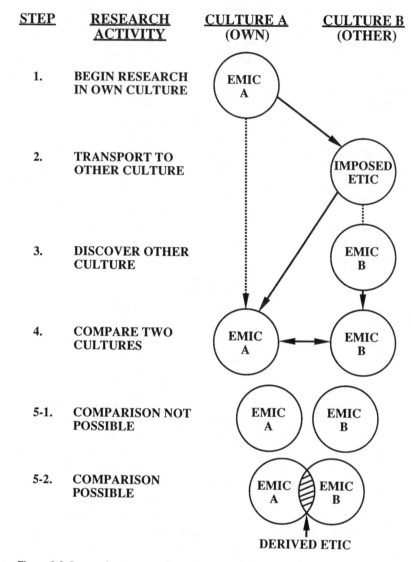

Figure 9-3 Steps taken to operationalize emics and etics. (After Berry, 1989.)

much evidence that it can be reasonably concluded that a psychological characteristic is universally present. So far this conceptual scheme has not been strictly implemented in an empirical project, although the underlying rationale has guided many researchers who are concerned about the cultural idiosyncrasies of their work.

Triandis (e.g., Triandis, 1978; Hui & Triandis, 1985) has recommended the "combined etic-emic" approach, which is similar to the strategy advocated by

Berry. The researcher begins with a construct that appears to be etic and then develops emic (culture-appropriate) ways of measuring it. This implies that instruments are constructed locally in each cultural setting. It is claimed that with such an instrument an emically defined etic construct is obtained that can be used for comparisons. There is empirical research conducted along these lines (cf. Davidson, Jaccard, Triandis, Morales, & Diaz-Guerrero, 1976). However, it is not entirely clear how the validity of such claims can be established unambiguously if instruments differ in content from culture to culture (cf. Poortinga, 1979).

Concerns similar to those captured in the emic-etic distinction are reflected in the contrast between *cross-cultural* and *cultural* approaches. In the emic-etic literature shortcomings and pitfalls of the traditional psychometric and experimental methods are emphasized, but research projects are still guided by the principles of the experimental paradigm as described earlier in this chapter. This means that researchers tend to make a distinction between independent and dependent variables, and that they favor the use of standardized methods (so that studies can be replicated) when testing hypotheses bearing on the validity of their interpretations. In the cultural approaches this experimental orientation is rejected as essentially insufficient. The types of problems that lend themselves to experimental analysis are often seen as trivial for the analysis of behavior in context. Instead, cultural psychology recommends descriptive methods that find their roots in the philosophical tradition of phenomenology.

Methodologically cultural psychology can be summarized in three main points: First, the appropriate level of analysis is the cultural system in which the behavior occurs rather than the level of separate variables. The ethnographic literature abounds with examples showing that the meaning of behavior patterns is dependent on the rules and customs of the society in which it is observed. (Quasi-) experiments and measurement by means of standardized tests and questionnaires are hardly ever found in cultural approaches. Behavior is usually described on the basis of observations in natural settings.

Second, there is an emphasis on processes of individual development and change in interaction with the cultural environment. These dynamic aspects require longitudinal observation studies of interactions between the individual and the environment. Moreover, it is claimed that the dynamics of development cannot be captured in experiments, which essentially assume a static relationship between independent and dependent variables. In studies of development, as disussed in Chapter 2, development is inferred from differences in scores; it is not directly observed.

The third and most essential point is that in cultural psychology there is little place for comparison of data, since the meaning of behavior is relative to the cultural context. In terms of the emic-etic distinction behavior is seen as essentially emic.

As far as the first point is concerned we do not see analyses at the level of cultures as incompatible with an experimental orientation. In fact, there appears to be a complementary relationship. Ethnographies and other descriptive studies in many respects represent an exploratory phase in a research effort that should consist of both exploration and verification. The issue of validity also has to be addressed in exploratory studies. Jahoda (e.g., 1990b), who has argued in favor of the analysis of behavior as it functions in a cultural system, has given examples showing how ethnographers go through a process of postulating hypotheses on the meaning of certain field observations and then testing these by checking whether other observations fit. Although these validation procedures are *post hoc*, they reflect the same concern for validity that is being advocated in this book.

The status of the concept of development is a much debated theoretical issue. Valsiner (1987) is among those who have given prominence to the cultural context of development. In his view cross-cultural psychology leads to data that simply reflect differences between cultures; studies are needed that show how a given socioecological frame structures child development as an interactional process. However, the empirical data collected by Valsiner so far are limited to the socialization patterns of young children within the U.S. (Valsiner, 1987; Valsiner & Hill, 1989). These studies hardly bear on the question how cross-cultural context differences are related to development outcomes. An analysis of the methodological implications probably will have to wait until pertinent cross-cultural data are available. In this connection, it is important to separate two arguments. The first is against the relevance of experimental studies that have been conducted in the past. There is no disagreement that many experiments can be found that are of poor quality, both theoretically and from an applied perspective. The second argument is that development as a concept falls outside the realm of the experimental paradigm. In this book the opposite view is held: interactive conceptions like that of the developmental niche (see Chapter 2) are compatible in our view with the experimental approach.

The third point amounts to the most serious challenge. If behavior can only be understood within the context of a particular culture, there is no logical basis for comparative studies as conducted in cross-cultural psychology. This challenge, which has theoretical as well as methodological implications, will be dealt with in the next chapter. In the last two sections of this chapter we shall assume that psychological data collected in different cultures *can* but *need not* have the same meaning. It then becomes an important methodological problem how to distinguish between these two possibilities.

Analysis of comparability

"For a specific observation a belch is a belch and nepotism is nepotism. But within an inferential framework, a belch is an 'insult' or a 'compliment' and nepotism is 'corruption' or 'responsibility.'" This comment from Przeworksi and Teune (1970, p. 92) puts in a nutshell the view that the meaning of behavior is dependent on the cultural context in which it occurs.

This is not only true for behavior observed in daily life, but also for reactions elicited with instruments such as standardized interviews, questionnaires, and psychometric tests. When scores on identical instruments do not have the same psychological meaning in different contexts, they are called *noncomparable, inequivalent,* or culturally *biased.*[3]

In this section we shall briefly describe various psychometric approaches to analyzing whether or not data can be taken as comparable. In Box 9-2 an outline is given of the rationale underlying much of the presentation in this and the following section.

Analysis of stimulus content. The best way to begin with an analysis of comparability is to look at the content of the stimuli in an instrument. A close scrutiny of each stimulus is necessary to identify possible peculiarities in meaning or other reasons that a stimulus might be inappropriate in a particular culture and should not be used. There are two kinds of methods, namely *judgmental methods* and methods for *translation equivalence.*

In *judgmental methods* experts are asked to give an opinion about the content of stimuli. Usually they evaluate for each stimulus whether or not it belongs to the domain of behavior of interest and whether or not it presupposes specific knowledge or experiences more readily available in one of the groups to be compared.

For a proper evaluation the judges should have an intimate knowledge of the cultures in a comparative study as well as of the theory and notions behind an instrument. Judgmental methods have been mainly employed in the U.S. to trace items in educational achievement and intellectual ability tests that are biased against women or ethnic minority groups. A review can be found in Tittle (1982). Although judges can have fairly strong opinions as to which items are biased, these ideas quite often are not confirmed by empirical findings; it proves difficult to predict on which items a certain group will show a relatively low performance level. In cross-cultural studies it is often not easy to find qualified judges; the least that can be done to identify inappropriate stimuli is to consult with colleagues in each of the cultures involved in a project.

There is a need for a careful check on *translation equivalence* whenever

---

[3] In the cross-cultural literature there are a number of fairly loosely defined terms. Among them are incomparability, bias or cultural bias, functional equivalence, conceptual equivalence, and stimulus equivalence (e.g., Brislin, Lonner & Thorndike, 1973). We shall not deal with the finer nuances in meaning but restrict ourselves to the use of three terms, namely *comparability, equivalence,* and *bias.* The first two have a similar meaning and can sometimes be used interchangeably. Comparability is the more generic term; equivalence and bias refer predominantly to measurements. Bias and inequivalence imply the noncomparability of data as a consequence of some unwanted factor. Data are equivalent or unbiased when no such factor is present.

Box 9-2   Scale identity

In the main text it is postulated as a condition for comparison that scores should have the same meaning across cultures. This is a somewhat vague formulation. In this box a more precise description will be given, taking the logic of comparison as a starting point.

A comparison between two cultural populations, A and B, can be misleading for two reasons. First, the dimension measured in culture A may not be the same as that measured in culture B. This happens if, for example, length in A would be compared with weight in B. Second, the scale units for a common dimension may not be the same for A as for B. This happens if length in A measured in centimeters would be compared with length in B measured in inches. In the first instance one may say that *qualitatively* different dimensions are compared. In the second instance the *quantitative* units of measurement are not the same for the entities that are compared.

Obviously, any meaningful comparison presumes a qualitatively and quantitatively identical scale of measurement, even though such a scale often is not observable and may not even be stated explicitly by the researcher who makes a comparison.

It is necessary to distinguish sharply between the scale of a concept and the scale of measurement. Let us say we want to compare two cultural populations on some cognitive ability. This is a hypothetical construct for which only a hypothetical scale can be postulated, but this hypothetical scale is the actual comparison scale we are interested in. The instrument that provides the data forms a measurement scale. Thus, in a sense we are dealing with two scales. One is the scale of the theoretical concept. The other is the measurement scale; in our example this is the scale of the ability test score variable. Whenever an instrument has validity for a concept, this can be thought of as a mathematical function to express the relationship between the two scales. Data are incomparable or inequivalent when the function expressing this relationship is not the same in the cultures to be compared.

The distinction between the measurement scale and the scale of comparison opens the possibility of a formal definition for incomparability or inequivalence of data. *A lack of equivalence implies that an observed difference on a measurement scale* (for example, a test or questionnaire) *is not matched by a corresponding difference on the comparison scale* (for example, a hypothetical concept or domain of behavior). A further elaboration of the ideas presented in this box can be found elsewhere (Poortinga, 1983, 1989; Malpass & Poortinga, 1986).

The most important points of this box can be summarized as follows.

1. Any cross-cultural comparison presupposes a cross-culturally identical scale or comparison standard.
2. The identical scale is often a hypothetical scale and as such is unobservable.
3. Data obtained in different cultures are called incomparable or biased when they show differences for which there are no corresponding differences on the comparison standard. (How this can be empirically determined will be discussed later in this section.)
4. Incomparability is not a fixed property of a measurement scale. The same data set can be comparable for one comparison standard but incomparable with respect to some other standard.

---

verbal items or instructions are used cross-culturally. Usually researchers are satisfied that translation equivalence has been attained when, after translation from the original language in the target language, followed by independent back-translation, the original wording is reproduced more or less precisely. The procedure requires that translators are available who are fluent in both the original language and the target language. The forward translation and back translation procedure sometimes has to be repeated by an independent team before the original version is reproduced with sufficient precision. Brislin (1976, 1980, 1986) pointed out that it is often necessary to change the original stimulus, because it is found to be simply untranslatable. He recommends that both the original and the modified version in the source language be administered to a group of subjects to check whether the changes have had any systematic effect on the scores.

The process of translation is closely linked to what O. Werner and Campbell (1970) have called "decentering." Since an instrument is developed within a particular cultural context, it will contain certain features characteristic of that culture. These have to be avoided in cross-cultural comparison, with the consequence that the original instrument also has to be modified. This may imply that not only a change in wording, but also a change in stimulus content is needed.

Thus we have to reckon with the possibility that what is referred to in a stimulus does not exist at all in some other culture. Elimination of the stimulus concerned is the only solution. If this happens for more than an occasional stimulus, cultural decentering raises a more fundamental question, namely whether the nonequivalence of stimuli points to the cross-cultural nonidentity of the trait being measured by the instrument. We shall come back to this point in the next section.

Another difficulty the researcher has to face in establishing linguistic equivalence is that bilinguals, when filling out a questionnaire in a certain language, adapt their answers to some extent according to the stereotypes that they hold about the culture concerned (e.g., Bond, 1983). Brislin (e.g., 1986) has pointed out that for the assessment of translation equivalence monolinguals as well as bilinguals are needed; the latter usually form a subgroup that is not representative of the total population.

Psychometric analyses. The psychometric analysis of comparability is based on a presumed order or structure. For example, attitudes can be ordered from positive to negative; items in an ability test range from easy to difficult. For comparable scores it is reasonable to expect that cross-culturally the same order of item difficulty or preference will be observed. Similarly, it is to be expected that correlations between variables in one culture should also be found in other cultures. This kind of consideration can lead to the formulation of conditions that should be met by comparable data, but are unlikely to be satisfied by noncomparable data.

In the analysis of *stimulus inequivalence*, usually referred to as *stimulus bias* or *item bias*, it is assumed that the results from the stimuli together (from an entire test) have approximately the same meaning cross-culturally. If there is a certain overall pattern of cross-cultural differences across stimuli, any particular stimulus that does not fit this pattern is likely to be biased. Given this assumption, psychometric requirements can be formulated to differentiate between biased and unbiased stimuli. One such requirement is that the relative difficulty of a stimulus (compared to the other stimuli in an instrument) should be the same across cultures. For more information on the available psychometric techniques to identify biased stimuli we refer to reviews of the relevant literature (e.g., Van de Vijver & Poortinga, 1991).

There is *instrument bias* if a large proportion (or all) of the stimuli in an instrument are biased against one group. In such a case most statistical techniques of item bias will lead to the elimination of the *unbiased* items because they are the ones that do not fit the general pattern of results. Consequently, there is a need to investigate noncomparability at the level of the instrument as a whole as well as at the level of the separate stimuli.

Correlational techniques were applied in the 1960s to demonstrate that a variable was "tapping" the same construct. For this purpose the product-moment correlation of that variable with other variables was computed. Similarity in correlation patterns across cultures was seen as positive evidence of scale identity (e.g., Berrien, 1967). The correlation coefficient provides information on the *qualitative* aspects of the meaning of scores (that is, is the same dimension being measured), rather than on the *quantitative* aspects (that is, are the measurements in identical scale units). Similarity in correlation values leaves open the possibility that quantitative differences in scores are noncomparable (cf. Box 9-2). This becomes obvious when one considers the following. If a constant is added to all the scores on a variable, the correlation of that variable with other variables does not change in value. Similarly, if a biasing effect influences all scores in one group, this will not change the value of correlations. In short, the similarity across cultures in the correlations between tests is insufficient to guarantee their comparability.

Another shortcoming of early correlational analyses was the vagueness of the notion of similarity. Sometimes the mere fact that a correlation was positive in two groups was seen as important evidence for comparability; this despite the fact that in certain areas of psychology the *a priori* probability of a correlation coefficient being positive is rather high (e.g., D. W. Fiske, 1971). Over the last twenty years more sophisticated correlational techniques have become available. The use of linear structural models is a development along these lines (e.g., Jöreskog & Sörbom, 1984; Watkins, 1989). Compared to correlational analyses these models also allow a better evaluation of the quantitative (in addition to the qualitative) aspects of comparability.

There are various kinds of factors that can cause nonequivalence of an entire instrument. All the stimuli in an instrument may be affected by the administration procedure (such as ethnicity of the interviewer), the stimulus and response format (for example, familiarity with multiple choice), and the subjects' internal state (such as a lack of motivation). In general, when an instrument is constructed within a particular culture, it is far less likely that a stimulus will be biased against members of that culture than against subjects who belong to some other culture.

Classification of inferences

In an extensive study in East Africa, Drenth and his co-workers (Drenth, Van der Flier, & Omari, 1983; Bali, Drenth, Van der Flier, & Young, 1984) found that Tanzanian children had a lower mean score than children from Kenya and Uganda on most of the fifteen ability tests that were administered. Most psychologists interpret differences in such scores between individual subjects *within* the same cultural group as indicative of differences in cognitive aptitudes, but will not conclude from differences between countries that there are differences between populations in aptitudes. Drenth and his colleagues considered two possible explanations for differences among the East African school populations. One was the use of the Kiswahili language in primary schools in Tanzania. In Kenya and Uganda the language of instruction at all levels is English, which was also the language of testing. The second was a difference in the quality of schools in the three countries. If pupils in Tanzania perform less well on the tests, it may indicate that they have learned less at school.

In this section we shall introduce a classification scheme that is meant to facilitate the distinction between valid and invalid inferences in cross-cultural psychology. The scheme is similar to one developed by Poortinga and Malpass (1986). The point of departure is that a psychological instrument usually represents a much larger set of stimuli than those it actually contains. The test stimuli form a *sample* from this larger set, to which we shall refer as a *domain* of behavior.[4] The interest is not so much in the sample per se, but in

---

[4] The commonly used term is "universe" of behavior rather than "domain" of behavior. The term *universe* has been avoided here to prevent confusion with the notion of "universal," that is, a concept that has validity in all cultures (see Chapter 10).

the domain of behaviors it represents. In other words, *an inference based on test scores can be seen as a generalization to some domain* (cf. Cronbach, Gleser, Nanda, & Rajaratnam, 1972).[5]

At the same time, there is more than one domain to which a single measurement can be generalized. For the scores on the ability tests administered in Africa, two possible domains of generalization were mentioned by Drenth et al. (1983): school achievement and knowledge of the English language. From the perspective that any inference is a generalization to a domain of behavior, two distinctions can be made that are relevant for cross-cultural comparison. The first distinction is between cross-culturally *identical and non-identical* domains. For example, the lexicon (that is, all the words in a language) is a domain that obviously differs from language to language. This is also the case for subdomains, like the set of color names in different languages. Similarly, it seems likely that the set of situations that provoke anxiety is partly different from culture to culture and thus does not form a cross-culturally identical domain. In contrast, examples of identical domains are the tones in the pitch scale (expressed in Hz) and the colors defined by the wavelength of the light. Note that the latter examples are defined in terms of physical scales.

The second distinction has to do with the *extent of empirical control* over the validity of inferences. Imagine a continuum; at one end are placed generalizations that are fully accessible to empirical control and at the other end are generalizations that are not open to control at all. (As discussed in the first section of this chapter, the notion of empirical control includes all techniques available to the researcher to investigate by empirical means the correctness of inferences; the experiment is the most important of these techniques.) To illustrate the continuum we shall describe three levels of generalization, corresponding to a low, a medium, and a high level of inference, respectively.

The three levels of inference and the presence versus absence of domain identity lead to six types of generalizations, presented in Table 9-3. The Table has three columns, which we shall discuss from left to right.

Low-level inferences (measurements as samples). First, there are generalizations to domains of which all the elements, at least in principle, can be listed. In other words, it is clearly known what does and what does not belong to the domain. A measurement instrument can be constructed by selecting a sample of stimuli from the appropriate set of elements. An example is an arithmetic test for young children consisting of items representing the major operations of addition and subtraction with one-digit numbers.

---

[5] The idea that inferences can be seen as generalizations to a domain has been systematically developed in Generalizability Theory (Cronbach, Gleser, Nanda, & Rajaratnam, 1972; Cronbach, Rajaratnam, & Gleser, 1963). The theory is concerned with the psychometric analysis of test data, but has some conceptual underpinnings that are relevant for the interpretation of cross-cultural differences.

Table 9-3. *Scope for valid cross-cultural comparisons of psychological data with inferences considered as generalizations* (after Poortinga, 1989)

	Level of inference		
	Low	Medium	High
Domain identity	Measurement as sample	Measurement as index	Unconstrained domain
Identical	Comparison generally possible	Comparison uncertain	Not measurable
Non-identical	No valid comparison	No valid comparison	No valid comparison

Perhaps another example is an attitude scale for intergroup relations in which all important areas of contact, such as intermarriage, social situations, and commercial dealings are included. A characteristic of low-level inferences is that they are limited to a domain from which the instrument concerned contains a more or less *representative sample* of all the relevant stimuli.

The upper left-hand cell of Table 9-3 refers to domains of generalization that are identical across cultures. A comparison is valid if the instrument on which a comparison is based is truly representative of the domain of generalization.

In practice a comparison should be carried out with an eye open for culturally specific effects, which make scores incomparable. Some of the stimuli can contain unexpected difficulties for subjects in one culture. For example, it is possible that the recognition time for the word "pig" in a tachistocopically presented reading task would be high among Muslim children, to whom this is a "dirty" word. Similarly, the expression of negative attitudes may be subject to stricter norms in one culture than in another. This means that even at a low level of generalization, comparability of scores should not be taken for granted. However, with the methods discussed in the previous section, checks on comparability can be carried out. This implies that at this level it is usually possible to decide with sufficient accuracy whether or not scores have the same meaning cross-culturally.

The lower left-hand cell of Table 9-3 refers to domains that are nonidentical for the cultures to be compared. Strictly speaking there is no basis for comparison. Suppose a vocabulary test is constructed for each of two languages by random selection of words from the lexicon. A difference in the average number of words recognized may well have to do with some psychological difference, but this is by no means sure. For example, if there are 50,000 words in one language and 100,000 words in the other, a difference in vocabulary scores is likely to be a function of the inequality of the domains rather than of vocabulary skills in the subject populations.

Medium-level inferences (measurements as indices). The second type of generalization is to domains defined in terms of unobservable psychological traits of individuals. When we talk about cognitive abilities, personality traits, or moral values, we refer to unobservable characteristics, often called hypothetical constructs, which are assumed to underlay certain behaviors. Theoretical and empirical relationships, as established in validation research, determine the range of behaviors in a domain at this level. For this type of inference instruments are not constructed with a view to obtain a representative sample of all possible elements. Rather, stimuli are selected that supposedly capture the essence of a trait or ability. A test of spatial relations may consist only of items in which the subject has to reconstruct three-dimensional figures from two-dimensional projections. The mental manipulations needed for correct solutions are seen as the essential core of spatial ability. At this medium level of inference a measurement can be said to serve as an *index* of the domain of generalization.

At this level of generalization it can be difficult to decide whether domains of behavior are identical across cultures. For example, we have seen in Chapter 4 that the universal identity of unblended emotions is fairly well established. At the same time it appeared that the expression of emotions is governed by display rules that may vary from culture to culture. This means that scores on an instrument using expressions of emotion to assess an underlying emotional state may not have the same meaning cross-culturally and thus may be psychometrically inequivalent. For reasons given in Chapter 4 we would place emotions in the top row of Table 9-1. However, we also mentioned in Chapter 4 that a perspective on folk taxonomies of emotions as nonidentical meaning systems has been advocated, especially by cultural anthropologists (e.g., Lutz & White, 1986). This implies that emotions can have an essentially different meaning in various cultures. It is a logical consequence of such a viewpoint that a comparison of scores on some psychological instrument would be quite meaningless and that emotion concepts should be located in the bottom row of Table 9-3.

High-level inferences (unconstrained domains). High-level inferences involve generalizations to domains that cannot be properly defined in terms of measurement procedures. In this third category it is not clear which instruments provide valid indices of the domain of interest and which do not. A large variety of observed differences can be explained post hoc in terms of a broad conceptual label. Hence, we speak about *unconstrained domains*.

Examples of high-level concepts are "intelligence A," adaptation, and adaptability. Biesheuvel (1972) introduced the concept of adaptability (i.e., the capacity of a population to cope with the demands of a changing environment) to replace the concept of intelligence. A difficulty is that adaptability is contingent upon different environmental requirements in each group. How are we to establish that one group has adapted better psychologically to its environment than a second group to another environment? For any answer to a general question like this some evidence can be mustered, but it would be hard to be sure about its validity. Therefore, we have marked in Table 9-3 generalizations to unconstrained domains as unmeasurable. These generalizations go beyond what can be reasonably inferred on the basis of psychological data.

We have maintained a distinction in Table 9-3 between identical and non-identical high-level concepts although it is more or less beyond empirical scrutiny. Still, if non-identity is postulated for a domain at this level, it is obvious that also conceptually there is no basis for any meaningful cross-cultural comparison of scores.

There is one concept on which positions in the literature exist that vary across most of the cells in Table 9-3, namely the concept of intelligence. The distinction between intelligence A, intelligence B, and intelligence C (see Chapter 5) comes fairly close to that between the three columns in the table of high-, medium-, and low-level inference. The two rows in the table correspond to the two positions on "intelligence" as a cross-culturally identical and as a non-identical concept respectively.

Let us consider once more the question about how empirical analyses of a data set can help to decide on the *identity* or *non-identity* of a domain of generalization across certain cultures. The starting point for such an analysis is the tentative assumption of domain identity. When evidence is found of data inequivalence, there is an interpretation dilemma. The incomparability can reflect bias in the instrument, but it can also point to non-identity of the domain of generalization.

The evidence for bias in an unobservable variable can only be circumstantial. Strictly speaking, there is no direct evidence to distinguish between inequivalence of data and the non-identity of a domain. However, a persistent failure to construct instruments with which equivalent data can be obtained ultimately should lead a researcher to give up the tentative assumption of domain identity and to argue that non-identity is a more profitable course for further research. A redefinition of theoretical concepts to bring out what is common to cultures is a plausible first step on this new course (Poortinga, 1975). This idea will be further elaborated in the next chapter.

Conclusions

In this chapter we have emphasized constraints on cross-cultural comparison, since in our opinion empirical studies often reinforce existing notions about the psychological significance of all kinds of intergroup differences. First the question has to be examined whether the results can support the inferences a researcher wants to make.

In the final analysis the methodological problems of cross-cultural psychology do not differ in principle from those of general psychology. If there are more variables that need to be controlled, this only means that the difficulties are greater. However, by using a wide range of methods and by taking context variables into account the degree of accuracy that is required for a valid interpretation of cross-cultural differences ultimately should be within our reach.

In this chapter we draw together various theoretical and methodological issues discussed in previous chapters, beginning with a systematization of the various inferences that can be drawn from data. Two major distinctions will be taken up again, that between interpretations in terms of genetic transmission and cultural transmission and that between various levels of inferences or generalizations. In the second section we link three major categories of interpretations that are developed in the first section to three general orientations in the ways cross-cultural psychologists may approach the issue of human variation: *absolutism*, *relativism*, and *universalism*. The third section contains a theoretical discussion of the concept of culture and how it is variously employed by cross-cultural psychologists. The phenomena that scientists study, the way in which they set up their studies, and their interpretation of the data are guided to a large extent by their prior conceptions. We shall see that this is also the case in cross-cultural psychology.

During the last forty years we think that much progress has been made in the understanding and explanation of cultural influences on behavior. Nevertheless, a critical attitude about the validity of our present insights remains as necessary as ever. To invoke such an attitude, Box 10-1 portrays some earlier preferred explanations for behavioral differences across cultures.

Inferred antecedents of differences in behavior

In Chapter 9 various difficulties in the interpretation of cross-cultural data were discussed. We presented a categorization of inferences or generalizations that was based mainly on methodological considerations. Here we want to look at interpretations from a more theoretical perspective. In Figure 1-3 psychological outcomes were presented as the consequences of four classes of antecedent variables: ecological influences, genetic transmission, cultural transmission, and acculturation influences. These four classes of variables correspond to four classes of inferences about the antecedent conditions that may have led to certain behaviors of persons belonging to culturally distinct groups.

Ecological influences were mentioned in Chapter 2, where we discussed the relationship between socialization practices and modes of subsistence; in

Box 10-1   Climate, race, and culture as explanatory concepts

In a review article on "the nature and amount of race differences" C. W. Mann (1940), a psychologist from the U.S., argued as follows: "In some respects the quest for a solution has resembled the classic game of 'passing the buck.' During the early part of the Nineteenth Century clergymen and others, impressed by the obvious differences in the physical appearances and in the customs of races and feeling the need for a justification of slavery as a social institution, rationalized that these differences were innate and produced indubitable evidence in favor of the superiority of the white race" (p. 366). According to Mann, the theologians passed the buck to social philosophers and anthropologists. The former soon produced additional armchair evidence for white superiority, while the latter adhered more to the principle of the "psychic unity of mankind." However, researchers in these fields soon turned their attention to societal problems and passed the buck of the problematic mental differences to the psychologists. "Showing little reluctance," Mann (1940, p. 367) wrote, "the psychologists took up the problem and either because they were less astute or more tenacious have stayed with it ever since. . . . The literature of the last 30 years is full of the results of comparative tests of racial differences."

Mann could have gone further back in history to show that preconceptions about human differences can mould "scientific" arguments. Boorstin (1985) relates that in 1550 the Habsburg emperor Charles V announced a special congregation in Valladolid on the question whether the Indians in America were or were not inferior to the Spaniards. Despite lengthy sessions and arguments, no vote was taken on the issue. However, this probably did not matter too much as the conclusion was reached "that expeditions of conquest were desirable on condition that they be entrusted to captains zealous in the service of God and the king who would act as a good example to the Indians and not for the gold" (Boorstin, 1985, p. 634). Boorstin adds that Philip II, who succeeded Charles V, banned the word "*conquest*," which in the future had to be replaced by "*pacification*."

In the eighteenth century, during the Enlightment, a quite different explanation was in vogue. Rather than involving personal qualities as a reason for cultural differences, reference was made to the external condition of climate (Glacken, 1967). It was argued that the temperate climates of the Middle East and Western Europe were more conducive to attaining a high level of civilization than the tropical areas where the heat would stifle human effort.

Since 1940, when Mann wrote his review, psychologists have not passed the buck to another discipline, although it would appear that some sociobiologists are eager to tackle the problem of racial differences. Rather, psychologists have changed the locus of the interpretation of perceived differences in cognition or other behaviors by naming "culture" rather than "race" as the presumed antecedent factor.

Many behavior differences between major population groups in the world may at face value fit quite well an interpretation in terms of either climate or race. For example, the correlation between the distance of nation-states to the equator and per capita income is equal to 0.71.[1] This makes a climatic interpretation statistically as good as most cultural interpretations and more parsimonious in conceptual terms. The same applies when we take "race" as an explanatory factor: any contrast between north and south that is correlated with climate is also likely to correlate with skin color.

The largely mythical explanations in terms of climate and race could become popular because of an insufficient distinction between covariations that are coincidental and covariations that reflect a causal or functional relationship. For all we know, the examples we give here may well refer to coincidences. For cohesive explanation theories are needed that cover a wide range of phemonena, but allow strict tests of postulated relationships. Such theories are not available. This means that high-order concepts such as climate and race, but also culture, can only serve as labels that indicate a general orientation. However, more specific concepts are needed for a scientifically acceptable explanation. This does not make the choice between the three general labels a trivial matter. Each has its own connotative meaning and because of the social implications as well as its utility in psychology, we consider the notion of culture a better starting point on the road to the explanation of differences than either climate or race.

The lesson to be learned from this box is that climate and race functioned in many respects as justifications of ethnocentric prior beliefs. In the future will the contemporary emphasis on culture and cultural differences in behavior also be seen as ethnocentrism in disguise? The philosophers and theologians in Valladolid did not have to settle the question of the equality or inferiority of the Indians as long as the "pacification" of America was not impeded. Could it be that the behavioral and social scientists of today need not provide answers about the nature of cross-cultural differences as long as they do not create impediments for economic expansion that helps to maintain a high standard of living in the West at the cost of environmental pollution everywhere, and for the transfer from "north" to "south" of Western-styled education, which may function as a cloak for continued cultural dominance?

---

[1] This is the product-moment correlation between the per capita GNP of 101 countries and the latitude of their capitals. The GNP data are taken from Table 1 in The World Development Report, 1985. Data from high-income oil-exporting countries were omitted.

Chapter 5, where we discussed studies of cognitive abilities; and in Chapter 6, where we referred to the relationship between visual illusions and the environment, both natural and manmade. We saw that cross-cultural differences in human development have been attributed by various authors to conditions in the ecological context.

The principle of genetic transmission was discussed in Chapter 8. There we indicated that differences in genetic makeup between cultural populations are small, but that their impact on cultural variables is difficult to estimate because of our limited knowledge about gene-behavior relationships.

Cultural transmission was given explicit attention in Chapter 2, where we elaborated on socialization and enculturation; it has permeated into most of the other chapters as well. This is not surprising since it is considered by many to be the most important, if not the sole, principle through which psychologically relevant cultural variations in behavior come about. Variables in the last category – acculturative influences – have only received minor attention so far. They will be elaborated in Chapter 11.

In Figure 1-3 the categories of ecological influences and acculturation are directly linked to, respectively, the ecological and sociopolitical contexts. For genetic and cultural transmission these links are not direct, but they go via an intermediate category labeled as biological and cultural adaptation. The distinction between the indirect and direct link is an essential one. It is not meaningful to study behavior as a function of genetic or cultural factors without postulating a pool of genetic information and a pool of cultural information at the population level. To illustrate: the rate of color blindness is a function of the gene pool in the (breeding) population; and the custom that children live in their mother's family reflects a collective norm in the population concerned. With respect to ecological influences and acculturation, direct reference to, respectively, the ecological and sociopolitical contexts can be quite meaningful: changes in behavior during acculturation can be explained in terms of the requirements of a given sociopolitical situation, and customs of dress can be explained partly as a function of the environmental temperature.

On the other hand acculturation and ecological influences can also be mediated by cultural variables; not every cultural group reacts in the same way to the requirements of a given ecological or sociopolitical environment. This is illustrated in Figure 1-3 by the two arrows linking population-level adaptation to acculturation and ecological influences. Examples of these links are the inadequate use of available foods that sometimes leads to malnutrition and the variation in the speed of acculturation of migrants to a new society as a function of certain variables in their culture of origin, such as the similarity of their language to that of the new society.

The four categories of antecedent variables are the process variables in Figure 1-3, and they all play a role in group-level as well as individual-level psychological phenomena. Starting from the behavior outcomes that serve as data in psychological research, the four categories correspond to the four major categories of inferences about the cause of behavioral differences that can be distinguished in the literature. This is illustrated in Figure 10-1. At the left-hand side of the figure there is a data set. The four categories of antecedent variables are represented by the four boxes in the middle. In the case of each category low-, medium-, and high-level inferences can be made. As outlined in the previous chapter, these range from staying near to being far away from the observed behavior (data).

Theoretical concerns in cross-cultural psychology have been mainly with behavior outcomes that are mediated by population-level transmission processes (both cultural and genetic in Figure 1-3) and less with outcomes that can be directly traced to the ecological or sociopolitical contexts. Since ecological and acculturative influences can have direct effects on human behavior, and population-mediated mechanisms are not involved, behavior should not show systematic cross-cultural differences, but only differences that result directly from these background variables. However, in population-mediated phenomena cross-cultural differences will likely become apparent. There is another reason for the theoretical emphasis on genetic and cultural transmission, namely the long-standing conflicts about the relative importance of these two mechanisms that have repeatedly emerged in the previous chapters.

The two population-mediated transmission mechanisms and their relationship to inferences are presented in more detail in Figure 10-2. The two axes demarcate a field in which the various inferences about the nature of cross-cultural differences can be located. The figure builds on the two distinctions made earlier between genetic and cultural transmission and between the three levels of inference.

The two axes represent the two principles of genetic transmission and cultural transmission postulated by Boyd and Richerson (1985). The shaded area in the lower left corner of the field is the location of the body of information (usually a data set) from which an inference is derived. The field is divided by two curved arcs (broken lines) that define the three levels of inference or generalization that we distinguished in Chapter 9: low-level inferences to domains of which the data form a more or less representative sample; medium-level inferences to domains for which the data have some demonstrated validity; and high-level inferences to virtually unconstrained domains.

We have also divided Figure 10-2 into three sectors. To the sector nearest the vertical axis belong inferences that are defined in terms of irreversible properties of human behavior. Where such properties are inferred, reference is made to the genetic basis of behavior even when a precise mechanism has not (yet) been identified. To the sector nearest the horizontal axis belong interpretations that are defined predominantly in terms of the subjective outlook of the members of a cultural group and the way in which they organize their world. Between these two sectors is a third kind of interpretation referring to interactions between properties of the vertical and the horizontal sector. In this sector lie interpretations that postulate some

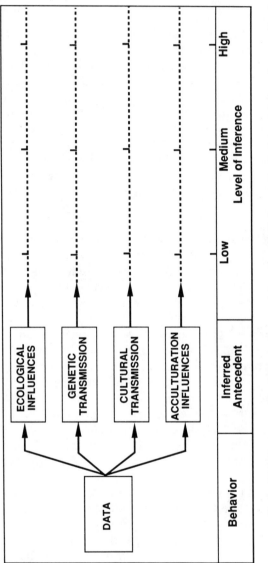

Figure 10-1 Four categories of antecedents and three levels of inference for the interpretation of cross-cultural psychological data.

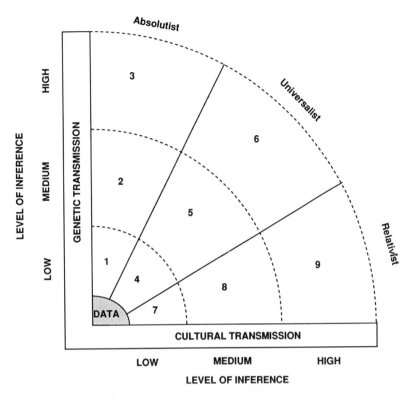

Figure 10-2 A classification of inferences according to level of inference and two transmission principles. The numbers refer to examples given in Box 10-2. (After Poortinga, 1985.)

biological basis for behavior and some cultural impact on its development and display. The three kinds of interpretation can be associated with three general orientations in cross-cultural psychology that will be discussed in the next section under the terms (respectively) *absolutism*, *relativism*, and *universalism*.

Together the straight lines and the arcs delineate nine areas, which correspond to nine different types of inferences about the nature of antecedent variables in cross-cultural studies. Examples illustrating the meaning of the figure are given in Box 10-2.

In the vertical sector of Figure 10-2 are placed inferences to psychological processes that have been acquired through genetic transmission. These by and large determine the behavioral potential of an individual. We believe that *within* a cultural group differences exist between individuals with respect to (hypothetical) traits postulated in this sector. To what extent such differences exist *between* cultural populations is rather unclear. In an environment with heavy restrictions on the development of some trait the range of variation

---

Box 10-2   Illustrations of the categories of inferences in Figure 10-2

We shall take an example from the literature that more or less fits each of the nine areas in Figure 10-2. The numbers are those found in the figure.

1. Differences in the rate of red-green color blindness inferred from scores on color blindness plates (Post, 1962; Chapter 8).
2. Differences in extraversion – introversion (Fuller & Thompson, 1978; Chapter 8).
3. Differences on the r/K dimension of parental reproduction strategy (Rushton, 1988; Chapter 8).
4. Differences in depth perception skills, inferred from depth perception tests (Deregowski, 1989; Chapter 6).
5. Differences in extraversion inferred from personality questionnaire scores (H. J. Eysenck & S. B. G. Eysenck, 1983; Chapter 4).
6. Differences in modal personality as inferred by the culture and personality school (Benedict, 1934; Chapter 7).
7. Differences in social representations (Moscovici, 1982; Chapter 7).
8. Unequal socialization practices for boys and girls as a function of mode of economic subsistence (Barry, Bacon, & Child, 1957; Chapter 2).
9. Deficiency formulations based on general sociocultural indices (cf. Howard & Scott, 1981; Chapter 12). (In the most extreme form this type of inference occurs when a group's behavior is "explained" with reference to its "culture" without further specification.)

It goes without saying that the categorization of these inferences is our judgment and that the original authors probably would be inclined to argue, particularly about the examples at a high level of inference.

---

between individuals may well be smaller than when no restrictions are exerted, but we do not know of any examples of well-established genetically-based intercultural differences in psychological variables. There are such differences in physical variables (for example, skin color, lactose intolerance) and direct derivatives of physical variables (for example, color blindness; see Chapter 8). Physical variables can also be of great psychological importance, but only in specific sociocultural conditions. That is, physical factors will be psychologically important, not in *all*, but only in *some* cultural environments.[2] A dark or a light skin color is only important for the selection of a marriage partner or for acquiring a job in those countries where skin color forms a basis for social distinctions. Admittedly, the claim (in Chapter 8) that genetically based diversity in psychological traits between cultural populations is so

---

[2] Note the word "cultural"; skin color can also have psychological significance in relation to specific ecological conditions, for example, via physical health. The high incidence of skin afflictions among light-skinned people in tropical areas is an example.

limited as to be virtually nonexistent may be partly due to a lack of precise information on gene-behavior relations and is not shared by everyone (e.g., Jensen, 1985). However, an important justification can be found in the plasticity of human behavior. In nonhuman species (even among primates) behavior patterns are rather rigidly fixed, while the range of variation found for human behavior in most situations is considerably larger. Plasticity is an essential feature of the behavior of human beings (Warren, 1980b). Except for the impaired, any human infant can learn to live in any society if the minimal experience needed for unstunted psychological development is provided.

In the horizontal sector of Figure 10-2 belong inferences to culturally defined domains of behavior. An interpretation of behavior emphasizing the cultural transmission component will refer to aspects of the sociocultural context in which that behavior occurs. Inferences in this horizontal sector of Figure 10-2 are based on other than biological or psychological knowledge. It could be argued that from a psychological perspective all behavior is an expression of underlying hypothetical traits or mechanisms, but this is not informative unless the relationship between overt action and traits can be specified. Take, for example, the observation that in India many parents prefer to have a son rather than a daughter, while in France such a preference is far less evident, if it exists at all. For a difference like this there should be some reason that makes it psychologically meaningful, but the observation as such contains no reference to a psychologically lawful relationship between cultural conditions and behavioral variables.

The example can be amplified, and it will make sense *psychologically*, when we know that in India daughters are to be given dowries and move to live with their in-laws, while sons are expected to look after their parents in old age. In many Western countries the obligations of children are less well defined and do not differ much for sons and daughters. This additional information leads to a shift in the interpretation. We can understand both the Indian and the French attitudes as well as the differences between them from a general principle, for example that behavior tends to be self-serving. However, by invoking such psychological principles we have moved to the middle sector of the diagram.

More broadly speaking, in the horizontal sector historical antecedents will determine relationships between psychological variables. Where cultures have a different history, there is no reason to expect that the same relationships should be found. There are two implications to this argument. First, inasmuch as behaviors are dependent on shared knowledge and common beliefs and attitudes, only small interindividual differences are to be expected, at least in homogeneous cultures. Second, to the extent that relationships between variables are dependent on a specific context, substantial variation across cultures can be expected. In other words, to this sector belong behaviors that typically will show relatively low within-group variation and high between-group variation.

In the middle sector belong such phenomena as cognitive abilities and personality traits. These concepts tend to refer, as we have seen in Chapter 9, to an intermediate level of generalization. For the present argument it is not important to separate the three levels of generalization within this sector. What matters here is that behavior is seen as a function of psychological structures and processes, implying that individual differences should be anticipated. At the same time, specific features of a culture play a role and this means that important differences between cultures will also be found. Characteristic of psychological traits is that they are modifiable under the influence of the environment. Genetic traits also undergo change in the process of biological maturation, but this happens in a more or less fixed and predictable manner. In contrast, abilities can be learned, within certain limits, and personality traits can be shaped to fit social norms and expectations.

Relativism, absolutism, and universalism

The three sectors of Figure 10-2 show a fairly close correspondence with three general orientations in cross-cultural research. Although they have been named differently by various writers, we will identify them in this text by the terms *relativism*, *absolutism*, and *universalism*. Each of these has been broached numerous times in previous chapters, but here we attempt to define and elaborate the terms. To help our exploration of these orientations, Table 10-1 outlines a number of features of the three orientations under three headings: general orientation, theoretical perspectives, and methodological perspectives.

As we noted in Chapter 7, the *relativist* position (right-hand column of Table 10-1) was first identified in anthropology by Herskovits (1948), but was based on an earlier set of ideas advanced by Boas (1911). This general orientation seeks to avoid all traces of ethnocentrism by trying to understand people "in their own terms," without imposing any value judgments or *a priori* judgments of any kind. It thus seeks not just to avoid derogating other peoples (an evaluative act), but to avoid describing, categorizing, and understanding others from an external cultural point of view (a cognitive act). "In their own terms" thus means both "in their own categories" *and* "with their own values." There is the working assumption that explanations of psychological variations across the world's peoples are to be sought in terms of cultural variation with little recourse to other factors. Theoretically, relativists do not show much interest in the existence of similarities across cultures, except to assume a general egalitarian stance (for example, "all people are equal") and to explain any cultural differences that they do observe as being due to cultural contexts that influence individuals' development. Differences are typically interpreted qualitatively: for example, people differ in their form or style of intelligence rather than in intellectual competencies. Methodologically, comparative studies are avoided, because they are considered so problematic and ethnocentric as to render valid comparison impossible. All

Table 10-1. *Three orientations to cross-cultural pyschology*

	Absolutist	Universalist	Relativist
1. *General orientation*			
a) Factors underlying behavior:	Biological	Biological and cultural	Cultural
b) Role of culture in behavior variation:	Limited	Substantial	Substantial
2. *Theoretical perspectives*			
a) Similarities due to:	Species-wide basic processes	Species-wide basic processes	Generally unexamined
b) Differences due mainly to:	Non-cultural factors	Culture-organism interactions	Cultural influences
c) Emics and etics:	Imposed etic	Derived etic	Emic
d) Context-free definition of concepts:	Directly available	Difficult to achieve	Usually impossible
3. *Methodological perspectives*			
a) Context-free measurement of concepts	Usually possible	Often impossible	Impossible
b) Assessment procedures:	Standard instruments	Adapted instruments	Local instruments
c) Comparisons:	Straight-forward, frequent, evaluative	Controlled, frequent, non-evaluative	Usually avoided, non-evaluative

psychological assessment should take place with procedures (tests and so on) developed within the local culture's terms. These practices clearly place relativists in the *emic* and cultural psychology approaches, as discussed in Chapter 9.

In sharp contrast, the *absolutist* position seems little concerned with the problems of ethnocentrism or of seeing people "in their own terms." Rather, psychological phenomena are considered to be basically the same across cultures: the essential character of, for example, "intelligence," "honesty," or "depression" is assumed to be the same everywhere, and the possibility is ignored that the researchers' knowledge is rooted in their own cultural conceptions of these phenomena. Methodologically, comparisons are considered to create no essential problems and are carried out easily and frequently, based on the use of the same instruments (presumed to have the same psychological meaning) in many cultures. These instruments are employed in a standard fashion; at most, linguistic equivalence is checked, but this is often the only nod in the direction of recognizing the possible role of cultural influences. Since instruments are likely to be biased, both procedurally and conceptually, this approach clearly leads to *imposed etics*, as outlined in Chapter 9. Theoretically, it is based on the assumption that psychologically people everywhere are pretty much alike. Where differences do occur, they are quantitative differences on the assumed underlying common construct; different people are just "less intelligent," "less honest," or "more depressed."

The *universalist* position adopts the working assumption that basic psychological *processes* are likely to be common features of human life everywhere, but that their *manifestations* are likely to be influenced by culture. That is, variations are due to culture "playing different variations on a common theme"; basic processes are essentially the same, but they are expressed in different ways. Methodologically, comparisons are employed, but cautiously, heeding the safeguards described in Chapter 9; they are neither avoided nor carried out at whim. Assessment procedures are likely to require modification. While the starting point may be some extant theory or test, one's approach to their use should be informed by local cultural knowledge.

Universally applicable concepts will have to come about by reformulation of existing concepts, giving them *derived etic* status as outlined in Chapter 9. Theoretically, interpretations of similarities and differences are made starting from the belief that basic psychological processes are panhuman and that cultural factors influence their *development* (direction and extent) and *deployment* (for what purposes, and how, they are used). Thus the major questions are to what extent and in what ways cultural variables influence behavior. Quantitative interpretations can be validly made along dimensions that fall within a domain in which the phenomena of interest are similar. For example, in cultures that share the same conception and encourage the same expression of depression differences on a test of depression may be interpreted quantitatively. At the same time, in cultures that differ in conception and expression of depression it may be impossible to obtain comparable measurements. Differences that are of a qualitative nature require theoretical analysis to define a common dimension on which they can be captured as quantitative differences before a comparison can be made (Poortinga, 1971).

Combining the outlook contained in Figure 10-2 and Table 10-1, the following summary can be given. In the absolutist view a definition of psychological concepts free of cultural context effects is judged to be within reach of the researcher. Such context-free measurement requires the avoidance of pitfalls in the formulation of items and careful translation, but there are no barriers that should prove to be insurmountable. Relativists believe that there can only be context-bound definition of psychological concepts in such areas as personality, cognition, and social behavior. It follows that context-free psychological measurement should not even be attempted. In the universalist perspective context-free definition of psychological concepts is seen as a goal that has to be, and can be, achieved through the modification of culture-specific concepts. The expression of behavior in many respects is culture-bound, and context-free measurement of certain kinds of variables may well be a goal that can never be fully reached.

The three positions have implications for the theoretical definition of psychological concepts as well as for the psychometric definition of cross-cultural similarities and differences. They also have implications for the definition of universality. In general terms a *universal* is a psychological concept or a relationship between concepts that can be validly used to describe the behavior of people in any culture. According to Triandis (1978), it is "a psychological process or relationship which occurs in all cultures" (p. 1). This definition is rather imprecise and will apply to almost any concept. Jahoda (1981) suggests "invariance across both cultures and methods" (p. 42) as a requirement for universality. This is a description that would fit an absolutist orientation, but also can be used by a relativist to indict the absolutist approach, because of imposing conditions that rarely can be met.

Lonner (1980) has noted considerable variation in approaches to universals in cross-cultural psychology. One orientation is derived from the psychometric tradition. Van de Vijver and Poortinga (1982) have argued that the universality of concepts can be defined at several levels of psychometric precision and that more cross-cultural similarity in behavior is implied as the definition becomes more precise. Their definitions are given in terms of invariant properties of the scale used to express a concept:

1. Conceptual universals are concepts at a high level of abstraction without any reference to a measurement scale. They correspond to concepts at the highest level of inference in Figure 10-2. Concepts at this level are broad labels to convey a general meaning, but the universality of these concepts cannot be tested for lack of precise empirical referents. A term such as *modal personality* is often used in this sense.
2. Weak universals are concepts for which measurement procedures have been specified and for which validity has been demonstrated in each culture investigated. At this level qualitatively identical aspects of behavior are measured. From the universalist perspective any concept in a psychological theory should meet this requirement, otherwise it needs reformulation. Generally, a claim to this level of universality is implicitly held for virtually all current concepts in psychology even without a much-needed analysis of its validity (see Amir and Sharon, 1987).
3. Strong universals are concepts that can be measured with a scale that has the same metric across cultures, but a different origin. This kind of scale is required for comparisons in the absolutist tradition, but also in the universalist tradition whenever quantitative comparisons are being made. In

Chapter 9 we argued that comparisons of concepts (referring to identical domains of behavior) at a low level of inference should not create great difficulties, implying that they can meet the demands for strong universals.

4. Strict universals are concepts that have the same metric scale and origin in each culture. According to Van de Vijver and Poortinga (1982) the same distribution of scores can be expected in all cultures for universals of this kind.

It should be noted that Van de Vijver and Poortinga (1982) do not accept a dichotomy between universal and culture-specific phenomena. They argue that it seems meaningful "to consider the degree of invariance of data across cultural groups as a function of the similarity in cultural patterns or background variables between them" (p. 393). This argument fits with the idea of universalism as an approach that tries to move toward invariant definitions of behavior cross-culturally. However, it seems useful to have a definition in more precise terms. We shall consider *a concept (or relationship) to be a universal when on theoretical grounds there is reason to accept it as invariant across all cultures, when there is empirical evidence to support this claim and when there is no empirical evidence to refute it.*

We have already seen that concepts at a high level of abstraction cannot meet the necessary empirical conditions. On the other hand, low-level concepts are not very informative for contemporary psychological theories that usually require at least a medium level of inference. In a long-term perspective the universalist's research agenda is to move progressively from more loosely defined to more strictly defined psychological concepts.

Culture as a psychological concept

In various chapters we have seen that the concept of culture apparently encompasses a wide range of phenomena. This makes culture of questionable value as an explanatory concept for behavior. Not surprisingly, the need for well-defined theories from which we can derive testable hypotheses has been repeatedly emphasized (e.g., Malpass, 1977). At the same time the formulation of such theories presupposes certain *a priori* notions about culture. In this section we shall look at three theoretical analyses and add some comments of our own.

An Action Theory approach. Eckensberger (1979; Eckensberger & Burgard, 1983) has given a methodological evaluation of psychological and cross-cultural psychological theorizing. He distinguishes five paradigms, which are hierarchically ordered, a higher one being more inclusive than a lower one. Most comprehensive is the *paradigm of the reflexive human being*. As indicated by the name the reflection of humans on themselves and on their own actions, goals, and intentions is characteristic of theories within this paradigm. A brief discussion of what is meant with the word *action* can be found in Box 10-3.

Box 10-3   Action as behavior in context

Action, in action theory, is not a property of the individual; it is placed between the individual and the environment. Eckensberger (1987) argues that it is "this change in the focus on the action, instead of a focus on the culture or the individual (so common in psychology), which exactly neutralizes the opposition between the individual and the culture, which connects the environment with the individual, and which therefore opens psychology as a discipline to other social sciences such as sociology and anthroplogy ..." (p. 18).

An example taken from Eckensberger and Meacham (1984, p. 169) may illustrate the meaning of the concept of action and show the basic concerns of the action theorists:

... imagine a tree. Standing next to the tree is a man. The man has an axe. What is happening here? How can we as social scientists understand the situation?

We can begin by assuming that the chopping of the tree relates to a future goal of the man, for example, so that the tree can be cut into boards to build a house. Further, we can assume that the man has considered various means by which he might chop down this tree. For example, he may have used a saw instead of an axe. After considering these and other means for chopping down the tree, the man made a free choice among these, and he chose the axe. Now the man is chopping. He may be thinking about many things, ... [but when asked] he will be able to set aside his thoughts of other things, and become conscious of the fact that he is chopping down the tree ... he understands that if, as an unintended consequence of his chopping down the tree, the birds lose their home, then he would be responsible for this, for he has made the decision that he will chop down the tree.

The description contains four essential aspects of action theory:

1. The behavior is structured by some future goal.
2. There is a choice among alternative means to reach the goal.
3. The acting person can be aware of the goal and the means employed.
4. The person can anticipate the consequences, intended as well as unintended, and will acept the responsibility for these.

The action theorist tries to cope with behavior in all its phenomenal complexity. Means and goals are hierarchically structured. Going to work is a goal, but it is also a means of earning a salary. Different stages are often distinguished in the course of an action.

The action theorist attempts to *understand* the structure of reasons in which the chopping of the tree takes place. Eckensberger and Meacham demonstrate how minor changes in the situation, particularly when interpersonal interactions are involved, can lead to major changes in its meaning. They also point out that a proper understanding requires knowledge about the cultural and the historical context of the action.

Action refers to the most central concept in action theories. These theories, of which particularly the one by Boesch (1976, 1980) has a strong cultural flavor, are claimed to offer a solution for the major problems that causal-experimental theories cannot cope with. Change and development of the individual, issues rarely studied by experimental psychologists, can be understood as the outcome of dialectical transactions with the physical and especially the social environment. We are not only shaped by our environment but we also form it; we reflect on it and can change the course of events through our actions. Eckensberger (1979) opts for the paradigm of the reflexive human being, because it pertains to the understanding of the unique aspects of a behavioral event. Not only the sociocultural context of an action falls within the scope of action theories, but even the understanding of the idiosyncratic interpretation of a particular situation by a specific person. Eckensberger recommends this paradigm for the study of cultural influences on behavior within a society as well as across societies. It places culture in the interface between person and environment; culture is an ingredient of any action by any person in any situation.

Despite the strong appeal of action theories, it should be realized that they do not provide analytic procedures or methodological prescriptions to distinguish between correct and incorrect (or valid and invalid) interpretations of data. This methodological problem is recognized by Eckensberger (e.g., Eckensberger, Krewer, & Kasper, 1984), but he arrives at a different evaluation of this shortcoming, expecting that an acceptable solution may be worked out within an action theoretical context.

Since the point has both theoretical and methodological implications, we would like to elaborate a little. First of all, antecedent-consequent relationships of other than a mechanistic nature fall under the paradigm of experimentation as we have described it in Chapter 9. This is obvious in ethology, where experimental manipulation and observation of behavior in natural settings are treated as complementary methods (see Chapter 8). In fact, we think that the approach outlined in this chapter covers most of Eckensberger's concerns. However, there remains an important difference of opinion. Action theoretical analyses are based on subjective understanding. In a phenomenological approach a plausible account can be given of a sequence of behaviors that form an action. But subjective plausibility remains the sole criterion, even in the context of scientific research. We agree that most ideas in psychology are initially based on subjective experience. However, experimental analysis is needed to separate more valid from less valid ideas. A unique event, by definition, cannot be subjected to experimental manipulation. Experimentation presupposes that even if from an historical perspective an event is unique, it is only unique in some respects. In other respects it reflects general laws of behavior, and as such an event can be replicated and compared with other events. Here we draw a sharp distinction between the application of science, which of course can help explain an event in retrospect, and basic research, for which the requirement of replicability is essential. It is questionable whether action theories can be placed in Figures 10-1 and 10-2. An essential feature of these figures is generalization. An approach in which the uniqueness of an event is emphasized does not fit this framework.

In summary, an approach based on understanding is important in the "context of discovery," but in our view it has to be complemented by less-subjective methods in the "context of scientific justification," where the unique aspects of an event have to be transcended by lawful general aspects.

Two other approaches to the conceptualization of culture are reflected in a special issue of the *Journal of Cross-Cultural Psychology*. An anthropological perspective was given by Rohner (1984) in which culture is defined as a symbolic meaning system. Segall (1984) suggested that culture is such a diffuse and abstract concept that it cannot be used as such to explain empirical findings. Jahoda (1984) occupied an intermediate position. He argued that Segall's orientation is only adequate for a limited set of problems and that Rohner's ideas, although possibly more promising, are not at present very useful for empirical research.

Culture as a set of conditions. Within this orientation a particular sociocultural environment is seen as a condition or treatment in the sense of a lifelong natural laboratory experiment. The members of a culture have been assigned by birth to that culture in the same sense that subjects are allocated to one condition in an experiment where the effects of various conditions are being compared. However, according to Segall (1983, 1984) culture is a high-order factor that cannot have the status of an independent variable; it is too diffuse to be measurable. Rather, culture has to be dissected into separate contextual factors (compare B. B. Whiting's (1976) notion of "unpackaging cultural variables and Berry's (1980a) proposal for "ecological analyses," discussed in Chapter 9). These include social institutions such as schools, language, rules governing interpersonal relationships, and features of the physical environment. It is common for cross-cultural research to start with the observation of some important behavioral difference and then try to find an antecedent variable that can explain this difference. In other words we start with the dependent variable rather than with the independent variable. First, we have to find a phenomenon that is important or interesting and only thereafter can we start to search for an explanation of it (cf. LeVine, 1970).

Poortinga, Van de Vijver, Joe, and Van de Koppel (1987) have expanded on Segall's conception. They suggest that the analysis of cultural variables can be illustrated with the metaphor of peeling an onion. One can take off more and more layers until in the end no onion is left. In the same sense, these authors claim that a cross-cultural study has only been completely successful when all variation in behavior between cultures has been fully explained in terms of measurable variables.

The view of culture as a set of conditions has two implications. First, the notion of culture is not more than a general label and cannot have the status of a theoretical concept. Segall has pointed out that in the literature authors tend not to make references to culture *per se*, but only to specific variables (on which the groups investigated show variation) when explaining cross-cultural behavioral differences. The second implication is that psychological laws and concepts, by definition, should have universal validity. If support for a theoretical statement is found in some cultures but not in others, that statement is falsified and the theory from which it has been derived should be rejected. Of course, in actual practice evidence is often not very straight-forward. Results can be suggestive of cultural bias in instruments or of the need to reformulate concepts.

Culture as a system. In this perspective on culture relationships among its various aspects within a group are emphasized. Culture is seen as an organized whole; the study of isolated variables taken from the complex fabric is considered a highly questionable practice by those who work from this perspective; we have seen in Chapter 7 that this is characteristic for cultural anthropologists. Often they refer to culture as a system in which the cultural context is inseparable from the way in which psychological traits and functions are organized.

Rohner (1984) has reviewed some of the current issues in anthropology on the conceptualization of culture that are relevant for cross-cultural psychology. One of these points is whether culture has an existence in its own right or whether it is only an abstraction made by observers. In Chapter 7 we have seen that anthropologists like Kroeber postulate culture as a superorganic entity. It has an existence in its own right, because it is governed by its own laws and is not dependent on specific individuals for its existence. Other anthropologists, including Rohner, hold the view that culture has no concrete reality, but that it is a construct inferred from observations of the behavior of individuals.

A second point of controversy is whether culture should be defined in terms of customs and behaviors ("explicit culture") or in terms of ideas and meanings ("implicit culture"). In the former case material products of be-havior and cultural artifacts are part of culture. In the latter case the concept of culture refers to symbolic meanings, such as beliefs, values, and prefer-ences. This so-called "ideational" view is held, among others, by the structur-alists, who with Lévi-Strauss conceive of culture "as shared symbolic systems that are cumulative *creations of mind*" (cf. Rohner, 1984, p. 119). Rohner's own choice is for culture as a symbolic meaning system, with particular emphasis on learning, with "equivalent and complementary learned mean-ings" transmitted from one generation to the next. Complementarity implies that not every member of a culture has to have learned everything that forms part of the symbolic meaning system. But there has to be a certain sharing of meaning to maintain the system. In Rohner's view there is nothing against the use of the term "culture" in a loose and generic sense.

An important question raised in Chapter 9 concerns the identity or non-identity of system parts (structural aspects) and system properties (functional aspects) across distinct populations. At an abstract level the psychological identity of all humans, anchored in the biological substrate, is not disputed. Malinowski (1944), for example, postulated this commonality in biological needs such as hunger and thirst. This commonality is most clearly expressed in the phrase "psychic unity of mankind." In an approach like that of Rohner there is no identity of culture systems at the level of empirical enquiry. Since culture and behavior (whether defined in terms of overt behavior or learned meanings) are closely linked, there is not much basis to postulate universal identity of psychological concepts.

Systems as such cannot be compared, but only parts and properties of systems. We cannot compare flies and flying machines unless some dimension or scale is specified, such as speed or maneuverability. Comparisons presuppose properties that can be attributed to each of the systems; jet fuel consumption does not apply to flies. It is not accidental that analyses following a systems approach to culture tend to take a relativist position and to emphasize relationships within a single culture rather than comparisons between cultures. In Chapter 7 we have seen that these analyses tend to be descriptive and that the postulated relationships are often complex. The validity of explanations hinges on the understanding of the culture by the researcher rather than on research procedures that allow validity checks independent of the observer.

Narrowing the gap? The highly discrepant views on such a central point as the nature of culture obviously require some resolution. Jahoda (1984) has argued that the notion of culture as a collection of independent variables has only a limited application, namely to fairly simple processes that can be captured in an antecedent-consequent relationship. For more complex behavior he accepts, with Rohner, that culture constitutes a system and is not a random assortment of parts. Jahoda refers in this context to a study that showed that the introduction of steel axes in one society not only had economic effects but also affected social relationships. Although he favors a system conception, Jahoda questions its present utility. In his opinion cross-cultural psychology does not have the means to transform the system notion so that it can be handled empirically, an opinion with which we entirely agree.

We would like to add three comments that should help to take away some of the sharper edges of the controversy. In the first place it may be possible to identify progressively more common properties in different systems. To take up our earlier example, jet fuel consumption does not apply to flies but only to flying machines. For comparative purposes a common variable may be defined; energy consumption per kg/m can be an appropriate alternative. We admit that this suggestion is limited to the extent that such a reformulation is possible in principle and feasible in practice. From the universalist point of view the definition of an identical scale for different cultures can be fraught with difficulties, as we have seen earlier in this chapter, but it is likely to add significantly to our understanding.

The second point to be made is that Rohner's and Segall's approaches can be seen as complementary rather than as direct opposites. As noted before, in the continuing process of science there are phases of discovery in which description and observation of spontaneous events are more appropriate and phases of justification during which the validity of competing explanations is investigated.

The third point to note is that in all three orientations (Eckensberger's, Rohner's, and Segall's) close relationships between culture (however defined) and behavior are assumed. Perhaps such a close correspondence should be questioned (Poortinga, 1986). The plasticity of human behavior implies a choice between alternative courses of action in a large number of specific instances. There are boundaries to the set of available alternatives imposed by biological factors, by the natural environment (the context in a physical sense), by the economic and technological means that are available, and by sociocultural constraints (the context in a social sense). An explanation can be perfect only if the set of available responses contains only a single alternative. If it is assumed that within cultures choices in a number of situations are to some extent ritualized (shared norms and values) but that between cultures these rituals differ, the boundaries of the deterministic explanation and predictability of behavior *across* cultures are more limited than *within* cultures.

To clarify this point we can refer to *conventions*. These are explicitly or implicitly accepted agreements among the members of a group as to what is appropriate in social interactions or in some field of activity (for example, in art). Conventions are not trivial. They can make a certain situation very strong (Mischel, 1973) so that (almost) all members of a culture will show the same reaction, while in some other culture some other reaction is equally prevalent. Think of traffic rules in countries with right-hand and left-hand traffic. Despite virtually lifelong practice a switch can be made practically at once as international travelers know and as the Swedes demonstrated a few years ago when they changed from left-hand to right-hand traffic overnight. The example illustrates that conventions contain little information about the functioning of people beyond the very limited domain in which they apply. That is, conventions cannot be related to broader psychological processes or traits on which groups differ (Shweder, 1984; Van de Koppel & Schoots, 1986). They cannot be related to some antecedent psychological factor or to some systems property of a culture. Still, conventions can exercise a strong effect on the total behavior repertoire, because they occur in large numbers. Conventions lead to reliable cross-cultural differences for which there is no explanation either in terms of any psychologically meaningful independent variable or in terms of some cultural system property.

Until we know better how to define the object of cross-cultural psychology it will remain difficult to decide on the most appropriate definition of culture. The incomplete correspondence between culture (in the objective sense) and behavior is difficult to handle in any of the three analyses discussed in this section. Still, it imposes limits on lawful relationships that a universalist can expect to find.

It should be noted that this concern does not much affect the relativist, who sees the essence of a culture in the subjective experience of reality by the members of that culture and who would be disinclined to accept that seriously incomplete correspondences occur in a cultural system. Moreover, functional relationships between variables need not be the same across cultures, because the relativist is not seeking cross-cultural invariance of relationships.

The concern is also not of great importance to the absolutist, who will dismiss conventions as trivial variations. For example, in a sociobiological perspective the scope for conventions is only small, as they have to fit the allegedly narrow constraints imposed by the genetic code.

The universalists are caught in the middle. They may acknowledge the triviality of conventions because these cannot be linked to broader principles in the explanation of cross-cultural differences. At the same time the principles cannot be assessed without taking into account the conventions that are inherent in the behavior repertoire of members of a culture.

Conclusions

In this chapter we have tried to integrate some major theoretical issues in cross-cultural psychology. The primary problem is the derivation of valid inferences from cross-cultural data. A related issue is the relationship between the two principles of transmission (genetic and cultural), both of which are basic to psychology. Three major orientations were distinguished, relativism, absolutism, and universalism. We explained why we think that universalism is the most fruitful orientation for cross-cultural psychology. In the last section of the chapter we discussed three conceptualizations of culture as a psychological phenomenon, adding some comments that may point the way to future convergence.

PART III

Applying Research Findings Across Cultures

11   Acculturation and culture contact

As we discussed in Chapter 2, there is an important distinction to be made between the processes of *enculturation* and *acculturation*. The former is the process that links developing individuals to their cultural contexts, while the later is a process that individuals undergo (usually later in life) in response to a changing cultural context. We have also noted (in Chapter 10) that acculturation is one of the inferred antecedents of observed variation in behavior. Related to acculturation is the more general phenomenon of *culture change* (see Segall et al., 1990; Chapter 13). Acculturation is only one form of culture change, namely that due to contact with other cultures (the *socio-political context* in Figure 1-3). In practice it is often difficult to separate the actual causes of change due to external forces from those due to internal forces. This is because many factors are usually operating simultaneously, including contact, diffusion, and innovation from within the cultural group.

Acculturation

The first major study of *acculturation* was that of Herskovits (1938), which was followed quickly by others (e.g., Linton, 1940). Together with Redfield, they defined the concept:

Acculturation comprehends those phenomena which result when groups of individuals having different cultures come into continuous first-hand contact, with subsequent changes in the original culture patterns of either or both groups ... under this definition acculturation is to be distinguished from culture change, of which it is but one aspect, and assimilation, which is at times a phase of acculturation. It is also to be differentiated from diffusion, which while occurring in all instances of acculturation, is not only a phenomenon which frequently takes place without the occurrence of the types of contact between peoples specified in the definition above, but also constitutes only one aspect of the process of acculturation. (Redfield, Linton & Herskovits, 1936, pp. 149–152).

In cross-cultural psychology it is important to distinguish between group levels and individual levels of acculturation. T. D. Graves (1967) has coined the term *psychological acculturation* to refer to the changes that an individual experiences as a result of being in contact with other cultures and as a result of participating in the process of acculturation that his cultural or ethnic group is

271

undergoing. The distinction between group-level acculturation and psychological acculturation is important for two reasons. One is that the phenomena are different at the two levels, as we shall see later in the chapter: for example, at the population level changes in social structure, economic base, and political organization frequently occur, while at the individual level the changes are in such phenomena as identity, values, and attitudes. A second reason for distinguishing between the two levels is that not every acculturating individual participates in the collective changes that are under way to the same extent or in the same way. Thus, if we want eventually to understand the relationships between culture contact and psychological outcomes for individuals, we will need to assess (using separate measures) changes at the population level, and participation in these changes by individuals, and then relate both of these measures to the psychological consequences for the individual.

To illustrate the process of acculturation, we may consider two concrete cases of individuals experiencing psychological change as a result of their membership in a changing cultural group. While there are many categories of such individuals (these types of groups are considered in Chapter 12), we may take first the case of an immigrant going to set up a new life in another country; this would be an example of acculturation, since external culture contact is involved, followed by both cultural and individual changes. First, the decision to emigrate is often based upon some prior contact, knowledge, and influence. Perhaps other individuals, even members of one's own family, have already settled in the new country and this has led to some changes in one's home culture, such as a foreign language being taught in the schools, new industries being established, and the presence of mass media showing the way of life in the new country. On immigration to the new country, there can be some dramatic and sometimes overwhelming contact experiences followed by psychological reactions: differences in climate, language, work habits, religion, and dress are examples of challenges for the immigrant to which response is required. These cultural differences may be accepted, interpreted, or denied, and the individual may ride with them or be overrun by them.

For a second illustration, we may take the case of a person whose country and culture have been colonized. In this case there is no choice made to enter into culture contact, since dominant cultures have a history of entering uninvited into many parts of the world, especially in Africa and the Americas. Precontact experiences and positive motivation to acculturate are therefore lacking. However, once the process has started individuals and communities may vary greatly in how they deal with the acculturative influences. Some may turn their backs, others may embrace, while yet others may selectively engage the new, while merging it with the old. Many options are possible (as we shall see later in this chapter), but in all cases the intercultural contact and the individual psychological response will be related to each other. It is the task of cross-cultural psychology to examine these relationships, to understand them, and finally to attempt to find systematic features in order to produce some generalizations about the processes involved in psychological responses to culture contact and change.

From the definition of acculturation presented earlier we may identify some key elements that are usually studied in cross-cultural psychology. First there needs to be continuous and firsthand *contact* or interaction between cultures; this rules out short-term, accidental contact, and it rules out diffusion of single cultural practices over long distances (see Bochner, 1982). Second, the result is some *change* in the cultural or psychological phenomena among the people in contact, usually continuing for generations down the line. Third, taking these first two aspects together, we can distinguish between a *process* and a *state*: there is dynamic activity during and after contact and there is a result of the process that may be relatively stable; this outcome may include not only changes to existing phenomena, but also some novel phenomena that are generated by the process of cultural interaction.

These distinctions can be considered in a general system of acculturation, in which there are two cultures in contact. In principle each could influence the other equally, but in practice one tends to dominate the other, leading to a distinction between the "dominant group" and the "acculturating group." For a complete picture mutual influence should be studied; however, for the balance of this chapter we will focus on the culture receiving the greater influence. This is not say that changes in the dominant culture are uninteresting or unimportant: acculturation often brings about population expansion, greater cultural diversification, attitudinal reaction (prejudice and discrimination), and policy development (for example, in the areas of immigration, cultural pluralism, bilingualism, and schooling).

One result of the contact and influence is that aspects of the acculturating group become transformed so that cultural features are not identical to those in the original group at the time of first contact. Of course, if contact is still maintained, further influence from the dominant culture is experienced. A parallel phenomenon is that individuals in the acculturating group undergo psychological changes (as a result of both influences from their own changing group and from the dominant group), and again if there is continuing contact, further psychological changes may take place.

The course of change resulting from acculturation is highly variable and depends on many characteristics of the dominant and nondominant groups. For both groups it is important to know the purpose, length, permanence of contact, and policies being pursued. Cultural and psychological characteristics of the two populations can also affect the outcome of the acculturation process.

Acculturative changes at the group level include political, economic, demographic, and cultural changes that can vary from relatively little to substantial alterations in the way of life of both groups. While these population-level changes set the stage for individual change, we have noted previously that there are very likely to be individual differences in the psychological characteristics a person brings to the acculturation process; and not every person will necessarily participate to the same extent in the process. Taken together, this means that we need to shift our focus away from general characterizations of acculturation phenomena to a concern for variation among individuals in the group undergoing acculturation.

We also need to be aware that individual acculturation (as well as group-level phenomena) do not cohere as a nice neat package (Olmeda, 1979). Not only will groups and individuals vary in their participation and response to acculturative influences, some domains of culture and behavior may become altered without comparable changes in other domains. For example, attitudes toward the value of traditional technology may change without a parallel change in beliefs and behaviors associated with it. That is, the process of acculturation is an uneven one and does not affect all cultural and psychological phenomena in a uniform manner.

We have noted that acculturation is a process that takes place over time and results in changes both in the culture and in the individual. The measurement of change between two or more points in time is a topic that has a considerable literature in developmental and educational psychology, but not much in anthropology or in cross-cultural psychology. This lack has been highlighted for anthropology by a volume devoted to conducting long-term, even continuous, field work (Foster, Scudder, Colson, & Kemper, 1978), but no similar treatment exists for cross-cultural psychology.

Culture change *per se* can only be noted and assessed when sets of data collected at different points in time are compared. While this is ideal, in practice such longitudinal research is difficult and time-consuming. Instead, a more usual practice is that many of the features of an acculturating group are identified from other sources (for example, earlier ethnographic accounts) or are partially reconstructed from reports of the older and/or less-acculturated members of the community. Similarly, longitudinal research is often plagued with problems of loss through death or out-migration and by problems of the changing relevance of theoretical conceptions and the associated research instruments.

A common alternative to longitudinal research is cross-sectional research in which a time-related variable such as length of residence or generational status is employed. Generally among immigrants those who have resided longer in the dominant society may have experienced more acculturation than those residing for a shorter period (usually controlling for present age and age of arrival). Similarly, it is common to classify group members by their generation (the first generation are themselves immigrants, the second generation are their immediate offspring, and so on). An assumption here is that acculturation is a unidirectional process over time, an assumption we will challenge later.

One longitudinal study (Berry, Wintrob, Sindell, & Mawhinney, 1982) that employed both a longitudinal and cross-sectional design, was concerned with how the Cree Indian communities and individuals of James Bay (northern Canada) would respond to a large-scale hydroelectric project constructed in their midst. Initial field work with adults and teenagers was carried out before construction began. Eight years later (after construction), about half the original sample was studied again; this sample was supplemented by an equal number of new individuals who were the same ages as the original sample was eight years earlier. This provided a longitudinal analysis for one group (who were compared at two points in time) and a cross-sectional analysis to maintain an age control.

Other designs may be needed in other acculturation arenas. For example, where longitudinal work is not done a respondent's age may be a suitable surrogate, since the younger are usually more exposed to current acculturative influences from the dominant culture, while the older have a longer history of enculturation in their culture of origin and hence may be more resistant. The key point, though, is to ensure that both the design and the measures match as well as possible the local acculturation phenomena. This view corresponds to the ones proposed earlier regarding methods, theories, and measurement in cross-cultural psychology. Indeed, the position adopted in this book is that all of the methodological and theoretical perspectives developed in cross-cultural psychology are necessary for the valid study of acculturating ethnic and minority groups and individuals.

Contact and participation

The central issue here is the extent to which a particular individual has engaged in the acculturation process. Some are highly involved (and become experts, according to Bochner, 1981), while others are quite uninvolved in the process. Numerous indicators may be sought from a variety of sources (the individual, an informant, or by direct observation). Some of these indicators are: level of formal schooling; participation in wage employment; extent of urbanization, mass media use, and political participation; and change in religion, language, daily practices, and social relations. These numerous variables are likely to be interrelated (Szapocznik, Scopetta, & Kurtines, 1978). Thus we find in the literature attempts to develop scales or indices of contact and participation that sum across these various experiences. Two examples of these follow.

An Index of Contact (de Lacey, 1970) was developed as a general index for Australian Aboriginal children in white Australian society. It contains two sections: *exposure variables* and *adaptation variables*. Exposure was assessed by the proportion of the school-going population and of the whole community which is Euro-Australian, by visits to Euro-Australian houses, shopping experiences of children, travel to Euro-Australian towns, use of English, access to mass media, and to Euro-Australian artifacts. Adaptation was assessed by ratings of persistence of aboriginal culture, use of Euro-Australian games and hobbies, use of Euro-Australian food, the home physical environment (Euro-Australian versus Aboriginal), and community organization (primarily tribal versus virtually Euro-Australian). Total scores were then calculated for each child. This index illustrates how acculturation may be assessed at the individual level, but of course the actual items will vary depending on population and research goals.

Another contact scale (Berry et al., 1986b) was developed for use in Central Africa with Biaka Pygmy and Bangandu villagers. It consists of eight variables: number of local languages spoken; knowledge of French; knowledge of Sango (the national lingua franca); ownership (with items for knives, pottery, ornaments, outside goods); employment and technology (scaled from traditional hunter or farmer through to wage earner); religion (animism through to Islam); adoption of clothing (in European style); and travel (to towns and cities). All these variables were positively and (in most cases) significantly correlated and were used to create a single standardized index for each person.

It should be emphasized that these scales and indices are not ready-made or standard instruments that can be taken "as is" for use in any field setting. Some variables are clearly more relevant to Pygmies than to a community of Italian-Americans (for example adoption of clothing), while others may be more relevant to an ethnic group undergoing acculturation (such as the language spoken in the family) than to a linguistically homogeneous community in Central Africa.

Attitudes toward acculturation

There are three distinct approaches to attitudes held during culture contact that appear in the literature: intergroup relations, psychological modernity, and acculturation attitudes. Since intergroup relations work is considered in Chapter 12, we will not deal with it further here except to note the obvious fact that the attitude that an acculturating individual has toward the dominant society will have some bearing on how an individual enters into the acculturation process. If own-group attitudes are very positive and out-group attitudes are very negative (the classical ethnocentrism orientation), then acculturative influences are more likely to be screened out, resisted, rejected, or otherwise rendered less effective. On the other hand, if the reverse attitude pattern is prevalent among acculturating individuals, then acculturative influences are more likely to be accepted.

Attitudes toward modernity are fully considered by Segall et al. (1990) and little will be said here on the topic. However, it needs to be recognized that both the modernity and acculturation attitudes research traditions attempt to understand how an individual is oriented toward social and cultural change. A major difference between the two approaches stems largely from their distinct disciplinary roots: modernity in sociology and acculturation in anthropology.

Three approaches to studying attitudes toward acculturation and modernity can be distinguished (see Figure 11-1). In one (A) there is assumed to be a single root to such attitudes in all acculturating groups called "traditionalism"; it is further assumed that there is a single outcome of acculturation

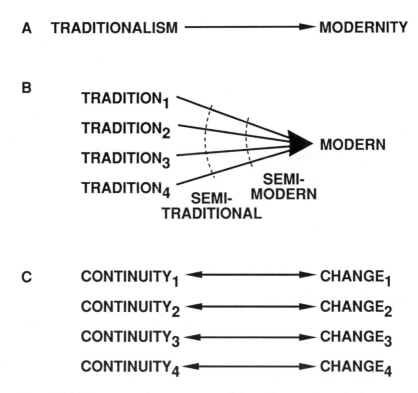

Figure 11-1 Three approaches to conceptualizing and measuring attitudes toward acculturation.

called "modernity" and that acculturating individuals hold attitudes that lie somewhere on this dimension. Research on "Overall Modernity" by Inkeles and Smith (1974) is an example of this approach. In another (B) different roots are recognized, since acculturating peoples have usually originated in different cultures; however, it is still assumed that there is a single outcome (becoming more modern) to the process. The various "T-M" scales of Dawson (1967, 1969) are examples of this approach. In this work four subscales are used: Traditional, Semi-Traditional, Semi-Modern, and Modern.

However, the valued goals of acculturation are not necessarily toward modernity or any other single alternative. There can be preference for continuity with one's heritage culture or toward various kinds of changes (C in Figure 11-1). The goal of change as articulated by the dominant society in their policy statements may not be the preferred course among the leaders or individuals in the acculturating group. In Australia (Sommerlad & Berry, 1970) an attempt was made to discover what the attitudes of Aborigines were to their relations with the dominant society; the government proposed assimilation, but others were not so sure. Since then the argument has been

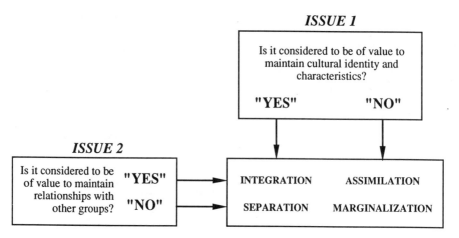

Figure 11-2 Four varieties of acculturation, based upon orientations to two basic issues. (From Berry, 1980a.)

made (Berry, 1980a) that acculturation can be viewed as a multilinear phenomenon; there is assumed to be a set of alternative outcomes rather than a single dimension ending in assimilation or absorption into a "modern" society.

The ways in which an acculturating individual (or group) wishes to relate to the dominant society have been termed *acculturation strategies* (see Berry, Kim, Power, Young, & Bujaki, 1989, for a review of the reliability, validity, and correlates of these attitudes). They are conceptually the result of an interaction between ideas deriving from the culture change literature and the intergroup relations literature. In the former the central issue is the degree to which one wishes to remain culturally as one has been (for example, in terms of identity, language, way of life) as opposed to giving it all up to become part of a larger society; in the latter the central issue is the extent to which one wishes to have day-to-day interactions with members of other groups in the larger society as opposed to turning away from other groups and relating only to those of one's own group.

When these two central issues are posed simultaneously, a conceptual framework (Figure 11-2) is generated that posits four varieties of acculturation. It is, of course, recognized that each issue can be responded to on an attitudinal continuum, but for purposes of conceptual presentation a dichotomous response ("yes" or "no") is shown. When an acculturating individual does not wish to maintain culture and identity and seeks daily interaction with the dominant society, then the *assimilation* path or strategy is defined. In contrast, when there is a value placed on holding onto one's original culture and a wish to avoid interaction with others, then the *separation* alternative is defined. When there is an interest in both maintaining one's original culture and in daily interactions with others, *integration* is the option; here there is some degree of cultural integrity maintained, while moving to participate as an integral part of the larger social network. Integration is the strategy that attempts to "make the best of both worlds." Finally, when there is little possibility or interest in cultural maintenance (often for reasons of enforced cultural loss), and little possibility or interest in relations with others (often for reasons of exclusion or discrimination), then *marginalization* is defined.

It should be noted that the term *integration* as used here is clearly distinct from the term *assimilation* (although the two sometimes appear in the literature as synonyms); cultural maintenance is sought in the former case, while there is little or no interest in such continuity in the latter. It should also be noted that acculturation may be "uneven" across domains of behavior and social life; for example, one may seek economic assimilation (in work), linguistic integration (by way of bilingualism), and marital separation (by endogamy). We will return to a consideration of these four varieties of acculturation in Chapter 12, when another element is added: the policies and practices of the dominant society, which can place important constraints on the choices made by acculturating groups and individuals. There may also be "flux" over time in which different strategies are employed: for example, one may begin with a preference for assimilation, switch to separation, and finally settle on integration.

Each of these four conceptual alternatives has been assessed with individuals in a variety of groups that are experiencing acculturation. The original study (Sommerlad & Berry, 1970) primarily sought to measure attitudes to assimilation and integration; other studies (e.g., Berry et al., 1982) assessed all four attitudes among James Bay Cree, while work with other groups (such as French-, Portuguese-, Korean- and Hungarian-Canadians; see Berry et al., 1989) has demonstrated the usefulness of the approach not only with Native peoples, but also with other acculturating groups.

While four possible outcomes are conceptualized and measured by Berry, et al. (1989), other researchers propose a different number of alternatives, and with different names. For example, Clark, Kaufman, and Pierce (1976) propose six types (based upon profiles of ethnic identity), while Triandis et al. (1986) and Pettigrew (1988) suggest three. For Triandis et al. there can be a movement of the acculturating group toward the dominant society ("accommodation"), a movement continuing *past* the dominant society ("overshooting"), or a movement away from it ("ethnic affirmation"). For Pettigrew the notions of "assimilation," "pluralism," and "integration" are used, but for differing kinds of acculturating groups in the U.S. The first two are used when discussing immigrant groups, while the latter is used when referring to blacks.

Scales to assess individual preferences for the four acculturation strategies are developed by selecting a number of topics (for example, endogamy, ethnic media) that are relevant to acculturation in the particular group. Then four statements (one for each alternative) are generated with the help of informants. Usually it is possible to establish face validity for the statements by asking judges who are familiar with the model (as depicted in Figure 11-2) to sort them into the four alternatives; those statements with good interrater agreement are then kept. Administration involves either a Likert scale response to each statement or a statement of preference for one of the four statements within a topic. Four scores are then calculated for each person by summing across topics within each alternative. Reliability (internal consistency) is enhanced by item selection, and validity is checked against behavioral measures (for example, high separation scorers read only ethnic newspapers, high assimilation scorers read only newspapers in the language of the dominant society, high integration scorers read both).

Further work will be necessary to bring the various measures together. In particular, the way in which the political and cultural context of acculturation (usually determined by the power of the dominant society) acts as an antecedent variable to acculturation will require further analysis.

Behavior change

In this section we focus on what happens to individuals as a result of acculturation. It is not always possible to maintain a clear separation between contact measures and attitude measures when we examine a particular acculturation study. Moreover, not all observed changes take place immediately; some effects may be delayed in time and some may even bring about acculturation in a continuing antecedent-consequent chain. For example, more contact sometimes results in a more positive attitude to assimilation; thus the attitude could be classified as a "consequence of acculturation." Conversely, an initially positive attitude toward assimilation may result in a person seeking out more contact; here the contact could just as well be classified as a consequence. Despite these qualifications, a number of studies have attempted to comprehend the results of acculturation and have developed instruments specifically to measure them.

Another distinction can be found in the literature between two kinds of consequences (Berry 1976a, 1980c). One refers to the relatively conflict-free changes in behavior, such as an individual gradually taking on wage employment and giving up another economic role; these have been termed *behavioral shifts* and are characterized by a continuity in quality, but a change in quantity (for example, from a pattern of 20 percent wage employment/80 percent farming at time 1 to 90 percent wage employment/10 percent farming at time 2). The other refers to new phenomena that often accompany acculturation, which appear to result from psychological conflict and social disintegration, such as an increase in homicide, spouse abuse, or a decline in mental health status; this type of consequence has been termed *acculturative stress*[1] and is characterized by a qualitative change in the life of an individual

---

[1] The term *acculturative stress* is employed here rather than *culture shock* (Furnham & Bochner, 1986; see Chapter 14) to emphasize its theoretical links to contemporary theories and models of stress in the health psychology literature (e.g., Selye, 1976; Lazarus & Folkman, 1984). The opposite outcome, successful *adaptation* to acculturative change, is used in this text as it is elsewhere in the literature (e.g., Ekstrand, 1978; Y. Y. Kim, 1988; Y. Y. Kim & Gudykunst, 1987). The *culture learning* alternative to *adaptation* as a theoretical approach is outlined in Bochner (1986a) and Chapter 14.

or community. Once again it is possible to challenge the distinction; after all, homicide, aggression, and neglect are present in most societies prior to acculturation, but we frequently encounter new forms as well as new rates, such that rather than being regarded as deviant and negatively sanctioned in the group they become common.

Virtually any behavior studied by psychology is a candidate for a shift during acculturation. Of course, this challenges the basic notions of personality trait and behavioral stability (see Chapter 4), which posit continuity over time and across situations. However, the field of cross-cultural psychology has established fairly solid linkages between how individuals act (including thoughts, feelings, and motives) and the culture that nurtured them; it should not be difficult to accept, then, that when the culture changes, individuals may change as well. What may be stable over time is the culture-behavior linkage rather than the behavior itself.

The amount of behavior change with acculturation and the way in which it relates to the two cultures can vary a great deal. Figure 11-3 illustrates a general framework for examining behavior change (vertical axis) as a function of the phase[2] of acculturation (horizontal axis) and as a function of the acculturation strategy that an individual uses.

On the vertical axis greater change is higher on the dimension, while little or no change is lower. Along the horizontal axis the phase moves from precontact, through initial contact, often through a period of rising feelings of psychological and cultural conflict, sometimes resulting in a crisis, followed by three possible acculturation outcomes or forms of adaptation. In the case of the assimilation outcome behavioral change is maximal, while in the case of the separation mode there is a return to more traditional (similar to minimally changed) behaviors; integration represents an outcome on which there is a relatively stable balance between behavioral continuity with one's traditional culture and change toward the new culture. In the case of marginalization the individual is suspended, often in a state of personal and social conflict, between the two cultures. It is in this last situation that the greatest levels of acculturative stress are to be found; this phenomenon will be considered in detail in the next section. Among the many behaviors that could be considered in this examination of change, only a few will be presented. We begin with identity, move to aspects of cognition, then to personality, and finally (to come full circle) consider acculturation attitudes as psychological characteristics that themselves shift as a result of acculturation.

Identity (or how one usually thinks of oneself) can be in terms of cultural (including ethnic and racial) or other (for example, age, sex, location) factors (Aboud, 1981). Here we are primarily interested in ethnic identity and how it may change over the course of acculturation. There is widespread evidence (de Vos, 1980) that cultural identities do change. At the beginning of contact there is usually little question; one thinks of oneself as a member of the group

---

[2] Although the phases generally follow the order in which they are placed on the horizontal axis of Figure 11-3, the duration of each phase can vary greatly. Hence, no standard "stage" theory can be advanced.

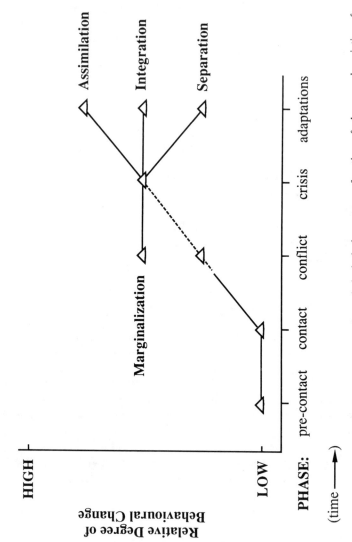

Figure 11-3 Degree of cultural and psychological change as a function of phases and varieties of acculturation. (Modified from Berry & Kim, 1988.)

into which one was enculturated, be it small in scale (a village or a band) or large (a state or country). As contact continues, identity changes may be monitored by a variety of techniques that can provide evidence for simple shifts and for identity conflict and confusion (e.g., Malewska-Peyre, 1982). Changes in ethnic identities and the role they play in the life of ethnic groups and minorities will be discussed in Chapter 12.

Cognitive shifts are also frequently observed in studies of acculturation. Indeed these shifts are often the very goal of acculturation, as in the case of educational or religious missions in many parts of the world. Here we are primarily interested in the intellectual changes that may occur with acculturation. A major focus (e.g., Scribner & Cole, 1973; Rogoff, 1981) has been on the cognitive consequences of formal education with an associated interest in the consequences of literacy (Scribner & Cole, 1981).

Perhaps the most common finding is that performance on cognitive tests becomes "better" (that is, more like the test maker or test administrator) as the test taker becomes more acculturated to the society of origin of the tests. The use of such tests among cultural groups in various parts of the world and among ethnic groups in plural societies continues, and continues to be criticized (e.g., Samuda, 1983), and the results continue to be open to numerous interpretations. One point of view about such results is that there is no substantive shift in cognitive functioning, only a superficial change in performance due to learning some "test taking tricks" (for example, familiarity with the language of the test or with testlike situations). Another point of view is that there may indeed be new cognitive qualities or operations that develop with acculturative influences such as literacy or industrialization. While this view is held by many who work in the field of modernization research (e.g., Inkeles and Smith, 1974) and in literacy (e.g., Goody and Watt, 1968), the evidence for such fundamental changes is rather sparse, as we saw in Chapter 5, where there was very little in the way of general cognitive consequences of literacy.

The evident conclusion to be drawn is one that follows from the discussion of methodological concerns in Chapter 9, namely that the search for cognitive consequences of acculturation is very difficult to carry out if one wants unambiguous results on cognitive variables. If the point is to demonstrate that over time or over generations beliefs, abilities, or even general intelligence (as defined and measured by the larger society) change in the acculturating group in the direction of the norms in the larger society, then the task is rather easy. However, the meaning (or "depth") of these cognitive changes is difficult to specify.

Personality shifts have also been claimed to result from acculturation. Hallowell (1955b) argued that with increasing Eurocanadian influence the personality of Ojibwa, while retaining some of the modal characteristics, shifted toward Eurocanadian personality, However such a "linear gradient" may not always be evident. Peck et al. (1976) have found that some individuals may show this pattern, but others may not change at all or indeed may show a reverse pattern. One way of interpreting these variations is to argue that those who follow the assimilation strategy may show a linear change, while those who are separating or integrating may not exhibit this pattern.

Acculturation attitudes, as we have seen, may predispose contact and hence lead to acculturative change. To come full circle, then, we should remind ourselves that the consequences of acculturation can be changes in acculturation attitudes and changes in contact-participation. Evidence does indeed show that there is a complex interrelationship among many variables. For example, a preference for assimilation has often been observed to increase as a result of acculturation experience and in turn to lead to even more contact and participation by acculturating individuals (Berry, Kim, Power, Young, & Bujaki, 1989). However, lest there be left the impression that there is a continuous linear skid toward assimilation and cultural and psychological homogeneity, we may remind ourselves that conflict, reaction, and other resistive strategies also frequently occur during acculturation. These are important factors in acculturative stress phenomena, to which we now turn.

Acculturative stress

One of the most obvious and frequently reported consequences of acculturation is that of societal disintegration and personal crisis (see Sanua, 1970, for an early review of these problems). The old social order and cultural norms often disappear, and individuals may be disturbed by the change. At the group level previous patterns of authority, civility, and welfare no longer operate; and at the individual level hostility, uncertainty, identity confusion, and depression may set in. Taken together these changes constitute the negative side of acculturation, changes that are frequently, but not inevitably, present. The opposite, successful *adaptation*, may also take place. As we shall see, the outcome appears to vary as a function of a complex set of cultural and psychological variables in which personal and situational factors interact to produce a particular level of adaptation (Kealey, 1989).

The concept of *acculturative stress* refers to one kind of stress, that in which the stressors are identified as having their source in the process of acculturation; in addition, there is often a particular set of stress behaviors that occur during acculturation, such as lowered mental health status (especially anxiety, depression), feelings of marginality and alienation, heightened psychosomatic symptom level, and identity confusion. Acculturative stress is thus a phenomenon that may underlie a reduction in the health status of individuals (including physical, psychological, and social aspects). To qualify as *acculturative* stress, these changes should be related in a systematic way to known features of the acculturation process as experienced by the individual.

In a recent review and integration of the literature Berry and Kim (1988) attempted to identify the cultural and psychological factors that govern the relationship between acculturation and mental health. It was concluded that

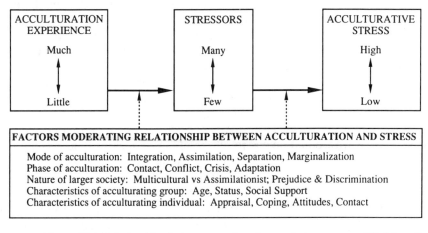

Figure 11-4 Relationships between acculturation and stress, as modified by other factors. (Modified from Berry et al., 1987.)

mental health problems often do arise during acculturation; however, these problems are not inevitable and seem to depend on a variety of group and individual characteristics that enter into the acculturation process. That is, acculturation sometimes enhances one's life chances and mental health and sometimes virtually destroys one's ability to carry on; the eventual outcome for any particular individual is affected by other variables that govern the relationship between acculturation and stress.

This conception is illustrated in Figure 11-4. On the left of the figure *acculturation* occurs in a particular situation (for example, migrant community or native settlement) and individuals participate in and experience these changes to varying degrees; thus, individual acculturation experience may vary from a great deal to rather little. In the middle *stressors* may result from this varying experience of acculturation; for some people acculturative changes may all be in the form of stressors, while for others they may be benign or even seen as opportunities. On the right, varying levels of *acculturative stress* may become manifest as a result of acculturation experience and stressors.

The first crucial point to note is that relationships among these three concepts (indicated by the solid horizontal arrows) depend upon a number of moderating factors (indicated in the lower box), including the mode and phase of acculturation, the nature of the larger society, the type of acculturating group, and a number of demographic, social, and psychological characteristics of the group and individual members. In particular, one's appraisal of the acculturation experience and one's coping skills in dealing with the stressors can affect the level of acculturative stress experienced. That is, each of these factors can influence the degree and direction of the relationships between the three variables at the top of Figure 11-4. This influence is indicated by the broken vertical arrows drawn between this set of moderating factors and the horizontal arrows.

Archival, observational, and interview methods have been employed to assess acculturative stress. Archival approaches can provide collective data for the society or community as a whole: rates of suicide, homicide, family and substance abuse can provide important information about the acculturation context in which an individual is operating. In particular, rates of psychiatric attention have been employed often in the literature (e.g., Murphy, 1982). However, all of these archival records require an organized social system with equal access to all members of society. The system may itself be suffering from disintegration; thus such macroindicators may not always be available or if available may not be reliable.

Interviewing samples of individuals in acculturating communities has been a particularly important source of evidence about stress both in western urban groups undergoing change (e.g., Srole, Langer, & Michael, 1962) and in specific cultural groups experiencing acculturation (e.g., Wintrob & Sindell, 1972). Because of the popularity of this approach, some fairly concise self-report measures have been developed, of which we will consider two.

One scale, which exists in a number of versions, is the Cornell Medical Index (Brodman et al., 1952). The full scale consists of 195 items concerned with somatic functioning and 51 items concerned with psychological life, arranged into six subscales (Inadequacy, Depression, Anxiety, Sensitivity, Anger, and Tension). Work in Alaska by Chance (1965) revealed somewhat heightened levels of psychological problems among acculturating Inuit compared to American norms. A twenty-item version was developed by Cawte, Bianchi, and Kiloh, (1968) containing ten somatic items and ten psychological items. This version was first employed with an Australian Aboriginal group that had experienced both relocation and acculturation. Later use was made of the scale by Berry (1976a) with various acculturating Canadian Indian groups, while Blue and Blue (1984) have employed it with Canadian Indian university students. The full 51-item psychological scales have also been employed with various groups, including Vietnamese refugees (Masuda, Lin, & Tazuma 1979, 1980; Berry & Blondel, 1982), and international students (Berry et al., 1987).

A second scale has been devised by J. Mann (1958) to assess the concept of marginality. The essence of being marginal is being "poised in psychological uncertainty between two worlds" (Stonequist, 1935), being unable to participate fully in either culture. The scale consists of fourteen items, such as "I feel that I don't belong anywhere" and "I feel that nobody really understands me." Respondents indicate those statements with which they agree, and the total score is the number of items agreed with.

A major problem with these scales is that all the items are phrased in a positive direction; thus, those with a tendency to agree will score higher than others. Another problem is that self-report of these disorders may not bear any relationship with their actual presence. However, cross-validation with other tests and with observational data tend to support their continued use in studies of acculturation as indicators of the stresses and strains being experienced by individuals (Berry et al., 1987).

Results of studies of acculturative stress have varied widely in the level of difficulties found in acculturating groups. Early views were that culture contact and change inevitably led to stress; however, as we have noted, current views are that stress is linked to acculturation, but the level of stress experienced will depend on a number of factors.

There is evidence (Berry et al., 1987) that mode of acculturation is one important factor: those who feel marginalized tend to be highly stressed, and those who maintain a separation goal are also stressed; in contrast those who pursue integration are minimally stressed, while assimilation leads to intermediate levels.

Similarly, the phase of acculturation (see Figure 11-3) is also a factor. In many studies (reviewed by Berry, 1985b, and by Furnham & Bochner, 1986) there have been attempts to link levels of acculturative stress to a particular phase of acculturation (using an inverted U function). Evidence to support such a simple relationship with length of acculturation is slight, probably because acculturative stress is also influenced by so many other factors. While those in first contact and those who have achieved some later stable adaptation tend to be minimally stressed, those in the intermediate phases may or may not exhibit stress, depending on the numerous other factors that are outlined in this discussion.

Another factor is the way in which the host society exerts its acculturative influences. One important distinction is the degree of pluralism accepted in the larger society (Murphy, 1965). Culturally plural societies (see Chapter 12), in contrast to culturally monistic ones, are likely to have two important characteristics: one is the availability of a network of social and cultural groups that may provide support for those entering into the experience of acculturation (that is, provide a protective cocoon); the other is a greater tolerance for or acceptance of cultural diversity (termed "multicultural ideology" by Berry, Kalin, & Taylor, 1977). Related to this general tolerance for ethnic diversity is the pattern of specific ethnic and racial attitudes in the larger society: some acculturating groups may be more accepted and placed higher in the prestige hierarchy, while others may occupy the lower ranks in the societies' prejudice system. Taken together, one might reasonably expect the stress of persons experiencing acculturation in plural societies to be lower than those in monistic societies who pursue a forced inclusion or assimilationist ideology (cf. Murphy, 1965).

A related factor, paradoxically, is the existence of policies that are designed to *exclude* acculturating groups from full participation in the larger society; to the extent that acculturating people wish to participate in the desirable features of the larger society (such as adequate housing, medical care, political rights), the denial of these may be cause for increased levels of acculturative stress.

There are also many social and cultural qualities of the acculturating group that may affect the degree to which acculturative stress is experienced by its members. The list of possible factors identified in the literature (Berry & Kim, 1988) is extremely long; thus we attempt here only a selective overview. It is useful to distinguish between original (precontact) cultural characteristics and those that evolve during the process of acculturation. However, some factors involve the interaction of variables from these two sets (pre- and postcontact).

One basic cultural factor that appears in the literature is the traditional settlement pattern of the group: nomadic peoples, who are usually hunters or gatherers, may suffer more negative consequences of acculturation than peoples who were sedentary prior to contact (Berry, 1976a). A complex set of factors has been suggested to account for this finding: nomadic peoples are adapted to relatively large territories, small population densities, and unstructured sociopolitical systems; during acculturation, they experience sedentarization into relatively dense communities with new authority systems; these changes are thought to induce relatively greater tension among nomadic peoples than among others.

Status is also a factor, even when one's origin is in a relatively stratified society. For example, one's "entry status" into the new society is often lower than one's "departure status" from the home society; this relative loss of status may result in stress and poor mental health. Another factor is one's status mobility in the larger society, whether to regain one's original status or just to keep up with other groups. In addition, some specific features of status (such as education and employment) provide one with resources to deal with the larger society, and these likely affect one's ability to function effectively in the new circumstances.

Some standard indicators, such as the age and gender group one belongs to, may also play a role: relatively older persons, and often females, have frequently been noted to experience more stress, as have those who are without a marriage partner (either because of loss or unavailability).

Perhaps the most comprehensive variable in the literature is that of social supports; this refers to the presence of social and cultural institutions for the support of the acculturating individual. Included here are such factors as ethnic associations (national or local), residential ethnic enclaves, extended families, availability of one's original group (by visits to, vitality of, or alienation from the culture), and more formal institutions such as agencies and clinics devoted to providing support.

A final set of social variables refers to the acceptance or prestige of one's group in the acculturation setting. Some groups are more acceptable on grounds of ethnicity, race, or religion than others; those less acceptable run into barriers (prejudice, discrimination, exclusion) that may lead to marginalization of the group and that are likely to induce greater stress. The point here is that even in plural societies (those societies which may be generally

more tolerant of differences) there are still relative degrees of social accepta-
bility of the various acculturating groups.

Beyond these social factors numerous psychological variables may play a
role in the mental health status of persons experiencing acculturation. Here
again a distinction is useful between those characteristics that were present
prior to contact and those that developed during acculturation. In the
precontact set of variables are included certain experiences that may predispose one to function more effectively under acculturative pressures. These
include prior knowledge of the new language and culture, prior intercultural
encounters of any kind, motives for the contact (voluntary *versus* involuntary
contact), and attitudes toward acculturation (positive or negative). Other
prior attributes that have been suggested in the literature are one's level of
education and employment, values, self-esteem, identity confusion, rigidity/
flexibility, and cognitive style (see Berry & Kim, 1988).

Contact experiences may also account for variations in acculturative stress.
Whether one has many or few contacts with the larger society, whether they
are pleasant or unpleasant, whether they meet the current needs of the
individual or not, and in particular whether the first encounters are viewed
positively or not may set the stage for all subsequent ones and ultimately
affect mental health. A recurring view is that the congruity between contact
expectations and actualities will affect mental health; individuals for whom
there is a discrepancy, such that they aspire to or expect more than they
actually obtain during acculturation, may have greater acculturative stress
than those who achieve some reasonable match between them.

Among factors that appear during acculturation are the attitudes toward
the various modes of acculturation. As noted in the previous section, individuals within a group do vary in their preference for assimilating, integrating, or rejecting. These variations, along with experiences of marginalization,
are known to affect one's mental health status (Berry et al., 1987).

A key psychological variable in dealing with acculturative stressors is that
of *coping* (Taft, 1977). Not all individuals deal with these pressures in the
same way, leading to highly variable stress outcomes. In the empirical work of
Taft the psychological variables of learning, social skills, values, attitudes,
and self-concept are employed to investigate how immigrants have adapted to
life in Australia. His review of this research program (Taft, 1986) incorporates these variables into a theoretical framework with five explanatory
constructs: social-emotional adjustment, ethnic and national identity, cultural
competence, social absorption, and role acculturation. The concept of "coping" is employed as a generic one to unify these five psychological processes.
Those who cope well adapt successfully, and those who do not experience
greater acculturative stress.

Elsewhere Bond and King (1985), drawing on Tajfel's (1978) Social Identity Theory, examined three possible coping strategies in Hong Kong: individual mobility, social competition, and social creativity. In the terms being

used in this chapter the first strategy is similar to assimilation (or "passing"), in which individuals identify with the dominant (Western, British) culture and seek to enter it. The second involves rejecting the dominant culture, seeking to remain separate and distinctive. The third, the one favored by most respondents in the Bond and King study, involves taking useful aspects from both cultures: "Chinese learning for the essentials; Western learning for practical applications" (p. 354). This integrative strategy involved a further psychological mechanism: use of the external-internal distinction. Most respondents easily distinguished modernization from Westernization by noting that the former "involves technology, behavior or material progress, whereas Westernization involves values, thinking or traditions from the West" (p. 357). Thus, as noted before, when confronted by two cultures, individuals develop attitudes and adopt coping strategies that lead to the best personal adaptations.

Another variable is the *appraisal* that one makes of the acculturation experience (cf. Lazarus & Folkman, 1984). The sense of cognitive control that an individual has over the acculturation process also seems to play a role; those who perceive the changes as opportunities they can manage may have better mental health than those who feel overwhelmed by them. In essence, then, the attitudinal and cognitive perspectives espoused here propose that it is not the acculturative changes themselves that are important, but how one sees them and what one makes of them.

Conclusions

Applications of findings reported in this chapter, especially after further evaluation and validation in a variety of cultures,[3] should contribute to helping the millions of individuals who find themselves in a situation of culture contact and change. Refugees, immigrants, and guest workers can all be provided with information, counseling, and other forms of psychological assistance based on these findings. Receiving countries can develop policies and programs, and public education of the host population may also be attempted. Enough information is now available about the process of acculturation and about factors affecting various psychological outcomes that there could, with better programs, be a reduction in problems experienced by acculturating peoples (C. L. Williams & Berry, 1991). However, with the possibility that there will be increasing numbers of refugees in the world, and

---

[3] As in the case of all research, these further studies should be *comparative*. An explicit framework for such comparisons has been presented by Berry et al. (1987). They propose a program of research that examines the psychological acculturation of a variety of groups (for example, immigrants, refugees) coming from a variety of cultures (for example, Vietnamese, Ethiopians) to a variety of settlement countries (for example, Australia, Britain, Canada) using some standard concepts (for example, contact indices, acculturation attitudes, and acculturative stress) and as much as possible standard instruments. Only within such a comparative framework will it be possible to produce valid generalizations about acculturation phenomena.

perhaps increasing numbers of temporary migrants (out-migration followed by return migration), the problem potential is not likely to diminish. Hence the findings reported in this chapter and the basic principles they point to urgently require interpretation and transfer to those responsible for managing acculturation in both donor and receiving countries.

Cross-cultural psychology can be done "abroad" and "at home"; that is, differences between cultural groups can be found and employed in making psychological analyses across either broad or narrow ranges of cultural variation. One of the positions taken in this book is that the study of ethnic groups and minorities within culturally plural societies is just as much a part of cross-cultural psychology as the study of widely varying and geographically dispersed cultural groups. At the same time, the theoretical and methodological approaches that are rooted in the broadly comparative traditions of cross-cultural psychology (see Chapters 9 and 10) need to be taken into account. In the last chapter the process of acculturation was examined along with some of the outcomes for individuals. In this chapter we carry some of these issues further by examining the results of the acculturation process and the issues that they pose for cultural groups and individuals living in plural societies. First, however, we need to consider some theoretical and methodological issues concerning plural societies.

Plural societies

Most societies do not contain a single cultural tradition, but are made up of a number of cultural groups interacting in various ways within a larger national framework. Indeed, it is difficult to find a nation-state at the present time that is culturally homogeneous. Plural societies have come about as a result of a variety of historical events, including colonization (of one culture by another), nation building (by placing borders around a number of distinct cultural groups), and migration (of individuals and groups to settle in other countries).

In the last chapter a framework (Figure 11-1) was presented to help our understanding of the ways in which individuals may orient themselves to the process of acculturation and four strategies or alternatives were discussed: assimilation, integration, separation, and marginalization. All are ways of describing not only individual preferences, but also the actual relationships among the various groups making up the plural society and the policies being pursued by them.

Here it is useful to add a third issue to the two raised in Figure 11-1: that of *who* is making the decisions about the course of acculturation and the long-term policy goals. When we focus on the preferences or choices being made by members of the acculturating group, the four terms in Figure 11-1 are appropriate. However, if these decisions are made by the dominant society about how groups *should* acculturate, then some other terms are required (see Berry 1974b). Voluntary assimilation is captured by the term *melting pot*, but forced assimilation may better be termed a *pressure cooker*.

To some extent integration implies a degree of voluntary cooperation on the part of both the acculturating and the dominant groups, and hence no new distinguishing term is required. In contrast, marginalization usually implies little voluntariness on the part of the acculturating group; it usually happens to them at the hands of the dominant group, but no distinctive term seems to be required. The counterpart to the case of *separation* (when it is desired by the acculturating group) is that of *segregation* (when imposed by the dominant group).

It should be obvious that if assimilation and separation run their full course, the society will no longer be plural. In the case of assimilation one homogeneous culture will eventually evolve, while in the case of separation the plural society may break apart into smaller, probably more homogeneous, independent societies. In the case of marginalization and segregation the societies remain in principle plural, but in practice there is only minimal interaction and participation among the groups. Clearly, the situation that has been termed integration represents the situation in a continuing plural society, where groups retain their distinctiveness and yet at the same time participate together in many of the major institutions of the larger society.

A term related to pluralism is *multiculturalism*. In our view a multicultural society is a plural society in which the pluralism is valued (by the population generally, by the various acculturating groups, and by government policy) and in which the diversity is likely to remain. In contrast, a plural society that is not multicultural is one in which there are governmental or political efforts to homogenize the population (via assimilation), to break it up (via separation), or to segment it (via marginalization or segregation). In short, a multicultural society is one in which integration is the generally accepted way of dealing with cultural diversity. Later we will introduce the notion of "multicultural ideology" to describe this generally positive orientation toward the maintenance of pluralism. A number of research questions arise in plural societies concerning the kinds of groups that often populate them, the implicit models employed in carrying out research in plural societies, and some of the assumptions contained in these models.

Plural societies are made up of a variety of groups. These groups usually distinguish themselves and are distinguished by others on the basis of *ethnicity*; they are sometimes referred to as *ethnocultural groups* and can be defined as follows. First, as a *group* there must be an identifiable set of individuals who socially interact and who maintain themselves over time; there also needs to be some social structure and some system of norms governing the

VOLUNTARINESS OF CONTACT

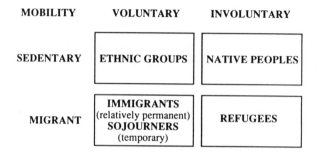

Figure 12-1 Kinds of groups in plural societies as defined by mobility, voluntariness, and permanence.

conduct of members. Thus, any category of people who merely share a common origin (for example, all persons in Brazil whose ancestors came from Italy) does not suffice to define an ethnocultural group. Second, the group needs to be *ethnic* in character (as distinct, for example, from a hobby, sports, or political group). The meaning of *ethnicity* is not easy to specify precisely (see Isajiw, 1974), but two aspects appear in most definitions. One is an *objective* facet, which refers to *descent* from an earlier cultural group in two distinct senses: being offspring and being derivative. People who are biological and cultural offspring can usually be defined by objective indicators such as name and genealogy; and ethnocultural group life can usually be studied objectively by social scientists to demonstrate that such things as food, dress, language, and religion are not exact replicas of original cultural phenomena, generation after generation, but are derivative in the sense of being versions of the original culture modified over time and space. The other key aspect is *subjective* in character, involving a sense of *identity* with or *attachment* to the group; people feel they belong and work to maintain the group and their membership in it. Both the objective and subjective aspects are usually considered necessary for the definition of an ethnocultural group.

Figure 12-1 illustrates five kinds of ethnocultural groups that are frequently studied; they are arranged according to two dimensions (mobility and voluntariness of contact), with a further distinction (that of permanence) added for one of the categories.

Some groups change their location, resulting in contact; *immigrants* and *refugees* do so with some degree of permanence while *sojourners* do so usually on a temporary basis. Others stay in their own place and have contact there; *native* or *indigenous peoples* are a clear example, while established *ethnic groups* usually have contact with others in their daily lives. The second dimension distinguishes those in voluntary contact, such as immigrants, sojourners, and ethnic groups, from those who usually have little choice in the matter (native peoples and refugees).[1]

It should be stressed that this typology is presented not to suggest that all peoples can be fitted into such a neat scheme, but to point out that the factors of voluntariness, mobility, and permanence may have important psychological consequences for individuals. Moreover, while these three factors are likely to be important in group relations in all plural societies, the terms used to refer to the various groups are likely to differ. The choice of terms to refer to these five types of groups probably reflects a bias rooted in one particular society (Canadian), and alternative terms may need to be employed in other plural societies. For example, "national group" may be used instead of "ethnic" or "indigenous" group in Europe, while "tribal group" continues to be used elsewhere (for example, in India).

One consequence of viewing work with ethnocultural and minority groups as an integral part of cross-cultural psychology is that research with such groups should be informed by the cross-cultural method (in which culture is taken seriously and represented fully in the research) rather than by methods that have served an acultural (or culture-blind) psychology (Berry, 1979b). It can be argued that methods employed in an "ethnic psychology" should parallel as much as possible those used in cross-cultural psychology (Berry, 1985a), so that ethnicity is taken as seriously as culture. A contrast between two implicit models of research is evident in the literature: one is the "mainstream-minority" model, the other the "multicultural" model. In the former there is assumed to be a single dominant culture (the "mainstream"), a number of satellite or subordinate groups ("minorities"), and perhaps some "fringe" groups (such as native peoples or refugees), while in the latter there is assumed to be a more complex pattern in which no single group is dominant in all regions (or in all social spheres), and smaller groups are incorporated in (and involved with) other groups in a variety of important ways. The first essential point to make is that the implicit model we employ in cross-cultural psychology should match as closely as possible the social and cultural reality in which we are working. Clearly, it would be inappropriate to study French-Canadians, French-Belgians, or French-Swiss from a "mainstream-minority" position, since these groups constitute full-scale national societies within their respective countries. Just as clearly, it is inappropriate to study Punjabis and Tamils in India or Yorubas and Ibos in Nigeria from this position. Why? Because although they may be numerically and politically in a nondominant or "minority" position they have viable cultures and identities within their respective plural societies. To carry out research with such peoples from the "mainstream-minority" point of view would be to allow political and demographic variables to override cultural and psychological ones.

---

[1] Others who were previously not in voluntary contact were, of course, slaves. Since slavery has now formally ended, it is not included as a category in Figure 12-1. Most descendants of slaves in the Western Hemisphere now make up ethnocultural or minority groups, and in some places (for example, Haiti, Jamaica) form the national society.

One consequence of working within the "mainstream-minority" framework is the frequent assumption that "minorities" are somehow deficient and need to become more like the "mainstream." Implicit is the view that they need to be "gently polished and reclaimed for humanity" (to quote Montaigne's phrasing of early French policy toward native peoples in their colonies). While we are aware that such views may be held by some citizens in dominant societies ("If they come here, they should learn to behave like the rest of us"), this does not require researchers to automatically carry out research from such an assimilationist point of view. Howard and Scott (1981) have argued that the failure to recognize the reality of cultural differences in plural societies has led to a *deficiency formulation* of difference. This kind of formulation leads in turn to judgments about ethnic minority groups in such terms as "disorganized," "normless," and "unstable," and to their individual members as being "ego-deficient," "immature," or "lacking in motivation." We have noted (in Chapter 11) that while acculturative stress may sometimes give rise to such social and psychological phenomena (particularly when there is a situation of marginalization), these outcomes are not inevitable. Clearly, our research concepts and models should reflect the multicultural alternative to these mainstream-minority views.

There is also an implicit bias in the "direction" of research. In the mainstream-minority model studies typically carry out analyses of mainstream attitudes to minorities; rarely in evidence are minorities' attitudes to the mainstream or attitudes of one minority to another. In the multicultural model, it has been argued (Berry & Kalin, 1979), there should be a full matrix of attitudes assessed; each group is capable of holding attitudes toward all groups (including itself), and these should be fully represented in the research (cf. Brewer & Campbell, 1976). Similarly, in acculturation research from the mainstream-minority point of view studies usually limit themselves to examining the changes in the minority groups as they gradually become more like the mainstream. In contrast, in the multicultural model *mutual* influences leading to changes in *both* groups in contact should be allowed for in research designs.

It can be argued that the constant pairing of the terms "ethnic" and "minority" (as in "ethnic minority") does not serve us well scientifically. It is obvious that in most plural societies there are ethnic groups that are not minorities in any sense of the term (cultural, demographic, or political), and just as obviously there are minorities that are not ethnic in character (for example, the handicapped, the aged). Thus the pairing of the two terms excludes two important sectors of the population. We cannot hope to understand the situation of an "ethnic minority" in a plural society unless we also understand the "ethnic majority" and their mutual relationships. Such an exclusive focus on ethnic minorities gives us only part of what we need to know and perhaps reinforces the implicit view that it is *they* who need "fixing" rather than *us*; this focus can also lead to ignoring the common fact that it is the *relationship* between "them" and "us" that should be of key scientific interest. Moreover, by studying only the *ethnic* minorities, excluding the *other* minorities, we cannot disentangle their position or treatment in society that may be due to being ethnically distinct from their being in a "minority" status.

Despite this preference for pluralistic alternatives to assimilation (which is based on the evidence presented in Chapter 11 with respect to acculturative stress) and our related preference for the "multicultural" model (which is rooted in the theoretical and methodological traditions in anthropology of accepting each cultural entity its own terms), we employ the term "minority" in the title of this chapter alongside the notion of "ethnic group." We do this because so much of the research in this area has been rooted in the mainstream-minority tradition and cannot be ignored.

Multiculturalism

A central issue to be addressed by cultural groups and governments in plural societies is how to manage their cultural diversity. While this issue can be addressed from a variety of perspectives, including political science, law, and economics, the approach taken here is predominantly psychological. Multiculturalism is meant to create a sociopolitical context within which individuals can develop healthy identities and mutually positive intergroup attitudes. Policies with respect to the continuation of pluralism are usually present; sometimes these are only implicit, but they can also be explicit. Those that explicitly favor pluralism are termed *multiculturalism policies*. We turn now to an examination of such policies in a few countries.

In Canada as in most immigrant-receiving countries early policies favored assimilation. However, this gradually changed, leading to the view that assimilation had not worked anywhere in the world and that it was impracticable as a general policy. In 1971 the Canadian Federal Government announced a national multiculturalism policy that was intended to:

break down discriminatory attitudes and cultural jealousies. National unity, if it is to mean anything in the deeply personal sense, must be founded on confidence in one's own individual identity; out of this can grow respect for that of others and a willingness to share ideas, attitudes and assumptions. A vigorous policy of multiculturalism will help create this initial confidence. It can form the base of a society which is based on fair play for all. The Government will support and encourage the various cultures and ethnic groups that give structure and vitality to our society. They will be encouraged to share their cultural expression and values with other Canadians and so contribute to a richer life for all. (Government of Canada, 1971, p. 3)

In essence the policy asserts that in Canada "although there are two official languages, there is no official culture, nor does any ethnic group take precedence over any other" (p. 1). Further, the policy asserts that the other cultural communities "are essential elements in Canada and deserve government assistance in order to contribute to regional and national life in ways that derive from their heritages, yet are distinctively Canadian" (p. 3).

Similar policies have also been proposed in other plural societies. In

Australia early views were largely assimilationist but evolved toward integrationist views recently (Poole, de Lacey, & Randhawa, 1985). In the late 1960s the Australian Minister for Immigration argued that "We must have a single culture ... I am quite determined we should have a monoculture, with everyone living in the same way, understanding each other, and sharing the same aspirations. We don't want pluralism" (quoted by Bullivant, 1985, p. 12). Within a few years, another Minister for Immigration had set the country on a multicultural course, claiming that "Australia is a multicultural society ... one of the most cosmopolitan societies on earth" (quoted by Bullivant, 1985, p. 17). Later, in 1978, a policy of multiculturalism was formally endorsed by the Australian government.

In Israel, where thousands of Jewish people have emigrated from both western (Europe and Western Hemisphere) and eastern (North Africa and Middle East) cultural traditions, and where a large Arab population was already resident, there is clearly a plural society in operation. However, a policy of westernization of eastern Jews was proposed: "the Israeli national leadership adopted the approach (supported by social scientists) that Middle Easterners should become Westernized through a process of resocialization ... facilitated by such factors as common Jewish nationality, religious tradition, and the relative similarity in physical appearance. Ethnic, cultural and economic differences were considered to be temporary and of only superficial importance" (Amir, 1986, p. 3). This assimilationist policy now seems to be diminishing in force and a "more genuine integration" is taking its place (Amir, 1986, p. 8). However, there is a clear de facto segregation between Jews and Arabs: "90% of Arab Israelis reside in separate towns and villages. Even the 10% who live in mixed cities occupy separate residential areas" (Amir, 1986, p. 11). Thus, we find a sharp contrast in policy toward different sectors of a population within a single plural society.

In Sweden an explicit multicultural policy was adopted in 1975 with three goals: equality, freedom of choice, and partnership:

The goal of *equality* implies continued work to give immigrants the same living standard as the rest of the population. The goal of *freedom of choice* implies that public initiatives are to be taken to assure members of ethnic and linguistic minorities domiciled in Sweden a genuine choice between retaining and developing their cultural identity and assuming a Swedish cultural identity. The goal of *partnership* implies that the different immigrant and minority groups on the one hand and the native population on the other both benefit from working together. (Lundström, 1986, p. 10)

This policy is implemented in various domains of public life, including libraries, drama, newspapers, broadcasting, and education, where many languages and cultural traditions are increasingly being represented.

Elsewhere in Europe the recent addition of guest workers and of immigrants from former colonies has directed the attention of many social scientists to the issue of pluralism. Most European countries have tended to favor an assimilationist orientation and much of the research has been cast in a similar mould. However, some recent thinking and research has shifted more to a pluralistic point of view. For example, Van Oudenhoven and Willemsen (1989), reviewing the evidence from intergroup relations in Europe, concluded that "in our opinion, some form of pluralism is to be preferred over complete assimilation. One of the negative consequences of full assimilation is that a cultural vacuum among minority groups members may develop. The second generation of immigrants in particular may lose their ethnic, linguistic, or religious roots, while not being rooted in the majority culture either" (p. 248).

Ethnic relations

The field of ethnic relations is a vast one; our intention here is simply to refer to the core concepts and attempt to illustrate how they can be incorporated into cross-cultural psychology and applied to the understanding and resolution of problems that arise in culturally plural societies.

Stereotypes. If we look upon stereotypes simply as cognitive categories that are necessary to bring order to diversity (D. L. Hamilton, 1981), then stereotypes may be useful psychological tools to have available in multicultural societies; individuals, in order to keep track of the numerous groups around them, may develop and share these generalizations as a normal psychological process (Berry, 1970). These acts of categorization are in essence benign; the difficulty lies with the overgeneralizations and the often negative evaluations (attitudes and prejudices) that are directed toward members of the categories. Thus, while stereotypes that are inaccurate or that carry negative evaluations are a problem, they can also make us aware of, and keep readily available, information that is important to have handy in day-to-day multicultural interactions.

Similar arguments have been elaborated by Taylor (1981), who has examined some of the "socially desirable" aspects of stereotyping in multicultural societies. These exist in "situations where intergroup stereotypes reflect mutual attraction, even though the members of each group maintain, through stereotypes, their own ethnic distinctiveness" (Taylor, 1981, p. 164). This situation, where a desire for both positive relations *and* group distinctiveness exists, we have identified (in Chapter 11) as the integration mode of relations in plural societies.

Attitudes. A fundamental feature of plural societies is that ethnic attitudes are likely to exist between in-group and out-group members. These may be relatively independent of ethnic stereotypes: one study (Gardner, Wonnacott, & Taylor, 1968) has demonstrated their factorial independence; that is, the degree of stereotyping of an ethnic group was unrelated to the evaluation (positive or negative) of that group. This finding lends support to the argument made above that ethnic stereotypes may be relatively benign in a plural society, since they are not inevitably linked to ethnic attitudes (which may not be benign).

A basic argument in our earlier discussion was that there should be a consideration of *reciprocal* attitudes (in a two-group case) or of the *matrix* of ethnic attitudes among *all* interacting groups in a plural society rather than a focus on just what the mainstream thinks of various minorities (see Box 12-1).

The first study to take this approach was that of Brewer and Campbell (1976) in East Africa (see Segall et al., 1990). In another study Berry and Kalin (1979) drew data from a national survey in Canada (Berry, Kalin, & Taylor, 1977) and extracted attitudes toward the five most numerous ethnic groups in the sample. The data in the five-by-five matrix have each group's *own group* rating on the diagonal, while the two halves of the matrix contain the particular pairs of *intergroup* ratings. Three questions may be asked of such a matrix: first, does the ethnocentric tendency to rate one's own group relatively high hold for all groups; second, does the tendency to rate all other groups in a consistent hierarchy also hold; and third, is there a balanced relationship (Heider, 1958) among the mutual attitudes held by a pair of groups?

Berry and Kalin (1979) found there to be a consistent tendency toward ethnocentrism (own group ratings always being higher than other group ratings), a high degree of commonality (a tendency to share a view of the "place" of each group in the plural society), and a moderate degree of reciprocity or balance in mutual evaluations. From a mainstream-minority perspective we might have learned only that English-Canadians (the presumed mainstream) are on top of the attitudinal hierarchy and that all others (examined only in relation to the English group) are located somewhere lower in attitudinal space. With the multicultural perspective we can better appreciate the complexity of multiple intergroup attitudes in such a society. We also may be able to advance social psychological theory in general by providing new insights into the nature of ethnocentrism and the applicability of Heider's (1958) balance theory beyond individual relations to the realm of intergroup relations.

As we noted earlier, the fourfold model proposed in Chapter 11 to conceptualize acculturation attitudes of members of nondominant groups can also be employed to describe the attitudes of individuals in the dominant society. To do this we can ask a sample of individuals in the larger society to indicate how they think the acculturation of others (for example, immigrants, native peoples) should proceed. Thus we may replace the items in scales designed to assess acculturation attitudes among acculturating groups so that they can be posed to these others; now the issue is whether others think that assimilation, integration, marginalization, and segregation *should be* the proper mode of acculturation and of eventual group relations.

When we examine the more objective aspects (structural features, policies, programs, and so on) or the more subjective aspects (attitudes toward how acculturation should take place), we are assessing the *multicultural ideology*

Box 12-1   Ethnocentrism and causal attributions in Asia

One approach to studying ethnic relations is that of attribution (Hewstone, 1989). The act of attribution involves inferring the causes of a person's behavior as being *internal* (due to some personal quality of the individual) or as *external* (due to some situational or environmental factor). Much research on attribution has shown that one tends to attribute causes of one's own behavior to internal factors when the behavior is positively evaluated and to external factors when one's behavior is negatively evaluated. Conversely, attributions of causes of the behavior of other individuals are to external factors when the behavior is positive but to internal factors when it is negative. This pattern has been called the "egocentric assumption" by Kelley (1973).

A first study, using the attribution concept in ethnic relations, was carried out by Taylor and Jaggi (1974) with Hindu participants in India. They were given a series of one-paragraph descriptions of an actor behaving in a social situation. In some cases the actors were Hindu, in others they were Muslims; in some cases the behaviors were socially desirable, in others they were undesirable. For example, in one paragraph a shopkeeper was either generous in a transaction or cheated the customer; sometimes the shopkeeper was identified as a Hindu, sometimes as a Muslim. Judgments were requested about the reasons for the behavior, using a set of alternatives that were internal (for example, the shopkeeper is generous), or external (for example, the shopkeeper was compelled by rules of commercial transactions).

Results showed that in all four situations, the Hindu participants were more likely to make internal attributions for positive behaviors of Hindu actors than for negative behaviors. Conversely, in two of the four situations they were more likely to make external attributions for Muslim actions for positive behaviors but internal ones for negative behaviors.

This pattern of results on interethnic attributions is consistent with the original work on interpersonal attributions. However, it is one-sided in the sense that Muslim participants were not included, and hence the reciprocal pattern could not be examined. Such a study was conducted by Hewstone and Ward (1985), using both Malay and Chinese participants in Malaysia. As expected, Malays made attributions in keeping with the theory. However, Chinese participants favored Malay actors over their own group, not supporting expectations. A follow-up study in Singapore raised further doubts about the generalizability of the original findings: while the Malays made internal attributions for positive behaviors of their own group, they did not make significantly different attributions for positive and negative behavior by the Chinese, nor did the Chinese attributions favor either group.

Hewstone (1989) interpreted the differences in findings across the three studies as due to the differing character of the sociopolitical context between the countries. Since the Indian study was not a reciprocal one, only the Malaysia-Singapore differences were commented on specifically. The key factor, according to Hewstone, is the more assimilationist ideology in Malaysia in contrast to the more tolerant multicultural one in Singapore. In Malaysia Malays tend to see themselves as the "mainstream" (and in positive terms), while the Chinese are considered a minority to be assimilated (and are less positively evaluated); the Chinese tend to share this less positive view of themselves. In contrast, a more tolerant multicultural policy and ideology in Singapore may be responsible for the minimal differences obtained there.

(Berry et al., 1977) of the larger society. At the policy and program levels, we have seen that some countries (for example, Canada, Australia) have made attempts to promote an integration mode of acculturation and to avoid assimilation, segregation, and marginalization; others (for example, the U.S.) are officially assimilationist (the U.S. national motto remains "E Pluribus Unum"), while a *de facto* pluralism is obvious; still others are clearly segregationist (for example, South Africa). At the attitudinal level, multicultural ideology has been assessed by creating a scale that loads pro-integration items as positive and the other three options as negative (Berry et al., 1977). In a national Canadian sample the mean ideology score was moderately in favor of multiculturalism, a finding that is consistent with the national policy discussed earlier.

Discrimination. A concrete outcome of these various cognitive and evaluative variables is, of course, the level of *discrimination* to be found in a multicultural society. Indeed, critics (e.g., Rocher, 1973) of multiculturalism as a general policy often claim that it has as its real motive the wish "to keep people in their place" by more easily identifying them as different and perhaps of lower value in society. In terms of the two issues raised in Figure 11-2 it is indeed possible that culturally distinct peoples are encouraged by the larger society to *maintain* their differences in order to *exclude* them from day-to-day participation in the economic, political, and educational life of the society. This danger has been recognized by many observers of multiculturalism and has been identified by Jayasuriya (1984) as the possibility of one's "lifestyle" limiting one's "life chances" in Australian society.

Note that discrimination is used here to refer not only to acts of forceful exclusion (such as in segregation and marginalization), but also to forceful inclusion (as in assimilation). Only in the integration mode, where a society is open to and accepting of the wishes of an individual or group, and where individuals are free to choose their preferred degrees of cultural maintenance and participation in the larger society, do we consider there to be no discrimination.

There is reason to believe that external factors like discrimination are an important determinant of the position of a group in society. In research on intergroup relations in India and The Netherlands (DeRidder & Tripathi, in press) a questionnaire was used in which subjects were asked to indicate what behavior they expected in reaction to various norm violations. These researchers worked with pairs of groups that are ethnically distinct and with pairs that are socially distinct (that is, managers and workers in industry). Subjects indicated how their own group would react to a norm violation by the other group as well as how the others would react to a norm violation by the subject's own group. Patterns of reactions tended to be similar across pairs of groups. In other words, if subordinates expected a stronger reaction from managers than from their own group, then managers would show a similar response pattern.

Ethnic identity

We saw earlier that an important aspect of belonging to an ethnocultural group is the sense of attachment to or identification with the group by its individual members. In monocultural societies such an identity is neither a distinguishing feature of a member nor likely to pose a problem. However, in plural societies one's ethnic identity serves to signal who one is; it can also sometimes be confused or even be lost.

For Aboud (1981, 1988) ethnic identity is one aspect of one's overall identity that can include personal (for example, name), social (for example, family) as well as cultural referents: "ethnic self-identity means knowing that oneself is defined in part by attributes which are in turn used to define an ethnicity" (Aboud, 1981, p. 39).

Perhaps the most influential theory of identity has been proposed by Tajfel (1978, 1982), known as "Social Identity Theory." For Tajfel (1978) one's social identity is "that *part* of an individual's self-concept which derives from his knowledge of his membership in a social group (or groups), together with the value and emotional significance attached to that membership" (p. 63). By extension, for our present purposes one's ethnic identity derives from the ethnocultural group to which one belongs. Further, social identity theory postulates that people strive for a positively valued social identity by comparing themselves to members of other groups and that they attempt to categorize and differentiate themselves from these others in a positive direction. These processes of categorization, differentiation, and positive valuation have been examined in a host of studies of intergroup relations, many of them with artificial experimental groups, called "minimal groups" by Tajfel. Others have extended this research tradition to natural groups, such as ethnolinguistic and racial groups (see Taylor & Moghaddam, 1987), revealing the probable universal status of the three processes. While full-scale cross-cultural replications have not yet been attempted, it is likely that such extensions will prove to be fruitful.

Extensions of Tajfel's ideas have been made by Boski (1987) in studying the national self-identity of Polish immigrants to Canada. Tajfel (1978) distinguished between two aspects of categorization: *criterial* attributes that split the population into discrete categories with definite boundaries and *correlated* attributes that are continuous qualities varying across individuals within a category. For example, an individual may form categories (Muslim/ Christian/Hindu) and then assign varying degrees of a quality (smart, lazy, and so on) to all members of the category. In Boski's view both category and quality measures need to be taken in order to fully understand an individual's ethnic identity.

This proposal stands in contrast to the more usual emphasis on category self-assignment alone. For example, among immigrants and their descendants (in country C) a typical approach is to ask for one's ancestral country of origin on both the father's (F) and mother's (M) side and then to pose the question: "How do you usually think of yourself? The options can be: As a "F"; as a "M"; as a "F-C"; as a "M-C"; as a "C"; or some other identity. Work in this mode (e.g., O'Bryan, Reitz, & Kuplowska, 1976; Berry et al., 1977) has usually found a significant change over time or over generations: immigrants themselves often identify as "F" or "M", second and third generations as "F-C" or "M-C" (an integrationist response), and later generations as "C" (an assimilationist outcome). Identity shifts are also common among non-dominant native peoples undergoing acculturation, but are usually more resistant to change toward an identification with the dominant society (Sommerlad & Berry, 1970).

In new nation-states identity shifts tend to be away from small-scale or local cultural identities toward larger nationwide identities. In one study (Segall, Doornbos, & Davis, 1976) Banyankore men in Uganda were interviewed before a new national constitution was enacted and again three years later. When asked "What are you?", the local cultural identity predominated over the national (Ugandan) identity. However, when asked "How should the Banyankore think of themselves?", the majority responded with a Ugandan identity. Segall et al. (1976) concluded that while the typical Munyankore man knew it was appropriate to identify with the new nation-state, few had yet come to do so.

Psychometric testing, using a variety of techniques, has also been employed (see Brand, Ruiz, & Padilla, 1974; Aboud & Skerry, 1984; Phinney, 1990, for reviews). The most common instrument has been the doll-choice technique among children, where a range of dolls of different skin color or in different cultural costumes are presented; the child is asked a series of questions about the dolls. The first studies were carried out by Clark and Clark (1939) with black children in the U.S.; subsequent studies have included Amerindian, Mexican American, and Maori children. The original study found that black children frequently chose a white doll to play with (rather than a black doll) and evaluated white dolls more positively than black dolls. Most of the subsequent studies have confirmed these original findings, but interpretations have varied: Clark and Clark considered the choices to reflect black self-rejection, but others considered alternative interpretations (such as the effect of race and language of the experimenter and the child's lack of familiarity with nonwhite dolls). Much of this work has been criticized for theoretical confusion and methodological inadequacies (see Aboud & Skerry, 1984). However, recent work with Native Indians in Canada that attempts to avoid these problems (Annis & Corenblum, 1986) confirms the most common findings: children who are of a minority racial group tend to be "accurate" (in distinguishing and correctly labeling the "Indian" and "White" dolls); to show a low degree of "self-identification" (in selecting the one that "looks like me"); and to exhibit a strong "white bias" (when picking the one that "looks nice"). Whether this pattern can be interpreted as self-rejection, however, continues to be disputed.

Language issues

Language is often at the heart of the dual questions of cultural maintenance and participation in the larger society. As one of the most distinctive and fundamental of cultural phenomena (see Chapter 7), for many people loss of language is equated with loss of culture. Language is also one of the most useful vehicles for participating in the social and economic institutions of the larger society. The most important issues surrounding language in plural societies are *language maintenance* (including the topics of language attitudes, language loyalty, and linguistic vitality) and *bilingualism* (including its psychological effects and the place of bilingualism in the school, the workplace, and other public institutions).

Language maintenance depends on a number of factors that are of psychological interest. First is the wish on the part of speakers to maintain their language in the new society by using it themselves and teaching it to their offspring. These language attitudes and behaviors have been widely researched (see, e.g., Fishman, 1966; O'Bryan et al., 1976; Clyne, 1982) among those peoples who use a language other than the dominant one in a particular society. The most impressive outcomes of this research are first the relatively strong (but variable) support in attitudes toward maintenance (exhibiting both individual and group differences) and second the discrepancy between attitudes and actual language behavior. For example, in the O'Bryan et al. (1976) report (Canada) and the Clyne (1982) study (Australia), relatively strong support for language maintenance was exhibited by many ethnic groups (for example, French, Greek, Italian, Ukrainian). However, for some ethnocultural groups (for example, Dutch and some Scandinavians) there is relatively little attitudinal support for language maintenance. Perhaps the variability that has been found within and across groups in general acculturation attitudes (Chapter 11) is a factor in the distribution of these language maintenance attitudes. Some indirect evidence for this link has been noted by Berry et al. (1987): those favoring the assimilation mode of acculturation tended to read newspapers, listen to radio, and to join clubs where the language of the dominant society was used; in contrast those favoring the integration and separation modes tended to read, listen, and join where their mother tongue was used.

However, individuals who hold positive attitudes toward language maintenance do not always know or use the language. This lack of correspondence is particularly noticeable in groups where most members are of second, third, or later generations (knowledge and use eroding with time in country). Thus, we may say that the issue of language maintenance is of central importance to many individuals who reside in plural societies, even though they do not always agree about the extent of language maintenance that is desirable or exhibit a degree of knowledge and use that is consistent with their preferences.

Attitudes held by others in the society are also an important part of the equation: in societies that are explicitly multicultural and display a multicultural ideology language maintenance will likely be far easier than where users are routinely denied rights to use their mother tongue. This factor helps to explain, in part, the attitude-behavior discrepancy noted above: language preferences cannot always become language practices when individuals and institutions in the dominant society consistently place obstacles in the way. The interruption of private conversations between two members of an ethnic group is not unknown; switching to the use of the dominant language at the insistence of a dominant group member is well-documented (e.g., Bourhis, 1983); and the denial of the right to educational institutions that operate in a nondominant language is a frequent occurrence in plural societies (see later section on schooling). On the other hand, support for language maintenance is often a keystone in a nation's multicultural policy: the teaching of "heritage languages" both in regular classes and in "extra" classes (evenings, weekends) is a common practice in societies that have adopted a multicultural arrangement.

Among those who are members of a particular group, but who do not know the group's ancestral language (and also among those who are not members), the motivation to learn it has been shown to be of central importance. In the work of R. C. Gardner (1985) language learning motives are considered to be more important than aptitudes. In a long series of studies Gardner has developed a comprehensive model to account for the acquisition of a second language, whether it is one's heritage language or that of another group. He distinguishes between two different motives: *instrumental* and *integrative*. When the major reason is to attain occupational or another type of advancement, the motive is said to be instrumental; when the major reason is a wish to learn more about the group and perhaps even to enter into the cultural life of (or even join) the group the motive is integrative. Both motives have been shown by Gardner to be important in second-language acquisition, and by measuring them independently he has assessed their separate contributions. Linking these language learning motives and the acculturation attitudes approach, Young and Gardner (1990) have demonstrated that for Chinese-Canadians a fear of linguistic assimilation is associated with separation attitudes and a sense of marginality. Conversely, support for maintaining their Chinese language and culture is associated with a preference for integration and a rejection of assimilation. This study nicely illustrates how the two distinct research traditions (language learning motives and acculturation attitudes) can be brought together theoretically and empirically to provide a more general insight into language behavior during acculturation.

The second main area of research has dealt with the question: if a language is maintained (as well as a second language being learned), how will bilingualism affect the language user? In answering this question there have been two main categories of research dealing respectively with the *cognitive* and the *social* consequences. A key research program in dealing with both these issues is that of W. E. Lambert (1967, 1977, 1980). Early studies of the academic, intellectual, and social achievements of bilingual children generally showed that they were "behind in school, retarded in measured intelligence and socially adrift" when compared to monolingual children (Lambert, 1977, p. 15). However, Lambert observed that these comparisons did not control for social class or educational opportunities, and when these factors were controlled in his own studies, bilingual children were ahead on both verbal and non-verbal measures of intelligence (Peal & Lambert, 1962; Lambert & Anisfeld, 1969).

Since then this picture has been broadened to include bilingual children from Singapore, Sweden, Switzerland, South Africa, and Israel, in addition to the original samples from Montreal. In particular, bilingual children (even when matched on IQ) appeared to be advanced in cognitive flexibility, divergent thinking, and creativity, possibly resulting from the perspective gained from knowing and using a whole new set of linguistic signs and categories (see Segalowitz, 1980, for a review). These studies, Lambert (1977) has noted, all involve bilingualism in two languages that are socially valued in their particular context; that is, the learning of the second language was not likely to threaten the survival of the first language. This situation has been termed *additive bilingualism* by Lambert in contrast to *subtractive bilingualism* where learning a second language often implies a loss of the mother tongue (because of national linguistic or educational policies). It is an important research question to discover whether the positive cognitive consequences of bilingualism are also evident in subtractive situations.

Social consequences of bilingualism, particularly effects on personal identity, have also been examined. In a parallel series of studies in the U.S. (Louisiana) and Canada (Quebec) Lambert and his colleagues (Gardner & Lambert, 1972; Aellen & Lambert, 1969) noted wide individual differences in identities of bilingual children: some identified with one or the other language group, some with both, and some with neither. This pattern corresponds rather closely to the four general modes of acculturation presented in Chapter 11.

Because so much of the work on these language issues has been conducted in Western societies, it is essential for cross-cultural psychologists to examine them in other plural societies in the world. The legacy of the colonial era has yielded many nation states (for example, Nigeria, India) where numerous indigenous languages exist and are used regionally, while one or more national languages (sometimes including that of the former colonial power) are being advocated. As we have argued throughout this book, it is inappropriate to attempt to generalize these (mainly) Western findings to other societies, and it would be foolhardy to develop educational or other programs on their basis.

Educational issues

Everyone agrees that one of the main functions of the school is to transmit important aspects of culture from one generation to another (Camilleri, 1986); as such it is a central institution in the processes of socialization and enculturation (see Chapter 2). In a plural society the questions naturally arise: *whose* culture is to be transmitted by the schools, using *whose* language, and incorporating *whose* values, knowledge, and beliefs? Until quite recently in most countries the answer was clear: the dominant culture's interests held sway, and there was little tolerance for pluralism in the nation's classrooms.

Most plural societies are grappling with these issues, and numerous volumes have been published in the past few years (e.g., Eldering & Kloprogge, 1989; Modgil, Verma, Mallick & Modgil, 1986; Lynch, 1986; Ouellet, 1988; Poole, de Lacey, & Randhawa 1985; Samuda, Berry, & Laferrière, 1984). Societies range from those that have rejected pluralistic alternatives to those that have embraced "multicultural education" and are experimenting with a variety of options (see, e.g., Banks & Lynch, 1985). The key components in multicultural education are the *educational system* (which often reflects only the culture of the larger or dominant society), the *teacher* (who may or may not be culturally part of the larger society), and the *student* (who in the present analysis is culturally *not* a member of the larger society). There is a complex triangular relationship among these components (cf. Chodzinski, 1984), within which cultural similarities and differences need to be understood. The most common situation is one in which the school and teacher share the heritage of the larger society but the student does not. However, other patterns are also evident. For example, in areas of large-scale immigration both the teachers and students can share a particular heritage that is different from the school and the larger society; or there may be some individual students of the dominant society in a school where another ethnocultural heritage is dominant among teachers and other students. In all cases of cultural dissimilarity, however, issues of both school curriculum and assessment arise; we now turn to these two issues.

Schooling. According to one analysis (McLeod, 1984), there are three main types of multicultural schooling: ethnic-specific, problem-oriented, and intercultural. In the first type the cultural content (history, values, religion, language) of a particular ethnic group is emphasized by the group, who operate a school for their own members, sometimes full-time but sometimes part-time. Such schools have existed in most plural societies for a long time and are not *in and of themselves* multicultural; in fact, they are unicultural and provide for each group the educational services that a public school does for the majority group. But *taken together* the educational system in which such schools operate may be termed multicultural, since more than a single cultural group is catered to by the system as a whole. Indeed, they may be an important first step on the road to full multicultural education, since such schools provide a vehicle for culture and language maintenance; however, they clearly do not provide a vehicle for intergroup participation.

The problem-oriented type of education is directed toward some identified difficulty being experienced by particular groups. These include poor achievement in learning a second language (usually the dominant language) and compensatory programs for the "culturally disadvantaged." As we have seen, full participation in the national society usually requires functional fluency in the national language(s); thus, solutions to the first of these problems may be of fundamental importance. However, as we have also seen, such second-language acquisition should be attempted in an "additive" rather than a "subtractive" way if other problems (both cognitive and social) are to be avoided. In contrast, the second problem usually being addressed (that of "cultural disadvantage") requires a further distinction. Sometimes it resides mainly in the historical prejudices of the dominant society. As Feuerstein (1979, p. 39) has cogently argued, this concept should only be employed when a person or group no longer has access to their *own* cultural traditions and supports; it should not be used when they are functioning outside the dominant culture. Put in terms of our own framework, marginalized persons and groups may be "culturally disadvantaged" and perhaps also those who are on the route toward assimilation (prior to full incorporation in the new culture), but not those who pursue cultural distinctiveness by separation or integration strategies. The other aspect of "cultural disadvantage" is that it is often used as a euphemistic term for "economic disadvantage"; that is, when there is unequal access to the common resources of a society (see D. Sinha, 1990).

The third type, which emphasizes intercultural knowledge and competence, comes closest to a multicultural education in its most common usage. Here there are educational materials that represent, if not all the world's peoples, then the major cultures, especially if they are represented in the plural society. In addition to learning *about* a variety of peoples, there is an emphasis on learning to *live with* cultural differences; that is, the cognitive is supplemented by an emphasis on the social and affective aspects of education (McLeod, 1984).

What is common among all of these forms is an acceptance of the view that cultural variation should be represented and transmitted in the school system in order for children to accept it in society. At the same time there is a recognition that the school should build links for the children to others outside their own group with whom they will eventually live and work. Thus the hallmarks of a multicultural education are both cultural maintenance *and* participation; the former without the latter leads to encapsulation (of both the dominant group and the various ethnic groups), while the latter without the former leads to enforced assimilation.

Experience varies in different plural societies. For example, in Europe, where many countries have become increasingly plural with the arrival of "guest workers," the Council of Europe and the European Conference of Ministries of Education have tended to adopt more pluralist policies over the past fifteen years (see, e.g., Rey, 1988). In 1970 the Ministries passed a resolution that favored the integration of children of guest workers into the host country schools and that promoted the maintenance of their cultural and linguistic links with their home countries, so that on their (presumed and anticipated) eventual return they would not find themselves strangers in their own lands. However, schools have continued to be largely assimilationist in orientation, with the exception of Sweden (where, as we have seen, there is provision for own-culture schools for immigrants if they so wish), and The Netherlands (where parents have the constitutional right to have their children educated in a school which teaches their religious or cultural values). In recent years an emphasis has shifted from cultural to intercultural issues; that is, from ethnic-specific and problem-orientations toward mutual understanding of host country and guest worker populations. This shift seems to have accompanied the gradual realization that eventual return is not likely for a large proportion of the guest workers and that a longer-term educational arrangement needs to be worked out (Rey, 1988).

Because of the central role of language in education, a great deal of research has been conducted on linguistic aspects of formal schooling in plural societies (J. Edwards, 1984). In addition to language being the practical vehicle for much of what transpires in the school, it also has great political and symbolic value for its users (Laferrière, 1984). The central issue surrounds the concept of *bilingual education*. As Edwards (1984), puts it:

bilingual education is primarily education for minority groups – either indigenous or immigrant – and, as such, it has something to do with the assimilation or nonassimilation of these groups into the larger society . . . Is bilingual education to serve the cause of an enduring cultural pluralism or multiculturalism, or is it actually to expedite the smooth assimilation of disparate groups into the mainstream? (p. 184)

In response to this central question two distinct forms of bilingual education have developed: *transitional* and *maintenance*. The first is a bridging operation, in which both the child's mother tongue and the dominant languages are used, but with the goal of phasing out the former and replacing it with the latter once functional competence has been developed to a level sufficient to carry the curriculum to the child. The second form has the goal of developing fluency in the language of the dominant society without diminishing competency in the mother tongue.

As we noted in the previous section on language issues, both positive and negative consequences of bilingualism are possible but they depend on a number of psychological, sociocultural, and policy factors. For example, if the language learning motives are integrative, acculturation attitudes are assimilative, and there is no interest in language maintenance, then transitional bilingual education may provide an easy route toward full participation without any cognitive or social difficulties. On the other hand such a program may have disastrous consequences for a group that is proud of its language and wishes to have full cultural maintenance (perhaps by pursuing separation) or partial maintenance (by pursuing integration).

Language policies and practices in schools vary considerably across plural societies and across ethnic groups within the same plural society (e.g., Malewska-Peyre, 1988). For example (Skutnabb-Kangas, 1981), in Sweden Finnish-speaking students have maintenance programs, but smaller groups (mainly of guest worker origin) may not. In Canada some French and English speakers have maintenance programs for learning the other "official" language in optional bilingual programs, but transitional programs only are available for most other groups; in principle Native Peoples have the choice to operate their own schools in their own way. In Australia, the U.S., and the U.K. only transitional programs are generally available, while in Switzerland moving to another language area requires schooling in that language only.

Of particular interest is the *immersion* type of program for acquiring a second language. Initiated by the work of Lambert and his colleagues (Lambert & Tucker, 1972), this approach places the child immediately and completely in a classroom where the second language only is used; the child often has no prior exposure to or knowledge of that language. In Canada these programs have been employed mainly to provide native English speakers with French fluency, but the system has been extended to other countries. Careful evaluation by Lambert generally shows no lag in native language competency or in general academic progress; but there is a large-scale improvement in second-language competency. As Edwards (1984) points out, however, these studies have taken place (and have been evaluated) in a particular social, cultural, and political context: this is where the two languages involved both have "official" status, where the second language (French) is usually that of the local majority, and where the mother tongue (English) is that of the national majority. All of these factors point to an additive form of bilingualism, with substantial opportunity for daily use of the second language and the possible operation of both integrative and instrumental motives to learn the second language. Whether the same generally positive outcome will be present in other sociopolitical contexts is largely an open question. Once again, it would be unwise to pursue immersion-type bilingual education programs in other plural societies (or even with other groups, in other regions in the same plural society) without considering the potential influence of these contextual factors.

Assessment. Children from minority groups who are not well-integrated in society typically obtain low scores in school examinations and on school achievement tests. When mental ability tests are administered that presumably are less dependent on curriculum-bound knowledge, a somewhat more diversified picture emerges, but low achievements still prevail. Since educational and economic advancement is often dependent on good school results, low scores tend to have negative consequences, not only for the child as an individual but also for the group as a whole. The lack of advancement means that existing social status differences are likely to be continued from generation to generation.

Suggested remedies for such a situation are dependent on what is seen as the reason for the low scores of minorities. Generally speaking, antecedents can be sought with the persons concerned, with the society and its institutions, and with the assessment instruments. If the persons are the focus of attention, emphasis will be placed on improving the opportunities of children within the existing educational system. Enrichment programs, sometimes even directed at the home environment of the preschool child (Lombard, 1981), are carried out to raise the performance of children at school. These programs take existing educational standards as a given and try to improve the adaptation of individuals to the prevailing demands of the society. Authors who see characteristics of the social system as the main reason take low scores as evidence that the society and, more particularly, the schools need to be changed so that aspects of all cultures represented in a society are integrated into a new multicultural educational system (e.g., McDermott & Goldman, 1983). The perspective of authors on assessment instruments is dependent on their outlook on the position of minorities in the educational system as a whole.

Instruments can be criticized because they are psychometrically biased against members of minority groups. For example, item content can reflect typical experiences of children of the dominant group. In numerous bias analyses (see Chapter 9) items have been identified on which a minority group was at a disadvantage. Preferably tests should be used that have been screened for bias, but if such tests are not available, at least the user should be aware of the possibility that scores of minority children may be suppressed.

The elimination of biased items does not necessarily lead to a substantial increase in the level of performance of minority groups. In the U.S. research on bias has shown that the low scores of children from the black community remain largely unaffected. More important, test score differences by and large correspond to differences in criteria, such as success in higher education (Jensen, 1980).

There is a wide range of opinions on the question of what consequences such findings should have. In the U.S. there has been strong criticism of the practice of applying the same cut-off on IQ scores for black and white children when placement in special educational programs is considered. In many regions the proportion of black children in special education programs is much higher than for white children. This has been claimed to be a clear indication that the tests used are insensitive to minority cultures and cannot serve as a common standard for the diverse ethnic communities (cf. Jones & Jones, 1988).

Some researchers, notably Mercer (cf. Lewis & Mercer, 1978), have designed scoring systems in which the IQ score of a child is compensated for adverse social circumstances, such as a broken home and low socioeconomic status of the family. Mercer assumes that the distribution of "intelligence" in all groups ultimately is the same. The performance of a child should be measured against that of children in similar circumstances. The score that is derived in this way has been named the "Estimated Learning Potential" by Mercer. This approach may be suitable to identify children that are disadvantaged (that is, have relatively high scores given their environment). However, it has not been demonstrated that the ELP score is valid in the sense that children can live up to the potential that is ascribed to them in this way. In other words, Mercer is likely to be right in seeing depressed scores as the effect of adverse social conditions. But this effect may well persist over time and certainly cannot be compensated for by a manipulation of test scores.

A more creative approach is the direct assessment of learning potential advocated by Feuerstein (1979). In this approach the current level of knowledge of a child is established first. Thereafter the rate of learning (for example, number of trials or cues needed) and the highest attainable level of performance is assessed. In line with the intuitive appeal of this approach end scores of learning potential tests tend to have a higher validity than the traditional IQ tests when school performance is used as a criterion (Lutje Spelberg, 1987).

So far tests have been treated as a means of assessment. Through the choice of item content they can also be used as a means of influencing the school curriculum, since teachers are apt to teach what their pupils are required to know. Authors like Samuda (1975, 1988) have no doubt that existing instruments promulgate social inequality and discrimination in Western societies. By changing the nature and the content of instruments educational assessment can be used to change school education.

It appears that earlier views that sought to put the blame for unequal test scores primarily on the tests have lost much of their momentum. However, a serious concern about cultural bias has become and will remain an inherent aspect of assessment, just as there is continuing concern for validity and the establishment of norms (American Educational Research Association, 1985). It is now generally recognized that within a society intergroup differences in test scores often are a reflection of a real state of affairs. These differences constitute evidence that points to the need for compensatory measures. Political decisions are required to determine which measures should be taken.

The choice between quota selection of minority groups, school enrichment, or home enrichment goes beyond the competence of assessment experts. Still, tests can provide important information that can form the basis for decisions both at the individual level and at the group level.

Conclusions

The cross-cultural psychological study of ethnic groups and minorities in culturally plural societies should be informed by what we have learned from the more conventional international approach. It should emphasize the cultural characteristics that support individuals and groups who remain ethnically distinct and should recognize the importance of understanding such distinctiveness from the point of view of the people themselves. While in principle the cross-cultural approach is also comparative, the examination to date has tended to be limited to a few Western industrial societies that have been migrant-receiving over the past few centuries. An urgent need, if the universality of current knowledge is to be established, is to draw a wider range of plural societies (for example, China, India, Nigeria, USSR) into this field of study. Until then, while we believe that the perspective and approach taken in this chapter are sound, the conclusions that can be drawn must remain tentative.

13 Organizations and work

As we have seen in Part I of this book, cross-cultural psychologists maximize the range of variation in the phenomena they study by including in their projects groups far removed from urbanized industrial ways of life. In contrast, organizational or industrial psychology, because of its main interest (human behavior in the contemporary industrial or administrative work setting), has focused on societies that have been industrialized or are in the process of industrialization. Interest in cultural factors has increased with intercultural contacts in industry, science, and technical-assistance programs. An impetus to cross-cultural organizational research came from the realization that in countries with similar technological conditions the productivity of employees is not always at the same level. This led to a search for psychocultural factors that could account for the discrepancies. Many American researchers were especially fascinated with the industrial growth of Japan in the 1960s and 1970s.

This chapter is centered around three themes where cultural differences and organizational variables mesh. First, we discuss whether the formal characteristics of organizations are the same everywhere or whether there are systematic differences across cultures in the way organizations tend to be structured. Then we deal with what is perhaps the most well-known topic of cross-cultural organizational research, namely differences in management behavior. The third section is concerned with differences in workers' needs, motives, and values across cultures.

Organizational structure

The most important characteristic of complex organizations is the distribution of tasks. Not every employee has the same responsibilities and the same kind of work. The total body of work that has to be performed is assigned to different divisions and subdivisions. The structural aspects of an organization can be represented on an organizational chart.[1] The question we pose is whether or not organizations in different countries have similar structures.

Lammers and Hickson (1979) studied cultural variation in organizational

---

[1] It is assumed that the reader is familiar with such charts.

structure. They suggest three types of organizations: "Latin," "Anglo-Saxon," and "Third World." The Latin type is more of a classical bureaucracy with (among other things) a centralized structure and a large number of hierarchical levels. It is found in southern and eastern Europe. The Anglo-Saxon type is more flexible, with decentralization and a relatively small number of hierarchical levels as important features. This flexible type is prevalent in northwest Europe and in North America. For third world countries the traditional organization is characterized by central decision-making, little formalization of rules, and paternalistic leadership. The features of the traditional organization according to Lammers and Hickson are also found in small firms and family businesses in West European countries. Lammers and Hickson believe that Hofstede's study (to be discussed later in this chapter) supports their categorization, although in their opinion a fourth type emerges from his results, namely an inflexible bureaucracy with strong rule orientation but limited hierarchy. Germany and Israel are among the countries where this type is found relatively frequently. Lammers and Hickson present their typology as tentative; it is based on a limited number of studies. For example, the data underlying the traditional organization come from a single but extensive interview study by Negandhi and his colleagues (cf. Negandhi, 1979, for a summary), in which U.S. subsidiaries were compared with local firms in six South American and Southeast Asian countries.

Udy (1970) has carried out one of the very few comparative studies of organizations over a wide range of preindustrial societies. He analyzed data from 125 societies in the HRAF (Murdock, 1975). In Udy's view there is a shift from *production*-determined (associated with hunter-gatherers) to *socially* determined (associated with agriculturists) forms of work in preindustrialized societies. In a production-oriented form of organized work the objectives of how and what to produce are given by the environmental setting. The buffalo hunt of some Native American groups is an example. The socially determined work context leads to a relatively stable organization that continues to exist when production does not demand it. An example is the family unit doing agricultural work. This form of organization is, according to Udy, low in effectiveness, efficiency, and innovative capacity.

Udy's study addressed the question to which extent subsistence variables are responsible for differences in organizational types. In many respects the shifts in types coincide with shifts in industrial development. At the same time the traditional organization that Lammers and Hickson consider characteristic of the Third World can still be found in industrial societies, for example in small agricultural communities of many regions in Western Europe. As we shall see later, structural aspects of organizations are correlated with other aspects of technological development, and this makes it difficult to disentangle the various variables.

In the 1970s and early 1980s the importance of political factors was emphasized, in particular the contrast between (Marxist) socialism and capitalism. As far as industrial organizations are concerned the main distinction is between public and private ownership. The latter leads to hierarchical domination and exploitation of the workers, according to Marxist theory. In Box 13-1 political factors are briefly discussed.

Political variables are mentioned here because in cross-cultural comparisons of organizations they are confounded with other cultural variables like values, beliefs, and customs. This is particularly evident in the orientation that has had the most significant impact on the discussion of the role of cultural factors in organizations, namely the *contingency* approach.

Modern organizational theory distinguishes dimensions of organizational structure from the determinants of this structure. According to Robbins (1987) there are three important dimensions: complexity, formalization, and centralization. *Complexity* refers to the degree of differentiation in an organization, that is, the diversity of groups of specialists, the number of levels in the management hierarchy, and the number of different locations at which the organization is actually operating. *Formalization* refers to the degree of standardization in tasks, ranging from almost total absence of any rules to a high degree of programming of what to do and how to do it. *Centralization* refers to the concentration of decision-making, which can be concentrated at a single point in the organization or widely dispersed.

The structure is contingent upon variables such as the size (number of employees), technology, resources, and history of the organization. In a broader sense contingency variables also include the environment in which the organization is functioning; environmental conditions affect the organization, but fall largely outside its sphere of control. Some aspects of the environment are directly relevant, for example, attitudes of customers, government regulations, and prices of commodities. The broader environment of an organization also encompasses the form of government of the country, the level of education of the work force, and even technological progress in some other part of the world insofar as it affects the market for an organization's product. The explanatory status of contingency variables is a matter of debate. They are seen by some authors as direct determinants of structure, by others as constraints that limit the range of potential structures of an organization.[2]

One form of the contingency approach, reminiscent of the absolutist perspective outlined in Chapter 10, is the "culture-free hypothesis." It maintains that situational demands are the sole determinants of organizational change and that theories about organizations have validity independent of the culture in which an organization functions. The effects of technology are so strong that they suppress the more subtle effects of cultural variables. Consequently, the relationships between structural or contextual variables

---

[2] Related to this are differences of opinion as to how important contingency variables are. For example, Robbins (1987) argues that they act as constraints that narrow decision-making choices and emphasizes that the structure of an organization to a considerable extent is the outcome of a battle for power; those in power want a structure that allows them to keep maximal control.

Box 13-1   The influence of the political context

The most extensive politically inspired changes in organizations have occurred in the People's Republic of China (e.g., Laaksonen, 1988). The Workers' Congress, legally established in 1950, gave the rank-and-file workers of an organization some influence in management, although much of the authority remained with members of the Communist Party.

Perhaps the most far-reaching experiments concerned participation, (that is, involvement in activities outside the immediate sphere of one's own task). In the West participation usually refers to influence on the decision-making processes higher *up* the hierarchical ladder or to co-operation between various departments (for example, technical and marketing). In the PRC the Workers' Congresses represent such a system of participation up the line. But in China there is also participation *down* the line. After the Cultural Revolution of the 1960s, managers and administrators were required to do physical work one day per week. Students and teachers, including university professors, were sent to rural areas to do manual work. These practices may have had some advantages (managers learn to know the work of their subordinates and communication is improved), but they were mainly inspired by the political ideal of a more egalitarian society. Later on technical expertise and knowledge (including academic knowledge) became again a respected reason for social and economic (salary) inequality in the PRC.

Political changes usually were followed by staff changes at the managerial level, For example, after 1978, there was a trend toward more influence of employees in the election of managers (Lockett, 1983). Despite the upheavals, the Chinese economy has developed rather well. Laaksonen (1988) suggests: "Perhaps, taken as a whole, the changes after all only rubbed the surface structure of Chinese society, and the basic structure, leaning upon the old culture, has not been destroyed too much" (p. 233). The majority of the Chinese still live in the rural areas, which were largely untouched by the political changes.

A major study on the distribution of power and influence in organizations as a consequence of differences in legislation was carried out in eleven (mainly Western) European countries and Israel by an international research group called Industrial Democracy in Europe (IDE, 1981). The goal of this project was to find out whether state regulations and legislation are related to organizational structure and behavior, particularly as far as workers' participation is concerned. It was found that participation, especially at the collective level through labor unions, indeed is influenced by the extent to which regulations concerning participation are entrenched in the law.

Individual rank and file workers were found to have little influence in the West European democracies; most organizations in these countries could be characterized as centralized and undemocratic. Individual employees, especially at low levels of the hierarchy, also felt little involved with decision-making processes in the organization. In Yugoslavia, the only socialist state in the IDE study, workers' influence was clearly more substantial.

According to the IDE group their results indicate that democracy in industries is influenced by sociopolitical factors rather than by requirements of a technological or structural nature. They expect that modification of the hierarchical characteristics of the work organization can lead to more democracy. However, this requires a complex of changes that is not easily realized.

Finally it may be noted that no effect was found of cultural values (cooperation and equality in power) on the extent to which participation promoting legislation existed in various countries. In other words cultural values did not appear to become manifest indirectly in laws and regulations.

are supposed to be invariant across cultures (e.g., G. A. Miller, 1987). The optimal structure of an organization can be derived from the technological and political conditions under which it has to operate. Adaptation of a given technology will have the same structural consequences in all national settings. Countries at approximately the same level of industrial development should show strong similarities in organizations. The idea that technological development will have a homogenizing effect on organizations is known as the *convergence* hypothesis (Ronen, 1986).

However, in some international comparative studies with companies of similar size operating in the same branch of industry major differences have been claimed to emerge. Maurice (1979) adheres to a relativist position (see Chapter 10), claiming that cross-national comparisons within the contingency approach are no more than extensions of studies within a single country. One might say that the convergence approach, according to Maurice's views, is based on imposed etics (see Chapter 9). In such comparisons, Maurice argues, culture is treated merely as something accidental that happens to be as it is, but also could have been different. He maintains that culture is part of the essence of an organization; it cannot be understood separate from the culture in which it is situated.

In a comparison of the hierarchical structure of matched pairs of firms from France and the (then) Federal Republic of Germany, two neighboring countries of similar technological advancement and political orientation, considerable differences were found in salary between employees low and high in the hierarchy. There were also differences in the number of hierarchical levels and opportunities for advancement on the basis of technical experience as opposed to formal education, with France having the more hierarchical structures. Maurice has explained these differences in terms of cultural background variables, such as the educational system and social stratification variables, which differ between France and Germany. In another study with data from Great Britain, France, and Germany similar variations between the countries were reported (Maurice, Sorge, & Warner, 1980).

While convergence may occur at the level of organizational structure and technology (macro-level variables), individual attitudes and values (micro-level variables) will remain culturally distinct. According to J. Child (1981) external factors impose certain limits within which organizations develop in harmony with the culture of a country. Cultural variables can moderate the effects of an existing political and economic system as well as organizational characteristics. Thus, differences exist where contingency theory would predict uniformity. However, Child noted that the influence of situational factors on variables of organizational structure is weaker and less consistent than on process variables at the behavioral level such as decision-making processes and managerial roles. The results with which he illustrated his argument, like those of Maurice, came from Western Europe (a study with 137 executives in 18 British firms and 50 executives in 26 West German firms).

Drenth and Groenendijk (1984) also question the assumption underlying the convergence hypothesis that technological requirements (which lead to convergence) should be more important than cultural factors. They see little reason to assume strong cultural influences on structural characteristics, because clear patterns of interrelationships between cultural variables and organizational structure have not been established. Drenth and Groenendijk argue that although cultural variables do not have much to do with how an organization is structured, they may have much to do with how it functions. With respect to a structural variable such as formalization (that is, the presence of formal rules and procedures) there are few cultural prescriptions, but the extent to which employees adhere to the rules will differ between cultures. Similarly, in respect of centrality of decision-making there can be large differences between cultures in the actual influence of lower echelons, even if structurally the decision-making power is in the hands of top executives everywhere.

Concern for social psychological variables is reflected in the notion of *organizational culture*, in which an organization is conceived of as a kind of miniculture with its own system of values and meanings, different from other organizations. Some conceptual and empirical difficulties with the notion of organizational culture are discussed in Box 13-2.

Our discussion has revealed little consensus on the significance of cultural variables. Opinions differ along two main dimensions. The first concerns the contrast between institutional-level and individual-level variables. Organizational structure is primarily a concept from organizational sociology and

---

Box 13-2 Organizational culture

Culture is usually defined at the level of populations that show differences on a large array of social and psychological variables. Organizational culture is defined at the level of organizations. The underlying assumption is that organizations differ from each other not only on variables such as production techniques, marketing, and attitudes of their employees, but also with respect to deep-rooted beliefs and values. Deal and Kennedy (1982) write about the "inner values," "rituals," and "heroes" of an organization as determinants of its success. Heroes are significant figures (the company founder or other senior executives with a large influence). Organizational culture refers to the subjective, sometimes called "soft," aspects of the organization.

The concept of organizational culture is based on the observation that organizations in some countries have a much better performance record than in others. Japanese industries particularly have shown a rapid rate of development from the 1950s through the 1980s. This success has been ascribed largely to social policies and management practices that allegedly find their origin in Japanese culture (e.g., Ouchi, 1981). The step from the national level to the level of separate organizations was easily made. The popularity of the concept of organizational culture results largely from best sellers written for managers. Despite strong criticism of its methodology, a book by Peters and Waterman (1982) has been most influential. It contained analyses of a number of American industries that were highly successful, despite the depressed economy of the late 1970s and early 1980s. Peters and Waterman give two reasons for this success, namely strong leadership and a complex of values that is shared by those who belong to the organization.

To capture the essence of an organization's culture anthropological research methods have been prominent. An analogy with ethnographic research, including "thick description" as advocated by Geertz (1973), has been suggested repeatedly (e.g., Allaire & Firsiotu, 1984; Frost, Moore, Louis, Lundberg, & Martin, 1985). Authors with a background in psychology such as Schein (1985) emphasize intangible aspects, like the "feel" of an organization and recommend the use of more subjective methods, such as interviewing, observation (without standardized schedules), and group discussion.

The limited volume of empirical research based on more objective methods so far has shown few promising results. For example, P. D. Reynolds (1986) developed a questionnaire for fourteen aspects of organizational culture described in the literature. A presumably excellent company differed from two others on only four of the fourteen dimensions. Lens and Hermans (1988) distinguished four types of organizational climate, which they saw as corresponding with four types of individual motivation. No significant correlations were found between questionnaire scores for organizational climate and motivational orientations of senior managers.

An important study has been reported by Hofstede, Neuijen, Ohayv, & Sanders (1990). Twenty organizations in Denmark and The Netherlands participated. First, interview data (guided by a checklist) were collected from key informants. Then an extensive questionnaire was administered to a stratified sample in each organization. Finally, the findings were checked in feedback discussions. Employee values were found to differ more on demographic variables (such as nationality, age, and education) than on organization membership. The main differences between organizations were found in daily practices as they are perceived by the employees. The core of an organizations's culture appeared to lie more in shared daily practices than in shared values. Hofstede et al. argue that cultural values are acquired fairly early in life and are difficult to change later on; in contrast, organizational practices are learned at the workplace. From this study organizational culture and culture at the level of nations emerge as phenomena of a different order. Hofstede and his colleagues point out that the use of the same term at both levels can be misleading. Still they do not abandon the term *organizational culture*. In fact, they propose six dimensions to describe the differences in perceived practices. However, it should be clear that the meaning of the term has changed considerably.

Summarizing the evidence, it appears to us that caution is needed in drawing parallels between national and organizational culture. Apart from terminological confusion there is the problem whether culture at the societal level can have (approximately) the same meaning as at the level of an organization. Organizational culture is a label derived from research that employs mainly impressionistic and subjective methods. The findings in the popular literature were based on *post hoc* and impressionistic interpretations of industrial success. There is little evidence collected with more objective methods that point to major differences in values between employees of various organizations within a more or less culturally homogeneous country. Differences that have been mentioned are not so much a matter of cultural values or meanings, but, more superficially, a matter of style.

tends to be defined at the institutional level. The cross-national typology by Lammers and Hickson (1979) is an example. Among psychologists (for example, Drenth and Groenendijk) there is a tendency to emphasize the importance of organizational processes and individual behavior. The second dimension concerns the role of culture; two contrasting viewpoints were identified, corresponding roughly to the contrast between absolutism and relativism described in Chapter 10.

This lack of consensus reflects first and foremost the lack of a clear conception of culture. Some of the problems are: the range of cultural variables is poorly defined; technology, political conditions, and economic constraints are not properly distinguished from other cultural variables such as beliefs and values; and nation-states tend to be treated as homogeneous cultures. Tayeb (1988, p. 41) has asked: "How is one to know, for instance, that the 'British' organization which is compared with, say, an Indian company, is not in fact staffed largely by immigrants from the sub-continent?" In many reviews the poor conceptualization of culture is cited as a weakness (e.g., Bhagat & McQuaid, 1982; Ronen 1986).

Design and methods of data collection contribute to the problems of interpretation. Many studies of organizational structure are based on interviews with most subjects in executive positions. The interviews tend to be extensive, covering a wide range of variables. The number of organizations and, particularly, the number of countries has to be limited because of the amount of work involved. "Cultural differences" are then introduced *post hoc* to explain the differences. Under these circumstances extensive and critical replication is needed before findings can be accepted as definitive.

Managerial behavior

This section deals with two topics. For one of these (leadership styles) the discussion will be restricted to the organizational behavior literature. On the other topic (decision-making) cross-cultural evidence from outside the organizational domain will be taken into consideration. Both choices have been inspired by the presence of cross-cultural research traditions.

Leadership styles. In the American literature two behavior categories have emerged in various forms as typical of effective leaders. In the Ohio State Leadership studies they were called *consideration* and *initiating structure* (cf. Wexley & Yukl, 1984). Consideration has to do with the concern and support of the leader for subordinates. Initiating structure refers to the definition and structuring by leaders of the various roles and tasks to be performed by themselves and other employees. Blake and Mouton (1964) expressed these dimensions as "concern for people" and "concern for production," while Likert (1967) distinguished between "exploitative" (or authoritive) and "participative" behavior. Cross-cultural variations of these categories have been described by J. P. B. Sinha (1980) for India and by Misumi (1985) for Japan.

J. B. P. Sinha (1980) proposes the concept of the *nurturant-task leader*. This management style has two components: concern for the task and a nurturant orientation toward subordinates. The nurturant-task leader creates a climate of purposiveness and maintains a high level of productivity. But he also shows care and affection for the well-being of his subordinates and is committed to their professional growth. The nurturant-task leadership style is flexible and as a subordinate needs less guidance and direction it should change to a more participative style. The personal character of the relationship with a father-like role for the leader appears to be the most outstanding feature of the nurturant-task leader. Sinha (1980) writes, for example, that the nurturant-task leader "understands the expectations of his subordinates. He knows that they relish dependency and personalized relationship, accept his authority and look towards him for guidance and direction"(p. 63).

The nurturant-task leadership style is an authoritative but not an authoritarian style according to Sinha. He proposes a continuum from authoritarian (which often is seen as related to the task-oriented leadership style in the U.S. literature) to participative, with nurturant-task leadership in the middle. Sinha considers participative management as the ideal, but is of the opinion that it can only function under certain social conditions that often are not (yet) present in India. Sinha cites historical antecedents, such as the domination by the Moguls and the British, and also refers to Indian values and dispositions that are not compatible with a people-oriented management style. One of the factors that Sinha listed is the preference for personal over contractual relationships. Rules and regulations can be sidestepped to accommodate a friend or relative. Other examples are a dependence proneness in Indian society, a lack of team orientation, and the conspicuous use of resting time (late arrival at work and long lunches) as a sign of status. These and similar factors make an authoritative leadership style necessary.

In a series of studies in which employees of Indian organizations were interviewed extensively, Sinha identified a profile of the nurturant-task leader distinct from both a participative and an authoritative leadership style. Evidence was found for a superior performance record of Indian managers who adhere to the nurturant style compared to those who apply other styles. However, it should be noted that Sinha's views are not shared by all Indian researchers. Others have been arguing for the positive effects of a democratic participative leadership style (cf. Khandwalla, 1988).

Another conceptualization, this time by a Japanese author, is Misumi's (1985) PM leadership theory. He distinguishes two main functions in a group; one is contributing to the group's goal achievement and problem solving, the other is promoting the group's self-preservation and strengthening the group processes. The achievement function is called Performance or P by Misumi and the self-preservation function is called Maintenance or M[3]. M

---

[3] Note that the Japanese researcher Misumi, though trained in the U.S., postulates a dimension for the continued existence of the *group*, while in the Western literature the corresponding dimension emphasizes concern for the *individual*.

leadership is aimed at increasing interpersonal encouragement and support and reducing conflict and strife (which leads to disintegration of the group when unchecked). Both the P and the M functions play a role in any leadership process. How these functions manifest themselves varies, depending among other things on the degree of structural differentiation in the organization. The two functions are not independent, but are interacting dimensions: the meaning of P amounts to "pressure for production" with (low) M and to "planning" with (high) M. Misumi makes a distinction between general characteristics of leadership and specific situational expressions. This distinction pertains to both the form (morphology) and the causes (dynamics) of managerial behavior.

The theory leads to a typology with four basic types, namely PM, Pm, pM and pm leadership (a capital indicates a high value on a dimension and a small letter a low value). A finer grading is possible by a further division of the types into subtypes. The scheme has been validated not only in survey research, but also in experimental studies within organizational settings in Japan, varying from schools and government departments to industrial firms. In the latter setting the effectiveness of leadership types has been assessed in terms of objective variables (such as long-term achievement, work motivation, accident rates, and turnover) as well as self-report criteria (such as satisfaction and norms for one's own performance). There is a consistent order in the effectiveness of the four types of leadership, namely PM, pM, Pm and pm. Only for subjects with a low task motivation has the Pm leadership style been found to be the most effective.

Misumi sees his typology as an extension of (classical) Western theories, which often emphasized a single dimension and were operationalized in a standard (survey) instrument. In his opinion new measures are required for the P and M aspects for each setting in which leadership is being studied. He expects that the PM theory as such will be found to have universal validity because the morphology and dynamics of leadership elsewhere should be similar to those in Japan.

Studies that support these expectations have been summarized by Smith and Peterson (1988). Data from Britain, Hong Kong, the U.S., and India show positive correlations between subordinates' ratings of their work situation and ratings on P and M scales for their supervisors. From these studies another result has emerged. In a set of questions pertaining to specific behaviors some correlated consistently with general leadership dimensions in all the countries studied, but for other items the correlations differed between countries. For example, a supervisor who talks about a subordinate's personal difficulties to his colleagues is seen as inconsiderate in Britain and the U.S. but considerate in Hong Kong and Japan. These results support Misumi's claim that a distinction has to made between general attributes of leadership and specific manifestations.

Heller (1985) has also pointed to the importance of the generality of items in survey instruments. In his opinion broad questions rather than specific ones lead to fairly clear cultural differences. Examples of general items are those used in the classical studies by Haire, Ghiselli, and Porter (1966) and by Hofstede (1980), which will be discussed later on. Reactions to items on specific aspects of day-to-day decision-making used by Heller and Wilpert (1981) were found to be contingent upon situational demands rather than on cultural (national) differences between Western countries. The reason is perhaps that the items of Heller and Wilpert were more task-related, while those in the studies mentioned by Smith and Peterson were primarily person-oriented.

For *ad hoc* samples (managers who attended a course) from mainly West European countries, Laurent (1983) reports substantial differences in factors such as political outlook (concern with managerial power), outlook on authority (need for clear lines of authority), and outlook on formal roles (need for a clear definition of employee's functions). Laurent used only a single questionnaire in which managers answered fairly broad statements. In his view the results show that the "collective mental maps" about organizations are clearly different for managers from various European countries. He writes (1983): "It may well be that the management process in these Western countries is as much culture-bound as their cooking and that international management has to avoid the trap of international cuisine"(p. 95).

Many researchers as well as managers (cf. N. J. Adler, 1986) share views like those of Laurent and appear to be convinced that for managerial practices cultural factors do play an important role. In a review Triandis (in press) mentions several examples. Doktor (1983) found that Japanese managers spend a much longer time period on a single task than Americans; for tasks that occupy more than an hour the percentages are 41 and 10 respectively. In contrast, 18 percent of the Japanese and 49 percent of the American managers are busy with tasks that take less than 9 minutes to complete. In Triandis's opinion this reflects the tendency of the Japanese to engage in long-time planning. J. B. P. Sinha (1984a) observed that in India more emphasis is placed on job satisfaction than on productivity, a finding that fits with the collectivistic tendencies of Indian societies. A third example by Triandis is the role of "face" in the sense of "losing face" or "gaining face" among the Chinese. This is considered an important value in business interactions (Redding & Ng, 1982).

This last example can serve to illustrate that the pattern of relationships between day-to-day practices and underlying cultural variables is almost never straightforward. Chinese business organizations, particularly in Hong Kong, have been described as resembling families with autocratic leadership. A condescending attitude toward subordinates and even scolding in public is not uncommon. Apparently the principle of "face" is less important in the personnel area than in other interpersonal dealings (cf. Redding & Wong, 1986). The cultural insider knows when issues of face apply and when not, but to the outsider with only partial knowledge professed values and actual practices may seem quite contradictory.

Decision-making. Research on decision-making varies from descriptive accounts to experiments in which probabilities of outcomes of imaginary bets are manipulated. An example of a rich descriptive analysis with low emphasis on theoretical formalization can be found in Janis and Mann (1977). Their work includes analyses of the decision-making process in single but historically important events. The use of biographical information next to knowledge derived from field studies and experiments allows the consideration of emotional and personal factors. There can be no doubt that these factors influence decision outcomes. At the same time it is evident that there are regularities in decision-making processes. The question is whether systematic cross-cultural differences can be discovered in these regularities.

Heller and Wilpert (1981) analyzed managerial decision-making at the top levels of 129 organizations in the U.S., five West European countries, and Israel. They postulated a continuum of power sharing that reaches from unshared unilateral decision-making by the superior via shared (participatory) decision-making to the delegation of all power for certain decisions to the subordinate.[4] Most managers greatly vary their behavior on the continuum, depending on the situation they are facing. Differences between countries were far less important than between situations. The extent of power sharing was found to be relatively high in France and Sweden and low in Israel and Spain. The overall trend in the results is that certain conditions foster participative decision-making and that these conditions are quite similar across the range of countries studied. The balance between situational contingencies that lead to cultural convergence on the one hand and values and practices that lead to cultural divergence clearly leans to the former side in this study. Another interesting result was that superiors not only valued participation as a means of improving the quality of decisions, but also to improve communication and to train their subordinates. These reasons are reminiscent of Sinha's nurturant task-leadership style.

Much of the cross-cultural research on decision-making has been summarized by Wright (1985). He discusses research within organizational settings as well as experimental research. In organizations the most extensively studied topic is the supposed superiority of Japanese over American organizational efficiency. This has been attributed to a more consultative style of decision-making that finds its expression in the *ringi* process, described in Box 13-3. In descriptive studies based on impressions and clinical-style interviews (for example, Abegglen, 1958) differences tend to emerge that can be explained in terms of cultural factors. In studies with more systematic data collection (for example, Pascale, 1978) striking similarities tend to be found. Wright concludes that the picture is still unclear.

In cross-cultural experimental research convergent evidence is also scarce. One of the issues studied is the so-called "risky-shift" phenomenon. This

---

[4] This dimension extends further then the usual continuum, which ends with participation (e.g., Vroom & Yetton, 1973).

Box 13-3   Decision-making by consensus

Martyn-Johns (1977) describes how a Javanese manager's decision style in the Indonesian subsidiary of an organization was seen by his international superiors as extremely authoritarian. Decisions were promulgated in instructions that were not to be questioned by anyone. A manager from Europe with a democratic style took over at a certain moment. He discussed issues at meetings, and decisions were often taken by majority vote. However, his subordinates found this new manager more coercive and authoritarian. They objected that certain relevant matters could not be mentioned in an open discussion and that there was coercion of the minority by the majority, because even those who had expressed disagreement were held responsible for a decision once it had been taken.

According to Martyn-Johns there is extensive deliberation (*musjawarah*) in Java until everybody agrees what the best decision is under given circumstances and in the light of the various prevailing opinions. The ideal is to reach consensus rather than to take a decision against the explicit opinion of a minority. Once consensus has been reached a decision made by the manager is supported by everyone and its implementation is not considered authoritarian.

Typical of decision-making in Japanese organizations is the *ringi* procedure, whereby plans are drafted at the lower levels of an organization and employees are encouraged to develop their own ideas into a plan. Occasionally the initiative comes from a higher-ranking person, but this is by no means the rule. A draft plan is circulated among the departments involved and can be changed repeatedly in the process. It gradually moves up the chain of command for approval. In this way the knowledge and experience of many employees is used and consensus is promoted. The *ringi* system fits in with the practice of broad consultation (*nemawashi*) in Japan. It is a bottom-up procedure of decision-making that is supposed to lead to more involvement of employees with the organization and to a sense of commitment to the success of plans because everyone shares the responsibility. Also, the implementation of decisions tends to take little time. In the management literature the *ringi* procedure has been hailed occasionally as the key to the economic success of Japan. However, it also has weaknesses, such as the long time it can take for a plan to get through a bureaucracy and the large amount of paper work that results from it (e.g., E. F. Vogel, 1975; Misumi, 1984).

The examples of *musjawarah* and *ringi* show that there are alternatives to the democratic system of decision-making adopted and glorified in the West. Whatever their disadvantages they do not so easily lead to a situation where the majority imposes its will without regard for the opinion of a minority as in the case of decisions based on majority vote.

refers to the tendency that group discussions lead to more hazardous decisions being reached than when individuals make them on their own. Brown (1965) has suggested that risk taking is valued in Western societies. Individuals want to take at least as much risk as their peers and in the course of a discussion they move to a more extreme position so as not to lag behind others. If this is correct, a "cautious shift" could be anticipated in cultures where caution is valued. Initially support was found for this idea by Carlson and Davis (1971), who studied the effect of group discussions on decisions in the U.S. and Uganda, the latter presumably a country where caution is seen as positive. Their results were criticized because of the possible culture inappropriateness of the American designed stimuli (e.g., L. Mann, 1980). With more suitable methods Gologor (1977) found no tendencies of risky shift in Liberia. Group decisions tended to be more extreme than individual decisions, but there was about as much polarization toward more caution as toward more risky decisions. An interesting finding by Harrison (1975) is that whites in Zimbabwe shifted to more caution and blacks to more risk when race track bets had to be agreed upon in a small-group discussion.

The confidence that subjects have in their decisions has been an important topic in research on cross-cultural differences in individual decision-making under uncertainty. Poortinga and Spies (1972) worked with samples of white and black South African truck drivers. To reduce the effects of prior educational experience Poortinga and Spies did not use cognitive tasks (as usually is the case), but tasks of perception and motor skills in which the level of difficulty (and thus the expected outcome) was adapted to the level of performance of a subject. In this way the probability of success was set at an equal level for each subject. The results of both groups fell well short of the maximum earnings because subjects were overconfident and took too high risks. But no significant intergroup difference was found with any of three different methods.

A more consistent difference in probabilistic thinking has been reported between Western (mainly British) and Southeast Asian subjects, including Malaysians, Indonesians, and Chinese (Wright, Phillips, & Wisudha, 1983). In their studies Wright and his colleagues asked subjects to answer a question and then to indicate how confident they are about the correctness of their opinion. Scales include factual items (for example, whether New York or London is farther north) and items on possible events, (for example, whether subject expects to catch a cold in the next three months). Subjects are usually overconfident, but Westerners less so than Asians. Asian subjects more often used absolute (yes/no) and less often intermediate judgments than Western subjects. Wright and Phillips (1980) ascribed this to a cultural difference in the tendency to use nonprobabilistic as opposed to probabilistic thinking. To support this claim a variety of (mainly impressionistic) cultural antecedents were mentioned (Wright, 1985). Still, the meaning of the differences remains unclear. Wright et al. (1983) found that the extent of cross-cultural differences varies between tasks and that the correlations between tasks were low.

This points to situational specificity in dealing with uncertainty. Therefore, differences in scores may well be limited to a narrow range of situations. Also, a speculation by Wright that the Japanese would be nonprobabilistic thinkers was not confirmed by Yates et al. (1989).

In summary, the results from cross-cultural research confirm the observation that management practices are influenced by the sociocultural environment. It remains to be seen to what extent these practices reflect underlying patterns of culture and to what extent they are pragmatic reactions to (different) here-and-now situations. However, this brief exploration of one aspect of managerial behavior (decision-making) has not uncovered cultural antecedents that affect a wide range of decision-making situations.

Work values and motives

In the area of motivation and related concepts two categories of variables will be distinguished: work-related values and traitlike individual dispositions (needs, motives, and attitudes). The discussion in this section will range from broad concepts that are relevant in a wide range of situations to more situation specific variables.

Values. The landmark study on work-related values was carried out by Hofstede (1980, 1983b) in the national subsidiaries of a multinational company.[5] At the end of the 1980s this work was the most frequently cited source in the cross-cultural literature, with references not only in psychology and cultural anthropology, but also in the literature on management and on communication. The major report on forty countries was published in 1980. Later, Hofstede (1983b) included the results of another ten countries and three regions from which small or uneven samples had been tested. Data were collected twice, around 1968 and around 1972. Seven different levels of occupation were distinguished, ranging from managers to administrative personnel. Altogether there were more than 116,000 questionnaires in twenty languages. The survey instrument included some 160 questions, of which 63, mainly pertaining to values, were used in the cross-cultural analysis (cf. Hofstede, 1980, p. 66).

In Chapter 3 Hofstede's work was discussed because of its relevance for social psychology. We now come back to it with a somewhat more critical emphasis, informed by the discussion in Part II of this book. In Chapter 3 we saw that Hofstede identified four dimensions, namely *power distance, uncertainty avoidance, individualism-collectivism*, and *masculinity-femininity*. It is important to consider how these were derived. At the stage of pilot studies it had already become clear that items dealing with hierarchical relationships

---

[5] The company was IBM. In Hofstede's book it is called HERMES, because it did not want its name associated with the research project. Later there was a change of policy and IBM can now be mentioned freely (Hofstede, personal communication).

showed differences among countries. "How frequently are employees afraid to disagree with their managers?" became a core question to assess power distance. The index of uncertainty avoidance was developed along similar lines, following theoretical distinctions in the literature. The indices for individualism and masculinity resulted from a factor analysis of twenty-two (later fourteen) items inquiring about the importance of various work goals. These items more or less fitted Maslow's need hierarchy (see below). Various factor analyses were carried out both at the individual level and at the level of countries (with data aggregated over individuals within countries). To distinguish between individuals or between occupations, Maslow's framework made sense. However, a meaningful distinction between countries could only be obtained with factor analysis on a data matrix of work goals by countries. This country level, or ecological, factor analysis yielded the two factors of individualism and masculinity.

To confirm the picture that had emerged factor analyses were carried out on the items relevant to all four factors. After some readjustments, thirty-two items provided a three-factor solution explaining 49 percent of the variance at country level. The first factor was a combination of individualism and power distance (with reversed sign), the second factor represented masculinity, and the third factor corresponded to uncertainty avoidance. For conceptual reasons Hofstede maintained a distinction between the two dimensions of individualism and power distance that together constituted the first factor. He justified this with the argument that the correlations between the two dimensions ($r = -0.67$) virtually disappear if variance due to national wealth is controlled for. It has often been suggested that Hofstede's dimensions are derived empirically (e.g., Ronen, 1986), but this is only partially true.

For each of the four dimensions country scores were computed. Hofstede sees these scores as reflecting broad underlying dimensions of culture.

The power distance index, based on three items (fear of employees to disagree with manager, perceived nondemocratic decision-making, and preference for consultative decision-making), is summarized by Hofstede (1983b) as "the extent to which the members of a society accept that power in institutions and organizations is distributed unequally" (p. 336).

The uncertainty avoidance index similarly is computed on the basis of three items (not breaking company rules, staying with the company, and feeling nervous or tense at work). According to Hofstede (1983b), it is "the degree to which the members of a society feel uncomfortable with uncertainty and ambiguity, which leads them to support beliefs promising certainty and to maintain institutions protecting conformity" (p. 336).

Of the fourteen work goals that were used to identify the last two factors, nine had a loading ≥ 0.35 on the individualism factor, including availability of time for personal and family life, freedom to adopt one's own approach to work, opportunity for training, and good physical working conditions (the latter two with a negative sign). In Hofstede's summary (1983b) individualism "stands for a loosely knit social framework in society in which individuals are supposed to take care of themselves and their immediate families only" (p. 336). It is contrasted with collectivism, "a preference for a tightly knit social framework in which individuals can expect their relatives, clan or other in-group to look after them, in exchange for unquestioning loyalty" (p. 336).

There were also nine work goals with substantial loading on the masculinity factor, including a good relationship with one's manager, good cooperation with others, high earnings, and getting recognition (the latter two with a negative sign). Hofstede (1983b) describes masculinity as a "preference for achievement, heroism, assertiveness and material success" (p. 337). It is opposed to femininity, that is, a "preference for relationships, modesty, caring for the weak, and quality of life."

The definitions of the four dimensions are much broader than could be justified given the limited number of items, especially for power distance and uncertainty avoidance. The interpretations are bolstered by extensive references to the literature about cross-cultural differences and by the use of data from other studies. In addition, data were collected with other value questionnaires on *ad hoc* samples of managers from various countries. The four dimensions were also correlated with seven economic, geographic, and demographic indicators. For example, the power distance dimension showed a correspondence with conformity versus independence and with higher versus lower authoritarianism. Subordinates in low-power distance countries negatively evaluate close supervision and prefer consultative decision-making. The strongest predictor of the power distance scores across forty countries was geographical latitude. Hofstede explained this relationship as due to the higher need for technology in realizing human survival in colder countries. He did not postulate a direct causal relationship between environmental temperature and the power distance index, but sees the climatic factors at the beginning of a causal chain that through a long process of adaptation leads to cross-cultural differences in social structure.

Another example is the high correlation ($r = 0.82$) between individualism and economic wealth (per capita GNP). In countries low on individualism conformity is liked and autonomy is rated as less important, while in countries with high individualism variety is aspired to and security is seen as less important.

Apart from the small numbers of items on which two of the factors were based, Hofstede's study gives rise to some other questions. Subjects were drawn from a single company and although Hofstede rightly points to the advantage that samples are matched on a number of variables (Hofstede, 1979, p. 392), there is the disadvantage that they are not representative of the national populations to which the results are generalized (see Chapter 9). There is another methodological problem. Hofstede's dimensions are identified at the group level. He sees a value as "a broad tendency to prefer certain states of affairs over others" (1980, p. 19). This is an individual-level rather than a society-level conceptualization, and in addition the main data set was collected on individuals. It is not immediately clear why in analyses with individual subjects a value dimension valid at the group level should not be identifiable at the individual level given these premises (see Chapter 10). The most serious difficulty is that in other studies patterns expected on the basis of Hofstede's analysis could not be found. This is the case with the IDE (1981) study mentioned in Box 13-1. Ellis (1988) failed to find patterns of differences on value ratings between American and German subjects predicted on the basis of their country scores. In the study of sex stereotypes by J. E. Williams and Best (see Chapter 3) three components of affective meaning were distinguished. On none of these was the sex difference significantly correlated with Hofstede's masculinity index over the twenty-one countries that the two studies had in common.

Still, Hofstede's results provide a better basis for clustering countries than earlier studies. A large number of countries was included and patterns can be defined in terms of scores on not less than four dimensions. Hofstede (1980) has reported the results of a cluster analysis. After some modifications of the outcome (on the basis of historical arguments), eight clusters remained: More Developed Latin, Less Developed Latin, More Developed Asian, Less Developed Asian, Near Eastern, Germanic, Anglo, and Nordic, while Japan forms a cultural area on its own. These clusters as well as those found in some studies of motivational and attitudinal variables tend to group countries by geographical proximity (cf. Ronen, 1986; Griffeth & Hom, 1987).

The fact that the clusters by and large coincide with regions gives face validity to the instruments on which they are based. In view of the fact that broad economic and technology-related variables and geographic variables such as the latitude of a country provide the best explanations of between-country variance, reservation as to their cultural meaning is still necessary.[6]

Hofstede (1983a) has drawn implications for managerial behavior from his findings. For example, harmony is important in countries with low individualism and paternalistic management should be more acceptable in countries high on power difference. Such statements are open to empirical testing and can lead to gradual refinement of our understanding of cultural influences. Hofstede's dimensional framework has also been found useful for training and communication. The need for information on cultural aspects of organizations is high, and Hofstede has made a commendable effort toward a thorough empirical analysis in an area where impressionistic attribution and stereotyping occur too frequently.

---

[6] The meaning of country clusters can also be questioned for more specific reasons. First there are no unambiguous rules for indentifying the number of clusters in cluster analysis and related techniques. Second, there is a lack of consistency in findings over studies. For example, The Netherlands is located with England and Canada in an Anglo cluster (Griffeth & Hom, 1987), with Latin Europe (Ronen, 1986, based on Griffeth, Hom, De Nisi, & Kirchner, 1980), and in a North European cluster (Hofstede, 1980) respectively, in three studies in which subjects from this country participated. A third problem is sampling. In all the studies mentioned Japan emerges as a separate cluster. But even in Hofstede's major study the selection of countries has limitations. The reason for Japan's separate position may well be that in none of the studies mentioned were subjects from neighboring countries (Koreans, Chinese) included.

Motives and needs. Among the motivation (or need) theories that have inspired cross-cultural researchers the most prominent are those of McClelland (1961) and Maslow (1954). The basic argument in McClelland's work is that economic development cannot be explained without reference to social and psychological variables. He was struck by the apparent role that a motivation to get ahead plays in the process of national development, and he proposed the idea that achievement motivation is in part responsible for this. To an impressive degree McClelland has been able to demonstrate, usually with some temporal lag, correlations between economic development and the frequency of themes of achievement in a culture's literary products. An example is a significant correlation between country-level achievement scores derived from an analysis of the stories in children's books and estimates of economic growth (in per capita income and electricity production). More information on cross-cultural studies of achievement motivation can be found in Segall et al. (1990).

Maslow's need hierarchy has served as the theoretical basis for the first major international survey of motivation conducted by Haire, Ghiselli, and Porter (1966). They slightly modified Maslow's scheme and investigated the following needs: security, social esteem, autonomy, and self-actualization. The questionnaire on motivation was one of three scales, the other two were on leadership styles and managerial roles. Haire et al. (1966) obtained data from samples of at least some 200 managers in 14 countries, 9 from Europe, the U.S., Argentina, Chile, India, and Japan. Subjects were recruited through employer's associations, universities, training centers, and individual companies. By comparing between-group and within-group variation the authors estimated that for most variables national differences comprised approximately one-quarter of the total variation in the subject pool. According to Haire et al. (1966), "Managers are so similar that countries find themselves, perforce, in the same region of the scale. However, in this considerable unanimity, a real diversity among countries exists" (p. 10).

Of the various needs, self-actualization (that is, realizing one's capacities) was rated as the most important in all countries, followed in most countries by the need for autonomy (that is, the opportunity to think and act independently). Between-country differences in the importance of needs were quite small; apparently managers are quite alike in what motivates them in their work situation. Relatively large differences were found in the satisfaction of needs. In all countries the two most important needs were the least satisfied. The most satisfied managers (on all needs combined) came from Japan and the cluster of Nordic European countries. Managers from developing countries (which formed a separate cluster in this study) and from Latin European countries were the most dissatisfied.

Apart from the clusters already mentioned, there was an Anglo-American cluster, while Japan stood alone. Haire et al. interpreted the similarity of response patterns as a reflection of a uniform industrial culture. They attributed the differences between clusters to (unspecified) factors of national culture. At the same time they acknowledged another important factor, namely the level of industrialization that in their view led to a single cluster for three culturally diverse developing countries (Argentina. Chile, and India).

In recent studies there has been a shift away from research on general needs and motives that are satisfied by work to the activity of working and the outcomes of work. The analysis of the meaning of working has a long history in social philosophy and more recently in the social sciences. Most famous is Weber's (1905/1976) treatise on the rise of capitalism as a result of Protestant religious dogma and work ethic. The most significant recent study (which did not support Weber's theory) has been reported by the Meaning of Working International Research team (MOW, 1987)[7]. The leading concept in this project was *work centrality*. This is defined as "a general belief about the value of working in one's life" (MOW, 1987, p. 17). To assess this concept subjects were asked directly how important working is for them and also how important it is in relation to other life roles (leisure, community life, religion, and family). The importance of working is best illustrated by two findings. Eighty-six percent of all subjects indicated that they would continue to work even if they had sufficient money to live in comfort for the rest of their lives. The second finding is that working was second in importance among the five life roles; only family was rated higher.

The MOW study was based on a complex model with work centrality as the core. Societal norms are intermediate and valued working outcomes and preferred working goals form a peripheral layer. To the model were further added antecedents and consequents of work centrality. Social norms (which can show cross-cultural differences) are seen as the basis for normative evaluations about work. A distinction is made between *entitlements* (the right to meaningful and interesting work) and *obligations* (the duty to contribute to society by working).

The study involved subjects from eight countries listed here in the order in which working was considered important (from high to low); they were: Japan, Yugoslavia, Israel, U.S., Belgium, Netherlands, West Germany, and Britain. Two kinds of samples were drawn in each country, a national sample (n = 450 or more) that was taken as representative for the country and various target groups (n = 90 approximately). These target groups were homogeneous with respect to demographic or work-related characteristics such as age or occupation. In Yugoslavia there was no national sample; for this country estimates were derived from the results of the target groups.

The importance of working varied between occupations, with the highest scores for professionals and the lowest for temporary workers. Skilled workers and the unemployed had medium scores on centrality of working. Except

---

[7] Among the members of the team who are also mentioned elsewhere in this chapter are Drenth, Heller, Misumi, and Wilpert. Most members of the MOW group were also involved in the IDE study (cf. Box 13-1).

in Belgium and the U.S. women scored significantly lower than men, with the most noticeable gender difference in Japan. Differences between countries were about $1\frac{1}{2}$ times larger than between occupational groups. The Japanese had by far the highest score, a finding expected by the MOW team; the score was lowest in Britain. The second-lowest position of the Germans and the second-highest position of the Yugoslavs were considered surprising. A tentative explanation for this pattern suggested by the MOW team is that the centrality of working is a nonlinear function of the length of time since industrialization. The West European countries, with Britain in the lead, have the oldest history in this respect; Japan and Yugoslavia have only more recently become industrialized.

Meaningful differences were found for both the entitlements and the obligations aspects of societal norms. On the entitlements side the U.S. scored low and The Netherlands, Belgium, and Germany high. The Netherlands was low on obligations, Yugoslavia and Israel scored high. Of particular interest is the balance between these two variables, that is, between the right to work and one's duty to do so. In Japan, Britain, Yugoslavia, and Israel these two variables were approximately balanced. In the U.S. there was more endorsement of duties than of rights. In the remaining three countries, The Netherlands, West Germany, and Belgium, entitlements are more emphasized than obligations. The MOW team believes (on intuitive grounds) that a balance between rights and duties would seem the most preferable state of affairs. Going a step further one could speculate that an overemphasis on rights when it is coupled with a low work centrality (as in The Netherlands) may well adversely affect the level of economic activity of a nation in the long run.

There are numerous studies in which a significant difference on one or more *attitudinal* variables between countries has been found. Most general trends point to cultural similarities rather than differences. For example, job satisfaction tends to be higher among older than among younger employees, and employees in a higher position are more satisfied than rank-and-file workers (Tannenbaum, 1980). The most extensive body of research on job attitudes in a single industrializing country has been conducted in India. From reviews by D. Sinha (1972) and Padaki (1988) one gains the impression that more often than not the same variables as identified in the West differentiate between more and less satisfied employees. However, there can be some doubt whether the emergence of indigenous variables is not suppressed by the use of Western theories and instruments (e.g., Bhagat & McQuaid, 1982).

Among the concomitant variables of between-country differences in job attitudes the most important is per capita GNP (Ronen, 1986). As noted before, this index is confounded with industrialization, level of education, and other variables and as such has limited value for an analysis of the cultural context of job satisfaction. The consistent correlation between industrialization and job security (e.g., Haire et al., 1966; Inkeles, 1960; G. V. Barrett &

Bass, 1976) lends itself more to psychological interpretation. Loss of work in an industrialized society with relatively low unemployment rates and a social welfare system usually has less alarming consequences than in a developing country.

The dominance of Western notions in the area of study discussed in this section is evident. The need for emic conceptualizations has been expressed by various authors. Munro (1986) has issued a plea for indigenous work-related value constructs valid in Africa. Differences in the factorial structure of (American) job satisfaction scales, for example, between Singapore and the U.S. (Spector & Wimalasari, 1986) provide support for such suggestions. Nevis (1983) has even proposed a specific hierarchy of needs for the People's Republic of China, in which most basic is the (social) need of belonging. In a value survey among small samples of students and workers items with clear political meaning were included, such as "belief in communism" and "to realize the four modernizations." These were among the highest-ranking values in a nine-item scale. Because this pattern of needs appears to be quite unusual the possibility cannot be ruled out that it reflects the ideals of the prevalent political system rather than personal values. Empirical evidence for a culture-specific value (Confucian work dynamism) among Chinese was found by the Chinese Culture Connection (1987). Nevertheless, the overall impression one gains is that cross-cultural differences as discussed in this section can be explained quite adequately as quantitative shifts on variables that are common to at least all industrial and industrializing countries.

Conclusions

When detecting some cross-cultural difference in organizational data, one may be wise to heed the advice of Drenth (1983, p. 570). "The researcher is still faced with ruling out other explanatory factors within the national context, such as economic conditions, level of national development, level of employment, type of product, etc. Clearly, not all *national* differences are caused by *cultural* factors...." A summary presenting this difficulty more systematically while at the same time making suggestions for the future has been given by Bhagat and McQuaid (1982, pp. 697–680). They make the following recommendations:

1. Researchers should examine in sufficient detail the rationale for doing their research cross-culturally.
2. Researchers should commit themselves to some theory in order to solve the methodological problems.
3. Researchers should be seriously concerned about suitable methodological strategies.
4. There is an obvious need for pooling of resources into multicultural research teams.

The elusiveness in the meaning of cultural variables remains a problem, but one that has received considerable attention. Researchers appear to be in a much better position now than ten or fifteen years ago to identify issues that are threatening valid comparisons. International research on organizations has become an important area of study. In view of the amount of ongoing research it carries the promise of contributing increasingly to our insight into cross-cultural differences in behavior.

The intercultural communication literature has roots in linguistics (especially sociolinguistics), sociology, cultural anthropology, and psychology. Of these, psychology is probably the most obvious parent discipline, and it is not surprising that there are many overlaps with cross-cultural psychology. This is evident from books representing the area of intercultural communication, for example, by Asante and Gudykunst (1989) and by Gudykunst and Ting-Toomey (1988). Rather than reviewing the whole intercultural communication literature, we focus on a few topics that are particularly relevant to cross-cultural psychologists and that have not been covered in other chapters of this book.

The first section is on sojourners: the difficulties they experience in adjusting to the new cultural environment as well as difficulties in communication. The second section is concerned with a topic that has received wide attention in the field of intercultural communication: communication training, or the preparation of sojourners (and migrants) to deal with people from a different cultural background. The last section is on international negotiations; illustrations are given of cross-cultural differences that have been reported in literature on this subject and some social psychological studies are discussed that can perhaps help explain these differences.

Intercultural communication

Concern for cultural factors in interpersonal communication has been increasing rapidly. The expansion over the last forty years of international business and trade, exchange of students, technical assistance programs, and tourism has brought about a corresponding increase in relatively short-term intercultural contacts. Apart from tourists and permanent migrants, there is a growing group of people who spend a limited time period abroad, from a number of months to a number of years, for purposes of study, work, or leisure.

Sojourners. As we have seen in Chapter 12, these temporary migrants are collectively referred to as *sojourners* or as *expatriates*. The relevant literature has been reviewed by Furnham and Bochner (1986) in a book called

339

Culture Shock. As noted in Chapter 11, this term has a meaning very similar to *acculturative stress*. Its origin is credited to the anthropologist Oberg (1960), who used it to indicate problems that arise during exposure to an unfamiliar environment. Among other things Oberg referred to the strain of making new adaptations, a sense of loss, confusion about one's role, and feelings of anxiety. Other authors have described the experience of going to another culture in similar terms. Guthrie (1966) mentions the frustration of subtle cultural differences that impede social interactions. In an extensive project with foreign students from 139 nations studying in eleven countries (Klineberg & Hull, 1979) a quarter of the subjects reported feelings of depression. The difficulties experienced are not the same for all sojourners. Major variables include the distance between home culture and host culture, the type of involvement, the duration of contact, and the status of the visitor in the host country (cf. Bochner, 1982).

Torbiörn (1982) carried out a study with 800 Swedish expatriates stationed abroad. He obtained data from approximately thirty subjects, businessmen and their wives, in each of twenty-six different countries by means of a postal survey. Among the more important findings are that only 8 percent of the respondents reported being unhappy. This is a surprising result in view of the allegedly large proportion of overseas assignments that turn out unsuccessfully (up to 30 percent in the U.S., according to Tung, 1981). It should be realized that Torbiörn had a biased sample, because business people are repatriated when they fail in their assignments. Torbiörn found no evidence that accompanying spouses were more frequently unhappy than the workers. However, it was confirmed that one cannot have a successful sojourn when one's family is unhappy.

Perhaps the most salient result of Torbiörn's study was that having friends among the nationals of the host country, rather than having contacts only with fellow expatriates, is an important determinant of satisfaction. Initially those who only mix with expatriates may have more positive experiences, but in the long run personal friendships with members of the host society are very important for the sojourner. This is a consistent finding also with other groups of expatriates, including students (Klineberg & Hull, 1979) and technical advisers (Kealey, 1989). A stay in a foreign country does not automatically lead to more positive attitudes toward the host country's people. Available evidence suggests that there is more often a negative than a positive change during a sojourn, at least among university students (Stroebe, Lenkert, & Jonas, 1988).

The adjustment of sojourners to the new culture over the course of time has been found to follow a U-shaped curve in a number of studies (though by no means always; Church, 1982). This could mean that sojourners initially have few problems. They are enthusiastic and fascinated by new experiences. After some time, feelings of frustration, loneliness, and anxiety take over. Still later, as the sojourner learns to cope, well-being increases again. The U-curve has been extended to a double U, or W, curve to include a period of adjustment after the return of sojourners to their homeland (cf. Brein & David, 1971). Initially there is the thrill of being back in the known environment and of meeting family and friends. Then disappointments occur because some of the more positive aspects of the life abroad are lost. Finally, after some time readjustment follows.

Furnham and Bochner (1986) question the empirical validity of the U or W curves, because they have been derived from cross-sectional rather than longitudinal studies and because of the many uncertainties concerning the precise form and the time period of the curves. More generally, they object to the clinical overtones of the culture shock notion in many writings. They also criticize theoretical approaches that presume negative or even pathological effects. Instead Furnham and Bochner advocate a social skills approach. Newcomers to a culture have problems because they are unfamiliar or not at ease with the social norms and conventions. Gradually sojourners will learn what they need to know in order to handle social encounters competently. A major advantage of this orientation is that it opens the way for culture training. If one lacks certain skills, they can presumably be learned.

Taking Bochner and Furham's culture learning approach as the point of departure, one may ask what sojourners or expatriates should learn and whether training programs can be designed to facilitate entry into a new country.

Communication difficulties. At various places in earlier chapters we have indicated that modes of communication and the underlying processes are essentially universal. However, this does not preclude a variety of differences in actual communication patterns. In this context it is important to distinguish failures of communication that are obvious to the interacting persons from subtle errors that easily escape one's notice.

Most important for human communication is language. It is also a very culture-specific medium. If two people do not share a common language, their interactions are much restricted and they realize this. Less obvious are communication difficulties when command of a language is less than perfect. Variations in pronunciation and usage of English have long been a point of concern in air traffic control (Ruffell Smith, 1975). Prosodic aspects of language, including stress and intonation contours, can occasionally lead to misunderstandings. An example from the work of Gumperz (1982) may illustrate this. Indian and Pakistani women working in a staff cafeteria in Britain were seen as surly and uncooperative. Gumperz observed that the few words they said could be interpreted negatively. When serving food, a British assistant would say "gravy?" with a rising intonation. The Indian women would use the same word, but pronounce it with a falling intonation. To the people they served this sounded like a statement of fact that under the circumstances was redundant and sometimes rude. Listening to taped sequences of this type, the migrant women at first could not hear any differences. After some training, they began to recognize the point. Gumperz claims quite far-reaching effects; during the training it also became clear to the women why attitudes toward them had often been negative and they regained confidence in their ability to learn.

Similar complications can occur in pragmatic aspects of language, including the taking of turns in conversations, exchange of compliments, politeness, and an indirect versus a direct style of communication (cf. Blum-Kulka, House, & Kasper, 1988, for a summary). Barnlund and Araki (1985) have found Japanese to be less direct in paying compliments and more modest in expressing them verbally than Americans. Findings by Tannen (1981) indicate that Greek-Americans who no longer speak Greek still follow Greek cultural norms about indirectness and may be misunderstood by Americans who state their true intentions directly rather than in a roundabout way.

Much the same can be said about nonverbal behavior, a mode of communication that we briefly reviewed in Chapter 4. Despite the overall similarities, there are cross-cultural differences, for example, in the meaning of specific gestures. Even within our own culture we may misinterpret the intended meaning of an emblem (that is, a gesture that can replace a verbal expression and is supposed to have a fairly clearly described meaning). Morris et al. (1979) found differences between subjects in the meaning attributed to specific emblems, even within the same region of various European countries.

At this stage it is not yet very clear how often and how seriously intercultural encounters are disrupted by an insufficient feeling for prosodic and pragmatic aspects of language or by errors of nonverbal communication. Still, it seems to us that unfamiliarity with aspects of culture bearing on *social* behaviors are a more important source of ignorance and the consequent ineptness of the stranger. The range of relevant variables includes stereotypes and prejudices, as well as customs, norms, and values about interpersonal interaction held by both sojourners and members of the host culture. We shall not review the evidence on cross-cultural differences in social behavior that have been touched upon repeatedly in this text. However, we would like to make two points. First, one has to realize that many differences are in the eye of the beholder. As we shall see later, one of the more important goals of training is to open people's minds to this. Second, misunderstandings often arise out of concrete conventions in everyday social situations. Triandis (1975) reports the example of the Greek villager inviting someone to dinner and mentioning that he is welcome "any time." For an American this amounts to a non-invitation; the vagueness of the time makes it noncommittal. The Greek literally means that his guest will be welcome at any time. More generally, Triandis states that effective intercultural communication requires "isomorphic attributions," that is, participants in an interaction have to give the same interpretation to behavior.

Intercultural competence. Which characteristics of the individual are correlates of effective communication? In the literature on intercultural competence or communication competence there are more holistic answers to this question that lean toward broad concepts, such as the adjustment and personal growth of the sojourner; there are also more behavior-oriented answers in which more narrowly described domains such as attitudes, knowledge about other cultures, and directly observable behavior find favor. A further issue is whether competence is a quality of the communicator, of the perceiver, or of the dyadic system that they form together. This is related to the question whether an individual who is competent in one culture is also competent in another culture or, in other words, whether the correlates of competence are the same everywhere (cf. Brislin, Landis, & Brandt, 1983; Hammer, 1989; Ruben, 1989).

Empirical research on intercultural competence, or communication competence, mainly started in the 1960s with Peace Corps volunteers from the U.S. At the time the trait-orientation in personality research was fashionable and several attempts were made to find the traits relevant for the prediction of successful volunteer candidates by means of self-report personality inventories. Kealey and Ruben (1983) have listed the traits claimed in a number of studies. Most of them, including honesty, empathy, display of respect, and flexibility, are rather vague and reflect general socially desirable interpersonal characteristics. The predictive success of these traits turned out to be disappointing. It was realized that part of the problem was the absence of well-defined criteria. The potential range of situations that sojourners are confronted with is very large, and the question can be asked whether intercultural competence over the whole range can be adequately predicted from personality variables.

Kealey and Ruben also found situational variables mentioned in the literature; these included job conditions, living conditions, health problems, realistic project objectives, political interference, and language difficulties.[1] In addition they listed criterion variables used to assess effectiveness. Apart from personality concepts such as strength of personality, one finds variables like social participation, local language ability, and appreciation of customs. Kealey and Ruben distinguish three main components: (1) personal and family adjustment and satisfaction, (2) professional competence, and (3) cordial relations with members of the host country.

Despite the poor predictive value found for personality trait measures, Kealey and Ruben maintain that the evidence presented supports the existence of what they call an "overseas type." They base this assertion on the similarity in personality traits that are thought relevant by various authors. The resulting profile is of a person who, among other things, is open and interested in others, with positive regard, self-confident, flexible, and professionally competent. In one respect Ruben and Kealy distance themselves

---

[1] Situational analysis has hardly been explored systematically. A broad range of situational variables has been collected by Detweiler, Brislin, and McCormack (1983). They used more than one 100 descriptors, which were sorted according to situational similarity by samples of American students. However, this project does not appear to have had a cross-cultural follow-up.

from the traditional trait approach. They are of the opinion that behavior-based assessment techniques rather than self-report inventories have to be used in view of the poor predictive value of the latter.

The evaluation of the literature by Kealey and Ruben shows a fairly close correspondence to their own empirical work (Ruben & Kealey, 1979; Hawes & Kealey, 1980; Kealey, 1989). In the latest of these studies (Kealey, 1989) the effectiveness of 277 Canadian technical advisers working in twenty different developing countries was investigated. Some of the subjects were tested prior to departure, so that the predictive validity of personality variables could be investigated better than in most earlier studies. Another feature of this project was that interviewers went into the field and that data were obtained from peers of the advisers and of their host country counter-parts in the various countries. Kealey's design included fourteen outcome variables, including difficulties in adjustment and stress, contacts with hosts, understanding, and effectiveness in transferring knowledge and skills. There were three situational variables: living conditions, job constraints, and hardship level. As predictors Kealey had twenty-one variables that included ratings by self on personality dimensions and interpersonal skills, ratings by peers on interpersonal skills, motives and attitudes, and work values.

The traditional personality variables assessed by self-reports and work values did not prove to be good predictors; motives and attitudes and interpersonal skills rated by others did clearly better. In a discriminant analysis 85 percent of the expatriates could be correctly classified as successful or unsuccessful on the basis of the predictor scores. The situational variables correlated with both predictor and outcome scores. Kealey interpreted this evidence as fitting a person by situation interactional model. However, the person variables were more important than the situation variables. Kealey argued that his results should serve to reestablish the value of personality traits for the prediction of success as an expatriate, with the understanding that motives and attitudes and ratings by others rather than by self are the appropriate predictor variables.

A somewhat different interpretation can also do justice to the findings. Kealey includes ratings by others plus motives and attitudes as indices of personality traits. However, such variables are quite compatible with the social skills approach outlined by Furnham and Bochner, if it is understood that not everybody is equally good at learning the skills concerned.

Communication training[2]

A large number of programs and training techniques exist in North America and Western Europe to prepare prospective expatriates for living and work-ing in another culture. Some last for weeks or even months, others a few

---

[2] An extensive source of information on this topic is the three-volume *Handbook of Intercultural Training* edited by Landis and Brislin (1983).

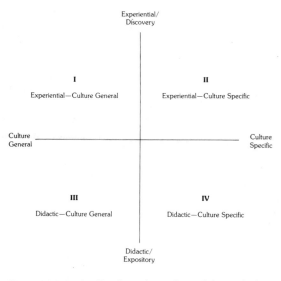

Figure 14-1 A classification scheme for training techniques (Gudykunst & Hammer, 1983).

hours. The longer programs usually include an intensive course in the language of the host country. Beyond language, much of the content of these programs is inspired by ideas and knowledge from intercultural communication studies. Descriptions of various techniques can be found in Weeks, Pedersen, and Brislin (1982) and Hoopes and Ventura (1979).

There have been various attempts to create some order in the diversity of available techniques. A convenient and simple scheme has been presented by Gudykunst and Hammer (1983). They propose a classification with two major distinctions, namely didactic versus experiential and culture-general versus culture-specific. The scheme can be presented as a figure with four quadrants (cf. Figure 14-1).

In the first quadrant are placed techniques in which personal experiences of the trainees are considered important. The effects presumably improve the communication competence in any culture. To this quadrant belong first of all programs with sensitivity training and T-group sessions. The objectives of this kind of training, widely practised in the 1960s and 1970s, are an increase in self-awareness and personal growth; a person with self-knowledge presumably can also understand others independent of their culture. A second kind of technique emphasizes more direct experience with people from various other cultures. This is realized in intercultural workshops with participants of various cultural origins where one learns to become more aware of the ways in which one's own cultural background and values influence perceptions and interactions with others.

A third kind of technique is the culture-general simulation game. There are a large number of these games, all based on similar principles. Imaginary "cultures" with contrasting values are specified in brief descriptions. The group of trainees is divided over the cultures; the subgroups receive one of the descriptions and have to familiarize themselves with their role. Then follows some kind of interaction (for example, bargaining for trade or a treaty). The games are designed so that the interactions are problematic and are likely to fail. At the end of the simulation there is a debriefing during which the reasons for the difficulties are discussed. Many of the games have been developed by training institutes for their own use and have not been published.

There are two important training techniques that belong to the second quadrant. First, there are those that involve real bicultural contacts. They can take the form of sensitivity training on an existing international conflict with members of the nations concerned in attendance. The limited evidence that is available shows that such programs have few long-lasting effects because of the strong identification of participants with the views of their own group. The second group of techniques is that of international workshops in which participants from two countries together discuss critical incidents in interactions between people from their respective cultures.

The bottom half of Figure 14-1 refers to didactic programs, where trainees are taught by instruction. To the left quadrant (on culture-general didactic methods) belong the traditional academic courses in cross-cultural psychology or intercultural communication. There are also more focused techniques. Gudykunst and Hammer (1983) mention as an example work by Kraemer (1974), who prepared videotapes (role played by actors) of conversations between an American and a non-Western person. After each episode, trainees are to indicate which cultural values and assumptions are reflected by the American on the tape. The technique is meant to increase the trainees' cultural self-awareness.

The most important form of didactic culture-specific training (the lower right quadrant of Figure 14-1) are language courses. In addition there is a variety of briefings for trainees about the country they are going to visit, including information concerning the economic and political situation, problems that an expatriate is likely to face, and major customs and attitudes.

The technique that has been used most systematically for intercultural training is the *culture assimilator*, first developed by Fiedler, Mitchell, and Triandis (1971). It consists of a large number of short episodes describing interactions between people belonging to two different cultures — the target culture and the trainee's culture. Usually some critical incident is described, such as an interaction in which something goes wrong. Each episode is followed by four or five possible reasons for the communication failure. The trainee has to choose the correct answer. In the ideal case there is one interpretation that is typically selected by members of the target culture. The other three or four are based on attributions likely to be made by members of the trainee's culture. After their choice, the trainees are given feedback on why their answer was correct or incorrect. In a good assimilator this feedback contains much culturally relevant information. Most culture assimilators have been constructed for Americans who are trained for an assignment abroad (Albert, 1983). Initially they were all culture-specific, but Brislin, Cushner, Cherrie, & Yong (1986) have constructed a culture general assimilator that should increase the effectiveness of trainees independent of their cultural background and the culture they intend to visit. In Box 14-1 one of the 100 items of this instrument is presented. Although we have no systematic evidence on this point, we have little doubt that non-Westerners will find the topics and the concerns of the items rather "American." Nevertheless, this attempt is a first step toward multicultural assimilators.

The construction of an assimilator is a tedious effort. It requires the collection of several hundred incidents. For each of these, likely attributions about the causes of miscommunication have to be found. The correct answer has to be identified. The items have to be validated by checking whether the distributions of answers by subjects from different cultures are indeed different (that is, whether the attributions are nonisomorphic). Finally, feedback has to be written for each answer explaining why it is correct or incorrect.

After the completion of a training program, trainees are usually asked for their opinion. Their satisfaction and that of the organizations that pay the costs for their employees are the main determinants of the future of any program. There is only a limited amount of more objective research on the effectiveness of the various types of techniques and programs in intercultural communication. Gudykunst and Hammer's (1983) review shows that the outcome evaluation studies often have not been very positive. Certain techniques, such as sensitivity training, have lost much of their popularity, although this probably reflects changing trends in counseling and training more than the direct impact of negative findings in evaluation studies.

Some systematic evaluation research has been conducted with the culture assimilators. From the available data, summarized by Albert (1983), it appears that the culture-specific assimilator is an effective training technique for improving intercultural communication skills. So far the culture-general assimilator by Brislin et al. (1986) is the only instrument of its kind. It carries a promise of making the assimilator technique more international. However, judgment has to be reserved in view of the still very limited amount of research (cf. Cushner, 1989).

International negotiations

The field of international negotiations would provide an inexhaustible source of anecdotal evidence if we felt the need to convince our readers of the importance of cultural factors in behavior. Many people who have been involved in international negotiations, especially of a commercial nature, can relate incidents that in their opinion illustrate in dramatic fashion the crucial importance of "culture." A telling example is the West European

Box 14-1 A culture assimilator item

The following item has been reprinted from Brislin, Cushner, Cherrie, and Yong (1986, pp. 212, 213, 223):

The Eager Teacher. Upon graduating college with a degree in English education with a Spanish minor, Rick Meyers accepted a position teaching English in a fairly large and progressive coeducational school in Merida, Mexico, capital city of the state of Yucatan. He had met the language director earlier that year while on a spring recess tour of Mexico and felt quite comfortable with him.

Eager to start the new school year off right, Rick spent a considerable amount of time in preparation of lessons and materials and in extra-help sessions with students. It seemed as if he was always doing something school related, often spending his lunch, free periods, and after-school hours with small groups of students.

Although his relationships with the students were growing, after the first few weeks, Rick noticed that his fellow teachers seemed cold and removed. He was seldom invited to after-school and weekend get-togethers or sought out during free times at school. Not sure what to make of this, Rick kept more and more to himself, feeling increasingly lonely and rejected.

What is the major issue of concern for Rick?

(1) It is not common or acceptable for teachers in Mexico to show so much personal attention to students.
(2) Rick has not spent the requisite amount of social time with his fellow workers.
(3) The other teachers were resentful as Rick was seen as someone special and was given attention by most of the students.
(4) Rick expected to be perceived as an expert. When this was not the case, he was disappointed that his talents were not utilized by all.

Rationales for the alternative explanations. After subjects have thought about the answers and made a choice, they are referred to another page of the book where a rationale is given for each of the four alternatives. (It has been found that subjects usually not only read the text with their own answer, but go over all the alternatives.) The following explanations are given about the item you just read:

(1) While our validation sample suggested this as a possibility, one of the writer's first-hand experiences demonstrates otherwise. Especially in the larger and more progressive schools, contact between teachers and students is quite frequent and in many ways expected. Please choose again.

---

(2) This is the best answer. Although skillful in his teaching and quite successful on the job, Rick's participation with other staff has been minimal. In many places, the degree of one's socializing with others is of critical importance. Although contrary to most Americans' desire to perform the task efficiently and well, attention must also be paid to social norms and expectations with colleagues to ensure success in the workplace.

(3) There is no indication in the story that the students were responding to anything more than Rick's genuine offer of time and assistance. There is a better response. Please try again.

(4) Although this may result in problems for some people in some situations, there is no indication that this is an issue for Rick. There is a better answer. Please choose again.

---

businessman who allegedly lost an important transaction in an Arab country even after the papers had been signed because he handed the contract over with his left hand.

The outsider is inclined to see "odd" practices as a reflection of broader and more systematic differences. Whatever phenomenon is being observed tends to be incorporated in a more general characterization best indicated with the term *national character* (see Chapter 4). Statements to the effect that one has to be careful with the X-people because they are easily offended, or that you have to be patient with the Y-people because they are slow in reaching a decision, form the heart of the literature on negotiations that pays attention to cultural factors. This does not mean that negotiators are ill at ease in cross-cultural settings. It is our impression that there tends to be considerable uncertainty among beginners. Experienced negotiators appear to be more confident that they can handle cross-cultural interactions, that through their experience they know how to avoid offending the X-es and show the patience required in Y-land.

Negotiators are virtually unanimous in considering the substantive issues that are on the table as the most important determinants of the outcome of a negotiation process. Opinions differ on the relevance of cultural factors, but many negotiators, from business as well as international diplomats (e.g., Kaufmann, 1989), believe that an understanding of these factors is essential.

Impressionistic observations.[3] Much of the literature consists of recommendations on how to behave in negotiations with people in other cultures. There is a good deal of similarity with the literature on cross-cultural

---

[3] Over the next few pages readers may wish to consider to what extent the statements on other nations reflect *desirable* or *undesirable* characteristics.

communication training discussed before. A distinction can also be made here between guidance on how to behave in other cultures in general and how to behave in specific cultural settings.

In a chapter called "Foreigners and Foreign Cultures" Posses (1978) gives a host of general statements about culture as an influence on behavior. For example: "Across the foreign border, the negotiator must observe and note the alien movements carefully and distinguish them from his own in order to evaluate their positive or negative relation to the actions and responses of his foreign adversary" (p. 25). A little later we learn: "Sometimes we may be thrust back by an apparent indifference. It may be a cultural convention, as it is in certain Oriental countries, for the Japanese or Chinese representative to appear impassive. Whereas in the Latin countries, the Spanish, the Portuguese or South American negotiators may be volatile about apparently irrelevant matters" (p. 29). These quotes contain both tips and general descriptions as well as descriptions of national characteristics of people in specific countries or regions of the world.

On the question to what extent nationals of various countries feel bound by commitments Posses comments:

In other countries, the striking of hands to seal the agreement carries a solemn undertaking that will be taken solemnly, as amongst Germans. Yet the striking of hands, as amongst the Italians, should not be relied upon as an absolute come-hell-or-high-water promise. Here too we may encounter the plea of "you didn't understand what I meant you to understand," and if the plea for modification or total exculpation is rejected, Italians can be adept at finding ways and means to delay, defer and deter the ultimate execution on their part of what was intended by both sides to be a waterproof contract. (p. 36)

The book by Posses deals with various aspects of negotiations (including legal and economic factors) but does not have any references, nor is the reader informed how the author has collected the information he is relying on. We call this kind of work *impressionistic*.

In some instances anthropological theory provides the background for culture-general recommendations. A distinct example is an article by the anthropologist Hall (1960) in which he relates an imaginary story of an American negotiating an industrial contract with a state minister in a Central American country. Hall mentions time (speed of action, coming to the point), interpersonal space, orientation toward material wealth, interpersonal relations (friendship), and the status and meaning of agreements (including contracts) as important points to keep in mind. The article was largely based on an earlier book by Hall (1959). Inasmuch as the advice is based on Hall's theory we would not call it impressionistic, but his recommendations go beyond the theory and no systematic empirical validation data are mentioned.

Recommendations relevant to specific cultures form the bulk of the literature on cultural differences in negotiations. Much of it is written from the perspective of the businessman or diplomat from the U.S. who has dealings with some other country. Examples can be found in a reader edited by

Binnendijk (1987). It contains chapters, mainly written by political scientists and diplomats, on six countries. In addition to existing literature their *personal experiences* as negotiators with the culture they describe appear to be a main source of information. Numerous statements are made about the "national character" of the countries described. This serves as a background to explain national negotiation styles. About the Chinese one learns among other things that "The most fundamental characteristic of dealings with the Chinese is their attempt to identify foreign officials who are sympathetic to their cause, to cultivate a sense of friendship and obligation in their official counterparts, and then to pursue their objectives through a variety of stratagems designed to manipulate feelings of friendship, obligation, guilt, or dependence" (Solomon, 1987 p. 3). In the case of Japan it is important to recognize that negotiation implies social conflict and that the Japanese have been socialized to avoid conflict. The development of personal relationships is critical as they form the basis for future, often long-lasting contacts (Thayer & Weiss, 1987). With the Egyptians "three elements — a sense of national pride and historical continuity, acceptance of the need for a strong ruler, and a highly developed bureaucratic tradition — are essential" for the understanding of their politics, nationally as well as internationally (Quandt, 1987, p. 106).

These few examples cannot do justice to the extensive body of writings that exist. We hope that some of the general flavor of the impressionistic literature is reflected in the quotations presented here. The readers of this literature, most often from the business and diplomatic communities, find prescriptions on how to behave and what to expect in foreign countries. In our opinion the main function is that the various comments serve to provide marker points in an inherently complex domain.

A problem to which hardly any attention has been paid is that of the validity of these descriptions. We would argue that descriptions of other cultures can be likened to descriptions of an individual's personality. Almost independent of their objective value they strike the reader as plausible, especially when they are couched in general terms. The absence of evidence on validity may not be surprising in view of the intended readership. However, in a text like the present one where the validity of presumed cultural differences is of concern precise and testable evidence is critical for an evaluation.

Since there are quite a few publications on some countries, it is possible to carry out consistency checks between them. Let us consider an article by Pye (1986) on trade with the People's Republic of China from an American perspective. The author, a political scientist with a research record of negotiations with the Chinese (e.g., Pye, 1982), has no hesitation in praising them for their knowledge of the "subtle art of negotiating." A few quotes may be given for comparison with the comments by Solomon, mentioned above.

According to Pye: "At the heart of Chinese bargaining, a predictable psychological dimension takes the form of getting the other party to exaggerate its capabilities while the Chinese reserve the right to ask for more. Flattery is too crude a description for this process. Instead, the Chinese use the advantage a weaker party has in extracting favours from the strong — all the while maintaining its dignity. The Chinese approach calls for elaborate courtesy, gestured humility, and high sensitivity to perceived insult" (p. 77). With respect to contracts Pye argues as follows: "The American goal is a binding agreement secured by a stable and enduring legal system, a contract with all the power and mystique we associate with the law. The Chinese see stability not in the power of the law but in the strength of human relationships. A contract establishes what is essentially a personal relationship" (p. 79).

There is obviously a resemblance between the quotations of Solomon and those of Pye, but this does not settle the validity problem. First, there is the possibility of confounding because both authors have made use of the same sources of information. Someone who writes on negotiations with the Chinese is likely to have read much of what has been written on the subject. Second, there is a problem of discriminant validity. Pye's comments also resemble the quotes we took from Thayer and Weiss on the Japanese, this despite the opinion of Binnendijk (1987) that the Japanese negotiation style differs fundamentally from the Chinese. A lack of differentiation between (presumably) dissimilar cultures is as detrimental to validity as a lack of coherence in observations on the same culture (D. T. Campbell & Fiske, 1959; cf. also Chapter 9).

Of course, there are large differences in the extent to which authors document their statements. We have already noted that Posses (1978) provides no identifiable references. On the other hand, McCreary and Blanchfield (1986) in a chapter on Japanese negotiations present broad principles of national culture, namely *amae* (see Chapter 4) and *haragei* (translated as "intuitive communication"), as well as the use of language, including the use of specific terms that are likely to be misunderstood in their implications. Similarly, there are large differences in the level of abstraction of the points raised. Hall (1960) offers broad principles on which cultures differ in an explanation of the "mistakes" the American in his imaginary story is making. McCreary and Blanchfield include in their review practical recommendations, such as not to put your feet on the table and to dress conservatively. However, it is not evident in their text how these concrete points are derived from the broader characteristics of Japanese culture. To the best of our knowledge, of all the peoples in the world, only some North Americans and Europeans would put their feet on a table except in their own home or club.

The search for validity. Because of the confidential character of most international negotiations it is difficult to carry out experimental studies in real life settings. Available research is mainly based on archival data, self-reports of negotiators, and simulation studies. Other, indirect, evidence can be derived from the experimental literature on psychological functions and processes that play a role in negotiations.

Personal accounts of diplomats were used by R. Cohen (1987) in a study of intercultural communication in Egyptian-American diplomatic relations. He obtained his materials largely from autobiographies of diplomats and interviews. Cohen uses a theoretical framework to describe his results, namely a theory of conflict and culture by Ting-Toomey (1985). He is quite explicit that one can never know to what extent intangible cultural factors have harmed relationships. Still, he points to a series of disruptive events in Egypt-U.S. relationships (for example, the Arab-Israeli wars of 1967 and 1973) where the recollections of some of the diplomats involved make it plausible that cultural incompatibilities and misapprehensions played a contributory if not a decisive role. Cohen's main problem is that each event in real life is embedded in a complex context from which it is difficult to extract a decisive factor retrospectively.

Moving to the literature in cross-cultural psychology, we find a large number of studies on basic processes that are potentially relevant to negotiations. Examples are decision-making (referred to in the previous chapter) and cooperation versus competition, especially with the Prisoners Dilemma Game and the Maximizing Difference Game (L. Mann, 1980; Madsen, 1971). Cross-cultural work on procedural justice can also be mentioned here. Leung (1987) found that students from (collectivistic) Hong Kong tend to prefer bargaining and mediation in a conflict situation while students from the (individualistic) U.S. lean more toward an adversary style in which the parties directly confront each other.

However, culture as a variable is usually manipulated by replication of the same study in various cultural groups; hardly any research has been carried out where subjects from different cultures have been actually interacting with each other. Consequently, this research has not been *inter*cultural, but rather *cross*-cultural. The same limitation applies to simulation studies where subjects were brought into laboratory situations to negotiate as buyers or sellers of certain commodities (Graham, 1983; Graham, Kim, Lin, & Robinson, 1988; N. C. G. Campbell, Graham, Jolibert, & Meissner, 1988).[4]

With the virtual absence of cross-cultural studies on mixed samples of subjects, the contributions of cross-cultural psychology to the understanding of international negotiation processes can only be tentative. We can anticipate further developments along two lines.

The first is theory development. Hofstede (1989) has proposed a set of

---

[4] A study of Graham and Andrews (1987) is one of the exceptions. It describes laboratory simulations of business negotiations between pairs of subjects. There were six American-Japanese dyads. The limited data set does not allow any firm conclusion. However, it may be interesting to note that language and communication problems were reported to create most difficulties.

hypotheses on the basis of the dimensions that have emerged from his earlier research (Hofstede, 1980) and that of Bond and colleagues (Chinese Culture Connection, 1987). The testable predictions include, for example, that large power distance will correlate with more centralized control and decision-making, and that negotiators from countries high on uncertainty avoidance will prefer structured and ritualistic procedures. A theory by Ting-Toomey (1985) elaborates on Hall's (1976) distinction between low-context and high-context cultures. Within high-context cultures much of the information in communication processes is shared by the sender and receiver of a message or is present in the context. Within low-context cultures much of the information is in the transmitted message. Most Western countries can be qualified as low-context cultures, while Japan, Korea, and Vietnam are high-context cultures. Ting-Toomey has derived a set of propositions. For example, she expects that in low-context cultures conflicts are more likely to arise when individual norms and expectations are being violated. In high-context cultures this is more likely to happen when collective norms and expectations are not met. In another pair of propositions she suggests individuals in low-context cultures will assume a confrontational attitude in conflicts, while those from high-context cultures will be more passive and non-confrontational.

The second line of development is an analysis of claims about differences in the light of other available cross-cultural psychological evidence. Present knowledge provides a reasonable basis for a critical evaluation of impressionistic observations. Such an analysis was carried out by Hendriks (cf. Poortinga & Hendriks, 1989) on the possible role of attribution processes in international negotiations. In Chapters 4 and 12 (Box 12-2) we have referred to intergroup research based on attribution theory and the finding that negative behavior of a member of one's own group tends to be explained with reference to situational constraints, while the same behavior of a member from another group is attributed to internal dispositions. Jaspars and Hewstone (1982; Hewstone & Jaspars, 1982) related these findings to Tajfel's (1978) Social Identity Theory, which postulates that the own-group identity is strengthened by a differentiation between own-group and other groups. Actors will interpret situations so that a positive social identity is preserved. An internal cause of undesirable behavior in a member of one's own group will be detrimental to a positive identity. For desirable behaviors the mechanisms work in the opposite direction; a situational explanation will be more prevalent for other groups and explanation in terms of internal dispositions more prevalent in the case of own-group members. Supportive laboratory evidence has been obtained (Hewstone, Bond, & Wan, 1983; Bond, Chiu, & Wan, 1984), but the generalization to real life interactions remains tentative.

We are only at the beginning of the systematic analysis of national differences in negotiation styles as they are reported by negotiators. Despite apprehension about the validity of many claims about cultural variables one cannot ignore the experience of many negotiators that these variables do play a significant role.

Conclusions

There is still a persistent belief that someone who is effective at home will also be effective in coping with members of other cultures. The available data, mainly from the U.S., are not compatible with this viewpoint (e.g., Copeland & Griggs, 1985). Training methods in cross-cultural communication and all kinds of advice are available to the prospective sojourner or international negotiator who wants to know more about the idiosyncrasies found in some other nation. The effectiveness of these interventions is still largely unknown. This is not surprising, as there is still so much uncertainty on questions surrounding the nature and extent of psychological differences between various cultures. As a consequence, the area of intercultural communications offers many challenges to cross-cultural researchers.

15   Health behavior

In the 1970s and 1980s there was a revolution in the way many people thought about health. As indicated in the unanimous acceptance of the Alma Ata Declaration of "Health for All by the Year 2000" (World Health Organization, 1978) and in the "Ottawa Charter" (World Health Organization, 1988) there has been a shift away from "curing disease" once it has occurred to the "prevention of disease" (through public health measures such as primary health care), and even more fundamentally to the "promotion of health" (through such factors as appropriate diet and exercise and the avoidance of unhealthy substances).

With this shift in goals, there came as well a shift in approach away from a high-technology biological- and equipment-oriented strategy to one that recognizes the potential role of the social and behavioral sciences in the health area. In public education, mass communication, and behavior modification there was seen a possibility of guiding the development of healthy behaviors or changing unhealthy ones. In the analysis, improvement, and control of social and environmental conditions (such as poverty, crowding, technological change, and forced migration) there was seen a way to prevent some major health problems. Of course, medical technology has remained an important element in health, both in prevention and cure, but it is now more a matter of "appropriate technology" where the local population can understand, use, and sustain the technology provided to them. For example, sanitation and safe water can prevent, and oral rehydration can reduce, the effects of diarrheal disease; and the control of parasites and infections are often within reach for most populations.

During this period not only was the approach to attaining health redefined, the actual definition of health was extended. In the Alma Ata Declaration (WHO, 1978) health was defined as a "state of complete physical, mental and social well being, and not merely the absence of disease or infirmity." That is, there are positive qualities to health, and these go beyond the physical into the realms of one's psychological and social life. At the same time, health was viewed as a prerequisite for human development, both individual and national (see Chapter 16) and was construed as the responsibility of everyone, not just as a professional responsibility of medical specialists.

In the light of this movement and the development of medical anthropology

356

(Alland, 1970; Lieban, 1973) cross-cultural psychology, attuned as it is to variations in culture and individual behavior, is well-placed to play an important and useful role in this newly redefined field. Psychology has already developed a number of new subfields ("behavioral medicine," "health psychology," "illness behavior," "community mental health") and there is a definable set of contributions that can be made to health by these fields (Holtzman, Evans, Kennedy, & Iscoe, 1987). Cross-cultural psychology has just begun to take a similar step (e.g., Draguns, 1990; Ilola, 1990), and while major strides have not yet been accomplished, it has been argued that the potential contribution is rather substantial (Dasen et al., 1988). In some cases, for example in the culturally sensitive delivery of mental health services, the process of application has already yielded some benefits (Pedersen, Sartorius, Marsella, 1984; Comas-Diaz & Griffith, 1988). We will be examining the evidence for these statements in this chapter.

It should be made clear at the outset that the social and behavioral science role is not limited solely to *mental* health; the approach taken here is that psychology and cross-cultural psychology are just as relevant for *physical* and *social* health issues. This position is one that is shared with the World Health Organization (1982), which makes it quite explicit that:

psychosocial factors have been increasingly recognized as key factors in the success of health and social actions. If actions are to be effective in the prevention of diseases and in the promotion of health and well being, they must be based on an understanding of culture, tradition, beliefs and patterns of family interaction. (p. 4)

Some specific ways in which cross-cultural psychology can contribute to such understanding are through the study of people's health beliefs (what health is), their attitudes and values (the importance attached to health), and their actual health-related behaviors.

We begin this chapter with an examination of the two central mental health issues confronting cross-cultural health psychologists (psychopathology and psychotherapy) and then turn to other health domains, including cultural aspects of physical health.

Psychopathologies across cultures

Frequent reference was made in Chapter 7 to the concern of the culture and personality school of anthropology for abnormal psychological phenomena. Over much the same period psychiatrists and clinical psychologists who were not associated with this school were developing an interest in similar phenomena; this activity has come to be known variously as the field of "cultural psychiatry," "transcultural psychiatry," "comparative psychiatry," "culture and mental health," or "culture and psychopathology." It is a difficult area to comprehend, partly because of the specialist nature of the topic. There are a few integrated treatments of the field (see Yap, 1974; Leff, 1981; Murphy, 1981) and numerous edited volumes that illustrate the range and depth of the material (e.g., Al-Issa, 1982; Foulks, Wintrob, Westermeyer, & Favazza, 1977; Marsella & White, 1982; Mezzich & Berganza, 1984).

By "abnormal behaviors and states" psychologists and psychiatrists usually mean those features of an individual's behavior or experience that have been classified as an "illness" or a "disorder" (not just "eccentricities") and are judged as strange or bizarre by others who interact with the individual in his daily life. While more formal definitions are provided in the psychiatric literature, this everyday definition will allow us to designate the domain with which we are concerned. A listing of such mental disorders is provided in Box 15-1; a more complete description of each category is available in textbooks of abnormal psychology (e.g., Coleman, Butcher, & Carson, 1980).

The main issue regarding psychopathology cross-culturally (see Chapter 10) is whether these phenomena are *absolute* (invariant across cultures in origin, expression, and so forth), *universal* (present in some form in all cultures, but subject to cultural influence on the factors that bring them on, expression, and so on), or *culturally relative* (unique to some cultures and understandable only in terms of that culture); this last view is also known as *ethnopsychiatry* (Devereux, 1980; Fourasté, 1985). In reviewing the evidence we will focus on some selected areas of research that cover the range of disorders identified in Box 15-1, beginning with the major organic disorders and ending with some of the "culture-bound syndromes."

The most likely candidates for supporting the absolutist position are those disorders that are clearly rooted in some basic biological functions: organic disorders and substance disorders (categories 1 and 2 in Box 15-1). While this position remains a logical possibility, there is little research actually available that would substantiate it, and those studies that are available suggest that cultural factors may affect rates and forms of expression. The physiological response to alcohol appears to vary across groups (Wolff, 1972), presumably for genetic reasons, but cultural norms about what, where, and how much alcohol to drink vary, leading to quite different expressions of alcohol use across groups (e.g., Korolenko, 1988; Mala, 1985). We may conclude that it makes little sense to even consider a culture-free abnormal behavior, since cultural factors appear to affect at least some aspects of mental disorders, even those that are so closely linked to human biology. The universalist (rather than the absolutist) position seems to be the more tenable one at this point in the presentation, and such a conclusion is clearly indicated by studies of the two major psychoses: schizophrenia and depression (categories 3 and 4 in Box 15-1).

Schizophrenia. This disorder has been identified in cross-cultural studies since the beginning of the twentieth century, using a variety of standard indicators (Draguns, 1980; Leff, 1981; Murphy, 1982). It is the most common mental disorder in the world. Usually, the signs of the disorder are a lack of insight, auditory hallucinations, delusions of reference, and flatness of affect (WHO, 1973). There is evidence that to some degree it is inherited,

---

Box 15-1 A classification of mental disorders

To facilitate the international reporting of psychiatric illness, the World Health Organization (1990) has developed an "International Classification of Diseases" (ICD-10). Mental Disorders are placed in the following categories:

1. *Organic mental disorders*: such as Alzheimer's disease and dementia (due to such organic factors as Huntington's and Parkinson's disease).
2. *Mental disorders due to psychoactive substance use*: such as alcohol, tobacco, cannabis, sedatives, cocaine, and hallucinogens.
3. *Schizophrenia and delusional disorders*: such as paranoia, catatonic schizophrenia, and delusions.
4. *Affective disorders*: such as manic and depressive mood disorders.
5. *Neurotic disorders*: such as phobia, anxiety, obsession, amnesia, multiple personality, hypochondriasis, and neurasthenia (fatigue syndrome).
6. *Physiological dysfunction*: such as anorexia, obesity, insomnia, sleep walking, and sexual dysfunctions (lack of desire, enjoyment, or response).
7. *Personality disorders*: such as impulsive, dependent personality, problems of gender identity, pathological gambling, fire-setting, and stealing; also included are abnormalities of sexual preference (fetishism, exhibitionism, voyeurism, pedophilia, but *not* homosexuality).
8. *Mental retardation*: such as arrested mental development (low IQ).
9. *Developmental disorders*: such as language, aphasia, and reading problems; autism, and hyperkinesis.
10. *Childhood disorders*: such as sibling rivalry, tics, bedwetting, and stuttering.

(see Chapter 8), but also that certain experiences may precipitate its onset. Murphy (1982) proposes that culture can affect the risk of developing schizophrenia in four ways: through mistraining regarding the processing of information; through the complexity of information given to people; through the expectations about making decisions when information is unclear; and through the degree to which schizophrenia-bearing families are discouraged or encouraged to have children. In addition to cultural factors affecting the *prevalence* of the disorder, Murphy (1982) proposes that culture can affect the *definition*, *recognition*, *acceptance*, and *symptomatology* of the disorder (the signs or behaviors through which the disorder is expressed); it can also affect the *course* of the disorder (changes over time) and the *response* of the disorder to treatment.

In the research of Murphy (1982) there is evidence that Irish Catholics have much higher hospitalization rates for schizophrenia than others: rates in Eire are four times those in England, with rates in Northern Ireland falling in between. However, rates within Northern Ireland for Roman Catholics are double those for non-Catholics (whose rates resemble those in England). Murphy concluded that the differences are real, but that the actual cultural sources of the differences are difficult to specify. However, two appear to have some validity: "the verbal agility and sometimes savage wit that Irish culture encourages; ... and the ambivalence toward individual independence" (Murphy, 1982, p. 225). For the first factor the frequency of "double-think" and "double-speak" in Ireland "increases the complexity and reduces the clarity of information to which people are exposed, while the particular type of ridiculing imposes on the victim a demand that he respond to that unclear information" (Murphy, 1982, p. 226). For the second factor a tendency by Irish psychiatrists to avoid returning schizophrenic patients to isolated cottages, but instead keeping them in a secure and dependent situation in hospital, may account for higher rates in Ireland. There is also evidence that cultural factors (in definitions and diagnostic preferences) may affect the *apparent* prevalence, and this may partially account for reported differences in rates across cultures. This subtle interaction between "true" rates in schizophrenia in different cultures and variations in diagnostic procedures has been highlighted in the work of Cooper et al. (1972) and in a major study by WHO (1973, 1979). In a detailed analysis of the Cooper et al. study Leff (1977) has shown that there are differences in diagnoses of schizophrenia by hospital psychiatrists in New York and London (61.5 percent versus 33.9 percent of psychiatric patients respectively), but that this difference disappears when diagnoses are made by trained members of a research project who used the same standard of diagnosis (29.2 percent versus 35.1 percent respectively).

   The WHO studies went further afield and included psychiatrists in nine centers (Columbia, Czechoslovakia, Denmark, India, Nigeria, Taiwan, U.K., U.S., and USSR) who were trained to use a standard diagnostic instrument (the "Present State Examination"). Over 100 psychiatric patients were examined in each center, and of the 1202 patients, 77.5 percent were diagnosed as schizophrenic. A "core of common symptoms" appeared in all sites, including social and emotional withdrawal, delusions, and flat affect. However, profiles of symptoms did differ substantially from center to center. For example, the U.S. schizophrenics differed from the Danish and Nigerian on symptoms of lack of insight and auditory hallucinations (fewer of both), while Nigerians had more frequent "other hallucinations" than the other two groups. Given this "common core" (and the partial reduction of variation in diagnosis when common instruments are employed) it has been concluded by the authors of the original studies, and by reviewers alike, that schizophrenia is a *universal* disorder, one that is recognizably present in all cultures, but that it appears to respond to different cultural experiences in prevalence rates and modes of expression. However, two cautions are necessary: first, the studies involved instruments, concepts, and researchers who were all Western-oriented; and second, the patient populations are not a representative sample of world cultural variation (and were to some extent themselves acculturated to Western life). Hence, one cannot exclude entirely the possibility that the definition of schizophrenia will have to be further informed by cultural variations that are insufficiently studied so far.

Depression. The other major disorder that has been studied cross-culturally is depression (category 4 in Box 15-1). While less common than schizophrenia, it has nevertheless received considerable empirical and theoretical effort (see Engelsmann, 1982, and Marsella, 1980, for overviews). "Depression," in the nonpsychotic sense, occurs often and for almost everyone; however, as a psychopathology it is characterized by a large set of problems and symptoms, including a sad mood and a lack of energy, interest, and enjoyment. It is often accompanied by emotional changes (such as feelings of guilt, anger, and anxiety), physical changes (such as sleep disturbance, tiredness, and loss of appetite, weight, and strength), behavioral changes (such as crying, withdrawal, and agitation) and changes in self-evaluation (low self-esteem, pessimism, and feelings of hopelessness and worthlessness); severe depression may be accompanied by suicidal tendencies (Engelsmann, 1982).

Depression was included along with schizophrenia in the Cooper et al. (1972) U.S.-U.K. study and the further analysis by Leff (1977). Once again there was a significant difference in hospital diagnosis (4.7 percent versus 24.1 percent in the U.S. and U.K. respectively), but this difference again largely disappeared when the research project psychiatrists carried out the diagnosis (19.8 percent versus 22.3 percent). Does this mean that apparent differences in rates and display of depression across cultures generally are due solely to the differential use of the depression diagnosis by psychiatrists? According to the comprehensive analysis of Marsella (1980), the answer is probably "no." The local cultural meaning of "being depressed" varies widely both with patient's language family and differentiation of emotional terminology (Leff, 1977); experience of acculturation to Western life-style also tends to increase the prevalence of depression (Prince, 1968).

Going beyond these observed cultural correlates of depression, there are a number of elaborated theories that are proposed to account for both the origin of and variation in depression. These refer to aspects of family structure (extended families providing more elaborate social support, close mother-child relationships, and reduced risk of loss of loved ones) and mourning rituals (low depression may result from ritualized and overt expressions of grief). Marsella's (1980) own theory involves a cultural dimension of "epistemic orientations" (that is, objective versus subjective orientation). In the relatively "objective" type of cultures there is an abstract language and individuated self-structure; in contrast, in "subjective" types of culture there is a metaphorical language and more communal structure. According to Marsella, depression takes a primarily affective and cognitive form in cultures with objective orientations (and is experienced as a sense of isolation), while it takes a primarily somatic form in cultures with subjective orientations.

Despite these variations, most observers believe that, as in the case of schizophrenia, there is a "common core" of symptoms of depression that allows the disorder to be recognized in all cultures. It thus qualifies as a universal, but like all other universals at the present time the Western bias in research approach and in the populations studied may well have affected the conceptualization.

Culture-bound syndromes. Culturally relative studies of psycho-pathology abound in the literature; there is apparently nothing more intriguing in this field than discovering another apparently unique way of "being mad"! The rich reports of "culture-bound syndromes" have fueled the relativist position and have led to the claim that there are unique, local forms of psychosis not known outside a particular culture. A sample of these conditions is provided in Box 15-2 in order to obtain a sense of their special and interesting qualities.

While many of these phenomena are limited to particular cultures, and while there are rich local interpretations and meanings for each condition, recent efforts in cultural psychiatry have been made to discover some underlying similarities between them and the major disorders recognized by psychiatry generally (Simons & Hughes, 1985; Prince & Tcheng-Laroche, 1987). That is, the question is raised whether these exotic and apparently culturally relative syndromes may be local expressions of some universal disorders already known and classified. An early proposal of such a "classification" was made by Yap (1969) and later elaborated by him (Yap, 1974). However, there are claims (e.g., Arieti & Meth, 1959) that they are "unclassifiable." There is also an assertion that any such attempt would yield categories that are "qualitatively of so diverse a nature that they cannot be systematically integrated but by distortion" (Pfeiffer, 1982, p. 202).

Yap begins by distinguishing between unusual behaviors and those that may signal an underlying disorder; this is similar to Honigmann's (1967) distinction between the *socially abnormal* and the *psychiatrically abnormal.* One is merely eccentric, while the other is dysfunctional for the society and the individual. By concentrating on those exotic behaviors that are in the dysfunctional category we can recognize that much of the unusual behavior reported in various parts of the world is culturally patterned, even culture-bound. Yap's distinction provides a basis for the search for similarities in the various reports. Yap is able to subsume, using his clinical judgment, many of the apparently culture-bound syndromes within established diagnoses. For example, *latah* and *susto* are judged to be local cultural expressions of a "primary fear reaction," while *amok* is a "rage reaction," and *witiko* is a "possession state," all conditions recognized and described by general psychiatry.

Yap recognizes that his classification may be premature and even wrong in

Box 15-2 Culture-bound syndromes

In the literature of cultural psychiatry numerous "exotic" mental disorders have been described and interpretations given in local terms, often with the indigenous name for the disorder entering into the medical literature (Yap, 1969; Pfeiffer, 1982; Simons & Hughes, 1985). A sampling of some of the better-known syndromes follows.

Amok involves wild, aggressive behavior of limited duration (usually among males) in which there are attempts to kill or injure a person. It has been identified in southeast Asia (Malaysia, Indonesia, Thailand). Amok is a Malay term meaning "to engage furiously in battle" (Westermeyer, 1973). It has obvious relations to the Viking behavior *berserker* practised just prior to entering battle (Leff, 1981). The terms "running amok" and "going berserk" are now in common usage.

Brain fag involves problems of academic learning, headache, eye fatigue, and an inability to concentrate. It appears widely in West African students often just prior to school and university examinations (Prince, 1960) and is virtually unknown outside that culture area!

Koro involves the sensation that one's penis is retracting into the abdomen and the belief that when fully retracted death will result. Panic attempts to keep the penis from retracting can lead to severe physical damage.

Latah involves imitative behavior (usually among women) that seems beyond control; movements and speech are copied, and individuals in this state are compliant to commands to do things outside their usual range of behavior (for example, to utter obscenities). Its onset is often the result of a sudden or startling stimulus. The term *latah* means "ticklish" in the Malay language.

Pibloqtoq involves an uncontrollable urge to leave one's shelter, tear off one's clothes, and expose oneself to the Arctic winter weather. It has been identified in Greenland, Alaska, and the Canadian Arctic and has been linked both to isolated environmental conditions and to limited calcium uptake during long sunless winters.

Susto involves insomnia, apathy, depression, and anxiety, often among children, usually brought on by fright. Among the people of the Andean highlands, it is believed to result from contact with supernatural forces (witches, the evil eye) and to result in soul loss.

Witiko involves a distaste for ordinary food and feelings of depression and anxiety, leading to possession by the *witiko* spirit (a giant man-eating monster) and often resulting in homicide and cannibalism. It occurs among Canadian Indians and has been interpreted as an extreme form of starvation anxiety. If a cure is not attained, the *witiko* sufferer often pleads for death to avoid his cannibalistic desires.

> The hallmark of all these syndromes is their exotic (to Western[1] observers) qualities; each is usually given an interpretation within the terms of their own culture. The issue for cultural psychiatry is whether they are also comprehensible within a universal framework of psychopathology.

some respects. However, he argues that the goal of organizing the mass of reports of exotic syndromes is a scientifically valid one and should be pursued. In Yap's view:

Once this idea is accepted, the way is open to the use of various tested clinical research techniques to explore the nature of these syndromes ... Undoubtedly modifications in tools and methods will have to be made. It is important that first steps be taken in an effective direction ... From such studies, a consistent definition of each disorder in terms of modal symptomatology, and eventually, psychopathology, can be arrived at and provide a firm basis for further clinical research. (1969, p. 49)

To draw this section on psychopathology to a close, it should be clear that evidence points in the direction of a universalist position. On the one hand there appears to be important cultural patterning of those disorders that are most evidently biologically rooted (making the absolutist position untenable), while on the other hand initial attempts to discover some "common core" of symptoms of the major psychoses across cultures and to identify underlying categorizing principles for the apparently "culture-bound" syndromes have both yielded some success. Of course, such a conclusion must be a tentative one, awaiting further research from points of view that are less clearly rooted in a single (Western) cultural tradition.

Cultural factors in psychotherapy

Just as there are cultural factors involved in the development and display of psychopathology, so too are there cultural factors involved in the process of attempting to alleviate these problems. There is a triangular relationship between the client, the therapist, and the society that serves as a useful point of departure to identify similarities and differences. The essential similarity is that cultural beliefs and practices prevalent in a society enter into the psychotherapeutic process because they form part of both the therapist's and patient's definitions and understandings of the problem. The essential difference is that in the case of *indigenous psychotherapy* all three elements share a common culture, since there is no intercultural situation involved. However, in the case of *cross-cultural psychotherapy* (as in the case of intercultural

---

[1] Not all culture-bound syndromes have been proposed for non-Western cultures. For example, *anorexia nervosa* is sometimes seen as a disorder of eating found almost exclusively among younger females in Western countries (Swartz, 1985).

counseling; see Sue, 1981; Samuda & Wolfgang, 1985) since Western-based theory and method are frequently used to assist persons of other cultures, serious misunderstandings may result.

The term *psychotherapy* is a general term that is employed to refer to any practice that involves a patient and a healer in a personal relationship whose goal is to alleviate the patient's suffering due to a psychological problem or disorder. According to Doi (1984) this interpersonal relationship is usually based upon a dependency need, although Prince (1980) questions whether this is an essential element in all forms of psychotherapy found across cultures. Note that the form of the therapy is usually *psychological* rather than *physical*, although this distinction is not always easy to maintain in practice (Prince, 1980, pp. 292–293). What is common to all psychotherapeutic practices in Prince's view (1980, p. 297) is that they serve to "mobilize the healing forces within the patient"; that is, coping mechanisms and other psychological resources (such as resting, withdrawing, expectation, and hope) of the individual are drawn out: "most of the treatments that the healers offer are simply an exaggeration or extra development of . . . endogenous mechanisms" (p. 297). Prince (1984) has proposed that there may be a biological endogenous mechanism as well, noting that "there is now considerable experimental and circumstantial evidence that endogenously generated neurohormones produce analgesia, euphoria, amnesia, and altered states of consciousness" (p. 62). These neurohormones "are also generated by religious and other rituals that constitute an important element in many indigenous psychotherapeutic systems" (Prince, 1984, p. 62).

Indigenous or culture-bound psychotherapy can be found in virtually any society. In Western industrialized societies it tends to take the form of psychoanalytic therapy (deriving from the ideas of Sigmund Freud and his followers) or a number of other forms based on various theoretical positions in psychology (learning theory, gestalt theory, humanist theory, and so on). In this chapter we will not treat such therapies as *indigenous* therapies, although they are important, because they are the most frequent basis for *cross-cultural* psychotherapy (which occurs when Western clinical psychology is used with people of other cultures). Instead, we will focus on a few indigenous therapies that have been used as traditional forms in non-Western cultures.

Indigenous psychotherapy. Among the range of these indigenous psychotherapies are those rooted in Japanese culture and thought: *Morita* therapy (Miura & Usa, 1970) and *Naikan* therapy (Tanaka-Matsumi, 1979). According to Murase (1982, p. 317), both of these therapies are "revivalistic, and oriented towards a rediscovery of the core values of Japanese society." These core values are *amae* and *sunao*, and are related to *Morita* and *Naikan* respectively, although both values are thought to enter to some extent into both therapies.

Morita therapy was developed in Japan by the psychiatrist S. Morita

(1874–1938) during the 1920s to treat psychoneurotic problems and is based upon isolation and rest rather than verbal interactions. Morita therapy lasts between four and eight weeks and is divided into four stages:

1. Total bed rest and isolation for four to ten days; the patient is totally inactive and not permitted to converse, read, write, or listen to the radio.
2. For the next seven to fourteen days he is out of bed and allowed in the garden where he does light work; the patient begins to write a diary for the doctor but other human contact is forbidden.
3. For a further week or two he is instructed to do heavier work, continue the diary and attend lectures from the doctor on self-control, the evils of egocentricity, and so forth.
4. Finally, the patient gradually returns to full social life and his former occupation; the patient continues contact with the doctor and attends group sessions with other patients on an out-patient basis. (Prince, 1980, p. 299)

As we have seen in Chapter 4, *amae* is a dependency need that is thought to be highly valued in Japanese life and is opposite to the independence and control over one's own fate that is promoted during Western psychotherapy (Doi, 1984). Its relationship to Morita therapy is that one goal of Morita is to have the patient accept the realities of one's life rather than attempt to bring reality into line with one's own needs and desires (Pedersen, 1981).

Naikan therapy is a kind of introspection and comes from the Japanese terms *Nai* ("inside") and *kan* ("looking"). Its goals are:

(1) the discovery of personal, authentic guilt for having been ungrateful and troublesome to others in the past, and
(2) the discovery of a positive gratitude towards individuals who have extended themselves on behalf of the client at some time in the past. In short, guilt and gratitude. When these goals are attained, a profound change in self-image and interpersonal attitude occurs. (Murase, 1982, p. 317)

The procedure involves the patient sitting quietly from 5:30 A.M. to 9 P.M. for seven days introspecting the whole time except for brief visits from an "interviewer" every ninety minutes. The patient is instructed to look at himself and his relationships with others from three perspectives:

(1) Care received. The first instruction is to "recollect and examine your memories on the care and kindness that you received from a particular person during a particular time in your life." The client usually begins with an examination of his relationship to his mother, proceeds to talk about relationships with other family members, and then moves on to close persons, always following a progression from childhood to the present. For example, in the first day he may remember how his mother cared for him when he was sick in grammar school.
(2) Repayment. During that particular period "recollect what you have done for that person in return."
(3) Troubles caused. "Recollect what troubles and worries you have caused that person in that same period." (Murase, 1982, p. 317)

This examination is conducted in "a boldly moralistic manner, placing the burden of blame on the client rather than 'on others.' Only in the earlier meetings when the interviewer is more lenient and tends to listen to what the client describes to him, are excuses, rationalizations or aggressions toward others permitted" (Murase, 1982, p. 318). The interviewer's role is not like that of a therapist, but serves merely to supervise the patient's introspection and self-examination.

The value of *sunao* is widespread in Japan and has a variety of meanings, but at its core (in the interpersonal realm) it refers to being obedient or docile, accepting (rather than being assertive), in harmony with one's social environment (rather than egocentric), open minded, honest and free from antagonism and rivalry. In the intrapersonal realm it refers to being relaxed, flexible, gentle, free from conflicts and frustrations, without bias and in tune with joy and gratitude (Murase, 1982, p. 321). While this is a rather broad "core," it does form a set of values that include being at peace with oneself and one's surroundings.

A case has been made (Murase, 1982, p. 322) that *sunao* is also relevant to Morita therapy. In Morita's view the nonacceptance of their own reality by the patients is a main source of their psychological problems, and becoming more *sunao* is one way to reestablish harmony or peace:

if they had a *sunao* mind it would be obvious to them that they have been trying to achieve the impossible. With a *sunao* mind they would be able to endure their anxiety and dissatisfaction. Accepting oneself means admitting one's weaknesses, demerits, discomforts, and undesirable feelings as they are. (Murase, 1982, p. 323)

While considerable attention has been devoted to these two Japanese forms of indigenous psychotherapy in the recent literature, most societies have examples of their own. In the survey by Prince (1980) there is a paradoxical redefinition of phenomena that in the West are often considered to be psycho*pathological* to be psycho*therapeutic* in many other cultures. These include altered states of consciousness (see Chapter 4), dream experience, trance (dissociation states), and various mystical states, including ecstasy. Since space does not permit a full review, we focus our attention on a single example, that of *voodoo* as practised in Haiti (Bourguignon, 1984).

Voodoo is a synthesis of African, Roman Catholic, and local beliefs and practices into a folk religion that has served to give the people of Haiti a sense of unique identity. It has also served the purpose of healing (among other purposes), thus exhibiting the not uncommon link between religion and medicine found in many parts of the world. One of the most spectacular features of *voodoo* is ritual possession trance, in which saints (*loa*) enter into and "possess" the practitioner, who can either be a believer (with no special psychological problem), a patient, or a priest/doctor who seeks to heal.

Many varieties of possession have been identified by Bourguignon (1984), including the *patient* being possessed by *harmful spirits* of a dead person, the patient being possessed by *protecting spirits*, and the *voodoo priest* being possessed by spirits that assist in the *diagnosis* and *cure* of the patient. Thus, in *voodoo* healing there is an intimate matrix of relationships involving not just a patient and a therapist, but a patient-believer, a therapist-priest, and a variety of good and evil spirits, all set in a complex medico-religious belief system; this system in turn is rooted in a culture contact (acculturation) situation that led to its development and set the stage for its widespread acceptance in the population.

What are we to make of these indigenous psychotherapies? Are they merely local superstitions that have no value, or do they perhaps only work to the extent that the superstitious believe in them? Or do they each have a status with respect to their sociocultural systems that parallels, for example, that of Freudian psychoanalysis in some Western societies? For some critics these practices may be dismissed as mere superstitions that work to some extent because and only because people believe they will work. Without "scientific foundations" or "proof" they could be dismissed easily by sceptics. However, rather than being dismissed as unscientific, a wide range of such indigenous psychotherapies (or their derivatives) are now being accepted into Western medical thought as supplementary to other psycho-therapeutic practices (Jilek, 1971, 1988). This more open-minded approach to psychotherapy parallels the acceptance by Western medicine of such practices as acupuncture (from Chinese medicine) and holistic theories (from *ayurvedic* medicine of India and elsewhere). Perhaps, as Prince (1980) suggests, *all* of these practices are effective to some extent precisely because they are believed in, are accepted as part of one's all-encompassing cultural belief system. This belief permits the "mobilization of endogenous resources" noted earlier, leading to relief for the sufferer; it may matter little what these beliefs and resources are as long as they are accepted by the patient and his own community.

Cross-cultural psychotherapy. This conclusion draws our attention to the second main question posed in this section: to what extent can cross-cultural psychotherapy work? That is, can medical beliefs and practices from one culture be effective in the healing process in another culture? Once again, it is useful to consider the absolute, universal, and relativist positions as points of view from which to approach the question. In the discussion of indigenous psychotherapies we noted the existence of culturally unique ideas and practices that were part of a larger complex of cultural beliefs and values; and the claim in the literature is that they may have a positive effect in their local settings. We also noted some common dimensions to all of these approaches; the mobilization of one's own resources through medico-religious practices one believes in seems to be a central thread. Thus, it would be a reasonable but tentative conclusion that there may be some underlying universal basis for the healing process. A common core to psychotherapeutic practices may exist, but with different historical and cultural roots and with highly varied cultural expressions.

Approaching the issue from the absolutist position, we may consider the attempts to employ Freudian psychoanalytic theory and practice in non-

Western cultures "as is," unmodified from its middle European Victorian-era roots. Prince (1980) has asked the question:

Are psychoanalytic formulations etic principles of human development and psychopathology? Psychoanalysts certainly believe this to be the case (Fenichel, 1955), but one crucial problem obstructs its verification. To validate psychoanalytic theory, it is necessary to apply the psychoanalytic technique cross-culturally, but this technique is impossible to employ beyond a very limited Western-educated elite. (p. 335)

If Prince's judgment is correct,[2] we can dismiss psychoanalytic theory as a candidate for an absolute approach to psychotherapy (cf. Kakar, 1985). One may attempt cultural adaptations of various psychotherapies (see Draguns, 1981, for a discussion of these attempts), but in so doing one shifts from an absolutist position to at least a universalist one as new cultural phenomena are taken into account. Thus, as in the case of the discussion of psychopathologies across cultures, we may venture the tentative conclusion that the universalist position is the most tenable in approaching psychotherapy across cultures.

Cultural factors in health behavior

At the beginning of this chapter we noted that cultural factors (including many behavioral, social, and environmental factors) play an important role in health generally, not just in mental health. At this point we turn more explicitly to these relationships, focusing as much on the promotion of health and the prevention of illness as on the curative aspects.

In an overview by Dasen, Berry, and Sartorius (1988) a number of specific topics were addressed, including the way in which socialization practices, education, nutrition, acculturation, public health programs, and the organization of health services can help to promote health and prevent health problems. Many of these factors are given specific coverage in this text (for example socialization in Chapter 2 and acculturation in Chapter 11) and so do not need full attention here.

The new focus on health promotion and disease prevention has created a role for social and behavioral scientists in the development and implementation of public health programs. For example, campaigns for the reduction of substance abuse, and of drinking and driving, and the advocacy of low-fat diets and exercise are clearly activities in which social psychologists' expertise in attitude change and clinical psychologists' expertise in behavior modification could play a major part. In developing countries similar roles have also been identified in such problem areas as parasite and other disease transmission and in increasing child survival (Harkness, Wyon, & Super, 1988). While these potential roles are self-evident for cross-cultural psychologists, Harkness et al. (1988) note that there have been "only a handful of reports

---

[2] Evidence that psychoanalysis can be used successfully in Africa has been presented by Parin, Morgenthaler, and Parin-Matthey (1966) and Ortigues and Ortigues (1966).

incorporating psychological, cultural, or social considerations into the design of research or intervention projects on disease prevention and control in developing countries" (p. 240). Two successful examples may help to establish the legitimacy and usefulness of this involvement.

Malaria. This is a major health problem in many tropical areas of the world, with some 150 million clinical cases of the disease reported every year; they constitute up to 12 percent of all medical cases in some areas of Africa, but are thought to represent only a fraction of actual incidence (due to under-reporting or nonreporting). Malaria is transmitted by a parasite that requires mosquitoes as a host and mosquitoes require stagnant water as a breeding environment.

Treatment of individuals with quinine or other drugs (the "cure" orientation) has been the most common attack on the disease, although some individual "prevention" measures were widely used (for example, the use of mosquito nets) as well. New, more effective drugs for individual treatment and the development of insecticides (notably DDT) for mosquito control made it possible since the 1950s to mount a worldwide campaign to eradicate the disease.

While some regions became virtually malaria-free, there has been a recent large-scale resurgence of the disease due to a growing resistance of mosquitoes and parasites to chemical treatment (both insecticides and drugs). Alternative approaches to controlling the disease employing social and behavioral techniques have been advocated (L. Miller, 1984). For example, the "Sarvodaya Project" in Sri Lanka has promoted public participation in the attempt to control mosquito population and in self-monitoring of one's own health. Local volunteers are trained to be on the lookout for stagnant water, to be vigilant about mosquito-human contacts, and to identify and report actual cases of malaria. This approach is in sharp contrast to the "vertical" approach, which involves large-scale control spraying by "outsiders" and drug administration by professionals; the local population is encouraged to be responsible for their own health rather than leaving it to others. Of course, "experts" are involved in teaching and training volunteers to use some basic technology (for example, parasite and human surveys, draining of ponds), and in bringing about changes in attitudes toward health through public education, but it is clearly a program "belonging to" the local population. The project:

has been organized as an alternative route to malaria control as part of a broad approach to community development through self-help. In contrast to the centrally organized, high-technology national malaria control program, the project was designed to put responsibility for malaria control with the villagers themselves. In contrast to the large regional groupings which are the administrative units of the national program, the project works through individual, culturally homogeneous villages. In this approach, the role of the behavioral sciences was conceived as important for understanding human behavior in relation to the transmission of malaria and in the organization of malaria control programs. (Harkness et al., 1988, p. 244)

Three behavioral factors were identified as important by the project researchers. First, villagers did not see malaria initially as a major or even as a solvable problem; the perception of malaria as a "disease" (rather than just one of life's ordinary problems) and the recognition that something could be done about it (rather than accepting it as part of one's "bad luck" or "fate") are specific areas of change that could be attempted using psychological techniques. Second, the perception of the earlier "vertical" control program (spraying and drug administration by outsiders) was examined; research showed that it was seen as heavy-handed and noxious, requiring costly countermeasures based on traditional *ayurvedic* medicine. Third, the symbiotic relationship between human behavior and mosquito behavior can be clarified by behavioral science research; initial findings revealed patterns of mosquito habitat preference and territory and of blood preference (animal blood is in fact preferred to human blood), but for a fuller understanding research is required to establish the behaviors on which to base effective control programs.

Child survival. As a second example, Harkness et al. (1988) examined "child survival" (a more positive orientation than "child mortality"). The "GOBI strategy" (an acronym for the four points listed below) of UNICEF is aimed at improving child survival rates throughout the world and concentrates on four techniques:

1. Growth monitoring to identify early cases of growth failure and malnutrition.
2. Oral rehydration therapy for infants and children with severe diarrhea in order to reduce the high rate of mortality from fluid loss.
3. Breastfeeding promotion, for the direct nutritional and immunologic benefits as well as the indirect reduction of contamination from unsanitary bottle feeding.
4. Immunization against major infectious diseases of childhood. (Harkness et al., 1988, pp. 245–246)

While initial results have been impressive, there have also been some evident failures, and social-behavioral analysis of these problems has been instructive. For example, *merely knowing* about the nature and causes of a child health problem (such as neonatal tetanus caused by unsterile umbilical cord cutting) is apparently not sufficient to correct the problem. In addition, as research in Bangladesh by Chen, Rahman, and Sardar (1980) has shown, *motivation to accept* the antitetanus injections by the mothers proved to be critical. After a major effort, only 22 percent of mothers actually agreed to the inoculation, probably because:

some mothers may have mistakenly associated the vaccinations with more familiar contraceptive injections; others feared harm to the fetus; and this biologically flawless procedure was perceived locally to be ineffective because the Bangla disease terms that cover tetanus also include other, unaffected, neonatal syndromes. (Harkness et al., 1988, p. 247)

Fertility behavior. The growth of the world's population has been identified both by international groups (e.g., World Bank, 1984) and by many societies as a major problem. For example, in China (Ching, 1984), concern about their rate of population increase has led to a national policy of limiting families to one child (along with other measures), in order to achieve "the four modernizations" (in industry, agriculture, science and technology, and defense). Generally, while the population in most economically developed countries is increasing only minimally, there is a rapid increase in developing countries (Salk & Salk, 1982). Are there social and behavioral factors that might help to explain these dramatic trends, and if so, can these same factors be employed to help control the increase?

At the outset, of course, the role of a number of other factors needs to be acknowledged: improved health care including curative and preventative measures and improved nutrition (see later section) have both changed the pattern of infant survival and longevity. But beyond these, are there other factors that can be understood and managed by social and behavioral scientists? For many, the answer is "yes."

For example, an early compendium by Fawcett (1973) on *Psychological Perspectives on Population* highlighted a wide variety of factors, including the value of children to parents, family structure (including forms of marriage), knowledge and use of birth control technology, values and beliefs regarding abortion, and ability to plan for one's future. These factors (and other, nonpsychological social variables) have begun to be considered as part of large systems, in which demographic, political, social, cultural, and psychological variables interact to affect population growth.

One psychological variable is the fundamental reasons adults give for having children. The question of why people have children has been the focus of a major international collaborative study called the "Value of Children Study." It involved nine countries (Germany, Indonesia, Korea, Philippines, Singapore, Taiwan, Thailand, Turkey, and the U.S.) with a total of over 20,000 adult respondents. While these societies are not representative of world cultural variation, they do include a range of countries, and in most of these (all except Indonesia and Germany) nationally representative samples were drawn.

A basic approach taken in the study was that the "values attributed to children are conceptualized as intervening between antecedent background and social psychological variables and consequent fertility-related outcome" (Kagitcibasi, 1984). Two issues are of interest here: one is the reasons given for wanting children and the other is the qualities one would like to see in one's children.

With respect to the first question, the "old age security value" of children is dominant for many societies; that is, children will provide for parents in their old age, not only materially, but socially and psychologically as well. The two relevant reasons posed were "To have someone to depend on when you are old" (as a reason for having a child) and "To be sure that in your old age you will have someone to help you" (as a reason for wanting *another* child). Clear differences appeared across samples in response to both items. In Germany and the U.S. these reasons are generally judged to be "unimportant" (about 75 percent responded so) but in Indonesia, Philippines, Taiwan, Thailand, and Turkey, the responses ranged between about 70 percent and 98 percent judging them to be "very important"; Korea and Singapore were in between these two extremes.

With respect to the question about characteristics that are valued in children, there was again wide cultural variation. For example, "obedience" is valued highly in Indonesia, Philippines, Turkey, and Thailand, while "independence and self-reliance" are valued least in those countries. In contrast, "independence" is valued more in Korea, Singapore, and the U.S. and "obedience" less. These values (and their distribution) correspond to some extent with the "compliance-assertion" dimension presented in Chapter 2 on socialization practices; here, however, industrialized and industrializing nations are exhibiting child-rearing values similar to those of hunter-gatherer societies noted earlier. Analyses of such reasons for having children, when taken into account along with economic, political, and nutritional factors, should provide a better basis for national and international programs in population planning.

Malnutrition and psychological development. One purpose of research on malnutrition and psychological development is to seek a better understanding of the links between biological and psychological aspects of human development. As we shall see, the theories in this respect have changed drastically over a very short time: in the early 1970s the predominant hypothesis was a simple effect of reduced food intake onto the number of brain cells, while now it is recognized that we are dealing with a very complex model of multiple interactions. The ultimate purpose of such research is to understand better the causes of malnutrition (that go well beyond lack of food) and the mechanisms of its effects on psychological development in order to be able to prevent malnutrition altogether or at least minimize its ill effects. Since malnutrition occurs in a complex ecological, economic, social, and cultural system, the solution is rarely as simple as providing more food, even though that may well have to be the first and most urgent measure (Barba, Guthrie, & Guthrie, 1982).

Before research on malnutrition and psychological functioning can even begin, a great deal of effort has to be devoted to the difficult question of the definition and measurement of nutritional status and protein-energy malnutrition (PEM). Most accurate would be a direct biochemical assessment of cell metabolism, but it has proven difficult to establish reliable methods that are practicable in field situations. The assessment of clinical signs, on the other hand, is notoriously unreliable and is applicable only to severe malnutrition. More indirect but practical are anthropometric growth measures. To simplify to the extreme, weight (in relation to age or height) indicates wasting, or current malnutrition, and height (for age) indicates stunting, or the effects of long-term (chronic) malnutrition. Nutritionists use these anthropometric measures (as well as others, such as head, chest, and arm circumference) to classify nutritional status into normal, mild, moderate, and severe malnutrition.

Problems related to the use of anthropometry are the choice of suitable reference norms and the choice of the cutoff points for the various categories (Keller & Fillmore, 1983; McLaren, 1984; Johnston & Lampl, 1984). In practice the norms used are often from Western industrial countries, especially the American "Harvard standards" (Nelson, Vaughan, & McKay, 1969). Local reference data are often either unavailable or are inevitably based on populations containing significant proportions of chronically undernourished individuals.

A large number of studies have attempted to assess the impact of malnutrition on intellectual development (for reviews, see Pollitt & Thomson, 1977; Brozek & Schürch, 1984; Ricciuti, 1979). While results vary a great deal from study to study, it may be said that children recovering from severe clinical PEM (that is, malnutrition needing hospitalization to avoid death), especially if it has occurred in the first two years of life and has lasted for several months, show a marked retardation in their intellectual development (in psychometric terms on the order of 10 IQ points). The effect may be long-lasting if the child returns from the hospital to the same unfavorable environmental circumstances, while there is complete resilience if the milieu is favorable to intellectual growth. Some caution is needed, however, when interpreting the results of these studies: they all suffer from the same limitations, insofar as they are unable to demonstrate the impact of malnutrition *per se*.

Chronic moderate or mild malnutrition also has a measurable effect on cognitive development; in one West African study (Dasen et al., 1978), for example, the development of sensorimotor intelligence was delayed by about two months in moderately malnourished children aged 9 to 30 months when compared to a group of children (matched on sex and age) with normal nutritional status. Comparing the developmental curves to French norms, this meant that the malnourished group was on par with French children, while the comparison group showed an advance of about two months. All children eventually reached the last substage of sensorimotor intelligence, and no structural differences in cognitive processes were found; it is therefore doubtful whether such minor lags in development have any functional importance.

In considering the impact of malnutrition on behavior two possible routes have been proposed. The first route is a direct influence of undernutrition on the development of the central nervous system (CNS) and on its functioning (number of cells or number of connections). Until the early 1970s this mechanism was thought to be the sole or major one, in both animal and man; the implications for the intervention were that food supplementation during pregnancy and the early periods of life would be sufficient to ensure optimal development. This proved to be a simplistic or at least insufficient model. A second, more indirect, route of influence of malnutrition on behavior is the functional isolation (Levitsky & Strupp, 1984) that occurs when social interactions, activity level, exploratory behavior, attention, and motivation are reduced because of the state of malnutrition; this functional isolation reduces learning opportunities and thus hinders psychological development.

These two mechanisms are not mutually exclusive, of course, and they may interact, but it is currently thought that the second route is the most important one. For intervention programs, it implies that greater attention be paid to social and behavioral aspects in addition to food supplementation. Empirical data in favor of the second model come from studies of the impact of malnutrition in the emotional and motivational spheres. D. E. Barrett (1984), for example, reviewed eight studies, all published after 1975, that show that malnutrition produced attentional impairments, reduced social responsiveness, poor state control, difficulties in tolerating frustration, low activity levels, and lack of initiative and independence, and this even in the absence of measurable cognitive impairment.

The findings of an impairment in social responsiveness, activity level, affect, attention, and interest in the environment are extremely important, because, in addition to suffering the direct consequences for reduced psychological activity and learning, the malnourished child becomes a different type of stimulus both to peers and to caregivers. The research of Chavez, Martinez, and Yaschine (1975) and P. L. Graves (1979), among others, shows that the latter tend to respond to the malnourished child less often and with less enthusiasm; the child in turn withdraws further from social interaction, and a sort of behavioral vicious circle is generated (Galler, Ricciuti, Crawford, & Kucharski, 1984).

It is now widely recognized that malnutrition is usually part and parcel of an ecologico-economico-socio-cultural system that includes, in addition to the biological factor of suboptimal nutrition, other adverse environmental conditions, such as poverty, poor housing and sanitation, repeated exposure to infectious and parasitic diseases, inadequate health care, and poor feeding and child-care practices. Research mainly based on anthropological, sociological, and epidemiological methods designates these characteristics as risk factors, a combination of which is likely to cause malnutrition, or to increase its ill-effects (Ricciuti, 1982; Ricciuti & Dorman, 1983; Grantham-McGregor, 1984).

The syndrome of malnutrition and poverty therefore occurs amidst macro-environmental factors linked to the social and political systems (for example, unequal distribution of wealth, lack of land ownership, agricultural policies favoring cash crops), and more generally speaking to the world's unbalanced economy (otherwise undernutrition would not be restricted mainly to the southern parts of the world).

A combination of unfavorable macroenvironmental factors is usually found to indicate a high risk of malnutrition, but even in the same unfavorable conditions, malnutrition does not occur in all families or all individuals. This indicates that other risk factors are linked to the family and home environment (for example, large number of children in the family, absence or lack of involvement of father, stress in marital relationships, alcoholism) and to the mother or caretaker characteristics (for example, mother's age below 19 or above 35, unwanted pregnancy, birth spacing below two years, early weaning and bottle feeding in unfavorable circumstances, anxiety, stress, depression, and apathy). Some children are also more prone to suffer from malnutrition than others because of constitutional factors or their own medical history (premature birth, low birth weight, perinatal medical complications, infectious and parasitic disease, and so forth).

It is important to consider the interaction among these risk factors, which can be additive or even multiplicative. The risk factors can also be compensated for by positive ones, interacting to prevent the occurrence of malnutrition or to alleviate its ill effects. Fernandez and Guthrie (1983) have argued that programs designed to support and encourage breastfeeding and supplementary feeding must take indigenous belief systems into account. However, educational programs designed to eradicate traditional beliefs and practices considered to be harmful by modern medicine are notoriously inefficient; mothers may well accept many of the beliefs and practices of modern medicine and hold traditional beliefs at the same time. "Cultural factors such as learned helplessness, a reluctance to compare the growth of babies, alternative explanations for poor growth, and a limited concept of prevention imposed alternative contingencies on the mothers to limit the effectiveness of a program designed to teach and support improved dietary practices" (Guthrie & Guthrie, 1982, p. 624). In a successful intervention study in the Philippines Fernandez, Estrera, Barba, Guthrie, and Guthrie (1983) used external reinforcements (praise, exhortations, lottery tickets, health coupons to be traded in against goods, or color photographs of the child or other family members) to induce mothers to continue breastfeeding, use food supplementation adequately, obtain a regular gain in the weight of the child, plant green leafy vegetables, and to visit the health center monthly.

Dasen and Super (1988) have argued that because it is demonstrated that malnutrition is not distributed uniformly among families living in the same high-risk conditions it may be a wise strategy to concentrate future research on those that somehow manage to cope, instead of (or in addition to) those that do not. In terms of applications to prevention and intervention programs it could be argued that a scheme based on the transfer of culturally familiar and acceptable coping mechanisms (Marsella & Dash-Scheuer, 1988) from one sector of a population to another within the same cultural group should be more efficient and more cost-effective than programs based on foreign models. Any intervention program should take into account the populations's own strengths.

Conclusions

Applications of cross-cultural psychological perspectives and findings to issues of health can be seen as an extension of the movement to bring social and behavioral science to bear on promotion and prevention strategies now under way nationally and internationally. While the volume edited by Dasen et al. (1988) argued that there is much valuable knowledge now available, it concluded that little of it is ready for immediate use and application. There were two reasons advanced for this conclusion. One was that much cross-cultural psychological research has been conducted with a view to scientific discovery rather than to application; hence, a process of bridging or translating is necessary in order to move from one activity to the other. The second reason is rooted in a perspective espoused in the present book, that of the culture-bound character of most human behavior:

a "fact" that has been found to be successfully applicable in one particular context may well be quite irrelevant in another; any list of applications would look rather suspect to a cross-cultural social scientist. Is it not against too easy generalizations that the cross-cultural approach is raising a word of caution? While this point of view might be seen as a negative one, it can also be seen as an important advance: Cross-cultural psychology informs us that there are definite limits to the transcultural portability of knowledge (thereby reducing our potential for making mistakes), and it provides us with a set of perspectives, procedures, and methods that are helpful in carrying out work in other cultures. (Dasen et al., 1988, p. 299)

We therefore conclude that applications of cross-cultural psychology to health must proceed cautiously and with a concern for validation in each cultural setting.

As is clear to everyone involved in psychology internationally, the discipline and the profession are overwhelmingly rooted in and practised in Western industrialized societies. The rest of the world has often assumed the roles of "consumers" or "subjects"; psychology is "sold to" or "tried out on" other peoples. The evidence for this state of affairs has been clearly presented by D. Sinha and Holtzman (1984) and Sloan and Montero (1990).

These roles, of course, are unlikely to be very useful for developing countries, since there may be a serious mismatch between what is available in Western psychology and what is needed by the third world (Jahoda, 1973). Part of the answer to the problem is the development of a psychology that is sensitive to cultural variation; and so one could take the emergence of cross-cultural psychology as an important move in the right direction. While this is partly true, it is also the case that cross-cultural psychology has been guilty of using the third world as a kind of "natural laboratory" and has been known to exploit its human resources in various other ways (Warwick, 1980). Indeed, for Warwick (1980), "From the choice of topic to the publication and dissemination of the findings, cross-cultural research is inescapably bound up with politics" (p. 323); the cross-cultural work may involve differences in goals, differences in power, and differences in intended use (even to the extent of misuse) of the results. For others, the comparative method is inherently ethnocentric (Nisbet, 1971) and is rooted in the tradition of "social Darwinism," complete with its overtones of "racism and ethnocentrism" (Mazrui, 1968, pp. 69–70). These critical comments and some more positive alternatives have been well summarized by Schwendler (1984, p. 4), who considered how psychology and knowledge more generally can be made relevant to the needs of individuals and nations in the developing world.

It is possible to attempt to address these problems by employing some distinctions that have been made in cross-cultural psychology. We start with the observation that psychology can be *exported* and *imported* "as is" (from Western cultures to developing countries). This represents a kind of "scientific acculturation" and has been referred to as psychology being done *in* a particular culture (Berry, 1978); it clearly resembles the imposed etic strategy. Second, there are the parallel processes of developing *indigenous* psychologies locally or adapting imported ones by *indigenizing* them; this

378

we refer to as a psychology *of* a particular culture and resembles the emic strategy. Third, there are attempts to integrate all available psychologies into a *universal* psychology; this resembles the derived etic strategy. In this chapter we address the issues of doing psychology *in* and doing psychology *of* a culture.

Impact of western psychology

Psychology is clearly a science rooted in Western culture and like much of Western science and technology psychology has been spread widely over the globe during the course of the twentieth century. While we argue in the next section that psychology need not be Western in character, that all societies can (and probably should) develop their own psychologies, the present state of affairs is one in which there is widespread *scientific acculturation*; others, both psychologists and the populations at large, have come to understand themselves in terms derived from Western pyschological science. This export and import of psychology has led to psychology being done *in* other countries without much regard for local cultural circumstances or needs.

For example, Lagmay (1984) for the Philippines, Melikan (1984) for the Gulf States, Salazar (1984) for Venezuela, Diaz-Guerrero (1984) for Mexico, and Durojaiye (1984) for Nigeria have all analyzed how Western psychology has in various ways changed aspects of their respective societies. Lagmay (1984, p. 31) argues that the entry of Western (mainly American) psychology was a case of "cultural diffusion" and was part of a more general flow of cultural elements that included language, educational and legal systems, and the media. The overall impact of this 50-year period of American colonization was that "Western Science and cultural concepts became part of the educated speech and thinking of all who went through the schools ... the language of research, interpretation and construction in the social sciences in the Philippines ... has been definitely American and Western" (p. 32). Such export and import of Western psychology is not likely to constitute an "appropriate psychology" for developing countries (Moghaddam & Taylor, 1986). Indeed confusion can result when "the techniques and ideology of modern psychology are ... overlaid, in some cases in considerable haste, upon an ideological background composed variously of Hinduism, Islam, Buddhism, Taoism, Confucianism, Shintoism and Marxism and Leninism, themselves occurring in a range of combinations" (Turtle, 1987, p. 2).

In Valenzuela, Salazar (1984) has argued that "psychological technology is an imported commodity, like automobiles, computers and airplanes" (p. 114) and is part of the overall problem of developing world's socioeconomic dependence (see also Montero & Sloan, 1988). However, unlike in the Philippines, Salazar (1984, p. 113) is sceptical that there has been any substantial value change in the culture as a whole and wonders "whether psychological knowledge can affect value systems at all."

Between these two contrasting views probably lies the experience of most developing countries. On the one hand psychology is only a small part of Western thought and may not have direct and widespread impact on a functioning culture. On the other hand psychology may be part of a broader package of acculturative influences that affect many of the core institutions (educational, work, religious) through which all or most people pass in the course of their development. While substantial acculturation may indeed take place (as outlined in Chapter 11), it may be very difficult to specify the particular contribution of psychology to this process.

One important role, however, is that psychologists (and other social scientists) are called upon to explain or interpret the behavior of people to themselves. In opinion surveys, assessment for educational and work selection, and in clinical practice psychologists are often in a position to be influential both with the public at large and with key decision makers in government and other institutions. We may ask: if their training, values, and technology are rooted in Western psychological science and are minimally informed by local cultural and psychological knowledge, what likelihood is there that this influence will be culturally appropriate? Unless this likelihood is substantial, psychologists in developing countries may end up playing the role of inadvertent acculturators. Such training may be all the more unsuitable when it is so specialized (focused on local Western topics) that the psychologist is ill-equipped to deal with broader issues set in complex local cultural settings (Moghaddam, 1989). The alternative to working with an imported psychology is to attempt to develop one locally, an enterprise to which we now turn.

Indigenous psychologies

By *indigenous psychology* we mean a system of psychological thought and practice that is rooted in a particular cultural tradition (see Enriquez, 1990; U. Kim, 1990). This notion can be linked to a number of other ones, including *ethnopsychology* (see the discussion of ethnoscience in Chapter 7), *common sense*, or *naive psychology* (as proposed by Heider, 1958), or *folk psychology* (as developed by Wundt, 1912; see Chapter 5). The roots of ethnopsychology lie in the intellectual tradition of *Geisteswissenschaften* (cultural sciences) rather than the *Naturwissenschaften* (natural sciences). For Heelas and Lock (1981) indigenous psychology is to be understood in contrast to *specialist psychology*, "those developed by academic psychologists who favour scientific experiments" (Heelas, 1981, p. 3); and is rooted in "the cultural views, theories, conjectures, classifications, assumptions and metaphors – together with notions embedded in social institutions – which bear on psychological topics" (Heelas, 1981, p. 3).

It is possible to discern some common threads among these various conceptions. First is the idea that cultural traditions give rise to psychological knowledge (including theories, methods, and data); second is the belief that the real stuff of psychology lies in the daily, mundane activity of people rather than in contrived experimentally induced behavior; third is the implied emic orientation, requiring indigenous psychological knowledge to be achieved and interpreted in terms of the local frames of reference. Taking these three themes together, we consider indigenous psychology to be a psychology of a cultural group based on the day-to-day behavior of its members, for which local points of view provide the paradigms that guide the collection and interpretation of psychological information.

Of course, Western psychology is one such indigenous psychology, but because it has taken on the role and status of *the* psychology, the term is usually reserved for those psychologies that reflect the traditions, beliefs, and ideologies of non-Western societies. At the same time the term reflects not only *other* psychologies, but also *counter* psychologies that stand in some opposition to Western psychology. This has come about because to a certain extent indigenous psychologies have developed as a reaction to or rejection of the dominance of Western psychology in a culture (D. Sinha, 1981).

Indigenous psychology attempts to develop a behavioral science that matches the sociocultural realities of one's own society. Indian scholars (D. Sinha, 1986; Sahoo, 1988) have sought the development of a psychology that reflects their historical and cultural traditions. In a comprehensive treatment D. Sinha (1986) has identified the transfer of Western psychology to India "as part of the general process of Modernization" (p. 10), characterizing it as "completely isolated from the Indian tradition, and alien to the local intellectual soil" (p. 11), leading to endless "repetitions of foreign studies" (p. 33). Historically, Sinha notes four phases, beginning with a preindependence period during which Indian psychology "remained tied to the apron strings of the West, and did not display any sign of maturing" (p. 36). Then came a period of post-independence expansion; however, according to Sinha, not all was well:

There is a good deal of academic research that is traditional and conventional with very little relation to the realities of the contemporary situation. The academic community is not generally concerned with what may be called research for policy, but more with research for prestige which is largely theory-oriented and academic. The tendency has been for the social psychologist to look to the West and be more concerned about the recognition of his researches by the western social psychologists rather than by the fact of their relevance to the crucial needs of the country. (1986, pp. 41–42)

The third period was one of problem-oriented research during which concerns for breaking the dependency were joined with those for more applied research. Finally came the period of *indigenization*, in which the imported Western psychology underwent a process of cultural transformation to become more informed by Indian social and cultural traditions and relevant to Indian economic and political needs (see Box 16-1).

A more radical approach than making modifications by a process of indigenization is that of developing an indigenous psychology from cultural basics. Diaz-Guerrero (1975, 1982) has developed a Mexican psychology

---

Box 16-1   The surveys of psychological research in India

Of all developing countries India has by far the largest number of psychologists, the most universities and colleges with curricula in psychology, and the largest volume of research. A convenient overview can be found in three surveys of research on Indian psychology. The overall structure of scientific psychology is the same as in Euroamerican countries; the topics for the chapters in the first survey even followed the categorization of the Psychological Abstracts and authors leave no doubt that Indian psychology finds its roots in the West. With respect to terminology, methods, and theories, the contents of the surveys are easily recognizable to the Euroamerican reader.

The three editors of the surveys have each addressed the issue of the relevance of Indian psychology to the Indian context and social reality. The first editor (Mitra, 1972) noted that after the initial development of the discipline a stage of consolidation had been reached at the end of the 1960s. Two directions for further research were indicated: social and applied issues, and the development of a "hard-headed" science in the traditions of experimental psychology. It is perhaps significant that Mitra only elaborates on the first direction for research, noting several social problems that demand attention, preferably in an interdisciplinary context. The editor of the second survey (Pareek, 1981) noted a shift toward applied issues during the 1970s and he emphasized the potential of psychology to contribute to the solution of social problems. The summary chapter in the third survey on emerging trends in the 1980s by Pandey (1988) is largely devoted to the question of how the sociocultural context is being taken into account by Indian researchers. The various chapters still cover the whole area of psychology, but the table of contents of the Psychological Abstracts is no longer followed. The emphasis on applied issues is evident not only from the distribution of chapters, but also from the attention given to social relevance by various chapter authors.

The trends that Pandey describes in his summary chapter are very much compatible with the notion of a universal psychology, as it has been developed in this book. He mentions the need for "outgrowing the alien framework" (p. 341), but argues that the emphasis on sociocultural context does not amount to a secessionist movement; the aim is rather to integrate the emerging Indian psychology into a more universal psychology. One area where this orientation is becoming visible is that of psychological assessment, where translated tests from the West instead of restandardized or locally constructed instruments have long been dominant (cf. Kulkarni & Puhan, 1988). Another area is socio-

---

economic change as it relates to national development (cf. Tripathi, 1988; Muthayya, 1988).

In the personality and clinical psychology area there have been attempts to construct theories and approaches to treatment that find their roots in the religious and philosophical traditions of Hinduism as laid down in the ancient scriptures. In some accounts (e.g., Kakar, 1982) the folkloristic and mythical aspects are hard to separate from scientific exploration; in other work, like that of Paranjpe (1984), an analytic and scientific orientation is followed and relationships and differences with Western conceptions are outlined. We have touched on Indian conceptions of personality in Chapter 4, where it was noted that so far there are only a few indigenous theories that lend themselves to a critical analysis of their validity. Still, it is particularly in this area that we expect a significant and lasting impact of Indian psychologists on the discipline.

---

rooted in "historico-sociocultural premises." He defined these as "a set of culturally significant statements that are held by a majority of persons in a culture" (1982). In Mexico these themes include affiliative obedience, machismo, respect, protection of women, and virginity.

Perhaps the most substantial set of writings on indigenous psychology has been produced by Enriquez (1981, 1982, 1989, 1990), who has consistently criticized Western influences on Filipino intellectual life. The alternative is to develop a *Sikolohiyang Pilipino* that is rooted in local culture and history. It emphasizes four areas of concern:

1) identity and national consciousness, specifically looking at the social sciences as the study of man and *diwa* [consciousness and meaning], or the indigenous conception and definition of the psyche, as a focus of social psychological research; 2) social awareness and involvement as dictated by an objective analysis of social issues and problems, 3) national and ethnic cultures and languages including the study of early or traditional psychology, called *kinagisnang sikolohiya* . . . ; and 4) bases and application of indigenous psychology in health practices, agriculture, art, mass media, religion, etc. but also including the psychology of behavior and human abilities as demonstrated in Western psychology and found applicable to the Philippine setting. (Enriquez, 1989, p. 21)

The indigenous psychology movement has three primary areas of protest: it is against a psychology that perpetuates the colonial status of the Filipino mind; it is against the imposition on a third world country of psychologies developed in and appropriate to industrialized countries; and it is against a psychology used for the exploitation of the masses.

For Enriquez:

The new consciousness, labelled *Sikolohiyang Pilipino* reflecting Filipino psychological knowledge, has emerged through the use of the local language as a tool for the
identification and rediscovery of indigenous concepts and as an appropriate medium
for the delineation and articulation of Philippine realities together with the development of a scientific literature which embodies the psychology of the Filipino people.
(1989, p. 21)

While it is difficult for a non-Filipino to comprehend some of the cultural
meanings, it is relatively easy to understand both the underlying sentiments
and the long-term implications of these views for a psychology of the
Philippines.

In addition to these integrative approaches, a number of volumes have
appeared that draw together a variety of research findings that are relevant to
particular culture areas (e.g., Wober, 1975, for Africa; Blowers & Turtle,
1987, for Asia) or to specific countries (e.g., Bond, 1986, for China). These
clearly represent an important and growing trend to achieve a psychology that
is relevant to local cultural and regional phenomena (Moghaddam, 1987).

An obvious advantage of an indigenous psychology is that there is likely to
be a reasonable match between the psychological phenomena to be understood and the description and interpretation of the phenomena. Numerous
mismatches can be found in the literature, such as the attempt to understand
Japanese or Indian achievement on the bases of American achievement
motivation theory (e.g., de Vos, 1986). Historically, such mismatches have
been the use of Freudian theory to comprehend father-son conflicts in
Melanesia and the use of Western intelligence tests to assess the cognitive
competence of individuals in other cultures (see Chapter 5).

A common criticism of indigenization is that there will be a proliferation of
psychologies; if every population had its own psychology, an infinite regress
to an individual psychology (for a population of one) is possible; or if not so
minute, then regress to provincial, city, or village psychologies are envisaged.
Our view is that a balance has to be found. On the one hand it does not make
sense to ignore the achievements of (a mainly) Western psychology and to
reinvent the wheel in each culture. On the other hand the ethnocentrism of
Western psychology makes it necessary to take other viewpoints on human
behavior into account. One of the goals of cross-cultural psychology is
the eventual development of a *universal* psychology that incorporates all
indigenous (including Western) psychologies. We will never know whether all
diverse data and cultural points of view have been incorporated into the
eventual universal psychology unless we cast our net as widely as possible in
order to gather all the relevant information.

Psychology and national development

In Chapter 11 we addressed the issue of change at both the population level
and the individual level; we distinguished between internal (dynamics) and
external (culture contact) antecedents to change and between these antece-

dents and some consequents (again at both the population and individual levels). Within this framework, we can locate "national development" as change at the population level (in economic, political, and social indicators) and at the individual level (in attitudes, values, motives, and so on); for these changes to constitute *development* they need to be in the direction of some more valued end state than was present at the beginning of the process (see Box 16-2). This definition of development fits generally into those views that have been expressed in the psychological literature over the past two decades (see D. Sinha, 1984, 1989, for reviews).

Box 16-2 Psychology and development

The potential contribution of psychology to research and application in the area of national development is rather large. If we define development as the process of individuals and groups moving from some present state to some more valued end state, then psychology can contribute in the following ways:

1. *Understanding the present state.* This is the obvious starting point for development and many psychological constructs are relevant to its description: *skills* (cognitive, technical, social, and so on); *attitudes* to change; *personality characteristics* that may assist or prevent change; *values* concerning maintaining the past (or present) state of affairs; and *interests* in various change alternatives. That is, constructing a "psychological profile" or a study of the distribution of psychological characteristics in a population should provide an understanding of the human resources upon which development may take place. Of course, there are political factors (such as the social organization and distribution of these resources) and economic factors (such as natural resources) that must enter into this present state description, but psychology does have something to contribute to the overall understanding of the current situation.
2. *Understanding the valued end state.* In the discussion of the local cultural meaning of "development" we saw that psychological research can draw out the local or indigenous meanings of a concept; this approach is one possible contribution of psychology to the study of national development. What, in fact, are the meanings assigned to "development" in various societies? Is it always associated with increased urbanization, industrialization, and organization (as the Western notion of "development" implies) or are there important cultural variations? The valued end state can also be studied by psychologists employing the conventional notions of *aspirations*, *needs*, *values*, and *preferences*. In short, "what do people want (if anything) out of life?" is a question that psychology can help to answer.
3. *Understanding the process of change.* How do people get from the present state to the future valued end-state? In addition to the human and material resources mentioned earlier, people have *motives*, *drives*, *coping mechanisms*, and so on, all of which have an established place in psychology. Examining these dynamic factors, including the possibility

of increasing their level and the effectiveness of their organization in a
population, is an important potential contribution of psychology to
national development.
4. *Design, implementation, and evaluation of development programs.*
   Psychologists have usually enjoyed a solid training in research methods
   on human behavior. Cultural variations in behavior have usually been
   ignored. As a result of ignoring this human factor many development
   programs have ended in failure. A psychology background can also be
   of immense help in a development team that is attempting to understand whether a particular development program is having its intended
   effects. In such areas as *sampling, interviewing,* the use of *control
   groups,* the *statistical evaluation* of change over time (including an
   informed choice between longitudinal and cross-sectional designs)
   psychology has a significant contribution to make.

However, criticism of such a definition also abounds in the literature. For
example, Rist and Sabelli (1986) have questioned the very notion of development, particularly its universality. Referring to development as one of the
Western world's favorite myths, they systematically attack most of the
accepted truths about development held by Western "developers." They
assert that not every culture has a concept for "development" and that if
there is, it may not be at all like the one in the "developer's" program.
However, if the procedures outlined in Box 16-2 are followed, misunderstandings about development should be discovered prior to the commence-
ment of development programs. The very existence (or nonexistence) and
important variations in the meaning of development should be revealed early
in psychologically oriented research, and appropriate decisions can be made
on these bases.

Others (e.g., Jahoda, 1974; Zaidi, 1979; Boesch, 1986) have seriously
questioned the role that psychologists can play in third world development. In
particular, Mehryar (1984) has argued that psychology may not be capable of
making a contribution to national development for a number of reasons. First
is the very limited role that psychology has played so far in the development
process in industrialized countries; how can it then presume to make a
contribution to the process in the developing world? Second, the problems of
development are "by their very nature and etiology, unlikely to be solved by
psychology, or other scientific disciplines ... any effort to 'psychologise'
these problems will not only be unproductive in terms of relieving the misery
and backwardness of the people concerned, but it may in fact be misused by
certain interest groups to obscure the real obstacles to development"
(Mehryar, 1984, p. 161). According to Mehryar (quoting Ardila, 1982) the
problems to be solved are not psychological, but are basically political and
economic. However, as we argued earlier, the role of psychology can be best
viewed as a partner with or supplement to political and economic sciences,
not as the only or best orientation to the promotion of national development.

A consideration of a range of possible ways to apply psychology is presented in Box 16-3.

Such a collaborative interdisciplinary effort has proved fruitful for Ugorji and Berman (1974, psychologist and political scientist), who assessed the orientations of Igbo Nigerian villagers toward development (*oganihu*) and structural aspects of socioeconomic and political processes. At the psychological level interviews focused on beliefs about what makes for the "good life," understanding of notions such as "development" and "progress," attitudes toward change, knowledge of national development policy, and attitudes toward government officials and institutions. *Oganihu* was judged to have both positive and negative aspects. On the positive side were better housing, modern consumer goods, piped water, electricity, and improved roads and hospitals. On the negative side were feelings of ambivalence, alienation, powerlessness, dependency, and dissatisfaction with government. It was believed that the most effective route to *Oganihu* was by obtaining a formal education, leading in turn to well-paid jobs. While life now was judged to be better than previously (in material terms), there was also a sense that moral decay had set in. This elaborate view of development in a Nigerian village is both a challenge to critics of the concept (who claim it to be only a Western notion) and an easily recognizable and probably widely shared orientation to life in many parts of the world.

The role of psychology in studying and promoting national development has been advocated particularly in India. For example, a journal entitled *Psychology and Developing Societies* has begun (1989) under the editorship of Durganand Sinha. His interests have been directed toward the issue of poverty and its relationship to national development (D. Sinha, 1990). Another Indian psychologist who has made a particularly important contribution to the study of national development is J. B. P. Sinha (1970, 1980, 1984b). His approach is an integrative one in which psychology is seen as a "partner in development," both with other disciplines and between psychologists from industrialized and developing countries. He has traced the evolving meaning of "development" and along with this change the evolution of the roles played by psychologists. In the 1950s national development was generally "taken as being synonymous to economic development, which was naturally the domain of economists ... however ... economic development of the newly independent nations did not obey the rational formula of saving, investment, and growth, because of the interfering effects of the socio-cultural features of the traditional societies (J. B. P. Sinha, 1984b, p. 169).

Western views of "development" continued to hold sway, because Western psychologists and other social scientists tended to dominate any collaborative relationships that were forged (see Blackler, 1983, for substantial evidence of this point of view). It was only with the realization in the 1960s by some developing world psychologists that local or indigenous perspectives were necessary in order to study local problems that some progress began to be made. For example, Singh (1967) was able to show that Weber's theory

Box 16-3   The utilization of psychology

There is a wide range of approaches to application in psychology from the purely scientific to the client-dominated. Heller (1986) has provided an overview. He distinguishes the following categories:

1. *The traditional approach: science only*. This includes experimental research, theory, and model building. Application is not a necessary outcome and diffusion of knowledge is mainly through academic books and journals.
2. *Building bridges between researcher and user*. Projects are developed by researchers but are meant to have practical applications. Sometimes the researchers will be involved in the implementation of findings. Apart from diffusion through academic channels, there is also more popular dissemination.
3. *Researcher-client equality*. Researcher and client discuss a problem area and formulate a research project. Initiative and active collaboration by the client is presumed. When the emphasis is on implementation rather than fact-finding, the method of "action research" is employed. Academic publications (usually requiring permission from the client) take second place to diffusion of knowledge via the client.
4. *Client-professional exploration*. Advice or assistance is given to the client on the basis of knowledge and expertise available to the scientific adviser. Diffusion through publications is limited; the recommendations should lead to training or the implementation of changes in policy.
5. *Client-dominated quest*. The client calls on a specialist (for example, counselor or personnel manager) or even someone untrained in the behavioral or social sciences. The best current knowledge as seen by this person is the basis for action. This kind of knowledge tends to be heavily influenced by personal experience and popular notions, called "common sense." Diffusion outside the client system is minimal.

The five categories differ along a number of dimensions. Basic research is usually paid for by universities or research foundations, while more applied research and client-dominated requests for help tend to be paid by the client. Basic research takes a long time to complete and the outcome is uncertain, while advice and interventions based on current insights are available immediately. As funds are more limited and the immediate needs more urgent, the scope for basic research becomes more restricted.

There is a persistent inequality between richer and poorer nations in the resources available for research as well as the number of professionals who possess scientific expertise. Since basic research is formulated primarily by scientists, it is the responsibility of the global scientific community to take other than local or national needs into account.

The application of knowledge based on research is primarily the concern of local experts. In the social and behavioral sciences where intimate knowledge of local circumstances is an essential requirement, the international community (which for any given developing society largely consists of outsiders) has a limited role to play. In the economically poorer countries the small numbers of local experts, the lack of facilities such as a good library, and the often overburdening workload impose serious limitations on the diffusion of scientific information and its use.

In our view Heller's scheme leaves room for the incorporation of concerns such as those expressed by Mehryar and other third world authors. In some of Heller's categories the client and the researcher cooperate, or the client has the initiative. Appropriate discourse with the client (which may well be a society represented by local psychologists, who can express their society's concerns and check suggested solutions for their suitability) is an essential step on the road to useful research outcomes. This does little to alleviate the problems of unequal power in a political sense between societies, but it should help to create at least a mutual dependency between the psychologists involved in this process.

linking the Protestant (Christian) ethic to economic growth (and its converse, that Hinduism restricted economic growth) was inappropriate if one looked at the relationship between religious ideology and economics from a Hindu perspective. For Indian scholars "the Western models of development were embedded in Western values ... where the individual was and still is the agent as well as the recipient of social change" (J. B. P. Sinha, 1984b, p. 171). From a Western perspective this individual is open to new experience, relatively independent of parental authority, concerned with time and planning, willing to defer gratification, assumes mastery over nature, believes in determinism and science, has a wide cosmopolitan perspective, uses broad in-groups, and competes with standards of excellence (Triandis, 1984). Such individuals are not common in many developing countries and so the question arises: "are these individuals necessary for national development?" According to J. B. P. Sinha (1984b), the answer is "no"! There are alternative psychological profiles that can serve as a basis for development. For example, cooperative behavior (rather than competition) carried out within a "nurturant" dependency relationship with the leader (Kakar, 1971; J. B. P. Sinha, 1980; see Chapter 13) can be a productive and satisfying form of economic activity. For J. B. P. Sinha (1984b) "an effective way of human resource mobilization in India is to focus on key individuals who are embedded in social groups, and collectives, which in essence are the instruments of change" (p. 173).

Armed with this indigenous redefinition of psychological qualities capable of engaging in development, J. B. P. Sinha (1984b) has argued that:

massive evidence has accumulated to prove that material affluence beyond a point may *not* lead to better quality of life either for individuals or social aggregates. Neither can we visualize development in any sense of the term unless the basic needs of food, shelter, health, and education of people are reasonably satisfied. If affluence beyond a point desensitizes us to others, acute poverty dehumanizes even to a more alarming extent. It appears that *economic growth has a curvilinear relationship with human development.* (pp. 173–174)

With this proposal we can observe one of the important contributions of cross-cultural psychology: knowledge and points of view gained from working in other cultures can give a much-needed perspective and provide alternative modes of action for Western psychological research and application. To be of most value cross-cultural psychology should be the two-way street exemplified in this discussion of national development.

Conclusions

The application of cross-cultural psychology to problem-solving in diverse cultures has been the central theme of Part III of this book. In principle, the discipline is poised to be of use in a number of domains (acculturation, intergroup relations, education, work, communication, and health). However, in this chapter we have attempted to establish some conceptual and practical limits to this enterprise. In particular, the need to make sure that the science and the problem are matched is paramount. Armed with basic knowledge from Part I and with methodological and theoretical tools from Part II, we believe that matching is possible. To accomplish this, however, working partnerships and two-way exchanges of psychological knowledge are required.

Epilogue

The reader will have realized that this book offers a selective presentation of a diverse field. Necessarily many important points of view, empirical research studies, and programs of application have not been mentioned, never mind given substantive treatment. Our attention, however, has not been random, but guided by an ecocultural framework that was made explicit at the outset. Central to this framework has been the view that individual human beings develop and exhibit behaviors that are adaptive to the ecological and socio-political contexts in which they and their group find themselves.

We have also taken the position that psychological processes are shared species-wide characteristics. These common psychological qualities are nurtured and shaped by enculturation and socialization, sometimes further affected by acculturation, and ultimately expressed as overt human be-haviors. While set on course by these transmission processes relatively early in life, behaviors continue to be guided in later life by direct influence from ecological, cultural, and sociopolitical factors. In short, we have considered culture in its broadest sense to be a major source of human behavioral diversity producing variations on some underlying themes. It is these common qualities that make comparisons possible and these variations that make comparisons interesting.

Our enterprise has some clearly articulated goals, and it is reasonable to ask whether the field of cross-cultural psychology generally, and this book in particular, has met them. In our view the third goal, as expressed in Chapter 1, has *not* been achieved: we are nowhere close to producing a universal psychology through the comprehensive integration of results of comparative psychological studies. However, we have taken some important steps toward this goal, both in terms of demonstrating some psychological universals and by pursuing the more basic "transport and test" and the "explore and discover" goals that were outlined in Chapter 1. Let us consider these claims.

In Chapters 2 and 11 human development and the transmission processes of enculturation, socialization, and acculturation were examined. Conceptual and empirical studies revealed both similarities in their essential character and differences in how they took place. All peoples engage in these activities, and the dimensions along which variation takes place appear to be common, but the actual practices and the outcomes for individuals are highly variable.

391

Our review of the psychological outcomes of these processes in Chapters 3 to 6 has brought us to a similar conclusion. In social behavior and personality, in cognition and perception, there is evidence for both panhuman psychological qualities and variation in the development and overt display of these qualities across cultures.

In Part II of the book we considered four areas of thinking and research that define the four corners of the terrain within which cross-cultural psychology has largely operated: culture, biology, method, and theory. This section essentially provided an interpretive frame for the materials reviewed earlier by linking them to cognate disciplines and to fundamental issues of comparative science. By so doing we have intended to lift the whole of the first section above the level of description to the level of possible (and alternative) interpretations. Central to this activity was the distinction between *absolutism*, *relativism*, and *universalism* as ways of thinking about the often subtle and complex interplay between psychological similarities and differences across cultures. While we have opted for a universalist stance, it is possible that future advances in the biological and cultural sciences will reinforce allegiance to absolutism or to relativism, at least for some behaviors.

Cross-cultural psychological findings can be assessed not only against disciplinary, methodological, and theoretical criteria, but also against practical criteria in the world of day-to-day problems. In Part III, again selectively, we considered areas of real concern to many people in many parts of the world. Using the findings, tools, and ideas drawn from basic research in cross-cultural psychology, we saw that the cross-cultural approach can begin to make a difference. In a rapidly changing and increasingly interconnected world concerns about acculturation and ethnic relations, about education, work, communication, health, and national development, have all come into the foreground of cross-cultural psychology and have stimulated many to direct their research toward these issues. Answers are partial and much remains to be done; but the evidence we have marshalled points, we believe, to a central and important role for cross-cultural psychology in helping to deal with some of the major problems facing the world.

To live up to such a promise will require three major changes to the field: the development of persistent and collaborative work on particular topics; the incorporation of psychologists from *all* societies into this enterprise; and the convincing of our students and colleagues to accept the view that culture is indeed one of the most important determinants of human behavior. If this book stimulates any of these changes, we will consider ourselves to be rewarded.

References

Abegglen, J. C. (1958). *The Japanese factory*. Glencoe, IL: Free Press.

Aberle, D. F., Cohen A. K., Davis, A., Levy, M., & Sutton F. X. (1950). Functional prerequisites of society. *Ethics*, *60*, 100–111.

Aboud, F. (1981). Ethnic self-identity. In R. C. Gardner & R. Kalin (Eds.), *A Canadian social psychology of ethnic relations* (pp. 37–56). Toronto: Methuen.

Aboud, F. (1988). *Children and prejudice*. Oxford: Basil Blackwell.

Aboud, F., & Skerry, S. (1984). The development of ethnic attitudes: A critical review. *Journal of Cross-Cultural Psychology*, *15*, 3–34.

Abrahamson, A. S., & Lisker, L. (1970). Discriminability along the voicing continuum: Cross-language tests. In *Proceedings of the Sixth International Congress of Phonetic Science* (pp. 569–573). Prague: Academia.

Adler, L. L. (Ed.). (1982). *Cross-cultural research at issue*. New York: Academic Press.

Adler, N. J. (1986). *International dimensions of organizational behavior*. Boston, MA.: Kent.

Adorno, T., Frenkel-Brunswik, E., Levinson, D. J., & Sanford, R. N. (1950). *The authoritarian personality*. New York: Harper and Row.

Aellen, C., & Lambert, W. E. (1969). Ethnic identification and personality adjustments of Canadian adolescents of mixed English-French parentage. *Canadian Journal of Behavioural Science*, *1*, 69–86.

Ainsworth, M. D. S. (1967). *Infancy in Uganda. Infant care and the growth of love*. Baltimore: Johns Hopkins University Press.

Aitkin, M., & Longford, N. (1986). Statistical modelling in school effectiveness studies. *Journal of the Royal Statistical Society*, *A*, 149, 1–43.

Albas, D. C., McCluskey, K. W., & Albas, C. A. (1976). Perception of the emotional content of speech. *Journal of Cross-Cultural Psychology*, *7*, 481–490.

Albert, R. D. (1983). The intercultural sensitizer or cultural assimilator : A cognitive approach. In D. Landis & R. W. Brislin (Eds.), *Handbook of intercultural training* (Vol. 2, pp. 186–217). New York: Pergamon.

Alcock, J. (1984). *Animal behavior: An evolutionary approach* (3rd ed.). Sunderland, Mass: Sinauer Associates.

Al-Issa, I. (Ed.). (1982). *Culture and psychopathology*. Baltimore: University Park Press.

Allaire, Y., & Firsiotu, M. E. (1984). Theories of organizational culture. *Organization Studies*, *5*, 193–226.

Alland, A. (1970). *Adaptation in cultural evolution: An approach to medical anthropology*. New York: Columbia University Press.

Allison, A. C. (1964). Polymorphism and natural selection in human populations. *Cold Spring Harbor Symposium in Quantitative Biology*, *24*, 137–149.

Allport, G. W., Vernon, P. E., & Lindzey, G. (1960). *A study of values*. Boston: Houghton Mifflin.

Altman, I., & Chemers, M. M. (1980). Cultural aspects of environment-behavior relationships. In H. C. Triandis & R. W. Brislin (Eds.), *Handbook of cross-cultural psychology* (Vol. 5, pp. 335–394). Boston: Allyn & Bacon.

393

American Educational Research Association, American Psychological Association, & National Council on Measurement in Education (1985). *Standards for educational and psychological testing*. Washington DC: American Psychological Association.

Amir, Y. (1986). *Intergroup cleavage in Israel*. Paper presented to International Congress of Applied Psychology, Jerusalem.

Amir, Y., & Sharon, I. (1987). Are social psychological laws cross-culturally valid? *Journal of Cross-Cultural Psychology, 18*, 383–470.

Anand, B. K., Chhina, G. S., & Singh, B. (1961). Some aspects of electroencephalographic studies in yogis. *Electroencephalography and Clinical Neurophysiology, 13*, 452–456.

Anastasi, A. (1988). *Psychological testing* (6th ed.). New York: Macmillan.

Andor, L. E. (1983). *Psychological and sociological studies of the black people of Africa, south of the Sahara: An annotated select bibliography*. Johannesburg: National Institute for Personnel Research.

Annis, R. C., & Corenblum, B. (1986). Self identification and race preference among Canadian Indian children. In L. Ekstrand (Ed.), *Ethnic minorities and immigrants in a cross-cultural perspective* (pp. 79–86). Lisse: Swets and Zeitlinger.

Anwar, M. P., & Child, I. L. (1972). Personality and aesthetic sensitivity in an Islamic culture. *Journal of Social Psychology, 87*, 21–28.

Archer, J. (1988). *The behavioural biology of aggression*. Cambridge: Cambridge University Press.

Ardilla, R. (1982). Psychology in Latin America. *Annual Review of Psychology, 33*, 103–122.

Argyle, M. (1988). *Bodily communication* (2nd ed.). London: Methuen.

Arieti, S., & Meth, J. (1959). Rare, unclassifiable, collective, exotic syndromes. In S. Arieti (Ed.), *American handbook of psychiatry* (Vol. 1, pp. 546–563). New York: Basic Books.

Armstrong, R. E., Rubin, E. V., Stewart, M., & Kuntner, L. (1970). *Susceptibility to the Müller-Lyer, Sander parallelogram, and Ames Distorted Room illusions as a function of age, sex and retinal pigmentation among urban Midwestern groups*. Research report. Northwestern University, Department of Psychology.

Asante, M. K., & Gudykunst, W. B. (1989). *Handbook of international and intercultural communication*. Newbury Park: Sage.

Asch, S.E. (1956). Studies in independence and conformity. *Psychological Monographs, 70*, (Whole No. 416), 1–70.

Asthana, H. S. (1988). Personality. In J. Pandey (Ed.), *Psychology in India: The state of the art* (Vol. 1, pp. 93–152). New Delhi: Sage.

Au, T. K. (1983). Chinese and English counterfactuals: The Sapir-Whorf hypothesis revisited. *Cognition, 15*, 155–187.

Bacon, M., Child, I., & Barry, H. (1963). A cross-cultural study of correlates of crime. *Journal of Abnormal and Social Psychology, 66*, 291–300.

Bali, S. K., Drenth, P. J. D., Van der Flier, H., & Young, W. C. E. (1984). *Contribution of aptitude tests to the prediction of school performance in Kenya: A longitudinal study*. Lisse: Swets and Zeitlinger.

Baltes, P. B. (1983). Life-span developmental psychology: Observations on history and theory revisited. In R. M. Lerner (Ed.), *Developmental psychology: Historical and philosophical perspectives* (pp. 79–111). Hillsdale, NJ: Erlbaum.

Bandura, A. (1977). *Social learning theory*. Englewood Cliffs, NJ: Prentice-Hall.

Banks, J., & Lynch, J. (Eds.). (1985). *Multicultural education in Western societies*. London: Holt, Rinehart and Winston.

Barba, C. V. C., Guthrie, H. A., & Guthrie, G. M. (1982). Dietary intervention and growth of infants and toddlers in a Philippine rural community. *Ecology and Nutrition, 11*, 235–244.

Barker, R. (1969). *Ecological psychology*. Stanford: Stanford University Press.

Barker, R. (1978). *Habitats, environments and human behavior*. San Francisco: Jossey-Bass.

Barnlund, D. C., & Araki, S. (1985). Intercultural encounters: The management of compliments. *Journal of Cross-Cultural Psychology, 16*, 9–26.

Barnouw, V. (1973). *Culture and personality*. Homewood, IL: Dorsey.

Barrett, D. E. (1984). Malnutrition and child behavior: Conceptualization, assessment and an empirical study of social-emotional functioning. In J. Brozek & B. Schürch (Eds.), *Malnutrition and behavior* (pp. 280–306). Lausanne: Nestlé Foundation.

Barrett, G. V., & Bass, B. M. (1976). Cross-cultural issues in industrial and organizational psychology. In M. D. Dunnette (Ed.), *Handbook of industrial and organizational psychology* (pp. 1639–1686). Chicago: Rand McNally.

Barry, H. (1980). Description and uses of the Human Relations Area Files. In H. C. Triandis & J. W. Berry (Eds.), *Handbook of cross-cultural psychology, Vol. 2, Methodology* (pp. 445–478). Boston: Allyn & Bacon.

Barry, H., Bacon, M., & Child, I. (1957). A cross-cultural survey of some sex differences in socialization. *Journal of Abnormal and Social Psychology, 55*, 327–332.

Barry, H., Child, I., & Bacon, M. (1959). Relation of child training to subsistence economy. *American Anthropologist, 61*, 51–63.

Barry, H., Josephson, L., Lauer, E., & Marshall, C. (1976). Agents and techniques for child training: Cross-cultural codes 6. *Ethnology, 16*, 191–230.

Barry, H., & Paxson, L. (1971). Infancy and early childhood: Cross-cultural codes. *Ethnology, 10*, 466–508.

Barry, H., & Schlegel, A. (Eds.). (1980). *Cross-cultural samples and codes*. Pittsburgh: University of Pittsburgh Press.

Bates, J. (1986). The measurement of temperament. In R. Plomin & J. Dunn (Eds.), *The study of temperament: Changes, continuities and challenges* (pp. 1–12). Hillsdale, NJ: Erlbaum.

Bayley, N. (1969). *Bayley scales of infant development*. New York: Psychological Corporation.

Benedict, R. (1932). Configurations of culture in North America, *American Anthropologist, 34*, 1–27.

Benedict, R. (1934). *Patterns of culture*. New York: Mentor.

Benedict, R. (1946). *The chrysanthemum and the sword*. Boston: Houghton Mifflin.

Berlin, B., & Berlin, E. A. (1975). Agueruna color categories. *American Ethnologist, 2*, 61–87.

Berlin, B., & Kay, P. (1969). *Basic color terms: Their universality and evolution*. Berkeley, CA: University of California Press.

Berlyne, D. E. (1960). *Conflict, arousal and curiosity*. New York: McGraw-Hill.

Berlyne, D. E. (1971). *Aesthetics and psychobiology*. New York: Appleton-Century-Crofts.

Berlyne, D. E. (1975). Extension to Indian subjects of a study of exploratory and verbal responses to visual patterns. *Journal of Cross-Cultural Psychology, 6*, 316–330.

Berlyne, D. E. (1980). Psychological aesthetics. In H. C. Triandis & W. J. Lonner (Eds.), *Handbook of cross-cultural psychology* (Vol. 3, pp. 323–361). Boston: Allyn & Bacon.

Berlyne, D. E., Robbins, M. C., & Thompson, R. (1974). A cross-cultural study of exploratory and verbal responses to visual patterns varying in complexity. In D. E. Berlyne (Ed.), *Studies in the new experimental aesthetics* (pp. 259–278). New York: Wiley.

Berman, J., Berman, V., & Singh, P. (1985). Cross-cultural similarities and differences in perception of fairness. *Journal of Cross-Cultural Psychology, 16*, 55–67.

Berrien, F. V. (1967). Methodological and related problems in cross-cultural research. *International Journal of Psychology, 2*, 33–43.

Berry, J. W. (1966). Temne and Eskimo perceptual skills. *International Journal of Psychology, 1*, 207–229.

Berry, J. W. (1967). Independence and conformity in subsistence-level societies. *Journal of Personality and Social Psychology, 7*, 415–418.

Berry, J. W. (1969). On cross-cultural comparability. *International Journal of Psychology, 4*, 119–128.

Berry, J. W. (1970). A functional approach to the relationship between stereotypes and familiarity. *Australian Journal of Psychology, 22*, 29–33.

Berry, J. W. (1971a). Ecological and cultural factors in spatial perceptual development. *Canadian Journal of Behavioural Science, 3*, 324–336.

Berry, J. W. (1971b). Müller-Lyer susceptibility: Culture, ecology or race? *International Journal of Psychology, 6*, 193–197.

Berry, J. W. (1972). Radical cultural relativism and the concept of intelligence. In L. J. Cronbach and P. J. D. Drenth (Eds.), *Mental Tests and Cultural Adaptation* (pp. 77–88). The Hague: Mouton.

Berry, J. W. (1974a). Canadian psychology: Some social and applied emphasies. *Canadian Psychologist, 15*, 132–139.

Berry, J. W. (1974b). Psychological aspects of cultural pluralism. *Topics in Culture Learning, 2*, 17–22.

Berry, J. W. (1976a). *Human ecology and cognitive style: Comparative studies in cultural and psychological adaptation.* New York: Sage/Halsted.

Berry, J. W. (1976b). Sex differences in behaviour and cultural complexity. *Indian Journal of Psychology, 51*, 89–97.

Berry, J. W. (1978). Social psychology: Comparative, societal and universal. *Canadian Psychological Review, 19*, 93–104.

Berry, J. W. (1979a). A cultural ecology of social behaviour. In L. Berkowitz (Ed.), *Advances in experimental social psychology*, (Vol. 12, pp. 177–206). New York: Academic Press.

Berry, J. W. (1979b). Research in multicultural societies: Implications of cross-cultural methods. *Journal of Cross-Cultural Psychology, 10*, 415–434.

Berry, J. W. (1980a). Acculturation as varieties of adaptation. In A. Padilla (Ed.), *Acculturation: Theory, models and some new findings* (pp. 9–25). Boulder, CO: Westview.

Berry, J. W. (1980b). Ecological analyses for cross-cultural psychology. In N. Warren (Ed.), *Studies in cross-cultural psychology* (Vol. 2, pp. 157–189). London: Academic Press.

Berry, J. W. (1980c). Social and cultural change. In H. C. Triandis & R. Brislin (Eds.), *Handbook of cross-cultural psychology* (Vol. 5, Social, pp. 211–279). Boston: Allyn & Bacon.

Berry, J. W. (1983). Wundt's *Völkerpsychologie* and the comparative study of human behaviour. In G. Eckardt and L. Sprung (Eds.), *In Memoriuam: W. Wundt* (pp. 92–100). Berlin DDR: Deutscher Verlag der Wissenschaften.

Berry, J. W. (1984a). Multicultural policy in Canada: A social psychological analysis. *Canadian Journal of Behavioural Science, 16*, 353–370.

Berry, J. W. (1984b). Toward a universal psychology of cognitive competence. *International Journal of Psychology, 19*, 335–361.

Berry, J. W. (1985a). Cultural psychology and ethnic psychology: A comparative analysis. In I. Reyes-Lagunes and Y. Poortinga (Eds.), *From a different perspective* (pp. 3–15). Lisse: Swets and Zeitlinger.

Berry, J. W. (1985b). Psychological adaptation of foreign students in Canada. In R. Samuda & A. Wolfgang (Eds.), *Intercultural counselling* (pp. 235–248). Toronto: Hogreffe.

Berry, J. W. (1986). The comparative study of cognitive abilities: A summary. In S. E. Newstead, S. H. Irvine, & P. L. Dann (Eds.), *Human assessment: Cognition and motivation* (pp. 57–74). Dordrecht: Nijhoff.

Berry, J. W. (1989). Imposed etics-emics-derived etics: The operationalization of a compelling idea. *International Journal of Psychology, 24*, 721–735.

Berry, J. W. (1990). Cultural variations in cognitive style. In S. Wapner (Ed.), *Bio-psycho-social factors in cognitive style* (pp. 289–308). Hillsdale, NJ: Erlbaum.

Berry, J. W., & Bennett, J. (1989). Syllabic literacy and cognitive performance among the Cree. *International Journal of Psychology, 24*, 429–450.

Berry, J. W., & Blondel, T. (1982). Psychological adaptation of Vietnamese refugees in Canada. *Canadian Journal of Community Mental Health, 1*, 81–88.

Berry, J. W., & Cavalli-Sforza, L. L. (1986). *Cultural and genetic influences on Inuit art.* Unpublished Report.

Berry, J. W., & Dasen, P. (Eds.). (1974). *Culture and cognition*, London: Methuen.

Berry, J. W., & Irvine, S. H. (1986). Bricolage: Savages do it daily. In R. Sternberg & R. Wagner (Eds.), *Practical intelligence: Nature and origins of competence in the everyday world* (pp. 271–306). New York: Cambridge University Press.

Berry, J. W., Irvine, S. H., & Hunt, E. B. (Eds.). (1988). *Indigenous cognition: Functioning in cultural context.* Dordrecht: Nijhoff.

Berry, J. W., & Kalin, R. (1979). Reciprocity of inter-ethnic attitudes in a multicultural society. *International Journal of Intercultural Relations, 3,* 99–112.

Berry, J. W., Kalin, R., & Taylor, D. (1977). *Multiculturalism and ethnic attitudes in Canada.* Ottawa: Supply and Services.

Berry, J. W., & Kim., U. (1988). Acculturation and mental health. In P. Dasen, J. W. Berry, & N. Sartorius (Eds.), *Cross-cultural psychology and health: Towards applications* (pp. 207–236). London: Sage.

Berry, J. W., Kim, U., Minde, T., & Mok, D. (1987). Comparative studies of acculturative stress. *International Migration Review, 21,* 491–511.

Berry, J. W., Kim, U., Power, S., Young, M., & Bujaki, M. (1989). Acculturation attitudes in plural societies. *Applied Psychology, 38,* 185–206.

Berry, J. W., Lonner, W. J., & Leroux, J. (Eds.). (1973). *Directory of cross-cultural research and researchers.* Bellingham, WA: Center for Cross-Cultural Research.

Berry, J. W., Trimble, J., & Olmeda, E. (1986a). The assessment of acculturation. In W. J. Lonner and J. W. Berry (Eds.), *Field methods in cross-cultural research* (pp. 291–324). London: Sage.

Berry, J. W., Van de Koppel, J. M. H., Sénéchal, C., Annis, R. C., Bahuchet, S., Cavalli-Sforza, L. L., & Witkin, H. A. (1986b). *On the edge of the forest: Cultural adaptation and cognitive development in Central Africa.* Lisse: Swets and Zeitlinger.

Berry, J. W., Wintrob, R. M., Sindell, P. S., & Mawhinney, T. A. (1982). Culture change and psychological adaptation. In R. Rath, H. Asthana, D. Sinha, & J. B. P. Sinha (Eds.), *Diversity and unity in cross-cultural psychology* (pp. 157–170). Lisse: Swets and Zeitlinger.

Bertino, M., Beauchamp, G. K., & Jen, K. C. (1983). Rated taste perception in two cultural groups. *Chemical Senses, 8,* 3–15.

Beveridge, W. M. (1935). Racial differences in phenomenal regression. *British Journal of Psychology, 26,* 59–62.

Beveridge, W. M. (1940). Some differences in racial perception. *British Journal of Psychology, 30,* 57–64.

Bhagat, R. S., & McQuaid, S. J. (1982). Role of subjective culture in organizations: A review and directions for future research. *Journal of Applied Psychology (Monograph), 67,* 653–685.

Biesheuvel, S. (1943). *African intelligence.* Johannesburg: South African Institute of Race Relations.

Biesheuvel, S. (1954). The measurement of occupational aptitudes in a multi-racial society. *Occupational Psychology, 28,* 189–196.

Biesheuvel, S. (1972). Adaptability: its measurement and determinants. In L. J. Cronbach and P. J. D. Drenth (Eds.), *Mental tests and cultural adaption,* (pp. 47–62). The Hague: Mouton.

Bijnen, E. J., Van der Net, T. Z. J., & Poortinga, Y. H. (1986). On cross-cultural comparative studies with the Eysenck Personality Questionnaire. *Journal of Cross-Cultural Psychology, 17,* 3–16.

Binnendijk, H. (Ed.). (1987). *National negotiating styles.* Washington, DC: Foreign Service Institute.

Birdwhistell, R. L. (1970). *Kinesics and context.* Philadelphia: University of Philadelphia Press.

Blackler, F. (Ed.). (1983). *Social psychology and developing countries.* Chichester: Wiley.

Blake, R. R., & Mouton, J. S. (1964). *The managerial grid.* Houston, TX: Gulf Publishing.

Bleichrodt, N. (1986). Mentale en ontwikkelingsstoornissen als gevolg van jodiumdeficientie: Een onderzoek in twee culturen [Mental and developmental disturbances as a consequence of iodine deficiency: A study in two cultures]. *Nederlands Tijdschrift voor de Psychologie en haar Grensgebieden, 41*, 165–178. '

Bleichrodt, N., Drenth, P. J. D., & Querido, A. (1980). Effects of iodine deficiency on mental and psychomotor abilities. *American Journal of Physical Anthropology, 53*, 55–67.

Bloom, A. (1981). *The linguistic shaping of thought: A study on the impact of language on thinking in China and the West*. Hillsdale, NJ: Erlbaum.

Blowers, G., & Turtle, A. (Eds.). (1987). *Psychology moving East*. Sydney: Sydney University Press.

Blue, A., & Blue, M. (1984). The trail of stress. In R. Samuda, J. W. Berry, & M. Laferrière (Eds.), *Multiculturalism in Canada: Social and educational perspectives* (pp. 301–308). Toronto: Allyn & Bacon.

Blum-Kulka, S., House, J., & Kasper, G. (1988). Investigating cross-cultural pragmatics: An introductory overview. In S. Blum-Kulka, J. House, & G. Kasper (Eds.), *Cross-cultural pragmatics: Requests and apologies* (pp. 1–34). Norwood, NJ: Ablex.

Boas, F. (1911). *The mind of primitive man*. New York: Macmillan.

Bochner, S. (1980). Unobtrusive methods in cross-cultural experimentation. In H. C. Triandis & J. W. Berry (Eds.), *Handbook of cross-cultural psychology, Vol. 2. Methodology* (pp. 319–387). Boston: Allyn & Bacon.

Bochner, S. (1981). The social psychology of cultural mediation. In S. Bochner (Ed.), *The mediating person: Bridges between cultures*. Cambridge, MA: Schenkman.

Bochner, S. (1982). The social psychology of cross-cultural relations. In S. Bochner (Ed.), *Cultures in contact* (pp. 5–44). Oxford: Pergamon.

Bochner, S. (1986a). Coping with unfamiliar cultures: Adjustment or culture learning? *Australian Journal of Psychology, 38*, 347–358.

Bochner, S. (1986b). Observational methods. In W. J. Lonner & J. W. Berry (Eds.), *Field methods in cross-cultural research* (pp. 165–201). London: Sage.

Bock, P. K. (1980). *Continuities in psychological anthropology: An historical introduction*. San Francisco: Freeman.

Bock, P. K. (1988). *Rethinking psychological anthropology: Continuity and change in the study of human action*. New York: Freeman.

Boesch, E. E. (1976). *Psychopathologie des Alltags* [Psychopathology of everyday]. Bern: Huber.

Boesch, E. E. (1980). *Kultur und Handlung* [Culture and action]. Bern: Huber.

Boesch, E. E. (1986). Science, culture and development. In M. Gottstein & G. Link (Eds.), *Cultural development, science and technology in Sub-Saharan Africa* (pp. 19–29). Berlin: German Foundation for International Development.

Boldt, E. D. (1978). Structural tightness and cross-cultural research. *Journal of Cross-Cultural Psychology, 9*, 151–165.

Boldt, E. D., & Roberts, L. (1979). Structural tightness and social conformity: A methodological note with theoretical implications. *Journal of Cross-Cultural Psychology, 10*, 221–230.

Bolinger, D. (1978). Intonation across languages. In J. H. Greenberg (Ed.), *Universals of human language* (Vol. 2, pp. 471–524). Stanford: Stanford University Press.

Bolles, R. C. (1970). Species-specific defense reactions and avoidance learning. *Psychological Review, 77*, 32–48.

Bolton, C., Bolton, R., Gross, L., Koel, A., Michelson, C., Munroe, R., & Munroe, R. (1976). Pastoralism and personality: An Andean replication. *Ethos, 4*, 463–482.

Bond, M. H. (1983). How language variation affects inter-cultural differentiation of values by Hong Kong bilinguals. *Journal of Language and Social Psychology, 2*, 57–76.

Bond, M. H. (Ed.). (1986). *The psychology of the Chinese people*. Hong Kong: Oxford University Press.

Bond, M. H. (Ed.). (1988). *The cross-cultural challenge to social psychology*. Newbury Park, CA: Sage.

Bond, M. H., Chiu, C. K., & Wan, K. C. (1984). When modesty fails: The social impact of group-effacing attributions following success or failure. *European Journal of Social Psychology, 14*, 335–338.

Bond, M. H., & King, A. Y. C. (1985). Coping with the threat of westernization in Hong Kong. *International Journal of Intercultural Relations*, *9*, 351–364.

Boorstin, D. J. (1985). *The discoverers*. New York: Vintage Books.

Born, M., Bleichrodt, N., & Van der Flier, H. (1987). Cross-cultural comparison of sex-related differences on intelligence tests: A meta-analysis. *Journal of Cross-Cultural Psychology*, *18*, 283–314.

Bornstein, M. H. (1973). Colour vision and colour naming: A psychophysiological hypothesis of cultural differences. *Psychological Bulletin*, *80*, 257–285.

Bornstein, M. H., Kessen, W. H., & Weiskopf, S. (1976). The categories of hue in infancy. *Science*, *191*, 201–202.

Boski, P. (1987). Retention and acquisition of national self-identity: Criterial and correlated attributes. In J. W. Berry & R. C. Annis (Eds.), *Ethnic psychology* (pp. 179–197). Amsterdam: Swets & Zeitlinger.

Boucher, J. D., & Carlson, G. E. (1980). Recognition of facial expression in three cultures. *Journal of Cross-Cultural Psychology*, *11*, 263–280.

Bourguignon, E. (1976). *Possession*. Corte Madera, CA: Chandler and Sharp.

Bourguignon, E. (1979). *Psychological anthropology: An introduction to human nature and cultural differences*. New York: Holt, Rinehart and Winston.

Bourguignon, E. (1984). Belief and behaviour in Haitian folk healing. In P. Pedersen, N. Sartorius, & A. Marsella (Eds.), *Mental health services: The cross-cultural context* (pp. 243–266). London: Sage.

Bourguignon, E., & Evascu, T. (1977). Altered states of consciousness within a general evolutionary perspective: A holocultural analysis. *Behavior Science Research*, *12*, 197–216.

Bourhis, R. (1983). Cross-cultural communication in Montreal. *International Journal of the Sociology of Language*, *9*, 33–47.

Bowlby, J. (1969). *Attachment and loss: Attachment* (Vol. I). New York: Basic Books.

Boyd, R., & Richerson, P. J. (1985). *Culture and the evolutionary process*. Chicago: The University of Chicago Press.

Bradshaw, J. L., & Nettleton, N. C. (1981). The nature of hemispheric specialization in man. *Behavioral and Brain Sciences*, *4*, 51–91.

Bragg, B. W. E., & Crozier, J. B. (1974). The development with age of verbal exploratory responses to sound sequences varying in uncertainty level. In D. E. Berlyne (Ed.), *Studies in the new experimental aesthetics* (pp. 91–108). Washington, DC: Hemisphere Publishing Corporation.

Brand, E., Ruiz, R., & Padilla, A. (1974). Ethnic identification and preference: A review. *Psychological Bulletin*, *81*, 860–890.

Brandt, M. E., & Boucher, J. D. (1985). Judgements of emotions from antecedent situations in three cultures. In I. Reyes Lagunes & Y. H. Poortinga (Eds.), *From a different perspective: Studies of behaviour across cultures* (pp. 348–362). Lisse: Swets and Zeitlinger.

Brazelton, T. B. (1973). *Neonatal behavioural assessment scale*. London: National Spastics Society.

Brein, M., & David, K. H. (1971). Intercultural communication and the adjustment of the sojourner. *Psychological Bulletin*, *76*, 215–230.

Brewer, M., & Campbell, D. T. (1976). *Ethnocentrism and intergroup attitudes: East African evidence*. London: Sage.

Bril, B., & Lehalle, H. (1988). *Le développement psychologique: Est-il universel? Approches interculturelles*. Paris: Presses Universitaires de France.

Bril, B., & Sabatier, C. (1986). The cultural context of motor development: Postural manipulations in the daily life of Bambara babies (Mali). *International Journal of Behavioural Development*, *9*, 439–453.

Bril, B., & Zack, M. (1989). Analyse comparative de l' "emploi du temps postural" de la naissance à la marche. In J. Retschitzki, M. Bossel-Lagos, & P. R. Dasen (Eds.), *La recherche interculturelle* (Vol. 2, pp. 18–30). Paris: L'Harmattan.

Brislin, R. W. (1974). The Ponzo illusion: Additional cues, age, orientation and culture. *Journal of Cross-Cultural Psychology*, 5, 139–161.

Brislin, R. W. (Ed.). (1976). *Translation: Applications and research*. New York: John Wiley/Halsted.

Brislin, R. W. (1980). Translation and content analysis of oral and written material. In H. C. Triandis and J. W. Berry (Eds.), *Handbook of cross-cultural psychology* (Vol. 2, pp. 389–444). Boston: Allyn & Bacon.

Brislin, R. W. (1983). Cross-cultural research in psychology. *Annual Review of Psychology*, 34, 363–400.

Brislin, R. W. (1986). The wording and translation of research instruments. In W. J. Lonner & J. W. Berry (Eds.), *Field methods in cross-cultural research* (pp. 137–164). Beverly Hills, CA: Sage.

Brislin, R. W., Cushner, K., Cherrie, C., & Yong, M. (1986). *Intercultural interactions: A practical guide*. Beverly Hills, CA: Sage.

Brislin, R., & Keating, C. (1976). Cultural differences in the perception of a three-dimensional Ponzo illusion. *Journal of Cross-Cultural Psychology*, 7, 397–411.

Brislin, R. W., Landis, D., & Brandt, M. E. (1983). Conceptualizations of intercultural behavior and training. In D. Landis & R. W. Brislin (Eds.), *Handbook of intercultural training* (Vol. 1, pp. 1–35). New York: Pergamon.

Brislin, R. W., Lonner, W. J., & Thorndike, R. M. (1973). *Cross-cultural research methods*. New York: Wiley.

Brodman, K., Erdmann, A., Lorge, I., Gershenson, C., & Wolff, H. (1952). The Cornell Medical Index health questionnaire: 3. The evaluation of emotional disturbances. *Journal of Clinical Psychology*, 8, 119–124.

Brown, R, (1965). *Social psychology*. New York: Free Press.

Brown, R. W., & Lenneberg, E. H. (1954). A study of language and cognition. *Journal of Abnormal and Social Psychology*, 49, 454–462.

Brozek, J., & Schürch, B. (Eds.). (1984). *Malnutrition and behavior: Critical assessment of key issues*. Lausanne: Nestlé Foundation.

Brunet, O., & Lézine, I. (1951). (3ème édition, 1971). *Le développement psychologique de la première enfance*. Paris: PUF.

Brunswik, E. (1956). *Perception and the representative design of psychological experiments*. Berkeley: University of California Press.

Brunswik, E. (1957). Scope and aspects of the cognition problem. In A. Gruber (Ed.), *Cognition: The Colorado Symposium*. Cambridge: Harvard University Press.

Bullivant, B. (1985). Educating the pluralist person: images of society and educational responses in Australia. In Poole, M., deLacey, P., & Randhawa, B. (Eds.), *Australia in transition: Culture and life possibilities*. Sydney: Harcourt Brace Jovanovich.

Bundy, R., & Mundy-Castle, A. (1984). Looking strategies in Nigerian infants: A cross-cultural study. In H. V. Curran (Ed.), *Nigerian children: Developmental perspectives* (pp. 12–33). London: Routledge & Kegan Paul.

Burridge, K. (1979). *Someone, no one: An essay on individuality*. Princeton: Princeton University Press.

Burstein, L. (1980). The analysis of multilevel data in educational research and evaluation. In D. Berlinger (Ed.), *Review of research in education* (pp. 158–233). Washington, DC: American Educational Research Association.

Butcher, J. N., & Pancheri, P. (1976). *A handbook of cross-national MMPI research*. Minneapolis: University of Minneapolis Press.

Camilleri, C. (1986). *Anthropologie culturelle et éducation*. Lausanne: Delachaux et Niestlé.

Campbell, D. T. (1960). Blind variation and selective retention in creative thought as in other knowledge processes. *Psychological Review*, 67, 380–400.

Campbell, D. T. (1969). Reforms as experiments. *American Psychologist*, 24, 409–429.

Campbell, D. T. (1970). Natural selection as an epistemological model. In R. Naroll & R. Cohen (Eds.), *A handbook of method in cultural anthropology* (pp. 51–85). New York: Natural History Press.

Campbell, D. T. (1975). On the conflicts between biological and social evolution and between psychology and moral tradition. *American Psychologist, 30*, 1103–1126.

Campbell, D. T., & Fiske, D. W. (1959). Convergent and discriminant validation by the multitrait-multimethod matrix. *Psychological Bulletin, 56*, 81–105.

Campbell, N. C. G., Graham, J. L., Jolibert, A., & Meissner, H. G. (1988). Marketing negotiations in France, Germany, the United Kingdom and the United States. *Journal of Marketing, 52*, 49–62.

Carlson, J. A., & Davis, C. M. (1971). Cultural values and the risky-shift: A cross-cultural test in Uganda and the United States. *Journal of Personality and Social Psychology, 20*, 392–399.

Carrithers, M., Collins, S., & Lukes, S. (Eds.). (1985). *The category of the person: Anthropology, philosophy, and history*. Cambridge: Cambridge University Press.

Carroll, J. B. (1983). Studying individual differences in cognitive abilities: Implications for cross-cultural studies. In S. H. Irvine and J. W. Berry (Eds.), *Human assessment and cultural factors* (pp. 213–235). New York: Plenum.

Carroll, J. B., & Casagrande, J. B. (1958). The function of language classifications in behavior, In E. Maccoby, T. Newcomb, & E. L. Hartley (Eds.), *Readings in social psychology* (3rd ed., pp. 18–31). New York: Holt, Rinehart & Winston.

Casati, I., & Lézine, I. (1968). *Les étapes de l'intelligence sensori-motrice. Manuel*. Paris: Centre de Psychologie Appliquée.

Case, R. (1985). *Intellectual development: Birth to adulthood*. New York: Academic Press.

Cavalli-Sforza, L. L., & Bodmer, W. (1971). *The genetics of human populations*. New York: Freeman.

Cavalli-Sforza, L. L., & Feldman, M. (1981). *Cultural transmission and evolution: A quantitative approach*. Princeton: Princeton University Press.

Cawte, J., Bianchi, G., & Kiloh, L. (1968). Personal discomfort in Australian Aborigines. *Australian and New Zealand Journal of Psychiatry, 2*, 69–79.

Chance, N. A. (1965). Acculturation, self-identification, and personality adjustment. *American Anthropologist, 67*, 372–393.

Chandra, S. (1973). The effects of group pressure in perception: A cross-cultural conformity study in Fiji. *International Journal of Psychology, 8*, 37–40.

Chavez, A. A., Martinez, C., & Yaschine, T. (1975). Nutrition, behavioral development, and mother-child interaction in young rural children. *Federation Proceedings, 34*, 1574–1582.

Chen, L., Rahman, M., & Sardar, A. (1980). Epidemiology and causes of death among children in a rural area of Bangladesh. *International Journal of Epidemiology, 9*, 25–33.

Child, I. L. (1969). Esthetics. In G. Lindzey & E. Aronson (Eds.), *The handbook of social psychology* (Vol. 3, pp. 853–916). Reading, MA: Addison-Wesley.

Child, I. L. & Iwao, S. (1968). Personality and esthetic sensitivity. Extensions of findings to younger age and to different culture. *Journal of Personality and Social Psychology, 8*, 308–312.

Child, J. (1981). Culture, contingency and capitalism in the cross-national study of organizations. In L. L. Cummings & B. M. Staw (Eds.), *Research in organizational behavior* (Vol. 3, pp. 303–356). Greenwich, CT: JAI Press.

Chinese Culture Connection (1987). Chinese values and the search for culture-free dimensions of culture. *Journal of Cross-Cultural Psychology, 18*, 143–164.

Ching, C. C. (1984). Psychology and the four modernizations in China. *International Journal of Psychology, 19*, 57–63.

Chodzinski, R. T. (1984). Counselling ethnic minorities. In R. Samuda, J. W. Berry, & M. Laferriere (Eds.), *Multiculturalism in Canada: Social and educational perspectives* (pp. 396–410). Toronto: Allyn & Bacon.

Chomsky, N. (1965). *Aspects of a theory of syntax*. Cambridge, MA: MIT Press.

Chomsky, N. (1980). *Rules and representations*. Oxford: Blackwell.

Church, A. T. (1982). Sojourner adjustment. *Psychological Bulletin, 91*, 540–572.

Cissé, Y. (1973). Signes graphiques, représentations, concepts et tests relatifs à la personne chez les Malinka et les Bambara du Mali. In *Colloques internationaux, La notion de personne en Afrique Noire*. Paris: Editions du CNRS.

Claeys, W. (1967). Conforming behavior and personality variables in Congolese students. *International Journal of Psychology*, *2*, 13–24.

Clark, K., & Clark, M. (1939). The development of consciousness of self and the emergence of racial identification in Negro preschool children. *Journal of Social Psychology*, *10*, 591–599.

Clark, M., Kaufman, S., & Pierce, R. C. (1976). Explorations of acculturation: Toward a model of ethnic identity. *Human Organization*, *35*, 231–238.

Clyne, M. (1982). *Multilingual Australia*. Melbourne: River Seine Publications.

Cohen, J. (1988). *Statistical power analysis for the behavioural sciences* (2nd ed.). Hillsdale, NJ: Erlbaum.

Cohen, J., & Cohen, P. (1983). *Applied multiple regression/correlation analysis for the behavioral sciences* (2nd ed.). Hillsdale, NJ: Erlbaum.

Cohen, R. (1970). Entree into the field. In R. Naroll & R. Cohen (Eds.), *Handbook of method in cultural anthropology* (pp. 220–245). New York: Natural History Press.

Cohen, R. (1987). Problems of intercultural communication in Egyptian-American diplomatic relations. *International Journal of Intercultural Relations*, *11*, 29–47.

Cole, M. (1975). An ethnographic psychology of cognition. In R. Brislin, S. Bochner, & W. Lonner (Eds.), *Cross-cultural perspectives on learning* (pp. 157–175). Beverly Hills, CA: Sage.

Cole, M., & Cole, S. (1989). *The development of children*. New York: Freeman.

Cole, M., Gay, J., & Glick, J. (1968). A cross-cultural study of information processing. *International Journal of Psychology*, *3*, 93–102.

Cole, M., Gay, J., Glick, J., & Sharp, D. (1971). *The cultural context of learning and thinking*. New York: Basic Books.

Cole, M., & Scribner, S. (1974). *Culture and thought*. New York: Wiley.

Cole, M., & Scribner, S. (1977). Developmental theories applied to cross-cultural cognitive research. *Annals of the New York Academy of Sciences*, *285*, 366–373.

Coleman, J., Butcher, J., & Carson, R. (1980). *Abnormal psychology and modern life*. Glenview, IL: Scott Foresman.

Comas-Diaz, L., & Griffith, E. (Eds.). (1988). *Clinical guidelines in cross-cultural mental health*. New York: Wiley.

Cook, T. D., & Campbell, D. T. (1979). *Quasi-experimentation: Design and analysis issues for field settings*. Chicago: Rand McNally.

Cooper, J. E., Kendell, R. E., Gurland, B. J., Sharpe, L., Copeland J. R. M., & Simon, R. (1972). *Psychiatric diagnosis in New York and London*. London: Oxford University Press.

Copeland, L., & Griggs, L. (1985). *Going international*. New York: Random House.

Corman, H. H., & Escalona, S. K. (1969). Stages in sensori-motor development: A replication study. *Merrill-Palmer Quarterly*, *15*, 351–361.

Cronbach, L. J., & Drenth, P. J. D. (Eds.). (1972). *Mental tests and cultural adaptation*. The Hague: Mouton.

Cronbach, L. J., Gleser, G. C., Nanda, H., & Rajaratnam, N. (1972). *The dependability of behavioral measurements*. New York: Wiley.

Cronbach, L. J., Rajaratnam, N., & Gleser, G. C. (1963). Theory of generalizability: A liberalization of reliability theory. *British Journal of Mathematical and Statistical Psychology*, *16*, 137–163.

Cushner, K. (1989). Assessing the impact of a culture-general assimilator. *International Journal of Intercultural Relations*, *13*, 125–146.

Dabbs, J. M., & Morris, R. (1990). Testosterone, social class and antisocial behavior in a sample of 4,462 men. *Psychological Science*, *1*, 209–211.

Daly, M., & Wilson, M. (1983). *Evolution and behavior* (2nd ed.). Boston: Willard Grant Press.

D'Andrade, R. G., Quinn, N. R., Nerlove, S. B., & Romney, A. K. (1972). Categories of disease in American-English and Mexican-Spanish. In A. K. Romney, R. N. Shepard, & S. B. Nerlove (Eds.), *Multidimensional Scaling* (Vol. 2, pp. 9–54). New York: Seminar Press.

Danziger, K. (1983). Origins and basic principles of Wundt's *Völkerpsychologie*. *British Journal of Social Psychology*, 22, 303–313.

Dasen, P. R. (1972). Cross-cultural Piagetian research: A summary. *Journal of Cross-Cultural Psychology*, 7, 75–85.

Dasen, P. R. (1984). The cross-cultural study of intelligence: Piaget and the Baoulé. *International Journal of Psychology*, 19, 407–434.

Dasen, P. R. (1988). Les activités quotidiennes d'enfants africains dans leur contexte naturel: La méthode des observations ponctuelles. *Enfance*, 41, 3–24.

Dasen, P. R., Berry, J. W., & Sartorius, N. (Eds.). (1988). *Cross-cultural psychology and health: Towards applications*. Newbury Park, CA: Sage.

Dasen, P. R., Berry, J. W., & Witkin, H. A. (1979). The use of developmental theories cross-culturally. In L. H. Eckensberger, W. J. Lonner, & Y. H. Poortinga (Eds.), *Cross-cultural contributions to psychology* (pp. 69–82). Lisse: Swets and Zeitlinger.

Dasen, P. R., & de Ribaupierre, A. (1987). Neo-Piagetian theories: Cross-cultural and differential perspectives. *International Journal of Psychology*, 22, 793–832.

Dasen, P. R., Dembele, B., Ettien, K., Kabran, K., Kamagaté, D., Koffi, D. A., & N'Guessan, A. (1985). N'glouèlê, l'intelligence chez les Baoulé. *Archives de Psychologie*, 53, 293–324.

Dasen, P. R., & Heron, A. (1981). Cross-cultural tests of Piaget's theory. In H. C. Triandis & A. Heron (Eds.), *Handbook of cross-cultural psychology. Vol. 4: Developmental psychology* (pp. 295–342). Boston: Allyn & Bacon.

Dasen, P. R., Inhelder, B., Lavallée, M., & Retschitzki, J. (1978). *Naissance de l'intelligence chez l'enfant Baoulé de Côte d'Ivoire*. Berne: Hans Huber.

Dasen, P. R., Ngini, L., & Lavallée, M. (1979). Cross-cultural training studies of concrete operations. In L. Eckensberger, Y. Poortinga, & W. Lonner (Eds.), *Cross-cultural contributions to psychology* (pp. 94–104). Lisse: Swets & Zeitlinger.

Dasen, P. R., & Super, C. M. (1988). The usefulness of a cross-cultural approach in studies of malnutrition and psychological development. In P. R. Dasen, J. W. Berry, & N. Sartorius (Eds.), *Health and cross-cultural psychology: Towards applications*. (pp. 112–138). Newbury Park, CA: Sage.

Davidson, A. R., Jaccard, J. J., Triandis, H. C., Morales, M. L., & Diaz-Guerrero, R. L. (1976). Cross-cultural model testing: Toward a solution of the etic-emic dilemma. *International Journal of Psychology*, 11, 1–14.

Davis, C. M., & Carlson, J. A. (1970). A cross-cultural study of the strength of the Müller-Lyer illusion as a function of attentional factors. *Journal of Personality and Social Psychology*, 16, 403–410.

Dawson, J. L. M. (1967). Cultural and physiological influences upon spatial perceptual processes in West Africa (Parts 1 and 2). *International Journal of Psychology*, 2, 115–128, 171–185.

Dawson, J. L. M. (1969). Attitude change and conflict among Australian Aborigines. *Australian Journal of Psychology*, 21, 101–116.

Dawson, J. L. M. (1971). Theory and research in cross-cultural psychology. *Bulletin of the British Psychological Society*, 24, 291–306.

de Lacey, P. R. (1970). An index of contact. *Australian Journal of Social Issues*, 5, 219–223.

DeRidder, R., & Tripathi, R. C. (Eds.). (in press). *Norm violation and intergroup relations*. Oxford: Oxford University Press.

de Vos, G. (1968). Achievement and innovation in culture and personality. In E. Norbeck, D. Price-Williams, & E. W. McCord (Eds.), *The study of personality* (pp. 348–370). New York: Holt, Rinehart & Winston.

de Vos, G. (1980). Ethnic adaptation and minority status. *Journal of Cross-Cultural Psychology*, 11, 101–124.

Deal, T. E., & Kennedy, A. A. (1982). *Corporate cultures: The rites and rituals of corporate life.* Reading, MA: Addison-Wesley.

Demetriou, A., & Efklides, A. (1987a). Experiential structuralism and neo-Piagetian theories: Toward an integrated model. *International Journal of Psychology, 22,* 679–728.

Demetriou, A., & Efklides, A. (1987b). Towards a determination of the dimensions and domains of individual differences in cognitive development. In E. De Corte, H. Lodewijks, R. Parmentier, & P. Span (Eds.), *Learning and Instruction* (pp. 41–52). New York: Pergamon Press/Leuven University Press.

Deregowski, J. B. (1968). Difficulties in pictorial depth perception in Africa. *British Journal of Psychology, 59,* 195–204.

Deregowski, J. B. (1980a). *Illusions, patterns and pictures: A cross-cultural perspective.* London: Academic Press.

Deregowski, J. B. (1980b). Perception. In H. C. Triandis, & W. Lonner (Eds.), *Handbook of cross-cultural psychology* (Vol. 3, pp. 21–115). Boston: Allyn & Bacon.

Deregowski, J. B. (1989). Real space and represented space: Cross-cultural perspectives. *Behavioral and Brain Sciences, 12,* 51–119.

Deregowski, J. B., & Bentley, A. M. (1986). Perception of pictorial space by Bushmen. *International Journal of Psychology, 21,* 743–752.

Deregowski, J. B., & Bentley, A. M. (1987). Seeing the impossible and building the likely. *British Journal of Psychology, 78,* 91–97.

Deregowski, J. B., & Byth, W. (1970). Hudson's pictures in Pandora's box. *Journal of Cross-Cultural Psychology, 1,* 315–323.

Deregowski, J. B., Muldrow, E. S., & Muldrow, W. F. (1972). Pictorial recognition in a remote Ethiopian population. *Perception, 1,* 417–425.

Detweiler, R. A., Brislin, R. W., & McCormack, W. (1983). Situational analysis. In D. Landis & R. W. Brislin (Eds.), *Handbook of intercultural training* (Vol. 2, pp. 100–123). New York: Pergamon.

Deutsch, M., & Gerard, H. (1955). A study of normative and informational social influences upon individual judgement. *Journal of Abnormal and Social Psychology, 51,* 629–636.

Devereux, G. (1980). *Basic problems of ethnopsychiatry.* Chicago: University of Chicago Press.

Diaz-Guerrero, R. (1975). *Psychology of the Mexican: Culture and personality.* Austin: University of Texas Press.

Diaz-Guerrero, R. (1982). The psychology of the historic-sociocultural premise. *Spanish Language Psychology, 2,* 382–410.

Diaz-Guerrero, R. (1984). Transference of psychological knowledge and its impact on Mexico. *International Journal of Psychology, 19,* 123–134.

Dittrich, A., Von Arx, S., & Staub, S. (1985). International study on altered states of consciousness (ISASC): Summary of results. *German Journal of Psychology, 9,* 319–339.

Dobzhansky, T., Ayala, F. J., Stebbins, G. L., & Valentine, J. W. (1977). *Evolution.* San Francisco: Freeman.

Doi, T. (1973). *The anatomy of dependence.* Tokyo: Kodansha International.

Doi, T. (1984). Psychotherapy: A cross-cultural perspective from Japan. In P. Pedersen, N. Sartorius, & A. Marsella (Eds.), *Mental health services: The cross-cultural context* (pp. 267–279). London: Sage.

Doise, W. (1982). *L'Explication en psychologie sociale.* Paris: Presses Universitaires de France.

Doktor, R. (1983). Culture and management of time: A comparison of Japanese and American top management practice. *Asia Pacific Journal of Management, 1,* 65–70.

Doty, R. L. (1986). Cross-cultural studies of taste and smell perception. In D. Duvall, D. Muller-Schwarze, & R. Silverstein (Eds.), *Clinical signals in vertebrates* (Vol. 4). New York: Plenum.

Dougherty, J. W., & Keller, C. (1982). Taskonomy: A practical approach to knowledge structure. *American Ethnologist, 9,* 763–774.

Draguns, J. (1980). Psychological disorders of clinical severity. In H. C. Triandis & J. Draguns

(Eds.), *Handbook of cross-cultural psychology. Vol. 6, Psychopathology* (pp. 99–174). Boston: Allyn & Bacon.

Draguns, J. (1981). Cross-cultural counselling and psychotherapy: History, issues, current status. In A. Marsella & P. Pedersen (Eds.), *Cross-cultural counselling and psychotherapy* (pp. 3–27). New York: Pergamon.

Draguns, J. (1982). Methodology in cross-cultural psychopathology. In I. Al-Issa (Ed.), *Culture and psychopathology* (pp. 33–70). Baltimore: University Park Press.

Draguns, J. (1990). Applications of cross-cultural psychology in the field of mental health. In R. Brislin (Ed.), *Applied cross-cultural psychology* (pp. 302–324). Newbury Park, CA: Sage.

Drenth, P. J. D. (1977). Prediction of school performance in developing countries: School grades or psychological tests? *Journal of Cross-Cultural Psychology*, *8*, 49–70.

Drenth, P. J. D. (1983). Cross-cultural organizational psychology: Challenges and limitations. In S. H. Irvine & J. W. Berry (Eds.), *Human assessment and cultural factors* (pp. 563–580). New York: Plenum.

Drenth, P. J. D., & Groenendijk, B. (1984). Work and organizational psychology in cross-cultural perspective. In P. J. D. Drenth, H. Thierry, P. J. Willems, & C. J. De Wolff (Eds.), *Handbook of work and organizational psychology* (Vol. 2, pp. 1197–1230). New York: Wiley.

Drenth, P. J. D., Van der Flier, H., & Omari, I. M. (1983). Educational selection in Tanzania. *Evaluation in Education*, *7*, 93–217.

Du Toit, B. M. (1966). Pictorial depth perception and linguistic relativity. *Psychologia Africana*, *11*, 51–63.

DuBois, C. (1944). *The people of Alor*. New York: Harper and Row.

Ducci, L., Arcuri, L. W., Georgis, T., & Sinseshaw, T. (1982). Emotion recogniton in Ethiopia. *Journal of Cross-Cultural Psychology*, *13*, 340–351.

Duncan, H. F., Gourlay, N., & Hudson, W. (1973). *A study of pictorial perception among Bantu and White primary school children in South Africa*. Johannesburg: Witwatersrand University Press.

Durham, W. H. (1982). Interactions of genetic and cultural evolution: Models and examples. *Human Ecology*, *10*, 289–323.

Durojaiye, M. (1984). The impact of psychological testing on educational and personnel selection in Africa, *International Journal of Psychology*, *19*, 135–144.

Dyal, J. A. (1984). Cross-cultural research with the locus of control construct. In H. M. Lefcourt (Ed.), *Research with the locus of control construct* (Vol. 3, pp. 209–306). New York: Academic Press.

Dziurawiec, S., & Deregowski, J. B. (1986). Construction errors as a key to perceptual difficulties encountered in reading technical drawings. *Ergonomics*, *29*, 1203–1212.

Eagly, A. (1978). Sex differences in influenceability. *Psychological Bulletin*, *85*, 85–116.

Eckensberger, L. H. (1972). The necessity of a theory for applied cross-cultural research. In L. H. Cronbach & P. J. D. Drenth (Eds.), *Mental tests and cultural adaptation* (pp. 99–107). The Hague: Mouton.

Eckensberger, L. H. (1979). A metamethodological evaluation of psychological theories from a cross-cultural perspective. In L. Eckensberger, W. Lonner, & Y. H. Poortinga (Eds.), *Cross-cultural contributions to psychology* (pp. 255–275). Lisse: Swets and Zeitlinger.

Eckensberger, L. H. (1987). Boesch dynamic action theory – A bridge between theory and practice, between general laws and context. *Arbeiten der Fachrichtung Psychologie*. Universität des Saarlandes, 113.

Eckensberger, L. H., & Burgard, P. (1983). The cross-cultural assessment of normative concepts: Some considerations of the affinity between methodological approaches and preferred theories. In S. H. Irvine & J. W. Berry (Eds.), *Human assessment and cultural factors* (pp. 459–480). New York: Plenum.

Eckensberger, L. H., Krewer, B., & Kasper, E. (1984). Simulation of cultural change by cross-cultural research: Some metamethodological considerations. In K. A. McCluskey & H. W. Reese (Eds.), *Life-span developmental psychology: Historical and generational effects* (pp. 73–107). Orlando, FL: Academic Press.

Eckensberger, L. H., & Meacham, J. A. (1984). Essentials of action theory: A framework for discussion. *Human Development, 27*, 166–172.

Eckensberger, L. H., & Reinshagen, H. (1980). Kohlbergs Stufentheorie der Entwicklung des moralischen Urteils. In L. H. Eckensberger & R. Silbereisen (Eds.), *Entwicklung sozialer Kognitionen: Modelle, Theorien, Methoden, Anwendung* (pp. 65–131). Stuttgart: Klett-Cotta.

Edgerton, R. (1971). *The individual in cultural adaptation: A study of four East African peoples.* Los Angeles: University of California Press.

Edgerton, R. (1974). Cross-cultural psychology and psychological anthropology: One paradigm or two? *Reviews in Anthropology, 1*, 52–65.

Edwards, A. L. (1970). *The measurement of personality traits by scales and inventories.* New York: Holt, Rinehart and Winston.

Edwards, C. P. (1985). Another style of competence. In A. Fogel & G. Melson (Eds.), *Origins of nurturance.* New York: Erlbaum.

Edwards, J. (1984). The social and political context of bilingual education. In R. Samuda, J. W. Berry, & M. Laferrière (Eds.), *Multiculturalism in Canada: Social and educational perspectives* (pp. 184–200). Toronto: Allyn & Bacon.

Efron, D. (1972). *Gesture, race and culture.* The Hague: Mouton. [Originally published 1941].

Eibl-Eibesfeldt, I. (1975). *Ethology: The biology of behavior* (2nd ed.). New York: Holt, Rinehart and Winston.

Eibl-Eibesfeldt, I. (1979a). Human ethology: Concepts and implications for the sciences of man. *Behavioral and Brain Sciences, 2*, 1–57.

Eibl-Eibesfeldt, I. (1979b). Ritual and ritualization from a biological perspective. In M. von Cranach, K. Foppa, W. Lepenies, & D. Ploog (Eds.), *Human ethology: Claims and limits of a new discipline* (pp. 3–55). Cambridge: Cambridge University Press.

Eimas, P. D. (1975). Auditory and phonetic coding of the cues for speech. Discrimination of the [r-1] distinctions by young infants. *Perception and Psychophysics, 18*, 341–347.

Ekman, P. (1973). Cross-cultural studies of facial expression. In P. Ekman (Ed.), *Darwin and facial expression* (pp. 169–222). New York: Academic Press.

Ekman, P. (1980a). *The face of man.* New York: Garland Press.

Ekman, P. (1980b). Three classes of nonverbal behavior. In W. von Raffler-Engel (Ed.), *Aspects of non-verbal communication* (pp. 89–102). Lisse: Swets and Zeitlinger.

Ekman, P. (Ed.). (1982). *Emotion in the human face* (2nd ed.). Cambridge: Cambrige University Press.

Ekman, P., & Friesen, W. V. (1969). The repertoire of nonverbal behavior: categories, origins, usage and coding. *Semiotica, 1*, 49–98.

Ekman, P., & Friesen, W. V. (1971). Constants across cultures in the face and emotion. *Journal of Personality and Social Psychology, 17*, 124–129.

Ekman, P., Friesen, W. V., O'Sullivan, M., Diacoyanni-Tarlatris, I., Krause, R., Pitcairn, T., Scherer, K., Chan, A., Heider, K., LeCompte, W. A., Ricci-Bitti, P. E., & Tomita, M. (1987). Universals and cultural differences in the judgements of facial expressions of emotion. *Journal of Personality and Social Psychology, 53*, 712–717.

Ekstrand, L. H. (1978). Migrant adaptation: A cross-cultural problem. In R. Freudenstein (Ed.), *Teaching the children of immigrants* (pp. 27–123). Brussels: Diden.

Ekstrand, L. H., & Ekstrand, G. (1986). Developing the emic/etic concepts for cross-cultural research. In L. H. Ekstrand (Ed.), *Ethnic minorities and immigrants in a cross-cultural perspective* (pp. 52–66). Lisse: Swets & Zeitlinger.

Eldering, L., & Kloprogge, J. (Eds.). (1989). *Different cultures, same school: Ethnic minority children in Europe.* Amsterdam: Swets and Zeitlinger.

Ellis, B. (1988). Hofstede's culture dimensions and Rokeach's values: How reliable is the relationship? In J. W. Berry & R. C. Annis (Eds.), *Ethnic psychology: Research and* practice with immigrants, refugees, native peoples, ethnic groups and sojourners (pp. 266–274). Lisse: Swets and Zeitlinger.

Engelsmann, F. (1982). Culture and depression. In I. Al-Issa (Ed.), *Culture and psychopathology*. Baltimore: University Park Press.

Enriquez, V. (1981). *Decolonizing the Filipino psyche*. Quezon City: Psychology Research and Training House.

Enriquez, V. (1982). *Towards a Filipino psychology*. Quezon City: Psychology Research and Training House.

Enriquez, V. (1989). *Indigenous psychology and national consciousness*. Tokyo: Institute for the Study of Languages and Cultures of Asia and Africa.

Enriquez, V. (Ed.). (1990). *Indigenous psychologies*. Quezon City: Psychology Research and Training House.

Eysenck, H. J. (1967). *The biological basis of personality*. Springfield, IL: Charles Thomas.

Eysenck, H. J. (1988). The biological basis of intelligence. In S. H. Irvine and J. W. Berry (Eds.), *Human abilities in cultural context* (pp. 70–104). New York: Cambridge University Press.

Eysenck, H. J., & Eysenck, S. B. G. (1975). *Manual of the Eysenck Personality Questionnaire*. San Diego, CA: Hodder and Stoughton.

Eysenck, H. J., & Eysenck, S. B. G. (1983). Recent advances in the cross-cultural study of personality. In J. N. Butcher & C. D. Spielberger (Eds.), *Advances in personality assessment* (Vol. 2, pp. 41–69). Hillsdale, NJ: Erlbaum.

Eysenck, H.J., & Iwawaki, S. (1971). Cultural relativity in aesthetic judgements: An empirical study. *Perceptual and Motor Skills, 32*, 817–818.

Eysenck, S. B. G., & Opolot, J. A. (1983). A comparative study of personality in Ugandan and English subjects. *Personality and Individual Differences, 4*, 583–589.

Francher, R. E. (1985). *The intelligence men: Makers of the IQ controversy*. New York: Norton.

Faucheux, C. (1976). Cross-cultural research in experimental social psychology. *European Journal of Social Psychology, 6*, 269–322.

Fawcett, J. T. (1973). *Psychological perspectives on population*. New York: Basic Books.

Feather, N. (1975). *Values in education and society*. New York: Free Press.

Feldman, D. (1975). The history of the relationship between environment and culture in ethnological thought: An overview. *Journal of the History of the Behavioural Sciences, 110*, 67–81.

Fenichel, O. (1955). Brief psychotherapy. In O. Fenichel, *Collected papers*, London: Routledge.

Ferguson, G. (1956). On transfer and the abilities of man. *Canadian Journal of Psychology, 10*, 121–131.

Fernandez, E. L., Estrera, N. O., Barba, C. V. C., Guthrie, H. A., & Guthrie, G. M. (1983). Reinforcing mothers for improving infants' diets with locally available food. *Philippine Journal of Nutrition, 36*, 39–48.

Fernandez, E. L., & Guthrie, G. M. (1983). Belief systems and breast feeding among Filipino urban poor. *Social Science and Medicine, 19*, 991–995.

Feuerstein, R. (1979). *The dynamic assessment of retarded performers*. Baltimore: University Park Press.

Fiedler, F. E., Mitchell, T., & Triandis, H. C. (1971). The culture assimilator: An approach to cross-cultural training. *Journal of Applied Psychology, 55*, 95–102.

Fishman, J. (1960). A systematization of the Whorfian hypothesis. *Behavioral Science, 5*, 323–338.

Fishman, J. (1966). *Language loyalty in the United States*. The Hague: Mouton.

Fiske, A. P. (1991). *Structures of social life: The four elementary forms of human relations*. New York: Free Press.

Fiske, D. W. (1971). *Measuring the concepts of personality*. Chicago: Aldine.

Flatz, G., & Rotthauwe, H. W. (1977). The human lactase polymorphism: Physiology and genetics of lactose absorption and malabsorption. *Progress in Medical Genetics, 2,* 205–249.

Flynn, J. R. (1987). Massive IQ gains in 14 nations: What IQ tests really measure. *Psychological Bulletin, 101,* 171–191.

Forgas J., & Bond, M. H. (1985). Cultural influences on the perception of interaction episodes. *Personality and Social Psychology Bulletin, 11,* 75–88.

Foster, G. M., Scudder, T., Colson, E., & Kemper, R. (1978). *Long-term field research in social anthropology.* New York: Academic Press.

Foulks, E., Wintrob, R., Westermeyer, J., & Favazza, A. (Eds.). (1977). *Current perspectives in cultural psychiatry.* New York: Spectrum.

Fourasté, R. (1985). *Introduction à l'ethnopsychiatrie.* Toulouse: Privat.

Frager, R. (1970). Conformity and anticonformity in Japan. *Journal of Personality and Social Psychology, 15,* 203–210.

Freedman, D. G. (1974). *Human infancy: An evolutionary perspective.* New York: Wiley.

Freeman, D. (1983). *Margaret Mead and Samoa: The making and unmaking of an anthropological myth,* Cambridge, MA: Harvard University Press.

Freud, S. (1938). *An outline of psychoanalysis.* London: Hogarth.

Frijda, N. H. (1986). *The emotions.* Cambridge: Cambridge University Press.

Frijda, N., & Jahoda, G. (1966). On the scope and methods of cross-cultural research. *International Journal of Psychology, 1,* 109–127.

Fromm, E. (1941). *Escape from freedom.* New York: Farrar and Rinehart.

Frost, P. J., Moore, L. F., Louis, M. R., Lundberg, C. C., & Martin, J. (Eds.). (1985). *Organizational culture.* Beverly Hills, CA: Sage.

Fuller, J. L., & Thompson, W. R. (1978). Foundations of behaviour genetics. St. Louis: The Mosby Company.

Furby, L. (1973). Implications of within-group heritabilities for sources of between-group differences: IQ and racial differences. *Developmental Psychology, 9,* 28–37.

Furnham, A., & Bochner, S. (1986). *Culture shock: Psychological reactions to unfamiliar environments.* London: Methuen.

Galler, J. R., Ricciuti, H. N., Crawford, M. A., & Kucharski, L. T. (1984) . The role of the mother-infant interaction in nutritional disorders. In J. Galler (Ed.), *Nutrition and behavior* (pp. 269–304). New York: Plenum.

Garcia, J., & Koelling, R. A. (1966). Relation of cue to consequence in avoidance learning. *Psychonomic Science, 4,* 123–124.

Gardner, E. J., & Snustad, D. P. (1984). *Principles of genetics* (7th ed.). New York: Wiley.

Gardner, R. C. (1985). *Social psychological aspects of second language learning.* London: Edward Arnold.

Gardner, R. C., & Lambert, W. E. (1972). *Attitudes and motivation in second language learning.* Rowley, MA: Newbury House.

Gardner, R. C., Wonnacott, E., & Taylor, D. (1968). Ethnic stereotypes: A factor analytic investigation. *Canadian Journal of Psychology, 22,* 35–44.

Gatewood, J. B. (1985). Actions speak louder than words. In J. W. D. Dougherty (Ed.), *Directions in cognitive anthropology.* Chicago: University of Illinois Press.

Gay, J., & Cole, M. (1967). *The new mathematics in an old culture.* New York: Holt, Rinehart & Winston.

Geber, M. (1958). The psycho-motor development of African children in the first year and the influence of maternal behaviour. *Journal of Social Psychology, 47,* 185–195.

Geber, M., & Dean, R. F. (1957). The state of development of newborn African children. *Lancet, 272,* 1216–1219.

Geertz, C. (1965). The impact of the concept of culture on the concept of man. In J. Platt (Ed.). *New views on the nature of man.* Chicago: University of Chicago Press.

Geertz, C. (1973). *The interpretation of cultures.* New York: Basic Books.

Geiger, L. (1880). *Contributions to the history of the development of the human race.* London: Trübner & Co.

Gesell, A. (1940). *The first five years of life: A guide to the study of the preschool child (Part I)*. New York: Harper.

Gesell, A., & Amatruda, C. (1947). *Developmental diagnosis*. New York: Harper Bros.

Gladstone, W. E. (1858). *Studies on Homer and the Homeric age*, Vol. III, Oxford: Oxford University Press.

Gibbs, J. C. (1977). Kohlberg's stages of moral judgement: A constructive critique. *Harvard Educational Review, 47*, 43–61.

Gibson, J. J. (1966). *The senses considered as perceptual systems*. Boston: Houghton Mifflin.

Glacken, C. J. (1967). *Traces on the Rhodian Shore*. Berkeley: University of California Press.

Goldberg, S. (1972). Infant care and growth in urban Zambia. *Human Development, 15*, 77–89.

Goldstein, A. P. (1983). Causes, controls and alternatives to aggression. In A. P. Goldstein & M. H. Segall (Eds.), *Aggression in global perspective*. Elmsford, NY: Pergamon.

Gologor, E. (1977). Group polarization in a non-risk-taking culture. *Journal of Cross-Cultural Psychology, 8*, 331–346.

Gombrich, E. H. (1977). *Art and illusion: A study in the psychology of pictorial representation* (5th ed.). Oxford: Phaidon Press.

Goodenough, N. (1980). Ethnographic field techniques. In H. C. Triandis & J. W. Berry (Eds.), *Handbook of cross-cultural psychology, Vol. 2, Methodology* (pp. 29–55). Boston: Allyn & Bacon.

Goody, J., & Watt, I. (1968). The consequences of literacy. In J. Goody (Ed.), *Literacy in traditional societies* (pp. 27–68). New York: Cambridge University Press.

Gorer, G., & Rickman, J. (1949). *The people of Great Russia*. New York: Norton.

Goto, H. (1971). Auditory perception by normal Japanese adults of sounds of "l" or "r". *Neuropsychologia, 9*, 317–323.

Graham, J. A., & Argyle, M. (1975). A cross-cultural study of the communication of extraverbal meaning by gestures. *International Journal of Psychology, 10*, 57–67.

Graham, J. L. (1983). Brazilian, Japanese, and American business negotiations. *Journal of International Business Studies, 14*, 47–61.

Graham, J. L., & Andrews, J. D. (1987). A holistic analysis of Japanese and American business negotiations. *Journal of Business Communications, 24*, 63–77.

Graham, J. L., Kim, D. K., Lin, C., & Robinson, M. (1988). Buyer-seller negotiations around the Pacific rim: Differences in fundamental exchange processes. *Journal of Consumer Research, 15*, 48–54.

Gough, H. G. (1969). *California Psychological Inventory*. Palo Alto, CA: Consulting Psychologists Press.

Gough, H. G., & Heilbrun, A. (1965). *Adjective check list manual*. Palo Alto, CA: Consulting Psychologists Press.

Gould, J. L., & Marler, P. (1987). Learning by instinct. *Scientific American, 256*, 1, 62–73.

Government of Canada. (1971). *Policy statement to House of Commons on multiculturalism*. Ottawa: Government of Canada.

Grant, G. V. (1970). *The development and validation of a classification battery constructed to replace the General Adaptability Battery*. Report C/Pers 181. Johannesburg: National Institute for Personnel Research.

Grantham-McGregor, S. (1984). Social background of childhood malnutrition. In J. Brozek & B. Schürch (Eds.), *Malnutrition and behavior: Critical assessment of key issues* (pp. 358–374). Lausanne: Nestlé Foundation.

Graves, P. L. (1979). Cross-cultural comparison of mothers and their undernourished infants in Asia. In J. Brozek (Ed.), *Behavioral effects of energy and protein deficits* (pp. 100–108). Washington, DC: NIH.

Graves, T. D. (1967). Psychological acculturation in a tri-ethnic community. *South-western Journal of Anthropology, 23*, 337–350.

Greenberg, J. H. (1957). The nature and uses of linguistic typologies. *International Journal of American Linguistics, 23*, 68–77.

Greenberg, J. H. (Ed.). (1963). *Universals of language*. Cambridge, MA: MIT Press.

Greenberg, J. H. (Ed.). (1978). *Universals of human language* (Vols. 1–4). Stanford: Stanford University Press.

Greenfeld, P. J. (1986). What is grey, brown, pink and sometimes purple: The range of "wild-card" color terms. *American Anthropologist, 88,* 908–916.

Greenfield, P. M. (1976). Cross-cultural research and Piagetian theory: Paradox and progress. In K. F. Riegel & J. A. Meacham (Eds.), *The developing individual in a changing world* (Vol. 1, pp. 322–333). The Hague: Mouton.

Gregory, R. L. (1966). *Eye and brain.* London: World University Library.

Griffeth, R. W., & Hom, P. W. (1987). Some multivariate comparisons of multinational managers. *Multivariate Behavioral Research, 22,* 173–191.

Griffeth, R. W., Hom, P. W., De Nisi, A. S., & Kirchner, W. (1980). A multivariate, multinational comparison of managerial attitudes. Paper presented at the Fortieth Annual Meeting of the Academy of Management, Detroit, August, 1980.

Griffiths, R. (1970). *The abilities of young children. A comprehensive system of mental measurement for the first 8 years of life.* London: Young & Son.

Gudykunst, W. B., & Hammer, M. R. (1983). Basic training design: Approaches to intercultural training. In D. Landis & R. W. Brislin (Eds.), *Handbook of intercultural training* (Vol. 1, pp. 118–154). New York: Pergamon.

Gudykunst, W. B., & Ting-Toomey, S. (1988). *Culture and interpersonal communication.* Newbury Park, CA: Sage.

Guilford, J. P. (1967). *The nature of human intelligence.* New York: McGraw-Hill.

Gumperz, J. J. (1982). *Discourse strategies.* Cambridge: Cambridge University Press.

Gussler, J. D. (1973). Social change, ecology, and spirit possession among the South African Nguni. In E. Bourguignon (Ed.), *Religion, altered states of consciousness and social change* (pp. 88–126). Columbus, OH: Ohio State University Press.

Guthrie, G. M. (1966). Cultural preparation for the Philippines. In R. B. Textor (Ed.), *Cultural frontiers of the Peace Corps.* Cambridge, MA: MIT Press.

Guthrie, G. M., & Guthrie, H. A. (1982). Cultural influence and reinforcement strategies. *Behavior Therapy, 13,* 624–637.

Guthrie, G. M., & Lonner, W. J. (1986). Assessment of personality and psychopathology. In W. J. Lonner & J. W. Berry (Eds.), *Field methods in cross-cultural research* (pp. 231–264). Beverly Hills, CA: Sage.

Gynther, M. D. (1978). Review of the California Psychological Inventory. In O. K. Buros (Ed.), *The eighth mental measurement yearbook* (Vol. 1, pp. 733–736). Highland Park, NJ: Gryphon Press.

Hagen, M. A., & Jones, R. K. (1978). Cultural effects on pictorial perception: How many words is one picture really worth. In R. D. Walk & H. L. Pick (Eds.), *Perception and experience* (pp. 171–209). New York: Plenum.

Haire, M., Ghiselli, E. E., & Porter, L. W. (1966). *Managerial thinking: An international study.* New York: Wiley.

Hall, E. T. (1959). *The silent language.* New York: Doubleday.

Hall, E. T. (1960). The silent language in overseas business. *Harvard Business Review, 38,* 87–96.

Hall, E. T. (1966). *The hidden dimension.* New York: Doubleday.

Hall, E. T. (1976). *Beyond culture.* Garden City, NY: Anchor Press.

Hallowell, A. I. (1946). Some psychological characteristics of Northeastern Indians. In F. Johnson (Ed.), *Man in Northeastern North America* (pp. 195–225). Peabody Foundation for Archaeology, *3.*

Hallowell, A. I. (1955a). The recapitulation theory and culture. In A. I. Hallowell, *Culture and experience* (pp. 14–31). Philadelphia: University of Pennsylvania Press.

Hallowell, A. I. (1955b). Sociopsychological aspects of acculturation. In A. I. Hallowell, *Culture and experience* (pp. 310–332). Philadelphia: University of Pennsylvania Press.

Hallpike, C. P. (1986). *The principles of social evolution.* Oxford: Clarendon Press.

Hamilton, D. L. (Ed.). (1981). *Cognitive processes in stereotyping and intergroup behavior.* Hillsdale, NJ: Erlbaum.

Hamilton, W. D. (1964). The genetical evolution of social behavior, I, II. *Journal of Theoretical Biology*, 7, 1–52.

Hammer, M. R. (1989). Intercultural communication competence. In M. K. Asante & W. B. Gudykunst (Eds.), *Handbook of international and intercultural communication* (pp. 247–260). Newbury Park, CA: Sage.

Haritos-Fatouros, M., & Child, I. L. (1977). Transcultural similarity in personal significance of esthetic interests. *Journal of Cross-Cultural Psychology*, 8, 285–298.

Harkness, S., Wyon, J., & Super, C. (1988). The relevance of behavioural sciences to disease prevention and control in developing countries. In P. Dasen, J. W. Berry & N. Sartorius (Eds.), *Cross-cultural psychology and health: Towards applications* (pp. 239–255). London: Sage.

Harrison, D. E. (1975). Race track shift: A cross-cultural study. *South African Journal of Psychology*, 5, 10–15.

Hawes, F., & Kealey, D. (1980). *Canadians in development*. Ottawa: Canadian International Development Agency.

Hays, W. L. (1988). *Statistics* (4th ed.). New York: Holt, Rinehart and Winston.

Hebb, D. O. (1949). *The organization of behavior*. New York: Wiley.

Hector, H. (1958). A new pattern completion test. *Journal of the National Institute for Personnel Research*, 7, 132–134.

Heelas, P. (1981). Introduction: Indigenous psychologies. In P. Heelas & A. Lock (Eds.), *Indigenous psychologies: The anthropology of the self*. London: Academic Press.

Heelas, P., & Lock, A. (Eds.). (1981). *Indigenous psychologies: The anthropology of the self*. London: Academic Press.

Heider, F. (1958). *The psychology of interpersonal relations*. New York: Wiley.

Heller, F. (1985). Some theoretical and practical problems in multinational and cross-cultural research on organizations. In P. Joynt & M. Warner (Eds.), *Managing in different countries* (pp. 11–22). Oslo: Universitetsforlaget.

Heller, F. (1986). Introduction and overview. In F. Heller (Ed.), *The use and abuse of social science* (pp. 1–18). London: Sage.

Heller, F. A., & Wilpert, B. (1981). *Competence and power in managerial decision-making*. Chichester: Wiley.

Hendrix, L. (1985). Economy and child training reexamined. *Ethos*, 13, 246–261.

Heron, A., & Kroeger, E. (1981). Introduction to developmental psychology. In H. C. Triandis & A. Heron (Eds.), *Handbook of cross-cultural psychology: Developmental psychology* (Vol. 4, pp. 1–15). Boston: Allyn & Bacon.

Herskovits, M. J. (1938). *Acculturation: The study of culture contact*. New York: Augustin.

Herskovits, M. J. (1948). *Man and his works: The science of cultural anthropology*. New York: Knopf.

Hewstone, M. (1989). Intergroup attribution: Some implications for the study of ethnic prejudice. In J. P. Van Oudenhoven & T. M. Willemsen (Eds.), *Ethnic minorities: Social psychological perspectives* (pp. 25–42). Amsterdam: Swets & Zeitlinger.

Hewstone, M., Bond, M. H., & Wan, K. C. (1983). Social facts and social attributions: The explanation of intergroup differences in Hong Kong. *Social Cognition*, 2, 142–157.

Hewstone, M., & Jaspars, J. M. F. (1982). Intergroup relations and attribution processes. In H. Tajfel (Ed.), *Social identity and intergroup behavior* (pp. 99–133). Cambridge: Cambridge University Press.

Hewstone, M., & Ward, C. (1985). Ethnocentrism and causal attribution in Southeast Asia. *Journal of Personality and Social Psychology*, 48, 614–623.

Heymans, G. (1932). *Inleiding tot de speciale psychologie* [*Introduction to special psychology*] (Vols. 1–2, 2nd ed.). Haarlem: Erven Bohn.

Hinde, R. A. (1982). *Ethology: Its nature and relations with other sciences*. Oxford: Oxford University Press.

Hofstede, G. (1979). Value systems in forty countries: Interpretation, validation and consequences for theory. In L. Eckensberger, W. Lonner, & Y. H. Poortinga (Eds.), *Cross-cultural contributions to psychology* (pp. 389–407). Lisse: Swets and Zeitlinger

Hofstede, G. (1980). *Culture's consequences: International differences in work-related values*. London: Sage.

Hofstede, G. (1983a). The cultural relativity of organizational practices and theories. *Journal of International Business Studies*, 14, 75–89.

Hofstede, G. (1983b). Dimensions of national cultures in fifty countries and three regions. In J. B. Deregowski, S. Dziurawiec, & R. C. Annis (Eds.), *Expiscations in cross-cultural psychology* (pp. 335–355). Lisse: Swets & Zeitlinger.

Hofstede, G. (1989). Cultural predictors of national negotiations styles. In F. Mautner-Markhof (Ed.), *Processes of international negotiations* (pp. 193–202). Boulder, CO: Westview Press.

Hofstede, G., & Bond, M. H. (1984). Hofstede's culture dimensions: An independent validation using Rokeach's value survey. *Journal of Cross-Cultural Psychology*, 15, 417–433.

Hofstede, G., Neuijen, B., Ohayv, D. D., & Sanders, G. (1990). Measuring organizational cultures: A qualitative/quantitative study across twenty cases. *Administrative Sciences Quarterly*, 35, 286–316.

Hofstede, G., & Spangenberg, J. (1987). Measuring individualism and collectivism at occupational and organizational levels. In C. Kagitcibasi (Ed.), *Growth and progress in cross-cultural psychology*. Lisse: Swets & Zeitlinger.

Holland, D., & Quinn, N. (Eds.). (1987). *Cultural models in language and thought*. Cambridge: Cambridge University Press.

Holland, P. W., & Rubin, R. B. (1983). On Lord's paradox. In H. Wainer & S. Messick (Eds.), *Principles of psychological measurement: A festschrift for Frederic M. Lord* (pp. 3–25). Hillsdale, NJ: Erlbaum.

Holtzman, W., Evans, R., Kennedy, S., & Iscoe, I. (1987). Psychology and health: Contributions of psychology to the improvement of health and health care. *International Journal of Psychology*, 22, 221–267.

Honigmann, J. J. (1967). *Personality in culture*. New York: Harper & Row.

Hoopes, D. S., & Ventura, P. (1979). *Intercultural sourcebook: Cross-cultural training methodologies*. Chicago: Intercultural Press.

Hopkins, B. (1977). Considerations of comparability of measures in cross-cultural studies of early infancy from a study on the development of black and white infants in Britain. In Y. H. Poortinga (Ed.), *Basic problems in cross-cultural psychology* (pp. 36–46). Lisse: Swets and Zeitlinger.

Hopper, P. J., & Thompson, S. A. (1984). The discourse basis for lexical categories in universal grammar. *Language*, 60, 703–752.

Horn, J. M., Loehlin, J. C., & Willerman, L. (1979). Intellectual resemblance among adoptive and biological relatives: The Texas adoption project. *Behavior Genetics*, 9, 177–207.

Howard, A., & Scott, R. A. (1981). The study of minority groups in complex societies. In R. H. Munroe, R. L. Munroe, & B. B. Whiting (Eds.), *Handbook of cross-cultural human development* (pp. 113–151). New York: Garland.

Hsu, F. L. K. (Ed.). (1961). *Psychological anthropology* (1st ed.). Homewood, IL: Dorsey/ (1972). (2nd ed.). Cambridge, MA: Schenkman.

Huang, L., & Harris, M. (1973). Conformity in Chinese and Americans: A field experiment. *Journal of Cross-Cultural Psychology*, 4, 427–434.

Hudson, W. (1960). Pictorial depth perception in sub-cultural groups in Africa. *Journal of Social Psychology*, 52, 183–208.

Hudson, W. (1967). The study of the problem of pictorial perception among unacculturated groups. *International Journal of Psychology*, 2, 89–107.

Hui, H. (1988). Measurement of individualism – collectivism. *Journal of Research in Personality*, 22, 17–36.

Hui, C. H., & Triandis, H. C. (1985). Measurement in cross-cultural psychology: A review and comparison of strategies. *Journal of Cross-Cultural Psychology*, 16, 131–152.

Hunt, E. B., & Banerjee, M. (1988). The Whorfian hypothesis revisited: A cognitive science view of linguistic and cultural effects on thought. In J. W. Berry, S. H. Irvine, & E. B. Hunt (Eds.), *Indigenous cognition* (pp. 57–84). Dordrecht: Nijhoff.

IDE (Industrial Democracy in Europe International Research Group). (1981). *Industrial democracy in Europe.* Oxford: Clarendon Press.

Ilola, L. M. (1990). Culture and health. In R. Brislin (Ed.), *Applied cross-cultural psychology* (pp. 278–301). Newbury Park, CA: Sage.

Inkeles, A. (1960). Industrial man: The relation of status to experience, perception and value. *The American Journal of Sociology, 66,* 1–31.

Inkeles, A., & Smith, D. (1974). *Becoming modern.* Cambridge, MA: Harvard University Press.

Irvine, S. H. (1979). The place of factor analysis in cross-cultural methodology, and its contribution to cognitive theory. In L. Eckensberger, W. Lonner, & Y. H. Poortinga (Eds.), *Cross-cultural contributions to psychology* (pp. 300–341). Lisse: Swets & Zeitlinger.

Irvine, S. H. (1983). Testing in Africa and America: The search for routes. In S. H. Irvine & J. W. Berry (Eds.), *Human assessment and cultural factors* (pp. 45–58). New York: Plenum.

Irvine, S. H., & Berry, J. W. (Eds.). (1983). *Human assessment and cultural factors.* New York: Plenum.

Irvine, S. H., & Berry, J. W. (Eds.). (1988). *Human abilities in cultural context.* New York: Cambridge University Press.

Irvine, S. H., & Carroll, W. K. (1980). Testing and assessment across cultures. In H. C. Triandis & J. W. Berry (Eds.), *Handbook of cross-cultural psychology* (Vol. 2, pp. 181–244). Boston: Allyn & Bacon.

Isajiw, V. (1974). Definitions of ethnicity. *Ethnicity, 1,* 111–124.

Izard, C. E. (1971). *The face of emotion.* New York: Appleton-Century-Crofts.

Jahoda, G. (1954). A note on Ashanti names and their relationship to personality. *British Journal of Psychology, 45,* 192–195.

Jahoda, G. (1971). Retinal pigmentation, illusion susceptibility and space perception. *International Journal of Psychology, 6,* 199–208.

Jahoda, G. (1973). Psychology and the developing countries: Do they need each other? *International Social Science Journal, 25,* 461–474.

Jahoda, G. (1974). Applying cross-cultural psychology to the Third World. In J. W. Berry & W. J. Lonner (Eds.), *Applied cross-cultural psychology* (pp. 3–7). Lisse: Swets & Zeitlinger.

Jahoda, G. (1975). Retinal pigmentation and space perception: A failure to replicate. *International Journal of Psychology, 97,* 133–134.

Jahoda, G. (1977). In pursuit of the emic-etic distinction: Can we ever capture it? In Y. H. Poortinga (Ed.), *Basic problems in cross-cultural pychology* (pp. 55–63). Lisse: Swets and Zeitlinger.

Jahoda, G. (1978). Cross-cultural study of factors influencing orientation errors in the reproduction of Kohs-type figures. *British Journal of Psychology, 69,* 45–57.

Jahoda, G. (1979). A cross-cultural perspective on experimental social psychology. *Personality and Social Psychology Bulletin, 5,* 142–148.

Jahoda, G. (1980). Theoretical and systematic approaches in cross-cultural psychology. In H. C. Triandis & W. W. Lambert (Eds.), *Handbook of cross-cultural psychology, Vol. I, Perspectives* (pp. 69–141). Boston: Allyn & Bacon.

Jahoda, G. (1981). Pictorial perception and the problem of universals. In B. Lloyd & J. Gay (Eds.), *Universals of human thought* (pp. 25–45). Cambridge: Cambridge University Press.

Jahoda, G. (1982). *Psychology and anthropology: A psychological perspective.* London: Academic.

Jahoda, G. (1983). The cross-cultural emperor's conceptual clothes: The emic-etic issue revisited. In J. B. Deregowski, S. Dziurawiec, & R. C. Annis (Eds.), *Expiscations in cross-cultural psychology* (pp. 19–38). Lisse: Swets and Zeitlinger.

Jahoda, G. (1984). Do we need a concept of culture? *Journal of Cross-Cultural Psychology*, *15*, 139–151.

Jahoda, G. (1986a). A cross-cultural perspective on developmental psychology. *International Journal of Behavioral Development*, *9*, 417–437.

Jahoda, G. (1986b). Nature, culture and social psychology. *European Journal of Social Psychology*, *16*, 17–30.

Jahoda, G. (1990a). Our forgotten ancestors. In J. J. Berman (Ed.), *Cross-cultural perspectives: Nebraska symposium on motivation*, *37* (pp. 1–40). Lincoln: University of Nebraska Press.

Jahoda, G. (1990b). Variables, systems, and the problem of explanation. In F. J. R. Van de Vijver & G. J. M. Hutschemaekers (Eds.), *The investigation of culture* (pp. 115–130). Tilburg: Tilburg University Press.

Jahoda, G., & McGurk, H. (1974a). Development of pictorial depth perception: Cross-cultural replication. *Child Development*, *45*, 1042–1047.

Jahoda, G., & McGurk, H. (1974b). Pictorial depth perception in Scottish and Ghanaian children: A critique of some findings with Hudson's test. *International Journal of Psychology*, *9*, 255–267.

Jahoda, G., & Stacey, B. (1970). Susceptibility to geometrical illusions according to culture and professional training. *Perception and Psychophysics*, *7*, 179–184.

Janis, I. L., & Mann, L. (1977). *Decision making: A psychological analysis of conflict, choice and commitment*. London: Free Press.

Jaspars, J., & Hewstone, M. (1982). Cross-cultural interaction, social attribution and intergroup relations. In S. Bochner (Ed.), *Cultures in contact: Studies in cross-cultural interaction* (pp. 127–156). Oxford: Pergamon Press.

Jayasuriya, L. (1984). *Whither multiculturalism?* 10th Annual Lalor Address. Canberra: Human Rights Commission.

Jensen, A. R. (1969). How much can we boost IQ and scholastic achievement? *Harvard Educational Review*, *39*, 1–123.

Jensen, A. R. (1973). *Educability and group differences*. London: Methuen.

Jensen, A. R. (1980). *Bias in mental testing*. New York: Free Press.

Jensen, A. R. (1985). The nature of black-white differences on various psychometric tests: Spearman's hypothesis. *Behavioral and Brain Sciences*, *8*, 193–263.

Jilek, W. (1971). From crazy witch doctor to auxiliary psychotherapist: The changing image of the medicine man. *Psychiatria Clinica*, *4*, 200–220.

Jilek, W. (1988). *Indian healing: Shamanic ceremonialism in the Pacific Northwest*. Vancouver, BC: Hancock House.

Joe, R. C. (1991). *Effecten van taaltonaliteit op het cognitief functioneren: Een cross-cultureel onderzoek*. [Effects of tonality in language on cognitive functioning]. Ph.D Thesis Tilburg: Tilburg University.

Johnston, E. F., & Lampl, M. (1984). Anthropometric assessment. In J. Brozek & B. Schürch (Eds.), *Malnutrition and behavior: Critical assessment of key issues* (pp. 51–70). Lausanne: Nestlé Foundation.

Jones, R., & Jones, J. M. (1988). Assessment and special education of minority and immigrant children in the United States. In J. W. Berry & R. C. Annis (Eds.), *Ethnic psychology* (pp. 219–233). Lisse: Swets and Zeitlinger.

Jöreskog, K. G., & Sörbom, D. (1984). *LISREL VI. User's guide*. Chicago: National Educational Research.

Kagitcibasi, C. (1984). Socialization in a traditional society: A challenge to psychology. *International Journal of Psychology*, *19*, 145–157.

Kagitcibasi, C. (1985). Culture of separateness – Culture of relatedness. *1984: Vision and Reality, Papers in Comparative Studies*, *4*, 91–99.

Kagitcibasi, C. (1987). Individual and group loyalities: Are they compatible? In C. Kagitcibasi (Ed.), *Growth and progress in cross-cultural psychology*. Lisse: Swets & Zeitlinger.

Kagitcibasi, C., & Berry, J. W. (1989). Cross-cultural psychology: Current research and trends. *Annual Review of Psychology*, *40*, 493–531.

Kakar, S. (1971). Authority patterns and subordinate behaviour in Indian organizations. *Administrative Science Quarterly*, *16*, 298–307.

Kakar, S. (1982). *Shamans, mystics and doctors*. New Delhi: Oxford University Press.

Kakar, S. (1985). Psychoanalysis and non-Western cultures. *International Review of Psychoanalysis*, *12*, 441–448.

Kalin, R., & Tilby, P. (1978). Development and validation of a sex-role ideology scale. *Psychological Reports*, *42*, 731–738.

Kalmus, H. (1969). Ethnic differences in sensory perception. *Journal of Biosocial Science, Supplement 1*, 81–90.

Kaplan, B. (Ed.). (1961). *Studying personality cross-culturally*. Evanston, IL: Row Peterson.

Kardiner, A., & Linton, R. (1945). *The individual and his society*. New York: Columbia University Press.

Kasamatsu, A., & Hirai, T. (1966). An electroencephalographic study of the Zen meditation. *Folia Psychiatrica et Neurologica Japonica*, *20*, 315–336.

Kashima, Y. (1987). Conceptions of person: Implications in individualism-collectivism research. In Kagitcibasi, C. (Ed.), *Growth and progress in cross-cultural psychology*. Lisse: Swets & Zeitlinger.

Kashima, Y., Siegel, M., Tanaka, K., & Isaka, H. (1988). Universalism in lay conceptions of distributive justice. *International Journal of Psychology*, *23*, 51–64.

Kashima, Y., & Triandis, H. C. (1986). The self-serving bias in attributions as a coping strategy. *Journal of Cross-Cultural Psychology*, *17*, 83–97.

Kaufmann, J. (1989). Towards an integral analysis of international negotiations. In F. Mautner-Markoff (Ed.), *Processes of international negotiations* (pp. 7–13). Boulder, CO: Westview Press.

Kay, P., & McDaniel, C. K. (1978). The linguistic significance of the meanings of basic color terms. *Language*, *54*, 610–646.

Kealey, D. J. (1989). A study of cross-cultural effectiveness: Theoretical issues, practical applications. *International Journal of Intercultural Relations*, *13*, 387–428.

Kealey, D. J., & Ruben, B. D. (1983). Cross-cultural personnel selection criteria, issues and methods. In D. Landis & R. W. Brislin (Eds.), *Handbook of intercultural training* (Vol. 1, pp. 155–175). New York: Pergamon.

Keating, C. F., Mazur, A., Segall, M., Cysneiros, P. G., Divale, W. T., Kilbride, J. E., Komin, S., Leahy, P., Thurman, B., & Wirsing, R. (1981). Culture and the perception of social dominance from facial expression. *Journal of Personality and Social Psychology*, *40*, 615–626.

Keefer, C. H., Dixon, S., Tronik E., & Brazelton, T. B. (1978). Gusii infants' neuromotor behavior. Paper presented at the International Conference on Infant Studies, Providence, R. I.

Keller, H., Schölmerich, A., & Eibl-Eibesfeldt, I. (1988). Communication patterns in adult-infant interactions in western and non-western cultures. *Journal of Cross-Cultural Psychology*, *19*, 427–445.

Keller, W., & Fillmore, C. M. (1983). Prevalence of protein-energy malnutrition. *World Health Statistics Quarterly*, *36*, 129–167.

Kelley, H. H. (1973). The process of causal attribution. *American Psychologist*, *28*, 107–128.

Kendon, A. (1984). Did gestures have the happiness to escape the curse at the confusion of Babel? In A. Wolfgang (Ed.), *Non-verbal behavior: Perspectives, applications, intercultural insights* (pp. 75–114). Lewiston: Hogrefe.

Kermoian, R., & Leiderman, P. H. (1986). Infant attachment to mother and child caretaker in an East African community. *International Journal of Behavioural Development*, *9*, 455–470.

Kettlewell, H. B. D. (1959). Darwin's missing evidence. *Scientific American*, *200*, 3, 48–53.

Khandwalla, P. N. (1988). Organizational effectiveness. In J. Pandey (Ed.), *Psychology in India: The state of the art* (Vol. 3, pp. 97–215). New Delhi: Sage.

Kilbride, P. L. (1980). Sensorimotor behavior of Baganda and Samia infants: A controlled comparison. *Journal of Cross-Cultural Psychology, 11*, 131–152.

Kim, U. (1990). Indigenous psychology: Science and applications. In R. Brislin (Ed.), *Applied cross-cultural psychology* (pp. 142–160). Newbury Park, CA: Sage.

Kim, Y. Y. (1988). *Communication and cross-cultural adaptation: An integrative theory.* Clevedon: Multilingual Matters.

Kim, Y. Y., & Gudykunst, W. B. (Eds.). (1987). *Cross-cultural adaptation: Current approaches.* Newbury Park, CA: Sage.

Kimmel, H. D., Van Olst, E. H., & Orlebeke, J. F. (Eds.). (1979). *The orienting reflex in humans.* New York: Wiley.

Kish, L. (1965). *Survey sampling.* New York: Wiley.

Klineberg, O. (1940). *Social psychology.* New York: Henry Holt.

Klineberg, O. (1980). Historical perspectives: Cross-cultural psychology before 1960. In H. C. Triandis & W. W. Lambert (Eds.). *Handbook of cross-cultural psychology, Vol. 1, Perspectives* (pp. 31–68). Boston: Allyn & Bacon.

Klineberg, O., & Hull, W. F. (1979). *At a foreign university: An international study of adaptation and coping.* New York: Praeger.

Kluckhohn, C. (1951). Values and value orientations in the theory of action. In T. Parsons & E. Shils (Eds.), *Toward a general theory of action.* Cambridge, MA: Harvard University Press.

Kluckhohn, C. (1957). *Mirror for man.* New York: Premier Books.

Kluckhohn, C., & Murray, H. A. (1948). *Personality in nature, society and culture.* New York: Knopf.

Kluckhohn, F., & Strodtbeck, F. (1961). *Variations in value orientations.* Evanston, IL: Row, Peterson.

Knapen, M. T., (1962). *L'enfant Mukongo. Orientation de base du système éducatif et développement de la personnalité.* Louvain: Ed Nauwelaerts.

Kohlberg, L. (1981). From *is* to *ought*: How to commit the naturalistic fallacy and get away with it in the study of moral development. In L. Kohlberg (Ed.), *Essays on moral development: The philosophy of moral development* (Vol. 1, pp. 101–189). San Francisco: Harper and Row.

Kohlberg, L. (1984). *Essays on moral development: The psychology of moral development* (Vol. 2). San Francisco: Harper and Row.

Kohlberg, L., Levine, C., & Hewer, A. (1983). Moral stages: A current formulation, and a response to critics. In J. A. Meacham (Ed.), *Contributions to human development* (Vol. 10). New York: Karger.

Konner, M. (1981). Evolution of human behavior development. In R. H. Munroe, R. L. Munroe, & B. B. Whiting (Eds.), *Handbook of cross-cultural human development* (pp. 3–51). New York: Garland.

Konner, M. (1988). The aggressors. *New York Times Magazine*, August 14, 33–34.

Kopp, C. B., Khoka, E., & Sigman, M. A. (1977). A comparison of sensorimotor development among infants in India and the United States. *Journal of Cross-Cultural Psychology, 8*, 435–452.

Kopp, C. B., & Sigman, M. (1972). UCLA revision of the administration manual: The stages of sensori-motor intelligence in the child from birth to two years by I. Casati and I. Lézine. Mimeo, UCLA.

Korolenko, C. P. (1988). The peculiarities of alcoholism in the North. In H. Linderholm (Ed.), *Circumpolar Health 87* (pp. 36–37). Oulu: Nordic Council for Arctic Medical Research.

Kraemer, A. (1974). *Workshop in intercultural communication.* Hum RRO Report.

Krech, D., Crutchfield, R., & Ballachey, E. (1962). *Individual in society.* New York: McGraw-Hill.

Kroeber, A. L. (1917). The superorganic. *American Anthropologist, 19*, 163–213.

Kroeber, A. L. (1939). *Cultural and natural areas of North America*. Berkeley: University of California Press.

Kroeber, A. L. (1949). The concept of culture in science. In A. L. Kroeber (Ed.), *The nature of culture* (pp. 118–135). Chicago: Chicago University Press.

Kroeber, A. L., & Kluckhohn, C. (1952). *Culture: A critical review of concepts and definitions*. Cambridge, MA: Peabody Museum, Vol. 47, No. 1.

Kulkarni, S. G., & Puhan, B. N. (1988). Psychological assessment: Its present and future trends. In J. Pandey (Ed.), *Psychology in India: The state of the art* (Vol. 1, pp. 19–91). New Delhi: Sage.

Kumagai, H. A., & Kumagai, A. K. (1986). The hidden "I" in Amae: "Passive love" and Japanese social construction. *Ethos*, *14*, 305–319.

Kuwano, S., Namba, S., & Schick, A. (1986). A cross-cultural study on noise problems. In A. Schick, H. Höge, & G. Lazarus-Mainka (Eds.), *Contributions to psychological acoustics* (pp. 370–395). Oldenburg: Universität Oldenburg.

Laaksonen, O. (1988). *Management in China during and after Mao in enterprise, government, and party*. Berlin: Walter de Gruyter.

Laboratory of Comparative Human Cognition. (1982). Culture and intelligence. In R. Sternberg (Ed.), *Handbook of human intelligence* (pp. 642–719). New York: Cambridge University Press.

Laboratory of Comparative Human Cognition. (1983). Culture and cognitive development. In P. H. Mussen & W. Kessen (Eds.), *Handbook of child psychology* (Vol. 1, pp. 295–356). New York: Wiley.

Laferrière, M. (1984). Languages, ideologies and multicultural education. In R. Samuda, J. W. Berry, & M. Laferrière (Eds.), *Multiculturalism in Canada: Social and educational perspectives* (pp. 171–183). Toronto: Allyn & Bacon.

Lagmay, A. (1984). Western psychology in the Philippines: Impact and response. *International Journal of Psychology*, *19*, 31–44.

Lambert, W. E. (1967). A social psychology of bilingualism. *Journal of Social Issues*, *23*, 91–109.

Lambert, W. E. (1977). The effects of bilingualism on the individual: cognitive and sociocultural consequences. In P. A. Hornby (Ed.), *Bilingualism: Psychological, social and educational implications*. New York: Academic Press.

Lambert, W. E. (1980). The social psychology of language: A perspective for the 1980's. In H. Giles, W. Robinson, & P. Smith (Eds.), *Language: social psychological perspectives* (pp. 415–424). Oxford: Pergamon.

Lambert, W. E., & Anisfeld, E. (1969). A note on the relationship of bilingualism and intelligence. *Canadian Journal of Behavioural Science*, *1*, 123–128.

Lambert, W. E., Hamers, J., & Frasure-Smith, N. (1979). *Child rearing values*. New York: Praeger.

Lambert, W. E., & Tucker, R. (1972). *Bilingual education of children: The St. Lambert study*. Rowley, MA: Newburg House.

Lammers, C. J., & Hickson, D. J. (Eds.). (1979). *Organizations alike and unlike: International and interinstitutional studies in the sociology of organizations*. London: Routledge and Kegan Paul.

Landis, D., & Brislin, R. W. (Eds.). (1983). *Handbook of intercultural training* (Vols. 1–3). New York: Pergamon.

Lantz, D., & Stefflre, V. (1964). Language and cognition revisited. *Journal of Abnormal and Social Psychology*, *69*, 472–481.

L'Armand, K., Pepitone, A., & Shanmugan, T. E. (1981). Attitudes toward rape: A comparison of the role of chastity in India and the United States. *Journal of Cross-Cultural Psychology*, *12*, 284–303.

Laurent, A. (1983). The cultural diversity of Western conceptions of management. *International Studies of Man and Organization*, *13*, 75–96.

Lawlor, M. (1955). Cultural influences on preference for designs. *Journal of Abnormal and Social Psychology*, *51*, 690–692.

Lazarus, R. S., & Folkman, S. (1984). *Stress, appraisal and coping*. New York: Springer.

Lefcourt, H. M. (1976). *Locus of control: Current trends in theory and research*. Hillsdale, NJ: Erlbaum.

Lefcourt, H. M. (Ed.). (1981). *Research with the locus of control construct* (Vol. 1). New York: Academic Press.

Leff, J. (1977). International variations in the diagnosis of psychiatric illness. *British Journal of Psychiatry*, *131*, 329–338.

Leff, J. (1981). *Psychiatry around the globe: A transcultural view*. New York: Dekker.

Leibowitz, H. W., Brislin, R., Perlmutter, L., & Hennessey, R. (1969). Ponzo perspective illusion as a manifestation of space perception. *Science*, *166*, 1174–1176.

Lenneberg, E. H. (1953). Cognition in linguistics. *Language*, *29*, 463–471.

Lenneberg, E. H. (1967). *Biological foundations of language*. New York: Wiley.

Lens, W., & Hermans, I. (1988). *Organizational climate and the individual motivational orientations of managers: A cross-national study*. Report, Louvain: University of Louvain.

Leung, K. (1987). Some determinants of reactions to procedural models for conflict resolution. *Journal of Personality and Social Psychology*, *53*, 898–908.

Leung, K. (1989). Cross-cultural differences: Individual-level vs. culture-level analysis. *International Journal of Psychology*, *24*, 703–719.

Leung, K., & Bond, M. H., (1989). On the empirical identification of dimensions for cross-cultural comparison. *Journal of Cross-Cultural Psychology*, *20*, 133–151.

Lévi-Strauss, C. (1962). *La pensée sauvage*. Paris: Plon. (Trans. 1966, *The savage mind*, London: Weidenfeld & Nicholson).

Levin, J., & Karni, E. S. (1970). Demonstration of cross-cultural invariance of the California Psychological Inventory in America and Israel by the Guttman-Lingoes Smallest Space Analysis. *Journal of Cross-Cultural Psychology*, *1*, 253–260.

LeVine, R. A. (1970). Cross-cultural study in child psychology. In P. Mussen (Ed.), *Carmichael's manual of child psychology* (3rd ed) (Vol. 2 pp. 559–612). New York: Wiley.

LeVine, R. A. (1977). Child rearing as cultural adaptation. In H. Leiderman, S. Tulkin, & A. Rosenfeld (Eds.), *Culture and infancy*. New York: Academic Press.

LeVine, R. A. (1982). *Culture, behaviour and personality* (2nd ed.) Chicago: Aldine.

LeVine, R. A., & Campbell, D. T. (1972). *Ethnocentrism*. New York: Wiley.

Levitsky, D. A., & Strupp, N. J. (1984). Functional isolation in rats. In J. Brozek & B. Schürch (Eds.), *Malnutrition and behavior: Critical assessment of key issues* (pp. 411–420). Lausanne: Nestlé Foundation.

Levy-Bruhl, L. (1910). *Les fonctions mentales dans les sociétés inférieures*. Paris: Alcan. (Trans: 1928, *How natives think*. London: Allen & Unwin.)

Levy-Bruhl, L. (1922). *Mentalité primitive*. Paris: Alcan. (Trans. 1923, *Primitive Mentality*, London: Allen & Unwin).

Lewin, K. (1936). *Principles of topological psychology*. New York: McGraw-Hill.

Lewis, J., & Mercer, J. (1978). The system of multicultural pluralistic assessment: SOMPA. In W. Coulter & H. Morrow (Eds.), *Adaptive behaviour: Concepts and measurement*. New York: Grune and Stratton.

Lewontin, R. C. (1972). The apportionment of human diversity. *Evolutionary Biology*, *6*, 381–398.

Lewontin, R. C. (1978). Adaptation. *Scientific American*, *239*, 3, 156–169.

Lewontin, R. C., Rose, S., & Kamin, L. J. (1984). *Not in our genes: Biology, ideology and human nature*. New York: Pantheon.

Lieban, R. (1973). Medical anthropology. In J. J. Honigmann (Ed.), *Handbook of social and cultural anthropology*. Chicago: Rand-McNally.

Likert, R. (1967). *The human organization: Its management and values*. New York: McGraw-Hill.

Lindzey, G. (1961). *Projective techniques and cross-cultural research*. New York: Appleton-Century-Crofts.

Linton, R. (1936). *The study of man*. New York: Appleton-Century-Crofts.

Linton, R. (1940). *Acculturation in seven American Indian tribes*. New York: Appleton-Century-Crofts.

Liu, L. A. (1985). Reasoning counterfactually in Chinese: Are there any obstacles? *Cognition, 21*, 239–270.

Lloyd, B. (1977). Culture and colour coding. In G. Vessey (Ed.), *Communication and understanding* (pp. 140–160). Sussex: Harvester Press.

Lockett, M. (1983). Organizational democracy and politics in China. In C. Crouch & F. Heller (Eds.), *Organizational democracy and political processes* (pp. 591–635). Chichester: Wiley.

Loehlin, J. C., Willerman, L., & Horn, J. M. (1985). Personality resemblances in adoptive families when children are late adolescent or adult. *Journal of Personality and Social Psychology, 48*, 376–392.

Lomax, A., & Berkowitz, N. (1972). The evolutionary taxonomy of culture. *Science, 177*, 228–239.

Lombard, A. D. (1981). *Success begins at home: Educational foundations for preschoolers*. Toronto: Lexington Books.

Longabaugh, R. (1980). The systematic observation of behavior in naturalistic settings. In H. C. Triandis & J. W. Berry (Eds.), *Handbook of cross-cultural psychology, Vol. 2, Methodology* (pp. 57–126). Boston: Allyn & Bacon.

Lonner, W. J. (1980). The search for psychological universals. In H. C. Triandis & W. W. Lambert (Eds.), *Handbook of cross-cultural psychology. Vol. 1, Perspectives* (pp. 143–204). Boston: Allyn & Bacon.

Lonner, W. J., & Berry, J. W. (Eds.). (1986a). *Field methods in cross-cultural research*. London: Sage.

Lonner, W. J., & Berry, J. W. (1986b). Sampling and surveying. In W. J. Lonner & J. W. Berry (Eds.), *Field methods in cross-cultural research* (pp. 85–110). London: Sage.

Lonner, W. J., & Sharp, D. (1983). Psychological differentiation in a rural Yucatec Mayan village. In S. H. Irvine & J. W. Berry (Eds.), *Human assessment and cultural factors* (pp. 191–209). New York: Plenum.

Lorenz, K. (1966). *On aggression*. London: Methuen.

Lucy, J. A., & Shweder, R. A. (1979). Whorf and his critics: Linguistic and nonlinguistic influences on color memory. *American Anthropologist, 81*, 581–615.

Ludwig, A. M. (1969). Altered states of consciousness. In C. C. Tart (Ed.), *Altered States of Consciousness* (pp. 9–22). New York: Wiley.

Lumsden, C. J., & Wilson, E. O. (1981). *Genes, mind and culture: The coevolutionary process*. Cambridge, MA: Harvard University Press.

Lundström, S. (1986). Opening address to IACCP Conference. In L. Ekstrand (Ed.), *Ethnic minorities and immigrants in a cross-cultural perspective* (pp. 9–13). Amsterdam: Swets and Zeitlinger.

Lutje Spelberg, H. C. (1987). *Grenzen testen [Testing boundaries]*. Groningen: Stichting Kinderstudies.

Lutz, C., & White, G. M. (1986). The anthropology of emotions. *Annual Review of Psychology, 15*, 405–436.

Lynch, J. (1986). *Multicultural education: Principles and practice*. London: Routledge and Kegan Paul.

Lynn, R. (1981). Cross-cultural differences in neuroticism, extraversion, and psychoticism. In R. Lynn (Ed.), *Dimensions of personality* (pp. 263–286). New York: Pergamon.

Ma, H. K. (1988). The Chinese perspective on moral judgement development. *International Journal of Psychology, 23*, 201–227.

Ma, H. K. (1989). Moral orientation and moral judgements in adolescents in Hong Kong, Mainland China, and England. *Journal of Cross-Cultural Psychology, 20*, 152–177.

MacArthur, R. S. (1967). Sex differences in field dependence for the Eskimo: Replication of Berry's findings. *International Journal of Psychology, 2*, 139–140.

Maccoby, E., & Jacklin, C. (1974). *The psychology of sex differences*. Stanford: Stanford University Press.

Maddieson, I. (1978). Universals of tone. In J. H. Greenberg (Ed.), *Universals of human language* (Vol. 2, pp. 335–365). Stanford: Stanford University Press.

Madsen, M. C. (1971). Developmental and cross-cultural differences in the cooperative and competitive behavior of young children. *Journal of Cross-Cultural Psychology, 2*, 365–371.

Magnus, H. (1880) Untersuchungen über den Farbensinn der Naturvölker. *Physiologische Abhandlungen*, Ser. 2, no 7. Jena: Fraher.

Magnusson, D., & Endler, N. S. (Eds.). (1977). *Personality at the crossroads: Current issues in interactional psychology*. Hillsdale, NJ: Erlbaum.

Maistriaux, R. (1955, 1956). La sous-évolution des Noirs d'Afrique. *Revue de Psychologie des Peuples, 10*, 167–191, 397–456; *11*, 81–90, 134–173.

Makinda, S. M. (1982). The African personality: Is it relevant in Africa? *Thought and Practice*, 4, 17–28.

Mala, T. (1985). Alcoholism and mental health treatment in circumpolar areas: traditional and non-traditional approaches. In R. Fortuine (Ed.), *Circumpolar health, 84* (pp. 332–334). Seattle: University of Washington Press.

Malewska-Peyre, H. (1982). *Crise d'identité et déviance chez les jeunes immigrés*. Paris: Ministère de la Justice.

Malewska-Peyre, H. (1988). *Le travail social et les enfants de migrants: Racisme et identité*. Paris: Harmattan.

Malinowski, B. (1944). *A scientific theory of culture*. Chapel Hill, NC: University of North Carolina Press.

Malpass, R. S. (1977). Theory and method in cross-cultural psychology. *American Psychologist, 32*, 1069–1079.

Malpass, R. S., & Poortinga, Y. H. (1986). Strategies for design and analysis. In W. J. Lonner & J. W. Berry (Eds.), *Field methods in cross-cultural research* (pp. 47–84). Beverly Hills, CA: Sage.

Mandell, A. J. (1980). Toward a psychobiology of transcendence: God in the brain. In T. Davidson & R. Davidson (Eds.), *The psychobiology of consciousness* (pp. 379–464). New York: Plenum.

Mann, C. W. (1940). Mental measurements in primitive communities. *Psychological Bulletin, 37*, 366–395.

Mann, J. (1958). Group relations and the marginal man. *Human Relations, 11*, 77–92.

Mann, L. (1980). Cross-cultural studies of small groups. In H. C. Triandis & R. W. Brislin (Eds.), *Handbook of cross-cultural psychology* (Vol. 5, pp. 155–209). Boston: Allyn & Bacon.

Mann, L. (1986). Cross-cultural studies of rules for determining majority and minority decision rights. *Australian Journal of Psychology, 38*, 319–328.

Manning, A. (1979). *An introduction to animal behavior* (3rd ed.). London: Arnold.

Markus, H., & Kitayama, S. (1991). Culture and self. *Psychological Review, 98*, 224–253.

Marsella, A. J. (1980). Depressive experience and disorder across cultures. In H. C. Triandis and J. Draguns (Eds.), *Handbook of cross-cultural psychology, Vol. 6. Psychopathology* (pp. 237–289). Boston: Allyn & Bacon.

Marsella, A. J., & Dash-Scheuer, A. (1988). Coping, culture, and healthy human development: A research and conceptual overview. In P. R. Dasen, J. W. Berry, & N. Sartorius (Eds.), *Health and cross-cultural psychology: Towards applications* (pp. 162–178). Newbury Park, CA: Sage.

Marsella, A. J., De Vos, G., & Hsu, F. L. K. (Eds.) (1985). *Culture and self: Asian and western perspectives*. London: Tavistock.

Marsella, A. J., Tharp, R., & Ciborowski, T. (Eds.). (1979). *Perspectives on cross-cultural psychology*. New York: Academic Press.

Marsella, A. J., & White, G. M. (Eds.) (1982). *Cultural conceptions of mental health and therapy*. Dordrecht: Reidel.

Martyn-Johns, T. A. (1977). Cultural conditioning of views of authority and its effect on the business decision-making process with special reference to Java. In Y. H. Poortinga, (Ed.), *Basic problems in cross-cultural psychology* (pp. 344–352). Lisse: Swets and Zeitlinger.

Maslow, A. H. (1954). *Motivation and personality*. New York: Harper.

Masuda, M., Lin, K., & Tazuma, L. (1979, 1980). Adaptation problems of Vietnamese refugees. *Archives of General Psychiatry, 36*, 955–961; *37*, 447–450.

Matsuda, N. (1985). Strong, quasi- and weak conformity among Japanese in the modified Asch procedure. *Journal of Cross-Cultural Psychology, 16*, 83–97.

Maurice, M. (1979). For a study of the "societal effect": Universality and specificity in organization research. In C. J. Lammers & D. J. Hickson (Eds.), *Organizations alike and unlike* (pp. 42–60). London: Routledge and Kegan Paul.

Maurice, M., Sorge, A., & Warner, M. (1980). Societal differences in organizing manufacturing units: A comparison of France, West Germany and Great Britain. *Organization Studies, 1*, 59–86.

Mazrui, A. (1968). From social Darwinism to current theories of modernization. *World Politics, 21*, 69–83.

Mazur, A. (1985). A biosocial model of status in face-to-face primate groups. *Social Forces, 64*, 377–402.

McClelland, D. C. (1961). *The achieving society*. Princeton, NJ: Van Nostrand.

McCluskey, K., Albas, D., Niemi, R., Cuevas, C., & Ferrer, C. (1975). Cross-cultural differences in the perception of the emotional content of speech. *Developmental Psychology, 11*, 551–555.

McCreary, D. R., & Blanchfield, R. (1986). The art of Japanese negotiation. In N. Schweda-Nicholson (Ed.), *Languages in the international perspective* (pp. 155–177). Norwood, NJ: Ablex.

McDermott, R. P., & Goldman, S. V. (1983). Teaching in multicultural settings. In L. Van den Berg-Eldering, F. J. M. de Rijcke, & L. V. Zuck (Eds.), *Multicultural education: A challenge for teachers* (pp. 145–163). Dordrecht: Floris Publications.

McGinnies, E., & Ward, C. D. (1974). Persuasability as a function of source credibility and locus of control: Five cross-cultural experiments. *Journal of Personality, 42*, 360–371.

McGurk, H., & Jahoda, G. (1975). Pictorial depth perception by children in Scotland and Ghana. *Journal of Cross-Cultural Psychology, 6*, 279–296.

McLaren, D. S. (1984). Forms and degrees of energy-protein deficits. In J. Brozek & B. Schürch (Eds.), *Malnutrition and behavior: Critical assessment of key issues* (pp. 42–50). Lausanne: Nestlé Foundation.

McLeod, K. A. (1984). Multiculturalism and multicultural education: Policy and practice. In R. Samuda, J. W. Berry, & M. Laferrière (Eds.), *Multiculturalism in Canada: Social and educational perspectives* (pp. 30–49). Toronto: Allyn & Bacon.

McLuhan, M. (1971). *The Gutenberg galaxy: The making of typographic man*. London: Routledge and Kegan Paul.

McNeill, N. B. (1972). Colour and colour terminology. *Journal of Linguistics, 7*, 259–268.

McNett, C. (1970). A settlement pattern scale of cultural complexity. In R. Naroll & R. Cohen (Eds.), *A handbook of method in cultural anthropology* (pp. 872–886). New York: Natural History Press.

McShane, D., & Berry, J. W. (1988). Native North Americans: Indian and Inuit abilities. In S. H. Irvine & J. W. Berry (Eds.), *Human abilities in cultural context* (pp. 385–426). New York: Cambridge University Press.

Mead, M. (1928). *Coming of age in Samoa*. New York: Morrow.

Meade, R., & Barnard, W. (1973). Conformity and anticonformity among Americans and Chinese. *Journal of Social Psychology, 89*, 15–25.

Mehryar A. (1984). The role of psychology in national development: Wishful thinking and reality. *International Journal of Psychology*, *19*, 159–167.

Melikan, L. (1984). The transfer of psychological knowledge to the Third World countries and its impact on development. The case of five Arab Gulf oil producing states. *International Journal of Psychology*, *19*, 65–78.

Mezzich, J., & Berganza, C. (Eds.). (1984). *Culture and psychopathology*. New York: Columbia University Press.

Miller, G. A. (1987). Meta-analysis and the culture-free hypothesis. *Organization Studies*, *8*, 309–325.

Miller, J. G. (1984). Culture and the development of everyday social explanation. *Journal of Personality and Social Psychology*, 46, 961–978.

Miller, J. G. (1988). Bridging the content-structure dichotomy: Culture and the self. In M. H. Bond (Ed.), *The cross-cultural challenge to social psychology* (pp. 266–281). Newbury Park, CA: Sage.

Miller, J. G., Bersoff, D. M., & Harwood, R. L. (1990). Perceptions of social responsibilities in India and the United States: Moral imperatives or personal decisions? *Journal of Personality and Social Psychology*, *58*, 33–47.

Miller, L. H. (1984). Malaria. In K. S. Warren & A. Mahmoud (Eds.), *Tropical and geographical medicine*. New York: McGraw-Hill.

Miller, N., & Dollard, J. (1941). *Social learning and imitation*. New York: Harper and Row.

Minturn, L., & Lambert, W. W. (1964). *Mothers of six cultures*. New York: Wiley.

Mischel, W. (1968). *Personality and assessment*. New York: Wiley.

Mischel, W. (1973). Toward a cognitive social learning reconceptualization of personality. *Psychological Review*, *80*, 252–283.

Misumi, J. (1984). Decision-making in Japanese groups and organizations. In B. Wilpert & A. Sorge (Eds.), *International perspectives on organizational democracy* (Vol. 2, pp. 525–539). Chichester: Wiley.

Misumi, J. (1985). *The behavioral science of leadership*. Ann Arbor, MI: University of Michigan Press.

Mitra, S. K. (Ed.). (1972). *A survey of research in psychology*. Bombay: Popular Prakashan.

Miura, M., & Usa, S. (1970). A psychotherapy of neuroses: Morita therapy. *Psychologia*, *13*, 18–34.

Miyawaki, K., Strange, W., Verbrugge, R., Liberman, A. M., Jenkins, J. J., & Fujimura, O. (1975). An effect of linguistic experience: The discrimination of [r] and [l] by native speakers of Japanese and English. *Perception and Psychophysics*, *18*, 331–340.

Modgil, S., Verma, G. K., Mallick, K., & Modgil, C. (Eds.). (1986). *Multicultural education: The interminable debate*. London: Falmer Press.

Moghaddam, F. (1987). Psychology in the three worlds: As reflected in the crisis in social psychology and the move toward indigenous Third World psychology. *American Psychologist*, *42*, 912–920.

Moghaddam, F. (1989). Specialization and despecialization in psychology: Divergent processes in the three worlds. *International Journal of Psychology*, *24*, 103–116.

Moghaddam, F., & Taylor, D. M. (1986). What constitutes an "appropriate psychology" for the developing world? *International Journal of Psychology*, *21*, 253–267.

Montero, M., & Sloan, T. (1988). Understanding behavior in conditions of economic and cultural dependency. *International Journal of Psychology*, *23*, 597–617.

Moore, F. W. (1971). The outline of cultural materials: Contemporary problems. *Behaviour Science Notes*, *6*, 197–189.

Morris, C. R. (1956). *Varieties of human values*. Chicago: University of Chicago Press.

Morris, C. R., Collett, P., Marsh, P., & O'Shaughnessy, M. (1979). *Gestures: Their origin and distribution*. London: Jonathan Cape.

Moscovici, S. (1972). Society and theory in social psychology. In J. Israel & H. Tajfel (Eds.), *The context of social psychology* (pp. 17–68). London: Academic Press.

Moscovici, S. (1982). The phenomenon of social representations. In R. M. Farr & S. Moscovici (Eds.), *Social representations* (pp. 3–70). Cambridge: Cambridge University Press.

Mounod, P. (1979). Développement cognitif: Construction de structures nouvelles ou construction d'organisations internes. *Bulletin de Psychologie, 343,* 107–118.

MOW (Meaning of Working International Research Team). (1987). *The meaning of working.* London: Academic Press.

Mundy-Castle, A. C. (1983). Are western psychological concepts valid in Africa? A Nigerian review. In S. H. Irvine & J. W. Berry (Eds.), *Human assessment and cultural factors* (pp. 81–94). New York: Plenum.

Munro, D. (1986). Work motivation and values: Problems and possibilities in and out of Africa. *Australian Journal of Psychology, 38,* 285–295.

Munroe, R. L. and Munroe, R. H. (1971). Effect of environmental experience on spatial ability in an East African society. *Journal of Social Psychology, 83,* 15–22.

Munroe, R. L., & Munroe, R. H. (1975). *Cross-cultural human development.* Monterey, CA: Brooks/Cole.

Munroe, R. L., & Munroe, R. H. (1986). Field work in cross-cultural psychology. In W. J. Lonner & J. W. Berry (Eds.), *Field methods in cross-cultural research* (pp. 111–136). London: Sage.

Munroe, R. H., Munroe, R. L., & Whiting, B. B. (Eds.). (1981). *Handbook of cross-cultural human development.* New York: Garland.

Murase, T. (1982). Sunao: A central value in Japanese psychotherapy. In A. J. Marsella & G. White (Eds.), *Cultural conceptions of mental health and therapy* (pp. 317–329). Dordrecht: Reidel.

Murdock, G. P. (1937). Comparative data on the division of labor by sex. *Social Forces, 15,* 551–553.

Murdock, G. P. (1949). *Social structure.* New York: Macmillan.

Murdock, G. P. (1967). *Ethnographic atlas.* Pittsburgh: University of Pittsburgh Press.

Murdock, G. P. (1975). *Outline of world cultures* (5th ed.). New Haven: Human Relations Area Files.

Murdock, G. P., Ford, C. S., & Hudson, A. E. (1971). *Outline of cultural materials* (4th ed.). New Haven: Human Relations Area Files.

Murdock, G. P., & White, D. (1969). Standard cross-cultural sample. *Ethnology, 8,* 329–369.

Murphy, H. B. M. (1965). Migration and the major mental disorders. In M. B. Kantor (Ed.), *Mobility and mental health* (pp. 221–249). Springfield, IL: Thomas.

Murphy, H. B. M. (1981). *Comparative psychiatry.* Berlin: Springer-Verlag.

Murphy, H. B. M. (1982). Culture and schizophrenia. In I. Al-Issa (Ed.), *Culture and psychopathology* (pp. 221–249). Baltimore: University Park Press.

Muthayya, B. C. (1988). Dynamics of rural development. In J. Pandey (Ed.), *Psychology in India: The state of the art* (Vol. 2, pp. 225–278). New Delhi: Sage.

Naidu, R. K. (1983). *A developing program of stress research.* Paper presented at the seminar on Stress, Anxiety and Mental Health. Allahabad, Dec. 1983.

Naroll, R. (1962). *Data quality control.* New York: Free Press.

Naroll, R. (1970a). The culture bearing unit in cross-cultural surveys. In R. Naroll & R. Cohen (Eds.), *Handbook of method in cultural anthropology* (pp. 721–765). New York: Natural History Press.

Naroll, R. (1970b). Galton's problem. In R. Naroll & R. Cohen (Eds), *Handbook of method in cultural anthropology* (pp. 974–989). New York: Natural History Press.

Naroll, R. (1983). *The moral order: An introduction to the human situation.* Newbury Park, CA: Sage.

Naroll, R., & Cohen, R. (Eds.). (1970). *Handbook of method in cultural anthropology.* New York: Natural History Press.

Naroll, R., Michik, G., & Naroll, F. (1980). Holocultural research methods. In H. C. Triandis & J. W. Berry (Eds.), *Handbook of cross-cultural psychology. Vol. 2, Methodology* (pp. 479–521). Boston: Allyn & Bacon.

Nebylitsyn, V. D., & Gray, J. A. (Eds.) (1972). *Biological bases of individual behavior*. London: Academic Press.

Neghandi, A. R. (1979). Convergence in organizational practices: An empirical study of industrial enterprises in developing countries. In C. J. Lammers & D. J. Hickson (Eds.), *Organizations alike and unlike* (pp. 323–345). London: Routledge and Kegan Paul.

Nelson, E. W., Vaughan, V. C., & McKay, R. J. (1969). *Textbook of pediatrics*. Philadelphia: Saunders.

Nevis, E. C. (1983). Using an American perspective in understanding another culture: Towards a hierarchy of needs for the People's Republic of China. *Journal of Applied Behavioral Science*, *19*, 249–264.

Ng, S. H., Akhtar Hossain, A. B. M., Ball, P., Bond, M. H., Hayashi, K., Lim, S. P., O'Driscoll, M. P., Sinha, D., & Yang, K. S. (1982). Human values in nine countries. In R. Rath, A. Asthana, D. Sinha, & J. B. P. Sinha (Eds.), *Diversity and unity in cross-cultural psychology* (pp. 196–205). Lisse: Swets & Zeitlinger.

Nisbet, R. (1971). Ethnocentrism and the comparative method. In A. Desai (Ed.), *Essays on modernization of underdeveloped societies* (Vol. 1, pp. 95–14). Bombay: Thacker.

Nisbett, R. E., & Ross, L. (1980). *Human inference: Strategies and shortcomings of social judgement*. Englewood Cliffs, NJ: Prentice Hall.

Nkounkou-Hombessa, E. (1988). *Le développement psycho-moteur du bébé Kongo-Lari. Environnement culturel et aspects cognitifs*. Thèse, Université René Descartes, Paris V.

Nursey-Bray, P. F. (1970). Négritude and the McLuhan thesis. *African Quarterly*, *10*, 237–250.

Oberg, K. (1960). Cultural shock: Adjustment to new cultural environments. *Practical Anthropology*, *7*, 177–182.

O'Bryan, K., Reitz, J., & Kuplowska, O. (1976). *Non-official languages*. Ottawa: Supply and Services.

Oliver, R. A. C. (1932). The musical talents of natives in East Africa. *British Journal of Psychology*, *22*, 333–343.

Oliver, R. A. C. (1934). The adaptation of intelligence tests to tropical Africa, I, II. *Overseas Education*, 1933, *4*, 186–191; *5*, 8–13.

Olmeda, E. (1979). Acculturation: A psychometric perspective. *American Psychologist*, *34*, 1061–1070.

Ombredane, A. (1954). *L'exploration de la mentalité des noirs au moyen d'une épreuve projective: Le Congo TAT*. Brussels: Institut Royal Colonial Belge.

Ombredane, A., Robaye, F., & Plumail, H. (1956). Résultats d'une application répétée du Matrix-Couleur à une population de noirs congolais. *Bulletin du Centre d'Etudes de Recherches Psychotechniques*, *5*, 129–147.

Ord, G. (1972). Testing for educational and occupational selection in developing countries. *Occupational Psychology*, *46*, 122–182 (Monograph Issue).

Orlansky, H. (1949). Infant care and personality. *Psychological Bulletin*, *46*, 1–48.

Ortigues, M. E., & Ortigues, E. (1966). *Oedipe africain*. Paris: Plon.

Osgood, C. E. (1977). Objective cross-national indicators of subjective culture. In Y. H. Poortinga (Ed.), *Basic problems of cross-cultural psychology* (pp. 200–235). Lisse: Swets and Zeitlinger.

Osgood, C. E. (1979). From yang and yin to *and* or *but* in cross-cultural perspective. *International Journal of Psychology*, *14*, 1–35.

Osgood, C. E. (1980). *Lectures on language performance*. New York: Springer-Verlag.

Osgood, C. E., May, W. H., & Miron, M. S. (1975). *Cross-cultural universals of affective meaning*. Urbana, IL: University of Illinois Press.

Osgood, C. E., Suci, G. J., & Tannenbaum, P. H. (1957). *The measurement of meaning*. Urbana, IL: University of Illinois Press.

Ouchi, W. G. (1981). *Theory Z: How American business can meet the Japanese challenge*. Reading, MA: Addison-Wesley.

Ouellet, F. (Ed.). (1988). *Pluralisme et école*. Montreal: Institut Québécois de Recherche sur la Culture.

Padaki, R. (1988). Job attitudes. In J. Pandey (Ed.), *Psychology in India: The state of the art* (Vol. 3, pp. 19–95). New Delhi: Sage.

Pandey, J. (Ed.). (1988). *Psychology in India: The state of the art* (Vol. 1–3). New Delhi: Sage.

Paranjpe, A. C., (1984). *Theoretical psychology: The meeting of East and West*. New York: Plenum.

Pareek, U. (Ed.). (1981). *A survey of research in psychology, 1971–76*. Bombay: Popular Prakashan.

Pareek, U., & Rao, T. V. (1980). Cross-cultural surveys and interviewing. In H. C. Triandis & J. W. Berry (Eds.), *Handbook of cross-cultural psychology: Vol. 2. Methodology* (pp. 127–179). Boston: Allyn & Bacon.

Parin, P., Morgenthaler, G., & Parin-Matthey, G. (1966). *Les blancs pensent trop: 13 entretiens psychoanalytiques avec les Dogons*. Paris: Payot.

Pascale, R. T. (1978). Communication and decision making across cultures: Japanese and American comparisons. *Administrative Science Quarterly, 23*, 91–110.

Pascual-Leone, J. (1970). A mathematical model for the transition rule in Piaget's developmental stages. *Acta Psychologica, 32*, 301–345.

Pascual-Leone, J. (1980). Constructive problems for constructive theories: The current relevance of Piaget's work and a critique of information-processing simulation psychology. In R. Kluwe & H. Spada (Eds.), *Developmental models of thinking* (pp. 263–296). New York: Academic Press.

Peabody, D. (1967). Trait inferences: Evaluative and descriptive aspects. *Journal of Personality and Social Psychology Monographs, 7* (Whole no. 644).

Peabody, D. (1985). *National characteristics*. Cambridge: Cambridge University Press.

Peal, E., & Lambert, W. E. (1962). The relation of bilingualism to intelligence. *Psychological Monographs, 76*, 1–23.

Peck, R., Manaster, G. J., Borich, G., Angelini, A. L., Diaz-Guerrero, R., & Kuso, S. (1976). A test of the universality of an acculturation gradient in three-culture triads (pp. 355–363). In K. Riegel & J. Meacham (Eds.), *The developing individual in a changing world*. The Hague: Mouton.

Pedersen, P. (1981). Alternative futures for cross-cultural counselling and psychotherapy. In A. Marsella & P. Pedersen (Eds.), *Cross-cultural counselling and psychotherapy* (pp. 22–58). New York: Pergamon.

Pedersen, P., Sartorius, N., & Marsella, A. (Eds.). (1984). *Mental health services: The cross-cultural context*. London: Sage.

Pedhazur, E. J. (1982). *Multiple regression in behavioral research* (2nd ed.). New York: Holt, Rinehart and Winston.

Pelto, P. J. (1968). The difference between "tight" and "loose" societies. *Transaction*, April, 37–40.

Pelto, P. J., & Pelto, G. H. (1973). Ethnography: The fieldwork enterprise. In J. J. Honigmann (Ed.), *Handbook of social and cultural anthropology*. Chicago: Rand McNally.

Pelto, P. J., & Pelto, G. H. (1981). *Anthropological research*. Cambridge: Cambridge University Press.

Pepitone, A. (1976). Toward a normative and comparative biocultural social psychology. *Journal of Personality and Social Psychology, 34*, 641–653.

Pepitone, A., & Triandis, H. C. (1987). On the universality of social psychological theories. *Journal of Cross-Cultural Psychology, 18*, 471–498.

Perera, M., & Eysenck, S. B. G. (1984). A cross-cultural study of personality: Sri Lanka and England. *Journal of Cross-Cultural Psychology, 15*, 353–371.

Pervin, L. A. (1975). *Personality theory, assessment and research* (2nd Ed.). New York: Wiley.

Peters, L. G., & Price-Williams, D. (1983). A phenomenological overview of trance. *Transcultural Psychiatric Review, 20*, 5–39.

Peters, T. J., & Waterman, R. H. (1982). *In search of excellence: Lessons from America's best run companies*. New York: Harper and Row.

Pettigrew, T. F. (1983). Group identity and social comparisons. In C. Fried (Ed.), *Minorities: Community and identity* (pp. 51–60). Berlin: Springer-Verlag.

Pettigrew, T. F. (1988). Integration and pluralism. In P. Katz & D. Taylor (Eds.), *Eliminating racism*. New York: Plenum.

Pfeiffer, W. (1982). Culture-bound syndromes. In I. Al-Issa (Ed.), *Culture and psychopathology*. Baltimore: University Park Press.

Phinney, J. (1990). Ethnic identity in adolescents and adults. *Psychological Bulletin, 108*, 499–514.

Piaget, J. (1936). *La naissance de l'intelligence chez l'enfant*. Neuchatel : Delachaux & Niestlé.

Piaget, J. (1937). *La construction du réel chez l'enfant*. Neuchatel: Delachaux & Niestlé.

Piaget, J. (1966). Nécessité et signification des recherches comparatives en psychologie génétique, *Journal International de Psychologie, 1*, 3–13. [Need and significance of cross-cultural studies in genetic psychology. In J. W. Berry & P. R. Dasen (Eds.), *Culture and cognition* (pp. 299–309). London: Methuen, 1974.]

Piaget, J. (1970a). *Genetic epistemology*. New York: Columbia University Press.

Piaget, J. (1970b). Piaget's Theory. In P. H. Mussen (Ed.), *Carmichael's manual of child psychology* (3rd ed., pp. 703–732). New York: Wiley.

Piaget, J. (1972). *The principles of genetic epistemology*. London: Routledge & Kegan Paul.

Piaget, J. (1975). La psychogenèse des connaissances et sa signification epistémologique. *Proceedings of the Royaumont conference on phylogenetic and ontogenetic models of development*.

Piaget, J., & Inhelder, B. (1966/1969). *La psychologie de l'enfant [The psychology of the child]*. Paris: PUF (London: Routledge & Kegan Paul).

Pike K. L. (1967). *Language in relation to a unified theory of the structure of human behavior*. The Hague: Mouton.

Plomin, R., DeFries, J. C., & McClearn, G. E. (1980). *Behavioral genetics: A primer*. San Francisco: Freeman.

Plotkin, H. C., & Odling-Smee, F. J. (1981). A multiple-level model of evolution and its implications for sociobiology. *Behavioral and Brain Sciences, 4*, 225–268.

Poggie, J., & Lynch, R. (Eds.). (1974). *Rethinking modernization*. New York: Greenwood.

Pollack, R. H. (1963). Contour detectability thresholds as a function of chronological age. *Perceptual and Motor Skills, 17*, 411–417.

Pollack, R. H., & Silvar, S. D. (1967). Magnitude of the Müller-Lyer illusion in children as a function of pigmentation of the fundus oculi. *Psychonomic Science, 8*, 83–84.

Pollitt, E., & Thomson, C. (1977). Protein-calorie malnutrition and behavior: A view from psychology. In R. J. Wurtmann & J. J. Wurtmann (Eds.), *Nutrition and the brain* (Vol. 2, pp. 261–306). New York: Raven.

Poole, M., de Lacey, P., & Randhawa, B. (Eds.). (1985). *Australia in transition: Culture and life possibilities*. Sydney: Harcourt Brace Jovanovich.

Poortinga, Y. H. (1971). Cross-cultural comparison of maximum performance tests: Some methodological aspects and some experiments *Psychologia Africana*, Monograph Supplement, No. 6.

Poortinga, Y. H. (1972). A comparison of African and European students in simple auditory and visual tasks. In L. J. Cronbach & P. J. D. Drenth (Eds.), *Mental tests and cultural adaptation* (pp. 349–354). The Hague: Mouton.

Poortinga, Y. H. (1975). Limitations on intercultural comparison of psychological data. *Nederlands Tijdschrift voor de Psychologie, 30*, 23–39.

Poortinga, Y. H. (1979). The achievements of cross-cultural research: Some critical comments. In L. H. Eckensberger, W. J. Lonner, & Y. H. Poortinga (Eds.), *Cross-cultural contributions to psychology* (pp. 276–286). Lisse: Swets and Zeitlinger.

Poortinga, Y. H. (1983). Psychometric approaches to intergroup comparison: The problem of equivalence. In S. H. Irvine, & J. W. Berry (Eds.), *Human assessment and cultural factors* (pp. 237–257). New York: Plenum.

Poortinga, Y. H. (1985). How and why cultural or ethnic groups are supposed to be different: A classification of inferences. Paper presented at IACCP conference, Malmö, June, 1985.

Poortinga, Y. H. (1986). *Psychic unity versus cultural variation: An exploratory study of some basic personality variables in India and The Netherlands.* Report. Tilburg University.

Poortinga, Y. H. (1989). Equivalence of cross-cultural data: An overview of basic issues. *International Journal of Psychology, 24,* 737–756.

Poortinga, Y. H., & Foden, B. I. M. (1975). A comparative study of curiosity in black and white South African students. *Psychologia Africana*, Monograph, Suppl. 8.

Poortinga, Y. H., & Hendriks, E. C. (1989). Culture as a factor in international negotiations: A proposed research project from a psychological perspective. In F. Mautner-Markhof (Ed.), *Processes of international negotiations* (pp. 203–212). Boulder, CO: Westview Press.

Poortinga, Y. H., & Malpass, R. S. (1986). Making inferences from cross-cultural data. In W. J. Lonner & J. W. Berry (Eds.), *Field methods in cross-cultural research* (pp. 17–46). Beverly Hills, CA: Sage.

Poortinga, Y. H., & Spies, E. (1972). An attempt to compare risk taking in two culturally different groups. *Psychologia Africana, 14,* 186–199.

Poortinga, Y. H., Schoots, N., & Van de Koppel, J. M. H. (1990). *Cross-cultural understanding of gestures as a function of distance between code and referent.* Report. Tilburg: Tilburg University.

Poortinga, Y. H., & Van der Flier, H. (1988). The meaning of item bias in ability tests. In S. H. Irvine & J. W. Berry (Eds.), *Human abilities in cultural context* (pp. 166–183). New York: Cambridge University Press.

Poortinga, Y. H., & Van de Vijver, F. J. R. (1987). Explaining cross-cultural differences: Bias analysis and beyond. *Journal of Cross-Cultural Psychology, 18,* 259–282.

Poortinga, Y. H., Van de Vijver, F. J. R., Joe, R. C., & Van de Koppel, J. M. H. (1987). Peeling the onion called culture. In C. Kagitcibasi (Ed.), *Growth and progress in cross-cultural psychology* (pp. 22–34). Lisse: Swets and Zeitlinger.

Popper, K. R. (1979). *Objective knowledge: An evolutionary approach* (rev. ed.). Oxford: Clarendon Press.

Porteus, S. D. (1937). *Primitive intelligence and environment.* New York: Macmillan.

Posses, F. (1978). *The art of international negotiations.* London: Business Books.

Post, R. H. (1962). Population differences in red and green color vision deficiency: A review, and a query on selection relaxation. *Eugenics Quarterly, 9,* 131–146.

Post, R. H. (1971). Possible cases of relaxed selection in civilized populations. *Human Genetics, 13,* 253–284.

Preiswerk, R., & Perrot, D. (1978). *Ethnocentrism and history.* New York: NOK. [Orig. French (1975). *Ethnocentrisme et histoire.* Paris: Anthropos.]

Prince, R. (1960). The "brain fag" syndrome in Nigerian students. *Journal of Mental Science, 106,* 550–570.

Prince, R. (1968). The changing picture of depressive syndromes in Africa. *Canadian Journal of African Studies, 1,* 177–192.

Prince, R. (1980). Variations in psychotherapeutic procedures. In H. C. Triandis & J. Draguns (Eds.), *Handbook of cross-cultural psychology: Vol. 6. Psychopathology* (pp. 291–349). Boston: Allyn & Bacon.

Prince, R. (1984). Shamans and endorphins: Exogenous and endogenous factors in psychotherapy. In P. Pedersen, N. Sartorius, & A. Marsella (Eds.), *Mental health services: The cross-cultural context* (pp. 59–77). London: Sage.

Prince, R., & Tcheng-Laroche, F. (1987). Culture-bound syndromes and international disease classifications. *Culture, Medicine and Psychiatry, 11,* 18–23.

Przeworski, A., & Teune, H. (1970). *The logic of comparative social inquiry*. New York: Wiley.

Pye, L. W. (1982). *Chinese commercial negotiating styles*. Cambridge, MA: Oelgeschlager, Gunn and Hain.

Pye, L. W. (1986). The China trade: Making the deal. *Harvard Business Review, 64*, 74–80.

Quandt, W. B. (1987). Egypt: A strong sense of national identity. In H. Binnendijk (Ed.), *National negotiating styles* (pp. 105–124). Washington, DC: Foreign Service Institute.

Rabain, J. (1979). *L'enfant du lignage*. Paris: Payot.

Rabain, J. (1989). Pratiques de soin et interaction mère-enfant dans un contexte d'émigration. In J. Retschitzki, M. Bossel-Lagos, & P. R. Dasen (Eds.), *La recherche interculturelle* (pp. 31–44). Paris: L'Harmattan.

Raven, J. C., Court, J. H., & Raven, J. (1982). *A manual for Raven's progressive matrices and vocabulary scales*. London: H. K. Lewis.

Ray, V. F. (1952). Techniques and problems in the study of human color perception. *South Western Journal of Anthropology, 8*, 251–259.

Redding, S. G., & Ng, M. (1982). The role of "face" in the organizational perception of Chinese managers. *Organization Studies, 3*, 201–219.

Redding, S. G., & Wong, G. Y. Y. (1986). The psychology of Chinese organizational behaviour. In M. H. Bond (Ed.), *The psychology of Chinese people* (pp. 267–295). Oxford: Oxford University Press.

Redfield, R., Linton, R., & Herskovits, M. J. (1936). Memorandum on the study of acculturation. *American Anthropologist, 38*, 149–152.

Resing, W. C., Bleichrodt, N., & Drenth, P. J. D. (1986). Het gebruik van de RAKIT bij allochtoon ethnische groepen. [The use of the RAKIT with allochthone ethnic groups]. *Nederlands Tijdschrift voor de Psychologie, 41*, 179–188.

Reuning, H., & Wortley, W. (1973). Psychological studies of the Bushmen. *Psychologia Africana* (Monograph Supplement No. 7).

Rey, M. (1988). L'éducation interculturelle: l'approche du Conseil de l'Europe. In F. Ouellet (Ed.), *Pluralisme et école*. Montreal: Institut Québécois de la Recherche sur la Culture.

Reynolds, P. D. (1986). Organizational culture as related to industry, position and performance: A preliminary report. *Journal of Management Studies, 23*, 333–345.

Reynolds, V. (1980). *The biology of human action* (2nd ed.). Oxford: Freeman.

Ricciuti, H. N. (1979). Malnutrition and cognitive development: Research issues and priorities. In J. Brozek (Ed.), *Behavioral effects of energy and protein deficits* (pp. 297–313). Washington, DC: NIH.

Ricciuti, H. N. (1982). Interaction of adverse environmental and nutritional influences on mental development. *Baroda Journal of Nutrition, 9*, 327–335.

Ricciuti, H. N., & Dorman, R. (1983). Interaction of multiple factors contributing to high-risk parenting. In R. A. Hoekelman (Ed.), *Minimizing high-risk parenting*. Media, PA: Harwal.

Rist, G., & Sabelli, F. (Eds). (1986). *Il était une fois le développement*. Lausanne: Editions d'en Bas.

Rivers, W. H. R. (1901). Vision. In *Physiology and psychology, Part I. Reports of the Cambridge Anthropological Expedition to Torres Straits* (Vol. 2). Cambridge: Cambridge University Press.

Robbins, S. R. (1987). *Organization theory: Structure, design and applications*. Englewood Cliffs, NJ: Prentice-Hall.

Rocher, G. (1973). Les ambiguités d'un Canada bilingue et multiculturel. Paper presented to Canadian Sociology and Anthropology Association.

Rogoff, B. (1981). Schooling and the development of cognitive skills. In H. C. Triandis & A. Heron (Eds.), *Handbook of cross-cultural psychology: Vol. 4, Development* (pp. 233–294). Boston: Allyn & Bacon.

Rohner, R. (1984). Toward a conception of culture for cross-cultural psychology. *Journal of Cross-Cultural Psychology, 15*, 111–138.

Rohner, R. (1986). *The warmth dimension: Foundations of parental acceptance-rejection theory.* Newbury Park, CA: Sage.

Rohner, R., & Rohner, E. (1976). *They love me, they love me not.* New Haven: Human Relations Area Files.

Rokeach, M. (1973). *The nature of human values.* New York: Free Press.

Ronen, S. (1986). *Comparative and multinational management.* New York: Wiley.

Rosch (Heider), E. (1972). Universals in color naming and memory. *Journal of Experimental Psychology, 93,* 10–20.

Rosch, E. (1977). Human categorization. In N. Warren (Ed.), *Studies in cross-cultural psychology* (Vol. 1, pp. 1–49). London: Academic Press.

Rosenthal, R., Hall, J. A., DiMatteo, M. R., Rogers, P. L., & Archer, D. (1979). *Sensitivity to nonverbal communication: The Pons test.* Baltimore: Johns Hopkins University Press.

Rotter, J. B. (1954). *Social learning and clinical psychology.* Englewood Cliffs NJ: Prentice-Hall.

Rotter, J.B. (1966). Generalized expectancies for internal versus external control of reinforcement. *Psychological Monographs, 80* (Whole no. 609).

Royal Anthropological Institute (1951). *Notes and queries on anthropology* (6th ed.). London: Routledge.

Ruben, B. D. (1989). The study of cross-cultural competence: Traditions and contemporary issues. *International Journal of Intercultural Relations, 13,* 229–240.

Ruben, B. D., & Kealey, D. J. (1979). Behavioral assessment of communication competency and the prediction of cross-cultural adaptation. *International Journal of Intercultural Relations, 3,* 15–47.

Ruffell Smith, H. (1975). Some problems of voice communication for international aviation. In A. Chapanis (Ed.), *Ethnic variables in human factors engineering* (pp. 225–230). Baltimore: Johns Hopkins University Press.

Rushton, J. P. (1988). Race differences in behaviour: A review and evolutionary analysis. *Personality and Individual Differences, 9,* 1009–1024.

Rushton, J. P., Fulker, D. M., Neale, M. C., Nias, D. K. B., & Eysenck, H. J. (1986). Altruism and aggression: The heritability of individual differences. *Journal of Personality and Social Psychology, 50,* 1192–1198.

Sahlins, M. (1976). Colors and cultures. *Semiotica, 16,* 1–22.

Sahlins, M. (1977). *The use and abuse of biology.* London: Tavistock.

Sahlins, M., & Service, E. (Eds.). (1960). *Evolution and culture.* Ann Arbor, MI: University of Michigan Press.

Sahoo, F. (Ed). (1988). *Psychology in Indian context.* Agra: National Psychological Corporation.

Sako, S. (1975). *An experimental approach to the cross-cultural study of conformity behavior,* unpublished thesis, University of Osaka, Japan.

Salazar, J. (1984). The use and impact of psychology in Venezuela. *International Journal of Psychology, 19,* 113–122.

Salk, J., & Salk, J. (1982). *World population and human values: A new reality.* New York: Harper.

Samuda, R. (1975). *Psychological testing of American minorities: Issues and consequences.* New York: Harper & Row.

Samuda, R. (1983). Cross-cultural testing within a multicultural society. In S. H. Irvine & J. W. Berry (Eds.), *Human assessment and cultural factors* (pp. 591–606). New York: Plenum.

Samuda, R. (1988). Psychometric abuse in assessing minority students: A Canadian perspective. In J. W. Berry & R. C. Annis (Eds.), *Ethnic psychology* (pp. 234–242). Lisse: Swets and Zeitlinger.

Samuda, R., Berry, J. W., & Laferrière, M. (Eds.). (1984). *Multiculturalism in Canada: Social and educational perspectives.* Toronto: Allyn & Bacon.

Samuda, R., & Wolfgang, A. (Eds.). (1985). *Cross-cultural counseling.* Toronto: Hogreffe.

Santa, I. L., & Baker, L. (1975). Linguistic influences on visual learning. *Memory and Cognition, 3,* 445–450.

Sanua, V. (1970). Immigration, migration and mental illness. In E. Brody (Ed.), *Behavior in new environments* (pp. 291–352). Newbury Park, CA: Sage.

Sapir, E. (1949). *Culture, language and personality*. Berkeley, CA: University of California Press.

Saxe, G. B. (1981). Body parts as numerals: A developmental analysis of numeration among remote Oksapmin village populations in Papua New Guinea. *Child Development, 52,* 302–316.

Saxe, G. B. (1982). Developing forms of arithmetical thought among the Oksapmin of Papua New Guinea. *Developmental Psychology, 18,* 583–594.

Saxe, G. B. (1983). Culture, counting and number conservation. *International Journal of Psychology, 18,* 313–318.

Saxe, G. B. (1985). Effects of schooling on arithmetical understandings: Studies with Oksapmin children in Papua New Guinea. *Journal of Educational Psychology, 77,* 503–513.

Saxe, G. B., & Moylan, T. (1982). The development of measurement operations among the Oksapmin of Papua New Guinea. *Child Development, 53,* 1242–1248.

Schachter, S., & Singer, J. (1962). Cognitive, social and physiological determinants of emotional state. *Psychological Review, 63,* 379–398.

Schein, E. H. (1985). *Organizational culture and leadership*. San Francisco: Jossey-Bass.

Scherer, K. R. (1981). Speech and emotional states. In J. Darby (Ed.), *Speech evaluation in psychiatry* (pp. 189–220). New York: Grune and Stratton.

Scherer, K. R., Matsumoto, D., Wallbott, H., & Kudoh, T. (1988). Emotional experience in cultural context: A comparison between Europe, Japan and the United States. In K. R. Scherer (Ed.), *Facets of emotion* (pp. 5–30). Hillsdale, NJ: Erlbaum.

Scherer, K. R., Wallbott, H. G., & Summerfield, A. B. (Eds.). (1986). *Experiencing emotion: A cross-cultural study*. Cambridge: Cambridge University Press.

Schlegel, A., & Barry, H. (1986). The cultural consequences of female contribution to subsistence. *American Anthropologist, 88,* 142–150.

Schmitt, N., & Noe, R. A. (1986). Personnel selection and equal employment opportunity. *International review of industrial and organizational psychology* 71–115.

Schwartz, S. H. (1990). Individualism and collectivism: Critique and proposed refinements. *Journal of Cross-Cultural Psychology, 21,* 139–157.

Schwartz, S. H., & Bilsky, W. (1987). Toward a universal psychological structure of human values. *Journal of Personality and Social Psychology, 53,* 550–562.

Schwartz, S. H., & Bilsky, W. (1990). Toward a theory of the universal content and structure of values: Extensions and cross-cultural replications. *Journal of Personality and Social Psychology, 58,* 878–891.

Schwendler, W. (1984). UNESCO's project on the exchange of knowledge for endogenous development. *International Journal of Psychology, 19,* 3–15.

Scribner, S., & Cole, M. (1973). Cognitive consequences of formal and informal education. *Science, 182,* 553–559.

Scribner, S., & Cole, M. (1981). *The psychology of literacy*. Cambridge, MA: Harvard University Press.

Segall, M. H. (1979). *Cross-cultural psychology: Human behavior in global perspective*. Monterey, CA: Brooks/Cole.

Segall, M. H. (1983). On the search for the independent variable in cross-cultural psychology. In S. H. Irvine & J. W. Berry (Eds.), *Human assessment and cultural factors* (pp. 127–138). New York: Plenum.

Segall, M. H. (1984). More than we need to know about culture, but are afraid not to ask. *Journal of Cross-Cultural Psychology, 15,* 153–162.

Segall, M. H. (1986). Culture and behavior: Psychology in global perspective. *Annual Review of Psychology, 37,* 523–564.

Segall, M. H., Campbell, D. T., & Herskovits, M. J. (1966). *The influence of culture on visual perception*. Indianapolis, IN: Bobbs-Merrill.

Segall, M. H., Dasen, P. R., Berry, J. W., & Poortinga, Y. H. (1990). *Human behavior in global perspective: An introduction to cross-cultural psychology*. New York: Pergamon.

Segall, M. H., Doornbos, M., & Davis, C. (1976). *Political identity: A case study from Uganda*. Syracuse: Maxwell Foreign and Comparative Studies/East Africa, *24*.

Segalowitz, N. S. (1980). Issues in the cross-cultural study of bilingual development. In H. C. Triandis & A. Heron (Eds.), *Handbook of cross-cultural psychology: Vol. 4, Developmental* (pp. 55–92). Boston: Allyn & Bacon.

Selye, H. (1976). *The stress of life*. New York: McGraw-Hill.

Serpell, R. (1976). *Culture's influence on behavior*. London: Methuen.

Serpell, R., & Deregowski, J. B. (1980). The skill of pictorial perception: An interpretation of cross-cultural evidence. *International Journal of Psychology*, *15*, 145–180.

Shanmugam, T. E. (1972). Personality. In The Indian Council of Social Science Research, *A survey of research in psychology* (pp. 266–335). Bombay: Popular Prakashan.

Sherif, M. (1935). A study of some social factors in perception. *Archives of Psychology*, No. 187.

Shuey, A. (1958). *The testing of Negro intelligence*. New York: Social Science Press.

Shweder, R. A. (1979a). Rethinking culture and personality theory. Part I: A critical examination of two classical postulates. *Ethos*, *7*, 255–278.

Shweder, R. A. (1979b). Rethinking culture and personality theory. Part II: A critical examination of two more classical postulates. *Ethos*, *7*, 279–311.

Shweder, R. A. (1980). Rethinking culture and personality theory. Part III: From genesis and typology to hermeneutics and dynamics. *Ethos*, *8*, 60–94.

Shweder, R. A. (1984). Anthropology's romantic rebellion against the enlightenment, or there's more to thinking than reason and evidence. In R. A. Shweder & R. A. LeVine (Eds.), *Culture theory: Essays on mind, self and emotion* (pp. 27–66). Cambridge: Cambridge University Press.

Shweder, R. A., & Bourne, E. J. (1984). Does the concept of the person vary cross-culturally? In R. A. Shweder, & R. A. LeVine (Eds.), *Culture theory* (pp. 158–199). New York: Cambridge University Press.

Shweder, R. A., Mahapatra, M., & Miller, J. G. (1990). Culture and moral development. In J. Stigler, R. A. Shweder, & G. Herdt (Eds.), *Cultural psychology: Essays in comparative human development* (pp. 130–204). New York: Cambridge University Press.

Sieye, A. (1975). *Le développement psychobiologique de l' enfant Ouest-africain*. Thèse de 3ème cycle, Université René Descartes, Paris V.

Silk, J. B. (1980). Adoption and kinshhip in Oceania. *American Anthropologist*, *82*, 799–820.

Silvar, S. D., & Pollack, R. H. (1967). Racial differences in pigmentation of the fundus oculi. *Psychonomic Science*, *7*, 159–160.

Simons, R., & Hughes, C. C. (Eds.). (1985). *The culture-bound syndromes*. Dordrecht: Reidel.

Singh, A. K. (1967). Hindu culture and economic development in India. *Conspectus*, *1*, 9–32.

Sinha, D. (1972). Industrial psychology. In Indian Council for Social Science Research, *A survey of research in psychology* (pp. 175–237). Bombay: Popular Prakahashan.

Sinha, D. (1979). Perceptual style among nomads and transitional agriculturalist Birhors. In L. Eckensberger, W. Lonner, & Y. H. Poortinga (Eds.), *Cross-cultural contributions to psychology* (pp. 83–93). Lisse: Swets & Zeitlinger.

Sinha, D. (1981). Non-western perspectives in psychology: Why, what and whither? *Journal of Indian Psychology*, *3*, 1–9.

Sinha, D. (1984). Psychology in the context of Third World development. *International Journal of Psychology*, *19*, 17–29.

Sinha, D. (1986). *Psychology in a Third World country: The Indian experience*. New Delhi: Sage.

Sinha, D. (1989). Research in psychology in the developing world. *Psychology and Developing Societies*, *1*, 105–126.

Sinha, D. (1990). Interventions for development out of poverty. In R. Brislin, (Ed.), *Applied cross-cultural psychology* (pp. 77–97). Newbury Park, CA: Sage.

Sinha, D., & Bharat, S. (1985). Three types of family structure and psychological differentiation. *International Journal of Psychology*, *20*, 693–708.

Sinha, D., & Holtzman, W. (Eds.) (1984). The impact of psychology on Third World develop-
    ment. *International Journal of Psychology*, *19* (Special Issue, Nos. 1 & 2).
Sinha, G. (1988). Exposure to industrial and urban environments and formal schooling as factors
    in psychological differentiation. *International Journal of Psychology*, *23*, 707–719.
Sinha, J. B. P. (1970). *Development through behaviour modification*. Bombay: Allied Publishers.
Sinha, J. B. P. (1980). *The nurturant task leader*. New Delhi: Concept Publishing House.
Sinha, J. B. P. (1984a). A model of effective leadership styles in India. *International Studies of
    Management and Organization*, *14*, 86–98.
Sinha, J. B. P. (1984b). Towards partnership for relevant research in the Third World.
    International Journal of Psychology, *19*, 169–177.
Skutnabb-Kangas, T. (1981). Guest worker or immigrant — different ways of reproducing an
    underclass. *Journal of Multilingual and Multicultural Development*, *2*, 89–115.
Sloan, T., & Montero, M. (Eds). (1990). Psychology for the Third World. Special issue of
    Journal of Social Issues, *46*, No. 3.
Smith, P. B., & Peterson, M. F. (1988). *Leadership, organizations and culture: An event
    management model*. London: Sage.
Snarey, J. R. (1985). Cross-cultural universality of social-moral development: A critical review of
    Kohlbergian research. *Psychological Bulletin*, *97*, 202–232.
Solomon, R. H. (1987). China: Friendship and obligation in Chinese negotiation style. In
    H. Binnendijk (Ed.), *National negotiating styles* (pp. 1–16). Washington, DC: Foreign
    Service Institute.
Sommerlad, E., & Berry, J. W. (1970). The role of ethnic identification in distinguishing between
    attitudes towards assimilation and integration of a minority racial group. *Human
    Relations*, *23*, 23–29.
Soueif, M. I., & Eysenck, H. J. (1971). Cultural differences in aesthetic preferences. *Internation-
    al Journal of Psychology*, *6*, 293–298.
Soueif, M. I., & Eysenck, H. J. (1972). Factors in the determination of preference judgments
    for polygonal figures: A comparative study. *International Journal of Psychology*, *7*,
    145–153.
Sow, I. (1977). *Psychiatrie dynamique africaine*. Paris: Payot.
Sow, I. (1978). *Les structures anthropologiques de la folie en Afrique noire*. Paris: Payot.
Spearman, C. (1927). *The abilities of man*. London: Macmillan.
Spector, P. E., & Wimalasari, J. (1986). A cross-cultural comparison of job satisfaction
    dimensions in the United States and Singapore. *International Review of Applied
    Psychology*, *35*, 147–158.
Spielberger, C. D., & Diaz-Guerrero, R. (Eds.). (1983). *Cross-cultural anxiety* (Vol. 2).
    Washington, DC: Hemisphere.
Spindler, G. (Ed). (1978). *The making of psychological anthropology*. Berkeley, CA: University
    of California Press.
Srole, L., Langer, T. S., & Michael, S. T. (1962). *Mental health in the metropolis*. New York:
    McGraw-Hill.
Sternberg, R. J. (1985). *Beyond IQ: A triarchic theory of human intelligence*. New York:
    Cambridge University Press.
Sternberg, R. J., & Wagner, R. (Eds.). (1986). *Practical intelligence: Nature and origins of
    competence in the everyday world*. New York: Cambridge University Press.
Stewart, V. M. (1973). Tests of the "carpentered world" hypothesis by race and environment in
    America and Zambia. *International Journal of Psychology*, *8*, 83–94.
Stonequist, E. V. (1935). The problem of the marginal man. *American Journal of Sociology*, *41*,
    1–12.
Strange, W., & Jenkins, J. J. (1978). Role of linguistic experience in the perception of speech.
    In R. D. Walk & H. L. Pick (Eds.), *Perception and experience* (pp. 125–169). New
    York: Plenum.
Strodtbeck, F. (1964). Considerations of meta-method in cross-cultural research. In A. K.
    Romney & R. D'Andrade (Eds.), Transcultural studies of cognition. *American
    Anthropologist*, *66*, 223–229.

Stroebe, W., Lenkert, A., & Jonas, K. (1988). Familiarity may breed contempt: The impact of student exchange on national stereotypes and attitudes. In W. Stroebe, A. W. Kruglanski, D. Bar-Tal, & M. Hewstone (Eds.), *The social psychology of intergroup conflict* (pp. 167–187). Berlin: Springer-Verlag.

Sturtevant, W. (1964). Studies in ethnoscience. *American Anthropologist, 66*, 99–124.

Sue, D. W. (1981). *Counselling the culturally different: Theory and practice.* New York: Wiley.

Sumner, W. G. (1906). *Folkways.* New York: Ginn.

Super, C. M. (1973). Infant care and motor development in rural Kenya: some preliminary data on precocity and deficit. Paper presented at the 1st Pan-African IACCP Conference, Ibadan, Nigeria.

Super, C. M. (1976). Environmental effects on motor development: The case of "African infant precocity." *Developmental Medicine and Child Neurology, 18,* 561–567.

Super, C. M. (1981a). Behavioural development in infancy. In R. Munroe, R. Munroe, & B. B. Whiting (Eds.), *Handbook of cross-cultural human development* (pp. 181–270). New York: Garland.

Super, C. M. (1981b). Cross-cultural research on infancy. In H. C. Triandis & A. Heron (Eds.), *Handbook of cross-cultural psychology: Vol. 4. Development* (pp. 17–53). Boston: Allyn & Bacon.

Super, C. M. & Harkness, S. (1982). The infant's niche in rural Kenya and metropolitan America. In L. L. Adler (Ed.), *Cross-cultural research at issue* (pp. 47–55). New York: Academic Press.

Super, C. M., & Harkness, S. (1986a). The developmental niche: A conceptualization at the interface of child and culture. *International Journal of Behavioral Development, 9,* 545–569.

Super, C. M., & Harkness, S. (1986b). Temperament, development and culture. In R. Plomin & J. Dunn (Eds.), *The study of temperament: Changes, continuities and challenges* (pp. 131–149). Hillsdale, NJ: Erlbaum.

Sussman, N. M., & Rosenfeld, H. M. (1982). Influence of culture, language and sex on conversational distance. *Journal of Personality and Social Psychology, 42,* 66–74.

Swartz, L. (1985). Anorexia nervosa as a culture-bound syndrome. *Social Science and Medicine, 20,* 725–730.

Symons, D. (1979). *The evolution of human sexuality.* Oxford: Oxford University Press.

Szalay, L. R., & Deese, J. (1978). *Subjective meaning and culture: An assessment through word associations.* Hillsdale, NJ: Erlbaum.

Szapocznik, J., Scopetta, M., & Kurtines, W. (1978). Theory and measurement of acculturation. *Interamerican Journal of Psychology, 12,* 113–130.

Taft, R. (1977). Coping with unfamiliar cultures. In N. Warren (Ed.), *Studies in cross-cultural psychology* (pp. 121–151). London: Academic Press.

Taft, R. (1986). Methodological considerations in the study of immigrant adaptation in Australia. *Australian Journal of Psychology, 38,* 339–346.

Tajfel, H. (Ed.). (1978). *Differentiation between social groups.* London: Academic Press.

Tajfel, H. (Ed.). (1982). *Social identity and intergroup relations.* Cambridge: Cambridge University Press.

Tanaka-Matsumi, J. (1979). Cultural factors and social influence techniques in Naikan therapy: A Japanese self-observation method. *Psychotherapy: Theory, Research and Practice, 16,* 385–390.

Tannen, D. (1981). Indirectness in discourse: Ethnicity as conversational style. *Discourse Processes, 3,* 221–238.

Tannenbaum, A. S. (1980). Organizational psychology. In H. C. Triandis & R. W. Brislin (Eds.), *Handbook of cross-cultural psychology* (Vol. 5, pp. 281–334). Boston: Allyn & Bacon.

Tayeb, M. H. (1988). *Organizations and national culture: A comparative analysis.* London: Sage.

Taylor, D. M. (1981). Stereotypes and intergroup relations. In R. C. Gardner & R. Kalin (Eds.), *A Canadian social psychology of ethnic relations* (pp. 151–171). Toronto: Methuen.

Taylor, D. M., & Jaggi, V. (1974). Ethnocentrism and causal attribution in a South Indian context. *Journal of Cross-Cultural Psychology*, 5, 162–171.
Taylor, D. M., Moghaddam, F. M. (1987). *Theories of intergroup relations: International social psychological perspectives*. New York: Praeger.
Ten Doesschate, G. (1964). *Perspective, fundamentals, controversials, history*. Nieuwkoop: De Graf.
Textor, R. (1967). *A cross-cultural summary*. New Haven: Human Relations Area Files.
Thayer, N. B., & Weiss, S. E. (1987). Japan: The changing logic of a former minor power. In H. Binnendijk (Ed.), *National negotiating styles* (pp. 45–74). Washington, DC: Foreign Service Institute.
Thompson, W. R. (1980). Cross-cultural uses of biological data and perspectives. In H. C. Triandis & W. W. Lambert (Eds.), *Handbook of cross-cultural psychology* (Vol. 1, pp. 205–252). Boston: Allyn & Bacon.
Thouless, R. H. (1932). A racial difference in perception. *Journal of Social Psychology*, 4, 330–339.
Thurstone, L. L. (1938). Primary mental abilities. *Psychometric Monographs*, No. 1.
Tinbergen, N. (1969). Ethology. In R. Harré (Ed.), *Scientific thought 1900–1960* (pp. 238–268). Oxford: Clarendon Press. (Reprinted in Tinbergen, N. (1973). *The animal and its world* (Vol. 2, pp. 130–160). London: Allen and Unwin.
Ting-Toomey, S. (1985). Toward a theory of conflict and culture. *International and Intercultural Communication Annual*, 9, 71–86.
Titchener, E. B. (1916). On ethnological tests of sensation and perception. *Proceedings of the American Philosophical Society*, 55, 204-236
Tittle, C. K. (1982). Use of judgemental methods in item bias studies. In R. A. Berk (Ed.), *Handbook of methods for detecting test bias* (pp. 31–63). Baltimore: Johns Hopkins University Press.
Torbiörn, I. (1982). *Living abroad*. New York: Wiley.
Triandis, H. C. (1972). *The analysis of subjective culture*. New York: Wiley.
Triandis, H. C. (1975). Culture training, cognitive complexity and interpersonal attitudes. In R. Brislin, S. Bochner, & W. Lonner (Eds.), *Cross-cultural perspectives on learning* (pp. 39–77). Beverly Hills, CA: Sage.
Triandis, H. C. (1978). Some universals of social behavior. *Personality and Social Psychology Bulletin*, 4, 1–16.
Triandis, H. C. (1980). Introduction to Handbook. In H. C. Triandis & W. E. Lambert (Eds.), *Handbook of cross-cultural psychology: Vol. 1, Perspectives* (pp. 1–14). Boston: Allyn & Bacon.
Triandis, H. C. (1984). Toward a psychological theory of economic growth. *International Journal of Psychology*, 19, 79–95.
Triandis, H. C. (1988). Collectivism *vs* individualism: A reconceptualization of a basic concept in cross-cultural social psychology. In C. Bagley & G. K. Verma (Eds.). *Personality, cognition and values* (pp. 60–95). London: Macmillan.
Triandis, H. C. (1989). The self and social behavior in differing cultural contexts. *Psychological Review*, 96, 506–520.
Triandis, H. C. (in press). Cross-cultural industrial and organizational psychology. In M. D. Dunnette, L. M. Hough, & H. C. Triandis. (Eds.), *Handbook of organizational psychology*. Vol. 4. Palo Alto: Consulting Psychologists Press.
Triandis, H. C., & Berry, J. W. (Eds.). (1980.) *Handbook of cross-cultural psychology: Vol. 2. Methodology*. Boston: Allyn & Bacon.
Triandis, H. C., Bontempo, R., Betancourt, H., Bond, M., & Leung, K. (1986). The measurement of the etic aspects of individualism and collectivism across cultures. *Australian Journal of Psychology*, 38, 257–268.
Triandis, H. C., Bontempo, R., Villareal, M. J., Asai, M., & Lucca, N. (1988). Individualism and collectivism: Cross-cultural perspectives on self-group relationships. *Journal of Personality and Social Psychology*, 54, 323–338.

Triandis, H. C., & Brislin, R. (Eds.). (1980). *Handbook of cross-cultural psychology: Vol. 5. Social.* Boston: Allyn & Bacon.

Triandis, H. C., & Draguns, J. (Eds.), (1980). *Handbook of cross-cultural psychology: Vol. 6. Psychopathology.* Boston: Allyn & Bacon.

Triandis, H. C., & Heron, A. (Eds.). (1981). *Handbook of cross-cultural psychology: Vol. 4. Developmental.* Boston: Allyn & Bacon.

Triandis, H. C., Kashima, Y., Shimada, E., & Villareal, M. (1986). Acculturation indices as a means of confirming cultural differences. *International Journal of Psychology, 21,* 43–70.

Triandis, H. C., & Lambert, W. W. (Eds.). (1980). *Handbook of cross-cultural psychology: Vol. 1. Perspectives.* Boston: Allyn & Bacon.

Triandis, H. C., Leung, K., Villareal, M. J., & Clack, F. (1985). Allocentric versus idiocentric tendencies: Convergent and discriminant validation. *Journal of Research in Personality, 19,* 395–415.

Triandis, H. C., & Lonner, W. J. (Eds.). (1980.) *Handbook of cross-cultural psychology: Vol. 3. Basic Processes.* Boston: Allyn & Bacon.

Triandis, H. C., Malpass, R., & Davidson, A. R. (1972). Cross-cultural psychology. *Biennial Review of Anthropology, 1,* 1–84.

Triandis, H. C., Malpass, R., & Davidson, A. R. (1973), Psychology and culture. *Annual Review of Psychology, 24,* 355–378.

Triandis, H. C., & Vassiliou, V. (1972). A comparative analysis of subjective culture. In H. C. Triandis, *The analysis of subjective culture* (pp. 299–335). New York: Wiley.

Tripathi, R. C. (1988). Applied social psychology. In J. Pandey (Ed.), *Psychology in India: The state of the art* (Vol. 2, pp. 225–278). New Delhi: Sage.

Tung, R. L. (1981). Selection and training of personnel for overseas assignments. *Columbia Journal of World Business,* Spring, 69–78.

Turtle, A. (1987). Introduction: A silk road for psychology. In G. Blowers & A. Turtle (Eds.), *Psychology moving East* (pp. 1–21). Sydney: University of Sydney Press.

Tylor, E. B. (1871). *Primitive culture* (2 Vols.). London: Murray.

Tzeng, O. C. S., Osgood, C. E., & May, W. H. (1980). Toward universal macro-denotative meaning systems via a cross-cultural multivariate quantification procedure. In P. R. Krishnaiah (Ed.), *Multivariate analysis – V* (pp. 651–671). Amsterdam: North-Holland.

Udy, S. H. (1970). *Work in traditional and modern society.* Englewood Cliffs, NJ: Prentice-Hall.

Ugorji, R., & Berman, B. (1974). Orientations of Umuaro Igbo villagers to development. In J. W. Berry & W. J. Lonner (Eds.), *Applied cross-cultural psychology* (pp. 52–57). Amsterdam: Swets & Zeitlinger.

Uzgiris, I. C., & Hunt, J. McV. (1975). *Assessment in infancy: Ordinal scales of psychological development.* Urbana, IL.: University of Illinois Press.

Valsiner, J. (1987). *Culture and the development of children's action.* New York: Wiley.

Valsiner, J., & Hill, P. E. (1989). Socialization of American toddlers for social courtesy. In J. Valsiner (Ed.), *Child development in cultural context,* (pp. 163–179). Toronto: Hogrefe.

Van Bezooijen, R., Otto, S. A., Heenan, T. A. (1983). Recognition of vocal expressions of emotion: A three-nation study to identify universal characteristics. *Journal of Cross-Cultural Psychology, 14,* 387–406.

Van de Koppel, J. M. H., & Schoots, N. H. (1986). Why are all trains painted yellow? Conventies in het acculturatieproces. *Nederlands Tijdschrift voor de Psychologie, 41,* 189–196.

Van de Vijver, F. J. R., & Poortinga, Y. H. (1982). Cross-cultural generalization and universality. *Journal of Cross-Cultural Psychology, 13,* 387–408.

Van de Vijver, F. J. R., & Poortinga, Y. H. (1991). Testing across cultures. In R. K. Hambleton & J. N. Zaal (Eds.), *Advances in educational and psychological testing: Theory and applications* (pp. 277–309). Dordrecht: Kluwer.

Van der Werff, J. J. (1985). Heymans' temperament dimensions in personality research. *Journal of Research in Personality*, *19*, 279–287.

Van Lancker, D., & Fromkin, V. A. (1973). Hemispheric specialization for pitch perception: Evidence from Thai. *Journal of Phonetics*, *1*, 101–109.

Van Lancker, D., & Fromkin, V. A. (1978). Cerebral dominance for pitch contrasts in tone language speakers and in musically untrained and trained English speakers. *Journal of Phonetics*, *6*, 19–23.

Van Leeuwen, M. S. (1978). A cross-cultural examination of psychological differentiation in males and females. *International Journal of Psychology*, *13*, 87–122.

Van Oudenhoven, J. P., & Willemsen, T. M. (Eds.). (1989). *Ethnic minorities: Social psychological perspectives*. Lisse: Swets and Zeitlinger.

Van Wattenwyl, A., & Zollinger, H. (1979). Color term salience and neurophysiology of color vision. *American Anthropologist*, *81*, 279–288.

Vernon, P. E. (1969). *Intelligence and cultural environment*. London: Methuen.

Vernon, P. E. (1979). *Intelligence, heredity and environment*. San Francisco: Freeman.

Vogel, E. F. (Ed.). (1975). *Modern Japanese organization and decision-making*. Berkeley, CA: University of California Press.

Vogel, F., & Motulsky, A. G. (1979). *Human genetics: problems and approaches*. Berlin: Springer-Verlag.

Vorster, J., & Schuring, G. (1989). Language and thought: Developmental perspectives on counterfactual conditionals. *South African Journal of Psychology*, *19*, 34–38.

Vroom V., & Yetton, P. (1973). *Leadership and decision-making*. Pittsburgh: University of Pittsburgh Press.

Vouilloux, D. (1959). Étude de la psychomotricité d'enfants africains au Cameroun: Test de Gesell et réflexes archaiques. *Journal de la Société des Africanistes*, *29*, 11–18.

Vygotsky, L. S. (1978). *Mind in society: The development of higher psychological processes*. Cambridge, MA: Harvard University Press.

Wagner, D. A. (1977). Ontogeny of the Ponzo illusion: Effects of age, schooling and environment. *International Journal of Psychology*, *12*, 161–176.

Wallace, A. F. C. (1959). Cultural determinants of response to hallucinatory experiences. *AMA Archives of General Psychiatry*, *1*, 58–69.

Wallace, A. F. C. (1970). *Culture and personality* (2nd ed). New York: Random House.

Wallbott, H. G., & Scherer, K. R. (1986). How universal and specific is emotional experience? Evidence from 27 countries on five continents. *Social Science Information*, *25*, 763–795.

Ward, C. (1989). (Ed.). *Altered states of consciousness and mental health*. Newbury Park, CA: Sage.

Warren, N. (Ed.). (1977). *Studies in cross-cultural psychology* (Vol. 1). London: Academic Press.

Warren, N. (Ed.). (1980a). *Studies in cross-cultural psychology* (Vol. 2). London: Academic Press.

Warren, N. (1980b). Universality and plasticity, ontogeny and phylogeny. The resonance between culture and cognitive development. In J. Sants (Ed.), *Developmental psychology and society* (pp. 290–326). London: Macmillan.

Warren, N., & Parkin, J. M. (1974). A neurological and behavioral comparison of African and European newborns in Uganda. *Child Development*, *45*, 966–971.

Warwick, D. (1980). The politics and ethics of cross-cultural research. In H. C. Triandis & W. W. Lambert (Eds.), *Handbook of cross-cultural psychology: Vol. 1. Perspectives* (pp. 310–371). Boston: Allyn & Bacon.

Wason, P. C., & Johnson-Laird, P. N. (1972). *Psychology of reasoning: structure and content*. Cambridge, MA: Harvard University Press.

Wassmann, J., & Dasen, P. R. (in press). Yupno number system and counting. *Journal of Cross-Cultural Psychology*.

Watkins, D. (1989). The role of confirmatory factor analysis in cross-cultural research. *International Journal of Psychology*, *24*, 685–701.

Weber, M. (1976). *The Protestant ethic and the spirit of capitalism*. (Originally published in 1905). New York: Scribners.

Weeks, W. H., Pedersen, P. B., & Brislin, R. W. (1982). *A manual of structured experiences for cross-cultural learning*. Chicago: Intercultural Press.

Werner, E. E. (1972). Infants around the world: Cross-cultural studies of psycho-motor development from birth to two years. *Journal of Cross-Cultural Psychology*, *3*, 111–134.

Werner, E. E. (1979). *Cross-cultural child development: A view from the planet earth*. Monterey, CA: Brooks/Cole.

Werner, H. (1957). The concept of development from a comparative and organismic point of view. In D. B. Harris (Ed.), *The concept of development* (pp. 125–148). Minneapolis: University of Minnesota Press.

Werner, O., & Campbell, D. T. (1970). Translating, working through interpreters and the problem of decentering. In R. Naroll & R. Cohen (Eds.), *A handbook of method in cultural anthropology* (pp. 398–419). New York: Natural History Press.

Westermeyer, J. (1973). On the epidemicity of Amok violence. *Archives of General Psychiatry*, *28*, 873–876.

Wexley, K. N., & Yukl, G. A. (1984). *Organizational behavior and personnel psychology* (rev. ed.). Homewood, IL: Irwin.

Whiting, B. B. (Ed.). (1963). *Six cultures: Studies in child rearing*. New York: Wiley.

Whiting, B. B. (1976). The problem of the packaged variable. In K. Riegel & J. Meacham (Eds.), *The developing individual in a changing world* (Vol. 1, pp. 303–309). The Hague: Mouton.

Whiting, B. B., & Whiting, J. W. (1975). *Children of six cultures: A psychocultural analysis*. Cambridge, MA: Harvard University Press.

Whiting, J. W. (1966). *Field guide for a study of socialization*. New York: Wiley

Whiting, J. W. (1968). Methods and problems in cross-cultural research. In G. Lindzey & E. Aronson (Eds.), *Handbook of social psychology* (Vol. 2, pp. 693–728). Reading, MA: Addison-Wesley.

Whiting, J. W. (1974). A model for psychocultural research. *Annual Report*, American Anthropological Association, Washington, DC.

Whiting, J. W. (1981) Environmental constraints on infant care practices. In R. H. Munroe, R. L. Munroe, & B. B. Whiting (Eds.), *Handbook of cross-cultural human development* (pp. 155–180). New York: Garland.

Whiting, J. W., & Child, I. (1953). *Child training and personality*. New Haven: Yale University Press.

Whiting, J. W., Kluckhohn, R., & Anthony A. (1958). The function of male initiation ceremonies at puberty. In E. Maccoby, T. Newcomb, & E. Hartley (Eds.), *Readings in social psychology* (3rd ed., pp. 359–370). New York: Holt.

Whorf, B. L. (1956). *Language, thought and reality*. J. Carroll (Ed.). Cambridge, MA: MIT Press.

Williams, C. L., & Berry, J. W. (1991). Primary prevention of acculturative stress among refugees: The application of psychological theory and practice. *American Psychologist*, *46*, 632–641.

Williams, J. E., & Best, D. L. (1982). *Measuring sex stereotypes: A thirty nation study*. London: Sage.

Williams, J. E., & Best, D. L. (1990). *Sex and psyche: Gender and self viewed cross-culturally*. Newbury Park, CA: Sage.

Williams, T. R. (1967). *Field methods in the study of culture*. New York: Holt, Rinehart and Winston.

Wilson, E. O. (1975). *Sociobiology: The new synthesis*. Cambridge, MA: Belknap Press – Harvard University Press.

Winkelman, M. (1986). Trance states: A theoretical model and cross-cultural analysis. *Ethos, 14*, 174–203.

Winter, W. (1963). The perception of safety posters by Bantu industrial workers. *Psychologia Africana, 10*, 127–135.

Wintrob, R. M., & Sindell, P. S. (1972). Culture change and psychopathology: The case of Cree adolescent students in Quebec. In J. W. Berry & G. J. S. Wilde (Eds.), *Social psychology: The Canadian context* (pp. 259–271). Toronto: McClelland and Stewart.

Wissler, C. (1923). *Man and culture.* New York: Thomas Y. Crowell.

Witkin, H., & Berry, J. W. (1975). Psychological differentiation in cross-cultural perspective. *Journal of Cross-Cultural Psychology, 6*, 4–87.

Witkin, H. A., Dyk, R. B., Paterson, H. F., Goodenough, D. R., & Karp, S. (1962). *Psychological differentiation.* New York: Wiley.

Witkin, H., & Goodenough, D. (1981). *Cognitive Styles: Essence and origins. (Psychological Monographs, 51)* New York: International Universities Press.

Witkin, H. A., Goodenough, D. R., & Oltman, P. (1979). Psychological differentiation: Current status. *Journal of Personality and Social Psychology, 37*, 1127–1145.

Wober, M. (1966). Sensotypes. *Journal of Social Psychology, 70*, 181–189.

Wober, M. (1967). Adapting Witkin's field independence theory to accommodate new information from Africa. *British Journal of Psychology, 58*, 29–38.

Wober, M. (1975). *Psychology in Africa.* London: International African Institute.

Wolff, P. H. (1972). Ethnic differences in alcohol sensitivity. *Science, 175*, 449–450.

Wolff, P. H. (1973). Vasomotor sensitivity to alcohol in diverse Mongoloid populations. *American Journal of Human Genetics, 25*, 193–199.

World Bank. (1984). *Consequences of rapid population growth: An overview.* Washington, DC: World Bank.

World Development Report. (1985). Washington, DC: World Bank.

World Health Organization. (1973). *Report of the International Pilot Study of Schizophrenia, Vol. 1.* Geneva: WHO.

World Health Organization. (1978). *Primary Health Care, Report of the International Conference at Alma Ata.* Geneva: WHO.

World Health Organization. (1979). *Schizophrenia: An international follow-up study.* New York: Wiley.

World Health Organization. (1982). *Medium term programme.* Geneva: WHO.

World Health Organization. (1988). *Charter for action to achieve health for all by the year 2000 and beyond.* Geneva: WHO.

World Health Organization. (1990). *International classification of diseases.* Geneva: WHO.

Wortley, W. W., & Humphriss, D. (1971). Study of acuity of vision of South African Whites, Bantu and Bushmen. *Psychologia Africana, 14*, 11–19.

Wright, G. N. (1985). Organizational, group and individual decision making in cross-cultural perspective. In G. N. Wright (Ed.), *Behavioral decision making* (pp. 149–165). New York: Plenum.

Wright, G. N., & Phillips, L. D. (1980). Cultural variation in probabilistic thinking: Alternative ways of dealing with uncertainty. *International Journal of Psychology, 15*, 239–257.

Wright, G. N., Phillips, L. D., & Wisudha, A. (1983). Cultural comparison on decision making under uncertainty. In J. B. Deregowski, S. Dziurawiec, & R. C. Annis (Eds.), *Expiscations in cross-cultural psychology* (pp. 387–402). Lisse: Swets and Zeitlinger.

Wundt, W. (1912). *Völkerpsychologie.* Leipzig: Englemann. (Trans. 1916, *Elements of folk psychology*, London: Allen & Unwin.)

Wyndham, C. H. (1975). Ergonomic problems in the transition from peasant to industrial life in South Africa. In A. Chapanis (Ed.), *Ethnic variables in human factors engineering* (pp. 115–134). Baltimore: Johns Hopkins University Press.

Yang, K. S., & Bond, M. H. (1990). Exploring implicit personality theories with indigenous or imported constructs: The Chinese case. *Journal of Personality and Social Psychology, 58*, 1087–1095.

Yap, P. M. (1969). The culture-bound reactive syndromes. In W. Caudill & T-Y. Lin (Eds.), *Mental health research in Asia and the Pacific.* Honolulu: East West Centre Press.

Yap, P. M. (1974). *Comparative psychiatry.* Toronto: University of Toronto Press.

Yates, J. F., Ying, Z., Ronis, D. L., Deng-Feng, W., Shinotsuka, H., & Toda, M. (1989). Probability judgment accuracy: China, Japan, and the United States. *Organizational Behavior and Human Decision Processes, 43,* 145–171.

Young, M. Y., & Gardner, R. C. (1990). Modes of acculturation and second language proficiency. *Canadian Journal of Behavioural Science, 22,* 59–71.

Zaidi, H. (1979). Applied cross-cultural psychology: Submissions of a cross cultural psychologist from the Third World. In L. Eckensberger, W. Lonner, & Y. H. Poortinga (Eds.), *Cross-cultural contributions to psychology* (pp. 236–243). Lisse: Swets and Zeitlinger.

Zavalloni, M. (1980). Values. In H. C. Triandis & R. Brislin (Eds.), *Handbook of cross-cultural psychology: Vol. 5. Social psychology* (pp. 73–120). Boston: Allyn and Bacon.

Zempléni-Rabain, J. (1970). L'enfant Wolof de 2–5 ans (Sénégal): Echanges corporels et échanges médiatisés par les objets. *Revue de Neuropsychiatrie Infantile, 18,* 785–798.

Zuckerman, M., & Brody, N. (1988). Oysters, rabbits and people: A critique of "race differences in behaviour" by J. P. Rushton. *Personality and Individual Differences, 9,* 1025–1033.

Author Index

Abegglen, J. C., 327
Aberle, D. F., 44, 68, 170
Aboud, F., 281, 303–305
Abrahamson, A. S., 144
Adler, L. L., 5
Adler, N. J., 326
Adorno, T., 182
Aellen, C., 307
Ainsworth, M. D. S., 31, 36
Aitkin, M., 232
Akhtar Hossain, A. B. M., 53, 55, 56
Al-Issa, I., 358
Albas, C. A., 83
Albas, D. C, 83
Albert, R. D., 347
Alcock, J., 207, 213
Allaire, Y., 321
Alland, A., 357
Allison, A. C., 198
Allport, G. W., 51
Altman, I., 88
Amatruda, C., 37
American Educational Research Association, 313
American Psychological Association, 313
Amir, Y., 42, 259, 298
Anand, B. K., 96
Anastasi, A., 111
Andor, L. E., 137
Andrews, J. D., 353
Angelini, A. L., 283
Anisfeld, E., 307
Annis, R. C., 129, 276, 305
Anthony, A., 67
Anwar, M. P., 157
Araki, S., 342
Archer, D., 88
Archer, J., 209
Arcuri, L. W., 82
Ardilla, R., 386
Argyle, M., 86–88
Arieti, S., 362
Armstrong, R. E., 149
Asai, M., 57
Asante, M. K., 339

Asch, S. E., 47
Asthana, H. S., 93
Au, T. K., 105
Ayala, F. J., 195, 206

Bacon, M., 21–24, 26, 29, 51, 66, 127, 254
Bahuchet, S., 129, 276
Baker, L., 104
Bali, S. K., 113, 241
Ball, P., 53, 55, 56
Ballachey, E., 167
Baltes, P. B., 31
Bandura, A., 216
Banerjee, M., 105
Banks, J., 308
Barba, C. V. C., 373, 376
Barker, R., 13, 229, 230
Barnard, W., 47
Barnlund, D. C., 342
Barnouw, V., 179
Barrett, D. E., 375
Barrett, G. V., 336
Barry, H., 21–27, 29, 51, 66, 67, 127, 175, 176, 254
Bass, B. M., 336
Bates, J., 202
Bayley, N., 37
Beauchamp, G. K., 135
Benedict, R., 180–182, 254
Bennett, J., 123, 124
Bentley, A. M., 153–155
Berganza, C., 358
Berkowitz, N., 46, 168
Berlin, B., 139–143
Berlin, E. A., 140
Berlyne, D. E., 157, 158
Berman, B., 387
Berman, J., 56
Berman, V., 56
Berrien, F. V., 240
Berry, J. W., 1, 2, 3–5, 11, 13, 18, 26, 34, 42, 43, 48–50, 65–67, 99, 100, 110, 111, 113–115, 117, 118, 120, 123–129, 146, 148, 169, 173, 185, 187, 204, 223, 224, 228, 229, 232–234, 263, 271, 276–280,

440

282, 284–290, 293, 294–296, 299, 300,
  302, 306, 308, 334, 357, 369, 377, 378
Bersoff, D. M., 33
Bertino, M., 135
Best, D. L., 59–64, 226, 333
Betancourt, H., 57, 58
Beveridge, W. M., 133
Bhagat, R. S., 323, 336, 337
Bharat, S., 128
Bianchi, G., 286
Biesheuvel, S., 113, 135, 136, 244
Bijnen, E. J., 75
Bilsky, W., 53
Binnendijk, H., 351, 352
Birdwhistell, R. L., 81
Blackler, F., 387
Blake, R. R., 323
Blanchfield, R., 352
Bleichrodt, N., 65, 66, 113, 134
Blondel, T., 286
Bloom, A., 104, 105
Blowers, G. H., 89, 384
Blue, A., 286
Blue, M., 286
Blum-Kulka, S., 342
Boas, F., 100, 169, 256
Bochner, S., 174, 273, 275, 280, 287, 339–341
Bock, P. K., 179–185
Bodmer, W., 193, 196, 200, 202
Boesch, E. E., 11, 262, 386
Boldt, E. D., 46–48
Bolinger, D., 107
Bolles, R. C., 208
Bolton, C., 29
Bolton, R., 29
Bond, M. H., 42, 53, 55–58, 94, 232, 240, 289,
  354, 384
Bontempo, R., 57, 58
Boorstin, D. J., 248
Borich, G., 283
Born, M., 65, 66
Bornstein, M. H., 142, 143
Boski, P., 304
Boucher, J. D., 82, 85
Bourguignon, E., 96, 97, 179, 367
Bourhis, R., 306
Bourne, E. J., 56, 94
Bowlby, J., 36
Boyd, R., 13, 20, 216, 217, 251
Bradshaw, J. L., 108
Bragg, B. W. E., 158
Brand, E., 304
Brandt, M. E., 85, 343
Brazelton, T. B., 37, 38
Brein, M., 341
Brewer, M., 296, 300
Bril, B., 5, 39
Brislin, R. W., 5, 60, 148, 149, 174, 237, 239,
  240, 343–345, 347, 348
Brodman, K., 286

Brody, N., 214
Brown, R., 329
Brown, R. W., 139
Brozek, J., 374
Brunet, O., 37
Brunswik, E., 13, 147, 229, 230
Bujaki, M., 278, 279, 284
Bullivant, B., 298
Bundy, R., 38
Burgard, P., 260
Burridge, K., 94
Burstein, L., 232
Butcher, J. N., 73, 358
Byth, W., 152

Camilleri, C., 308
Campbell, D. T., 8, 9, 10, 147–150, 169, 215,
  218, 220, 223, 224, 239, 296, 300
Campbell, N. C. G., 353
Carlson, G. E., 82
Carlson, J. A., 148, 329
Carrithers, M., 94
Carroll, J. B., 104, 116
Carroll, W. K., 171
Carson, R., 358
Casagrande, J. B., 104
Casati, I., 40
Case, R., 121
Cavalli-Sforza, L. L., 17, 18, 129, 193, 196,
  200, 202, 214–216, 276
Cawte, J., 286
Chan, A., 82
Chance, N. A., 286
Chandra, S., 47
Chavez, A. A., 375
Chemers, M. M., 88
Chen, L., 371
Cherrie, C., 347, 348
Chhina, G. S., 96
Child, I. L., 21–24, 26, 27, 29, 51, 66, 127,
  156, 157, 183, 254
Child, J., 320
Chinese Culture Connection, 232, 337, 354
Ching, C. C., 372
Chiu, C. K., 354
Chodzinski, R. T., 308
Chomsky, N., 106
Church, A. T., 340
Ciborowski, T., 5
Cissé, Y., 91
Clack, F. L., 54, 56
Claeys, W., 47
Clark, K., 304, 305
Clark, M., 279, 304, 305
Clyne, M., 305
Cohen, A. K., 44, 68, 170
Cohen, J., 226, 231
Cohen, P., 231
Cohen, R., 171, 173, 353

Cole, M., 30, 114, 115, 120, 122, 123, 149, 223, 283
Cole, S., 30
Coleman, J., 358
Collett, P., 87, 342
Collins, S., 94
Colson, E., 274
Comas-Diaz, L., 357
Cook, T. D., 220
Cooper, J. E., 360, 361
Copeland, J. R. M., 360, 361
Copeland, L., 355
Corenblum, B., 305
Corman, H. H., 40
Court, J. H., 112
Crawford, M. A., 375
Cronbach, L. J., 111, 242, 244
Crozier, J. B., 158
Crutchfield, R., 167
Cuevas, C., 83
Cushner, K., 347, 348
Cysneiros, P. G., 84, 211

Dabbs, J. M, 67
Daly, M., 213
D'Andrade, R. G., 188
Danzinger, K., 100
Dasen, P. R., 1, 3, 34, 39–41, 43, 66, 67, 99, 114, 115, 118, 120, 121, 146, 185, 189, 204, 232, 271, 276, 300, 334, 357, 369, 374, 376, 377
Dash-Scheuer, A., 376
David, K. H., 341
Davidson, A. R., 1, 5, 233, 235
Davis, A., 44, 68, 170
Davis, C., 304
Davis, C. M., 148, 329
Dawson, J. L. M., 32, 125, 277
de Lacey, P. R., 275, 298, 308
De Nisi, A. S., 333
De Vos, G., 94, 281, 384
de Ribaupierre, A., 121
DeRidder, R., 303
Deal, T. E., 321
Dean, R. F., 37
Deese, J., 80
DeFries, J. C., 193, 203
Dembele, B., 120
Demetriou, A., 121
Deng-Feng, W., 330
Deregowski, J. B., 136, 145–147, 149, 152–155
Detweiler, R. A., 343
Deutsch, M., 47
Devereux, G., 358
Diacoyanni-Tarlatris, I., 82
Diaz-Guerrero, R., 73, 235, 283, 379, 381, 383
DiMatteo, M. R., 88
Dittrich, A., 95
Divale, W. T., 84, 211

Dixon, S., 38
Dobzhansky, T., 195, 206
Doi, T., 91, 92, 365, 366
Doise, W., 43
Doktor, R., 326
Dollard, J., 183
Doornbos, M., 304
Dorman, R., 375
Doty, R. L., 135
Dougherty, J. W., 188
Draguns, J., 5, 228, 357, 358, 369
Drenth, P. J. D., 111, 113, 134, 241, 242, 320, 337
Du Toit, B. M., 103
DuBois, C., 180, 182
Ducci, L., 82
Duncan, H. F., 152
Durham, W. H., 215
Durojaiye, M., 379
Dyal, J. A., 72
Dyk, R. B., 125
Dziurawiec, S., 153

Eagly, A., 66
Eckensberger, L. H., 1, 11, 32, 260–262, 266
Edgerton, R., 6, 7, 29, 180
Edwards, A. L., 74
Edwards, C. P., 32
Edwards, J., 310, 311
Efklides, A., 121
Efron, D., 88
Eibl-Eibesfeldt, I., 34, 105, 208–211
Eimas, P. D., 144
Ekman, P., 81, 82, 86, 87
Ekstrand, G., 233
Ekstrand, L. H., 233, 280
Eldering, L., 308
Ellis, B., 56, 333
Endler, N. S., 76
Engelsmann, F., 361
Enriquez, V., 380, 383, 384
Escalona, S. K., 40
Estrera, N. O., 376
Ettien, K., 120
Evans, R., 357
Evascu, T., 96
Eysenck, H. J., 74, 75, 117, 157, 201, 202, 254
Eysenck, S. B. G., 74, 75, 254

Fancher, R. E., 116
Faucheux, C., 43
Favazza, A., 358
Fawcett, J. T., 372
Feather, N., 51, 53
Feldman, D., 13
Feldman, M. W., 17, 214–216
Fenichel, O., 369
Ferguson, G., 124
Fernandez, E. L., 376
Ferrer, C., 83

Feuerstein, R., 309, 313
Fiedler, F. E., 346
Fillmore, C. M., 374
Firsirotu, M. E., 321
Fishman, J. A., 103, 305
Fiske, A. P., 44, 45
Fiske, D. W., 223, 241, 352
Flatz, G., 206
Flynn, J. R., 204
Foden, B. I. M., 97, 158–160
Folkman, S., 280, 290
Ford, C. S., 175
Forgas, J., 56
Foster, G. M., 274
Foulks, E., 358
Fourasté, R., 358
Frager, R., 47
Frasure-Smith, N., 29
Freedman, D. G., 202
Freeman, D., 13, 181
Frenkel-Brunswik, E., 182
Freud, S., 20, 21
Friesen, W. V., 82, 86, 87
Frijda, N. H., 86
Fromkin, V. A., 108
Fromm, E., 182
Frost, P. J., 321
Fujimura, O., 144
Fulker, D. M., 202
Fuller, J. L., 201, 254
Furby, L., 204, 344
Furnham, A., 280, 287, 339–341

Galler, J. R., 375
Garcia, J., 208
Gardner, E. J., 193
Gardner, R. C., 299, 306, 307
Gatewood, J. B., 188
Gay, J., 115, 122, 149, 223
Geber, M., 31, 37, 38
Geertz, C., 170, 321
Geiger, L., 137
Gerard, H., 47
Gesell, A., 31, 37
Geser, G. C., 244
Ghiselli, E. E., 326, 334, 336
Gibbs, J. C., 32
Gibson, J. J., 145
Glacken, C. J., 248
Gladstone, W. E., 137
Gleser, G. C., 242, 244
Glick, J., 115, 122, 149, 223
Goldberg, S., 40
Goldman, S. V., 312
Goldstein, A. P., 66
Gologor, E., 329
Gombrich, E. H., 145
Goodenough, D. R., 125
Goodenough, N., 171
Goody, J., 123, 283

Gorer, G., 182
Goto, H., 144
Gough, H. G., 60, 73
Gould, J. L., 208
Gourlay, N., 152
Government of Canada, 297
Graham, J. A., 88
Graham, J. L., 353
Grant, G. V., 113
Grantham-McGregor, S., 375
Graves, P. L., 375
Graves, T. D., 271
Gray, J. A., 201
Greenberg, J. H., 107, 108, 188
Greenfeld, P. J., 143
Greenfield, P. M., 121
Gregory, R. L., 152
Griffeth, R. W., 333
Griffith, E., 357
Griffiths, R., 37
Griggs, L., 355
Groenendijk, B., 320
Gross, L., 29
Gudykunst, W. B., 339, 345–347, 380
Guilford, J. P., 116
Gumperz, J. J., 341
Gurland, B. J., 360, 361
Gussler, J. D., 97
Guthrie, G. M., 73, 340, 373, 376
Guthrie, H. A., 373, 376
Gynther, M. D., 73

Hagen, M. A., 152, 154
Haire, M., 326, 334, 336
Hall, E. T., 88, 350, 352, 354
Hall, J. A., 88
Hallowell, A. I., 99, 283
Hallpike, C. P., 169
Hamer, M. R., 343, 345–347
Hamers, J., 29
Hamilton, D. L., 299
Hamilton, W. D., 212, 213
Haritos-Fatouros, M., 157
Harkness, S., 31, 34, 202, 369–371
Harris, M., 47
Harrison, D. E., 329
Harwood, R. L., 33
Hawes, F., 344
Hayashi, K., 53, 55, 56
Hays, W. L., 225
Hebb, D. O., 116
Hector, H., 146
Heelas, P., 380
Heenan, T. A., 83
Heider, F., 300, 380
Heider, K., 82
Heilbrun, A., 60
Heller, F. A., 325–327, 388
Hendriks, E. C., 354
Hendrix, L., 25

Hennessey, R., 148
Hermans, I., 322
Heron, A., 5, 30, 121
Herskovits, M. J., 8, 18, 77, 147–150, 165, 169, 224, 256, 271
Hewer, A., 33
Hewstone, M., 76, 301, 302, 354
Heymans, G., 201
Hickson, D. J., 315, 316, 320
Hill, P. E., 236
Hinde, R. A., 207–209
Hirai, T., 96
Hofstede, G., 51, 54, 55, 57, 182, 226, 316, 322, 326, 330–333, 353, 354
Holland, D., 188
Holland, P. W., 223
Holtzman, W., 357, 378
Hom, P. W., 333
Honigmann, J. J., 362
Hoopes, D. S., 345
Hopkins, B., 38
Hopper, P. J., 107
Horn, J. M., 202, 204
House, J., 342
Howard, A., 223, 254, 296
Hsu, F. L. K., 94, 179, 183
Huang, L., 47
Hudson, A. E., 175
Hudson, W., 151, 152, 155
Hughes, C. C., 362, 363
Hui, C. H., 56, 57, 234
Hull, W. F., 340
Humphriss, D., 134
Hunt, E. B., 105, 110, 187
Hunt, J. McV., 40

IDE (Industrial Democracy in Europe International Research Group), 318, 333
Ilola, L. M., 357
Inhelder, B., 39–41, 374
Inkeles, A., 180, 277, 283, 336
Irvine, S. H., 110, 111, 114, 116, 118, 171, 187,
Isajiw, V., 294
Isaka, H., 57
Iscoe, I., 357
Iwao, S., 157
Iwawaki, S., 157
Izard, C. E., 82

Jaccard, J. J., 235
Jacklin, C., 65
Jaggi, V., 76, 301
Jahoda, G., 2, 7, 34, 42, 43, 70, 91, 124, 146, 148, 150, 152, 153, 155, 165, 180, 183, 185, 188, 223, 233, 236, 259, 263, 265, 378, 386
Janis, I. L., 327
Jaspars, J. M. F., 354
Jayasuriya, L., 302
Jen, K. C., 135

Jenkins, J. J., 144
Jensen, A. R., 203, 255, 312
Jilek, W., 368
Joe, R. C., 108, 263
Johnson-Laird, P. N., 100
Johnston, E. F., 374
Jolibert, A., 353
Jonas, K., 340
Jones, J. M., 313
Jones, R., 313
Jones, R. K., 152, 154
Jöreskog, K. G., 241
Josephson, L., 25, 26, 67

Kabran, K., 120
Kagitcibasi, C., 5, 56, 58, 372
Kakar, S., 369, 383, 389
Kalin, R., 63, 64, 287, 296, 300, 302, 304
Kalmus, H., 135
Kamagaté, D., 120
Kamin, L. J., 204
Kaplan, B., 179
Kardiner, A., 11, 180–182
Karni, E. S., 73
Karp, S., 125
Kasamatsu, A., 96
Kashima, Y., 56–58, 279
Kasper, E., 262
Kasper, G., 342
Kaufman, S., 279
Kaufmann, J., 349
Kay, P., 139–143
Kealey, D. J., 284, 340, 343, 344
Keating, C. F., 84, 211
Keefer, C. H., 38
Keller, C., 188
Keller, H., 34
Keller, W., 374
Kelley, H. H., 301
Kemper, R., 274
Kendell, R. E., 360, 361
Kendon, A., 87
Kennedy, A. A., 321
Kennedy, S., 357
Kermoian, R., 36
Kessen, W. H., 142
Kettlewell, H. B. D., 196
Khandwalla, P. N., 324
Khoka, E., 40
Kilbride, J. E., 84, 211
Kilbride, P. L., 39
Kiloh, L., 286
Kim, D. K., 353
Kim, U., 223, 278, 279, 284–287, 288–290, 306, 380
Kim, Y. Y., 280
Kimmel, H. D., 157
King, A. Y. C., 289
Kirchner, W., 333
Kish, L., 226

Kitayama, S., 94
Klineberg, O., 8, 81, 340
Kloprogge, J., 308
Kluckhohn, C., 51–53, 165–167, 180, 182, 186
Kluckhohn, F., 51, 52
Kluckhohn, R., 67
Knapen, M. T., 41
Koel, A., 29
Koelling, R. A., 208
Koffi, D. A., 120
Kohlberg, L., 31–33
Komin, S., 84, 211
Konner, M., 35, 36, 67
Kopp, C. B., 40
Korolenko, C. P., 358
Kraemer, A., 346
Krause, R., 82
Krech, D., 167
Krewer, B., 262
Kroeber, A. L., 165–167, 175, 264
Kroeger, E., 5, 30
Kucharski, L. T., 375
Kudoh, T., 85
Kulkarni, S. G., 382
Kumagai, A. K., 92
Kumagai, H. A., 92
Kuntner, L., 149
Kuplowska, O., 304, 305
Kurtines, W., 275
Kuso, S., 283
Kuwano, S., 135

Laaksonen, O., 318
Laboratory of Comparative Human
    Cognition, 31, 122, 124
Laferrière, M., 308, 310
Lagmay, A., 379
Lambert, W. E., 27, 29, 307, 311
Lambert, W. W., 5, 27, 28
Lammers, C. J., 315, 316, 320
Lampl, M., 374
Landis, D., 343, 344
Langer, T. S., 286
Lantz, D., 139
l'Armand, K., 76
Lauer, E., 25, 26, 67
Laurent, A., 326
Lavallée, M., 39–41, 120, 374
Lawlor, M., 156
Lazarus, R. S., 280, 290
Leahy, P., 84, 211
LeCompte, W. A., 82
Lefcourt, H. M., 71
Leff, J., 357, 360, 361
Lehalle, H., 5
Leibowitz, H. W., 148
Leiderman, P. H., 36
Lenkert, A., 340
Lenneberg, E. H., 103, 105, 139
Lens, W., 322

Leroux, J., 4
Leung, K., 54, 56–58, 232, 353
Lévi-Strauss, C., 110, 187
Levin, J., 73
Levine, C., 33
LeVine, R. A., 8, 20, 179, 180, 186, 187, 224,
    263
Levinson, D. J., 182
Levitsky, D. A., 375
Levy, M., 44, 68, 170
Lévy-Bruhl, L., 100
Lewin, K., 230
Lewis, J., 313
Lewontin, R. C., 196, 199, 200, 204
Lézine, I., 37, 40
Liberman, A. M., 144
Lieban, R., 375
Likert, R., 323
Lim, S. P., 53, 55, 56
Lin, C., 353
Lin, K., 286
Lindzey, G., 51
Linton, R., 11, 165, 166, 180–182, 271
Lisker, L., 144
Liu, L. A., 105
Lloyd, B., 138
Lock, A., 380
Lockett, M., 318
Loehlin, J. C., 202, 204
Lomax, A., 46, 168
Lombard, A. D., 312
Longabaugh, R., 174
Longford, N., 232
Lonner, W. J., 2, 4, 5, 73, 129, 170, 173, 224,
    228, 237, 259
Lorenz, K., 207, 209
Louis, M. R., 321
Lucca, N., 56
Lucy, J. A., 142
Ludwig, A. M., 95
Lukes, S., 94
Lumsden, C. J., 215
Lundberg, C. C., 321
Lundström, S., 298
Lutje Spelberg, H. C., 313
Lutz, C., 244
Lynch, J., 308
Lynch, R., 168
Lynn, R., 74, 75

Ma, H. K., 33
MacArthur, R. S., 65, 127
Maccoby, E., 65
Maddieson, I., 107
Madsen, M. C., 353
Magnus, H., 137, 138
Magnusson, D., 76
Mahapatra, M., 33
Maistriaux, R., 117
Makinda, S. M., 89

Mala, T., 358
Malewska-Peyre, H., 283, 311
Malinowski, B., 265
Mallick, K., 308
Malpass, R. S., 1, 85, 221, 222, 225, 226, 233,
    238, 241, 260
Manaster, G. J., 283
Mandell, A. J., 98
Mann, C. W., 248
Mann, J., 286
Mann, L., 57, 327, 329, 353
Manning, A., 207
Markus, H., 94
Marler, P., 208
Marsella, A. J., 5, 94, 357, 358, 361, 376
Marsh, P., 87, 342
Marshall, C., 25, 26, 67
Martin, J., 321
Martinez, C., 375
Martyn-Johns, T. A., 328
Maslow, A. H., 334
Masuda, M., 286
Matsuda, N., 47, 48
Matsumoto, D., 85
Maurice, M., 319, 320
Mawhinney, T. A., 279
May, W. H., 60, 78–80
Mazrui, A., 378
Mazur, A., 67, 84, 211
McClearn, G. E., 193, 203
McClelland, D. C., 334
McCluskey, K. W., 83
McCormack, W., 343
McCreary, D. R., 352
McDaniel, C. K., 143
McDermott, R. P., 312
McGinnies, E., 72
McGurk, H., 152, 153, 155
McKay, R. J., 374
McLaren, D. S., 374
McLeod, K. A., 309
McLuhan, M., 135
McNeill, N. B., 141
McNett, C., 46
McQuaid, S. J., 323, 336, 337
McShane, D., 117
Meacham, J. A., 261
Mead, M., 180, 181
Meade, R., 47
Mehryar, A., 386
Meissner, H. G., 353
Melikan, L., 379
Mercer, J., 313
Meth, J., 362
Mezzich, J., 358
Michael, S. T., 286
Michelson, C., 29
Michik, G., 177, 178, 227
Miller, G. A., 317
Miller, J. G., 33, 77, 94, 370

Miller, L. H., 370
Miller, N., 183
Minde, T., 223, 285–287, 289, 290, 306
Minturn, L., 27, 28
Miron, M. S., 60, 78–80
Mischel, W., 76, 266
Misumi, J., 323–325, 328
Mitchell, T., 346
Mitra, S. K., 382
Miura, M., 365
Miyawaki, K., 144
Modgil, C., 308
Modgil, S., 308
Moghaddam, F. M., 303, 379, 380
Mok, D., 223, 285–287, 289, 290, 306
Montero, M., 378, 379
Moore, F. W., 175
Moore, L. F., 321
Morales, M. L., 235
Morgenthaler, G., 369
Morris, C. R., 156
Morris, D., 87, 342
Morris, R., 67
Moscovici, S., 42, 43, 188, 254
Motulsky, A. G., 193, 197–199, 202, 206
Mounoud, P., 121
Mouton, J. S., 323
MOW (Meaning of Working International
    Research Team), 335
Moylan, T., 120
Muldrow, E. S., 145
Muldrow, W. F., 145
Mundy-Castle, A. C., 38
Munro, D., 337
Munroe, R. H., 25, 29, 30, 31, 35, 47, 65, 171
Munroe, R. L., 25, 29, 30, 31, 35, 47, 65, 171
Murase, T., 365–367
Murdock, G. P., 26, 46, 170, 175, 183, 227,
    316
Murphy, H. B. M., 286, 287, 357–360
Murray, H. A., 186
Muthayya, B. C., 383

Naidu, R. K., 93
Namba, S., 135
Nanda, H., 242, 244
Naroll, F., 177, 178, 227
Naroll, R., 66, 173, 175, 177, 178, 227
National Council on Measurement in
    Education, 313
Neale, M. C., 202
Nebylitsyn, V. D., 201
Neghandi, A. R., 316
Nelson, E. W., 374
Nerlove, S. B., 188
Nettleton, N. C., 108
Neuijen, B., 322
Nevis, E. C., 337
Ng, M., 326
Ng, S. H., 53, 55, 56

Ngini, L., 120
N'Guessan, A., 120
Nias, D. K. B., 202
Niemi, R., 83
Nisbet, R., 9, 168, 378
Nisbett, R. E., 76
Nkounkou-Hombessa, E., 39
Noe, R. A., 111
Nursey-Bray, P. F., 136

Oberg, K., 340
O'Bryan, K., 304, 305
Odling-Smee, F., 215
O'Driscoll, 53, 55, 56
Ohayv, D. D., 322
Oliver, R. A. C., 133
Olmeda, E., 126, 274
Oltman, P., 125
Omari, I. M., 113, 241, 242
Ombredane, A., 112, 135
Opolot, J. A., 74
Ord, I. G., 112
Orlansky, H., 184
Orlebeke, J. F., 157
Ortigues, E., 369
Ortigues, M. E., 369
Osgood, C. E., 60, 78–80, 108, 109, 226
O'Shaughnessy, M., 87, 342
O'Sullivan, M., 82
Otto, S. A., 83
Ouchi, W. G., 321
Ouellet, F., 308

Padaki, R., 336
Padilla, A., 304
Pancheri, P., 73
Pandey, J., 382
Paranjpe, A. C., 92, 383
Pareek, U., 171, 382
Parin, P., 369
Parin-Matthey, G., 369
Parkin, J. M., 38
Pascale, R. T., 327
Pascual-Leone, J., 121
Paterson, H. F., 125
Paxson, L., 25
Peabody, D., 73, 76, 88
Peal, E., 307
Peck, R., 283
Pedersen, P. B., 345, 357, 366
Pedhazur, E. J., 321
Pelto, G. H., 171, 174, 233
Pelto, P. J., 46, 171, 174, 233
Pepitone, A., 43, 76
Perera, M., 74, 75
Perlmutter, L., 148
Perrot, D., 9, 168
Pervin, L. A., 233
Peters, L. G., 98
Peters, T. J., 321

Peterson, M. F., 325
Pettigrew, T. F., 223, 279
Pfeiffer, W., 362, 363
Phillips, L. D., 329
Phinney, J., 118, 304
Piaget, J., 31, 40, 105, 115, 118–121
Pierce, R. C., 279
Pike, K. L., 232
Pitcairn, T., 82
Plomin, R., 193, 203
Plotkin, H. C., 215
Plumail, H., 112
Poggie, J., 168
Pollack, R. H., 148
Pollitt, E., 374
Poole, M., 298, 308
Poortinga, Y. H., 1, 3, 34, 43, 66, 67, 75, 85,
   87, 97, 99, 112, 115, 118, 136, 146, 158–
   160, 185, 204, 221, 224–226, 231, 232,
   235, 238, 240, 241, 243, 244, 250, 253,
   259, 260, 263, 266, 271, 276, 300, 329,
   334, 354
Popper, K. R., 218
Porter, L. W., 326, 334, 336
Porteus, S. D., 117
Posses, F., 350, 352
Post, R. H., 135, 205, 254
Power, S., 278, 279, 284
Preiswerk, R., 9, 168
Price-Williams, D., 98
Prince, R., 361–363, 365–369
Przeworski, A., 236, 237
Puhan, B. N., 382
Pye, L. W., 351, 352

Quandt, W. B., 351
Querido, A., 134
Quinn, N. R., 188

Rabain, J., 39, 41
Rahman, M., 371
Rajaratnam, N., 242, 244
Randhawa, B., 298, 308
Rao, T. V., 171
Raven, J., 112
Raven, J. C., 112
Ray, V. F., 139
Redding, S. G., 326
Redfield, R., 271
Reinshagen, H., 32
Reitz, J., 304, 305
Resing, W. C., 113
Retschitzki, J., 39–41, 374
Reuning, H., 112, 134, 146, 150, 210
Rey, M., 310
Reynolds, P. D., 321
Reynolds, V., 193
Ricci-Bitti, P. E., 82
Ricciuti, H. N., 374, 375
Richerson, P. J., 13, 20, 216, 217, 251

Rickman, J., 182
Rist, G., 386
Rivers, W. H. R., 131, 132, 134, 138
Robaye, F., 112
Robbins, M. C., 157
Robbins, S. R., 317, 324
Roberts, L., 48
Robinson, M., 353
Rocher, G., 302
Rogers, P. L., 88
Rogoff, B., 283
Rohner, E., 21
Rohner, R., 21, 262, 264–266
Rokeach, M., 53
Romney, A. K., 188
Ronen, S., 319, 323, 331, 333, 336
Ronis, D. L., 330
Rosch (Heider), E., 141, 142
Rose, S., 204
Rosenfeld, H. M., 88
Rosenthal, R., 88
Ross, L., 76
Rotter, J. B., 71
Rotthauwe, H. W., 206
Royal Anthropological Institute, 171
Ruben, B. D., 343, 344
Rubin, E. V., 149
Rubin, R. B., 223
Ruffell Smith, H. P., 341
Ruiz, R., 304
Rushton, J. P., 117, 202, 214, 254

Sabatier, C., 39
Sabelli, F., 386
Sahlins, M., 141, 168, 169, 214
Sahoo, F., 381
Sako, S., 47
Salazar, J., 379, 383
Salk, J., 372
Samuda, R., 283, 308, 313, 364
Sanders, G., 322
Sanford, R. N., 182
Santa, I. L., 104
Sanua, V., 284
Sapir, E., 180
Sardar, A., 371
Sartorius, N., 357, 369, 377
Saxe, G. B., 120, 189
Schachter, S., 98
Schein, E. H., 321
Scherer, K. R., 82, 83, 85, 86
Schick, A., 135
Schlegel, A., 26, 27, 175
Schmitt, N., 111
Schölmerich, A., 34
Schoots, N. H., 87, 266
Schürch, B., 374
Schuring, G., 106, 107
Schwartz, S. H., 53, 58
Schwendler, W., 378

Scopetta, M., 275
Scott, R. A., 223, 254, 296
Scribner, S., 114, 120, 122, 123, 283
Scudder, T., 274
Segall, M. H., 1, 3, 5, 34, 43, 66, 67, 84, 99,
    115, 118, 146–150, 169, 185, 204, 211,
    224, 232, 263, 266, 271, 276, 300, 304, 334
Segalowitz, N. S., 307
Selye, H., 280
Sénéchal, C., 129, 276
Serpell, R., 5, 155
Service, E., 168, 169
Shanmugam, T. E., 76, 93
Sharon, I., 42, 259
Sharp, D., 115, 122, 129
Sharpe, L., 360, 361
Sherif, M., 49
Shimada, E., 279
Shinotsuka, H., 330
Shuey, A. M., 117
Shweder, R. A., 33, 56, 94, 142, 179, 183, 184
Siegel, M., 57
Sieye, A., 40
Sigman, M. A., 40
Silk, J. B., 203
Silvar, S. D., 148
Simon, R., 360, 361
Simons, R., 362, 363
Sindell, P. S., 279, 286
Singer, J., 98
Singh, A. K., 387
Singh, B., 96
Singh, P., 56
Sinha, D., 53, 55, 56, 128, 309, 336, 378, 381,
    385, 387
Sinha, G., 129
Sinha, J. B. P., 323, 326, 387, 389
Sinseshaw, T., 82
Skerry, S., 304, 305
Skutnabb-Kangas, T., 311
Sloan, T., 378, 379
Smith, D., 277, 283
Smith, P. B., 325
Snarey, J. R., 32
Snustad, D. P., 193
Solomon, R. H., 351
Sommerlad, E., 277, 279, 304
Sörbom, D., 241
Sorge, A., 320
Soueif, M. I., 157
Sow, I., 89, 90
Spangenberg, J., 57
Spearman, C., 116
Spector, P. E., 337
Spielberger, C. D., 73
Spies, E., 329
Spindler, G., 179
Srole, L., 286
Stacey, B., 148
Staub, S., 95

Stebbins, G. L., 195, 206
Steffire, V., 139
Sternberg, R. J., 110, 116
Stewart, V. M., 149
Stonequist, E. V., 286
Strange, W., 144
Strodtbeck, F., 51, 52, 220
Stroebe, W., 340
Strupp, N. J., 375
Sturtevant, W., 187
Suci, G. J., 78, 226
Sue, D. W., 364
Summerfield, A. B., 85
Sumner, W. G., 8
Super, C. M., 31, 34, 38–40, 202, 369–371, 376
Sussman, N. M., 88
Sutton, F. X., 44, 68, 170
Swartz, L., 369
Symons, D., 213
Szalay, L. R., 80
Szapocznik, J., 275

Taft, R., 289
Tajfel, H., 183, 289, 303, 304, 354
Tanaka, K., 57
Tanaka-Matsumi, J., 365
Tannen, D., 342
Tannenbaum, A. S., 336
Tannenbaum, P. H., 78, 226
Tayeb, M. H., 323
Taylor, D. M., 76, 287, 299, 300–304, 379
Tazuma, L., 286
Tcheng-Laroche, F., 362
Ten Doesschate, G., 154
Teune, H., 236, 237
Textor, R., 175
Tharp, R., 5
Thayer, N. B., 351, 352
Thompson, R., 157
Thompson, S. A., 107
Thompson, W. R., 17, 193, 201, 254
Thomson, C., 374
Thorndike, R. M., 5, 237
Thouless, R. H., 132, 133
Thurman, B., 84, 211
Thurstone, L. L., 116
Tilby, P., 63, 64
Tinbergen, N., 207
Ting-Toomey, S., 339, 353, 354
Titchener, E. B., 138
Tittle, C. K., 237
Toda, M., 330
Tomita, M., 82
Torbiörn, I., 340
Triandis, H. C., 1, 5, 43, 54–58, 78, 80, 94, 233–235, 259, 279, 326, 342, 346, 389
Trimble, J., 126
Tripathi, R. C., 303, 383
Tronik, E., 38
Tucker, R., 29, 311

Tung, R. L., 340
Turtle, A. M., 89, 379, 384
Tylor, E. B., 165, 166
Tzeng, O. C. S., 79

Udy, S. H., 316
Ugorji, R., 387
Usa, S., 365
Uzgiris, I. C., 40

Valentine, J. W., 195, 206
Valsiner, J., 236
Van Bezooijen, R., 831
Van de Koppel, J. M. H., 87, 129, 263, 266, 276
Van de Vijver, F. J. R., 231, 240, 259, 260, 263
Van der Flier, H., 65, 66, 112, 113, 241, 242
Van der Net, T. Z. J., 75
Van der Werff, J. J., 201
Van Lancker, D., 108
Van Leeuwen, M. S., 26
Van Olst, E. H., 1157
Van Oudenhoven, J. P., 299
Van Wattenwyl, A., 143
Vassiliou, V., 78, 80
Vaughan, V. C., 374
Ventura, P., 345
Verbrugge, R., 144
Verma, G. K., 308
Vernon, P. E., 51 115, 116, 203, 204
Villarcal, M. J., 54, 56, 57, 279
Vogel, E. F., 328
Vogel, F., 193, 197–199, 202, 206
Von Arx, S., 95
Vorster, J., 106, 107
Vouilloux, D., 38
Vroom, V., 327
Vygotsky, L. S., 30

Wagner, D. A., 144
Wagner, R., 110
Wallace, A. F. C., 98, 179
Wallbott, H. G., 85, 86
Wan, K. C., 354
Ward, C. A., 76, 95
Ward, C. D., 72
Warner, M., 320
Warren, N., 5, 38, 255
Warwick, D., 378
Wason, P. C., 100
Wassmann, J., 189
Waterman, R. H., 321
Watkins, D., 241
Watt, I., 123, 283
Weber, M., 335
Weeks, W. H., 345
Weiskopf, S., 142
Weiss, S. E., 351, 352
Werner, E. E., 35, 38
Werner, H., 31

Werner, O., 239
Westermeyer, J., 358, 363
Wexley, K. N., 323
White, D., 175
White, G. M., 244, 358
Whiting, B. B., 2, 30, 35, 263
Whiting, J. W., 2, 11, 21, 27, 28, 36, 67, 180, 183–185
Whorf, B., 102, 103, 188
Willemsen, T. M., 299
Willerman, L., 202, 204
Williams, C. L., 290
Williams, J. E., 59–64, 226, 333
Williams, T. R., 171
Wilpert, B., 326, 327
Wilson, E. O., 212–215
Wilson, M., 213
Wimalasari, J., 337
Winkelman, M., 98
Winter, W., 145
Wintrob, R. M., 279, 286, 358
Wirsing, R., 84, 211
Wissler, C., 165, 166
Wisudha, A., 329
Witkin, H. A., 115, 120, 125–129, 276
Wober, M., 107, 135, 136, 384
Wolff, P. H., 135, 358
Wolfgang, A., 364
Wong, G. Y. Y., 326

Wonnacott, E., 299
World Bank, 372
World Development Report, 249
World Health Organization, 356–360
Wortley, W., 112, 134, 146, 150
Wright, G. N., 327, 329, 330
Wundt, W., 100
Wyndham, C. H., 134
Wyon, J., 369–371

Yang, K. S., 53, 55, 56, 94
Yap, P. M., 357, 362–364
Yaschine, T., 375
Yates, J. F., 330
Yetton, P., 327
Ying, Z., 330
Yong, M., 347, 348
Young, M., 278, 279, 284
Young, M. Y., 307
Young, W. C. E., 113, 241
Yukl, G. A., 323

Zack, M., 39
Zaidi, H., 386
Zavalloni, M., 51
Zempléni-Rabain, J., 41
Zollinger, H., 143
Zuckerman, M., 214

Subject Index

Aborigines, Australian, 275, 277, 286
Absolutism, 110, 120, 253, 256–260, 358, 364, 369
Accommodation, 119
Acculturation, 13, 18, 19, 62, 128, 152, 271–291
  attitudes, 276–280
  behavior change, 280–284
  contact, 275–276
  definition, 271–272
  modes, 277–278
  strategies, 278
Acculturative stress, 284–290
Achievement motivation, 334
Achievement training, 22–25
Action theory, 260–263
Activity (factor), 78–79, 108
Adaptation, 2, 13, 35–36, 196–199, 275, 284, 391
  biological, 13, 192, 196
  cultural, 13, 169
Adoption, 203
Aesthetics, 156–160
  appreciation, 156–157
  curiosity, 157
  perception, 157–159
  stimulus seeking, 157
Affective meaning, 77–81
Affective polarity, 108
African personality, 89–91
Aggression, 66–68, 202, 209
Aggression training, 38
Agriculture, 24, 35, 46, 126–128, 134, 316
Alcoholic flush, 134
Allele, 193–195
Allocentrism, 55–56
Alma Alta Declaration, 356
Altered states of consciousness, 95–98
Alternative explanations, 132, 219–222
Altruism, 201, 212
Amae, 91–92, 352, 365
American Indians, 98, 135, 139, 248
Amok, 362, 363
Analogies, 210
Antecedents of differences, 1, 247–256

Anthropology, 6–7, 165–191
  cognitive, 187–190
  psychological (*see also* Culture and personality), 179–187
  relationship with psychology, 6–7, 165
Arabs, 88, 298
Archaic reflexes, 37
Archival studies (*see also* Human Relations Area Files), 21–27
Ashanti, 70
Assertion, 46, 373
  training, 22–25
Assessment, 111, 312–314
Assimilation, 271, 278–280, 281, 284, 290, 292–293, 296, 297, 301, 302, 309
Assortative mating, 195
Atlas of Affective Meaning, 79, 226
Atman, 92–93
Attachment, 19–20
Attitudes
  acculturation, 276–280
  ethnic, 299–302
  work, 336
Attribution, 354
  dispositional, 77, 301
  external, 301
  internal, 301
  situational, 77, 301
Auditory predominance, 135
Authoritarian personality, 182
Ayoreo Indians, 210

Baby tests, 37, 39
Baganda, 39
Balance theory, 300
Bambara, 39, 91
Bangandu, 276
Baoulé, 40, 120
Basic color terms, 139
Bayley scale, 39
Behavior changes (with acculturation), 280–284
  cognitive, 283
  identity, 281
  personality, 283

451

Behavior genetics, 200–205
  adoption studies, 203
  heritability, 202
  intelligence, 201–204
  personality, 201–204
  twin studies, 203
Behavior outcomes, 229
Berserker, 363
Between vs within group differences, 253,
  255–256
Biaka, 129, 276
Bias, 72, 225, 237, 240–241, 242–245
  assessment of intelligence, 116–118
  instrument, 240
  item, 240
  observation, 101
  researcher (ethnocentrism), 8–10
  stimulus, 240
Bilingual education, 310
Bilingualism, 305–308
Biocultural synthesis, 34–35
Biological transmission (genetic transmission),
  11–13, 17, 192
Biological variables, 2, 7, 13
Birhor, 128
Black Americans, 72, 313
Block Design Test, 129
Brazelton Examination, 38
Breeding, 193
Bricolage, 110
Bushmen, 112, 134, 146

Cambridge Anthropological Expedition, 131
Canadian Indians, 286
Capitalism (and Protestant Ethic), 335
Caretaking (by mother), 28
Carpentered world hypothesis, 147–149
Child rearing (child training), 20–30
  dimensions, 22
  economy, 23–27
  sex differences, 22–23
Child survival, 371–372
Choice Reaction Times, 137
Chromosome, 194
Civilization, 166
Class, social, 30, 45
Climate, 248–249
  infant carrying, 36
Codability, linguistic, 103, 139
Cognition, 99–130
  every day cognition,
  history, 99–101
Cognitive anthropology, 187–189
Cognitive competence, 110
Cognitive style, 124–129
  acculturative influences, 129
  ecological influences, 126–127
  field-dependence/field-independence,
    125–129
  patterns of abilities, 124

  sex differences, 127
  socialization influences, 127
Cognitive tests, 111–113
Collective (social) representations, 188, 254
Collectivism, 56–58, 330–331
Color blindness, 134, 138, 205
Color perception, 103, 137–145
  color sensitivity, 137
  color terms, 137, 139–142
  focal colors, 140–145
  linguistic issues, 137–138
  physiological issues, 138, 142–143
  spectral sensitivity, 142–143
Communication, intercultural, 339–355
  competence, 342–344
  difficulties, 341–342
  effectiveness, 347
  training, 344–347
Comparability (see also Bias, Equivalence)
  analysis of, 236–241
  cultural categories, 178
  judgmental methods, 237
  psychometric analyses, 240–241
  scale identity, 238–239
  translation equivalence, 237–239
Comparative psychiatry (transcultural
    psychiatry), 357
Compensation hypothesis, 135
Complexity
  art, 157
  cultural, 48, 94
Compliance (in child rearing), 22–25, 27–28,
  46–48, 72, 373
Concrete operational stage, 119, 120
Conformity, social, 46–51, 217
Confucian work dynamism, 337
Connotative meaning, 78
Consciousness, 93–98
Constancies (see Phenomenal regression)
Constraints on behavior, 266
Context, 6, 8
  cultural, 11, 43–46, 228
  ecological, 11
  socio-political, 11
Context-free measurement, 258–259
Context specificity theory, 31, 122–124
Contexts, classification of, 228–232
Contingency approach, 317–320
Continuity assumption, 184
Controls in cross-cultural research, 222–224,
  242
  composite scores, 223
  elimination of variance, 223
  extension of data set, 223
  selection of population, 222
Conventions, 160, 266
Convergence hypothesis, 319–320
Convergent validity, 223–224
Coping, 285, 289, 376
Cornell Medical Index, 286

Counterfactuality, 104–106
Cree Indians, 83, 123, 274, 279
Creole English, 108
Critical periods, 208
Cross-cultural psychology
  definitions, 1–2
  framework, 10–14
  goals, 2–4
Cross-cultural psychotherapy, 368–369
Cross-national research, 2
Cultunit, 177, 227
Cultural anthropology, 6–7, 165–191
Cultural context, 11, 43–46, 228
Cultural development, 30
Cultural diffusion, 177, 227, 271, 379
Cultural diversity, 297
Cultural evolution, 168–169
Cultural inheritance, 218
Cultural materials, 175–177
Cultural psychology, 235–236
Cultural relativism, 8, 121, 169–170
Cultural transmission, 12–13, 42, 214–217,
  247–256
Cultural universals, 44, 170
Culture
  areas, 175, 227
  assimilator, 346–349
  change, 271
  contact, 13, 275–276
  conceptualizations of, 260–267
  definitions, 165–168
  explicit, 167–168, 264
  implicit, 167–168, 264
  shock, 280, 340–341
  superorganic, 167
Culture and personality (Psychological
  anthropology), 7, 11, 14, 179–187
  basic personality, 181
  configurationalism, 180
  cross-cultural approach, 182
  definition, 179
  modal personality, 181–182
  national character, 182
  psychoanalysis, 186
Culture-bound syndromes, 362–364
Culturegen, 215
Curiosity, 157–160

Dani, 82, 141
Decentering, 239
Decision making, 327–330
  cautious shift, 329
  confidence, 329
  consensus, 328
  democratic, 328
  managerial, 327
  probabilistic, 329
  risky shift, 327
  situational factors, 327
Deficiencies (deficit models), 8, 100, 117, 296

Denotative meaning, 78
Dependency, 19–20
Depression, 361–362
Depth cues, 151, 153, 154
  impoverished cues, 155
Depth perception, pictorial, 151–156
  gradient of texture, 154
  Hudson's test, 151–153, 155
  linear perspective, 153
  skills, 155
  three dimensional, 151–156
  two dimensional, 151–156
Design of cross-cultural studies, 220–228
  independent variable, 220
  quasi-experiments, 221
  selection of cultures, 224–227
  selection of individuals, 228
  selection of subgroups, 227
Detachment, 93
Developing world psychology, 378–390
Development
  concept, 30–35
  cultural, 30
  individual, 30–41
  infancy, 30–41
  national, 384–390
  ontogenetic, 30
Developmental niche, 31–35, 236
Developmental quotient, 37–39
Dialectical relationships, 11, 262
Dichotic listening, 108
Differentiation theory, 31, 124–129
Diffusion, cultural, 177, 227, 271, 379
Discrimination, 302–303
Display rules, emotions, 86–87
Distance, between cultures, 80
Diversity, genetic, 192–193
Division of labor, 26–27
DNA, 193–194
Dobuan Islanders, 181
Domain of behavior, 242–245
Dominance, 84
Down syndrome, 201
Dual inheritance model, 216–217

Ecocultural approach, 34, 110, passim
Ecocultural framework (model), 10–14,
  passim
Ecocultural index, 49
Ecological analysis, 125, 228–232, 263
Ecological context, 11, 230
Ecological cue validity, 147–149
Ecological factor analysis, 331
Ecological niche, 34, 36, 198, 208
Ecological psychology, 13, 229
Ecological variables, 2, 27, 127
Ecological validity, 230
Economy, 2, 13
  child rearing, 23–25
  roles, 26

women's contribution (*see also* Division of labor), 26–27
Education
  formal, 283
  informal, 283
  schooling, 124
  selection, 111–113
Eidolic perception, 154
Embedded Figures Test (EFT), 128–129
Emblems, 87
Emic-Etic distinction, 232–236, 337, 380
  combined emic-etic approach, 234
  derived etics, 233
  emics, 232–234
  imposed etics, 233–234
  iterative approach, 233
  pseudo etics, 233
Emotions, 81–86
  antecedents, 85
  appraisal, 85
  display rules, 86
  expression, 81–86
  inheritance, 81
Enculturation, 13, 17, 271
Enrichment programs, 312
Environmental determinism, 13
Environmental tracking, 198
Epigenetic rules, 215
Epinephrine, 98
Epitomic perception, 154
Equivalence, 237–241
Equivalence of measurements (*see* Comparability)
Estimated learning potential, 313
Ethnic psychology, 2, 295
Ethnic identity, 303–305
Ethnic relations, 299–303
Ethnicity, 293–294
Ethnocentrism, 8–10, 100, 117, 169, 301–302
Ethnocultural groups, 293–297
Ethnography, 20, 170–179
  archives, 21, 174–179
  collaboration, 171
  field work, 171–174
  informants, 174
  observations, 174
Ethnology, 170
Ethnopsychology (*see also* Indigenous psychology), 380
Ethnoscience (*see also* Cognitive anthropology), 187
Ethology, 205–214
Etic (*see* Emic-Etic distinction)
Evaluation (factor), 78, 108
Evolution, biological, 192–200
  cultural, 168–169
  linguistic, 140–141
Exchange students, 340
Expatriates (*see also* Sojourners), 339
Experimental approach, 7, 180

Experimental controls, 220–224
Experimental design, 220–221
Explicit culture, 168, 264
Export of psychology, 378–379
Expressive behaviors, 81–88
Extraversion – Introversion, 74–75
Eysenck Personality Questionnaire, 73, 74

Face, losing, 326
Facial expression (of emotion), 81–84, 86
Femininity, 54, 61, 330, 332
Fertility behavior, 372–373
  old age security, 372–373
  value of children, 372
Field dependence-independence (*see also* Cognitive Style), 124–129
  acculturation factors, 127–129
  ecological factors, 126–128
  patterns of abilities, 125
  sex differences, 127
  socialization factors, 126–127, 129
Field studies, 27–30, 171–174
Fishing, 24
Fixed action patterns, 207
Focal colors, 103, 140–143
Folk psychology (*see also* Indigenous psychology), 380–381
  Völkerpsychologie (Wundt), 99, 380
Food accumulation (subsistence economy), 24
Fore, 81–82
Formal operational stage, 119
Functional prerequisites, 44, 170

Galton's problem, 177, 227
Gender behavior, 58–68
Gender differences (*see* Sex differences)
Gender stereotypes, 59–62
Gene, 194
General Adaptability Battery, 113
General intelligence, 115, 116–118
  acculturation factors, 118
  antecedents, 117–118
  biological factors, 117
  deficit models, 117
  difference models, 117
  hierarchical models, 116
  intelligence A, B, & C, 116, 125, 245
  psychophysiological techniques, 117
Generalizability theory, 244
Genetic drift, 195
Genetic epistemology, 115, 118–121
Genetic transmission (biological transmission), 12, 13, 134–135, 192–196, 200–205, 208–217, 247, 251
Genotype, 116, 194
Gestalt psychology, 181
Gestures, 86–88
  adaptors, 87
  emblems, 87

illustrators, 87
universality, 87
Goals of cross-cultural psychology, 2–4
  exploration and discovery, 3
  integration, 3
  transport and test, 3
Golden Mean principle, 33
Good Will principle, 33
Gradient of texture (*see* Depth perception)
Green-blue confusion, 138
Greeting procedures, 8, 42, 208
Gross national product, 249
Guest workers, 298, 310

Hardy-Weinberg law, 193–195
  constant environment, 195
  gene frequencies, 193
Health behavior, 356–377
  behavioral science role, 356–357
  cultural factors, 369–376
  disease transmission, 369
  health promotion, 356
  prevention, 356–357, 369, 370
Hemispheric dominance (lateralization), 108
Heritability estimates, 201–204
  extraversion-introversion, 201
  intelligence, 203–204
  personality variables, 201–202
Heterozygous, 194
High contact cultures, 88
High context *vs* low context cultures, 354
High culture, 166–167
High inference variables, 118
Hindu concepts of personality, 93
Holocultural (hologeistic) approach, 36, 175
Homologies, 210
Homozygous, 194
Hopi Indians, 102–103
Horizontal cultural transmission, 17–18
Horizontal-vertical illusion, 147–148
Human ethology, 208–212
  phylogenetic adaptation, 210
  reductionism, 211
  rituals, 210–211
  similarities in behavior, 208–209
  symbolic behavior, 210
  universal motor patterns, 210
Human Relations Area Files (HRAF), 20–27,
    165, 170, 174–179
  coding rules, 178
  data quality, 178
  Galton's problem, 177, 227
  problems 175–178
  selection of cultures, 178–179
Hunter-gatherers, 13, 24, 35, 46, 97, 125–128,
    134, 205, 316
Hutterites, 48
Identity (*see also* Ethnic identity), 303–305
Identity of scales (*see also* Domain of
    behavior), 242–245

Idiocentrism, 55–58
Idiographic *vs* Nomothetic, 233
Illusion susceptibility, 147–149
Immigrants, 290, 294
Implicit culture, 167–168, 264
Importation of psychology, 379–380
Imposed etics, 233–234
Imprinting, 207
Independence training, 22–25
Independence *vs* conformity, 48
Indian personality, 92–93, 382–383
Indian survey of psychology, 382–383
Indigenous cognition, 110
Indigenous personality, 89–93
Indigenous psychology, 42, 380–384
  definition, 381
  emic orientation, 380
  phases, 381
  reactions to Western psychology,
    381
Indigenous psychotherapy, 365–369
Individualism-collectivism, 56–58, 94,
    330–331
Indo-European languages, 102
Indulgence, 92
Industrialization, 35, 129
Infant
  carrying, 36–37
  development, 35–41
Inferences, 241–245, 251–256
  behavioral potential, 253
  classification, 241–245
  cultural domains, 255
  low, medium, high, 242–245
  psychological traits, 255–256
Information transmission, 137
Ingroup–outgroup distinction, 57
Instinct, 207–208
Instrumental motives, 306
Instrumental values, 53
Integration, 278–281, 293
Integrative motives, 306
Intelligence (*see also* General intelligence),
    113–118
  A, B, and C, 116, 245
  culture-gene interactions, 204
  heritability estimates, 203–204
  increase in test scores, 205
Interactionism, 76
Intercultural competence, 342
Intercultural communication, 339–344
Intercultural counselling, 364
International negotiations, 347–354
Inuit, 36, 65, 103, 286
Invariance, 259–260
  color perception, 104, 138
  language, 109
  moral stages, 32
Iodine deficiency, 134
Isomorphic attributions, 342

Jiva, 92
Job satisfaction, 336
Job selection, 111, 113

Key informants, 174
Kipsigis, 34, 39
Koro, 363
Kpelle, 122, 149
Krishna, 79
Kurds, 87
Kwakiutl Indians, 181

Lactase, 206
Lactose intolerance, 206
Language
  attitudes, 306
  bilingualism, 305–308
  biological foundation, 105–106
  cognition, 101–109, 187–188
  cultural maintenance, 305
  minorities, 305–308
Latah, 363
Lateralization, 108
Leadership styles, 323–326
  authoritative, 323–326
  consideration, 323
  cultural specificity, 326
  initiating structure, 323
  maintenance, 324–325
  nurturant task leader, 323–324
  participative, 324
  people oriented, 323–325
  performance, 324–325
  task oriented, 323–325
Learning, 207–208
Learning potential, 313
Level of analysis, 6–7, 11, 52, 55–56, 73–76,
    179–180, 230–232, 235, 332
  individual, 11, 231, 271, 319–320
  institutional, 319–320
  population, 11, 231, 271
  statistical techniques, 231
Life span development, 31
Linear structural models, 241
Linguistic relativity, 101–105
Literacy
  cognition, 123–124
  general effects, 123
  schooling, 123–124, 283
  specific effects, 124
Locus of control, 71–73
Longitudinal research, 274
Low-contact cultures, 88
Low-inference variables, 118

M-power, 121
Mabuig, 138
Malaria, 370–371
  behavioral factors, 370–371
  control, 370–371
  self-help, 371

Malay, 301–302
Malnutrition, 373–376
  clinical signs, 373
  growth, 373–374
  intellectual development, 374
Managerial behavior, 323–330
Marginalization, 278–281, 285–286, 292–293,
    309
Masculinity, 54, 61, 330, 332
Maslow's need hierarchy, 331, 334
Maturation theory, 31
Maya Indians, 129
Measurement scale, 238–239
Mennonites, 48
Mental disorders, 201, 359
Mental health, 284–285, 356
Minorities, 292–314
Modal personality, 181–182
Modernity, 276–277, 283, 290
Monozygotic twins, 195
Moral development, 31–33
Morita therapy, 365–367
Mother-child interaction, 28, 41
Motives, 334–337
Motor development, 39
Müller-Lyer illusion, 147–150
Multiculturalism, 297–299
  definition, 293
  multicultural education, 308–310
  multicultural ideology, 300–302
  multicultural policies, 297–298
Munsell color system, 137, 139
Musical abilities, 133
Musjawarah, 328
Muslims, 63, 301
Mutations, 193

Naikan therapy, 365–367
National character, 73–76, 180, 182
National development, 384–390
National stereotypes, 73–76
Native American
  languages, 102–103
  mind, 100
  peoples, 294–295
Natural selection, 193–196
Naturalistic approach, 6–7, 180, 229
Nature-nurture distinction, 31, 34, 201
Navajo Indians, 104
Neo-Piagetian theories, 120–121
Neonatal development, 37–39
Neuromotor development, 35
Neuroticism, 74–75
Non-equivalent group designs, 221
Non-Representational Complexity Text,
    158–160
Non-verbal communication, 86–88
Non-western approaches, 10, 380–381
Norms, 43, 46–47
Null hypothesis, 225

Number systems, 189–191
Nurturance training, 22–25
Nurturant-task leader, 323–324
Nutrition, 134, 373–376

Obedience training, 22–25
Objective culture, 77
Ojibwa Indians, 283
Oksapmin, 120
Ontogenetic development, 30
Oraon, 128
Organism-environment interaction, 192–193
Organizational culture, 320–322
Organizational structure, 315–323
    democracy, 318
    hierarchy, 319
    political factors, 318–319
    preindustrial societies, 316
    task distribution, 316
    types, 316

P-M Leadership Theory, 324–325
Pandora's Box, 152
Papiamento, 107
Parasympathetic nervous system, 98
Parental ethnotheories, 39, 120
Participant observation, 171, 233
Participation of workers, 318–319
Pastoralism, 24, 29
Pattern perception, 145–156
    depth, 151
    idiosyncrasies, 145
    schooling, 145, 151
    symmetry, 145
Peace Corps, 343
Pedi, 106
Perception, 131–161
Personal space, 88
Personality, 23, 29, 69–98
    consistency, 71, 88
    definition, 186
    heritability estimates, 201–202
    indigenous theories, 89–93
    self, 94–95
    traits, 70–77
Phenomenal regression, 133
Phenomenology, 262
Phenotype, 194
Phenylketonuria, 201
Philotimous, 78–80
Phonemes, 144
Phonemics, 232
Phonetics, 232
Pibloqtoq, 363
Pigmentation, retinal, 138, 142–143
Plasticity of behavior, 35, 201, 255, 266
Pleiotropy, 199
Plural societies, 292–297
Poggendorff illusion, 147–150
Polypeptides, 194

PONS test, 88
Ponzo illusion, 147–150
Positions, 43
Possession, 96–98
Potency (factor), 78–79, 108–109
Power distance, 54–56, 330–333
Practical intelligence, 110
Precocity (African infant), 37–39
Preoperational stage, 119
Present State Examination, 360
Primary institutions, 181
Primates, 36, 67, 83–84
"Primitive" societies, 100, 166–167
Projective tests, 185
Psychic unity of mankind, 265
Psychoactive substances, 95, 98
Psycholinguistics, 101–109
Psychological acculturation, 271–272
Psychological anthropology (*see* Culture and personality)
Psychological Differentiation Theory, 31, 124–129
Psychometric approach
    comparability, 240–241
    intelligence, 116
Psychomotor development, 38
Psychophysiological measurements, 97
Psychotherapy, 364–369
Psychoticism, 74–75
Pueblo Indians, 181
Pygmies, 129, 276

Quasi-experiments, 221

r/k continuum, 214
"Race," 199–200, 248–249
Radical cultural relativism, 169
Raven's Progressive Matrices, 112, 123
Recapitulation theory, 101
Recognition of emotions, 81–84
Reductionism, 6
Reflexive human beings, 260–263
Refugees, 294–295
Regulatory genes, 200
Relativism, 8, 253, 256–260, 319, 358
Releasers, 207, 211
Replication, 9–10, 42–43
Representational Complexity Test, 158–160
Representative samples, 224–228
Resocialization, 18–19
Restricted literacy, 123
Retinal pigmentation, 138, 142–143
Ringi, 327–328
Risk factors (health), 375–376
Risky shift phenomenon, 327–329
Rokeach Value Survey, 53–56
Roles, 43
Role diversity, 45
Role obligation, 46
Rotter I-E Scale, 71–73

Samia, 39
Samoa, 85
Sampling, 224–228
  cultures, 224–227
  groups, 227
  individuals, 228
  stratified, 226
Samurai, 81, 182
Sander parallelogram illusion, 147–150
Sango, 276
Santhal, 129
Sapir-Whorf hypothesis (see Linguistic
  relativity)
Schizophrenia, 358–361
  cultural influences, 359
  diagnosis, 360
  prevalence, 360
  WHO studies, 360–361
Schooling,
  cognitive test performance, 118, 123, 283
  minorities, 309–312
  pictorial perception, 145–152
Scientific acculturation, 34, 379–381
Seashore Test for Musical Abilities, 133
Second language learning, 306–307
Secondary institutions, 182
Segregation, 293, 302
Self, 93–95
Self-rejection, 305
Self-reliance training, 22–25, 28–29
Semantic Differential Technique, 78–81
Semantic meaning, 108–109
Sensorimotor intelligence (stage), 39–41, 105,
  118
Sensory stimuli, 133–137
Sensotypes, 135
Separation, 278–280, 281, 290, 293, 309
Sex differences, 58–68
  abilities, 65–66
  aggression, 66–68
  conformity, 66
  physical, 26
  socialization, 22–30
  stereotypes, 59–63
Sex role ideology, 62–64
Shaman, 96
Sickle cell anemia, 197–198
Sikolohiyang Pilipino, 383–384
Similarities
  behavior, 2, 4, 186, 192, 210, 327
  cultures, 21, 28, 30
  language, 107–108
Size constancy (see Phenomenal regression),
  133
Skin color, 198–200
Smiling, 84
Snellen's E chart, 132
Social Darwinism (see Cultural evolution)
Social desirability, 74

Social Identity Theory, 303, 354
Social Learning Theory, 71–73
Social stratification, 24, 45
Social structure, 22, 45
Social support, 288
Socialization, 13, 17–20, 135, 183
Society (as distinct from culture), 167
Sociobiology, 212–214
Socio-political context, 11, 271, 302
Sojourners, 294, 339–341
Sotho, 106
Specific abilities, 113–115, 121–124
Specific evolution, 168–169
Speech perception, 143
Stage theory, 31
  cognitive development, 118–121
  color terminology, 141
  moral development, 31–33
  sensorimotor intelligence, 39–41
  universality, 40
Standard Average European (language), 102
Status, 46, 288
Stereotypes
  ethnic, 299
  national, 73
Structural genes, 200
Subjective culture, 77–80
Submissiveness, 25, 84
Subsistence mode (see Economy)
Susto, 362–363
Swaddling hypothesis, 182
Symbols, 210

Taste, 135
Temperament, 34, 70, 74, 210
Terminal values, 53
Test
  administration, 111–113
  bias, 219, 240, 313
  transfer, 111–113
Thick description, 321
Tight-loose dimension, 46–48
Tonal language, 107
Traditional-modern attitudes, 276–277
Traits (see also Personality), 70–77
Trance, 97, 367
Transcultural psychiatry, 357
Tribal groups, 295
Twin studies, 201–203
Typical personality, 23

Uncertainty avoidance, 54, 330–331
Universal laws, 3
Universal processes, 391
Universal psychology, 3, 382, 384, 391
Universal validity, 3, 10, 264
Universals, 2, 259–260, 391
  cognitive processes, 100, 110
  cultural, 170, 176–177

definition, 259–260
language, 105–109
meaning, 79
motor activity, 210
non-verbal communication, 87
perception, 160–161
psychopathology, 358–364, 368
social behavior, 44–45, 211
stereotypes (gender), 60
values, 53
Universalism, 69, 253, 256–260, 392
"Unpackaging" culture, 263
Utilization of psychology, 388–389

Validation, 14, 223, 224
Values, 51–56, 330–333
Variance
between cultures, 227, 253, 334
within cultures, 227, 253, 334
Vedanta, 93
Vertical transmission, 17–18
Visual acuity, 132

Visual illusions, 146–150
Visual predominance, 135
Vitamin A, 134
Vitamin D, 206
Voodoo, 367–368

Weaning, 21, 36, 39
Western psychology, 378–380
Westernization, 290
Whorf's hypothesis, 102–105, 138–139
Witiko, 362–363
Work
attitudes, 336
centrality, 335
motives, 334–337
values, 330–333

Yanomami, 210
Yoga, 93, 95–96
Yupno, 189

Zen, 96